'Romantic' and Its Cognates / The European History of a Word

EDITED BY HANS EICHNER

UNIVERSITY OF TORONTO PRESS

© University of Toronto Press 1972
Printed in Great Britain for
University of Toronto Press, Toronto and Buffalo
ISBN 0-8020-5243-6
Microfiche ISBN 0-8020-0077-0
Library of Congress Catalogue Card Number 77-163812

This book has been published with the help of a
grant from the Humanities Research Council of Canada,
using funds provided by the Canada Council.

'ROMANTIC' AND ITS COGNATES /

THE EUROPEAN HISTORY OF A WORD

Contents

ABBREVIATIONS OF PERIODICALS

BBMP	Boletín de la Biblioteca Menéndez Pelayo
BHS	Bulletin of Hispanic Studies
BSS	Bulletin of Spanish Studies (continued after 1948 as *BHS*)
DVLG	Deutsche Vierteljahrsschrift für Literaturwissenschaft und Geistesgeschichte
GRM	Germanisch-romanische Monatsschrift
JEGP	Journal of English and Germanic Philology
JHI	Journal of the History of Ideas
MLN	Modern Language Notes
MLQ	Modern Language Quarterly
MLR	Modern Language Review
NRFH	Nueva Revista de Filologia Hipánica
PEGS	Publications of the English Goethe Society
PMLA	Publications of the Modern Language Association of America
PQ	Philological Quarterly
RH	Revue Hispanique
RLC	Revue de Littérature Comparée
RR	Romanic Review
TLS	[London] Times Literary Supplement

'ROMANTIC' AND ITS COGNATES /
THE EUROPEAN HISTORY OF A WORD

Introduction

I

Ever since the word *romantic* and its many cognates in European languages began to be used self-consciously as technical terms towards the end of the eighteenth century, the quest for a satisfactory definition of their meanings has continued unabated. It has been estimated that in the last sixty years some seven hundred articles and treatises have been devoted to this quest, and there is no indication that scholarly concern with the problem is lessening. The vast majority of these articles are concerned with the word *romantic* as it is used in contemporary scholarly writing, where it refers to the authors or works constituting the 'romantic movements' in the various European literatures of the first half of the nineteenth century; they aim to explain and justify this usage by showing what features, styles, techniques, or convictions certain authors or works have in common. The present collection of essays intends to serve a more purely historical purpose – to show how the word and its cognates were first introduced, how their usage spread and their connotations proliferated, and how their present usage became established. In the first of these essays, Raymond Immerwahr surveys the history of the word *romantic* and its French and German cognates from their beginnings to about 1790. This history is then continued in individual essays on the groups of cognates in Germany, England, France, Italy, Spain, the Scandinavian countries, and Russia. In the last essay of this volume, Henry H. H. Remak – without attempting to close the gap between the point at which the authors of the preceding essays conclude their survey and the present – deals with the contemporary scene.

The limitations of the present work are somewhat arbitrary. The decision to exclude such languages as Polish and Portuguese, or, for that matter, the decision to ignore American literature, must be justified on the pragmatic ground that the editor wished to produce one volume rather than two or three. Also, there is no irrefutable logic in the arrangement of the individual essays. Because of the immense influence German writers and critics had throughout Europe, the history of *romantisch* in Germany is presented early in the volume; the Romance countries form a natural block, and Russia and Scandinavia could be fittingly placed at the end, as their influence on events in other countries was minimal. England, however, posed a special problem; although it passed through its romantic period very early – in the year of the first performance of *Hernani*, Byron, Keats, and Shelley were dead, and Wordsworth and Coleridge past their prime – the technical use of the word *romantic* became established in the homeland of the word much later than almost anywhere else, and our decision to place George Whalley's essay on 'romantic' in England early, immediately after that on Germany, seemed merely the lesser of two evils.

As few readers will be able to cope with the nine languages dealt with in the present volume – its editor certainly cannot – quotations from all foreign languages except French are accompanied by English translations. If the editor's belief that very few readers will have difficulties with the French quotations is found illusory, perhaps he will be forgiven more readily if it is kept in mind that he resides in Canada.

II

In the essays that make up the present volume, the history of the word *romantic* is told as clearly as could be done without oversimplification. Even so, the story is so complicated that a brief (and necessarily schematic) summary of it may be helpful.[1]

As far as we know, 'romantic' was used for the first time in 1650, 'romanesque' in 1661, 'romanisch' in 1663.* The adjectives were

---

* See the Chronology below. According to Grimm's *Deutsches Wörterbuch* VIII (Leipzig, 1893): 1155, the word *romanticus* was used as early as the fifteenth century, in a Latin tract against superstition by Jean Gerson. However, Germán Colón, in a short article entitled 'Latin médiéval "romanticus" ' (*Zeitschrift für romanische Philologie* LXXVII, 1961: 75–80), argues convincingly that the word in Gerson is *Romanciorum* (or *Romantiorum*), the genitive plural of

derived from nouns that were then still synonymous – English 'romance,' French 'roman,' and German 'Roman' – and their users were conscious of this derivation. It is probably no coincidence that the new words were coined at a time when critics were just beginning to look with disfavour on the wholly fictitious nature and the improbability of the world of romance, and the adjectives derived from 'romance' and 'roman' express some of their disapproval: as 'romantic' meant 'romance-like' or 'romancical,' it also meant 'fantastic,' 'exaggerated,' or even 'absurd.' These pejorative connotations clearly prevailed when the adjective was applied to books, or when it was applied to persons who (perhaps misled by such books) ill-advisedly behaved, spoke, or acted like characters in a book; hence such stock phrases as 'romantic (i.e., absurdly unrealistic, lying) fiction' or 'romantic (i.e., extravagantly devoted, chivalrous or naïve) love.' Romances were still read and enjoyed, however, and the word could also be used in a way that reflected that enjoyment. Fiction can be more pleasing than fact; and consequently, when an object rather than a person or book was called 'romantic' because of its resemblance to similar objects described in romances, the epithet was likely to imply praise.[2]

In the course of time, the positive use of 'romantic' gradually gained ground, particularly as applied to landscapes – be they idyllic country scenes that would appear 'romance-like' only to city dwellers, scenes of alpine grandeur, or the painted landscapes of a Nicolas Poussin (1594–1665), Claude Lorrain (1600–82), or Salvator Rosa (1615–73).

In the second half of the eighteenth century, when the change of sensibility began to set in that as a first result led to the victory of the English garden, with its semblance of naturalness and freedom from restraint, over its French competitor, the discovery of 'romantic' scenes such as might have been painted by Lorrain, Rosa, or Poussin became a fashion in England. When the cult of the English garden spread into France and Germany, 'romanesque' and 'romantisch' (which quickly, though not entirely, replaced the earlier 'romanisch') became truly popular epithets in France and Germany. 'Romantique' caught on in France, as an English import, in the late seventies, mainly in a positive sense, while 'romanesque' continued to look after such meanings as 'chimérique' and 'fabuleux,' although it **was** not confined to them.

romantium, which was Gerson's Latinization of the Old French romanz. Thus, Colón concludes, 'ce fameux *romanticus médiéval n'est qu'une erreur de lecture, devenue fantôme lexicographique.'

Meanwhile, the change in sensibility that had produced the English garden began to make itself felt in literature as well – at first in England, in such works as Warton's *Observations on the Faerie Queen* (1754), Macpherson's Ossianic forgeries (1760 *ff.*), Hurd's *Letters on Chivalry and Romance* (1762), and Bishop Percy's *Reliques of Ancient English Poetry* (1765).

It was Warton who – after beginnings reaching back as far as 1667–established the concept of a 'romantic poetry' that, embracing the medieval romances, Ariosto's and Tasso's *romanzi*, and similar works of the Middle Ages and the Renaissance, contrasted with the literary tradition of the ancients; and it was in Warton's *Observations on the Faerie Queen* that the words 'classical' and 'romantic' were juxtaposed (although more by accident than by design, and as yet without consequences) for the first time.[3] Warton's concept was taken over in Germany by such critics as Gerstenberg and Herder, who had none of Warton's neoclassicistic reservations and had an even clearer vision of the Middle Ages as an epoch to be judged on its own terms, and who prepared the ground for the next event in the development of our concept–the twist imparted to it by Friedrich Schlegel in his writings of 1798–1800. With Warton, the concept 'romantic poetry' had been primarily chronological and descriptive. Schlegel retained most of Warton's connotations, but reemphasized the etymology of the adjective, used it rather more consciously as a technical term, and enriched its meaning with important typological and descriptive implications.

For the purposes of a specific paper, Raymond Immerwahr has defined a 'pre-romanticist' as a writer prior to the romantic movement who 'took special delight in viewing objects [he] called romantic,' and a 'romanticist' as someone who thinks that 'everything that matters is or ought to be romantic.'[4] With F. Schlegel we pass from the first kind of person to the second. In his famous definition of romantic poetry in *Athenäums-Fragment 116*, Schlegel started out with a concept closely related to Warton's – the tradition of the romance, in the widest sense of that word – and pointed out what he considered to be the essential characteristics of that literary form. He urged that the tradition of the romance should be revitalized; and in claiming that 'in a certain sense all poetry ... ought to be romantic,' he added a new ambiguity to the concept: romantic poetry was for him both a concrete achievement of the past and an ideal to guide the poetic activities of the future.

F. Schlegel asserted that 'romantic poetry,' as he conceived it, was 'subject to no rules,' and thus enabled the phrase to become the password of the opposition to neoclassicism; but in 1798 he failed to make clear that the 'romantic' was the antithesis of the 'classical.' In his second important statement on the subject, the 'Gespräch über die Poesie' of 1800, he only partly made up for this deficiency. Here 'klassisch' and 'romantisch' are juxtaposed three times, but two of these instances are quite insignificant[5]; and while elsewhere in the essay he works with such equivalent pairs of opposites as *romantisch/ alt, romantisch/antik*, and *antik/modern*,[6] his explanations and definitions are obscure. Nonetheless, Schlegel's usage of the word caught on, and it became a fashion for German scholars, critics, and journalists to discuss *das Romantische*, contrast it with *das Klassische*, and offer definitions of 'romantic poetry.' In the first decade of the nineteenth century, the preoccupation with the romantic spread from Germany to Denmark and Russia, where the term was discussed long before there was any indigenous literature that could conceivably be called romantic, and before long, the nature, merits, and claims of romantic poetry were debated throughout Europe.

The man who more than anyone else contributed to the spread of the debate was Schlegel's elder brother, August Wilhelm, not nearly as original a thinker, but a more lucid and effective writer than Friedrich. A. W. Schlegel had begun to promote his version of his brother's ideas in a series of lectures held in Berlin in 1801–4; they were widely discussed, but remained unpublished during his lifetime.* In 1807, he began to campaign on behalf of his theories in articles written in French and addressed specifically to French readers, and in 1808 he gave his immensely influential Vienna lectures on *Dramatic Art and Literature*, published in the original German in 1809–11, in Dutch in 1810, in French in 1813, in English in 1815, in Italian in 1817, and in Polish in 1830.† Moreover, in 1804 he had become a close friend and adviser of Mme de Staël, who presented a theory of romantic poetry closely related to his own in *De l'Allemagne*, published both in the original and in English translation in 1813.

A. W. Schlegel's concept of romantic poetry was historical and typological: ancient literature was classical, modern literature (if it was not imitative) was romantic and had a right to be fundamentally different from the classical. Classical literature tended towards the purity of the *genres*, romantic literature towards 'indissoluble mixtures.' Ancient poetry was sculpturesque, devoted to the present

* Four of the lectures were published in Friedrich Schlegel's *Europa* II, 1 (1803): 3–95.
† The Dutch and Polish versions are incomplete.

and to the finite, and limited to a refined sensuality; modern poetry was picturesque, instilled with a sense of the past and the future, more spiritual and more capable of intimations of the infinite. Contemporary poetry presumably ought to be romantic, but both A. W. Schlegel and his brother were convinced that they lived in an *un*romantic age.[7] Admittedly, Friedrich Schlegel had called Tieck's novel *Franz Sternbald* (1798) 'romantic,'[8] while Tieck himself had published two volumes of *Romantische Dichtungen* (1799/1800) and had embodied in his *Kaiser Octavianus* (1804) most of the characteristics demanded by Friedrich Schlegel of romantic poetry; yet in their common view, romantic poetry had flourished above all in the period from Dante to Shakespeare or Calderón, and the contrast they thought of was not primarily that between a 'contemporary' romantic poetry and neoclassicism, but between an 'historical' romantic poetry and either the classical poetry of the ancients that was its equal and opposite or the non-poetry of the Enlightenment.

It was in A. W. Schlegel's historical and typological sense that the concept of 'romantic poetry' spread across Europe; but in every country it reached, the term subsequently had a history of its own, with its own shades of meanings and its own peculiar twists and turns. In England, Coleridge adopted A. W. Schlegel's usage, but there was almost no public debate on the issues that occupied so many minds on the continent. In France, the advocacy of the new ideas was confined for a few years to Mme de Staël and her circle at Coppet, and while she encountered massive opposition from conservatives who upheld the neoclassical canon, the debate had no contemporary French literature to refer to: it took place during the lull between the first emergence of a romantic literature at the beginning of the century (Chateaubriand, Senancour) and the second, more important wave of the movement in the 1820s (Lamartine, Stendhal, Vigny, Hugo). In Italy, the discussion among the critics (1814 *ff.*) was almost immediately followed by the publication of poems and plays in the new style (Pellico, Manzoni).* In Spain, twenty years elapsed between the beginning of the battle among the critics (Böhl von Faber, Mora) and the emergence of a group of important romantic poets (Rivas, Larra, Martínez de la Rosa, etc.). In Germany, as will be remembered, both the critical and the poetic activities had started almost twenty years earlier, before the turn of the century.

Needless to say, these chronological differences – the difference

* In fact, the first of Manzoni's *Inni sacri* had already been written in 1812.

in the times at which the concept of 'romantic' was debated by the critics, the difference in the times at which poems, plays, and novels reflecting the new sensibility were written, and consequently the difference of the extent to which the history of romantic theory and criticism was in step or out of step with the history of creative literature in the various countries – had a considerable bearing on the way in which the concept itself was understood. Also, the intellectual environment in which the discussion of the concept of 'romantic' flourished varied widely from country to country. In England, the pre-eminence of Shakespeare had been a perpetual reminder of the possibility of writing great poetry in defiance of the 'rules.' Neo-classicism had failed to produce a poet indubitably of the first rank, and the evolution of the new sensibility had been so gradual as almost to escape notice:* the English romantic movement was the only one that was hardly conscious of being a movement (and it may perhaps be doubted whether 'movement' is the right term for it). In Germany, the champions of romantic poetry emphatically opposed the piecemeal imitation of classical examples and championed the *mèlange des genres*, but the battle against French neoclassicism and its rules had been won by the previous generation, and the early romanticists owed much of their sense of identity to the common fight against the *Weltanschauung* and the criticism rather than the literature of the Enlightenment. The dichotomy between the romantics and Weimar classicism has been overstated by German scholars,†

* René Wellek (*Concepts of Criticism*, pp. 152–5) quotes Southey, Lord Jeffrey, and T. B. Macaulay saying respectively in 1807, 1816, and 1831 that 'the time which elapsed from the days of Dryden to those of Pope is the dark age of English poetry,' that the 'wits of Queen Anne's time have been gradually brought down from the supremacy which they had enjoyed,' and that the period from 1750 to 1780 was the 'most deplorable part of our literary history.' This corresponds exactly to Friedrich Schlegel's mockery, in 1800, of the so-called 'golden age' of English poetry during the reign of Queen Anne (*Kritische Friedrich-Schlegel-Ausgabe* II: 295); but it is typical that English observations of this type are scarce and that they were made so much later.

† The preferred meter of Schiller's and Goethe's 'classical' plays is blank verse – the meter of the 'romantic' Shakespeare; each of them wrote precisely one full-length play in which the unities are observed; one of Schiller's so-called classical plays has the sub-title 'Eine romantische Tragödie'; Schiller's celebrated quarrel with the Schlegels was largely a personal matter; Goethe's association with A. W. Schlegel was so close at one time that the former asked the latter – the classicist asked the romantic – for help in correcting his hexameters; the anonymously published manifesto of romantic aesthetics, *Herzensergiessungen eines kunstliebenden Klosterbruders* (by Wackenroder and Tieck, 1797) was held by its German readers in Italy to have been written by Goethe, who, in 1806, helped to defend Brentano's and Arnims' anthology, *Des Knaben Wunderhorn*, against its classicistic detractors; the latter, paradoxically, received support from Friedrich Schlegel. Evidently, this list of trivia cannot take the place of

and the second romantic generation in Germany owes much of its sense of cohesion to attacks on them, which were frequently directed against preoccupations (their interest in religious art and poetry, their concern with folksong and chapbooks, their cultivation of Romance verse forms) which they themselves had not considered to be particularly revolutionary. In the Romance countries, however, the neoclassicists still dominated the literary world around 1815.* This may or may not be a reason why drama, which (in spite of such works as Tieck's *Kaiser Oktavianus*, Byron's *Manfred*, or Pushkin's *Boris Godunov*) is of minor importance in English, German, and Russian romanticism, played such a major role in France, Italy, and Spain; it certainly is responsible for the fact that Schiller and Goethe, whose early plays flagrantly defy the rules of the classicistic canon, were regarded as important romantics in the Romance countries, where the continued strength of neoclassicism produced an entirely different alignment of forces. In the Romance countries – and, though this seems less significant, in Russia – the struggle against the unities (Hugo in France, Manzoni in Italy, Monteggia in Spain) was still an issue in the second and third decades of the nineteenth century. Hence, whereas 'romantic' in Germany had to be associated with positive issues, were they Fichteanism, Medievalism, Catholicism, or Primitivism, in order to have a recognizable profile, and whereas the concept failed to achieve critical importance in England, the association of the concept with positive issues in France, Italy, and Spain was rather in the nature of an additional attraction or a further point of departure: in the Romance countries, it could stir excitement enough as a rallying point of the opposition against the *ancien régime* in literature, and anyone siding with the new against the preceding generation was likely to use the word *romantic* for his purposes. When Berchet asserts that romantic poetry is the 'poetry of the living' and classical poetry that of the 'dead,'[9] or when Stendhal claims that '*Le romanticisme* [sic] *est l'art de*

reasoned argument, for which there is no space in the present connection; but it may help to suggest that matters are not as simple as the reader of most German histories of literature is led to believe.

* In the visual arts, there was far greater uniformity. In England, Horace Walpole had begun to prepare the ground for a more tolerant attitude to medieval art as early as 1750, and Goethe had written most enthusiastically about Gothic architecture in 1773, although he then quickly and radically changed his mind; yet at the beginning of the nineteenth century, neoclassicism still dominated the academies of art *throughout* Europe. Hence, the importance of painting and architecture in the writings of the early German romantics. It was in this field, and particularly through their emphasis on medieval religious painting, that they aroused Goethe's anger.

présenter aux peuples les œuvres littéraires qui, dans l'état actuel de leurs habitudes et de leurs croyances, sont susceptibles de leur donner le plus de plaisir possible. Le classicisme, *au contraire, leur présente la littérature qui donnait le plus grand plaisir possible à leurs arrière-grands-pères,*'[10] these formulations are typical of the Romance countries. Hence, romanticism has an open-endedness in these countries that it lacks elsewhere. The association of romanticism with realism that was attempted in France and Italy (Stendhal, Hugo, Vitet, Manzoni, Tommaseo: cf. Vyazemsky in Russia) would make no sense in England or Germany; and the claim that the romantic period extended far into the second half of the nineteenth century is found with particular frequency among students of French and Italian literature.

Such differences – and others could easily be added – lend support to the claim (made with particular eloquence by A. O. Lovejoy) that one should talk in terms of individual romantic movements rather than of a single, pan-European school. Yet surely, wherever the romantic debate was pursued, we find not merely differences (and no one ever maintained that all romanticists, or all romantic movements, were completely alike) but also, and more significantly, common concerns, convictions, and preoccupations.[11] Wherever the notion of a 'romantic poetry' came into vogue, the leading poets of the Middle Ages and the Renaissance were studied more intensively and judged more intelligently. The renewed interest in the old romances had an effect on the literature currently being written. There was a new and productive interest in folklore and folksong (although in Italy this led to little more than translations of some of Bürger's ballads) and, as writers began to turn to their own national heritage rather than to Athens and Rome for inspiration, historical plays and novels came into vogue. Above all, the concept of 'romantic poetry' had from its very beginnings emphasized the role of the marvellous, the imaginative, and the unashamedly fictitious in literature, and the romantic period is marked by an unprecedented faith not merely in the importance of the poetic imagination as the most indispensable quality of the writer, but as a source of vitally important insights not to be obtained through science or philosophy. Indeed, unless some such common core of preoccupations and beliefs had existed, it would hardly be credible that the same terms and slogans should have been pounced upon by so many writers throughout the continent.*

*   René Wellek has argued persuasively that two of the most significant features of the romantic period were the replacement of the 'mechanical philosophy' by an

To repeat, it was the typological and historical concept of 'romantic' as defined by A. W. Schlegel and Mme de Staël that was discussed throughout Europe in the second decade of the nineteenth century. But this concept could never have become a bone of contention if it had merely been asserted, as Warton had done half a century earlier, that writers long dead and gone had composed and had a right to compose in the romantic manner. What was contentious was the view that neoclassicism had been a mistake and that literature should become romantic again. Now, wherever this view was adopted by a group of writers, it was all but inevitable that the word which they used to describe their models should sooner or later be used of the writers themselves. When this happened, the typological and historical concept of 'romantic,' which referred to such poets as Dante, Cervantes, or Shakespeare and their manner of writing, changed into the 'contemporary' concept, which referred to such poets as Brentano, Manzoni, or Hugo.

By and large, the protagonists of the romantic manner themselves were reluctant to use the word in this new sense: one simply does not say 'Dante, Cervantes, Shakespeare, and I' (although Hugo came pretty close to doing so after 1850). Their enemies had no such inhibitions. Of course, nothing was further from their minds than to suggest that the contemporary champions of the romantic manner were nineteenth-century Shakespeares. On the contrary, they exploited the fact that 'romantic' had a long history as a deprecatory epithet; they made use of and delightedly added to the existing linguistic confusion and employed both the adjective and the corresponding nouns as terms of ridicule and abuse. This practice provided the romantics with a further reason for not applying the term to themselves, but the development could not be halted. The awareness of a 'new school' of poets and critics existed, the need for a name

organic view of nature and the emphasis on symbol and myth in literature. While these features do seem central to an understanding of the romantic period, they play only a peripheral role in the history of the *concept*. Perhaps the paradox can be explained by the fact that some of the writers who most emphatically insisted on the organic view of nature and on the importance of symbolism, e.g., the brothers Schlegel, found both features already present and united in classical mythology, and hence regarded them as constituents of all great art rather than as prerogatives of romantic poetry. Even so, there is a strong link between the typological concept of the romantic and that of symbolism. As it was widely held that romantic poetry, to a far greater extent than that of the ancients, was a 'poetry of the infinite' and that the infinite could be represented only symbolically, it would seem to follow that romantic poetry must be symbolic. This connection was suggested, for example, by A. W. Schlegel.

for it was felt, and the only convenient name available was 'roman-tic.' The transition from the typological to the 'contemporary' usage was so gradual that no precise date can be given for its completion, and there are such fine gradations between the two meanings that the editor of the present volume had to give up his original intention of distinguishing between them by the common device of spelling 'romantic' in the 'contemporary' sense with an initial capital. The transition, however, did take place, and unless the distinction be-tween the present usage and that prevalent in the early nineteenth century is kept clearly in mind, the writings of the romantics will inevitably be misinterpreted.*

In Germany, the shift towards the 'contemporary' reference of our word set in relatively early. In the winter of 1807–8, a group of writers of classicistic persuasion applied the adjective *romantisch* and the nouns *Romantik* and *Romantiker* extensively, as terms of abuse and in parodies, to Brentano, Achim von Arnim, and their friends. But it then took at least a quarter of a century for the terms to establish themselves as purely descriptive, non-vituperative designations of the 'new school' and its members, and (if only because most German writers and literary historians between 1830 and 1880 happened to dislike romanticism) a certain derogatory aura remained connected with the term even in scholarly works until about 1880.

In France, Stendhal referred to himself as a romantic in a letter of 14 April 1818 to Baron de Mareste,[12] but the 'contemporary' sense of the word did not catch on until the mid-twenties, when it was used extensively in polemics against the movement. Towards the end of that decade, this usage was adopted to a limited extent by the romantics themselves, for example, by Hugo; but one may generalize none the less that 'the major romantics no more called themselves *romantiques* than the authors of the seventeenth century had called themselves *classiques*.'[13]

In Italy, the enemies of the movement took the initiative with

---

* One example instead of many: in a recent article ('Friedrich Schlegel's Literary Manifesto,' *Acta Germanica* III, 1968; 99–109). Leonard Forster asserts without qualification that 'Romanticism is the first movement in German literature which adopted a name and a label' (p. 106) and proposes that in *Athenäums-Fragment 116* 'we are informed what Romantic poetry is and does – this at a time (1798) when practically no Romantic poetry had been published' (p. 103). Confusing the typological and historical meaning in which Schlegel used the term with the 'contemporary' meaning in which it is used at present, Forster constructs a paradox where none exists. In Schlegel's sense of the word, romantic poetry had been written for centuries when he explained 'what it is and does.'

such works as *La romanticomania, La romanticomachia, La romantea*, and *I romanticisti* before any Italian poet called himself a romantic; but perhaps because the term had come into use so very recently – *romantico* was used of literature before it was used of landscapes! – it was particularly pliable in Italy, and the transition to the 'contemporary' usage seems to have taken place more swiftly than elsewhere. In Spain, however, there was no indigenous romantic literature for twenty years after Böhl von Faber had introduced the term, and the concept of a *romanticismo actual* could not meaningfully arise before the return of the exiled poets in 1834. England, as we know, had one of the earliest romantic movements, but had the movement without the term; and in Denmark – to mention one of the more peripheral literatures – it is not settled even now who does and who does not qualify as a romantic.

Finally – but again at different times in different countries – the romantic movement lost its momentum and our group of words reached the final stage of its chequered career. They ceased to play a vital role in debates on contemporary poetry, drama, and fiction, and found a new home in the universities, in the writings of academic historians of literature. Here, 'romantic' continued to be used occasionally in its typological sense, and, although it must surely be evident by now that the word cannot be defined with any acceptable degree of precision in this sense, it seems impossible to eradicate the typological usage. For the last hundred years or so, however, the predominant use has been that familiar to every student of literature – the use in which it refers to the 'romantic movements' of the first half of the nineteenth century.

The extent to which the history of our cognates is continued forward into its 'academic' stage differs widely from essay to essay in the present work, partly because its editor, unwilling to run the risk of sacrificing quality to neatness and uniformity, deliberately refrained from laying down rigid guidelines, and partly because the divergent patterns of development and the different state of discussion and research in different countries demanded different procedures. The emphasis of the book rests, however, squarely on the period before the word settled down to its present meaning.

But what is this meaning? In one sense, this is an idle question. When we pick up a book on the 'History of the Romantic Movement in England' or read the announcement of a course of lectures on 'German Romanticism' in a university calendar, we know with quite satisfactory accuracy what the book or the lectures will be about (and this simple fact suffices to make certain that our group of words will continue to be used and to serve, quite satisfactorily, a limited practical purpose). Yet, even though in most European countries there is widespread agreement about which writers are held by habit and convention to belong to a given national romantic movement, and in spite of what has been said about a common core of characteristics earlier in this introduction, the fact remains that the questions of how much coherence these national movements have in themselves, how much they have in common with one another, and what precisely it is they have in common, can by no means be considered closed. In fact, even the roll-call of agreed names has its problems; to mention a single example, it augurs ill for the soundness and certainty of our knowledge that French historians of German literature call Schiller a romantic with the same air of inevitability with which German historians refuse to consider him under that heading. Thus, in a very important sense, we still do not know what 'romantic' means. Now it does seem to me that in recent years considerable progress has been made in finding answers to these questions, mainly along lines suggested by René Wellek. But the discussion continues, and, although so much has been and is being written about European romanticism that only a scholar of exceptional devotion and stamina can keep up with it, it is evident that a great deal of research still needs to be done. This situation has prompted the last essay of the present volume, which reports on the most recent attempts at coming to grips with the phenomenon of romanticism and suggests new avenues of exploration.

H. E.

NOTES

1 Inevitably, this summary will repeat information available with fuller details in the body of the present volume and in such essays as René Wellek, 'The Concept of "Romanticism" in Literary History,' *Comparative Literature* I (1949): 1–23, 147–72, reprinted in Wellek, *Concepts of Criticism* (New Haven and London, 1963), pp. 128–98 (hereafter cited as *Concepts*), and François Jost, 'Romantique: la leçon d'un mot,' *Essais de littérature comparée* II (Urbana, 1968): 181–258.
2 See Raymond Immerwahr, 'Reality as an Object of Romantic Experience in Early German Romanticism,' *Colloquia Germanica* II (1969): 134 *ff*. (hereafter cited as 'Reality').
3 See Wellek, *Concepts*, pp. 131 *ff*.
4 Immerwahr, 'Reality,' pp. 133 *ff*.
5 *Kritische Friedrich-Schlegel-Ausgabe*, ed. E. Behler et al., II (Paderborn, 1967): 298 *ff*., 338 (where 'klassisch' seems to be used in the sense of 'exemplary' or 'perfect'), p. 346.

6 Ibid., pp. 334, 335, 348, 351.

7 See, e.g., *Kritische Friedrich-Schlegel-Ausgabe* II: 330, and A. W. Schlegel's description of Calderón as 'the last pinnacle of romantic poetry,' *Europa* I, 2 (1803): 86.

8 *F. Schlegel, Literary Notebooks 1797–1801*, ed. H. Eichner (London and Toronto, 1957), no. 1342. Cf. p. 119 below.

9 Ragusa, p. 312 below.

10 *Racine et Shakespeare*, ed. Georges Eudes (Paris, 1954), p. 27. Cf. Shroder, pp. 282 *f.* below.

11 For what follows, cf. H. H. H. Remak, 'West European Romanticism. Definition and Scope,' *Comparative Literature: Method and Perspective*, ed. N. P. Stallknecht and Horst Frenz (Carbondale, 1961), pp. 223–59, and Wellek, *Concepts.*

12 Wellek, *Concepts*, p. 141.

13 M. Z. Shroder, p. 286 below.

RAYMOND IMMERWAHR

'Romantic' and its Cognates in England, Germany, and France before 1790*

ENGLAND

The Beginnings

The relation of the complex critical concept of the romantic that emerged in Germany in the last few years of the eighteenth century, with all its rich, fluid, and paradoxical connotations, to the simple term that had existed in popular usage for a century and a half has occupied scholarship for some time. It was investigated for Germany four decades ago in a comprehensive monograph by Richard Ullmann and Helene Gotthard[1] after briefer and more general studies by Sigmund von Lempicki[2] and Logan Pearsall Smith.[3] The title of the most recent contribution to this question, 'Was ist eigentlich romantisch?'[4] shows that the problem is still a formidable one. L. P. Smith's essay may well be considered the starting-point for research on the origins of the romantic. It stimulated that of Lempicki as well as Fernand Baldensperger's table of quotations in several languages, which illustrated the immediate contexts of the term in chronological sequence for the first 160 years of its existence.[5]

Although the word *romantic* emerged as a term of cultural history shortly after 1760 and almost simultaneously began to take on connotations for literary criticism as well, it has never become a definable concept. To quote L. P. Smith:

* Research for this paper was begun in 1956 with the aid of a fellowship from the Guggenheim Foundation. The English Goethe Society has kindly given me permission to use some passages from a paper read to it in March 1966, and published in *PEGS* xxxvi (1966): 1–33.

In the first place *romantic* is ... one of those modern words which describe, not so much the objective quality of things, as our response to them, the feelings they arouse in the susceptible spectator. And secondly, if we examine the special subjective feeling described by *romantic*, we see that it is a literary emotion (as indeed the derivation of the word from *romant* implies); it is Nature seen through the medium of literature, through a mist of associations, and sentiments derived from poetry and fiction.[6]

The challenge of this term for research lies, then, in doing justice to the subjective feelings, the 'mist' of literary associations, all the manifold and elusive connotations the term came to acquire, w hile at the same time discussing it meaningfully as a concept of criticism.

Baldensperger's synoptic table discloses that from the beginning the term *romantic* was associated with the expansive effect that romances exerted upon the imagination of their readers: transporting them out of their humdrum everyday experience into exotic settings and distant ages; introducing them to wonderful adventure, extraordinary virtue, and intense passion; affording the boundless freedom of wild nature and primitive society as a release from the regulated monotony of modern urban civilization. One is struck also by the very early emergence of the subjective response noted by Pearsall Smith, and one observes an increasing complexity and diversity in the range of experiences associated with the romantic as well as in the accompanying emotional overtones. These associations prove even more rich and disparate when we turn from the abridged and telescoped quotations of Baldensperger to his sources.

The first instance of our English adjective is found in 1650;[7] this date may therefore be regarded as the inception of the term in modern European languages. 'Romantic' and such other adjectival forms as 'romance,' 'romancicall,' 'romancial,' and 'romancy' that were at first used interchangeably with it all derived from the English noun 'romant' or 'romaunt,' which was in turn borrowed from French.[8] According to Curtius, 'In Old French, *romant, roman* means "courtly romance in verse," literally "popular book." '* And the seventeenth-century English adjectives, as Smith points out,

---

* *Curtius*, p. 32. The development of the Old French nouns *romanz, roman, romant* is traced in somewhat greater detail by Walther von Wartburg in his *Französisches Etymologisches Wörterbuch* x (Basel, 1962): 452 *ff*. They were applied in the twelfth century to texts translated or adapted from Latin. Since these texts were generally narratives, the nouns took on this latter meaning; from the thirteenth century the noun *roman* was increasingly applied to prose narratives.

simply meant 'like the old romances,' and [their appearance] shows that men at this time were becoming aware of certain qualities in these romances for which they needed a name – that they were becoming critical of them, and had begun to view them with a certain detachment. These romances were of two kinds: there were the medieval tales of chivalry and knight-errants, of 'The Palmerins of England and the Amadises of Gaul' ... and there were also those prolix French romances of intrigue and gallantry, which succeeded the earlier tales. The special characteristic of all these romances, for which a name was now needed, was their falseness and unreality, all that was imaginary or impossible in them, all that was contrary to the more rational view of life which was beginning to dominate men's minds.[9]

The literature in question had developed out of the chivalric romances of the high Middle Ages originating in the legends surrounding Roland and the Arthurian Knights, but had come to include some purely fictitious imitations, composed around 1500, of those older romances. The dangers of projecting such literature upon actual life had been foreseen by Dante in the fifth canto of his *Inferno*, where Paolo and Francesca are tempted to the enjoyment of carnal love by reading about Launcelot and Guinivere. But if courtly readers of the thirteenth century might risk the salvation of their souls, seventeenth-century readers were risking their judgment and good sense; in the intervening centuries the printing press had transformed romance into a 'mass medium' available to anyone who had learned to read and could pay a modest price. From the first emergence of the adjective *romantic*, the literature and everything else associated with the word reflected, in consequence, an essentially popular interest, and so it remained, a fact that has been somewhat obscured by the spread of the taste for the romantic to cultivated aristocrats like Horace Walpole and intellectuals like the Wartons and the Schlegels. Most certainly, the term acquired great cultural prestige in the course of the eighteenth century, but it never became severed from its popular roots, nor were these roots forgotten by the thinkers who elevated it to the status of a critical concept.

The instances of 'romantic' in the year 1650, from the subtitle of a tale by Thomas Bayly and from Lower's translation of a French romance, appear to mean nothing more than 'of romance,' analogous to our 'fictitious' or even 'fictional.' But the adjectives *romance* and *Romancial* in 1653 are concerned with behaviour and ideas that are exaggerated and impractical and hence have no place in life or in serious discussion.[10] The next instance of an unquestioned date is found in a work of the Cambridge Platonist, Henry More, *The Immortality of the Soul*: 'As for *Imagination*, there is no question but that Function is mainly exercised in the chief seat of the Soul, those purer Animal Spirits in the fourth Ventricle of the Brain. I speak especially of *that Imagination* which *is most free*, such as we use in *Romantick Inventions*, or such as accompany *the more severe Meditations* and *Disquisitions* in Philosophy ...'[11] Here again the adjective means fictitious, but such invention is considered to be made possible by the freedom of the imagination and is viewed as a constructive activity of the intellect.

As early as the 1660s, the romantic becomes extended from literature to landscape. This phenomenon is attested by a passage from the *Monumenta Britannica* of John Aubrey (1626–97), first published in the nineteenth century but written in 1663:

Our sport [hunting] was very good, and in a romantick country, for the prospects are noble and vast, the downs stockt with numerous flocks of sheep, the turfe rich and fragrant with thyme and burnet, –
  'Fessus ubi incubuit baculo, saxoque resedit
  Pastor arundineo carmine mulcet oves;'
nor are the nut-brown shepherdesses without their graces.[12]

The literary association in this instance is with Latin pastoral rather than medieval romance, but the vastness and rich fertility of a rural landscape have become romantic in their own right. Some twenty years later Aubrey conjectures that 'romancy plaines and boscages' in this same Wiltshire countryside stimulated the literary imagination of Sir Philip Sidney, who 'lived much in these parts,' where he conceived and in part wrote his pastorals. The immediate context attributes an enhancement of pastoral happiness to 'the pleasing meadows, shades, groves, green banks, stately trees, flowing springs, and the wanton windings of a river.'[13]

However, the most sensitive observer of romantic scenes in the seventeenth century is John Evelyn. 'Romantic' occurs in entries of his *Diary* for 1654, but we do not know whether he used the word then or added it when revising the *Diary* in the 1680s.[14] On a visit to Bath he is struck by the 'stupendious' rock of St. Vincent and finds its 'precipice ... equal to any ... I have seen in the most confragose cataracts of the Alpes.' Between them glides the river at 'an extraordinary depth,' and there is 'on the side of this horrid Alp, a very romantic seate.'[15] At Warwick he visits the grotto where a medieval knight did his penance and died. It is 'croun'd yet with venerable Oakes' and overlooks 'a goodly streame.' With some improvement it could be 'render'd one of the most romantique & pleasant places imaginable.'[16] Here an impressive concentration of qualities in the objects viewed and in their spatial and temporal relationship to the viewer have become romantic. His emotions are stirred, now to horror, now to admiration. Potentialities projected in the imagination are even more romantic than what is presently observable.

Unlike Evelyn, most writers of the late seventeenth and early eighteenth centuries deprecated the romantic. Thomas Shadwell, for example, contrasts Ben Jonson's 'perfect Representations of Humane Life' with the 'wilde Romantick Tales' of 'most other Authors,' who 'strain Love and Honour to that Ridiculous height that it becomes Burlesque,'[17] as well as with the 'senseless amorous Idolatry' of their sex which makes female spectators 'love a dull Romantick whining play.'[18] He charges most English dramatists with making 'true History ... Romantick and impossible.'[19] Elsewhere he uses the word *romancy* in the same sense.[20]

The distortion of life by literature is also a theme of Steele's comedies. The sentimental Niece in *The Tender Husband* 'has spent all her solitude in reading romances,' such as *Amadis*, *Palmerin*, Roger Boyle's *Parthenissa*, Sidney's *Arcadia*, and the French romances of d'Urfé, Mlle de Scudéry, and La Calprenède. Consequently 'her head is full of shepherds, knights, flowery meads, groves, and streams,' and she longs to lose herself 'in some pensive grove or to hang over the head of some warbling fountain,' lute in hand. Her suitor cajoles her by praising the 'flowery lawns ... gloomy shades ... embroidered valleys ... and ... transparent stream' of the country.[21]

The deprecatory use of the term *romantic* exemplified by Shadwell and implicit in Steele remained common throughout the entire period covered by this paper and even survives today. In contrast to the constantly developing and expanding connotations of the romantic applied to vistas, what was 'romantic' in ideas and actions remained the folly of allowing life to be influenced by imaginative literature. This latter use of the term will therefore be considered in the remainder of our investigation only occasionally and incidentally, where it happens to occur in writers primarily interested in the romantic vista. The by no means infrequent concurrence of favourable and unfavourable connotations in a single writer, indeed the very impossibility of using the term in a positive sense without some consciousness of its negative implications, ultimately contributed to the development of what was to be called 'romantic irony.' Moreover, the emergence of a programmatic romantic movement may be viewed as a a new synthesis of the two main senses of the term *romantic* in popular usage: the aesthetic qualities found in romantic vistas were incorporated in the critical platform of a movement that categorically affirmed the principle that life and thought in their totality could and should be patterned after imaginative literature.

Nevertheless, even in the late seventeenth century some writers apply the word *romantic* to life and literature more favourably. Quoting the charge of a certain Spaniard that *Don Quixote* had made his countrymen ridicule 'romantic honour and love' and thus undermined the national character, Sir William Temple regrets generally 'the vein of ridiculing all that is serious and good, all honour and virtue, as well as learning and piety'; he calls this tendency 'the itch of our age and climate.'[22] Sir William also calls an imaginary landscape in Homer, the garden of Alcinous on Phaeacia, romantic.[23] But the writer who contributes most to enhancing the prestige of the romantic at this period is Joseph Addison. He calls Milton's account of Thammuz (*Paradise Lost*, I, 446 *ff.*) 'finely romantic,'[24] and of the Mediterranean coast between Marseilles and Genoa, he writes: 'We were ... surprized to see the mountains ... covered with green Olive-trees, or laid out in beautiful Gardens, which gave us a great variety of pleasing prospects ... We were here shown at a distance the Deserts, which have been rendered so famous by the Penance of *Mary Magdalene*, who ... is said to have wept away the rest of her life among those solitary rocks and mountains. It is so Romantic a scene, that it has always probably given occasion to such Chimerical relations.'[25] Along with the elements of solitude and spatial and temporal remoteness from the observer already encountered in Evelyn, we note here the emphasis on variety and contrast and the association of landscape with a legendary account of intense human emotion. In this case, however, the observer suggests that the romantic qualities of the scene may actually have given rise to that legend. This awareness of a reciprocal relationship between literature and landscape, which he explains by their analogous appeal to the imagination, is characteristic of Addison. Fanciful episodes in literature and rich variety and primitive energy in landscape both give rise to 'Pleasures of the Imagination,' the subject of a series of letters Addison contributed to the *Spectator* in 1712. Here the *Iliad* is likened to an uninhabited country entertaining 'the Fancy ... with a thousand savage Prospects of Vast Desarts, wide uncultivated Marshes, huge Forests, misshapen Rocks and Precipices,' the *Aeneid* to a 'well ordered Garden,' Ovid's

Metamorphoses to 'inchanted Ground.'[26] Conversely, the sensations a viewer derives from the shifting scenes of nature resemble the 'pleasing Delusion' of the 'inchanted Hero in a Romance,' whose spell makes him see 'beautiful Castles, Woods, and Meadows' and hear 'the warbling of Birds and the purling of Streams,' but who finds himself back 'on a barren Heath' when the spell is broken.[27] In both literature and landscape Addison favours concentrated richness, variety, and contrast; immense, undetermined, wild, and sublime prospects; change and movement, and above all freedom from restraint.[28] He is therefore one of the earliest champions of both the untamed natural landscape and of informal and asymmetrical gardens.

Addison's contemporary, Shaftesbury, avows similar preferences for 'Things of a *natural* kind; where neither Art, nor the *Conceit* or *Caprice* of Man has spoil'd their *genuine Order*.' He admires 'rude Rocks, the mossy *Caverns*, the irregular unwrought *Grotto's*, and broken *Falls* of Waters, with all the horrid Graces of the Wilderness itself' more than 'the formal Mockery of Princely Gardens.' But he knows that in the eyes of his contemporaries, 'All those who are deep in this Romantick way, are ... out of their Wits or over-run with Melancholy and ENTHUSIASM.'[29]

A third writer of the early eighteenth century who prefers the irregular and primitive in landscape is Elizabeth Singer Rowe. The word *romantick* occurs several times in her *Letters Moral and Entertaining* (first published from 1729 to 1733 as an addition to her *Friendship in Death in Twenty Letters from the Dead to the Living*, 1728). To be sure, her departed souls generally use the term in the traditional sense of the preposterous or imaginary, as when they concede that their descriptions of celestial bliss will appear romantic to persons still on earth.[30] But even in such contexts the romantic may be associated with idyllic and fertile, but varied and changing, landscapes, or, as she once put it, with 'a sort of elegant disorder.'[31] On occasion, however, the correspondents apply the adjective directly to nature: 'I have found a romantick retreat, surrounded with a charming variety of woods, open lawns, and flowery vales, in their uncultivated beauty. Here I rove unattended and free ...'[32] In this passage and elsewhere the author manifests the same taste as Addison for the semblance of wanton irregularity characteristic of the new English style of gardening.[33]

A representative example of the conscious association of romantic landscape with literary tradition is to be found in Edward Wright's *Observations Made in Travelling Through France, Italy, &c. in the Years 1720, 1721, and 1722.*[34] As he journeys from St. Remo to Genoa 'along the Brinks of vast high Mountains, the Path very narrow ... the Precipices steep ... the vast Waves with a grumbling ... which ended with a Ratling like that of the Thunder-Clap,' he thinks 'the Stories I have formerly read much more probable, of the Cataracts of Nile deafening the Neighbouring Inhabitants.' He notes 'the variety of distant Prospects ... the nearer ones often romantick enough, and would have been fine Situations for enchanted Castles,' and is impressed by the mountain covered with olive groves, pine woods, and a profusion of myrtle, juniper, and fragrant herbs.[35] Near Naples he visits the hermitage of Camaldoli, the situation of which 'is the most romantick that can be ... on a very high Hill,' approached by a 'perfect Labyrinth of a Road ... all among Woods of Chestnuts,' and from the corner of a garden he enjoys a varied prospect 'of Sea and Land, Hills and Valleys, antique Ruins, fruitful Vineyards; and pleasant Pastures ...'[36]

How attentively Wright can observe his own subjective impressions and feelings may be seen from his passage on the Grotto of Paurilypo, where Virgil is buried: 'Gloominess yielded matter of Reflection. I felt a kind of Shock and Alternation in my Mind, tho without Fear, caus'd ... by the Novelty and Offensiveness of a thing so uncouth [quam insolitae rei]: – Again, at the first Glimpse of the returning Light a sudden Chearfulness return'd with it ... [The light coming through the top] strikes a sudden bright Spot on the Ground, which amidst the surrounding darkness, serves rather to dazzle than direct. The Passage ... is very romantick and uncommon.'[37]

In contexts of the romantic as rich as those of Wright, it is helpful to classify the impressions according to the qualities attributed to the objects, the perspectives and media through which the latter are observed, the subjective attitudes and moods of the viewer, and his association of the scene with literature, other arts, or historical tradition. We have already encountered these several elements together in Evelyn and in Addison. The pattern emerging from such a classification is to be observed again and again throughout the eighteenth century and well into the nineteenth, although with variations. In Wright's scenes the objects display grandeur and vastness in all dimensions, tremendous power, deafening sounds, labyrinthine curves, set off by pleasing richness, variety, fertility, and spicy fragrance. The remoteness of perspective is extended beyond the range of immediate vision as far as Africa and back in time to the ages when the ruins were built, Virgil lived, or the monastic order was founded. The vision is at one moment obscured by darkness, at the next dazzled by brilliant light. There are associations with the enchanted castles of romance, with accounts of explorers, and with Virgilian poetry. The viewer becomes absorbed in the contemplation of his own emotions: horror alternating with delight, shock with cheerfulness, bewilderment with the enjoyment of novelty.

The Literature of Exploration

Wright's passages belong to the category of travel literature, and one of them reflects the kindred literature of exploration. It is these two closely related categories that made the greatest contribution to the development of connotations of 'romantic' in the course of the eighteenth century. They comprise records of travel to European regions, notably the English Lake Country, Scotland, Ireland, Wales, the Alps, Italy, Spain, and southern France, and to distant continents as well as accounts of exploratory expeditions by sea, especially to the islands of the Pacific. Although most of the works in question were written during the eighteenth century, older works dating as far back as antiquity contributed indirectly.*

Starting with the more distant exploratory expeditions, we may take notice of three Pacific islands that successively captured the imagination of the European reading public in the course of the eighteenth century as embodiments of ideal seclusion, fertility, and primitive but paradisaical beauty. The shipwreck of Alexander Selkirk on Juan Fernandez off the coast of Chile at the beginning of the century not only inspired *Robinson Crusoe* and its unnumbered fictional progeny; it also conditioned subsequent navigators to find a romantic paradise on this island. Visiting it in 1720, the year after this novel's publication, Shelvocke found 'everything ... perfectly romantic' and singled out especially 'a certain savage, irregular beauty,' 'the many prospects of lofty inaccessible hills,' 'the solitariness of the gloomy narrow valleys...and the fall of waters,' all of which were especially to be commended to persons of a melancholy bent.[38] Twenty-one years later, the historian of Admiral Anson's expedition notes this island's 'great number of romantic vallies' which, with their clear streams, cascades, falls, woods, and overhanging rocks, demonstrate that 'the simple productions of

---

* In addition to its importance for the word *romantic*, the literature of travel and exploration was a rich source of symbolism and imagery for writers of the Romantic Age. Novalis, Wackenroder, and Friedrich Schlegel were avid readers of such literature, and it is strongly reflected in such works as Jean Paul's *Hesperus* and Mörike's shadow play, *Der letzte König von Orplid*. Scholarship has so far done justice to this source only in the case of Coleridge.

unassisted nature ... excel all the fictitious descriptions of the most animated imagination.'[39]

Some months later the Anson expedition came upon a new and even more remote island paradise, Tinian. The scurvy-ridden crews were delighted to find there 'a great number of the most elegant and entertaining prospects according to the different blendings of these woods and lawns,' and even the strangely white cattle seemed to 'partake in some measure of the romantic cast of the Island ...' On his final departure from Tinian, the expedition's historian called it 'an Island which, whether we consider the excellence of its productions, the beauty of its appearance, the elegance of its woods and lawns, the healthiness of its air, or the adventures it gave rise to, may in all these views be justly styled romantic.'[40]

When the expedition of Captain Cook saw similar prospects on New Zealand a generation later, one of its chroniclers, the young German, Georg Forster, remarked that such paradisaical descriptions owe something to the imagination and emotions of the navigators observing them: 'The view of rude sceneries in the style of *Rosa*, of antediluvian forests which cloathed the rock, and of numerous rills ... altogether conspired to complete our joy; and so apt is mankind, after a long absence from land, to be prejudiced in favour of the wildest shore, that we looked upon the country at that time, as one of the most beautiful which nature unassisted by art could produce.'[41] Forster and other chroniclers of Cook's voyages helped to eclipse the romantic glamour of Juan Fernandez and Tinian with that of the third island, Tahiti, which has kept its pre-eminence among romantic paradises down to our own time.

Among the explorers whose writings have been made famous by John Livingston Lowes' brilliant inquiry into the workings of Coleridge's creative imagination,[42] there are three who make significant use of the adjective *romantic*: Thomas Maurice and James Rennel, writing on India, and James Bruce, on Africa. Maurice is of interest as an example of the survival of the older derogatory use of the term, in a general sense and without application to landscape, as late as 1790. His *History of Hindostan*[43] vents its wrath upon all those who dared claim that anything in Judaeo-Christian tradition might have been anticipated by Greeks, Babylonians, Indians, or Chinese: their assertions are romantic, that is to say, wild, extravagant, visionary, and absurd.[44] But Maurice is none the less worried that some of his own ideas may seem absurdly romantic to his readers, and well he might be, for he resorts to a hypothesis that traditions of the *Old Testament* together with older 'antediluvian' knowledge he claims for the Hebrews were borrowed by the Phoenicians, projected by them upon the stellar constellations, and transplanted to Greece, the eastern Mediterranean, and India in the form of astronomical myths.[45] Whether on the attack or on the defense, this author characteristically pairs 'romantic' with some other, not quite commensurate, derogatory adjective: 'totally romantic and visionary,' 'romantic and remote,' 'wildest and most romantic,' and so on.

Unlike Maurice, James Bruce in his *Travels to Discover the Source of the Nile* applies the adjective to landscape, but not until he has come within a few thousand feet of the object of his quest (actually the source of the Blue Nile); then the conventional character of the immediate context suggests that the word is inspired not so much by the 'romantic situation' in question, an old church near an 'almost impenetrable wood,' as by the anticipation of the great goal to be reached soon afterwards.[46] Major James Rennell displays a much more poetic and sensitive temperament in his description of Cashmere. He attributes the celebrated 'romantic beauties' of this valley to its fertility, the steep mountains towering above it, and the river that in ancient times forced a passage through the mountains:

... only light showers fall there: these however ... feed some thousands of cascades, which are precipitated into the valley, from every part of the stupendous and romantic bulwark that encircles it. The soil is the richest that can be conceived ... A vast number of streams and rivers ... bring their tribute to the Chelum, ... in which we recognize the Hydaspes of Alexander ... Many small lakes are spread over the surface, and some of them contain floating islands. In a word, the scenery is beautifully picturesque; and a part of the romantic circle of mountains, makes up a portion of every landscape. The pardonable superstition of the sequestered inhabitants, has multiplied the places of worship of Mahadeo, of Beschan and of Brama. All Cashmere is holy land; and miraculous fountains abound.[47]

The most important connotations of the romantic (the word occurs three times in the one passage) are awesome power, miraculous vitality, ideal fertility, seclusion, and religious mystery; temporal perspective is added by the references to Alexander and the geological past. A comparison of this description with other instances of the adjective in the same work throws light upon the difference between its conceptual meaning and its wider connotations. At Rajemal on the Ganges 'the fancy is presented at best with nothing but a wild scene: which can only be relished by being contrasted with soft and beautiful ones.'[48] Wildness of itself may render a scene romantic for Rennell, but to be relished by the imagination wildness must contrast with the soft, the pleasant, the beautiful, or rich fertility.[49]

If luxuriant paradises, reminiscent of Eden and the Hesperides, were especially attractive to persons on hazardous sea expeditions or to those who had to cross deserts and perilous mountain ranges, visitors to scenes on the British Isles or the European Continent were more apt to stress the mysterious, the primitive, and the rugged in association with historical and literary traditions of the Middle Ages or more recent times. The mountains, lakes, and cascades of the Scottish Highlands and the mysterious, fantastic caves of the Hebrides, for example, were all the more romantic to eighteenth-century viewers for their associations with Macbeth or with the savage feuds and intense loyalties that still survived as a living vestige of the Middle Ages. Even the level-headed Dr. Johnson, on visiting the ancestral home of Boswell, had to concede that his imagination was 'excited by the view of an unknown and untravelled wilderness,' and that he was now convinced that 'the fictions of the *Gothick* romances' and of 'romantick chivalry' were credible and based on 'the real manners of the feudal times.'[50] While Johnson was thus impressed by the projection of the past into the present, his companion Boswell enjoyed conversely 'a most romantic' satisfaction in seeing Mr. Johnson 'actually in' Macbeth's Castle and 'walking among the romantic rocks and woods of my ancestors at Auchinlek.'[51]

The ambivalence of Dr. Johnson's attitude toward the romantic generally is reflected in a different kind of context, an excursus in his *Adventurer* on the temptation of readers weary of reality to take refuge in the 'romantic scene' as it is depicted in poetic literature. It is also interesting that by the date of this number, 17 November 1753, Johnson could consider the romantic scene an established poetic cliché comparable to the whispering zephyrs, verdant groves, warbling linnets, and gamboling herds in poetic evocations of spring, which he mentions in the context: 'When night overshadows a romantic scene, all is stillness, silence and quiet; the poets of the grove cease their melody, the moon towers over the world in gentle majesty, men forget their labours and their cares, and every passion and pursuit is for a while suspended. All this we know already, yet we hear it repeated without weariness; because such is generally the life of man, that he is pleased to think on the time when he shall pause from a sense of his condition.'[52] The same yearning for escape from the world of affairs is illustrated in Johnson's case-history, Euryalus, a well-to-do professional man who wearies of 'the drudgery of getting money.' Allowing his 'imagination to be fired by an unextinguishable curiosity,' he set out to enjoy the 'pleasures of travel ... and with all the eagerness of romantic chivalry crossed the sea in search of happiness,' only to die a few days after landing on the Continent.[53] Nevertheless, this is precisely the yearning which Johnson himself satisfied by travelling with Boswell to the Highlands and the Hebrides.

The delighted contemplation of romantic scenes and objects with literary and historical associations around the middle of the eighteenth century was not confined to men. The word occurs repeatedly in the correspondence of the Bluestocking poetess, Elizabeth Carter,[54] in reference to English scenes in association with literature, gardening, or picturesque landscape painting. Writing from Canterbury in 1745, she is distressed because her host 'talks of cutting down a set of trees that form a very pretty romantic gloom.'[55] In rustic isolation for a week, she fancies herself 'in the condition of some unfortunate damsel in a romance, confined to an enchanted palace.' One 'romantic chateau' she visits has a moat and looks 'as if a giant, or at least a score of knights armed cap-a-pié were to sally out over the drawbridge.'[56] At Lambeth in 1764, her 'romantic genius' is gratified at finding herself lodged in a separate tower and having to 'pass every night, under Gothic arches dimly lighted by pale lamps, with all the winds of heaven whistling round me, followed by the echo of my own steps, and the deep hollow sound of the closing doors.'[57] One may readily imagine that she has been reading Walpole's *Castle of Otranto*, the first 'Gothic novel,' which appeared that year.

The passage just quoted concludes with a reference to 'the sublime of the storm on the thirteenth.' From this time on the romantic and the sublime are so intimately associated in Mrs. Carter's letters that the two terms become virtually interchangeable. Commenting on a 'romantic adventure' of her friend Mrs. Vesey, she writes: 'The sublime views of wild uncultivated nature, the silence of a desert, and the melancholy repose of a ruin, strike the imagination with awful and affecting ideas. In such a situation the soul expands itself, and feels at once the greatness of its capacities, and the littleness of its pursuits ...'[58]

At this time some of Mrs. Carter's compatriots were finding wildly romantic and sublime scenes rich with historical and literary associations on the Continent. Visiting the ruins of Henry IV's castle at Pau in the Pyrenees in 1776, the popular historical memoirist Nathaniel William Wraxall delights in contemplating the intense passions and high spirit of this prince, of his mother, Joan of Navarre, and of other great figures of the Huguenot Wars. Henry's castle 'stands on one of the most romantic and singular spots' Wraxall has seen, a ridge of vine-covered hills overlooking the torrent of the Gave. At Vaucluse he observes vivid green meadows secluded from human view by lofty rocks. Through the recesses of one of these the streams run into a silent, unfathomable basin. 'The rocks themselves, which surround and invest this romantic spot, are worn by time and the inclemency of elements into a thousand extraordinary forms, to which fancy attaches shape and figure.' A ruined castle projecting over the water 'completes the wondrous scene ... The peasants call it "Il castello di Petrarca." ' Wraxall sits down here 'to consider the ... romantic assemblage of objects ... on every side.' This author, who regards 'with a mixt sensation of pleasure and of pain, the valley and the fountain which had been witnesses of Petrarch's complaints and hopeless passion,' illustrates other typical subjective elements as well in the pattern of romantic contemplation: the state of pensive revery in which the observer's imagination is free to roam at will; the accompanying emotions of wonder, awe, sympathy, and melancholy. But he is entranced by the contemplation of his own attitudes and moods, the workings of his own creative imagination, even more than by the scene before him. Indeed, he feels his own identity merging with that of Petrarch.[59]

In Search of the Picturesque

There are other accounts of romantic views in the second half of the eighteenth century without specific literary or historical associations. At times it appears as though the word *romantic* has taken on some fairly definite meaning in terms of a quality of landscape: wild and primitive; varied, changing, irregular, and contrasting; or secluded and paradisaical. Again, a single natural feature – rock, stream, waterfall, forest, oak, beech, etc. – may be termed 'romantic,' apparently because it is felt to be characteristic of romantic landscapes. The clue to these phenomena lies in that other analogous word, the *picturesque*, which stands in much the same relation to painting and sketching – truly popular arts in the eighteenth century – as the romantic does to literature. 'Just as *romantic* means Nature seen through a literary medium, so *picturesque* was used to describe scenes that were like pictures, and were seen through the medium of ... painting.'[60]

The close relationships of these two concepts with each other and with concepts of the English school of gardening has been traced in detail by Elizabeth Manwaring.[61] Around the time that the word *romantic* was coined in England, landscapes rich in literary associations and poetic feeling were being painted in Italy by Claude Gelée (known as Lorrain), Nicolas Poussin, Gaspard Dughet (known under the adopted name of 'Gaspard Poussin'), and Salvator Rosa. These four artists drew their inspiration largely from classical mythology and poetry, Biblical tradition, and Christian legend, rather than from romances of chivalry; but more important than any story enacted in their scenes is the poetic experience of landscape itself which their painting communicates. Salvator Rosa became best known for his depiction of the savage and sublime aspects of Alpine and Apennine landscapes: jagged peaks, dark caverns, startling contrasts of light and shade, in which there frequently appear figures of gypsies or brigands. We have already seen Georg Forster associate a scene in New Zealand with Rosa's style of painting. Claude Lorrain bathed his Arcadian landscapes in a dreamy glow. Poussin rediscovered the bliss of the Golden Age in ancient myths and scenes from Virgil.[62] 'Gaspard Poussin' was popular for his depiction of lush, hilly landscapes, grottoes, and waterfalls. The four painters and others who emulated them in oil, aquatint, or engraving enjoyed a tremendous vogue throughout the eighteenth century. The visual impressions of landscape that they projected were another channel affording the imagination release from the everyday world together with moods of yearning, nostalgia, melancholy, awe, and fascinated horror.

The single writer who was most influential in lending cultural prestige to the new currents of taste and criteria of value drawn from both literary romance and landscape painting was Horace Walpole.[63] His revival of what he understood to be Gothic architecture at Strawberry Hill, his incorporation there of gardening in the spirit of picturesque landscape painting, and his *History of Modern Taste in Gardening*;[64] his art collection and his *Anecdotes of Painting* in England; his Gothic novel; his active correspondence on all such subjects with contemporary poets, critics, and connoisseurs – all played a major part in bridging the gap between sophisticated English taste and the lower cultural strata from which the romantic

had sprung. The development of romantic and picturesque inclin-
ations in Walpole's youth is illustrated by a passage from the letters
he wrote to West while on a tour of the Alps in 1739:

From a hamlet among the mountains of Savoy ... Precipices, mountains,
torrents, wolves, rumblings, Salvator Rosa ... Here we are, the lonely
lords of glorious desolate prospects ... Yesterday I was a shepherd of
Dauphiné, today an Alpine savage; tomorrow a Carthusian monk ...

We rode three leagues to see the Grande Chartreuse ... The building
... has nothing remarkable but its primitive simplicity ... But the road,
West, the road! winding round a prodigious mountain, and surrounded
with others, all shagged with hanging woods, obscured with pines or lost
in clouds! Below, a torrent breaking through cliffs, and tumbling
through fragments of rocks! Sheets of cascades forcing their silver speed
down channelled precipices ... Now and then an old footbridge, with a
broken rail, a leaning cross, a cottage, or the ruin of an hermitage! This
sounds too bombast and too romantic to one that has not seen it, too cold
for one that has.[65]

This youthfully exuberant passage shows the imagination stimulated
by savage natural force, primitive forms of society, monastic solitude,
the frailty and mutability of man's creation, and the very rapidity
of changing impressions; the shade and clouds provide liberating
obscurity; with a hint of irony the viewer relishes his own succession
of literary and artistic poses. In the more restrained Walpole of later
years one finds 'sensations of romantic devotion' infused by the
'tombs, painted windows, gloom and perspective' of the 'venerable
and picturesque' creations of Gothic architecture, the 'well-applied
obscurity' of which is more conducive to religious devotion than
the beauties of St. Peter's for the same reason that 'a dark landscape,
savage with rocks and precipices, by Salvator Rosa, may be preferred to a serene sunshine of Claude Lorrain.'[66]

If Walpole could only wish he were a poet, Thomson was really
able to transform the picturesque romantic landscape back into
poetry. Familiar with landscape painting from collections he had
seen in Italy and in the homes of his English patrons, as well as from
his own collection of prints, he sought to make his readers visualize
'Whate'er *Lorrain* light-touch'd with softening Hue,/or savage *Rosa*
dash'd, or learned *Poussin* drew.'[67] He uses the word *romantic* in a
prose passage of 1725 and in several descriptions of landscape in *The
Seasons* and *Liberty*. The contexts include a 'solemn arch of ... em-
bowering trees,' 'moss-grown cascades,' Caledonian and Alpine
mountains, and the fanciful shapes of clouds. They are seen through

the media of 'glimmering shades,' 'sympathetic glooms,' and 'pensive dusk.' The poet views them in such psychological states as pensive contemplation, a 'tender trance,' a 'dream of waking fancy,' 'heart-thrilling meditation,' or 'melancholy.' Thomson's poetic scenes, in turn, are compared with landscape painting by Joseph Warton, who finds them 'frequently as wild and romantic as those of Salvator Rosa, varied with precipices and torrents, and "castled cliffs," and deep vallies, with piny mountains, and the gloomiest caverns.'[68]

Beginning about 1755, the picturesque romantic landscape really comes into its own in descriptions of Ireland and the English Lake Country. The adjective is applied a number of times to the environs of Lake Killarney in Charles Smith's book on *The Antient and Present State of the County of Kerry*.[69] A castle is 'pleasantly and boldly situated in a romantic manner on a high cliff, inaccessible from the sea, commanding ... a bay ... environed with craggy but stupendous mountains.'[70] High and irregular rocks, appearing 'like the prodigious ruin of a great city,' the frequent shifts of the scenery 'affording a pleasant novelty, that strikes the traveller with astonishment, at the rude kind of magnificence' – all of this elicits the comment: 'It is hardly possible, to meet with more romantic prospects anywhere ...'[71] Smith contrasts this agreeably varied landscape, similar to those in Italy depicted by Rosa and the 'Poussins,' with the monotonous regularity of the Netherlands depicted by Paul Bril and Breughel.[72] 'The grandeur, and magnificence of these mountains not only entertain and surprize the spectator, but he must also be agreeably amused, in contemplating the infinite variety of beautiful colouring they afford.'[73] All this natural beauty is enhanced by the 'strange romantic notion' of the common people that they see a carbuncle at the bottom of the lake, as well as by the 'extremely romantic and retired' remains of an 'antient religious house' on Innisfallen.[74]

A single passage saturated with connotations of the romantic was, like Smith's descriptions of Killarney, written in the 1750s about the English Lake country by a Dr. John Brown, but published a decade later. On one side of the Derwentwater, Brown sees a 'rich and beautiful landskip of cultivated fields ... in the most various and picturesque forms,' contrasting with 'rocks and cliffs of stupendous height, hanging broken over the lake in horrible grandeur.' Here, he continues: '... the eagles build their nests; a variety of waterfalls are seen pouring from their summits, and tumbling in vast sheets from rock to rock in rude and terrible magnificence: while on all sides of this immense amphitheatre the lofty mountains rise round, piercing the clouds in shapes ... spiry and fantastic ...' Amid such scenes, 'the eye is lost in agreeable perplexity.' The extent to which Keswick unites the 'three perfections' of 'beauty, horror, and immensity' could only be conveyed by 'the united powers of Claude, Salvator, and Poussin.' Of these, 'The first should throw his delicate sunshine over the cultivated vales, the scattered cots, the groves, the lake, and wooded islands. The second should dash out the horror of the rugged cliffs, the steeps, the hanging woods, and foaming waterfalls; while the grand pencil of Poussin would crown the whole, with the majesty of the impending mountains.' Perpetually changing, the woods, rocks, and mountains are 'now beautifully dreadful, and now ... [assume] new romantic shapes ... insensibly losing themselves in an azure mist.'[75]

Our classification of the elements of romantic experience according to the objective qualities observed, perspective and visual media, moods and psychological states, and associations with literature, popular tradition, and painting will by this time be sufficiently familiar to the reader so that he can apply it himself to the passages we have quoted from Smith and Brown. In doing so he will recognize that by the 1750s the viewing of romantic prospects and their description had become a popular game with its own familiar, if unwritten, rules. But as in other games, each new participant may introduce new plays. One independently introduced by both these writers is the apparent attempt of nature to imitate the human artist by creating a ruined city, pyramids, spiry and fantastic shapes. Dr. Brown is to be credited in addition with the classification of three main kinds of romantic landscape in the respective styles of Claude Lorrain (delicate beauty), Salvator Rosa (savage horror), and Poussin (majestic grandeur).

By the 1770s, however, some aspects of the game were coming to be painstakingly observed, analyzed, and creatively applied in the form of illustration. Some of the examples have been discussed in another paper[76] and may be passed over briefly here. The Reverend William Gilpin toured Great Britain with pencil and brush in hand, sketching and tinting each scene to achieve the maximum picturesque effect. The illustrations with their accompanying descriptions and evaluations were first circulated privately, later published under general titles usually beginning: 'Observations, Relative Chiefly to Picturesque Beauty,' with the region and date of the particular tour added to each. Like many devotees of the picturesque in eighteenth-century England, including his friend

Gray, the poet, Gilpin viewed the prospects from his carriage window through specially tinted 'Claude Lorrain' glasses intended to cast over the scene the soft glow characteristic of that artist. Gilpin is one of the first to feel the need for a differentiation between the romantic and the picturesque. Some prospects along the Severn that would not form an appropriate composition on canvas and hence cannot be called picturesque are nevertheless 'extremely romantic and give a loose to the most pleasing riot of imagination.'[77] Other scenes as well are romantic when the whole is created more by the imagination than by direct vision or when the pictorial is enhanced by literary associations.[78]

A less discriminating and sensitive traveller in search of the romantic was the agronomist Arthur Young. At the time of the French Revolution he became famous for his *Travels in France*, a few lines in which sufficed to inspire the setting and title of Jean Paul Richter's *Kampaner Tal*.[79] But the more exuberant *Tours* in the British Isles, which Young published in the early 1770s, afford more examples of romantic landscape description. In them, the romantic very nearly merges with both the picturesque and the sublime. The same scenes are frequently called both romantic and sublime and are associated with landscape painting, as when one of them elicits the wish that the author 'could unite in one sketch the chearfulness of Zucarelli with the gloomy terrors of Poussin, the glowing brilliancy of Claude with the romantic wildness of Salvator Rosa.'[80] Like Charles Smith and Dr. John Brown, Young is especially interested in those works of nature that resemble the sport of human fancy;[81] like Gilpin, he is aware that some romantic objects 'received a heightening from the fancy, which would be half dissipated by viewing the reality.'[82] His descriptions of the romantic abound in striking contrasts: 'Nor can any thing be more horribly romantic than the adjoining ground where you command this sweet view';[83] 'whimsical, yet frightful forms.'[84] The emotional moods aroused in him by the romantic are most commonly amazement, awe, and horror, but they also include melancholy and sweet enchantment. One might say that the greater part of the territory of the romantic for Young is occupied by the sublime, but it also extends into those areas of enchanted fantasy and sweet delight which were the special heritage of popular romance.

A writer who fuses the romantic with the sublime even more completely than Arthur Young at this period, the late 1770s, is Henry Swinburne. The following scene at Amalfi may serve as an example:

The ... view of the coast [was] sublime; the lofty mountains seemed to rise out of the bosom of the waves, covered with verdure to the very summit, except some rocky pinnacles ... On the boldest and most towering points, convents and churches are placed, and in the deep vales ... are jammed the principal towns ... The shore is rocky and bold, turned in many romantic forms, with dark caves, paths, and buildings hanging in a tremendous manner over the brow; while beneath lies a noble expanse of sea enlivened by crowds of light skiffs skudding across its surface.[85]

Romantic, Sublime, and Picturesque

Although we are concerned here primarily with connotations of the romantic in popular usage, where any precise delineation of this and related aesthetic concepts is impossible, we must devote further attention to the association of the romantic with the picturesque and the sublime. A common feature of the romantic and the sublime is the dual application of each to qualities in the observed object and to the reactions of the observing subject. This is not quite the case with the picturesque; it applies primarily to the object, but to the object as viewed by an observer conditioned by recollections of other scenes in nature and landscape painting. The sublime, for its part, has a much longer history than the other two concepts and has been enriched by long association with philosophy, religion, ethics, and rhetoric. The most important source for such associations was the late antique Greek work, *On the Sublime*, which had become increasingly popular since the Renaissance and was still attributed to Longinus in the eighteenth century; next most important was Burke's book *On the Sublime and Beautiful*.[86] These and later eighteenth-century investigations, both English* and German,† tended to accentuate the difference between the sublime and the beautiful. The scenes in nature generally called sublime were, on the one hand, noble, inspiring, and reminiscent of ancient poetry and mythology or the reflection of these in the paintings of Poussin; on

---

* See Samuel H. Monk, *The Sublime: A Study of Critical Theories in* XVIII-*Century England*, (New York, 1935); Christopher Hussey, *The Picturesque*, (London and New York, 1927); W. J. Hipple, Jr., *The Beautiful, The Sublime, & The Picturesque in Eighteenth Century British Aesthetic Theory* (Carbondale, 1957).

† Notably Kant's *Kritik der Urteilskraft* and Schiller's *Über Anmut und Würde* and *Über das Erhabene*. The application of the sublime and related philosophical concepts to landscape in and prior to German romanticism is the subject of the important study by Helmut Rehder, *Die Philosophie der unendlichen Landschaft* (*Deutsche Vierteljahrsschrift für Literaturwissenschaft und Geistesgeschichte*: Buchreihe, XIX, Halle, 1932).

the other hand, they could be associated with fierce energy, danger, and mystery, inspiring awe or fear. Examples are wild mountain prospects or the scenes of Ossianic poetry. Burke's idea of beauty could best be applied to landscapes like those of Claude Lorrain or of the eighteenth-century Venetian artist, Francesco Zuccarelli.

We have observed the tendency to associate the romantic particularly with the contrast of the sublime and the beautiful: the peaceful, verdant valley surrounded by stupendous crags and mountains; the calm surface of the lake and the waterfall; the rolling wooded hills with a background of bare peaks. But the romantic also was frequently associated with the wild and the savage, the changing and irregular, or the exotic; then the viewer would be reminded of Salvator Rosa or perhaps of 'Gaspard Poussin' (Dughet). The relationships are further complicated by the fluidity of the fourth concept, the picturesque, which tended to attract to itself certain aesthetic qualities *per se*. In general, the last quarter of the century witnessed both an increasing effort at conscious definition and discrimination of the romantic, the sublime, and the picturesque on the part of serious aesthetic thinkers and a tendency to merge them in popular literature. And it was this last tendency that was to prevail at the end of the century in the romantic movement, even with such sophisticated thinkers as Novalis and August Wilhelm Schlegel.

Problems such as these, which had been implicit in landscape description for some decades, were elucidated in the last decade of the century by a group of English writers concerned with the picturesque in both painting and landscape architecture: Humphrey Repton, Sir Uvedale Price, and Richard Payne Knight. Repton was the most influential landscape architect of the period, not only for England, but for Germany and the United States as well. As an amateur landscape painter, he was interested in the applicability of the picturesque to his own profession; it was here that he came into conflict with his good friend Price, who was likewise an amateur of painting and who practised landscape improvement on his own estate. Although the dispute revolved in part around the merits of the landscape gardening techniques of Launcelot 'Capability' Brown (which Repton practised in modified form and Price opposed[87]), its real crux was the meaning of the picturesque and its significance for landscape architecture. Price argued, not merely that this latter art should emulate painting more closely than was the practice of Repton, but that gardens and parks should share with landscape paintings a common objective: the expression of the picturesque as an aesthetic attribute in its own right, distinct on the one hand from the sublime, and on the other from the beautiful. For him, the picturesque was a quality that happened to be historically associated with painting but was not limited to this particular art.[88] This aesthetic quality, which renders objects especially suitable for painting, comprises 'roughness, sudden deviation and irregularity,' as opposed to the 'smoothness, undulation, and symmetry' which constitute beauty.* As Price himself admits, he is adopting Burke's distinction of the beautiful from the sublime and extending it to the differentiation of a third fundamental aesthetic quality, the picturesque: 'In the first place, greatness of dimension is a powerful cause of the sublime ... The picturesque has no connection with dimension of any kind, and is as often found in the smallest as in the largest objects. The sublime, being founded on principles of awe and terror, never descends to anything light or playful; the picturesque, whose characteristics are intricacy and variety, is equally adapted to the grandest and to the gayest scenery.'[89]

But Price is no less careful to distinguish picturesqueness from beauty. In landscape gardening, beauty is associated with 'smoothness, verdure, and gentle undulation,' picturesqueness with 'bold and sudden breaks, and varied tints of soil,' even with 'deformity.'[90] Beauty goes with 'youth, health, and vigour,' the picturesque with 'strongly marked peculiarity of character ... the variety produced by sudden and irregular deviation,' and 'the rich and mellow tints produced by various stages of decay.'[91] Although he is somewhat inconsistent in applying his concepts to landscape gardening, Price tends at times to associate the well-maintained Baroque garden with the sublime; the smooth undulations, oval belts, round clumps, and concealed 'ha-ha' fences of 'Capability' Brown with the beautiful; the Renaissance or Baroque garden in decay or viewed in moonlight with the picturesque.[92] The romantic for Price is usually that bold, wild irregularity characteristic of unimproved nature, but it still carries literary associations, and at one point these become fused with the picturesque. Approaching a fifteenth-century mansion in the moonlight, he experiences a heightened awareness of its 'solemn stillness' and of the religious awe it inspires.'

A few gleams had pierced the deep gloom of the avenue – a large massive tower at the end of it, seen through a long perspective, and half lighted by

* *On the Picturesque*, p. 160. The extent to which Price builds upon ideas of Gilpin is evident from the discussion of Gilpin's theory of the picturesque in Templeman (as in note 77), pp. 134 *ff.*

the uncertain beams of the moon, had a grand mysterious effect. Suddenly a light appeared in this tower – then as suddenly its twinkling vanished – and only the quiet silvery rays of the moon prevailed; again, more lights quickly shifted to different parts of the building, and the whole scene most forcibly brought to my fancy the times of fairies and chivalry. I was much hurt to learn ... that I might take leave of the avenue and its romantic effects, for that a death-warrant was signed.[93]

Price opposes the prevailing tendency to destroy the straight lines and avenues, the symmetry and artfulness, of the Renaissance or Baroque garden to replace them with undulating curves. He recalls nostalgically the Renaissance gardens he has seen at villas near Rome with their balustrades, fountains, statues, their remnants of antiquity, their pines and cypresses:

Those who admire undisguised symmetry ... will be most pleased with such gardens, when kept up according to their original design; ... those ... who may wish for an addition of more varied and picturesque circumstances, will find them in many of those old gardens whenever they have been neglected; for the same causes which give a picturesque character to buildings, give it also to architectural gardens. The first step towards it is the partial concealment of symmetry by the breaks and interruptions that arise from an irregular mixture of vegetation.[94]

Sir Uvedale Price's ideas have been considered here as a kind of expanded footnote to our general argument because they carry to its logical conclusion the tendency, elsewhere arrested, to establish the picturesque as an aesthetic concept in its own right. The elements he attributes to the picturesque – intricacy, variety, and irregularity; symmetry concealed and broken up by decay; the subjective enjoyment of surprise and the contemplation of mutability – comprise an important part of the area which other critics of the late eighteenth century were assigning to the romantic. As Repton was quick to point out, the deliberate neglect or contrived decay advocated by Price was not suitable for houses that were to be lived in or the estate over which they had to be approached.[95] But such principles were ideally applicable to the portrayal of houses and gardens in romantic literature; hence they strikingly anticipate the aesthetic effects of descriptive passages in Tieck and, especially, Eichendorff. It would almost seem as though the latter author had engaged Sir Uvedale Price to design the estate of Venus in *Das Marmorbild*!

A third English writer on aesthetic taste and its application to landscape gardening, Richard Payne Knight, attempted to compose and synthesize the views of Repton and Price, suggesting that additional fundamental aesthetic elements might be added to the beautiful, the sublime, and the picturesque: romantic, classical, sculpturesque, and grotesque. His definition of romantic scenery merits quotation: '... scenery, in which every object is wild, abrupt, and fantastic; – in which endless intricacies discover, at every turn, something new and unexpected; so that we are at once amused and surprised, and curiosity is constantly gratified, but never satiated ... we call *romantic*; not only because it is similar to that usually described in romances, but because it affords the same kind of pleasure ...'[96] Many years earlier, in 1777, Knight had travelled from Italy to Sicily in the company of Goethe's friend Philipp Hackert; Knight's journal of this voyage came into the possession of Goethe, who translated and incorporated it in his biographical sketch of Hackert, which he published in 1811. The term *romantisch* is applied here four times to scenes characterized by wild, luxuriant, and colourful foliage. They carry more literary and historical than pictorial associations, and objective contrast evoking subjective surprise and wonder is especially conspicuous.[97] All of them contain the element of seclusion stressed in Goethe's own much later definition of the romantic scene.[98]

The relationship between the romantic, the sublime, and the picturesque in the last three decades of the eighteenth century may be summed up by saying that the romantic and the picturesque largely overlap with variations chiefly in emphasis and in the relative prominence of associations with literature and the pictorial arts, respectively. There is much greater variation in the explicit or implicit association of the romantic with the sublime. Arthur Young and Henry Swinburne illustrate the maximum fusion of these concepts.[99] For them the romantic is more often than not sublime, and the sublime can always be romantic; even where the two are differentiated, each is heightened by the proximity of the other. Perhaps a more typical relationship between the two elements would be that found in Philip Thicknesse travelling in the Pyrenees[100] or William Coxe in Switzerland;[101] they call much mountain scenery both sublime and romantic, but when they are confronted with the dizzy terraces of Montserrat or the awesome heights and vast glaciers of Furka and Mont Blanc, they can only speak of sublimity. Coxe's descriptions of romantic scenes also allude to the picturesque and the grotesque; they abound in striking contrasts and in such superlatives as 'infinitely,' 'inconceivable,' and 'beyond expression.' In 1770 it is still possible to find a travel journal that consistently discriminates between the two attributes: Patrick Brydone's *Tour through Sicily and Malta*. Brydone calls those scenes romantic that are wildly beautiful, colourful, rich in variety and contrast, and picturesque, that is to say, reminiscent of 'our greatest landscape painters ... the school of Poussin and Salvator Rosa,' also others associated more with the mystery and magic of literary romance or with the illusion of the ancient past coming alive in the present.[102] But as he gazes out from the summit of Mount Aetna, even though he still feels a sense of enchantment, the intensity of his awe precludes the use of the word *romantic*.[103]

The English Garden

We have already touched upon the association of the picturesque landscape with the eighteenth-century English style of informal landscape gardening. Inspired in large measure by landscape painting, it began to assert itself in the second quarter of the century,* and in the 1760s and '70s it spread to the Continent. There has been much investigation of this subject, including an article by the present writer.[104] The informal English garden was important as the first triumphant reaction against the rigidity and symmetry of the late Baroque, exemplified in the creations of Le Nôtre at Versailles.[105] In addition to seventeenth-century painting, the sources of the new gardening style included Milton's descriptions of the Garden of Eden and reports of the irregular but extravagantly fanciful Chinese garden, carried to Europe in the early eighteenth century by French Jesuits, notably Frère Attiret. A passage in Sir William Temple's *Gardens of Epicurus* (1685) was frequently cited – contrary to the author's intention – to exalt the merits of Chinese gardens, and it popularized a name for them that sounds curiously un-Chinese, the *Sharawadgi*.† In this passage, Temple acknowledges the possibility that 'wholly irregular' gardens may excel in beauty by reducing 'many disagreeing parts into some figure, which shall yet, upon the

---

* Batty Langley, *New Principles of Gardening: on the Laying out and Planting Pastures, Groves, Wildernesses, Labyrinths, Avenues, Parks, &c. After a most Grand and Rural Manner* ... 2 vols. in 1 (London, 1728). The principles enunciated by Langley were championed in poetry by Alexander Pope in the Epistle on Riches he addressed to Burlington in 1731.

† A possible Japanese source, *sorowaji* ('not being regular') was suggested by E. V. Gatenby in a letter to *The Times Literary Supplement*, 15 February 1934. S. Lang and N. Pevsner conjecture that Temple may have invented the word himself with some assistance by scholars of Chinese ('Sir William Temple and Sharawaggi,' *The Architectural Review* CVI, July-December 1949: 391 f.).

whole, be very agreeable.' He has seen some examples and heard more 'from others, who have lived among the Chineses [sic]; a people whose way of thinking seems to lie as wide of ours in Europe, as their country does ... Their greatest reach of imagination is employed in contriving figures, where the beauty shall be great ... but without any order or disposition of parts that shall be commonly or easily observed.' Where the Chinese find this sort of beauty, 'they say the *sharawadgi* is fine, or is admirable ...'[106]

The spirit in which the English gentleman set out to 'improve' the landscape endowed his estate by nature is exemplified in a poem, 'The English Garden,' which William Mason, the friend of Walpole and Gray, wrote in the early 1770s:

> Stands he in blank and desolated state,
> Where yawning crags disjointed, sharp, uncouth,
> Involve him with pale horror? In the clefts
> Thy welcome spade shall heap that fost'ring mould
> Whence sapling oaks may spring; whence clust'ring crouds
> Of early underwood shall veil their sides,
> And teach their rugged heads above the shade
> To tower in shapes romantic: Nor, around
> Their flinty roots, shall ivy spare to hang
> Its gadding tendrils, nor the moss-grown turf,
> With wilde thyme sprinkled, there refuse to spread
> Its verdure.[107]

If gardening in general is the creative activity of nature fostered and guided by man, one might say that English gardening would limit the element of human direction, liberating nature wherever possible and creating the illusion of unguided and unlimited nature where necessary. But the kind of scene the eighteenth-century garden criticism calls romantic is found most often in wild, undirected nature. If the human landscape architect is to create an illusion of the romantic, he must operate both with unusual resources and with the greatest degree of subtlety and self-restraint. Often his task is simply to clear obstructions to romantic scenes already created by nature. Nevertheless, some garden critics, such as Joseph Heely, admit the possibility of an illusion of the romantic occurring where nature appears to imitate a human creation, as in our passages quoted from Charles Smith and Dr. John Brown, or when the gardener creates an idyllic scene reminiscent of Arcadian pastorals or enchanted sites in romance. The critical viewer may then consciously relish the artistic creation, much as was to be the case with the Schlegels admiring the work of Shakespeare, Cervantes, or Goethe. In his praise of romantic scenes in famous eighteenth-century English gardens, Heely stresses the principles of novelty, variety, irregularity, wild disorder, confusion, grotesqueness, the contrast of nature and art, of multiplicity with unity.[108]

Heely's emphasis on both unguided nature and artistically created illusion reflects an underlying dichotomy in English garden theory, a dichotomy reflected in the French term *le goût anglo-chinois*. On the one hand, there was the predominant stylized naturalism exemplified in the work of William Kent and Batty Langley in the first half of the century,* 'Capability' Brown in the middle, and Humphrey Repton at the end, as well as in the influential writing and practice of Walpole. But the third quarter of the century witnessed the rise of a minority movement favouring the imaginative and the exotic. This movement accentuated one important tendency of English gardening, its attempt to stimulate the viewer's imagination and elicit a variety of emotional moods through suitable arrangements of views, plantings, and emblematic structures. The champion of the new exotic movement was Sir William Chambers, royal architect under George ii and iii and designer of Kew Gardens. In two treatises on Chinese garden design,[109] he describes romantic gardens that could never occur in nature but remind us rather of enchanted scenes in Ariosto, Tasso, and the *Arabian Nights*. He claims that the Chinese classify 'three different species of scenes ... pleasing, horrid, and enchanted,' the last of which corresponds 'in a great measure, to what we call romantic.' These incorporate elaborate acoustic effects, 'extraordinary trees, plants, and flowers,' and 'monstrous birds and animals.' Sudden contrasts of luxuriant scenes confronting the viewer who has just passed 'through dark caverns and gloomy passages,' devices to stimulate curiosity and reward it with surprise, and the concealment of some elements of the scenes all aim at affording 'room for the imagination to work.'[110] Especially radical devices are attributed to Chinese gardeners in the later treatise: 'Their surprizing, or supernatural scenes, are of the romantic kind and abound in the marvellous.' The spectator is led 'to subterraneous vaults ... where lamps, which yield a faint and glimmering light, discover the pale images of antient kings and heroes ... flutes, and soft melodious

---

* Kent (1685-1748) was considered by Walpole and others to be 'the father of modern gardening.' He was the most influential landscape architect of his time but, unlike Langley (see note p. 41 above), he did not contribute to the literature on the subject.

organs, impelled by subterraneous waters, interrupt ... the silence ... and fill the air with solemn sacred melody.'[111] Chambers thus takes us far beyond the mere picturesque to a realm of enchanted romance, well on the way to Xanadu. Whether or not Chambers influenced Coleridge,* such exoticism was to become increasingly associated with the romantic in popular literature, although it could obviously contribute little to practical gardening.†

If Chambers in a sense anticipates Coleridge, the exponents of the more prevalent stylized naturalism in English gardening may be said to anticipate Wordsworth. One of these was Thomas Whately, author of *Observations on Modern Gardening*.[112] In seemingly diametrical opposition to the Chinese gardener-magician of Chambers, Whately insists that the arrangement of trees, for example, be 'absolutely free from all appearance of art.' He would avoid straight or even regularly curved lines, for 'regularity always suggest a suspicion of artifice; and artifice detected, no longer deceives.'[113] But when it comes to the romantic landscape created by nature, as in the wildly rockly Vale of Matlock,[114] the aesthetic effects with which Whately is concerned are not so far from those of Chambers after all: 'Nature proceeds ... beyond the utmost verge to which art can follow; and in scenes licentiously wild, not content with contrast, forces even contradictions to unite.' Her 'caprice does not stop' with 'grotesque discordant shapes ... confusedly tumbled together ... To mix with such shapes a form perfectly regular is still more extravagant; and yet the effect is sometimes so wonderful, that we cannot wish the extravagance corrected.'[115] From this description and those of other natural scenes, such as Dovedale, it becomes evident that the wild irregularity that may of itself suffice to constitute the romantic is heightened by chance resemblances to human creation and embodiments of the ideas of romance. In designing Dovedale, nature has worked 'absolutely free of restraint,' has employed fanciful wildness, paradoxical contrast, 'inexhaustible variety,' and 'infinite' change. She mystifies the imagination with grotesque forms, quick transitions, contrasts of gloom and radiance or roaring and gurgling, and manifestations of incredible power–all apparently to afford 'endless entertainment' to the human imagination and the pleasurable sensations of awe, mystery, and terror.[116] But human activity may enhance the romantic effects of nature. At New Weir on the Wye the rhythmic power of a forge vies with the untamed

* He is not mentioned in John Livingston Lowes, *The Road to Xanadu*.
† Chambers himself introduced nothing more exotic than a pagoda in Kew Gardens.

destructive force of the cascade; frail bridges and boats challenge natural perils. The imagination, already aroused by the primitive power of nature, gains further stimulus from the courage of the weak humans who have been defying this power from time immemorial. The human landscape architect can contribute to the effect of such romantic scenes in nature by adding reminders of human habitation that are not 'too mild for the ruggedness of the place,' developing 'a little inclination towards melancholy' or throwing 'just a tinge of gloom upon the scene.'*

The Limits of Eighteenth-Century Romantic Experience

Some of the tendencies we have observed in the criticism of landscape gardening continue in descriptions of romantic scenes in other contexts in the last two decades of the century: the comparison of natural configurations with the works of man, for example, and the delight in rich luxuriance with suggestions of the erotic. Literary associations are extended from chivalric romance and the fairy tale over more recent popular literature: the poems of Ossian (generally accepted, to be sure, as the relic of an age antedating medieval chivalry); the new category of Gothic romance; Rousseau's *Nouvelle Héloïse*; Goethe's *Werther*, to name a few. As an example we may take a letter written by Hannah More to Mr. Pepys in 1784. She tells of the 'gloriously idle life' she has enjoyed 'rambling about the romantic hills and delicious vallies of Somersetshire ... full of enchanting scenery.' She prefers to '*live* amongst' such 'gentle scenes,' which are 'rather interesting than magnificent':

... of this *I* am convinced, by a ride ... through the lofty cliffs of Cheddar so stupendously romantic that the shade of Ossian or the ghost of Taliessen himself might range, not undelighted, through them: my imagination was delighted, was confounded, was oppressed, and darted a thousand years back into the days of chivalry and enchantment, at seeing hang over my head, vast ledges of rock exactly resembling mouldered castles and

---

* *Observations on Modern Gardening*, p. 110. Here and elsewhere Whately develops the emblematic tradition common to English landscape architecture. Natural features and artificial improvements or structures were exploited to stimulate the imagination and emotions of the viewer in particular directions. Whately, however, distinguishes stereotyped garden emblems and the proper use of what he calls 'character,' impressions spontaneously suggested by the scene. They should be 'not sought for, not laboured; and have the force of a metaphor, free from the detail of an allegory.' Ibid., pp. 150 f. On the genealogy of the emblematic tradition, see Liselotte Dieckmann, *The Hieroglyph, History of a Symbol* (St. Louis: Washington University Press, 1970).

ruined abbeys. I had a delightful confusion of broken images in my head, without one distinct idea; but the delight was of so serious a nature that I could scarcely refrain from crying, especially when we sat down upon a fragment of rock, and heard one of Gray's odes ... sung with infinite feeling. I would have given the world to have heard my favourite Ode to Melancholy by Beaumont and Fletcher ... But these pensive pleasures should be repeated at long intervals; they ... infuse into the spirit a sentiment compounded of sadness and delight, which, though it may qualify one to write odes, yet indisposes one for a much more indispensable thing, the enjoyment of the intercourse of ordinary society.[117]

Hannah More is here giving explicit utterance to something implicit – because taken for granted – among other cultured people indulging the romantic imagination through travel, reading, sketching, and gardening at this period: the experience of the romantic was an intensely pleasurable pastime, but it had to be subordinated to really essential activities like 'the intercourse of ordinary society.' A dozen years later, when a Novalis could dream of recasting society in the mould of romantic imagination, the romantic movement would be underway.

Even in the 1780s we encounter one brilliant mind devoting nearly all its resources and energies to such indulgence. But the person in question, William Beckford, was disqualified by an abnormal emotional constitution from the intercourse of ordinary society and had the financial means to escape from the sober realm of English Enlightenment to the exotic and sensuous environment of Portugal or to the seclusion of his own Gothic abbey. Beckford is also the first English author of literary stature in whom erotic love becomes romantic. Prior to his time romantic love had been largely associated with literary romance and the age of chivalry or with the notion of impractical young people that love might actually be a path to marriage. In the English version of Beckford's Gothic novel, *Vathek* (1786), we find the adjective *romantic* applied, conventionally enough, to some cabins on the shore of a lake, but it is the scene where two lovers have just been magically revived from death. Nouronihar and Gulchenrouz are contemplating a gloomy penitential existence which must chastise for a time their 'indolent and voluptuous life.' The lake, with 'flames reflected from its glassy surface, the pale hues of its banks, the romantic cabins, the bulrushes that sadly waved their drooping heads, the storks' with their 'melancholy cries,' is a kind of purgatory,[118] associated by its imagery with the shores of the Island of Purgatory in Dante.

Beckford's *Journal in Portugal and Spain* (1787–8) shows the erotic imagination stimulated by romantic objects of both sexes. A 'lovely girl with eyes full of youthful gaiety and a turn of shape remarkably graceful' is seen 'as in a dream ... My imagination, lighted up by this romantic apparition, inspired me to play and sing ...'[119] Again and again lushly romantic and picturesque landscape imagery is combined with erotic revery, as in the following description of a Portuguese convent:

The building is irregular and picturesque, rising from a craggy eminence and backed by a thick wood ... A fountain playing in the middle and sprinkling a profusion of gillyflowers gave an oriental air to this little court ... Bindweed and dwarf aloes almost prevented my getting across it ... The trees, though bent by the winds into very grotesque shapes, still retain a luxuriance of foliage very seldom to be met with in the neighbourhood of Lisbon. Thanks to monkish laziness, the underwood remains unclipped and intrudes wherever it pleases upon the alleys, which hang over the sea in a bold romantic manner ... The waves ... broke softly on the shore. How I should enjoy stretching myself on its sands by moonlight and owning all my frailties and wild imagination to some love-sick languid youth reclined by my side and thrown by the dubious light and undecided murmurs into a soft delirium.[120]

Imagery appealing to all the senses, indefinite sounds and half-lights, the 'soft delirium' or erotic longings experienced near an 'irregular and picturesque' building amid grotesquely shaped trees – much of this recurs in other contexts of 'romantic' in this journal, sometimes with explicit literary associations and to the accompaniment of music. A few snatches may convey something of the abundance and variety of romantic associations at Beckford's disposal:

... a young romantic girl warbling to herself in the deepest recess of a forest ... I was thrown into a languor ... I am to meet her ... in the wild shrubberies ... and we shall sing like skylarks ... She may ... languish away at these soft sounds at the foot of a branching citron, half lost among tufts of fern. I think I see ... the old hairy *Conservador* in the shape of a satyr rousing her from her concealment and coursing her over the soft hills.[121]

The entertainment ... must have been highly romantic and magnificent. The villa and its flowery ornamented gardens is wrapped up in a wild forest of timber trees and boundless shrubberies of orange and myrtle. Choirs of musicians were stationed in the thickets, and glittering illuminated pavilions appeared emerging like fairy edifices from the gloom of impervious foliage.[122]

We were both in a romantic mood peculiarly calculated to enjoy the melancholy scenery of this ruined garden. The sun was just sinking ... and the thick shrubbery of myrtle looked black and dismal in the twilight The whole atmosphere was perfumed with the subtle odour of the jasmine. I gave way to enervating languid sensations, and found myself imperceptibly declaiming some of the most tender and passionate recitatives in my beloved opera *Quinto Fabio*.[123]

... a small square terrace overhung by a fantastic cork tree, which commands the most romantic point of view in Sintra: vast sweeps of varied foliage, banks with twisted roots ... and citrons clustered with fruits. Above ... tower three shattered pinnacles of rock, the middle one diversified by the turrets and walls of ... a Convent of Hieronymites frequently concealed in clouds ... I could hardly hold my head up when we arrived at the fair, which is held on a pleasant green lawn, bounded on the one side by picturesque buildings of [this] ancient convent ... and on the other by rocky hills shattered into a variety of uncouth romantic forms.[124]

The next to last passage is preceded by the outcry: 'When shall I cease acting the part of the Wandering Jew and being stared and wondered at as if I bore the mark of God's malediction on my countenance.' Prepared to flee anywhere before his countrymen, even to abjure his religion, Beckford knows that he will everywhere feel himself a stranger and an exile. But the role of the Wandering Jew is not simply forced upon him by other Englishmen; as in the case of Byron a generation later, it is a pose inflicted by his own Anglican conscience.[125]

Romantic as a Concept of Cultural History

But Beckford's case was exceptional. For the romantic to be transformed from a mere avocation to a cultural ideal, something more was required than experience of the romantic landscape. The original source of this experience, the imaginative literature of the late Middle Ages and the cultural ground of that literature, had to be re-evaluated, to acquire a new status and prestige. The re-evaluation of the imaginative qualities of romance and of the romantic cultural age, the Middle Ages and the Renaissance, was finally consummated in Germany in the last two decades of the eighteenth century. It had begun, however, some thirty years earlier in

England. There the process took place so gradually that even by the early nineteenth century it never quite occurred either to Coleridge or Keats or to their adversaries that it was their mission to revive the cultural values of a past romantic age.* Along with the progressive cultural rehabilitation of the Middle Ages and the Elizabethan period, the word *romantic* itself gradually took on more positive cultural and literary connotations, but the persons using it did not realize the extent to which they were making it a concept of cultural history. We have had a glimpse of this process in Dr. Johnson. Although he experienced the romantic primarily as a vista, what he viewed was not simply the landscape of the Highlands and the Hebrides but the age of feudalism and romantic chivalry surviving into his own time with cultural and ethical merits that he was forced to recognize.

Like Dr. Johnson, his younger contemporary, Bishop Richard Hurd, took an essentially negative attitude toward those elements of Gothic romance which had been revived in the poetry of the Renaissance, but he was keenly aware of the attractions which they held for poetic genius: 'The greatest geniuses of our own and foreign countries, such as Ariosto and Tasso in Italy, and Spenser and Milton in England, were ... charmed by the Gothic Romances. Was this caprice and absurdity in them? Or, may there not be something in the Gothic Romance peculiarly suited to the views of a genius, and to the ends of poetry?'[126] The 'romantic ideas of justice,' 'passion for adventures,' and 'eagerness to run to the succour of the distressed' typical of Gothic romance, Hurd explains sociologically as needs of a chaotic, continuously warring feudal world. On finding adventure in the aid of their own feudal lords, the knights undertook the more widely ranging quests of knight errantry, that 'wandering the word over in search of occasions on which to exercise their generous and disinterested valour,' which 'may truly be called *romantic*.'[127] When the social conditions justifying such practices disappeared, people were 'led ... to think and speak of them, as romantic, and unnatural.'[128] But such behaviour again became attractive to poets of the Renaissance and to rulers like Queen Elizabeth. 'This romantic spirit of the Queen may be seen as well in her *amours*, as military achievements.' The 'weak and romantic sense' characteristic of woman made her feel flattered at being

---

* See René Wellek, *Concepts of Criticism* (New Haven and London, 1963), pp. 147 *ff*. As noted by Wellek, the English romantics, as we now call them, were first termed romanticists or members of a romantic school in two critical works appearing in 1849 and 1852. Cf. Whalley, pp. 246 *ff*. below.

the object of a duel or having the spectacle of a 'Triumph' enacted in her honour by noblemen and poets like Sir Philip Sidney.[129] This 'romantic Spirit of the age ... brought into fresh credit, by the romantic Elizabeth,' encouraged Spenser to write the *Faerie Queene*. At this period, 'when reason was but dawning,' the revived 'Spirit of Chivalry made a shift to support itself for a time,' but the 'growing splendour' of the Enlightenment 'in the end, put ... to flight' these 'portentous spectres of the imagination.'[130]

Hurd's own attitude in these passages is ambivalent. The immediate intent of the word *romantic* is derogatory, and Hurd seems to exult in the ultimate triumph of rationalism in his own time, but he is aware that from the poetic standpoint the romance revived by Ariosto, Tasso, Sidney, Spenser, and Milton was superior to the plausibly realistic literature of the eighteenth century. Hurd was not prepared, like Friedrich Schlegel forty years later, to advocate a return to the spirit of Renaissance romance, but neither could he conceal his regret of the price paid for the triumph of reason.[131]

Just a year after Hurd's *Letters on Chivalry and Romance* were published, the romantic spirit was revived again by Macpherson's great forgery of the melancholy and nobly sentimental laments of Ossian. As Hugh Blair wrote in his *Critical Dissertation on the Poems of Ossian* (1763), this poetry is characterized by 'tenderness and sublimity ... [and] moves perpetually in the high region of the grand and the pathetic ... The scenery throughout, wild and romantic. The extended heath by the sea-shore; the mountain shaded with mist; the torrent rushing through a solitary valley; the scattered oaks, and the tombs of warriors overgrown with moss; all produce a solemn attention in the mind ... His poetry ... deserves to be styled, the *Poetry of the Heart* ... a heart that glows and kindles the fancy ...'* Blair especially praises the 'still pathetic, and the romantic scenery of several of the night adventures' in the Ossianic poem *Temora*.[132] And he notes that the ideal of chivalry is as strongly manifest in the Ossianic poems as among the Troubadors, 'whose songs ... first gave rise to those romantic ideas of heroism, which for so long a time enchanted Europe. Ossian's heroes have all the gallantry and generosity of those fabulous knights, without their extravagance; and his love scenes have native tenderness, without any mixture of

---

* In *Poems of Ossian*, tr. J. Macpherson (London, 1796), II: 291 f. The *Dissertation* was written for the first edition. The last phrase quoted might be compared with Friedrich Schlegel's formulations of the romantic, in his 'Gespräch über die Poesie' and numerous notebook entries, as a combination of sentiment and imagination (*Fantasie*).

those forced and unnatural conceits which abound in the old romances.'[133]

The critical publications of Thomas Warton began earlier than those of Blair and Hurd and continued longer, more widely influencing subsequent English and Continental thought. In his critical attitude toward the romantic in literary and cultural history Warton resembles Hurd more than Blair, for he shares the former's underlying ambivalence and transmitted it to other historians of culture, notably Herder. Both in the *Observations on the Faerie Queene of Spenser* (1754) and in the dissertation published two decades later, *Of the Origin of Romantic Fiction in Europe*, 'romantic' means extravagantly imaginative and is intended to be derogatory. At times this intention gets across clearly enough, as at the outset of the *Observations*: 'When ... every species of literature at last emerged from the depths of Gothic ignorance and barbarity; it might have been expected, that, instead of the romantic manner of poetical composition introduced and established by the Provençal bards, a new and more legitimate taste of writing would have succeeded...'[134] But elsewhere the charm in the sequence of improbable or miraculous events presented by romance is recognized: 'It is no less amusing to the imagination to bewilder itself in various conjectures, concerning the expedients by which these promised events were brought about, and to indulge the disquisitions of fancy, about the many romantic miracles that must have been effected by this wonderful steed ...'[135] Several times the romantic is explicitly or implicitly associated with the sublime. Thus, Chaucer 'abounds ... in strokes of ... pathos, and sublimity, not unworthy a more refined age. His ... romantic arguments ... transport us into some fairy region, and are all highly pleasing to the imagination.'[136] Indeed, it appears that sublimity itself lies in that boundless stimulus to the imagination which it shares with the romantic: 'If the poet had limited the depth of this cave to a very great, but to a certain number of fathoms, the fancy could still have supposed and added more; but, as no determinate measure is assigned, our imagination is left at liberty to ... add fathom to fathom, and depth to depth, till it is lost in its own attempt to grasp the idea of that which is unbounded or infinite ... From a *Concealment* of this kind arises the sublime ...'[137] Warton especially justifies his 'many references ... to Romances' by the sublime images which they evoke in the imagination: '... so magnificently marvellous are their fictions and fablings, that they contribute ... to rouse and invigorate all the powers of imagination: to store the fancy with those sublime and alarming images, which true poetry best delights to display.'[138] This amounts to saying that romantic poetry,* for all its incompatibility with the ideals of the Enlightenment, is to be valued as an image of a significant cultural epoch and for that effect of the sublime on the imagination which is characteristic of all true poetry.

At one point in the *Observations*, Warton alludes to the origin of romantic fiction in the Orient;[139] this Asiatic origin of romantic imagination is the special concern of his dissertation *Of the Origin of Romantic Fiction in Europe*, which he prefixed to his *History of English Poetry* in 1774. By going out of his way to ascribe an oriental source to the romantic, Warton lends to the literature of the European Middle Ages something parallel to that exoticism with which Chambers, Beckford, and even Whately were investing the romantic landscape. Research of the two centuries between his time and ours makes his argument sound quaint to us, and it can only be briefly summarized here. He believed that the 'extravagant inventions ... peculiar to [the] romantic and creative genius' of the Orient reached Europe by two principal routes: one by way of the Iberian Peninsula, France, Brittany, Wales, and Cornwall; and another with the Gothic migration from Georgia to Northern Europe. Of these, the Gothic transmission is the older; the Iberian route twice served as a channel for the imaginative creation of the Arabs. They first inspired the extravagant fictions of Arthurian romance at the beginning of the twelfth century, and a little later the cycle of romances revolving around Charlemagne and Roland.[140]

To the Gothic migration – in a direction opposite to that we ascribe to it today – Warton credits all the wealth of imagination in Norse, Icelandic, and Saxon British poetry. But he uses the word 'Goth' loosely of all the Germanic nations. Their 'Georgian' imagination inspired the poetry of Scandinavia, which, owing to a late conversion to Christianity, enjoyed 'an uninterrupted possession through many ages of the most romantic religious superstitions.' For the 'true religion' would have 'suppressed their wild exertions of fancy, and banished that striking train of imagery, which their poetry derived from a barbarous theology.[141] But the Goths also imparted their sublime oriental imagery to the ancient British poetry of Ossian and the Welsh poetry of Taliessin. The chronological gap between the Georgian Gothic wave and those of the Arabians by

* Although Warton does not himself use the term *romantic poetry*, he does at one point call Spenser 'a ROMANTIC Poet' (Warton, II: 88). On Warton's use elsewhere of 'classical' and 'romantic' together, see Wellek, *Concepts of Criticism*, p. 132.

way of Armorica accounts for a marked difference between the poetry of the older bards like Taliessin and Ossian and the later poetry revolving around Roland and Arthur. So beautiful a 'romantic fiction' as that of the transporting of wounded King Arthur to the 'land of Faery or spirits' to be healed and return at some future day could not be found in the compositions of the most 'ancient Welsh bards,' but only 'after the native vein of British fabling had been tinctured by these fairy tales, which ... the Welsh had received from their connection with [Armorica] ...'[142] But on the other hand: 'There is an air of barbaric horror in the incantations of the scaldic fablers,' a 'sublime solemnity ... awfully' displayed in their 'necromantic machinery,' by comparison to which the 'visions of pleasure and delight' conjured up by the later 'magicians of romance,' the 'flowery forests' through which they lead us and the 'palaces glittering with gold and precious stones' which they raise up often appear 'but mere tricks.'[143]

Although these writings contain many passages which could be taken as expressing Warton's unabashed preference for the age of Georgian-Gothic and Arabian-Armorican legend, he is after all an exponent of that true Christian religion – eighteenth-century enlightened style – which was so inimical to poetic imagination. The ambivalence of Warton's attitude was pointed out in the particular area of art and architecture by his contemporary, Reynolds, who accused him of only pretending to recant his preference for the Gothic style over the contemporary neo-classical.[144] But this ambivalence, far from being confined to Warton, could be pointed out in most writers of the eighteenth century fascinated by the imaginative release of the romantic, whether derived from the natural landscape, painting, gardens, literature, or cultural history. We have observed it already in the young Walpole, Elizabeth Singer Rowe, Thomas Maurice, Hurd, and Heely, among others. It is part of that 'romantic irony' which was not invented by Friedrich Schlegel in the 1790s, but was implicit from the start in the use of a derogatory term for an experience that was at once absurd and delightful, perilous and irresistible, an experience that was being objectified in an aesthetic quality depending on contrast and incongruity.

GERMANY

The development of the concept and word *romantisch* in Germany has been traced in the monograph of Richard Ullmann and Helene

Gotthard[145] from the first occurrence of the word until the 1820s. Although the present study is indebted to their investigation, the approach is quite different. For the most part, the German investigators did not organize their material by individual authors but by categories of usage at various historical periods. Because of the vast amount of materials they attempt to cover and the inherent difficulty in distinguishing such categories, their monograph encounters formidable organizational problems.[146] They distinguish an early 'invasion' of the romantic from England around 1700, introducing the concept in the sense 'untrue' (like the novel), and a second one, via the English sentimental novel, introducing two additional senses: an aesthetic sense associated with the wildness and primitive energy of the natural landscape and a psychological sense of the eccentric and exaggerated (*überspannt*).[147] To this it must be objected that the psychological meaning simply embraces certain aspects of the concept 'untrue' and that the association of the romantic with qualities of the natural landscape derived from English sources other than the sentimental novel. Samplings undertaken for the present study have shown that the sentimental novelists either make little use of the word at all (Sterne and Fanny Burney) or they use it almost exclusively to denote attitudes of persons whose good sense has been warped by the reading of romances and novels (Richardson).* The English influences associating the romantic with aesthetic qualities of landscape came from the literature of exploration and travel, from tours of sketchers and persons visiting collections of landscape paintings, as well as from the theory and criticism of landscape gardening. Except for a few personal diaries and letters, the majority of the writings discussed above were

---

* The one instance this investigator has found in *Tristram Shandy* (end of Chapter Five, vol. VII) means exciting, adventurous, and heroic and has nothing to do with the landscape. Typical instances from a Richardson novel, *Clarissa Harlowe*, are: 'the pretty romantic flight you have delighted in,' 'a romantic young creature,' 'a romantic girl,' 'a romantic contrivance of your wild-headed foolish brother,' 'a warm and romantic turn,' 'a little sprinkling of the romantic and contradictory,' 'romantic notions,' 'romantic friendship.' Once in this novel, when Richardson mentions the 'romanticness of the place' (of Clarissa's uncle, Antony), landscape connotations are probably included, but the author fails to develop them. Fanny Burney (Madame D'Arblay) brings out the role of the imagination in creating romantic associations more clearly when she writes of 'the fantastic regions of Romance, where Fiction is coloured by all the gay tints of luxurious imagination' or says 'their lively and romantic imaginations paint it to them as a paradise' (*Evelina*), but for romantic connotations of the landscape as such one must turn to her *Diary and Letters* (e.g. IV: 306 f., London, 1905), which were not available until after the period with which Ullmann and Gotthard are concerned.

published and promptly translated into German.* The one-sided emphasis on fiction, poetic literature, and literary criticism in the monograph of Ullmann and Gotthard results also in the neglect of some German writers interested in the romantic qualities of the natural landscape and of princely parks in the informal English gardening style, such as Johann Georg Zimmermann, Georg Forster, and C. C. L. Hirschfeld.

The first wave of English influence took place via Zurich, where the theologian, Gotthard Heidegger, in a work published in 1698[148] attacks the 'vain Romantic entertainments' of the erotically coloured fantastic romances for their lies and their corrupting effect on morals.[149] For the next half century Switzerland remains the focal area for our adjective, as indeed for German literary life generally, whereas the second English invasion in the 1760s and 70s takes place via northern Germany. In 1734 another Swiss author uses *romantisch* in a somewhat different derogatory sense, unhistorical.[150] For Bodmer and Breitinger around 1740 it means 'as in romances,' but the tone is more neutral, occasionally even favourable, for they recognize the legitimacy of the fantastic and improbable in romance.[151]

The first major German writer to make frequent use of the adjective *romantisch* was Wieland. During and for about six years after his early pietistic period he uses the then prevalent *romanhaft*; *romantisch* appears fairly frequently in the 1760s and increasingly thereafter. Without ever abandoning the older word or clearly differentiating the two, Wieland used both with conscious reference to literary romance and with the wider connotation of a rich stimulus to the imagination. He made an unparalleled contribution to the popularization of *romantisch* both through his own published works and through his journal, *Der Teutsche Merkur*, published from 1773, where the word occurs in articles, reviews, and extensive excerpts from a great variety of German and foreign authors. The contributors included Herder, Schiller, Goethe, Friedrich Jabobi, Heinse, and, later on, the romanticists and their adversaries.† Its excerpts from travel literature (e.g., from Georg

---

* E.g., the writings of Edward Wright, Admiral Anson, Arthur Young, William Gilpin, William Coxe, Patrick Brydone, Philip Thicknesse, James Rennell, Thomas Whately, Joseph Heely, and Sir William Chambers. For the titles and dates of German translations, see Mary Bell Price and Lawrence M. Price, *The Publication of English Humaniora in Germany in the Eighteenth Century* (Berkeley and Los Angeles, 1955).

† After 1790 it was published as *Der Neue Teutsche Merkur* and edited by Karl August Böttiger, a disciple of Wieland. Under both Wieland and Böttiger the journal afforded examples of the term *romantisch* in all kinds of contexts.

Forster's *Reise um die Welt* in 1778, III) afford examples of the romantic in the natural landscape, whereas Wieland's own landscapes are always scenes of romance or gardens contrived to resemble them. Wieland's role in establishing the idea of a romantic Middle Ages as an epoch with characteristic ethical and cultural values and a unique 'romantic epic' expression of them was comparable to that of Herder.[152] By creating new 'romantic poems' himself (as in *Idris und Zenide*, which had the sub-title *ein romantisches Gedicht**), he also established this special concept and was thus an important precursor of Friedrich Schlegel and Novalis.

The remarkable thing about Wieland's influence on that word *romantisch* is that he helped to strengthen the very tendencies that he was consciously opposing as he used it. Basically, the romantic for Wieland is what it was in England in the third quarter of the seventeenth century: an exalted view of life nurtured by the uncritical reading of popular fiction and the consequent acceptance of literary imagination as real. This realm of imagination he associated with enthusiasm (*Schwärmerei*), the impractical, idealistic, and sentimental view of life that had to be surmounted for the attainment of true maturity, as Wieland himself had done when he rejected pietism in the late 1750s.[153] In particular, Wieland's literary creations warn repeatedly against the notion that sentiment and idealism can triumph over the erotic impulses of human nature. It was of course this hedonistic denial that idealistic aspiration can or should triumph over the senses that made Wieland the object of such intense hostility by the German romanticists, notably Tieck and A. W. Schlegel. But that triumph of sober judgment and temperate hedonism over romantic enthusiasm for which Wieland strove was not fully achieved even in his mature creative writings.†

Moreover, Wieland's lasting interest in the themes and characters of late medieval popular romance, in the more sophisticated, semi-satiric verse romances of the Italian Renaissance, and in *Don*

---

*   This sub-title was added to the edition of 1784; the sub-title *romantisches Heldengedicht* was posthumously added to *Oberon* by the publisher Göschen in 1820, but Wieland applied this phrase to it in a review of a younger poet's romance in 1797, *Neuer Teutscher Merkur* (1797) III: 232 *ff*. *Der Teutsche Merkur* repeatedly applies such phrases to medieval and renaissance narrative poetry. See *Ullmann and Gotthard*, pp. 97 *ff*.

†   An example is the novel *Agathon*. Despite successive revisions, Wieland was unable to resolve the fundamental problems of its content and form. Disillusioned of his youthful idealism, the hero nonetheless remains dissatisfied with the hedonism of Aristippos and Hippias; the ultimate outcome of his development remains a question, and the novel itself a fragment. Cf. Sengle, *Wieland*, pp. 196 *ff*.

Quixote,* as well as his own continued use of chivalric and fantastic romance as a vehicle for satire, attest to an insurmountable fascination with the domains of poetic imagination inhabited by the Arthurian knights, by Amadis, by the fairy king Oberon, and by Don Quixote.† The invocation in the first two verses of *Oberon* might well be taken as the theme of Wieland's whole vast creation in the realm of poetic romance:

Noch einmal sattelt mir den Hippogryphen, ihr Musen,
Zum Ritt ins alte romantische Land!‡

His preface to the first edition of *Der neue Amadis* (1771) explains the choice of this name for poem and hero by the fact that it has an indefinable 'romantic sound' particularly appropriate for an adventure of such a special cast:

Caprice ... has also inspired the name, and it would hardly be possible to give any other reason why this poem might not be called the *New Esplandian* or the *New Florismarte* than because the name *Amadis* is better known and has some indefinable romantic sound.

Die Laune ... *hat ihm auch den Namen geschöpft, und es könnte schwerlich ein andrer Grund angegeben werden, warum dieses Gedicht nicht der* Neue Esplandian *oder der* Neue Florismarte *genannt worden, als weil der Name* Amadis *bekannter ist, und ich weiß nicht was für einen romantischen Klang hat* ...[154]

The comic muse evoked in the first strophe herself proceeds to apply the adjective to a grove in a princely park at Biberach where the song will be heard by the nymphs in the moonlight and momentarily arouse a drunken faun from his slumbers.[155]

The didactic aim of most of Wieland's writings is exemplified in the title of the original edition of one of his early prose satires: *Der Sieg der Natur über die Schwärmerei oder die Abenteuer des Don Sylvio de Rosalva* (1764).[156] By 'nature', Wieland means sensual impulse guided by calm judgment. The titular hero has allowed his good sense to be corrupted by romances of fairies just as that of Don Quixote was corrupted by chivalric romances. In the first volume the older *romanhaft* is associated with this theme, in the second

---

*   Sengle (p. 323) calls Wieland 'der deutsche Cervantes und Ariost.'
†   Half hidden in the playful mockery and serene hedonism of *Oberon* is a longing for an inward, divine ideal which, as Sengle (pp. 368, 370) points out, anticipates the ideals of German romanticism.
‡   Logan Pearsall Smith (p. 84) misinterpreted this phrase as a reference to romantic landscape. This and other egregious distortions in his hasty sketch of the romantic in German literary history are pointed out by *Ullmann and Gotthard*, footnote, pp. 13 *f.*

volume, *romantisch*. But in both instances the derogatory intention is accompanied by the author's recognition of the pleasure of such romantic imaginings.[157] What is directly termed *romantisch* in volume two is a garden, which has been contrived to resemble an enchanted scene of romance by means of an indiscriminate mixture of the whole repertory of baroque and rococo garden emblems. The hero, who by this time is being cured of his folly, recognizes that the scene of enchantment is really the deliberate creation of a poetically inspired imagination, which has skilfully combined varied elements of natural and artistic beauty into a pleasing whole:

He had become ... more deeply lost in the passages of the labyrinth. Its size and the variety of walks, arbors, little pleasure groves, cascades, Greek temples, pagodas, statues, and a hundred other things that gave it a romantic appearance made it the most pleasurable place in the world.

Er hatte sich ... in den Alleen des Labyrinths vertieft, welches wegen seiner Größe und der Mannigfaltigkeit der Gänge, Sommerlauben, kleinen Lustwäldchen, Cascaden, griechischen Tempeln, Pagoden, Bildsäulen und hundert Dingen, die geschickt waren, ihm ein romantisches Ansehen zu geben, den angenehmsten Ort von der Welt ausmachte.[158]

These contexts of the romantic in *Don Sylvio* exemplify a pattern which is rather frequently the context of the term in Wieland's literary creation: A sentimentally idealized conception of love (on the part of the male!) is confronted with the seductive sensual charms of the female, usually in an exotic and seemingly enchanted garden paradise; the male succumbs and the cure of his false idealism is either begun or consummated. In this situation the term *romantisch* may be applied to the idealistic male, to the hedonistic female (woman, nymph, or goddess), or to the garden which she contrives as the setting for her triumph. It is applied to the male, for example, in the little prose satire of Mexican primitivism entitled *Koxkox und Kikequetzel*.[159] In the comic verse narrative *Aurora und Cephalus*, it is used of the setting: a hall of mother-of-pearl adorned with rubies and covered with bowers of jasmine, where the goddess reclines like Titian's Venus on a bed of moss amid garlands of flowers; similarly in a stage direction of the lyric drama *Die Wahl des Herkules*.[160]

The most lushly exotic passage of this kind occurs in an excerpt of the philosophical novel *Peregrinus Proteus* first published in *Der Teutsche Merkur* in 1789. It is part of a dialogue between Peregrinus and Lucian in Elysium that serves as a frame for the whole work.

Here the word *romantisch* occurs four times in as many pages. Peregrinus recounts the experience he had in a temple of Venus Urania, where a statue of the goddess on whom he had been rapturously gazing suddenly came alive and embraced him. She was in reality a wealthy Roman widow who had conceived the 'unique romantic plan' of using her wealth to enjoy the erotic delights which the temple and surrounding gardens could attract for her. To give her pleasures 'a certain ideal of perfection,' she had transformed her villa 'into a veritable enchanted palace' filled with little boys and young girls culled from all the provinces of the Empire. Her 'imagination was attuned to ... a romantic enjoyment of life.' By the lavish resources at her disposal, Peregrinus was kept for some time 'in continual intoxication and delusion.' He was led 'through ... gleaming marble halls and rooms, richly and lavishly filled with everything ... conceived for the most voluptuous imagination and spoiled senses.' Finally, after slumbering a few hours, he awakened late in the afternoon to seek his goddess in a romantic setting, a narrow valley surrounded by rocks covered with shrubbery. Peregrinus had paid virtually no heed to any of this romantic beauty, because he finally caught sight of this goddess again, bathing in a grotto like Artemis surprised by Actaeon, her naked beauty lit up by the rays of the late afternoon sun.[161]

The theme of the sentimental idealist seduced by a sensual woman is, of course, not confined to those passages in Wieland which contain the work *romantisch*. Conversely, the word also occurs in other contexts, as in *Agathon*, where it does not apply directly to the seduction of the hero by Danae but to the sentimental and idealistic love of modern Europe – 'this romantic passion, this love which has been raised to a virtue by a whole series of novelists in Spain, Italy, France, and England.' In this passage – a relatively early instance of the concept 'romantic love' in German – modern sentimentality is contrasted with the 'beautiful and laughing imagination' of the Greeks that 'gave birth to the goddess of love, the Graces, and so many other gods of joy':

von dieser romantischen Leidenschaft, von dieser Liebe, welche von einer ganzen Folge von Romanschreibern in Spanien, Welschland, Frankreich und England zu einer Heldentugend *erhoben worden ist ... Von einer so abgeschmackten ... Liebe wußte diese geistreiche Nation nichts, aus deren schöner und lachender Einbildungskraft die Göttin der Liebe, die Grazien, und so viele andre Götter der Freude hervorgegangen waren.*[162]

As we have observed in *Peregrinus Proteus*, Wieland tends to associate the romantic more directly and explicitly with imagination than most other authors of his time, and the connotations are not always unfavourable. A story of medieval chess from a French romance in a collection published by La Curne de Sainte Palaye – the pieces are life-sized and magically animated, and any knight who loses two games out of three to the lady owning the set is led off to prison – elicits Wieland's comment that such a chess game 'would make no mean figure in a romantic poem.'[163] The adjective *romantic* is twice associated with the imagination in the *Briefe an einen Freund über J. J. Rousseau* in connection with Rousseau's accusing a servant girl of a theft he had committed himself: the story, already embellished by the 'romantic ... imagination' of Rousseau, is further enhanced by associations with 'twenty poetic and romantic Marianes' in the imagination of the friend to whom these letters are addressed.[164]

Wieland's predilection for the romance of chivalry has already been cited as an instance of an ambivalent attitude toward the romantic. In the case of *Oberon*, satire largely gives way to a poetic apotheosis, not merely of the ideals of chivalry but of the fantastic supernatural that had been parodied in *Don Sylvio*. Nor is the ambivalence confined to the poetic qualities which the romantic takes on in medieval and renaissance literature. We find it even where Wieland attacks romantic idealism and mysticism *per se*. Sengle points this out in *Peregrinus Proteus*: the titular hero is actually never cured of his *Schwärmerei* and the author has to concede that there is a legitimate place in life for such enthusiasts.* Ambivalence towards the belief in spiritual apparitions and magic associated with the neo-Platonic and theosophic traditions from antiquity through the Middle Ages to modern times is evident in an article on spiritualistic phenomena that Wieland wrote for *Der Teutsche Merkur* in 1781.[165] 'This romantic way of philosophizing,' Wieland maintains, satisfied a natural craving for the sublime, the marvelous, and for mysteries accessible only to a select few, to whom the prospect of natural powers heightened 'to the point of participation in the divine nature' is held out:

Diese romantische Art zu philosophieren, die zu gleicher Zeit der natürlichen Trägheit der Menschen, und ihrer Begierde nach erhabnen und wunderbaren Ideen schmeichelt, konnte nicht fehlen sich in eine desto größere Achtung zu setzen: da sie sich ... in ein heiliges Dunkel verbarg, in welches nicht einem jeden einzudringen

---

* Sengle (pp. 481 *ff*.) says that Wieland had Lavater in mind here.

erlaubt war ... Die Magische Philosophie *... versprach ... die größte Veredlung der Menschheit, Erhöhung ihrer natürlichen Kräfte bis zur Gemeinschaft mit der göttlichen Natur.*[166]

Even while denying the truth of the alleged supernatural events, the philosopher 'feels himself imperceptibly overcome by his own imagination.' The 'instinctive inclination to the marvelous' common to all men makes him want to be convinced of what he knows is unreal:

Ja, sogar der Philosoph, indem er die Wahrheit der Begebenheiten ... leugnet, fühlt sich unvermerkt von seiner eignen Phantasie überschlichen; und ist oft selten [sic!] von seinen Vernunftschlüssen überzeugt genug, daß nicht die instinktmäßige Neigung zum Wunderbaren, die er ... mit den Ungelehrtesten gemein hat, den leisen Wunsch, des Gegenteils durch unleugbare Tatsachen überführt zu werden, in ihm erregen sollte.[167]

Two other German authors who helped familiarize the notion of a romantically attractive medieval literature and culture were Gerstenberg and Herder.[168] In his *Briefe über die Merkwürdigkeiten der Litteratur* (1766), Gerstenberg transmitted and evaluated the views of Warton's *Observations on the Faerie Queene*. Whereas Warton was torn between his polemics against the romantic and his half-conscious fascination by it, Gerstenberg comes out unequivocally for the romantic poetry of Spenser, Ariosto, and Tasso as different in kind but equal in merit to the 'classical' beauties of Homer.[169] Although he scarcely introduced any new connotations of the terms, Gerstenberg placed the antithesis between the romantic and the classical in even sharper focus than Warton. Moreover, he was the first writer to uphold the romantic style and imagination of Ariosto as of equal merit of Homer and Virgil.[170] He also stresses two concepts associated with the romantic which were later to be especially developed by the Schlegels: the picturesque (*malerisch*) and Warton's 'various,'[171] rendered *mannigfaltig* by Gerstenberg. For his own part, he attributes the quality *romantisch* equally to Ariosto and to Homer, in the sense of the fictitiously imaginative.[172] The Twenty-Second Letter of the series describes a visit to

the happy places which were once the scene of so many immortal adventures ... which the hero of Mancha performed for the benefit of the queens and damsels and for the destructions of the magicians and giants of his time there.

Es war mir ... kein geringes Vergnügen ... auch die glückseligen Örter zu besehen, welche einst die Scene so vieler unsterblichen Abenteuer waren ... die der Held von Mancha zum besten der Königinnen und Fräuleins, und zum Verderben der Zauberer und Riesen seiner Zeit daselbst ausgeführt hat.[173]

Spain seems uniquely suited to be the scene of these exploits, for 'it has a singular variety of romantic regions,' and its very liabilities for agriculture and the economy 'give a much freer field to the imagination than the better institutions of any other European country':

... es hat eine sonderbare Verschiedenheit romantischer Gegenden, und die Fehler selbst, die dem Anbau und der Bevölkerung so nachteilig sind, verschaffen der Phantasie ein viel freieres Feld, als die bessern Einrichtungen irgend eines andern Reichs von Europa.[174]

Like Wieland and Gerstenberg, Herder starts using *romantisch* in the 1760s, although *romanhaft* continues to recur with similar connotations, once even *romanzisch*. Herder shares with Wieland an ambivalent attitude towards the romantic elements in medieval literature and culture (including in the Middle Ages what we now call the Renaissance),* but it is not expressed ironically. Because it was precisely the literary expression of medieval culture and ideals in prose and verse romances and folk literature that attracted him the most unequivocally, the medieval values which he associates with *romantisch* are more consistently favourable than those of *gotisch*, even though the latter term occurs much more frequently and is more crucial in his writings. If Herder could not, like Wieland, create new poetic embodiments of chivalric romance, he was, on the other hand, more accessible to the romantic experience of the natural landscape. The Gothic is not the only concept closely associated with the romantic in Herder's thought and sometimes overlapping it: the sublime (*erhaben*)[175] tends to carry richer associations, to evoke, so to speak, more pronounced emotional vibrations; the adventurous (*abenteuerlich*)[176] has more restricted connotations.

---

*   Cf. *Ullmann and Gotthard*, pp. 83 *ff.*, 91 *ff.* W. D. Robson-Scott, 'The Legend of Herder's Medievalism,' *PEGS* n.s. xxxiii (1963): 99–129, goes too far in limiting Herder's affirmation of medieval culture to the early 1770s, the period of *Auch eine Philosophie der Geschichte der Menschheit*, and reducing it there to a tactical maneuver in critical polemics. It may be granted that Herder's later writings attest the general superiority of his own age to the 'Gothic' Middle Ages, at all events in Germany. But precisely in the contexts of *romantisch*, Herder's lasting fascination with the poetic and aesthetic qualities of the age of chivalry is beyond dispute. As in the case of Wieland, one must distinguish between soberly considered value judgments and spontaneous aesthetic reactions. We have observed the same ambivalence in Hurd and Thomas Warton, who profoundly influenced Herder's view of the romantic Middle Ages. It is part of the irony inherent in the eighteenth century's experience of the romantic.

From his first use of *romantisch*,[177] Herder associates it not merely with medieval cultural and ethical values generally, but more especially with the influence of Arabic and Persian cultures and with southern Europe, by which – following Thomas Warton – he thinks this influence was transmitted. He soon applies the term also to the Welsh and Normans, who jointly introduced Arthurian romance into Europe. Herder frequently attributes to the romantic a certain 'sweetness,'* implicitly associated with love in chivalric romance and explicitly in the 'true, pure, tender, and romantic' love of such Shakespearean couples as Romeo and Juliet; it contrasts with the 'marital, unromantic love' that Shakespeare avoided: '*Ist diese Liebe nicht wahr, rein, zärtlich und Romantisch genug? Aber doch keine "eheliche, Unromantische Liebe?"*' [178] But the romantic is also associated with the religious piety manifested in pilgrimages, Crusades, and personal combat. The *Ideen zur Philosophie der Geschichte der Menschheit* accounts for the Normans' role in developing originally Welsh Arthurian romance by their 'romantic spirit of invention.' The Arthurian legends had a 'wonderful influence on human imagination,' which, however, had been exercising its creative capacities on saints' legends, tales, myths, and *fabliaux* since antiquity. The 'romantic character' of the Normans is also evident in their love of adventure, heroic legends, chivalric exploits, and in their 'Nordic' reverence for women, all qualities that coincided with the influence of the 'more refined chivalry of the Arabs' to produce romance:

Als ihr romantischer Charakter, ihre Liebe zu Abenteuern, Heldensagen und Ritterübungen, ihre nordische Hochachtung gegen die Frauen, mit dem feineren Rittertum der Araber zusammentraf, so gewann solches damit für Europa Ausbreitung und Haltung ... Das Denkwürdigste, was uns von den Kymren übrig geblieben und wodurch wunderbar auf die Einbildungskraft der Menschen gewirkt worden, ist ihr König Artus mit seinen Rittern der runden Tafel. [179]

Like Warton, Herder stresses the importance of Spain, an 'isolated romantic land of enthusiasm [*Schwärmerei*],'[180] as a channel of oriental influence.

Herder's attraction to the Orient is evident in several references to the Persians as a pre-eminently romantic people, more so than Arabs, Tartars, Mongols, or even Indians. The Persians are especially romantic for the richness of their imagination. The 'most fabulous' kind of poetry, the fairy tale, developed under an 'Oriental sky' among a people whose imagination was 'attuned to the exaggerated, the incomprehensible, lofty, and marvelous,' so

---

*   E.g., in references to the Rosamunda ballad in 1767, in *Suphan* II: 186.

that 'the commonplace [was] raised to strangeness, the unknown to the extraordinary.' 'The most pleasant creations of Oriental imagination seem to be of Persian origin. The happy loquacity of the Persians and their love of splendor [also] gave ... a peculiar romantic heroic form to their old legends ...':

Vorzüglich bildete sich unter dem morgenländischem Himmel der fabelhafteste Teil der Dichtkunst aus, das Märchen ... *Wenn die Einbildung des Volks, das [eine alte Stammessage] erzählet, fürs Uebertriebene, Unbegreifliche, Hohe und Wunderbare gestimmt ist, so wird auch das Gemeine zur Seltenheit, das Unbekannte zum Außerordentlichen erhoben ... wie in der Tat die angenehmsten Dichtungen der orientalischen Phantasie persischen Ursprunges zu sein scheinen. Die fröhliche Geschwätzigkeit und Prachtliebe der Perser gaben ihren alten Sagen ... eine eigne romantische Heldenform ...*[181]

But Herder finds popular literary tradition to be a rich source of romantic imagination in Europe as well. Indeed, 'a streak of romantic thinking runs across Europe.'* This is what gave rise to the Arthurian and Carolingian cycles of chivalric romance, and it is manifest in the boldness of language and vividness of imagery common to these poetic creations and to the shorter love ballads with their 'romantic trees, landscapes, plants ... wild song birds,' and so on, all of which 'gives the song a wild grace and romantic sweetness ...' '*Die Liebesromanze hat gewisse Naturbilder, eine Reihe Romantischer Bäume, Gegenden, Gewächse, eine Anzahl singender wilder Vögel ... Das alles aber gibt dem Liede eine wilde Anmut und Romantische Süßigkeit ...*'[182] These qualities are rooted in the sensuous imagination of the common people, which 'dreams because it does not know, believes because it does not see and operates with the whole, undivided, uncultivated soul':

Auch die gemeinen Volkssagen, Märchen und Mythologie gehören hieher. Sie sind gewissermaßen Resultat des Volksglaubens, seiner sinnlichen Anschauung ... wo man träumt, weil man nicht weiß, glaubt, weil man nicht siehet und mit der ganzen, unzerteilten und ungebildeten Seele würket ...[183]

This 'romantic streak' is to be found in German mythologies, folk legends, and folk songs as well, but unfortunately Germany lacked the Spenser or Shakespeare to develop its full artistic potential.

If, in such passages, Herder associates the romantic primarily

---

*   The identical sentence, 'Der Strich von Romantischer Denkart läuft über Europa: aber wie nun über Deutschland besonders,' is found with insignificant variants in two places: *Alte Volkslieder, Zweiter Teil,* and *Von Ähnlichkeit der mittlern englischen und deutschen Dichtkunst,* both published in 1774; see *Suphan* IX: 524, and XXV: 65.

with the wildness, sweetness, richness, and freshness of folk imagination, there are others in which he approximates it to the mystery, obscurity, and wonder of the sublime. In a simile he once alludes to the 'greater romantic form in which the setting sun, surrounded by the haze of the horizon, appears': '*Wie die Sonne im Niedergange von den Dünsten des Horizonts umringt, eine größere, romantische Gestalt hat: so hats die Staatskunst Griechenlandes in diesem Zeitpunkt ...*'[184] And it is as an obscure and vast but tremendously rich Gothic structure that he views the 'romantic adventure' of medieval civilization in *Auch eine Philosophie der Geschichte der Menschheit*.[185] Another passage in the same work compares Herder's own effort to survey the vast reaches of the Middle Ages with a fly examining a corner of a landscape painting in a vast darkened gallery.[186] This period of Herder's most positive appraisal of the Middle Ages is also that of his most intense personal experience of the romantic landscape; for it is the time when his imagination and emotions are warmed by the love of Caroline Flachsland, whom he is courting. In one letter of 1772 the countryside near Bückeburg becomes a symbol of Germany's historical past and of the German national character: 'the most beautiful, boldest, most German most romantic region of the world. The very field where Hermann fought and Varus was beaten; even now a dreadful, bold romantic valley, surrounded by strange mountains':

Ich bin jetzt ... in der schönsten, kühnsten, Deutschesten, Romantischten [sic!] *Gegend von der Welt. Eben das Feld, wo Hermann focht, und Varus geschlagen ward, noch jetzt ein fürchterliches kühnes Romantisches Tal, mit sonderbaren Gebürgen umgeben ...*[187]

The most vibrant reaction to romantic landscape in this correspondence is Herder's account of a moonlight ride to Lemgo in October 1771, a time when he was tormented by pain, melancholy, and worry over Caroline's health. The 'landscape full of hills and valley and wood and meadows' takes on 'a romantic charm of which we usually dream as only in Elysium.' Each time he comes over the crest of a hill or emerges from the forest to see the 'broad, radiant valley ... melting in the half-light,' he feels himself 'in a new world.' Then, when 'speechless and lost in dreams' he sees the first glow of dawn, the whole world becomes 'a silent, solemn, gentle temple of God':

Der Schmerz ... zusammt der schmelzenden Sorge für Sie ... gab im Mondenschein den schönsten Gegenden, voll Höhen und Tal und Wald und Wiesen, eine Romantische Anmut, als wir uns nur gemeiniglich in Elysium träumen! Allemal

wenn wir auf einer steilen Höhe hinauf, oder einen finstern Wald ... durch waren,
und sich dann ... ein weites Strahlental eröffnete, das in Dämmerung floß, war ich
allemal in Einer neuen Welt ... und so Sprachlos und Traumversenkt kamen wir
endlich auf halbem Wege an ... sahen die Morgenröte ...! Die ganze Welt war ein
stiller, feierlicher, sanfter Tempel Gottes ...[188]

After this the brilliance of the actual sunrise seems anti-climatic.
The next day, when he goes out to walk among the hills 'melting in
the silken mist of autumn and the evening sun,' he sees 'some clumps
of romantic black trees on a wild hill, by a waterfall,' surrounded by
willow brush and wildflowers. Nearby, a medieval knights' castle is
reflected in the water, and he hears first a sentry singing behind
him, then girls singing of joy and love. Here the reminder of the
Middle Ages, the singing, the landscape, and the flowers remind him
of Shakespeare's fairy and love songs, all blending in together as
connotations of the romantic:

> *Stellen Sie sich ... eine Kette kleiner Gebürge ... vor, die ... nun in dem seidnen*
> *Nebel des Herbstes und der Abendsonne flossen ... auf der andern Seite das*
> *Ritterliche, gräfliche Schloß, das sich im hellen, stillen Wasser spiegelt ... ich ...*
> *warf mich unweit einiger Kuppeln Romantischer, schwarzen Bäume auf einen*
> *wilden Hügel, an einen Wasserfall ... Um ihn viel wildes Weidengebüsche, um mich*
> *Alle wilden Blumen, die in Shakesp[eares] Feen- und Liebesliedern vorkommen ...*
> *Eine Schildwache sang hinter mir hinter den Bäumen ... und da kamen vom Walde*
> *her 3 Mädchenstimmen, die ihre Freuden- und Liebeslieder jauchzten.*[189]

One of the most widely read devotees of romantic and sublime
landscape in the last quarter of the eighteenth century was the Swiss,
Johann Georg Zimmermann. Best known for a series of books on the
pleasures of solitude,[190] Zimmermann is a representative example
of German rococo sentimentality. His four-volume work *Über die
Einsamkeit* begins with reminiscence on the delight the author had
enjoyed in youth 'in the escape to convents and cells, to untrod
mountains, awesome wooded heights, and ruined castles' and in
'communion with the dead':

> *In diesem unruhvollen Leben ... möchte ich noch Schatten ... hervorrufen ... aus*
> *jenen Tagen meiner Jugend ... in denen ich keine angenehmere Ausflucht kannte, als*
> *in Klöster und Zellen, in unbewanderte Gebürge, hohe schauervolle Wälder und*
> *zerstörte Schlösser ... und kein lebhafteres Vergnügen, als den Umgang mit den*
> *Toten.*[191]

If the heart should not be calmed in such solitude, it will 'gladly
bleed in silence' and sacrifice the pleasure of the earth for 'sweet

melancholy, for a single tear of love,' enjoyed in 'sublime nature,' for the delight in everything that 'melts away in gentle images':

Aber wäre auch das Herz nicht ruhig, so blutet es doch gerne im Stillen; um süße Melancholie gibt man gerne alles übrige Erdenglück hin, die ganze Welt um eine einzige sanfte Träne der Liebe. Solches Glückes ist das Herz empfänglich, wenn es Freude hat an erhabener Natur ... an allem wodurch wir die Seele erweitern, oder was sich in sanfte Bilder verschmelzt.[192]

For all that, the ambivalence we have noted in other writers is evident in Zimmermann's recognition that solitude may be a source of either desirable *Enthusiasmus* or dangerous *Schwärmerei.**

Like some of the English authors we have considered, Zimmermann tends to associate the sublime with grander natural objects and more intense emotions, the romantic with scenes of a more quiet charm; but for him, too, each is enhanced by the proximity of the other:

Reverent awe and sweet rapture are alternately aroused by the dark woodlands, the horribly steep rocky mountain ranges, and by every splendid and sublime scene combined with little glimpses of a smiling landscape.

Ehrfurchtsvolle Schauer und süßes Entzücken werden wechselweise erreget, durch das schwarze Gehölze, durch das fürchterlich abhängende Felsengebirge, und durch jede prachtvolle und erhabene Erscheinung, vereinigt mit kleinen Aussichten in eine lachende Landschaft.[193]

The Bernese Alps evoke 'sublime and dreadful' images in the soul / '... *ganz in der Nähe schien mir jedes Bild, das die Alpen in meiner Seele erregten, erhaben und fürchterlich,*'[194] but Switzerland also invites one to delights 'on its romantic hills, in many a lovely valley, on the banks of many a mirror-bright lake'/'*Aber zu welchem Genusse, ladet dann auch die Schweiz ein, auf ihren romantischen Hügeln, in so manchem lieblichen Tale, an den Ufern von so manchem spiegelhellen See ...*'[195]

For Zimmermann, solitude is not simply the absence of company but 'a state of the soul in which it gives itself over to its own imaginings' / '*Einsamkeit ist eine Lage der Seele, in der sie sich ihren eigenen Vorstellungen überläßt.*'[196] The imagination has an 'infinitely greater rule over man' than the intellect:

* Cf. ibid., ii: 82 *f.*; iii: 467 *f.* Lavater's patriotic Swiss songs serve as an example of *Enthusiasmus*, modern vestiges of neoplatonic mysticism 'in Werkstätten der Schuster und alchymistischen Küchen' and the Fakirs of India as examples of *Schwörmerei.*

The intellect is the capacity of clearly conceiving what is possible; a warm imagination, on the other hand, believes that it sees clearly an infinite number of things that the clearly visualizing, composed head does not see. To be sure, the imagination reproduces ideas like memory, but it alters, magnifies, weakens, or confuses them.

Einsamkeit wirket so mächtig auf die Einbildungskraft, weil die Herrschaft von dieser über den Menschen unendlich größer ist als die Herrschaft des Verstandes ... Der Verstand ist das Vermögen das Mögliche sich deutlich vorzustellen; eine warme Einbildungskraft hingegen glaubt unendlich viele Dinge deutlich zu sehen, die der reinsehende kaltblütige Kopf nicht sieht. Die Einbildungskraft wiederholet zwar auch Ideen wie das Gedächtnis, aber sie werden in ihr verändert, vergrößert, geschwächt, verwirret.[197]

That such activity of the imagination is associated alike with the sublime and the romantic is apparent from passages like the following:

Sometimes deep contemplation in solitary places arouses the highest forces of the intellect and the imagination and awakens the greatest feelings and convictions ... At every step the soul traverses boundless distances and glows with enthusiasm in this free self-enjoyment, striding ever higher in reflection upon great things and holding firmly to heroic decisions.

Tiefes Nachdenken erreget zuweilen an einsamen Örtern die höchsten Kräfte des Verstandes und der Imagination, und wecket zu den größten Empfindungen und Gesinnungen ... Bei jedem Fußtritt geht die Seele durchs Unermeßliche und glühet in diesem freien Genusse ihrer selbst von Enthusiasmus, und schreitet immer höher im Durchdenken großer Dinge, und im Festhalten heroischer Entschlüsse.[198]

Here it is evident that Zimmermann has sublimity in mind. So also when he describes the ardour aroused in Swiss peasants by his singing of Lavater's songs in praise of Tell and other national heroes, but in this case he says: 'This is romantic, I will be told, and romantic ideas never catch fire, except with people who live wholly in silence and seclusion'/'*Dies ist romantisch, wird man mir sagen, und romantische Ideen fangen nirgends Feuer, als bei Menschen die ganz in der Stille und in der Absonderung leben ...*'[199] In general, those human personalities whom Zimmermann terms romantic have elements of sublimity as well, even though this sublimity may have its ridiculous aspect:

Solitude and philosophy thus accustom one to modes of thought ... about which the world usually laughs ... Whoever has become acquainted with great people and great convictions from books readily takes on something romantic that often affords great material for laughter. Romantic minds, to be sure, would always have everything different from what it can be and what it is ...

Einsamkeit und Philosophie machen also Vorstellungsarten geläufig, ... über die gewöhnlich die Welt lacht ... Wer große Menschen und große Gesinnungen aus Büchern kennt, nimmt leicht etwas Romantisches an, das oft großen Stoff zum Lachen giebt. Romantische Köpfe möchten zwar immer alles anders haben, als es sein kann, und als es ist ...[200]

The above characterization of romantic nobility of soul is obviously inspired by the image of Don Quixote. At one point Zimmermann describes a contemporary Quixote, Count von Bückeburg, a warrior both romantic and sublime who was discussed in similar terms by Moses Mendelssohn and Herder.* Zimmermann had heard an account of the impression made by the Count when he led the Portuguese against the Spanish. On seeing him, the enemy generals cried out: 'Are the Portuguese commanded by Don Quixote?' Zimmermann explains:

Seen from the distance, he had a romantic quality, because of the heroic bearing of his body, his flying hair, his extraordinarily long, lean figure, and especially the unusually long oval of his head, which could indeed make one think of Don Quixote. But at close view ... sublimity ... spoke ... from his whole face.

Das Äußerliche dieses Grafen habe alle spanischen Generale ... so sehr frappiert, daß einer nach dem andern ausrief: sind denn die Portugiesen von Don Quichotte kommandiert? ... Es ist wahr, er hatte von weitem ein romantisches Wesen, wegen der heroischen Haltung seines Körpers, wegen seiner fliegenden Haare, wegen seiner außerordentlich langen hagern Figur, und zumal durch das ungewöhnlich lange Oval seines Kopfes, wobei man freilich an den Don Quichotte denken konnte. Aber in der Nähe sah und dachte man ganz anders. Erhabenheit, Scharfsinn, Feinheit, Milde, Güte und Ruhe, sprachen ... aus seinem ganzen Gesichte.[201]

Another writer whose literary career began with writings in

---

* See Herder's discussion, in his *Literarischer Briefwechsel* of 1782, of a passage in Mendelssohn's *Anmerkungen zu Abbts freundschaftlicher Korrespondenz.* Herder says here: 'Die Arme trug er edel und fast romantisch, so wie er etwas Romantisches in seiner ganzen Denkart und Lebensweise hatte.' He finds him to have surpassed all the rest of his countrymen in both physical and mental stature; a warrior by vocation, all his other interests were related to warfare. *Suphan* xv: 132.

praise of quiet country life was C. C. L. Hirschfeld.[202] However, he became better known for his works on garden theory, a one-volume *Theorie der Gartenkunst* published in 1775 and a five-volume work with the same title published from 1779 to 1785 in Leipzig. This work, as the present writer has pointed out elsewhere,[203] includes the first summation of the aesthetic qualities that constitute an artistic creation as romantic. Hirschfeld's books and a periodical he edited[204] are frequently mentioned by German classicists and romanticists alike, and his part in propagating associations of the romantic was substantial, but he was essentially an eclectic who systematically organized elements of the romantic that had been impinging on the German reading public from countless other sources. The essence of Hirschfeld's definition of the romantic object is that it 'is almost entirely a work of nature,' consisting not merely of the wild, huge, and powerful, but also of 'unusual combinations and juxtapositions ... extravagant irregularity, and ... surprising boldness and contrasts.'

[Der] Charakter des Romantischen ... ist fast ganz ein Werk der Natur. Sie bildet ihn nicht bloß durch gebirgigte Gegenden ... sondern auch durch ungewöhnliche Verbindungen und Gegenstellungen, durch eine ausschweifende Regellosigkeit der Anordnung und durch überraschende Kühnheiten der Kontraste.[205]

But when he discusses 'the romantic or enchanting in landscape,' it becomes evident that the romantic subsists in the contemplating subject as well, in the form of 'amazement, surprise, pleasurable astonishment, and sinking back into oneself'/'*Die Wirkungen des Romantischen sind Verwunderung, Überraschung, angenehmes Staunen und Versinken in sich selbst.*'[206] It 'transports the imagination out of its everyday sphere into a series of new images, lets it roam into the fairy world ...':

Alles, was die Einbildungskraft aus ihrer alltäglichen Sphäre heraus in eine Reihe neuer Bilder versetzt, sie in die Feenwelt, in die Zeiten der seltsamsten Bezauberung hinüberschweifen läßt – das ist hier an seinem Platze.[207]

The aesthetic objective of the romantic garden is to '*arouse the imagination* and *feelings*'/'*die Einbildungskraft und die Empfindung*'[208] strongly, even more strongly than the natural scene can do. Although Hirschfeld classifies the solemn (*feyerlich*) or sublime as a different category among gardens, it too is intended to stimulate the feelings and imagination, and conversely the ultimate goal of the romantic garden is to train the imagination to soar more easily ... far beyond the familiar stimulating elements by an intellectual contemplation of original beauty and grandeur in raptures elevated infinitely above the usual impressions of nature ...

Die Phantasie, die sich aus schönen Landschaften und Gärten erweitert und bereichert ... wird mit einem erleichterten Flug von einer Reihe neuer Bilder zu der andern sich erheben lernen, bis sie über die bekannten veranlassenden Vorwürfe hinaus, durch eine geistige Betrachtung der ursprünglichen Schönheit und Größe, in Entzückungen dahinschwebt, die über die gewöhnlichen Eindrücke der Natur auf die Organe der Empfindung unendlich erhaben sind.[209]

Goethe's systematic preoccupation with English garden style, which was to find its literary culmination in his *Wahlverwandtschaften,* began with his move to Weimar,[210] but the interest is already evident in *Werther.* The hero's favourite garden is in the English style. No sooner has one entered it than one is aware that it was designed by a gardener with a 'feeling heart that wanted to enjoy itself here'/ '... *Man fühlt gleich bei dem Eintritte, daß nicht ein wissenschaftlicher Gärtner, sondern ein fühlendes Herz den Plan gezeichnet, das seiner selbst hier genießen wollte.*'[211] It ends in a dark enclosure of beeches where one feels oneself enveloped by 'all the shudders of solitude,' and it is 'truly one of the most romantic' spots Werther 'has seen produced by art':

... Wie freuten wir uns, als wir ... die wechselseitige Neigung zu diesem Plätzchen entdeckten, das wahrhaftig eins von den romantischsten ist, die ich von der Kunst hervorgebracht gesehen habe ... ich habe dir ... schon viel davon geschrieben, wie hohe Buchenwände einen endlich einschließen und ... die Allee immer düsterer wird, bis zuletzt alles sich in ein geschlossenes Plätzchen endigt, das alle Schauer der Einsamkeit umschweben. [212]

Werther, Lotte, and Albert approach this secluded corner just as the moon is rising, and in this romantic setting Lotte is transported to an enraptured faith in immortality.

German authors of the late eighteenth century do not always expressly associate the word *romantisch* – as distinguished from *romanhaft* – with literature, but as a rule there is evidence that the author was conscious of the literary source of the term. Hirschfeld, for example, recommends that buildings to be erected at romantic sites have something of the supernatural element associated with local folk legends, fairy tales, or even with specific poetic works of Ariosto or Wieland.[213] An author in whom the literary associations of the romantic scene are unusually evident is Goethe's Strassburg friend, Heinrich Jung-Stilling. Among the works of imaginat ve literature that he came to associate with the romantic natural settings experienced in his childhood are the German folk novels *Kaiser Octavianus* and the *Historie von vier Haymonskindern* as well as H. A. von Ziegler's *Asiatische Banise* (1689). Left until his seventeenth year without companions of his own age but only such books with which to occupy himself, his 'imagination was heightened, because it received no objects other than ideal persons and acts.'[214] One morning, as they were walking out into the woods together, Stilling's grandfather asked him to tell him the story of Melusine. As he did so, the path was transformed for Stilling into a sheer paradise. With the help of the greenish light and the shade of a beech tree, 'the whole region immediately became an ideal of heavenly beauty in his eyes ... everything was new and ineffably alluring':

Eine recht düstere Maibuche ... mit ihrem schönen grünen Licht und Schatten, machte einen Eindruck auf ihn; alsofort war die ganze Gegend ein Ideal und himmlisch schön in seinen Augen ... alles war ihm neu und unaussprechlich reizend.[215]

Another time, when he sat down with his father and little sister by a spring in a clearing,

Heinrich saw in his mind ... the Egyptian desert, in which he would have liked to become St. Anthony. Soon afterwards he saw the spring of Melusine before him and wished that he were Raymund. Then the two ideas merged and became transformed into a reverent romantic sensation that made him savour everything beautiful and good in this solitary region with the highest rapture.

Heinrich ... sah in seiner Seele ... die ägyptische Wüste vor sich, worinnen er gern Antonius geworden wäre; bald darauf sah er den Brunnen der Melusine vor sich, und wünschte, daß er Raymund wäre; dann vereinigten sich beide Ideen, und es wurde eine fromme romantische Empfindung daraus, die ihm alles Schöne und Gute dieser einsamen Gegend mit höchster Wollust schmecken ließ.[216]

Another prospect rich in family memories, which included the ruins of a medieval castle, 'filled his soul with images illumined by the most splendid light; he stood as though intoxicated and gave himself over completely to his feelings.' Wishing like a prince to build a city on this site, it

immediately appeared before his imagination. He had his official residence at St. Anthony's Church. On the Heights he saw the castle of the city like Montalban in the woodcuts of the book of the fair *Melusine*.

*Da traten dann alle Szenen ... als so viele vom herrlichsten Licht erleuchtete Bilder
vor seine Seele ; er stand da wie ein Trunkener und überließ sich ganz der Empfindung
...Zuweilen wünschte er sich ... ein Fürst zu sein, um eine Stadt auf dieses Gefilde
bauen zu können; alsofort stand sie schon da vor seiner Einbildung; auf der*
Antonius-Kirche *hatte er seine Residenz, auf dem* Höchsten *sah er das Schloß
der Stadt, so wie* Montalban *in den Holzschnitten im Buch von der schönen*
Melusine.[217]

Romantic experience directly aroused by chap-books and
popular romances of the sixteenth and seventeenth centuries was no
longer a common phenomenon by Jung-Stilling's time. Such an
instance of ontogeny recapitulating a cultural philogeny was
possible only in an autodidactic imagination that had not been subject to the more usual literary influences of its age. But another,
quite similar example may be found in Karl Philipp Moritz. The
hero of his autobiographical novel *Anton Reiser* seeks escape from an
unhappy childhood environment in such romances as the *Asiatische
Banise*, the Robinson novel *Insel Felsenburg*, and the *Arabian Nights*.
By identifying himself with the patriarchal ruler of the Utopian
society on Felsenburg Island, he can compensate for the humiliation
he suffers in his own family. His imagination converts the city wall
to a mountain, a thicket to a forest, a mound in the moat to an
island. In walks of a few hundred yards he imagines himself in
forests, climbing high cliffs, coming upon uninhabited islands,
converting an ideal world of romance to reality.[218] In adolescence,
Reiser's imagination gains a great new stimulus from the discovery
of Shakespeare and *Werther*:

His reading, together with the impression made upon him by the beauty
of nature, had a wonderful effect upon his soul; everything appeared to
him in a romantic, enchanting light, wherever he stepped ... The walk on
the meadow along the river toward the waterfall was especially inviting
for his romantic ideas.

*Seine Lektüre, mit dem Eindruck, den die schöne Natur damals auf ihn machte
zusammengenommen, tat eine wunderbare Wirkung auf seine Seele; alles erschien
ihm in einem romantischen bezaubernden Lichte, wohin sein Fuß trat ... Nun war
... der Gang auf der Wiese, längst dem Flusse, nach dem Wasserfall zu, besonders
einladend für seine romantischen Ideen.[219]*

The rustic scenery round about him in the noonday stillness, with
the city, its walls and four towers appearing like a picture in a
camera obscura – all this evoked a wonderfully vivid sensation of the
reality of the immediate world about him at that moment: that this

place here and now was the same one he was used to conceiving in merely ideal terms. Recalling that the places of which he read in romances seemed all the more wonderful, the more distant they were, he suddenly realizes how the scenes around him would seem as imagined by an inhabitant of Peking.

This idea gives the real world immediately surrounding us an unaccustomed glow, making it appear to us just as strange and wonderful, as if we had just travelled a thousand miles to experience this moment.

Die uns umgebende wirkliche Welt bekommt durch diese Idee einen ungewohnten Schimmer, der sie uns ebenso fremd und wunderbar darstellt, als ob wir in dem Augenblick tausend Meilen gereist wären, um diesen Augenblick zu haben.[220]

Moritz-Reiser's discovery that the romantic perspective of remoteness can be projected back upon one's immediate experience to lend the 'dignity of the unknown to the familiar' anticipates Novalis' well known formulation of the process of 'romanticizing.'[221]

No writer of the period was more keenly aware of the workings of the imagination than Moritz. In his youth he had contemplated writing an essay on the contribution of distance and the unseen to the experience of the romantic, and in his *Reisen eines Deutschen in Italien in den Jahren 1786–1788* we find him reiterating the principle that the imagination loses its freedom of play when the object is actually visible.[222] In his *Anthousa* he notes the contribution of remoteness in time to the effect of historical traditions upon the imagination of those ancient Romans whose history, in turn, seems so romantic from our perspective.[223] It is understandable that in journeying to some of the most celebrated romantic scenes in England, he is thrilled by a view of Richmond from the valley in the moonlight but disappointed at the clear view from the hill the next morning:

Yesterday evening my sensations were much more lively and the impression much stronger and more romantic, when I looked up at this hill from the valley and imagined all sorts of splendid things, than this morning, when I looked out over the valley from the hill itself and knew what was there.

... Gestern Abend waren meine Empfindungen weit lebhafter, und der Eindruck weit stärker und romantischer, da ich aus dem Tale diesen Hügel hinauf blickte, und mir da allerlei Herrliches dachte, als heute Morgen, da ich von dem Hügel selbst das Tal überschaute, und nun wußte, was da war.[224]

The German creative writer who projects the image of romantic experience with the most dazzling intensity in the pre-romantic period is Wilhelm Heinse. His conscious literary and historical associations of the romantic are enriched by his vivid experience of music and painting. Very nearly fusing the romantic with the sublime and the beautiful, he experiences all three with an eroticism more intense than that of Wieland or even Beckford. He observes romantic aspects of such widely ranging objects as Alexander's expedition in Persia,[225] the bearing and costume of Venetian women,[226] Macpherson's fusion of eighteenth-century tenderness and gentility with the heroic freedom of a primitive people.[227] Heinse's description of a waterfall near Tivoli may serve as an example of his romantic landscape. Surpassingly 'picturesque,' the 'most charming' and 'sweetest' sight in the whole 'romantic valley,' it 'descends voluptuously' over amphitheatres of moss-covered rocks, 'framed by slender ashes and poplars, surrounded by walls of ivy and thousands of lower shrubs, as though conjured up by an omnipotent fairy.' The 'fresh whirlwind of spray,' held together 'in amorous splendour' by brilliant illumination, evokes 'an image of fresh, youthful beauty like a Phryne in the Bacchic dance.' Standing opposite this Cascatella, Heinse feels 'like a bride, passionately embraced by the whole of nature, his face soaked in a love-bath of kisses,' his senses 'dissolved in rapture':

Doch übertrifft diesen Hauptsturz des Teverone am malerischen, bei weitem ... die sogenannte große Cascatella ... Sie ist das Reizendste dieser Art, was ich je gesehen habe, und das Süßeste von dem ganzen romantischen Tale, das ... zwischen die Gebirge wollüstig sich hinsenkt. Ein grünes Doppeltheater über einander, von bemoosten Felsen, ... von schlanken Eschen und Pappeln eingefaßt, und von Epheuwänden und tausend niederm Gesträuch umlagert, wie von einer allmächtigen Fee hingezaubert, worauf das Wasser ... aus den Höhen herunterschäumt und ... in einem frischen Wirbelwind von Staub herumfliegt in glänzender Beleuchtung, die alles in verliebter Pracht zusammenhält, macht ein Bild von frischer jugendlicher Schönheit in die Seele, wie eine Phryne im bacchischen Tanze. Und, wenn man ... sich der Cascatella gegenüberstellt, und einen die ganze Natur da, wie eine Braut voll Leidenschaft umarmt, ein Liebesbad von Küssen das Gesicht benetzt ... wie das erquickt, ist unaussprechlich ... Wonne löst die Sinnen.[228]

In Heinse's novel *Ardinghello* (1787), similarly 'enchanting' views of Rome with 'pines, romantic villas, vineyards, and the splendid mountains in the distance' remind the characters of the transience of men and nations, the mystery of man's origin and

destiny,* much as was to be the case with Byron's Manfred a generation later. In several of Heinse's descriptions of Swiss landscape, the
romantic is presented in close geographical and emotional proximity
to the sublime.[229] The emotional experience of the sublime in a
romantic setting is illustrated by this passage on Civita Castellana:

The valley between [the town and the half of the volcanic mountain
split apart from it by an earthquake] is quite romantic, with the rocks
full of green shrubs and the clear brook which rushes past below, and the
acutely angled crevasses which attest to the terrifying force.

*Il ponte alto verbindet die Stadt mit der andern Hälfte des vulkanischen Bergs, der
einmal durch ein Erdbeden entzwei barst ... Das Tal dazwischen ist ganz
romantisch, mit den Felsen voll grünem Gesträuch und dem klaren Bach, der unten
vorbei rauscht, und den scharfwinklichten Felsenrissen, die von der entsetzlichen
Gewalt zeugen.*[230]

In *Ardinghello* the sublime is defined as

a higher being which penetrates us with feelings, thoughts, form, gesture,
action ... Sublime in the highest degree is that which infinitely surpasses
the forces of man. Everywhere it fills the soul with rapture, shuddering,
and amazement ...

*Erhaben ... ist ein höher Wesen, das in uns eindringt mit Empfindungen, Gedanken,
Gestalt, Gebärde, Handlung ... Erhaben im höchsten Grade, was die Kräfte des
Menschen unendlich übersteigt. Überall fühlt es die Seele mit Entzücken,
Schauder, und Erstaunen ...*[231]

Part of this definition is taken from the diary of the Italian journey
(1780-3), which further notes that 'the naked sublime darts into the
soul like lightening and transports man amid the gods,' where he is
'enchanted by sweet harmonies.'

*Das nackende Erhabene fährt wie ein Blitz in die Seele, und versetzt den Menschen
unter die Götter, und Geruch und Geschmack von Nektar und Ambrosia durch
entzücken ihn in süßen Harmonieen.*[232]

The next entry relates the sublime to beauty: 'The most beautiful
landscape is the one which gives the best sustenance to sublime

* 'Man hat hier reizende Aussichten hin überall, und verschiedne Landschaften
... zeigen immer neue bezaubernde Seiten mit Pignen, romantischen Villen,
Rebenhügeln und den herrlichen Fernen der Gebirge ... Wir fingen endlich an,
von Rom zu sprechen ... "Ach, alles geht auf und unter, Völker und wir, und
die Werke der Menschen! der Mensch ... weiß nicht von wannen er kömmt,
noch wohin er fähret ..." ' *Ardinghello, und die glückseeligen Inseln,* in *Sämtliche
Werke* IV: 202.

man' in terms of both physical nourishment and the sensuous enjoyment of variety. 'Man likes to lose himself in expanses of land and sea; this lifts him up, gives him a greater sphere, and sends a shudder of rapture through him.'

Die schönste Landschaft ... ist wohl die, welche dem erhabnen Menschen die beste Nahrung gibt, und seinen Sinnen die mannigfaltigsten Veränderungen der Erde zeigt, und wo er zugleich bequem leben kann ... der Mensch verliert sich gern in Weiten von Land und Meer; es erhöht ihn, und gibt ihm eine größere Sphäre, und schaudert ihn entzückend durch.[233]

The effect of the sublime upon the imagination and emotions is thus essentially identical with that of the romantic in other passages. In a discussion of Jomelli's opera *Il Vologeso* the two concepts are expressly linked together.[234]

Georg Forster, who had earlier helped to popularize the romantic beauty of the South Pacific,* also observed romantic vistas on his journey with Iffland down the lower Rhine and in England. A passage on the prospect from Mont Cassel in Flanders, noted for its 'romantic situation,' stresses the 'sublime perfection' the view would have afforded in clearer weather if the 'immeasurable blue horizon' over the dunes and sea had been added to the combination of picturesque forms, infinite wealth, and variety in the other direction:

Wir hielten unsere Mittagsmahlzeit zu Cassel [Mont-Cassel], das wegen seiner romantischen Lage auf einem Berge so berühmt ... ist ... Bei dieser üppigen Pracht des Frühlings entbehrten wir dennoch den Anblick der Dünen und des Meeres, den uns der Nebel neidisch verhüllte. Jener unermeßliche blaue Horizont ... muß der hiesigen Aussicht eine erhabene Vollkommenheit geben ...†

But in addition to the landscape, he and Iffland also experienced the romantic in the dark interior of the then unfinished Cologne Cathedral. Indeed, every time he visited Cologne, Forster entered the Cathedral 'to feel the shudders of the sublime. Before the daring of such masterpieces, the mind falls to the ground in amazement and enthusiasm, but then it soars proudly up over the achievement conceived by a kindred spirit.' A comparison of the columns with the trees of a forest approximates the sublime to the romantic; in either case the imagination is 'extended into infinity':

---

*   See the description of Tinian above, p. 26, and Georg Forster, *A Voyage Round the World* II: 168 f., 346 f., 474, 486, 589 ff.

†   Georg Forster, *Ansichten vom Niederrhein, Werke*, ed. G. Steiner, IX (Berlin, 1958): 232 f. See also the implicit association of the sublime with the romantic and the picturesque in his description of the Rhine valley near the 'romantic Mouse Tower,' ibid., p. 2.

So oft ich Köln besuche, geh ich immer wieder in diesen herrlichen Tempel, um die Schauer des Erhabenen zu fühlen. Vor der Kühnheit der Meisterwerke stürzt der Geist voll Erstaunen und Bewunderung zur Erde; dann hebt er sich wieder mit stolzem Flug über das Vollbringen hinweg, das nur Eine Idee eines verwandten Geistes war ... so liegt gleichwohl in diesem kühnen Emporstreben der Pfeiler und Mauern das Unaufhaltsame, welches die Einbildungskraft so leicht in das Grenzenlose verlängert.[235]

A little later, at Oxford, Forster substitutes the term 'romantic' for 'sublime' in an almost identical context.[236]

Two important German writers who still used the word *romantisch* with conscious reference to the influence of literature on the imagination and on life rather than with reference to vistas are Lenz and Schiller. Herz, the hero of Lenz's unfinished epistolary novel, *Der Waldbruder*,[237] conceives a 'romantic' love for a countess he knows only from letters, projects it upon another lady he has been led to confuse with her, and then withdraws as a hermit into the forest. He is described by another character as 'a new Werther [or] ... Idris' with 'something romantic in his expressions,' in consequence of either his innate temperament or the corrupting influence of his readings in Goethe and Wieland:

Wissen Sie auch wohl, daß wir hier einen neuen Werther haben, noch wohl schlimmer als das, einen Idris, der es in der ganzen Strenge des Wortes ist ... Kurz, es ist der junge Herz ... er war ... immer in seinen Ausdrücken etwas romantisch ... Er ... ist in den Odenwald gegangen und Einsiedler geworden.[238]

The experiences of his youth have given his soul

a wonderfully romantic tone. He lives and moves in sheer fantasies and cannot put anything in the real world ... in its right place ... He has simply acquired a certain skill ... at viewing all people and actions in an ideal light. All characters and opinions different from his own seem so grand to him ... that he believes himself surrounded by nothing but extraordinary people, gigantic heroes of virtue or villains ...

Sie sollten nicht glauben, was alle diese Schicksale ... seiner Seele für eine wunderbarromantische Stimmung gegeben haben. Er lebt und webt in lauter Phantasien und kann nichts, auch manchmal nicht die unerheblichste Kleinigkeit aus der wirklichen Welt an ihren rechten Ort legen ... Er hat sich nun einmal eine gewisse Fertigkeit gegeben ... alle Menschen und Handlungen in einem idealischen Lichte anzusehen. Alle Charaktere und Meinungen, die von den seinigen abgehen, scheinen ihm so groß, ... daß er mit lauter außerordentlichen Menschen, gigantischen Tugendhelden oder Bösewichtern umgeben zu sein glaubt ...[239]

Schiller, before incorporating the word *romantisch* in the subtitle of *Die Jungfrau von Orleans* (1801),[240] used it largely in historical contexts and in reference to his own historical drama *Don Carlos*. A passage on his character Marquis Posa in the *Briefe über Don Carlos*, published in *Der Teutsche Merkur* in 1788, traces Posa's development from an immature romantic attitude in youth to the 'sublime conception of *man as a whole*' that he ultimately achieved:

He has changed from an idle enthusiast into an active man. Those former dreams and intuitions that were still obscure and undeveloped in his soul have been refined into clear concepts ... in association with kindred spirits his ideas take on versatility and form; tested men of the world ... take the romantic quality from them and gradually tone them down to pragmatic utility.

Aus einem müßigen Enthusiasten ist ein tätiger, handelnder Mensch geworden. Jene ehemaligen Träume und Ahndungen, die noch dunkel und unentwickelt in seiner Seele lagen, haben sich zu klaren Begriffen geläutert ... im Umgange mit verwandten Geistern gewinnen seine Ideen Vielseitigkeit und Form; geprüfte Weltleute ... nehmen ihnen das Romantische und stimmen sie allmählich zu pragmatischer Brauchbarkeit herunter.[241]

But the next paragraph makes clear that this development does not involve any loss of emotional warmth and fervour: Posa has returned from the Netherlands with a glowing heart 'kindled with all the more ardour for the happiness of this great whole and burning with longing' to realize his ideals.

... mit geschäftigem Kopf, glühendem Herzen, von den großen begeisternden Ideen allgemeiner menschlicher Kraft und menschlichen Adels durchdrungen und feuriger für die Glückseligkeit dieses großen Ganzen entzündet ... so kommt er jetzt ... zurück, brennend von Sehnsucht, einen Schauplatz zu finden, auf welchem er diese Ideale realisieren ... könnte.[242]

Another passage in these letters brings the romantic imagination closer to the sublime:

[Posa's] whole imagination is filled and permeated with images of romantic grandeur, so that the heroes of Plutarch are alive in his soul and the first of two alternatives to offer itself to him must always be the heroic one.

Wer entdeckt nicht ... daß seine ganze Phantasie von Bildern romantischer Größe angefüllt und durchdrungen ist, daß die Helden des Plutarch in seiner Seele leben und daß sich also unter zwei Auswegen immer der heroische zuerst und zunächst ihm darbieten muß?[243]

The full development of Schiller's concept of the sublime in the great philosophical studies developed from Kantian premises took place a little later. At the period we are considering, romantic experience for Schiller is a spontaneous psychological phenomenon, whereas the sublime requires an intellectual and ethical discipline. But the fundamental elements are the same, and an imagination permeated with images of romantic grandeur and heroism is well on its way to sublimity.

A passage in Schiller's *Geschichte des Abfalls der vereinigten Niederlande*, also published in 1788, explains the failure of the Reformation in Italy by the romantic tendencies of that nation: a luxuriant and smiling landscape combined with 'the most varied enchantments of art' to render better suited to this 'romantic nation ... a religion whose splendid pomp captures the senses, whose mysterious enigmas open up an infinite range to the imagination, and whose principal doctrines flatter their way into the soul with picturesque forms':

Aber einem romantischen Volke, das ... durch eine üppige, immer junge und immerlachende Natur und die mannigfaltigsten Zaubereien der Kunst in einem ewigen Sinnengenusse erhalten wird, war eine Religion angemessener, deren prächtiger Pomp die Sinne gefangen nimmt, deren geheimnisvolle Rätsel der Phantasie einen unendlichen Raum eröffnen, deren vornehmste Lehren sich durch malerische Formen in die Seele einschmeicheln.[244]

From this we can see that Schiller was, after all, accessible to the romantic in landscape, aware of its nourishment by the pictorial arts and especially of that stimulating effect of mystery upon the romantic imagination expressed – as in so many other writers – through the metaphor of infinity.

If Schiller tends to absorb the romantic into the sublime, the more common opposite tendency is illustrated by the last German author we are to consider, Wilhelm von Humboldt; he also commands our attention for the unusual sensitivity and breadth of his imagination and his fascinated observation of its workings. This imagination is nourished by more varied and sophisticated literary associations than that of Jung-Stilling or Moritz: they include ancient and medieval traditions, Ossian and *Werther*,* and travel

---

*   See his reaction to his first reading of *Werther* in association with the 'wilde, schöne, romantische Gegend' near Göttingen from which he writes his fiancée Caroline. *Wilhelm und Caroline von Humboldt in ihren Briefen*, ed. Anne von Sydow, I, *Briefe aus der Brautzeit 1787–1791* (Berlin, 1906), p. 40.

literature such as the writings of Christian Meiners.[245] The reaction of Humboldt's imagination to romantic landscapes, particularly in Switzerland, is a concentration of most of the tendencies we have observed up to now. From the beginning of his travels to Paris and Switzerland in 1788–9, Humboldt is alert, not merely to the varied and contrasting scenes he observes,[246] but even more so to the effect of visual obscurity and uncertain historical tradition upon 'the ever active imagination' [*Einbildungskraft*],[247] and to the emotional states accompanying his contemplation: the 'expansion of his heart,' the 'anxious yearning' for friends left behind, and the 'sweet melancholy' into which this yearning plunges him. Such are his moods as he gazes out over the expanse of the Rhine valley at Mainz.[248]

The term *erhaben* occurs once in this travel diary associated with scenes in the Rhineland and the Swiss Alps,[249] but the qualities generally attributed to it are implicit in most of the vistas Humboldt calls romantic. In landscapes, he finds the romantic in contrasts of wild nature with fertility and regular planting.[250] In gardens, he calls ruins and irregular planting 'most romantic.'[251] Humboldt is one of the earliest writers to acclaim the romantic qualities of Heidelberg. The hills towering over the city on all sides and 'the ruins of the old castle ... make the view romantic ...' It is also 'exceedingly picturesque; it is a great, simple whole, it has character.' Although one may prefer to see more smiling and charming scenes more frequently, 'just as one reads a song by Wieland more often than an ode by Klopstock,' Heidelberg 'makes a deeper impression on the soul':

... [*Das über den Häusern hervorragende Gebirge*] *und die trümmern des alten schlosses auf dem schloßberge macht den anblick romantisch ... Dieser anblick ... ist überaus malerisch, es ist ein großes, einfaches ganze, es liegt charakter darin. Andre gegenden sind lachender, mannigfaltiger, reizender; man sieht sie vielleicht lieber oft als diese, so wie man ein Wielandsches lied öfter liest als eine Klopstocksche ode. Aber diese greift gewiß tiefer in die seele ein.*[252]

Humboldt finds the greatest number of romantic prospects as well as the most powerful effect on his imagination and emotions in the Swiss Alps, for example at Lake Lucerne.[253] The view at Beatenberg (north of the Thuner See) with its succession of steep rocks topped by forests, its solitary trails, and isolated huts is 'indescribably picturesque'; the 'trail along the lake on the mountain slope must be difficult but extremely romantic':

Bei Merlige[n] ... fängt der Beatenberg ... an, und nun wird der anblick un-
beschreiblich malerisch. Hohe steile felsen mit oft 80 bis 100 schuh hohen senk-
rechten wänden laufen ununterbrochen fort, und man erblickt auf ihnen nichts als
wald, einsame fußsteige, und einzelne hütten. Der fußsteig dem see entlang am
abhange des bergs muß freilich beschwerlich, aber äußerst romantisch sein ...[254]

On his second visit to the grotto of the hermit saint for whom this
mountain is named, his imagination grasps the feeling of ancient
peoples that such grottoes must be the seats of goddesses. There alone,
'far from all the botchings of art, would it be possible to understand
Homer and Ossian' / '*In solchen gegenden, den schönsten werken der natur*
nah, fern von allem machwerk der kunst, würde man erst Homer, und Ossian
verstehn.'[255] Proceeding up the narrow valley of a rushing stream
past waterfalls and heaps of fallen rocks, with his first view of the
Jungfrau, he enjoys at every step images of irresistible annihilating
power and defiantly resistant force. His soul feels the succession of
countless past centuries and

has a dim premonition of an immeasurably distant future, ever destroying and creating anew. Past and future, creation and ruin were the ideas
which seized control of my soul most intensely ... and never had human
destinies and human plans appeared more contemptibly small.

Kurz jeder schritt gibt bilder unwiderstehlicher alles zerschmetternder gewalt, und
widerstrebender trotzender stärke. Bei den spuren von verwüstungen die man in
jedem augenblick wahrnimmt, bei dem gefühl einer zahllosen reihe verfloßner
jahrhunderte ... dämmert in der seele ein ahnden unabsehbar ferner, wieder zertrüm-
mernder und wieder schaffender zukunft auf. Vergangenheit und zukunft, schöpfung
und untergang waren überhaupt die ideen, die sich meiner seele am heftigsten
bemeisterten ... und nie erschienen mir menschliche schicksale, menschliche plane in
einer verächtlicheren kleinheit.[256]

The impact of the Jungfrau is somewhat less than Humboldt had
expected from Meiners; but finally,

in the red glow of the sunset when all the other peaks were already enveloped in shade, the Jungfrau aroused ... ideas of lonely desolation, of
solitude ... keen expectations of what might lie behind those mountains ...
Only the past, future, the remote and uncertain hover before the dreaming imagination ... One can conceive nothing more romantic [than the
view one imagines one would see from the middle of the valley in the light
of the moon].

... [ich] wollte nun wie [Meiners] alle die gefühle in mir hervorgebracht sehn, die er
der wunderkraft der jungfrau zuschreibt ... Aber ... umsonst. Freilich wirkte die

jungfrau, vorzüglich als die scheidende abendsonne sie rötete, da schon alle andren gipfel in schatten verhüllt standen ... Ideen der einöde, der einsamkeit ... rege erwartungen des, was hinter jenen bergen, über jenen gipfeln hinaus ist. Dadurch verschwindet in der seele alles gegenwärtige, nahe, gewisse, und das vergangne, zukünftige, entfernte, ungewisse schwebt allein vor der träumenden phantasie ... Steht man nun draußen mitten im tal, so blickt man noch bis auf die Hunnen- und Eisenflühe zurück. Etwas romantischeres läßt sich kaum denken. Nichts bedaure ich so sehr, als daß wir jetzt keinen mondschein haben. Dann fehlte meiner wanderung hieher nichts.[257]

For this sophisticated viewer any actual vista carries a certain disappointment; to achieve the utmost in romantic experience he must project the romantic object in his imagination across a greater distance or through a more obscure and enchanting light than is actually afforded him.* The extent to which Humboldt absorbs the sublime into the romantic is especially evident in a passage on the valley of the Aar near Gutannen, where the 'most romantic part of the route' is precisely the one evoking the most awe, astonishment, and dread, where the rocks are the wildest, most naked, and irregular, the abyss below the trail the most precipitous, with an 'immense wall of rock' opposite and two snow-capped peaks visible to the right:

Noch mehr erstaunte ich, als ich selbst den weg erstieg. Er ist in den felsen, den man an mehreren orten gesprengt hat, gearbeitet, und wegen des fürchterlichen abgrunds mit einem geländer versehn. Die aussicht von der größten höhe ist eine der wildesten, die ich sah ... Gegenüber ist eine lange ungeheure felswand, und zur rechten sieht man die schneeberge ... Allein dies ist auch der romantischste teil des wegs. Der andre ist freilich auch noch wild, und schön, aber doch nicht in gleichem grade. Das tal ist breiter, die felsen regelmäßiger und weniger nackt.[258]

Much as Humboldt is partial to those qualities of the romantic object which most previous viewers of landscape had termed sublime, he is in the last analysis more concerned with subjective factors. Among numerous passages attesting this fact in his correspondence with his bride, Caroline, we may cite one written from his home in Tegel in May of 1790. The prospect here has 'something romantic' because he recollects his subjective reaction to it in childhood:

Longing swelled my breast then as now, but then the longing was so indefinite, so restless, now it is so definite, so harmonious, though even now

---

* For example, see the account of his journey to Grindelwald: of two routes, the one he did not take 'muß ungleich romantischer sein, und auch darum vorzüglich, weil man die jungfrau von ihrer andren schrecklichern seite sieht.' *Tagebücher*, ed. A. Leitzmann (Berlin, 1916 ff.), I: 71.

consuming and intense. At every step I find a scene of the past again ...

Die Gegend hat in der Tat etwas Romantisches ... Und ich, der ich von meiner ersten Kindheit an da war, von wie vielen Erinnerungen werd ich ergriffen bei jedem Anblick. Wie oft stand ich, wie neulich, auf dem Weinberg ...! Sehnsucht dehnte dann meinen Busen aus, wie jetzt, aber damals war das Sehnen so unbestimmt, so unruhvoll, jetzt so bestimmt, so harmonisch, wenngleich auch jetzt verzehrend und heftig. Bei jedem Schritt finde ich eine Szene der Vergangenheit wieder, und das fesselt mich wunderbar an die Gegend.[259]

Irregularity, contrast, wildness, power, and danger viewed in the object are less important to this observer than his own entranced contemplation, something stimulated best by the thought of the same scene viewed in the past, under different conditions of observation, or by that of other scenes not yet accessible to him.

FRANCE

The term *romantique* was introduced to France somewhat later than its cognate to Germany; but for a time, in the 1780s and 1790s, the taste for the romantic seemed to prevail almost as much there. It remained, however, largely a concept of criticism, never completely supplanting the earlier *romanesque* in general usage. Contexts of both French terms enriched the connotations of the romantic in other literatures.

The writer who contributed the most through his use of *romanesque* was probably Jean Baptiste la Curne de Sainte-Palaye,[260] who is frequently cited by Thomas Warton and Herder. La Curne is particularly interested in medieval chivalric love: '*Un amour romanesque avoit toujours ses rafinemens: plus il étoit plein d'idées fantastiques, plus il étoit sujet à des caprices bizarres.*'[261] Many troubadours made it their mission to address the tenderest and most daring wishes to princesses. '*Ces passions, souvent romanesques dans l'origine, devinrent souvent des passions réelles.*'[262] La Curne cites as an example Balaun, who was '*infatué des chimères les plus romanesques.*'[263] The contradictions between such 'romantic gallantry' and the religious reverence in which knights were supposed to hold their ladies are no greater than those between the violence perpetrated by Christians, even in the most enlightened centuries, and the sanctity of their faith.[264]

The term *romanesque* was extended to landscapes and gardens by Claude Henri Watelet in his *Essai sur les Jardins* (1774).* This treatise accepts somewhat cautiously the fundamental aesthetic principles

*   The title page says 'Paris, 1764,' but the approval of the censor is dated 1774.

of the informal garden with virtually no intimation of the latter's English origin and no explicit mention of English authors on the subject. It views the *romanesque* as a more piquant source of illusion than what it calls the poetic. A wild, rocky landscape with the sounds of torrents echoing from caverns and other concealed acoustic effects, such as might emanate from unseen forges or glass-works, may evoke impressions of moaning evil spirits and of 'a magic wilderness.' The imagination supplies the wanting visual impressions, and at the moment of dusk the gloom of the spreading shadows can almost make one believe that one sees 'Demons, Magicians, and monsters in the wilderness.' Like the English garden and landscape literature, this work regards the romantic (*romanesque*) as essentially a creation of nature; it is the function of the human artist to enhance it by contrast with opposite aesthetic impressions.* Another passage, to be sure, recognizes the possibility of elaborate contrivances to remind the viewer of the 'gardens of Alcinous,' 'the palace of Armida,' or Sybaris. In such 'fairy scenes' a prodigality of sense impressions may be derived from 'all times and nations,' particularly from China. Here the author lets himself be momentarily carried away in a description of exotic delights, lavish acoustic effects, and concealed machinery unmistakably influenced by Chambers, only to remind us of the difference between such enervating delights and the 'pure pleasure' to be enjoyed where 'the reserve of good taste' prevails:

C'est dans ces aziles absolument romanesques que l'Art, ministre des égaremens de l'imagination, affecte ... de maîtriser la Nature. Les jardins d'Alcine & le palais d'Armide sont les modèles qu'il s'efforce d'imiter; c'est à Sybaris qu'il faut se transporter; c'est aux enchantemens qu'il faut avoir recours. Aussi dans ces lieux de féerie, les artifices & les prodigalités l'emportent sur des perfections mesurées dont le naturel & la simplicité seroient les bases ...

Mais ce que tant d'artifice & de recherche ne pourront créer, c'est le plaisir pur que ne trouble point le remords, que ne trahit point la langueur, que ne détruit point la sassiété, le bonheur enfin dont on s'éloigne d'autant plus qu'on multiplie les efforts pour l'atteindre. La réserve du bon goût ne l'éfarouche point ...[265]

It is interesting that the need for the term *romantique*, derived

---

* *Essai sur les Jardins*, pp. 86 *ff.* The passage from which two phrases have been quoted is on pp. 88 *f.* and reads: 'Ces images d'un désert magique ... présenteroient un romanesque auquel la pantomime même ne seroit pas nécessaire. En effet l'imagination émue seroit prête à la suppléer; & dans l'instant où le jour s'obscurciroit, où les ombres de la nuit répandroient la tristesse qui leur est propre, & les illusions qui les accompagnent; peu s'en faudroit qu'on ne crût voir dans ce désert des Démons, des Magiciens & des monstres.'

directly from the English, came to be felt only when the English source of the new garden style was frankly acknowledged and that this development, in turn, coincided with the awakening of a new and more positive appraisal of Shakespeare. Two authors with these particular interests first introduced *romantique* to France in 1776, just two years after the appearance of Watelet's *Essai*: Pierre Letourneur, the translator of Shakespeare, and René Louis de Girardin, patron of Rousseau and exponent of English gardening.[266] Both call attention to their importation of the term from England. Although Letourneur applies it to the subjective experience of Shakespeare's genius, it is by analogy to the experience of romantic landscape: he who would really feel the genius of Shakespeare must '... *gravir sur la cime des rochers et des montagnes; que de là il porte sa vue sur la vaste mer, et qu'il la fixe sur le paysage aérien et Romantique des nuages, alors il sentira quel fut le génie de Shakespeare.*'[267] The French words previously available for a view that fixes the eyes and captivates the imagination, *pittoresque* and *romanesque*, cannot convey the 'tender feelings and melancholy ideas' which such a sensation evokes in the soul, so that a new term is needed:

Nous n'avons dans notre langue que deux mots ... pour exprimer une vue, une scène d'objets, un paysage, qui attache les yeux et captive l'imagination; si cette sensation éveille dans l'âme émue, des affections tendres et des idées mélancholiques, alors ces deux mots: Romanesque *et* Pittoresque *ne suffisent pas pour le rendre. Le premier ... est alors synonyme de chimérique et de fabuleux : il signifie à la lettre un objet de Roman qui n'existe que dans le pays de la féerie, dans les rêves bizzarres de l'imagination, et ne se trouve point dans la nature. Le second n'exprime que les effets d'un tableau quelconque, où diverses masses rapprochées forment un ensemble qui frappe les yeux et le fait admirer, mais sans que l'âme y participe, sans que le coeur y prenne un tendre intérêt. Le mot anglois est plus heureux et plus énergique. En même temps qu'il renferme l'idée de ces parties groupées d'une manière neuve ... il porte de plus dans l'âme le sentiment de l'émotion douce et tendre qui naît à leur vue ... Si ce vallon n'est que pittoresque, c'est un point de l'étendu qui prête au Peintre ... Mais s'il est Romantique, on désire de s'y reposer, l'oeil se plaît à le regarder et bientôt l'imagination attendrie le peuple de scènes intéressantes : elle oublie le vallon pour se complaire dans les idées, dans les images qu'il lui a inspirées. Les tableaux de Salvator Rosa, quelques sites des Alpes, plusieurs Jardins et Campagnes de l'Angleterre, ne sont point romanesques : mais on peut dire qu'ils sont plus que pittoresques c'est à dire touchans et Romantiques.*[268]

The function of the suggested new term, then, is to extend the limited area occupied by *romanesque* over the additional territory belonging to 'romantic' in England. Letourneur is demanding three things: first, the enlarging of the range of romantic objects to include painted landscapes; second, the ability of the imagination to expand beyond any object seen in nature or on canvas or described in a book, even to forget it altogether, soaring away to entirely different scenes; finally, that emotional overtones be set vibrating by the romantic object viewed or imagined. In short, he would draw a line of demarcation between the older literary associations of the romantic as understood in England and Germany and the pictorial, imaginative, and emotional connotations the English word had acquired in more recent decades. Perhaps it was this very demarcation – never made in either England or Germany – that tended to limit *romantique* to movements in taste and aesthetic criticism. We also note that in emphasizing the emotional aspect of romantic experience Letourneur is implicitly approximating the romantic to the sublime. But there is an underlying inconsistency in his argument: while pleading that romantic experience be severed from association with literary romance in the older, more narrow sense of fanciful popular narrative, he draws romantic inspiration from another kind of literature, Shakespearean drama, precisely the literature that was to be regarded as romance *par excellence* by Friedrich Schlegel.* Letourneur acclaims those aspects of Shakespeare's work which a Voltaire could admire but not recommend for emulation: its tremendous energy and wild irregularity, its bursting of the bounds set by critical rules. These are the very qualities that the late eighteenth century generally considered sublime when it encountered them in nature but which some writers, like Wilhelm von Humboldt, were now incorporating in the romantic.

Much of the foregoing also applies to the other French author, Girardin, who introduced *romantique* at about the same time as Letourneur.† Girardin, a financier with the avocation of landscape architecture, was well versed in the English criticism of this art and applied its principles at his estate in Ermenonville, where Rousseau spent his last years. His use of the term *romantique* is closer to the English sources than was the case with Letourneur. Like most English landscape theorists, Girardin held the romantic to be essentially a quality of the natural landscape. Like them also, he was especially concerned with the differentiation of the romantic from

---

* Cf. his 'Brief über den Roman,' *Kritische Friedrich-Schlegel-Ausgabe* ii, ed. Hans Eichner (Paderborn, 1967), pp. 335 ff.

† Baldensperger gives 1776 as the date of Girardin's *De la composition des paysages*. The work was first printed in Geneva in 1775, but it did not appear until later, bearing the date 1777. The author's name is spelled Gérardin on the title page.

the picturesque. A scene that 'enchants the eyes' he considers picturesque; one that evokes Arcadian literary associations is poetic; a romantic setting can be afforded by nature alone:

Mais si la situation pittoresque *enchante les yeux, si la situation Poëtique intéresse l'esprit & la mémoire, retraçant les scènes Arcadiennes en nous ... il est une autre situation que la nature seule peut offrir: c'est la situation* Romantique. *Au milieu des plus merveilleux objets de la nature, une telle situation rassemble tous les plus beaux effets de la perspective pittoresque, & toutes les douceurs de la scène Poëtique; sans être farouche ni sauvage, la situation* Romantique *doit être tranquille & solitaire, afin que l'âme n'y éprouve aucune distraction, & puisse s'y livrer toute entiere à la douceur d'un sentiment profond.*[269]

A footnote to this passage explains the choice of the word *romantique* instead of the customary French *romanesque* on the grounds that the latter 'denotes more the fictitious quality of romance,' whereas the English word 'denotes the situation and its impression on our feelings ...'/'*J'ai préféré le mot Anglois,* Romantique, *à notre mot François,* Romanesque, *parce que celui-ci désigne plutôt la fable du roman, & l'autre désigne la situation, & l'impression touchante que nous en recevons.*' The emphasis on feeling shared by Letourneur and Girardin does not imply an interest in intense emotional reactions such as the profound awe or terror relished by German *Sturm und Drang.* These French authors were rather more concerned with the emotions associated with tranquil revery. According to Girardin, even amid the wildest and most lofty Alpine scenery,

On se plaît à y rêver de cette rêverie si douce, besoin pressant pour celui qui connoît la valeur des choses, & les sentimens tendres; on voudroit y rester toujours, parce que le coeur y sent toute la verité, & l'énergie de la nature. Tel est à peu près le genre des situations Romantiques; *mais on n'en trouve gueres de cette espece que dans le seins* [sic] *de ces superbes remparts, que la nature semble avoir élevés, pour offrir encore à l'homme des asyles de paix, & de liberté.*[270]

It is thus not altogether a coincidence that the word *romantique* was first used by Girardin's protegé Rousseau precisely in a work on revery, the *Rêveries du promeneur solitaire* written during his sojourn at the Lac de Bienne in Switzerland in 1777. Midway between that date and the publication of his famous novel, *Julie, ou la Nouvelle Héloïse,* in 1760, Rousseau had spent several years at the fountainhead of the romantic, in England. Rousseau makes no effort to distinguish *romantique* from *romanesque,* applying both within a few pages to the natural setting:

Les rives du lac de Bienne sont plus sauvages & romantiques que celles du lac de Geneve, parce que les rochers & les bois y bordent l'eau de plus près; mais elles ne sont pas moins riantes. S'il y a moins de culture de champs & de vignes, moins de villes & de maisons, il y a aussi plus de verdure naturelle, plus de prairies, d'asyles ombragés de boccages, des contrastes plus fréquens & des accidens plus rapprochés.[271]

En sortant d'une longue & douce rêverie, me voyant entouré de verdure, de fleurs, d'oiseaux, & laissant errer mes yeux au loin sur les romanesques rivages qui bordoient une vaste étendue d'eau claire & cristalline, j'assimilois à mes fictions ous ces aimables objets; & me trouvant enfin ramené par degrés à moi-même & à ce qui m'entouroit, je ne pouvois marquer le point de séparation des fictions aux réalités; tant tout concouroit également à me rendre chere la vie recueillie & solitaire que je menois dans ce beau séjour.[272]

The text between these two passages in the Fifth Promenade presents unsurpassed examples of the more tranquil emotional overtones of romantic experience, free from the extravagances and resentments that are otherwise so common in Rousseau's writing. Here on the island of St. Pierre, Rousseau enjoyed for two months perfect seclusion from that society to which he was never able to adapt himself. Here he could become wholly immersed in the quiet, blissful enjoyment of a precious *far niente*. He collected botanical specimens and for hours on end reclined in a boat in the middle of the lake, his eyes turned toward Heaven, drifting wherever the current took him, 'plunged in a thousand confused but delicious reveries.'[273]

The contribution of these *Rêveries* to the literary associations of the romantic is attested, for example, by the Dano-German poet Jens Baggesen, who in 1795 visited the island of St. Pierre on the Lac de Bienne and called the island a 'Tinian' because of its variety of prospects and fertility, its 'romantic groves,' vineyards, flowering meadows, steep heights, avenues of trees, and arbors, everything 'alternating in a continuous labyrinth of enchantments':

Ich brachte den ganzen Tag mit dem Umherwandeln auf diesem Timan [sic] zu, das in dem Umfang von einer halben Meile nicht bloß das Auge mit allen möglichen Abwechslungen von Landschaften und Aussichten befriedigt, sondern aus seinem eigenen fruchtbaren Schoße eine Welt en miniature, *und jedes zur Notdurft und Bequemlichkeit des Lebens Erfoderliche hervorbringt. Romantische Haine von allerlei Bäumen ... die niedlichsten Weinberge, Blumenwiesen, steile Anhöhen, Buschwerke, Alleen, kleine Lauben, wechseln in einem beständigen Labyrinth von Bezauberungen mit einander ab.[274]*

But quite apart from these isolated occurrences of *romantique* and *romanesque*, Rousseau had long since rendered the shores of Lake Geneva and its surrounding mountains one of the favourite romantic settings of Europe through his *Nouvelle Héloïse* with its spiritually noble but self-enchanted characters, its contrasts of sublimely wild and smiling cultivated landscapes, its changing tones of light and shadow and their effect on the viewer, and its emphasis on the enjoyment of a past transfigured in recollection, of the pleasures of passion indulged in solitude.[275]

The failure of *romantique* wholly to absorb the more subjective connotations of *romanesque* illustrated in Rousseau's Fifth Promenade foreshadowed the ultimate failure of the former term to absorb its older precursor and establish itself in common usage apart from particular currents of landscape gardening and literary criticism. The examples cited by Baldensperger for the late 1770s and '80s[276] reflect similar tendencies: a general fluctuation between the two terms coupled with efforts to differentiate them and a special association of *romantique* with landscape. If in France the *romantique* could not long remain a vigorous part of the living language, in England *romantic* had become too important and too spontaneous a part of the language to be taken over by any programmatic literary or cultural movement. Only in Germany, where *romantisch* was firmly rooted, but at the same time especially coloured by its association with literary and cultural history, could a programmatic romantic*ism* originate and remain an important aspect of the national culture.

NOTES

1 Richard Ullmann and Helene Gotthard, *Geschichte des Begriffs 'Romantisch' in Deutschland* (Berlin, 1927).
2 Sigmund von Lempicki 'Bücherwelt und wirkliche Welt. Ein Beitrag zur Wesenserfassung der Romantik,' *DVLG* III (1925): 339–86.
3 Logan Pearsall Smith, 'Four Romantic Words,' in *Words and Idioms* (Boston and New York, 1925) (hereafter cited as *L. P. Smith*). First published in S.P.E. Tract, no. XVII (Oxford, 1924).
4 Arthur Henkel, in *Festschrift für Richard Alewyn*, ed. Herbert Singer and Benno von Wiese (Köln, Graz, 1967), pp. 292–308.
5 Fernand Baldensperger, ' "Romantique," ses analogues et ses équivalents: Tableau synoptique de 1650 à 1810,' *Harvard Studies and Notes in Philology and Literature* XIX (1937): 13–105 (hereafter cited as *Baldensperger*).
6 *L. P. Smith*, p. 82.
7 See *Baldensperger*, p. 16.
8 *L. P. Smith*, pp. 10 f.; E. R. Curtius, *European Literature and the Latin Middle Ages* (New York, 1953), pp. 30 f. (hereafter cited as *Curtius*)

9   *L. P. Smith*, p. 70
10 *Baldensperger*, p. 16.
11 Henry More, 'The Immortality of the Soul,' in *A Collection of Several Philosophical Writings* (London, 1662), p. 106. The work was first published in 1659. Throughout the present paper, italics in English quotations represent italics or otherwise differentiated type settings in the sources.
12 John Britton, *Memoir of John Aubrey* (London, 1845), pp. 32 *f.* Regarding the date, see pp. 38 *f.* and 91.
13 John Aubrey, *The Natural History of Wiltshire*, ed. John Britton (London, 1847) pp. 107 *f.*
14 See E. S. de Beer's introduction to his edition of Evelyn's *Diary* (Oxford, 1955), I: 71 *ff.*; also *L. P. Smith*, p. 67. note 1.
15 Evelyn's *Diary* III: 103, 27 June 1654.
16 Ibid., pp. 120 *f.*, August 1654.
17 Thomas Shadwell, Preface to *The Sullen Lovers*, in *Critical Essays of the Seventeenth Century*, ed. J. E. Spingarn, (Bloomington, 1957), p. 150; cf. *L. P. Smith*, pp. 70 *f.*
18 Thomas Shadwell, *Works* (London, 1720), I: 417.
19 Ibid., III: 110; See also p. 231.
20 Ibid., p. 342.
21 Steele, *The Tender Husband*, ed. G. A. Aitken, Mermaid Series, pp. 201, 222 *ff.*, 235; see also pp. 293 *ff.*
22 Sir William Temple, 'An Essay upon the Ancient and Modern Learning' (1690) in *Five Miscellaneous Essays by Sir William Temple*, ed. Samuel Holt Monk (Ann Arbor, 1963), p. 70 (hereafter cited as *Monk*).
23 Sir William Temple, 'Upon the Gardens of Epicurus; or, Of Gardening, in the Year 1685,' in *Monk*, p. 13.
24 *The Spectator*, Letter No. 303 (1712); see *L. P. Smith*, p. 76.
25 *The Miscellaneous Works of Joseph Addison*, ed. A. C. Gutkelch (London, 1914), II: 19. (From *On Italy*, 1705, describing Addison's journey of December 1699.)
26 *The Spectator*, Letter no. 417.
27 Ibid., no. 413.
28 Ibid., no. 412.
29 Shaftesbury, *Characteristicks* (6th ed., London, 1738), II: 394 *f.*
30 E. S. Rowe, *Friendship in Death* (5th ed. London, 1738), p. 170; cf. p. 409.
31 Ibid., pp. 451 *f.*
32 Ibid., p. 140.
33 Ibid., pp. 188, 344, 349 *f.*
34 Edward Wright, *Observations Made in Travelling Through France, Italy, &c. in the years 1720, 1721, and 1722* (London, 1730).
35 Ibid., I: 20 *f.*
36 Ibid., I: 163 *f.*
37 Ibid., I: 175 *f.*
38 Shelvocke, *Voyage Round the World* (London, 1828), p. 143. This work was first published in 1726.
39 George Anson, *A Voyage Round the World*, ed. Richard Walter (6th ed., London, 1749), p. 163.
40 Ibid., pp. 415 *f.*, 450.
41 George Forster, *A Voyage Round the World* (London, 1777), I: 124 *f.*
42 John Livinsgton Lowes, *The Road to Xanadu* (revised ed., New York, 1930). References will be to the Vintage Books edition, New York, 1959.
43 Thomas Maurice, *The History of Hindostan*, vol. I, 1795; vol. II, 1798. References will be to 2nd ed., London, 1820.
44 Ibid., I: 8 *f.*, 104 *f.*, 181.
45 Ibid., pp. 21, 397 *ff.*

46 James Bruce, *Travels to Discover the Source of the Nile*, Vol. v (3rd ed., Edinburgh, 1813), 261 *ff.* First published 1790. Cf. Lowes, *The Road to Xanadu*, pp. 338 *ff.*

47 James Rennell, *Memoir of a Map of Hindoostan; or the Mogul Empire* (London, 1808), pp. 104 *ff.* (hereafter cited as *Rennell*). Cf. Lowes, *The Road to Xanadu*, pp. 394 *ff.* (His references are from the 2nd ed., 1792; the work was first published in 1788.)

48 *Rennell*, pp. 60 *f.*

49 Ibid., pp. 111 *f.*

50 Johnson's *Journey to the Western Islands of Scotland* and Boswell's *Journal of a Tour to the Hebrides with Samuel Johnson* ... (London, 1930), pp. 35 *f.*, 69, 140 *f.*

51 James Boswell, *Journal of a Tour to the Hebrides* (London, 1939), p. 96.

52 Samuel Johnson, *Adventurer* (2nd ed., London 1754), 1 :17 *ff.* Cf. *L. P. Smith*, p. 79.

53 Johnson, *Adventurer*, p. 21.

54 *A Series of Letters between Mrs. Eliz. Carter, & Mrs. Catherine Talbot, 1741-1770* ... with *Letters of Mrs. Eliz. Carter to Mrs. Vesey, 1763-1787*, 2 vols. (London, 1808).

55 Ibid., 1: 71, 8 August 1745 .

56 Ibid., 1: 135, 14 May 1747; 1: 193 *f.*, 10 October 1748.

57 Ibid., ii: 100 *ff.*

58 Ibid., ii: 106 *f.*, 29 September 1764.

59 Nathaniel William Wraxall, *A Tour through the Western, Southern and Interior Provinces of France* (added to *Memoirs of the Kings of France*, London, 1777, vol. ii), pp. 286 *ff.*, 335 *ff.*, 341 *ff.* Cf. Immerwahr, 'The Ascending Romantic View in the Eighteenth Century,' *PEGS* xxxvi (1966): 10 *f.* (hereafter cited as *Immerwahr, Romantic View*).

60 *L. P. Smith*, p. 82.

61 Elizabeth Manwaring, *Italian Landscape in Eighteenth-Century England* (New York, 1925) (hereafter cited as *Manwaring*).

62 See *Great Centuries of Painting: Seventeenth Century*, ed. Jaques Dupont and François Mathey (Geneva, 1951), p. 97.

63 See W. S. Lewis, *Horace Walpole* (London, 1961).

64 See Isabel W. U. Chase, *Horace Walpole, Gardenist* (Princeton, 1943) (hereafter cited as *Chase*).

65 Horace Walpole, *Correspondence with Thomas Gray, Richard West and Thomas Ashton*, ed. W. S. Lewis, G. L. Lam, and C. H. Bennett (New Haven and London, 1948), 1: 181 *ff.*

66 Horace Walpole, *Anecdotes of Painting in England* iii (London, 1798): 94 *f.* and 95.

67 See *Manwaring*, pp. 101 *ff.*; the quotation is from p. 107.

68 Joseph Warton, *Essay on the Genius and Writings of Pope* (5th ed., London, 1806), 1: 41 *f.* See also his comment on *The Castle of Indolence*, ibid., p. 349, on Milton, pp. 6 f., and on Ariosto, p. 367.

69 Charles Smith, *The Antient and Present State of the County of Kerry* (Dublin, 1756).

70 Ibid., p. 80.

71 Ibid., p. 95.

72 Ibid., pp. 96 f.

73 Ibid., p. 123.

74 Ibid., pp. 127 *f.*

75 Published posthumously as a footnote to a poem in *A Collection of Poems*, printed for G. Pearch (London, 1768), 1: 36 *ff*; printed separately in 1767.

76 *Immerwahr, Romantic View* (as in note 59), pp. 16 *ff.*

77 William Gilpin, *Observations on the River Wye* ... (5th ed., London, 1800), pp. 58 *f.* On this author, see W. D. Templeman, *The Life and Work of William Gilpin*, Illinois Studies in Language and Literature, xxiv, nos. 3–4 (Urbana, 1939).

78 *Immerwahr, Romantic View*, p. 17.

79 *Jean Pauls Sämtliche Werke*, ed. E. Berend, Abt. i, vol. vii (Weimar, 1931). Young's passage on the Campan Valley is in his *Travels during the Years* 1787

1788, and *1789, Undertaken with a View of Ascertaining the Cultivation ... of France*, (London and New York, 1892), pp. 59 *f.* Young's work was first published in 1792 and the German translation published in Berlin, 1793-5.

80 Arthur Young, *A Six Months' Tour through the North of England* (London, 1770), II: 197 *ff.* See also III: 146 *f.*

81 Ibid., II: 197.

82 Ibid., p. 331.

83 Ibid., III: 153.

84 Arthur Young, 'A Tour in Ireland Made in the Years 1766 ... to ... 1779,' in John Pinkerton, *A General Collection of the Best and Most Interesting Voyages and Travels* III (London, 1809): p. 820.

85 Henry Swinburne, *Travels in the Two Sicilies in the Years 1777. 1778, 1779, and 1780* (London, 1790), III: 218 *f.*

86 Edmund Burke, *A Philosophical Enquiry into the Origin of Our Ideas of the Sublime and Beautiful* (London, 1757).

87 Uvedale Price, *On the Picturesque* (hereafter cited as *Price*). This essay first appeared in 1794 and included in later editions a letter by Repton written the same year and Price's rebuttal. References in the following are to the edition of London, 1842.

88 Ibid., pp. 94 *ff.*, 158 *ff.*

89 Ibid., p. 96.

90 Ibid., p. 150.

91 Ibid., pp. 158 *f.*

92 Ibid., pp. 181 ff.

93 Ibid., pp. 183 *f.*

94 Ibid., pp. 299 *f.*

95 'Letter to Uvedale Price, Esq.,' in *Price*, pp. 410 *ff.*

96 Richard Payne Knight, *An Analytical Inquiry into the Principles of Taste* (London, 1805), pp. 192 *f.* See also pp. 146 *ff.*, 189 *ff.*

97 *Weimarer Ausgabe*, Abt. I, vol. XLVI, pt. i, pp. 152 *f.*, 167 *f.*, 200 *f.*, 221.

98 'Maximen und Reflexionen,' *Weimarer Ausgabe*, Abt. I, vol. XLII, pt. ii, p. 129; *Hamburger Ausgabe* XII: 488, no. 868.

99 See above, pp. 35 *f.*

100 Philip Thicknesse, *A Year's Journey through France and Parts of Spain*, 2 vols. (London, 1771), I: 108 *ff.*; II: 63.

101 William Coxe, *Sketches of the Natural, Civil, and Political State of Swisserland* (2nd ed., London, 1786), pp. 3 *f.*, 14 *f.*, 28 *f.*, 56 *f.*, 131 *ff.* See also *Travels in Switzerland. In a Series of Letters to Wm. Melmoth*, 3 vols. (London, 1789).

102 Patrick Brydone, *A Tour through Sicily and Malta* (Edinburgh, 1840), pp. 38 *f.*, 47, 54. The work was written in 1770 and first published in London, 1773.

103 Ibid., pp. 28 *ff.*

104 In addition to the works cited above by *Chase* and *Manwaring*, see Marie Luise Gothein, *Geschichte der Gartenkunst* II (Jena, 1914); three articles by Arthur O. Lovejoy, 'The Chinese Origin of a Romanticism,' *JEGP* XXXII (1933): 1–20; 'Nature as Aesthetic Norm.' *MLN* XLII (1927): 444 *ff.*; 'The First Gothic Revival and the Return to Nature' *MLN* XLVII (1932): 419–46; and R. Immerwahr, 'The First Romantic Aesthetics,' *MLQ* XXI (1960): 3–26 (hereafter cited as *Immerwahr, Romantic Aesthetics*).

105 See especially the articles of Lovejoy cited above.

106 *Monk*, pp. 29 *f.*

107 William Mason, 'The English Garden,' quoted from edition of New York, 1783, pp. 34 *f.*; see also a similar context of the word *romantic*, pp. 79 *f.*

108 See Immerwahr, *Romantic Aesthetics*, pp. 8 *ff.*, where passages are quoted from Heely's *Letters on the Beauties of Hagley, Envil, and the Leasowes* (London, 1777).

109 Sir William Chambers, *Designs of Chinese Buildings, Furniture, Dresses, Machines, and Utensils* (London, 1757) (hereafter cited as *Designs of Chinese Buildings*), and

Dissertation on Oriental Gardening (London, 1772). Quotations are from the second edition, 1773.

110 *Designs of Chinese Buildings ...*, pp. 15 *ff*.
111 *Dissertation on Oriental Gardening*, pp. 39 *ff*. The passages from Chambers are quoted more fully in *Immerwahr, Romantic Aesthetics*, pp. 11 *ff*.
112 Thomas Whately, *Observations on Modern Gardening*. The first two editions were published in London, 1770, the third in the following year; a German translation, *Betrachtungen über das heutige Gartenwesen* (Leipzig, 1771). See the fuller discussion of this work in *Immerwahr, Romantic Aesthetics*, pp. 13 ff.
113 *Observations on Modern Gardening*, 2nd edition, pp. 18 *f.*, 59.
114 Ibid., pp. 98 *ff*. See *Immerwahr, Romantic Aesthetics*, pp. 13 *f*.
115 *Observations on Modern Gardening*, pp. 21 *f*.
116 Ibid., pp. 111 *ff*.
117 *The Letters of Hannah More*, ed. R. Brimley Johnson (New York, 1926), pp. 98 *f*.
118 *Vathek, an Arabian Tale* (London and Philadelphia, 1900), pp. 115 *f*. The novel was written in French and published in that language in 1787; the unauthorized English translation had appeared the previous year. The French original here reads 'ces cabanes bizarres.' See *Vathek* (Lausanne, 1962), p. 96.
119 William Beckford, *Journal in Portugal and Spain*, ed. Boyd Alexander (London, 1954), entry of 25 May 1787, p. 38.
120 Ibid., 29 May, pp. 46 *f*.
121 Ibid., 10 June, pp. 73 *f*.
122 Ibid., 5 July, p. 122.
123 Ibid., 6 July, pp. 124 *f*.
124 Ibid., 23 July and 15 August, pp. 142, 160.
125 Ibid., p. 124.
126 Richard Hurd, *Letters on Chivalry and Romance ...* ed. Edith J. Morley (London, 1911), p. 81. This work was first published in 1759. The edition cited includes notes from the 1788 edition.
127 Ibid., p. 87 and footnote 2 on that page.
128 Ibid., pp. 148 *f*.
129 Ibid., pp. 59 f. and footnote, p. 60.
130 Ibid., pp. 152 *f*.
131 See especially ibid., pp. 51 *f.*, 59 *f*.
132 *Poems of Ossian* II: 326.
133 Ibid., p. 337.
134 Thomas Warton, *Observations on the Faerie Queene of Spenser* (2nd ed., London, 1762), I: 1 (hereafter cited as *Warton*). Cf. pp. 57, 64 *ff*.
135 Ibid., p. 153.
136 Ibid., p. 197.
137 Ibid., II: 220 *f*.
138 Ibid., pp. 267 *f*.
139 *Warton*, I: 178 *f*.
140 Thomas Warton, *History of English Poetry* (London, 1871), I: 93 *ff.*, 109, 125 *ff*. First published in 1774.
141 Ibid., I: 125.
142 Ibid., p. 142.
143 Ibid., p. 141.
144 Quoted by *L. P. Smith*, p. 107, footnote.
145 Richard Ullmann and Helene Gotthard, *Geschichte des Begriffes 'Romantisch' in Deutschland* (Berlin, 1927) (hereafter cited as *Ullmann and Gotthard*).
146 Cf. Wellek, *Concepts of Criticism*. p. 130n.
147 *Ullmann and Gotthard*, pp. 55 *ff*.
148 Gotthard Heidegger, *Mythoscopia Romantica oder Discours von den so benannten Romans* (Zürich, 1698).
149 See *Ullman and Gotthard*, pp. 16 *ff*.

150 Ibid., pp. 18*ff.*
151 Ibid., pp. 19*f.*
152 See the excellent treatment of Wieland and Herder in *Ullman and Gotthard,* pp. 91*ff.*, 97.
153 See Friedrich Sengle, *Wieland,* (Stuttgart, 1949), pp. 89*ff.*
154 Wieland, in *Werke* (Berlin: Hempel, n.d.), LXVII: 7. This edition will be cited for all works not yet included in the *Gesammelte Schriften.*
155 Erster Gesang: 5. Strophe.
156 Wieland, *Werke* XIV: 7–172.
157 Ibid., p. 162.
158 Ibid., XV: 154.
159 Wieland, *Gesammelte Schriften,* herausgegeben von der Deutschen Akademie, Abt. I, vol. VIII, p. 349.
160 Wieland, *Werke* XI: 59; *Gesammelte Schriften,* Abt. I vol. IX, p. 421.
161 Wieland, *Werke* XXI: 93*ff.*; *Der Teutsche Merkur* (1789), II: 313 ff.
162 Wieland, *Agathon,* Neuntes Buch, 8. Kapitel, *Werke* II: 128.
163 Wieland, 'Über die ältesten Zeitkürzungsspiele,' in *Gesammelte Schriften,* Abt. I, vol. XIV, p. 311.
164 Ibid., pp. 204*ff.*
165 Wieland, 'Betrachtung über den Standpunkt, worin wir uns in Absicht auf Erzählungen und Nachrichten von Geistererscheinungen befinden,' *Der Teutsche Merkur* (1781), II: 226*ff.*
166 Ibid., p. 229.
167 Ibid., p. 227.
168 Cf. *Ullmann and Gotthard,* pp. 80*ff.*
169 Gerstenberg, *Briefe über die Merkwürdigkeiten der Literatur.* Erste Sammlung. Zweiter Brief [1766] (hereafter cited as *Gerstenberg*). Deutsche Literaturdenkmale 29/30 (Stuttgart, 1890), pp. 17*ff.*
170 Gerstenberg, p. 17.
171 *Warton* I: 15.
172 See, e.g., *Gerstenberg,* p. 19.
173 Ibid., Dritte Sammlung [1767], p. 258.
174 Ibid., p. 259.
175 See Herder, *Sämmtliche Werke,* ed. Suphan (hereafter cited as *Suphan*), IV: 439; V: 360, 601, and passim.
176 Ibid., V: 383*ff.*; XIV: 444, and passim.
177 In the draft of an essay, 'Vom gotischen Geschmack' [1763], in *Suphan* XXXII: 30.
178 *Suphan,* V: 316*f.*
179 *Suphan,* XIV: 462, 266.
180 Ibid., p. 348. See also top of p. 462 and V: 384.
181 Ibid., XIV: 440*f.* Novalis: 'Indem ich dem Gemeinen einen hohen Sinn, dem Gewöhnlichen ein geheimnisvolles Ansehn, dem Bekannten die Würde des Unbekannten ... gebe so romantisiere ich es.' *Schriften* II (Stuttgart, 1965), 545.
182 *Suphan* XXV: 66.
183 *Suphan* IX: 525; see also the following pages and XXV: 65.
184 Ibid., XIV: 141.
185 Ibid., V: 522*f.*; cf. also p. 360.
186 Ibid. p. 585.
187 *Schriften der Goethe-Gesellschaft* XLI (1928): 169*f.*
188 Ibid., XXXIX (1926): 323*f.*
189 Ibid., pp. 324*f.*
190 Johann Georg Zimmermann, *Betrachtungen über die Einsamkeit* (Zürich, 1756); *Von der Einsamkeit* (Leipzig, 1773); *Über die Einsamkeit,* 4 vols. (Leipzig, 1784–5; 2nd ed., Troppau, 1786). Quotations from vol. I are from the first edition, those from later volumes are from the second edition.
191 Ibid., I (1784): 1*f.*

192 Ibid., IV (2nd ed., 1786): 2.
193 Ibid., IV: 3 *f.*
194 Ibid., IV, 8 *f.*
195 Ibid., IV: 19 *f.*
196 Ibid., I: 3.
197 Ibid., II: 51 *f.*
198 Ibid., III: 324 *f.*
199 Ibid., III: 478.
200 Ibid., III: 468 *f.* ..
201 Zimmermann, *Über die Einsamkeit* III: 457 *f.*
202 Christian Cay Lorenz Hirschfeld, *Das Landleben* (Bern, 1767), with three more editions: Leipzig, 1768, 1771, 1776; *Versuch über den groß en Mann* (Leipzig,1768), *Der Winter* (Leipzig, 1769, 1775); *Betrachtungen über die heroischen Tugenden* (Kiel, 1770); *Anmerkungen über die Landhäuser* (Leipzig, 1773).
203 *Immerwahr, Romantic Aesthetics*, pp. 3 *ff.*
204 *Gartenkalender*, 8 vols. (Kiel, Dessau, Altona, Braunschweig, 1782–9).
205 Hirschfeld, *Theorie der Gartenkunst* IV: 90.
206 Ibid., I: 214.
207 Ibid., I: 193.
208 Ibid., I: 155 *f.*
209 Ibid., I: 158. A chapter, 'Feierlicher Garten,' with several examples is in vol. IV, pp. 116 *ff.*
210 See *Weimarer Ausgabe*, Abt. I, vol. XXXVI, pp. 233 *ff.*, and Abt. II, vol. VI, pp. 228 *ff.*
211 *Weimarer Ausgabe*, Abt. I, vol. XIX, p. 7.
212 Ibid., pp. 81 *f.*
213 Hirschfeld, *Theorie der Gartenkunst* IV: 112.
214 *Sämtliche Schriften* I (Stuttgart, 1835): 66; first published in 1777.
215 Ibid., p. 75.
216 Ibid., p. 86.
217 Ibid., p. 110.
218 *Deutsche Literaturdenkmale*, vol. VII, no. 23, pp. 91 *f.* (hereafter cited as *DLD*).
219 Ibid., pp. 254 *f.*
220 Ibid., pp. 254 *f.*
221 See above, Note 181, and below, pp. 124 *f.*
222 Karl Philipp Moritz, *Reisen eines Deutschen in Italien in den Jahren 1786 bis 1788* (Berlin, 1792), I: 5.
223 Karl Philipp Moritz, *Anthousa oder Roms Alterthümer* (Berlin, 1791), p. 197.
224 *DLD*, vol. XX, no. 126: 65 *ff.*; quotation from p. 67.
225 *Sämtliche Werke*, ed. Schüddekopf (Leipzig, 1902 *ff.*), IV: 358. Cf. Max L. Bäumer, *Das Dionysische in den Werken Wilhelm Heinses* (Bonn, 1964).
226 *Sämtliche Werke* VII: 183.
227 Ibid., III, ii: 570.
228 Letter to Gleim, in *Briefe zwischen Gleim, Wilhelm Heinse und Johann von Müller*, ed. W. Körte (Zürich, 1805–6), II: 409 *f.*
229 Cf. *Sämtliche Werke* VII: 44, 46 *f.*
230 Ibid., p. 91.
231 *Sämtliche Werke* IV: 177 *f.*
232 *Sämtliche Werke* VIII: 470.
233 Ibid., p. 473.
234 Ibid., p. 481.
235 Georg Forster, *Werke* IX (Berlin, 1958), p. 23.
236 Georg Forster, *Sämtliche Schriften* (Leipzig, 1843), III: 433.
237 It was published posthumously in Schiller's *Horen* in 1797. The word *romantisch* first occurs in Part One, Fourth Letter. (Jacob Michael Reinhold Lenz, *Werke*

und Schriften, ed. Britta Titel und Hellmut Haug, Stuttgart and Darmstadt, 1966–7, I: 286.)
238 Ibid., pp. 293 *f.*
239 Ibid., pp. 317 *f.* See also p. 310.
240 See *Ullmann and Gotthard*, pp. 156 *ff.*, and below, pp. 116.
241 *Sämtliche Werke*, ed. G. Fricke and H. G. Göpfert (2nd ed., München, 1960), II: 234.
242 Ibid., pp. 234 *f.*
243 Ibid., p. 265.
244 Ibid., IV: 66.
245 Christian Meiners, *Briefe über die Schweiz*, 4 vols. (Berlin, 1788–90).
246 See Wilhelm von Humboldt, *Tagebücher*, ed. A. Leitzmann (Berlin, 1916 *ff.*), I: 23 *f.*, 39.
247 Ibid., p. 16.
248 Ibid., pp. 23, 39.
249 Ibid., p. 95.
250 Ibid., p. 96.
251 Ibid., p. 143.
252 Ibid., pp. 144 *f.*
253 Ibid., p. 174.
254 Ibid., p. 183.
255 Ibid., p. 207.
256 Ibid., p. 185.
257 Ibid., pp. 186 *ff.*
258 Ibid., p. 200.
259 *Wilhelm und Caroline von Humboldt in ihren Briefen* I: 144.
260 Jean Baptiste la Curne, *Histoire littéraire des troubadours* (Paris, 1774).
261 Ibid., p. 45.
262 Ibid., p. 71.
263 Ibid., p. 124.
264 Ibid., p. 170.
265 Watelet, *Essai sur les jardins*, pp. 117 *ff.* The passage reminiscent of Chambers, omitted from the above quotation, is on pp. 118 *f.*
266 Cf. *Baldensperger*, p. 76.
267 Quoted by *Baldensperger*, from the *Discours* in front of *Shakespeare, traduit de l'Anglois* I (Paris, 1776): cxviii.
268 Quoted by Mary Gertrude Cushing, *Pierre Le Tourneur* (New York, 1908), p. 184n from the same page of the source as the passage above quoted by *Baldensperger*.
269 Girardin, *De la composition des paysages*, pp. 128 *f.*
270 Ibid., pp. 133 *f.*
271 *Collection complète des oeuvres de J. J. Rousseau* XX (Genève, 1782): 308 *f.* This is the first published edition, but *Les Rêveries* were written in 1777.
272 Ibid., pp. 325 *f.*
273 Ibid., p. 316.
274 'Rousseaus Insel oder St. Peter im Bielersee, Fragment aus Baggesens Reisen, aus dem Dänischen übersetzt,' *Neuer Teutscher Merkur* (1795), I: 31 *f.* Hirschfeld, *Theorie der Gartenkunst* (IV: 103 *f.*) also describes this island as an example of romantic scenery.
275 See the edition in Classiques Garnier, (Paris, n. d.), I: 52 *ff.*, 80 *ff.*, 326 *ff.* and *passim*.
276 *Baldensperger*, pp. 78. 80, 82, 84, 86.

HANS EICHNER

Germany /
Romantisch – Romantik –
Romantiker

I

At the cost of some oversimplification, the history of the adjective
romantisch and its cognates can be divided into four periods:
I   From the time of its first introduction in Germany in 1698*
until the founding of the first German romantic periodical, the
Athenäum, exactly one hundred years later, 'romantisch' acquired a
wide variety of connotations, all of which, however, are fairly
closely connected with the root meanings of the word: 'romance-
like,' 'reminiscent of romances,' or pertaining to the Romance
languages.
II   From 1798 onwards it became fashionable to theorize about a
'romantic poetry' – *romantische Poesie* – which was the characteristic
mode of expression of the moderns and stood in significant contrast
to the 'classical poetry' of the ancients.
III In the winter of 1807–8, opponents of those literary trends that
are now customarily grouped under the heading 'romanticism'
began to use *romantisch* and the nouns derived from it, *Romantik* and
Romantiker, as pejorative terms descriptive of these trends and their
protagonists, thus giving the terms a chronologically narrow, contemporary reference. For a few years, the nouns were used mostly,
and the adjective frequently, as terms of abuse.

*   See R. Immerwahr, p. 55 *ff.* above, and Richard Ullmann and Helene
       Gotthard, *Geschichte des Begriffes 'Romantisch' in Deutschland* (Berlin, 1927), p. 16.
       My indebtedness to this exhaustive study in the present article can hardly be
       overestimated; except where stated, however, I have not quoted from Ullmann
       and Gotthard without checking the full context in the original source.

iv When the quarrel between the classicists and the romantics began to abate, *romantisch* (in such phrases as *romantische Schule*), *Romantik*, and *Romantiker* gradually established themselves as the non-evaluative terms that they are now in histories of German literature. This process was probably completed by the middle of the nineteenth century.

The first of these periods was amply discussed by Raymond Immerwahr in the first essay of the present volume. Before we turn to the events of the late 1790s, it will be useful, however, to classify the meanings of *romantisch* that had by then become established.

1 As Immerwahr has shown, the most widespread use of *romantisch* was probably that in which the word referred to certain types of landscape; in fact, this is the only usage of the word recognized by the most influential German lexicographer of the late eighteenth and the early nineteenth centuries, J. C. Adelung:

Romantisch ... from the French *romantesque*, which is likewise [i.e., like the preceding entry, *romanenhaft*] derived from *roman*, but is only current in a narrower meaning, of particularly pleasant and, as it were, enchanting landscapes, as they are described in novels and chivalric romances.

Romantisch ... aus dem Französischen romantesque *[sic!], welches gleichfalls von Roman abstammet, aber nur in engerer Bedeutung von vorzüglich angenehmen und gleichsam bezaubernden Gegenden üblich ist, so wie sie in den Romanen und Ritterbüchern beschrieben werden.**

While less frequent than around 1800, this usage is still quite common. The following passage from Thomas Mann's *Buddenbrooks* (1901) is typical:

It was not long till they had reached the 'spring,' a pretty, romantic spot with a wooden bridge spanning a small ravine, rocky, precipitous slopes and overhanging trees, whose roots lay bare.

... es dauerte gar nicht lange, bis sie die 'Quelle' erreicht hatten, einen hübschen, romantischen Punkt mit einer hölzernen Brücke über einem kleinen Abgrund, zerklüfteten Abhängen und überhängenden Bäumen, deren Wurzeln bloßlagen.[1]

2 Whereas modern German strictly distinguishes between *romantisch* and *romanisch* (= 'Romance,' of the languages descended from Latin), these two adjectives were synonymous in the eighteenth and

* J. C. Adelung, *Versuch eines vollständigen grammatisch-kritischen Wörterbuches der Hochdeutschen Mundart* ... (Leipzig, 1777), III: 1475. This definition is repeated without change in the fourth edition of Adelung's dictionary (1808). His reference to *romantesque* is, of course, erroneous; there is no such adjective, and the *t* in *romantisch* points plainly to its English origin.

the early nineteenth centuries. Thus, Herder writes of the '*romanischer Geschmack*' (romantic taste) of the Spaniards and Italians;[2] F. Schlegel speaks of the 'system of the ... Provençal or romantic languages'/'... *des ganzen Systems der ... provenzalischen oder romantischen Sprachen*';[3] Görres holds that 'the French or romantic language' was not used in poetry prior to 1150/'... *da die französische oder romantische Sprache vor der Hälfte des zwölften Jahrhunderts nicht in die Poesie eingedrungen ist*';[4] and J. H. Voß refers to the Romance languages as 'romantic hybrids'/'... *romantische Bastardinnen*.'[5]

3 In accordance with the etymology of the word, *romantisch* was used in the sense of 'romance-like,' 'pertaining to romances,' 'as in a romance rather than in real life,' and consequently carried such connotations as 'fictitious,' 'untrue,' 'extravagant,' 'improbable,' or 'absurd.' The perfect illustration of this usage of the word *romantic* and its cognates in Europe is perhaps to be found in Richardson's *Pamela*, where the villainous B. says of the heroine, 'With all her pretended simplicity and innocence, I never knew so much romantic invention as she is mistress of. In short, the girl's head is turned by romances.'[6] With similar implications – although there is really no need to add further illustrations to those adduced by Immerwahr in the preceding essay – J. G. Eichhorn claims in 1799 that Sturla Thordarson had been the last scald to practise historical faithfulness, those after him having initiated the 'romantic falsification of the Icelandic sagas'/'...*die romantische Verfälschung der isländischen Sagen*.'[7] An anonymous reviewer in the *Jenaische Allgemeine Literatur-Zeitung* of 7 February 1801 enumerates as 'romantic ingredients' of a story an old castle whose owner has been murdered, a voluptuous abbot, and an affected niece whose manner of speaking is modelled on romances of chivalry;[8] and one year later, another reviewer defines 'romantic travelogues' as those whose authors are indifferent to the truth:

Die romantischen Reisebeschreibungen aber leitet Herr Manso aus dem, seit Xerxes ... rege gewordenen Hange nach der Kenntnis fremder Reiche und Völker ab, welcher eine Menge von Länderbeschreibern weckte, die, wenig um die Wahrheit bekümmert, die sonderbarsten Nachrichten zusammenrafften und so den Betrug und die Leichtgläubigkeit auf mannigfaltige Weise beförderten.[9]

These pejorative connotations have, of course, survived into the present; but as fiction can be more interesting than fact, the description of a book, a situation, or an event as *romantisch* in the sense of 'romance-like' can imply praise as well as censure. (It always implied praise when applied to landscapes.) Hence, when in the last third of the eighteenth century the taste for the unusual, exotic, and marvellous increased and a large percentage of the German reading public began once again to prefer books that provided them with an escape from their humdrum existence, the adjective *romantisch* became increasingly popular in contexts that gave it such positive connotations as 'imaginative,' 'eventful,' or 'stimulatingly unusual.' This development may be illustrated, to choose an exceptionally odd example, with Schiller's referring to plaster cast replicas of statues of Greek gods he saw in Mannheim as 'romantic gods.'[10] The most convincing evidence for it is, however, the ever increasing number of novels, histories, and collections of tales that displayed the word *romantisch* on the title page. Inevitably, of course, this advertising use of the word annoyed some fastidious readers. Thus Jean Paul, who intended in 1792 to give his novel *Die unsichtbare Loge* the sub-title *Romantische Biographie*, was urged by his friend Otto to leave out the word *romantisch*, because it had been 'used too often and ... had acquired a bad reputation,'

Jetzt fällt mir nur noch das ein, daß Du das Wörtchen: Romantisch, *wohl von dem Titel weglassen mußt, weil es zu verbraucht und durch das Romanschreiber-Wesen schon in zu schlechten Ruf gekommen ist* * –

and Jean Paul accepted this suggestion. In 1805, Garlieb Merkel explained the neglect of a work sub-titled 'A Romantic Picture of old German Freedom and National Grandeur' by pointing out

that its title is reminiscent of that of so many insipid historical novels and that the word 'romantic' has become almost notorious with the more tasteful public.

... daß sein Titel denen so vieler abgeschmackten historischen Romane ähnlich klingt, und das Wort romantisch bei dem geschmackvollern Publikum fast verrufen ist.[11]

But such strictures failed to change the fashion, and in 1815, a belated reviewer of Friedrich Majer's study, *Bertrand du Guesolin* (1801–2), sub-titled *Romantische Biographie*, could still claim that 'most people certainly expect something else from a romantic biography than mere history, and all expect something entertaining':

Unter einer romantischen Biographie denken sich die meisten gewiß etwas anders, als bloße Geschichte, alle aber erwarten etwas Unterhaltendes.[12]

---

* *Jean Pauls Briefwechsel mit seinem Freunde Christian Otto* (Berlin 1829), 1: 113. *Ullmann*, p. 124, erroneously ascribes the remark to Jean Paul himself.

4 As Adelung pointed out, *romantisch* was derived from the noun *Roman* (novel, romance), and most *Romane* were, as they still are, love stories:

Der Roman ... in the widest sense, any fictitious marvellous story, fictitious marvellous travelogues etc. being also known by this name ... In the narrowest sense, a *Roman* is a marvellous love story, or one with an intricate plot; these intricacies or marvels distinguish a *Roman* in all meanings of the word both from a tale and from any other kind of fiction.

Der Roman ... im weitesten Verstande, eine jede erdichtete wunderbare Geschichte, da denn auch erdichtete wunderbare Reisebeschreibungen u.s.f. diesen Namen führen ... Im engsten Verstande ist der Roman eine wunderbare, oder mit Verwirrungen durchwebte Liebesgeschichte; welche Verwirrungen, oder Wunderbares, einen Roman in allen Bedeutungen sowohl von einer Erzählung, als auch von einer andern erdichteten Geschichte unterscheiden.[13]

Roman, m. fictitious or poetically adorned story of some length in prose, whose centre is usually a love story.

Roman, m. *erdichtete oder dichterisch ausgeschmückte erzählung größeren umfanges in prosa, deren kern gewöhnlich ein Liebesvorgang ist.**

Consequently, *romantisch* had such overtones as 'erotic' or 'amorous'. In this sense, Herder spoke of the 'romantic time' he hoped to spend with his fiancée in 1771 in Darmstadt.[14]

5 Although modern German, like English, has well-established adjectives referring to the three classical genres – *episch, lyrisch*, and *dramatisch* – it has no such word referring to the novel (*Roman*). Around 1800, *romantisch* could be used to fill this gap, and – given a suitable context – was readily understood to have the same semantic relationship to *Roman* that *dramatisch* has to *Drama*. This meaning of *romantisch* has been ignored in all the German dictionaries I have been able to consult and was mentioned only casually by Ullmann and Gotthard; as we shall see, however, it is of crucial importance in the history of our word. It is present in the title of the work in which *romantisch* was first used in German – Heidegger's *Mythoscopia romantica oder Discours von den so benannten Romans* (1698). It is present when Schleiermacher in 1792 suggests that the 'greatest romantic

* Grimms *Deutsches Wörterbuch* VIII (Leipzig, 1893): 1152. The same implication is still present when Thomas Mann says of the third of his Joseph-novels, 'Der dritte "Joseph" ist durch seinen erotischen Inhalt der romanhafteste Teil des Werkes' (*Gesammelte Werke*, Frankfurt a.M. [1960], XI: 661).

and dramatic poets' – i.e., the greatest novelists and dramatists – let their villains express a fatalistic philosophy when they reflect about themselves/'*Daher die größten romantischen und dramatischen Dichter, wo sie einen Bösewicht über sich selber reflektieren lassen, ihm diese fatalische Ansicht geben ...*'[15] and it is present when, eight years later, he speaks of the 'usual comparison of the romantic and the dramatic.'[16] We find it again when Tieck intends to call a work in which narrative alternates with dramatic dialogue 'Romantic and Dramatic Representation'[17] (1797), or when F. Schlegel writes that 'in Shakespeare's tragedies the form is dramatic, the spirit and purpose romantic,'[18] or when, while working on his novel *Lucinde*, he writes to his niece: 'I am now devoting myself expecially to romantic [*die romantische*] science. Tell your mother about this and ask her how her little novel [*Romänchen*] is coming along'/'*Welche Wissenschaft treibst Du jetzt vorzüglich? – Ich lege mich vorzüglich auf die romantische. Sag das der Mutter, und frag sie, wie sich ihr Romänchen befindet?*'[19] (1798). In 1807, Goethe used the phrases 'romantische Motive' and 'romantische Sujets' of subjects that might be suitable for inclusion in a novel;* and in 1821, to end up with a rather late example of this usage, Jean Paul called his first novel, *Die unsichtbare Loge*, his 'romantic firstling' / '*Gegenwärtiger Schreiber ist ... im Begriffe ... ein Familienfest mit einem seiner liebsten Kinder – eben dem gegenwärtigen Buche, seinem romantischen Erstling – zu begehen.*'[20]

6 In literary contexts, *romantisch* – because of its etymological connection with such words as (Fr.) *roman*, (Sp.) *romance*, (It.) *romanzo*, etc. – referred to the poetry of the Middle Ages and the Renaissance or to the time when this poetry was written. The phrase *romantische Poesie* could occasionally be used with specific reference to Romance poetry and contrasted with the 'Northern' literature of the same time, but its primary reference was chronological, so that it included all poetry written in the European vernaculars (as distinct from classical Latin) from the earliest times through and beyond the sixteenth century and including such authors as Spenser and Shakespeare. In the 1790s, this usage of *romantische Poesie* was familiar to every reader of Herder,[21] and until 1797 Friedrich Schlegel employed the phrase exclusively in this sense.[22] Similarly,

---

*   'Früh am Brunnen ... Nachher romantische Motive überdacht, die von Pyramus und Thisbe und von der Mystification' (i.e., the story of *La folle en pélerinage*, which Goethe had translated three days before he made this note and which was subsequently incorporated in *Wilhelm Meisters Wanderjahre*). 'Verschiedene romantische Sujets überlegt. Verwandlung der Achilleis in einen Roman.' (Diary notes of 10 August 1807, *Weimarer Ausgabe*, Abt. III, vol. III, pp. 255, 256.)

given a suitable context, the phrase *die romantische Zeit* (the romantic age) would have been accepted by any reader at that time as a synonym of 'the Middle Ages' (including, as this concept did not yet exist, the Renaissance).*

Evidently, whenever 'romantic poetry' in the sense defined above was discussed, one must have been aware that it was different in form, style, and content from the poetry of the ancients, and such men as Warton in England and Gerstenberg and Herder in Germany urged that it should not be judged by standards abstracted from the ancients. Even so, there seems to be no clear-cut instance prior to 1800 were 'romantic poetry' was explicitly contrasted with 'classical poetry'. It was this contrast that dominated the history of the word *romantisch* in the second phase, which was ushered in by Friedrich Schlegel.

II

Before we can discuss the range of meanings that Friedrich Schlegel attached to the word *romantisch* around the turn of the century, we shall first have to take a brief look at some of his earlier writings.[23] The dominant aesthetic experiences of his youth had been Greek drama, which he read in the original at the age of sixteen, and Greek sculpture, which he got to know through a collection of plaster casts in Dresden. The enthusiasm for Greek art and letters thus kindled in him was strengthened by his study of the works of J. J. Winckelmann and led to his writing, while still in his early twenties, a series of articles on Greek poetry that culminated in a long treatise, 'Über das Studium der griechischen Poesie,' written in 1795 and published in 1797. This essay – a somewhat eclectic work, in which Schlegel tried to systematize views proposed by Winckelmann and a number of later writers – centres in the assertion that Greek and modern poetry are radically different, attempts to account for this difference, and prescribes the study of the Greeks as the panacea for all the aesthetic ills of the moderns. Reduced to bare essentials, Schlegel's argument may be summarized as follows.

Greek poetry was 'beautiful' and 'objective': its main purpose, to which every didactic, philosophical or sociological interest was

---

*   See, e.g., Friedrich Schlegel, *KFSA* xi: 85: 'Für die neueren dramatischen Dichter verdienen wohl die Gegenstände aus der romantischen Zeit den Vorzug. Sie liegt gerade in der Mitte' (between the ancients and the contemporary world). Anonymous review of *Bertrand de Guesolin* (as in note 12, col. 61): '*Krieg war offenbar nicht das einzige* Element, und ebensowenig die einzige Sphäre des Lebens in der romantischen Zeit.'

subordinated, was beauty, achieved – as Winckelmann had taught – through the idealized representation of the typical. Modern poetry, for the most part, was didactic, beauty being subordinated to the quest for goodness and truth, or – an even worse aberration in Schlegel's view – to the quest for originality. Hence, whereas Greek poets controlled their individual predilections for the sake of a common, impersonal ideal of beauty, the moderns portrayed interesting individuals in an individual, characteristic manner or gave free reign to their fancy: straying from the classical ideal of objectivity in all possible directions, modern poetry was 'characteristic,' 'fantastic,' and 'mannered.'

The difference between Greek and modern poetry, Schlegel maintained, was a result of the difference between the two civilizations themselves. The classical civilization was 'natural'; that is to say, its development was instinctive, the free gift of nature. The modern civilization was 'artificial,' its development being guided and controlled by the understanding. Now the Greeks – as Schlegel believed, in accordance with the Graecomania so widespread in Germany at that time–having been Nature's favourite children and having developed the 'most fortunate endowments' under ideal conditions,[24] their civilization – and consequently Greek poetry – reached perfection at every stage of its growth: 'Greek poetry as a whole is a maximum and a canon of natural poetry, and its every single product is the most perfect of its kind.'[25] Such perfection was, however, achieved at a price: like all natural things, the Greek civilization had to pass through the cycle of birth, youth, maturity, and decay. The destiny of the modern, 'artificial' civilization was in all respects the exact opposite. Unlike Nature, the human understanding is subject to error. The history of the moderns is, as it were, the history of these errors, but, guided by the understanding, the moderns can find their way back to the right path again. Hence, the modern civilization need not perish like all natural things. If the Greeks reached finite perfection, the moderns (and, hence, also their poetry) are imperfect at every stage, but they are infinitely perfectible. The ancient civilization was 'cyclical,' the modern civilization is 'progressive.' Our defects themselves are our hopes, and there is no limit to our prospects.

As Schlegel deduced the contrast between ancient and modern poetry from a fundamental and unalterable dichotomy between the two cultures, it seems hardly logical that he should have claimed that only the 'beautiful' and 'objective' poetry of the Greeks was aesthetically sound, or that he should have insisted, as he did time and again, that the moderns had pursued the wrong goals in poetry and must mend their ways by learning from the Greeks. Moreover, he wrote about some of the moderns, above all about Shakespeare, with such enthusiasm that it is difficult at times to persuade oneself that he really believed the harsh things his theoretical condemnation of modern poetry implied. His essay on the study of Greek poetry was, however, hardly in the hands of his publisher when he began to change his mind and to contemplate at least the possibility that modern poetry might after all have a claim to its own standards of excellence. One reason for this reversal was the publication, in the winter of 1795–6, of Schiller's treatise, 'Über naive und sentimentalische Dichtung.'

To summarize this complex and difficult work in a few sentences would be impossible; but its influence, not only on F. Schlegel, but on the whole debate concerning the classical and the romantic, was so great that at least a brief indication of some of its conclusions must be provided. Like Schlegel, Schiller distinguished between two types of poetry – 'naïve' poetry, which is the product of a natural and healthy society and is best represented by the Greeks, and 'sentimental' poetry, which is the product of a sophisticated and corrupt society and is typical of the moderns. The former is intuitive and harmonious, the latter reflective, self-conscious, and discordant. The naïve poet is objective in the sense in which this quality is traditionally ascribed to the Homeric epics; the sentimental poet is emotionally involved in his subject, intrudes in the narrative, and comments on the action. Naïve poetry can achieve perfect form, but is limited in its content; sentimental poetry is incapable of perfection, but unlimited in scope; inferior to naïve poetry in beauty, it surpasses it in sublimity.

The parallels between Schiller's and Schlegel's treatises are so striking that scholars have attempted to account for them in terms of direct influence, but this hypothesis is unwarranted. Schlegel had, however, read Schiller's *earlier* writings and learned a great deal from them, and the two men were subject to the same intellectual cross-currents. They both admired the Greeks; both had studied Winckelmann, Rousseau, and Kant, and both were oppressed by the awareness that they lacked the harmony and unspoilt intuition that were at that time commonly associated with the Greeks. Moreover, if the two essays resembled each other in some respects, they differed in others. Whereas Schlegel's starting point was the contrast between two stages in the history of mankind, Schiller vacillated between a systematic and a chronological approach. Schlegel regarded all literature written after the collapse of the Roman Empire, and much that had been written earlier, as essentially modern, whereas Schiller classed a large number of medieval and Renaissance poets as 'naïve.' Above all, Schlegel praised the Greeks at the expense of the moderns, whereas Schiller, although he too had yearned for the glory that was Greece, knew that the clock could not be turned back and argued with brilliant persuasiveness that the moderns had every right to be themselves: if the price they had to pay for the prospect of metaphysical freedom, which their divorce from nature held out to them, was heavy, it was nevertheless eminently worthwhile.

When the decisive second instalment of Schiller's treatise reached Schlegel, he was thrown into such a turmoil that he 'did nothing for several days but read it and make notes.'[26] And there were other forces at work as well that forced him to reconsider his views. For one thing, he continued his study of medieval and Renaissance poetry – particularly of Shakespeare and the great Italians from Dante to Tasso – and his fascination with it continued to increase. For another, prompted partly by his reading of Cervantes' *Don Quixote* and of Goethe's *Wilhelm Meisters Lehrjahre*, which was published in four instalments in 1795–6, he became increasingly interested in the modern novel and could not but realize the folly of evaluating works in this genre by standards abstracted from the dramas of Sophocles. By the fall of 1797, he was ready to recant publicly; he did so in some of the aphorisms published in the journal *Lyceum* with the title 'Kritische Fragmente':

My essay on Greek poetry is a mannered hymn in prose on objectivity in poetry. Its worst feature seems to me its total lack of that *sine qua non*, irony ...

The ancients are neither the Jews, nor the Christians, nor the Englishmen of poetry. They are neither the Lord's arbitrarily chosen people in matters of art, nor do they possess the sole true aesthetic faith or have a monopoly on poetry.

All classical genres of poetry in their strict purity are now ridiculous.

From what the moderns aspire to, we must learn what poetry ought to become; from what the ancients do, what it must be.

In the ancients, we see the perfected letter of the whole poetry; in the moderns, we surmise its evolving spirit.

Mein Versuch über das Studium der griechischen Poesie ist ein manierierter Hymnus in Prosa auf das Objektive in der Poesie. Das Schlechteste daran scheint mir der gänzliche Mangel der unentbehrlichen Ironie ...

Die Alten sind weder die Juden, noch die Christen, noch die Engländer in der Poesie. Sie sind nicht ein willkürlich ausgewähltes Kunstvolk Gottes; noch haben sie den alleinseligmachenden Schönheitsglauben; noch besitzen sie ein Dichtungs-monopol.

Alle klassischen Dichtarten in ihrer strengen Reinheit sind jetzt lächerlich.

Aus dem, was die Modernen wollen, muß man lernen, was die Poesie werden soll: aus dem, was die Alten tun, was sie sein muß.

In den Alten sieht man den vollendeten Buchstaben der ganzen Poesie: in den Neuern ahnet man den werdenden Geist.[27]

In these pronouncements, the literatures Schlegel contrasts are still referred to as 'ancient' and 'modern'; but these terms soon failed to satisfy him. As long as he had regarded the whole of post-classical literature as a chaos or system of aberrations – in his early essays he had considered both these possibilities – such chronological terms had served him well. But he was now beginning to undertake the task of distinguishing trends within this whole and of defining what seemed to him the essential nature of modern poetry – 'das Wesentlich-Moderne,' as he had called it already in 1794;[28] and to distinguish this essence from other trends and traditions that were also modern, but that he continued to disapprove of, he needed a term that was typological as well as chronological – a term that could be contrasted not only with the poetry of the ancients, but also with such 'merely' and (as he thought) undesirably modern pheno-mena as the imitation of the Greeks in the manner of French classicism or the literature of much of the German Enlightenment. It was the expression *romantische Poesie* that seemed ideally suited to fill this need: there was hardly a connotation of that phrase that did not somehow fit into the picture he was beginning to form of that great and essential tradition in modern literature, which – as he now felt – was the equal of Greek poetry while being utterly different from it.

As we have seen, *romantisch* could be used with reference to the Romance languages, and – at least until medieval German and English poetry became better known – it was in these languages that modern literature seemed to have come into its own. Its giants, as Schlegel never tired of proclaiming, were such Romance or 'romantic' poets as Dante, Petrarch, Boccaccio, Ariosto, and Cervantes. Moreover, English being a mixture of Romance and Germanic, even Shakespeare could, at a pinch, be called romantic in the linguistic sense.

Such works as the French medieval *romans*, the Italian *romanzi*, and the Spanish *romances* were obviously *romantisch* – this was the root meaning of the word; and if *romantisch*, from this root meaning, had acquired such connotations as 'imaginative,' 'fantastic,' or 'marvellous,' nothing could fit in better: in the essay on the study of Greek poetry, Schlegel had already found *das Fantastische* to be a distinguishing characteristic of post-classical poetry, and he had since developed a special predilection for poets who gave the reins to their imagination. Again, the romantic was associated with love, and its was rapidly becoming a commonplace that love played a different and more significant role in post-classical or 'romantic' poetry.

Finally, it will be remembered that *romantisch* could be used with reference to the *Roman*, in analogy with *dramatisch, lyrisch*, and *episch*; and it was this meaning, although probably least familiar, that became decisive for Schlegel's usage. As he told his brother in 1797, it was the *Roman* that, along with his work on a history of Greek poetry, abandoned upon completion of a first volume in 1798, occupied the centre of his interest. His literary notebooks in 1797–8 were predominantly concerned with a theory of the *Roman*; and it was in the *Roman* that Schlegel now discovered the central phenomenon of modern or 'romantic' poetry:

[There are] three dominant genres, 1 *Tragedy* with the Greeks. 2 *Satire* with the Romans. 3 *Roman* with the moderns. (1797)

Just as the *Roman* colours the whole of modern poetry, so satire ... colours the whole of Roman poetry. (1798)

Just as our poetry did with the *Roman*, so Greek poetry began with and finally again converged with the epic. (1800)

Drei herrschende Dichtarten. (*1*) Tragödie *bei den Griechen*. (*2*) Satire *bei den Römern*. (*3*) Roman *bei den Modernen*.[29]

Wie der Roman die ganze moderne Poesie, so tingiert auch die Satire ... die ganze römische Poesie.[30]

*Wie unsre Dichtkunst mit dem Roman, so fing die der Griechen mit dem Epos an und löste sich wieder drin auf.**

Evidently, these assertions reflect the fact that the novel had gained immensely in importance in the course of the eighteenth century and – as F. Schlegel realized with exceptional clarity – had a still more important future in store. It is essential to realize, however, that the German word for 'novel,' *Roman*, had a very much wider range of meanings at that time than it has now – a wider range, in fact, than the English 'novel' and 'romance' combined. (It is for this reason that the word cannot be translated in the present context; if its retention in an English context invites confusion with the English sense of the word, in which Cato was a Roman, this seems a far smaller risk than the confusion of German *Roman* and English *novel*, which would render Schlegel's theories absurd.) Around 1800, much of the original meaning of the word, in which it denoted any work of fiction in the vernacular, had been preserved, and it was not at all unusual to apply the word to such medieval epics as *Parzifal* or to Italian *romanzi* such as *Jerusalemme liberata*. In fact, the word could even be applied to plays intended to be read rather than performed and to plays whose form was radically un-Aristotelian, such as those of Shakespeare.† It was in this sense that Schlegel

---

*   *KFSA* II: 335. Cf. F. Bouterwek, *Geschichte der Poesie und Beredsamkeit* I (Göttingen, 1801): 197: 'In denjenigen dieser Schriften, die sich sämtlich unter dem Klassennamen der *Romane* begreifen lassen, entdeckt man leicht eine Manier, durch die sie zum Teil alle einander gleichen ... Diese Manier im Ganzen mag die *romantische* heißen, denn sie ist durch die Nachahmung der Werke entstanden, die sämtlich Romane in der weiteren Bedeutung genannt werden, vom berühmten *Roman von der Rose* ... bis herab zum deutschen Ritterroman.'

†   Whereas Furetière explained as early as 1666, in the first paragraph of his *Roman Bourgeois*, that 'un roman n'est rien qu'une poésie en prose,' Adelung did not specify in any edition of his dictionary that a *Roman* must be written in prose, and Manso, in his *Nachträge zu Sulzers allgemeiner Theorie der schönen Künste* I, i (Leipzig, 1791): 38, claimed that metrical form could not be the distinguishing characteristic between the epic and the *Roman*: there were 'Epopöen ohne Versifikation,' while the earliest French *Romane* were written in verse.

    In histories of literature of the last third of the eighteenth century, it was quite common to refer to such works as *Parzival*, the *Heldenbuch*, the *Nibelungenlied*, Ariosto's *Orlando Furioso*, or Spenser's *Faerie Queene* as *Romane* (see, e.g., J. G. Eichhorn, *Litterärgeschichte*, pp. 253 f.; *Über die Schicksale der Litteratur, aus dem Italienischen des Herrn Abt Denina, mit dessen Verbesserungen und Zusätzen durch F. G. Serben* I, Berlin und Leipzig, 1785, pp. 287, 414). Friedrich Schlegel called Dante's *Divina Commedia* a *Roman* and said of Shakespeare's plays that they are 'dem Wesen nach Romane' (*Literary Notebooks*, nos. 76, 357). A. W. Schlegel called the *Nibelungenlied* and the *Heldenlied* 'Sittenromane,' found in Shakespeare's

could claim in 1797 that the *Roman* was the dominant genre of the moderns, or explain, as he did ten years later, that 'the *Roman* is a genre comprising all innovations in poetry that do not fit into the old rubric'/'*Der Roman ist eine Gattung, die alle Neuerungen der Poesie in sich faßt, die in die alte Rubrik nicht passen.*'[31] To put things differently, in this sense of the word all the truly significant achievements of the moderns either were *Romane* or were at least 'coloured' by the *Roman* – were they the rhymed medieval epics, Shakespearean tragedies, or modern novels like *Wilhelm Meister*.

Now at first sight, it may be hard to see what a work like the *Divina Commedia* and a modern novel have in common, other than that they are both 'unclassical,' but Schlegel was by no means blind to this difficulty. He thought of all existing *Romane* or romantic poems as imperfect representatives of an ideal which modern, progressive poetry could only approximate without ever achieving. It was on the basis of this conviction that he attempted in his literary note-book of 1797–8 a kind of typology of the *Roman*, distinguishing, for instance, two main classes, the 'poetic *Roman*,' comprising two sub-classes, which he called 'fantastic' and 'sentimental,' and the 'prose *Roman*,' which was either 'philosophical' or 'psychological.' As examples of these four types, he named Ariosto's *Orlando Furioso*, Tasso's *Jerusalemme Liberata*, Diderot's *Jacques le Fataliste*, and Diderot's *La Religieuse*. A slightly later classification distinguishes between the 'fantastic,' the 'sentimental,' the 'political' and the 'mimic' *Roman*. All these types he regarded, however, merely as imperfect 'sub-genres' (*Nebenarten*); the ideal or perfect *Roman* this is the decisive point in Schlegel's theory – would be a synthesis of all of them, and thus contain verse and prose, the 'fantastic,' the 'sentimental,' and the 'mimic.' It would be the complete *Misch-gedicht*,[32] in which epic, dramatic and lyrical poetry, criticism, and philosophy would be mixed and combined with one another – a work universal in both form and content, presenting a complete picture of its age and utilizing all forms of literature. But such a work, of course, exceeded all human possibilities. Whereas Greek, 'classical' poetry had actually realized its supreme possibility in the

plays 'fast Annäherungen an den Roman,' and referred to them as 'Roman-spiele' (*Vorlesungen über philosophische Kunstlehre*, Leipzig, 1911, pp. 212, 219, 220). Schiller stated in his preface to *Die Räuber* that he had written a 'drama-tischer Roman,' not a 'theatralisches Drama' (*Nationalausgabe* III, Weimar, 1953, p. 244), and Wieland explained that he regarded Schiller's *Don Carlos* as a 'dramatischer Roman' because its length indicated that it was meant to be read rather than performed (*Anzeiger des Teutschen Merkur*, September 1787).

tragedies of Sophocles, modern 'progressive' poetry could only strive towards its ideal and approximate it in an infinite progression: the *Roman* was the progressive form *par excellence*, and the poetry whose ultimate goal was the ideal *Roman* was romantic.

Schlegel's theory of the *Roman* remained buried in his notebooks. The gist of it, however, became known through Schlegel's first – and probably still most famous – public statement on romantic poetry, the 116th of the 451 'Fragmente,' from the pen of both F. and A. W. Schlegel, Schleiermacher, and Novalis, published in the first volume of their periodical, the *Athenäum* (1798–1800):

> Romantic poetry is a progressive universal poetry. Its destiny is not merely to reunite all the separate genres of poetry and to put poetry in touch with philosophy and rhetoric. Its aim and mission is now to mingle, now to fuse poetry and prose, genius and criticism, the poetry of the educated and the poetry of the people; to make poetry living and social, life and society poetic; to poeticize wit, fill and saturate the forms of art with matters of genuine cultural value, and quicken them with the vibrations of humour. It embraces everything that is poetic, from the most comprehensive system of art that contains in itself further systems to the sigh or kiss which the child who writes verses expresses in artless song. It can lose itself so completely in its subject matter that one might think its supreme purpose the characterization of poetic individuals of every kind; and yet there is no form better suited to the complete self-expression of the spirit of the author, so that many an artist who wanted merely to write a *Roman* willy-nilly portrayed himself. It alone can, like the epic, become a mirror of the whole surrounding world, a portrait of the age. And yet it can, more than any other art form, hover on the wings of poetic reflection between the portrayed object and the portraying artist, free from all real and ideal interests; it can raise this reflection to higher and higher powers and multiply it, as it were, in an endless series of mirrors ... Other genres have been perfected and can now be completely analyzed. The romantic genre is in a state of becoming; indeed, it is its essential nature that it is eternally becoming and can never be perfected. No theory can exhaust it, and only a divinatory criticism could dare to attempt to characterize its ideal. It alone is infinite, as it alone is free; its supreme law is that the caprice [*Willkür*] of the author shall be subject to no law. The romantic genre is the only one that is more than a genre, but is, as it were, poetry itself; for in a certain sense, all poetry is or should be romantic.

> *Die romantische Poesie ist eine progressive Universalpoesie. Ihre Bestimmung ist nicht bloß, alle getrennte Gattungen der Poesie wieder zu vereinigen, und die*

Poesie mit der Philosophie und Rhetorik in Berührung zu setzen. Sie will, und soll auch Poesie und Prosa, Genialität und Kritik, Kunstpoesie und Naturpoesie bald mischen, bald verschmelzen, die Poesie lebendig und gesellig, und das Leben und die Gesellschaft poetisch machen, den Witz poetisieren, und die Formen der Kunst mit gediegnem Bildungsstoff jeder Art anfüllen und sättigen, und durch die Schwingungen des Humors beseelen. Sie umfaßt alles, was nur poetisch ist, vom größten wieder mehrere Systeme in sich enthaltenden Systeme der Kunst, bis zu dem Seufzer, dem Kuß, den das dichtende Kind aushaucht in kunstlosen Gesang. Sie kann sich so in das Dargestellte verlieren, daß man glauben möchte, poetische Individuen jeder Art zu charakterisieren, sei ihr Eins und Alles; und doch gibt es noch keine Form, die so dazu gemacht wäre, den Geist des Autors vollständig auszudrücken: so daß manche Künstler, die nur auch einen Roman schreiben wollten, von ungefähr sich selbst dargestellt haben. Nur sie kann gleich dem Epos ein Spiegel der ganzen umgebenden Welt, ein Bild des Zeitalters werden. Und doch kann auch sie am meisten zwischen dem Dargestellten und dem Darstellenden, frei von allem realen und idealen Interesse auf den Flügeln der poetischen Reflexion in der Mitte schweben, diese Reflexion immer wieder potenzieren und wie in einer endlosen Reihe von Spiegeln vervielfachen ... Andre Dichtarten sind fertig, und können nun vollständig zergliedert werden. Die romantische Dichtart ist noch im Werden; ja das ist ihr eigentliches Wesen, daß sie ewig nur werden, nie vollendet sein kann. Sie kann durch keine Theorie erschöpft werden, und nur eine divinatorische Kritik dürfte es wagen, ihr Ideal charakterisieren zu wollen. Sie allein ist unendlich, wie sie allein frei ist, und das als ihr erstes Gesetz anerkennt, daß die Willkür des Dichters kein Gesetz über sich leide. Die romantische Dichtart ist die einzige, die mehr als Art, und gleichsam die Dichtkunst selbst ist: denn in einem gewissen Sinn ist oder soll alle Poesie romantisch sein.

If the present reader finds this pronouncement obscure in some of its details, so did Schlegel's contemporaries.[33] The main outlines are, however, quite clear. The mainstream of modern (post-classical) poetry is 'romantische Poesie' or 'Romanpoesie.' (Given the vagueness of both terms, they may be regarded as virtually synonymous.) This poetry is universal in its form – a *mélange des genres* – and in its content: poetry, philosophy, and criticism – kept separate by the Greeks – are combined in it, so that it can both present a picture of its age and a self-portrait of its author. It is progressive in that it is eternally in a state of becoming, striving to approximate an unrealizable ideal; yet this ideal is of such a kind that it in no way interferes with the freedom (*Willkür*) of the romantic poet.*

Although the contrast between this concept of romantic poetry

---

*   Although the concept of *Willkür* is of great importance for other aspects of Schlegel's theory of literature, it need not be discussed in the present context.

and classical poetry is not made explicit in 'Athenäums-Fragmente,' no. 116, it is of course implied, as must have been obvious to anyone who was familiar with Schlegel's earlier writings: the major characteristics traditionally ascribed to Greek classicism – objectivity, the purity of the genres, the attainment of absolute perfection, 'naïveté' in Schiller's sense of the word, the self-limitation of the poet, the adherence to rules, the autonomy of the aesthetic, the simplicity of forms – are without exception incompatible with romantic poetry as described by Schlegel. If, none the less, Schlegel insists in his final sentence that 'all poetry is or should be romantic,' one is driven to the conclusion that he thought of romantic poetry both as one of two clearly distinct types of literature and as an ideal of all literature. This is a difficulty which no interpretation of his writings can explain away and which led to endless confusion. It is still present in Schlegel's next, and far more detailed, exposition of his theory, the 'Gespräch über die Poesie,' published in 1800 in the third and last volume of the *Athenäum*.

Like *Fragment* 116, the 'Gespräch über die Poesie' is to a considerable extent based on Schlegel's theory of the *Roman* of 1797–8 and contains, therefore, much that is already familiar to us. A brief summary of two parts of this essay – 'Epochen der Poesie' and 'Brief über den Roman' – will suffice for our purposes.

In 'Epochen der Poesie,' Schlegel laid down his and his fellow romanticists' view of the history of European literature – a view sharply contrasting with that of the earlier, neoclassicist generation. He begins with an enthusiastic summary of the history of Greek poetry, in which Sophocles is singled out as the 'eternal prototype of perfection'; the Romans, he declares, had only a 'brief paroxysm of poetry,' satire being their only original contribution. As Schlegel was as yet largely ignorant of French and German medieval poetry, he passed over the whole era from the fall of the Roman Empire to the early fourteenth century in a few sentences – an omission which he made good in later years – and resumed his survey with the great Italians from Dante to Ariosto and Guarini. Of Spain and England, we hear that the history of their poetry 'is concentrated in the art of two men, Cervantes and Shakespeare, who were so great that everything else, by comparison, appears to be merely a preparatory, explanatory, complementary environment.' (Subsequently, Calderón was added to the canon and ranked even above Shakespeare.) With the death of these men, the flame of poetic imagination is said to have been extinguished in their countries. The age of 'wrong trends' had set in: 'Out of superficial abstractions and arguments, misinterpretations of the ancients, and mediocre talents, there arose in France a comprehensive and coherent system of false poetry [i.e., the neoclassicism of Racine, Corneille, and Boileau] ... and from France, the imbecility of so-called good taste spread across almost the whole of Europe.' The 'Golden Ages' of literature in France and England and their feeble imitation in Germany spelt the death of true poetry – but not forever: Winckelmann's aesthetic theories, the writings of Goethe, and the philosophic idealism discovered, although by no means perfected, by Fichte had begun to usher in a new age in literature: romantic poetry was about to rise again from its ashes.[34]

Whereas 'Epochen der Poesie' offers an explanation of Schlegel's concept of romantic poetry only by implication, the other section of the 'Gespräch über die Poesie' deals with this topic explicitly. Most of it is devoted to a discussion of the modern novel, those novelists – particularly Lawrence Sterne and Jean Paul – being singled out for praise whose works, in Schlegel's view, resumed in their spirit or in their technique the great romantic tradition from Dante to Cervantes. The discussion culminates in a definition of *romantisch* which runs as follows: '... in my view and in my usage, exactly that is romantic which represents a sentimental content in an imaginative form' / '*Denn nach meiner Ansicht und in meinem Sprachgebrauch ist eben das romantisch, was uns einen sentimentalen Stoff in einer fantastischen Form darstellt.*'[35]

As Schlegel adds a few pages later that the romantic usually is 'historical,' that is, based on facts, this definition takes us straight back to his theory of the *Roman* of 1797–8, with its demand for a synthesis of the qualities of poetic *Romane*, which are imaginative or sentimental, with qualities of the prose novel. This time, however, Schlegel explains in somewhat greater detail what these qualities are. The sentimental, we are told, is

that which moves us, where feeling predominates; not sensual, but spiritual feeling. The source and soul of all these stirrings is love, and the spirit of love must hover everywhere, visibly-invisibly, in romantic poetry.

Was ist denn nun dieses Sentimentale? Das was uns anspricht, wo das Gefühl herrscht, und zwar nicht ein sinnliches, sondern das geistige. Die Quelle und Seele aller dieser Regungen ist die Liebe, und der Geist der Liebe muß in der romantischen Poesie überall unsichtbar sichtbar schweben ...

* *KFSA* II: 334. Evidently, Schlegel uses 'sentimental' neither in its ordinary sense nor in the specific sense assigned to it by Schiller.

The mystery of this love, which is something quite different from the 'gallant passions' described in so many books, can only be comprehended and portrayed by the imagination and is the source of imaginative or 'fantastic' form in poetry: '*Nur die Fantasie kann das Rätsel dieser Liebe fassen und als Rätsel darstellen; und dieses Rätselhafte ist die Quelle von dem Fantastischen in der Form aller poetischen Darstellung.*'[36] 'Sentimental' content and 'fantastic' form, or chaos and eros, as a notebook entry puts it, are complementary: "*Chaos und Eros ist wohl die beste Erklärung des Romantischen.*'[37]

The 'Gespräch über die Poesie' was by no means F. Schlegel's last attempt at defining romantic poetry, and, although Schlegel never radically departed from his concept of 1800, there are minor variations; in particular, as the years went by, he increasingly stressed the Christian element in romantic poetry, while at the same time he came to place far greater emphasis on the distinction between romantic and merely modern (realistic and unimaginative) literature than on that between the romantic and the classical. There will be no need for us, however, to investigate this development: after 1800, the intellectual leadership of the romantic movement gradually passed to other writers, although these, as we shall see, based their theoretical utterances on F. Schlegel's writings in the *Athenäum* more often than they cared to confess. It was certainly because of Schlegel that the word *romantisch*, which hitherto had been used as if everybody could be assumed to know what it meant, now attracted semantic attention from a sizable and varied group of writers – casually in many book reviews, and rather more systematically in articles, treatises on aesthetics, and histories of literature.

Thus, to mention a few titles only, August Wilhelm Schlegel discussed the term in the public lectures he gave in Berlin in the years from 1801 to 1804.[38] Brentano included a discussion of it in his novel, *Godwi*.[39] In 1802, Schiller published his play, *Die Jungfrau von Orleans*, with the sub-title 'Eine romantische Tragödie,' thus tempting most of his reviewers to reflect on the meaning of 'das Romantische.'[40] In the same year, J. J. Mnioch published a long, confused poem on the subject of 'Hellenik und Romantik.'[41] In 1804, Jean Paul devoted a chapter of his influential *Vorschule der Aesthetik* to a discussion of the nature of romantic poetry, and in the following year, the term was discussed at length in two further treatises – J. A. Eberhard's *Handbuch der Ästhetik* (Halle, 1803–5), vol. II, and Friedrich Ast's *System der Kunstlehre* (Leipzig, 1805). That there was a popular interest in discussions of this topic is shown by such articles as 'Vom Geiste des Romantischen' in the *Zeitung für die elegante Welt* of 12 June 1806 (no. 70, cols. 561–6; anon.), 'Über schön und romantisch' in the quarterly *Selene* (vol. 1, no. 1, Leipzig, 1807, pp. 12–29) by J. A. Apel,* and 'Klassische und romantische Kunst' in Cotta's *Morgenblatt für gebildete Stände* of 4 March 1808 (no. 55, pp. 217–19) by S. H. K. Michaelis.† These, for the most part, somewhat amateurish attempts at clarifying a subject of steadily increasing complexity were followed by A. W. Schlegel's masterly exposition in his Vienna lectures on *Dramatische Kunst und Literatur*, delivered in 1808 and published in 1809–11; and in 1813, Mme de Staël's *De l'Allemagne* produced a new wave of interest in the subject. To report on these discussions and on the countless more casual remarks on our subject in chronological order would result in hopeless confusion; rather, we shall list the types of explanations offered, although, needless to say, they all shade into each other, and few writers who commented on the subject at all were satisfied with a single explanation.

To begin with, it should be noted that, whereas prior to 1800 passages in which the romantic is *explicitly* contrasted with the classical were quite rare, they now began to occur frequently, and in the unlikeliest contexts. A particularly absurd example is an article on Polish women in the *Zeitung für die elegante Welt*, where 'Hellenic' is used for the more usual 'classical':

Here [in the case of Polish girls] education can achieve nothing unless it favours their native national character, which inclines far more to the Hellenic than to the romantic, more to the quick and frank look at things, to enjoyment, activity, and dominance than to leisurely examination, contemplation, hoping, and suffering.

The most interesting feminine characteristic of Polish women at the highest degree of culture is a marvellous, not disharmonious mixture of all these seemingly contradictory things. I see it in the image of an interim truce between Hellenism and romanticism.

Nichts vermag hier [bei polnischen Mädchen] die Erziehung, in sofern sie nicht den ursprünglichen National-Charakter begünstigt, und dieser neigt sich bei

---

*   The article is signed 'A. A.'; the identity of the author is evident from the reprint in Apel's collection of verse and prose, *Cicaden* (Berlin, 1810); another (partial) reprint appeared in the *Zeitung für die elegante Welt*, 1810, no. 168 (23 August), col. 1332 *ff.*

†   Signed 'F . . . . . . A . . . . . .' For the identification of the author, see Wilhelm Budde, 'Heidelberger Tagebuch,' *Neue Heidelberger Jahrbücher* xxii (1918–19): 292.

weitem mehr zum Hellenischen *hin als zum* Romantischen, *mehr zum schnellen und offnen Beschaun, zum Genuß, zum Wirken, zum Herrschen; als zum langsamen Betrachten, zur Kontemplation, zum Hoffen und Erdulden.*

Die interessevollste Weiblichkeit der Polinnen im höchsten Grad ihrer Kultur, ist eine wunderbare, nicht disharmonische Mischung aller dieser scheinbar wider-sprechenden Dinge. Mir schwebt sie vor unter dem Bilde eines interimistischen Waffenstillstandes zwischen Hellenik und Romantik.[42]

In 1814, F. Kohlrausch wrote of two epochs in the history of man-kind 'which one refers to with the usual names of the antique and the romantic age':

Wenn wir einen Blick auf den bisherigen Lauf der Weltgeschichte werfen, so bieten sich uns zwei große Epochen und Abschnitte derselben dar, welche längst vollendet sind; es sind die, welche man mit dem gewöhnlichen Namen der antiken und romantischen Zeit benennt.[43]

The same statement could have been made ten, but not fifteen, years previously. Yet, while there was widespread agreement on the existence (although not, as we shall see, the exact nature) of a fundamental difference between the romantic and the classical, an-tique, or Hellenic, there was no unanimity as to the possibility of a synthesis between these opposed manifestations of the human spirit. Among idealistic philosophers, of course, the conviction that the synthesis of opposites leads to a higher stage was common long be-fore Hegel. It corresponded to this conviction that Schiller envisaged the synthesis of naïve and sentimental poetry as an ideal. F. Schlegel discussed the synthesis of the classical and romantic in the 'Gespräch über die Poesie,' suggesting that a synthesis was both possible and desirable for the *spirit* of poetry, but that classical and romantic *forms* would have to remain distinct.[44] In 1803, he claimed that there was something unnatural about the 'separation of the classical and the romantic' in European poetry,[45] and in 1807, he asserted that there was only an historical, no theoretical or necessary, contrast between the two types of poetry and that all poetry ought to be both romantic and classical.[46] His faithful disciple, Friedrich Ast, not only advocated the synthesis, but claimed that it had actually been achieved in F. Schlegel's – preposterously bad – play, *Alarkos*.[47] Yet, as early as 1803, it was argued even by writers who largely depended on the brothers Schlegel for their critical terminology that a synthesis was altogether unthinkable.[48]

To agree that there was a difference between the classical and the romantic was one thing; to explain the nature of that difference was quite another. Yet it was on these explanations that the meaning attached to *das Romantische* depended. There was not even agreement as to where the most characteristically romantic poetry might be found. Thus, Tieck claimed in 1800 that Shakespeare and Cervantes had 'as if by an explicit arrangement' raised romantic poetry to its highest perfection;[49] three years later, the same author placed the period of highest achievement some four centuries earlier: '*Diese Zeit, in welche alle jene Erzählungen von Parzifal, Titurel, Tristan, Artus, Daniel von Blumental u.a. gehören, ist die Blütezeit der romantischen Poesie.*'[50] And in 1808, the theologian Molitor claimed that the romantic spirit had reached its most brilliant florescence in the tenth century.[51] Moreover, there is no shortage of passages in which the epithet *romantisch* was applied to works written after the death of Shakespeare and Cervantes – at one point, F. Schlegel considered *Don Quixote* and Tieck's *Franz Sternbald* the only truly romantic novels;[52] but at least until 1808 romantic poetry was *primarily* looked for in the past and only occasionally found in the present.

An obvious corollary of the dichotomy of the classical and the romantic was that the former was pagan, the latter Christian. Thus, already in his essay on the study of Greek poetry, F. Schlegel called the 'fables of the age of knights and Christian legendry the mythology of romantic poetry[53] – a view echoed in a review in the *Jenaische Allgemeine Literatur-Zeitung* of 28 February 1806, whose author calls the 'legends of Christian antiquity' the 'sources of romantic art and poetry' and regards them as a romantic mythology ('romantische Mythik'), that is, the modern equivalent of the pagan mythology of the ancients.[54] Friedrich Bouterwek, whose multi-volume *Geschichte der Poesie und Beredsamkeit seit dem Ende des dreizehnten Jahrhunderts* (1801–19) was widely read in its own day, saw the difference between the poetry of 'classical antiquity' and 'more recent' or – as he called it after 1801 – 'romantic' poetry in three factors, Christianity, chivalric love, and the (real or pretended) learning of the moderns.[55] Christian Schreiber, in his 'Aphorismen über das Romantische,' felt that 'what we call the romantic seems to have emerged from a combination of oriental [i.e., Christian] religion with poetry and the visual arts' /'... *daß aus der Vermischung der Orientalischen Religion mit der Poesie und bildenden Kunst, das hervorgegangen zu sein scheine, was wir das* Romantische *nennen*'[56] and – evidently drawing on F. Schlegel – defined that 'we call an event romantic if by delighting the imagination, it intensely arouses our emotion.' The sensibility which makes this possible is supposed to be a result of that oriental, supernatural religion:

Wir nennen eine Begebenheit romantisch, die, indem sie die Phantasie ergötzt, unser Gefühl in die höchste Mitleidenschaft setzt.[57]

Die Empfindsamkeit aber (die, den Griechen und Römern unbekannt, aus der modernen Kunst hervorgeht) ist eine Blüte des Orients, ein Erzeugnis jener übersinnlichen Religion.[58]

Friedrich Ast maintained that 'art being itself an element of religion, the contrast between ancient and romantic art resulted from the contrasting religions of the Greek and the romantic world,'[59] whereas Zacharias Werner, who used the word *romantic* in the sub-titles of many of his plays, insisted on the 'necessity of early Christian [*altchristliche*] mythology in romantic tragedy' and even spoke of a 'Christian-romantic' / '*christlich-romantische*' religion.[60]

A frequent variant of the view of the romantic as Christian is its association with mysticism. Thus, the anonymous reviewer of Novalis' *Schriften* (1802) in the *Jenaische Allgemeine Literatur-Zeitung* of 12 September 1803 suggests that 'one of the most charming fruits' that mysticism bore in Europe was romantic poetry, for example, that of Ariosto; that mysticism had begun to come into its own again towards the end of the eighteenth century; and that both as a romantic poet and as a mystic philosopher, Novalis occupied one of the first ranks:

Herrschend war die Mystik zuerst im Morgenlande. Nach Europa, wo sie in früheren Zeiten nur einzelne Pfleger gefunden hatte, wurde sie durch das Christentum verpflanzt. Eine der lieblichsten Früchte, welche sie hier trug, war die romantische *Poesie ... In beiden Eigenschaften, als romantischer Dichter und als mystischer Philosoph, behauptete ... Novalis ... eine der ersten Stellen.*[61]

Similarly, Jean Paul claimed that the 'origin and character of the whole of modern poetry can so easily be derived from Christianity that one might just as well call romantic poetry Christian poetry,' that Christianity was the 'common father of the romantic children,' and that mysticism was the 'sanctum sanctorum of the romantic.' If there were romantic literatures 'without Christianity,' such as the *Edda* or Sanscrit poetry, these were based on a similarly spiritual religion:

Ursprung und Charakter der ganzen neueren Poesie läßt sich so leicht aus dem Christentum ableiten, daß man die romantische ebensogut die christliche nennen könnte.[62]

Übrigens ergibt sich von selber, daß das Christentum, obwohl gemeinschaftlicher

*Vater der romantischen Kinder, andere im Süden, andere im Norden erzeugen muß
... Das Mystische ist das Allerheiligste des Romantischen.*[63]

*Wer ist nun die Mutter dieser Romantik? – Allerdings nicht in jedem Lande und
Jahrhunderte die christliche Religion; aber jede andere steht mit dieser Gottes-
Mutter in Verwandtschaft. Zwei romantische Gattungen ohne Christentum,
einander in Ausbildung wie in Klima fremd, sind die indische und die der Edda.
Die altnordische, mehr ans Erhabne grenzende fand im Schattenreich ihrer
klimatischen verfinsterten Schauernatur ... eine grenzenlose Geisterwelt, worin die
enge Sinnenwelt zerfloß und versank ... Die indische Romantik bewegt sich in
einer allbelebenden Religion, welche von der Sinnenwelt durch Vergeistigung die
Schranken wegbrach...*[64]

Christian Schreiber, as we have seen, linked the greater sensibility he ascribed to romantic poetry with its Christian origins – an
argument advanced also by other critics who believed that the
romantic was 'sentimental' in Schlegel's sense or who listed chivalric
love as one of its primary characteristics. Thus the reviewer of
Novalis' *Schriften* in the *Jenaische Allgemeine Literatur-Zeitung* argues
that

the conviction of the simple truth that the soul is more valuable than the
body ... that the spiritual realm is subject to other laws than the realm of
nature, and that the latter ... must obey the former ... [produced a] new
human passion, sentimental love.

*Die mannigfaltigen Mythen von einem guten und einem bösen Urwesen ... von
Zauberern ... Talismanen ... Propheten ... Wundertieren ... – alle diese Mythen
haben zur Quelle die Überzeugung von einer einfachen Wahrheit, daß die Seele
vortrefflicher ist als der Leib, und unabhängig von demselben, daß das Geisterreich
andere Gesetze anerkennt als das Naturreich, und daß dieses ohnmächtiger als jenes
ihm gehorchen muß, eine Überzeugung, welche der Denkart des Mittelalters sich so
tief einprägte, daß sie eine ganz neue menschliche Leidenschaft hervorbrachte, die
empfindsame Liebe, welche sich nicht begnügend mit dem Genusse körperlicher
Schönheit und Anmut, nach dem Besitze des Gemütes trachtete. Und eben in einer
solchen Darstellung der Begebenheiten, nach welcher ungleichartige verschiedenen
Welten angehörige Wesen zusammen oder einander entgegenwirken, besteht das
Eigentümliche der romantischen Poesie.*[65]

Bouterwek claimed that 'the light in which the genuine knight saw
his lady was as different from the shadow that Greek national
custom cast on all women as light is different from shadow in the
original sense of these words: and this difference is nothing less than

the soul of modern poetry.' In the heart of the knight who swore in the same breath to fight for God and his lady, love and religion merged in a common emotion:

Das Licht, in welchem dem echten Ritter seine Dame erschien, war von dem Schatten, den die Nationalsitte der Griechen auf alle Weiber warf, so durchaus wie Licht vom Schatten im eigentlichen Verstande, verschieden; und diese Verschieden-heit ist nichts geringeres als die Seele der neueren Poesie ... Von der fast religiösen Ehrerbietung, mit der ein europäischer Ritter sich seiner Dame nahte und an seine Dame dachte; von der wirklichen Verschmelzung der Liebe mit der Religion im Herzen des Ritters, der Gottes und der Damen Sache zugleich zu verfechten am Altare schwur; von solchen Empfindungen und Träumen ist in der arabischen Poesie schwerlich je die Rede gewesen ... Die neuere Poesie ist eine Tochter der romantischen Liebe.[66]

The association of romantic poetry with the marvellous (*das Wunderbare*), the extravagant (*das Abenteuerliche*), and the imagin-ative or fantastic (*das Phantastische*, spelt with an initial *F* by Friedrich Schlegel and with a *Ph* by most other writers) was, of course, given with the original meaning of the word, and the deviation from the faithful depiction of reality was named frequently as a defining characteristic of romantic poetry. Thus, the majority of the critics who felt called upon to explain why Schiller had sub-titled his *Jungfrau von Orleans* a 'romantic tragedy' pointed out the extent to which Schiller had departed from historic truth and the many miracles in the play, concluding, for instance, that a work is ro-mantic if 'the natural conditions of reality do not prevail [in it] and the imagination is given a free rein' or that Schiller 'probably intended to indicate with the epithet "romantic" that he had im-bued the story with the magic of his imagination':

Wer endlich von romantischen Gedichten spricht, denkt immer an einen Orlando, Oberon und ähnliche Gedichte: denn in ihnen werden die gewöhnlichen Bedingungen der Wirklichkeit aufgehoben, und die Phantasie herrscht nach Willkür ...[67]

Der Dichter hat ... durch das Beiwort romantisch vermutlich bezeichnen wollen, daß er den Zauber seiner Einbildungskraft über diese Geschichte ausgegossen.[68]

With Friedrich Schlegel and his school, who held that the imagina-tion was an important source of genuine knowledge not attainable by other means, the imaginative character of romantic poetry was of course valued particularly highly; but as they regarded the imagination to be the essential creative faculty of all genuine poets, they rarely used this category as the sole defining characteristic.*

Among writers of a more rationalistic cast of mind, this emphasis on the imaginative quality of poetry was frowned upon, and romantic poetry was condemned as extravagant and 'fantastic' in the pejorative sense of the word. Thus, a reviewer in the *Zeitung für die elegante Welt* complained in 1809 that

since a romantic poetry has been created, so many absurdities and immature abortions of a lawlessly rambling imagination have seen the light of day that give no pleasure to any man of sound sense;

Seit man eine romantische Poesie geschaffen hat, sind so viel Abgeschmacktheiten, so viel unreife Mißgeburten einer regellos umherschweifenden Phantasie an das Tageslicht gekommen, an welchen kein Mensch von gesundem Sinn Vergnügen finden kann;[69]

and Bouterwek distinguished in 1819 between the 'beautiful' enthusiasm of a Klopstock and the 'really romantic' enthusiasm that 'almost exclusively occupies the imagination and provides but little food for thought.'

Die schöne Schwärmerei, ohne die Klopstock nicht der Dichter der Messiade geworden wäre, ist sehr verschieden von der eigentlich romantischen, die fast nur die Phantasie beschäftigt und dem Verstande nur wenig Nahrung gibt.†

A third group of writers attempted to steer a middle course, either by prescribing strict limits to the extent to which romantic poetry was to be permitted flights of fancy or by claiming that it must *seem* to deviate from reality without really doing so. Thus, Garlieb Merkel explained in 1801, 'The romantic is the middle stage between complete reality and fabulous fiction, it is reality poetically treated, turned into the free art product of the spirit' /'*Das Romantische ist die Mittelstufe zwischen der vollen Wirklichkeit und der fabelhaften Dichtung, es ist die Wirklichkeit, poetisch behandelt, zum freien Kunstwerke des Geistes gemacht,*'[70] and repeated four years later in his journal, *Der Freimütige*:

* Cf., however, F. Schlegel, writing in 1823: 'Übrigens dürfte die Benennung der gotischen Baukunst ... für immer beizubehalten sein; so wie auch die scheinbar willkürliche und wenig passende Benennung des Romantischen, welche uns jetzt die vorherrschende Fantasie in der Dichtkunst des Mittelalters [!] so charakteristisch zu bezeichnen dient, nicht füglich entbehrt und durch kein andres historisch so bedeutsames Wort ersetzt werden kann' (*KFSA* iv: 161).

† Bouterwek, *Geschichte* xi (1819): 79 *f.* It is characteristic of Bouterwek that he found absurd flights of fancy in the *Divina Commedia*.

The romantic is reality elevated so as to have a poetic effect – and this elevation need not be brought about by the admixture of the marvellous. An object becomes romantic if it gains the semblance of the marvellous without losing its truth.

Das Romantische ist die zur poetischen Wirkung veredelte Wirklichkeit – und dieses Veredeln braucht nicht durch Beimischung des Wunderbaren zu geschehen. Romantisch wird ein Gegenstand, wenn er den Anschein des Wunderbaren gewinnt, ohne daß er seine Wahrheit verliert.*

The trouble with these definitions is that they hark back to an eighteenth-century commonplace about *all* poetry; thus, J. J. Breitinger, writing in 1740, strongly recommended to poets to exploit the fascination of the marvellous, but insisted that this must only have the 'semblance of the untrue and contradictory,' while being in fact 'based on real or possible truth.'

... das Wunderbare ... nimmt einen unbetrüglichen Schein des Falschen und Widersprechenden an sich ... Alleine dies ist nur ein ... Schein der Falschheit; das Wunderbare muß immer auf die würkliche oder die mögliche Wahrheit gegründet sein.[71]

Nonetheless, not only such enemies of the new school as Merkel, but some of its most prominent members used the semblance of untruth or strangeness as a defining characteristic of the romantic – above all Novalis, who, however, succeeded in investing the idea with a deeper significance:

The world must be romanticized. This is how one rediscovers its original significance ... When I give the common a high significance, the ordinary a mysterious appearance, the familiar the dignity of the unfamiliar, the finite the semblance of the infinite, then I romanticize it. (1789)

Die Welt muß romantisiert werden. So findet man den ursprünglichen Sinn wieder... Indem ich dem Gemeinen einen hohen Sinn, dem Gewöhnlichen ein geheimnisvolles

---

*   Editorial note protesting against Christian Schreiber's assertion that 'Das Romantische ist an und für sich wunderbar; alles Wunderbare an und für sich poetisch.' *Der Freimütige*, 1805, no. 20 (28 January), p. 78. Merkel's note almost literally repeats a definition given in the same journal seven months previously by one R. L.: 'Der Charakter des Romantischen besteht darin: daß die Wirklichkeit, ohne durch Wunderbares *entstellt zu werden*, zu der lebhaftesten Wirkung auf Phantasie und Gefühl veredelt wird.' *Der Freimütige*, 1804, no. 106 (28 May), p. 421.

*Ansehn, dem Bekannten die Würde des Unbekannten, dem Endlichen einen unendlichen Schein gebe, so romantisiere ich es.**

A number of ways of making familiar things look strange had already been suggested in 1740 by Breitinger, who saw, of course, no connection between this procedure and the romantic. The connection is made sixty years later, when a character in Brentano's novel, *Godwi*, explains that 'everything which stands between our eye and an object to be seen at a distance, making it seem closer to us but at the same time adding to the object something of its own, is romantic,' and gets the reply from the titular hero of the novel: 'The romantic is therefore a telescope, or rather the colour of the lens and the effect the form of the lens has on the object.'

Alles, was zwischen unserm Auge und einem entfernten zu Sehenden als Mittler steht, uns den entfernten Gegenstand nähert, ihm aber zugleich etwas von dem Seinigen mitgibt, ist romantisch. ... Das Romantische ist also ein Perspektiv oder vielmehr die Farbe des Glases und die Bestimmung des Gegenstandes durch die Form des Glases.[72]

But there is really no need of a telescope with coloured glasses: what is usual in a distant country or was familiar in the distant past might seem strange and therefore romantic to us, and 'romantic distance' soon became a cliché.† Italy,[73] the orient, and above all

---

* Novalis, *Schriften*, ed. Kluckhohn and Samuel (Leipzig [1929]), II: 335. Cf. L. Tieck: 'Von Jugend auf ist es unser Studium gewesen, uns alles *Fremde* ... *gewöhnlich* zu machen; wir sollten es nur einmal versuchen, uns das *Gewöhnliche fremd* zu machen ...' (*Peter Leberecht*, in *Frühe Erzählungen und Romane*, ed. M. Thalmann, Darmstadt, 1963, p. 124). *Nachtwachen von Bonaventura*: '... kommen ihm [Kreuzgang] doch ganz gewöhnliche Dinge höchst ungewöhnlich vor' (ed. R. Riemeck, Frechen-Köln, 1955, p. 44). Samuel Johnson: 'New things are made familiar [in *The Rape of the Lock*], and familiar things strange' (*The Life of Pope*, in *Rasselas, Poems, and Selected Prose*, ed. Bronson, New York, 1962, p. 394). S. T. Coleridge: 'Mr. Wordsworth ... was to propose himself as his object [in the *Lyrical Ballads*], to give the charm of novelty to things of every day, and to excite a feeling analogous to the supernatural, by awakening the mind's attention from the lethargy of custom ...' (*Biographia Literaria*, in *Complete Works*, ed. Shedd, New York, 1884, vol. III, p. 365). Shelley: 'Poetry ... strips the veil of familiarity from the world, and lays bare the naked and sleeping beauty, which is the spirit of its forms' (*A Defense of Poetry*, in *Complete Works*, ed. Ingpen and Peck, vol. VII, London, 1965, p. 137).

† See, e.g., Novalis, *Schriften* I: 109 ('romantische Ferne') and O. v. Loeben, *Guido* (Mannheim, 1808), p. 119: 'Die Geschichte beweist deutlich ... daß alles in der Welt romantisch, d.h. sublimiert werden soll. Die Ferne ist der Lebensreiz aller Geschichte ... Die Geschichte muß zum Gedicht werden, ehe sie eigentlich beginnt. Sie ist schon romantische Poesie, wie jede verklärte Gegend, wie das Waldhorn, die Minne und alle Entfernung des Geliebten, Nahen.'

India[74] seemed particularly romantic. The Middle Ages were, of course, *the* romantic age for more than one reason; but the future was almost as romantic as the past, and among the moods associated with the romantic, *Ahnung* or *Ahndung* (presentiment) is rarely missing. As Jean Paul put it, 'If poetry is presentiment, romantic poetry is the presentiment of a greater future than there is room for on earth'/'*Ist Dichten Ahnen: so ist romantisches das Ahnen einer größern Zukunft, als hienieden Raum hat.*'[75]

Another mood connected with distance is longing or yearning (*Sehnsucht*), which ranks second only to love in the closeness of its association with the romantic. As early as 1795, Friedrich Schlegel had claimed that in complete contrast to Greek poetry, many of the best works of the moderns were 'representations of ugliness,' and that, if they contained even a slight intimation of perfect beauty, this was to be found 'not in calm enjoyment, but in unsatisfied yearning.'

Dies [Das Schöne] ist so wenig das herrschende Prinzip der modernen Poesie, daß viele ihrer trefflichsten Werke ganz offenbar Darstellungen des Häßlichen sind ... Findet sich ja eine leise Ahndung vollkommner Schönheit, so ist es nicht sowohl im ruhigen Genuß, als in unbefriedigter Sehnsucht.[76]

Like so many of his aperçus, this remark was subsequently repeated by his brother in a more prominent context.[77] Friedrich Ast, drawing on both Schlegel and Schelling, reached similar conclusions from a slightly different basis: whereas the Greeks, he believed, had the unique advantage of an 'objective intuition of the absolute,' romantic poetry was based on a 'subjective knowledge of the divine, i.e., on love and yearning for the absolute.'

Ist aber die Poesie nicht die objektive Anschauung des Absoluten [as with the Greeks], sondern die Philosophie, der Geist der Erkenntnis vorherrschend, so entspringt der Idealismus der Poesie, die romantische Poesie, die in der subjektiven Erkenntnis des Göttlichen lebt, also in der Liebe und Sehnsucht nach dem Absoluten ...[78]

Yet another version of this argument is to be found in the anonymous essay 'Vom Geiste des Romantischen' in the *Zeitung für die elegante Welt*: living under ideal conditions, the Greeks were preoccupied with the present moment and knew no longing; the moderns turn their glance away from the unhappy present and direct it longingly to the future, the presentiment of which sheds its twilight on our sombre world:

... wir wenden von der unglücklichen Gegenwart unsern Blick hinweg und richten ihn mit Sehnsucht in die Zukunft ... Die dunkle Ahndung der Zukunft wirft über die vorher düstere Welt ein dämmerndes Halblicht ... Nicht ruhiger Genuß und einfache frohe Tätigkeit, sondern rastloses ungeduldiges Streben und kühnes nie sich genügendes Unternehmen ist das Element, worin der Geist lebt, der sich die begrenzte Welt, die als eine halbgebildete rohe seiner Freiheit widersprach, in eine unbegrenzte verwandelte. Und leuchtet nicht dieser Geist aus allen echt romantischen Dichtungen, und aus dem Zeitalter hervor, dem der Name des romantischen allein zukommt?[79]

For E. T. A. Hoffmann, to quote a last example, Beethoven's music evoked 'that infinite yearning which is the essence of romanticism'/ *'Beethoven's Musik ... erweckt aber jene unendliche Sehnsucht, welche das Wesen des Romantischen ist.'*[80]

Closely connected with the contrast between Greek enjoyment of the present and the modern inclination towards yearning and presentiment is another dichotomy that was often used in defining the romantic. A literature devoted to the here-and-now will present its figures clearly and concretely; it will be 'sculpturesque' (*plastisch*).* A literature of longing and foreboding will be evocative, shadowy, and given to mood-painting; it will be 'picturesque' or 'musical,' or both.

The dominance of sculpture among the Greeks and of painting among the moderns was pointed out in 1765 by F. Hemsterhuis, the Dutch philosopher who wrote in French and was much beloved by the German romantics – '*On peut dire que nos sculpteurs modernes sont trop peintres, comme apparemment les peintres Grecs étaient trop sculpteurs*'[81] – and there is no reason to assume that he was the first who was tempted thus to generalize. Greek sculpture was immensely admired in the eighteenth century, medieval and baroque sculpture was held in contempt, and the superiority of modern paintings over the pitiful remains of the ancients was as obvious as the comparison was unfair. Besides, the sculpturesque tendencies of Greek vase paintings are almost as obvious as the painterly tendencies of Baroque sculpture and architecture. Also, as we have seen, the association between the picturesque and the romantic was well established long before 'romantic' was used as a technical term. From such starting points, it was only a small step to conclude, as Jean Paul did in his *Vorschule der Ästhetik*, that

---

* Although inadequate, 'sculpturesque' seems a better rendering of the German *plastisch* than 'plastic.' The corresponding noun, *Plastik*, meant 'statuary' or 'the art of statuary' and can still be used in this sense.

'a statue, because of its definite and precise contours, excludes the romantic, whereas the art of painting approximates it through its groupings of figures and attains it without people in landscapes, e.g., by Claude Lorraine,'

Eine Statue schließt durch ihre enge und scharfe Umschreibung jedes Romantische aus; die Malerei nähert sich schon durch Menschen-Gruppierungen ihm mehr und erreicht es ohne Menschen in Landschaften, z.B.von Claude,[82]

or to use the contrast between 'pagan sculpture' and 'romantic painting' in describing the difference between classicistic and romantic poets, as did Friedrich Ast: '*Die* Goethische *Poesie hat ihr Gegenbild in der heidnischen Plastik, die* Tieckische *und* Novalische *in der romantischen Malerei.*'[83]

The distinction between sculpturesque and musical poets had been made by Schlegel in 1793, in a letter to his brother: '*... daß die modernen Dichter sich in zwei Klassen zu teilen scheinen, die musikalischen und die bildenden. Goethe neigt sich mehr zu der letzten. Bürger, Klopstock, und selbst Schiller sind ganz lyrisch.*'[84] In his essay on the study of Greek poetry, he made the distinction again and claimed to have found it in Plato: '*Man hat den Wink Platos nicht beachtet, der im Ion die Eigentümlichkeiten der* plastischen *und der* musikalischen *Begeisterung scharf und zart bestimmt.*'* In later years, when he used this terminology to explain the nature of the romantic, he usually described it as *both* picturesque and musical –

Was ist der eigentliche innerste Grundcharakter der romantischen Poesie? Die witzige Konstruktion des Fantastischen reicht noch nicht ganz zu; vielleicht aber der pictorielle und musikalische Charakter, der freilich bewußtlos ist, aber doch unverkennbar –†

but nowhere did he clearly explain what he meant by this. Meanwhile, however, Schiller – who at that time could not have known any of Schlegel's remarks on the subject – had furnished an explanation. Having, in his treatise on naïve and sentimental poetry, called Klopstock a 'musical poet,' he commented on this usage:

I say *musical* in allusion to the dual relationship of poetry to music and visual art. For, depending on whether poetry imitates a certain *object*, as

---

*   F. Schlegel, *Prosaische Jugendschriften* i: 62. The assertion seems to be based on a rather inaccurate reading of Plato's *Ion* (533–4).

†   F. Schlegel, *Literary Notebooks*, no. 2091. See also his Paris lectures of 1803–4: 'In Rücksicht der Form nennt man in der Poesie überall dasjenige romantisch, was in einem hohen Grade entweder musikalisch, oder pittoresk und farbig ist.' *KFSA* xi: 156.

do the visual arts, or whether, like music, it merely calls forth a certain *state of mind* without requiring a definite object for this purpose, it can be called visual (*sculpturesque*) or musical. The latter expression therefore refers not only to that in poetry which is really and in its substance music, but generally to all those effects of poetry that it can produce without limiting the imagination by a definite object.

Ich sage musikalischen, um hier an die doppelte Verwandtschaft der Poesie mit der Tonkunst und mit der bildenden Kunst zu erinnern. Je nachdem nämlich die Poesie entweder einen bestimmten Gegenstand *nachahmt, wie die bildenden Künste tun, oder je nachdem sie, wie die Tonkunst, bloß einen bestimmten* Zustand *des* Gemüts *hervorbringt, ohne dazu eines bestimmten Gegenstandes nötig zu haben, kann sie bildend (plastisch) oder musikalisch genannt werden. Der letztere Ausdruck bezieht sich also nicht bloß auf dasjenige, was in der Poesie wirklich und der Materie nach, Musik ist, sondern überhaupt auf alle diejenigen Effekte derselben, die sie hervorzubringen vermag, ohne die Einbildungskraft durch ein bestimmtes Objekt zu beschränken; und in diesem Sinne nenne ich Klopstock vorzugsweise einen musikalischen Dichter.*[85]

Needless to say, Schiller associated musical poetry with the sentimental and sculpturesque poetry with the naïve, and greatly contributed to the wide currency this dichotomy gained. Thus, in 1804, Jean Paul headed the chapter on Greek poetry in his *Vorschule der Ästhetik* 'Über die griechische oder plastische Dichtkunst,' and explained:

In the following, I shall adopt the usual [!] classifications. The most comprehensive is that between Greek or sculpturesque and modern or musical poetry ... It is well-known how all people in Greek poetry, like the statues in walking position by Daedalus, appear to us bodily on earth and full of motion, while the people in modern poetry change their shape like clouds in the sky ...

Ich werde mich im folgenden in angenommene Abteilungen fügen. Die breiteste ist die zwischen griechischer oder plastischer Poesie und zwischen neuer oder romantischer oder auch musikalischer ... Es ist bekannt, wie in den griechischen Gedichten alle Gestalten wie gehende Dädalus-Statuen voll Körper und Bewegung auf der Erde erscheinen, indes neuere Formen mehr im Himmel wie Wolken fließen, deren große, aber wogende Umrisse sich in jeder zweiten Phantasie willkürlich gestalten.*

---

*   Jean Paul, *Werke* v: 67, 71. Similarly, Hegel held that Greek sculpture represents the summit of classical art, whereas the key-note ('Grundton') of romantic art is musical (*Werke* x, ii, Berlin, 1843, pp. 124, 134); Hegel's views on the subject are, however, inseparable from his whole system and cannot be discussed in the present context.

The explanations of the romantic as the (musical or picturesque) opposite of the plastic did not remain unchallenged. Thus, one K.H.L. R – – – – dt, reviewing Jean Paul's *Vorschule* in *Der Freimütige*, called his definition of romantic poetry 'vague and unfounded,' complained that it was a mere rehash of Friedrich Schlegel's definition, and insisted that all poetry must be sculpturesque.

Jean Paul betet sie [die Definition des Romantischen] F. Schlegel nach, so viel ich weiß. Ist denn aber griechisch *und* plastisch *einerlei? und war denn die griechische Poesie nicht gar oft auch* romantisch? *Wenn sie uns nur selten so scheint; so kommt das bloß daher, weil uns der lebendige Glaube an die Wahrheit griechischer Mythen mangelt. Noch mehr: sollte es wirklich eine romantische Poesie geben, die nicht zugleich plastisch wäre? Meines Erachtens ist eine* nicht *plastische Poesie gar nicht denkbar.*[86]

But such criticisms proved of no avail. A. W. Schlegel, as we shall see, operated with the same dichotomy, Jean Paul only slightly modified his views in the second edition of the *Vorschule*, and in 1819 Grillparzer – who heartily disliked both Schlegels – felt just as provoked by all this as the reviewer in *Der Freimütige* had been fifteen years previously:

All great masters at all times from Shakespeare and Milton to Goethe were more or less sculpturesque, because just this sculpturesque and well-defined presentation with precise contours, being the most difficult thing in art, can be achieved only by the forceful master and is therefore also his foremost goal. The shapelessness that is a main ingredient of so-called romanticism has always been a sign of a weak, sickly spirit which can control neither itself nor its subject matter. – What does the expression 'romantic' really mean? If it is supposed to refer to the character that was impressed upon modern art by Christianity ... then I do not know how one can call Shakespeare a romantic poet ... Now what follows from this? ... It follows that there are no drawers into which one can lock ... the human spirit, classifying it like a collection of insects.

Alle großen Meister aller Zeiten von Skakespeare und Milton bis Goethe waren mehr oder weniger plastisch, weil eben dieses plastische, gesonderte Hinstellen mit scharfen Konturen, als das schwerste in der Kunst, nur dem kräftigen Meister gelingt und deshalb auch seines Strebens Hauptziel ist. Die Formlosigkeit, welche ein Hauptingrediens der sogenannten Romantik ist, war von jeher ein Zeichen eines schwachen kränkelnden Geistes, der sich selbst und seinen Stoff zu beherrschen nicht vermag. – Was heißt denn eigentlich der Ausdruck: romantisch? Soll er auf jenen Charakter hindeuten, den die neuere Kunst durch das Christentum erhielt ... so

weiß ich nicht, wie man Shakespeare einen romantischen Dichter nennen kann ...
Was folgt nun daraus? ... Daß es keine Schubfächer gebe, folgt daraus, in denen
man den menschlichen Geist ... einschließen kann und registrieren wie eine
Insektensammlung.[87]

Even this outburst, however, did not mend matters, and the musical
rather than sculpturesque nature of romantic poetry is still emphasized in as comparatively recent a work as Julius Petersen's
Wesensbestimmung der deutschen Romantik (Leipzig, 1926).

Another defining characteristic of the romantic that was
adduced very frequently was its connection with the 'infinite.' Here
again, Schiller was important. The ancient poets, he had claimed in
his treatise of 1795, derived their power from the 'art of limitation,'
the moderns from the 'art of the infinite' – a contrast that is closely
connected with that of the sculpturesque and the romantic;

And the very fact that the strength of the ancient artist ... consists in
limitation accounts for the great superiority of the visual arts of the
ancients over those of the moderns, and quite generally for the different
degree of excellence which modern poetry and modern visual art have
achieved as compared with the corresponding achievements of the
ancients. A work of art for the eye reaches perfection only through
limitation; a work for the imagination can attain it also through the
unlimited.

Jener [the ancient poet] ... ist mächtig durch die Kunst der Begrenzung; dieser ist es
durch die Kunst des Unendlichen. Und eben daraus, daß die Stärke des alten
Künstlers ... in der Begrenzung bestehet, erklärt sich der hohe Vorzug, den die
bildende Kunst des Altertums über die der neuern Zeiten behauptet, und überhaupt
das ungleiche Verhältnis des Werts, in welchem moderne Dichtkunst und moderne
bildende Kunst zu beiden Kunstgattungen im Altertum stehen. Ein Werk für
das Auge findet nur in der Begrenzung seine Vollkommenheit; ein Werk für die
Einbildungskraft kann sie auch durch das Unbegrenzte erreichen.[88]

Similarly Jean Paul, who had said that sculpture, because of
the precise limitation of its contours, was unromantic, defined the
romantic as 'the beautiful without limitation, or the beautiful infinite'/'*Das Romantische ist das Schöne ohne Begrenzung, oder das* schöne
Unendliche, so wie es ein erhabnes *gibt*,'[89] whereas Ast distinguished
the 'romantic epoch' from the preceding 'Indic' and 'Greek' epochs
by claiming that in it the 'spiritual love of the infinite' revealed itself.[90] Ludwig Uhland defined the romantic as the 'presentiment of
the infinite in one's intuitions'/'*Dies Ahnen des Unendlichen in den*

Anschauungen ist das Romantische,'[91] and E. T. A. Hoffmann, writing, as usual, about music rather than literature, established a nexus between yearning, the romantic, and the infinite:

Beethoven's music ... arouses exactly that infinite yearning which is the essence of romanticism.

[Music] is the most romantic of all the arts; one might almost say, it alone is genuinely romantic, for only the infinite is its subject.*

Beethovens Musik ... erweckt eben jene unendliche Sehnsucht, welche das Wesen der Romantik ist.

Sie [die Musik] ist die romantischste aller Künste, beinahe möchte man sagen, allein echt romantisch, denn nur das Unendliche ist ihr Vorwurf.[92]

Needless to say, the defining characteristics we have so far discussed – Christianity, mysticism, the spirit of chivalric or caritative love, the marvellous or fantastic, 'romantic distance,' subjectivity, a prevailing mood of yearning or presentiment, picturesque or musical tendencies, 'witty construction,' propensity towards the infinite – by no means exhaust the list, but only a brief sampling of some of the more far-fetched explanations can be given. Thus, J. A. Eberhard declared in his *Handbuch der Ästhetik* that

the romantic is generally, in nature and in art, grandeur mixed with loveliness, and more particularly, in art, the grandeur of the modern ideal tempered by loveliness.

Das Romantische ist also überhaupt in der Natur wie in der Kunst das mit Lieblichkeit gemischte Große und in der Kunst in Sonderheit das Große des modernen Ideals, durch Lieblichkeit gemildert.[93]

In a review of Kleist's *Amphitryon* we read that the dramatist had written 'in a romantic spirit' because his play is dominated by reflection /'*Der Verfasser ... hat ... durchaus im romantischen Geiste gedichtet, da in den ernsten und scherzhaften Partien die Reflexion überall gesetzgebend und bildend vorherrscht.*'[94] J. A. Apel opined that the beautiful was the sublime and the pleasing in complete synthesis ('dynamische Durchdringung'), whereas the romantic was the sublime and the pleasing mixed ('in mechanischer, oder auch harmonischer Verbindung'), and illustrated this theory with a remarkable collection of examples:

---

*   For a relatively recent investigation defining classicism and romanticism on the basis of perfection and infinity, see Fritz Strich, *Deutsche Klassik und Romantik oder Vollendung und Unendlichkeit* (München, 1922).

A spring day can be beautiful, a spring night is romantic; even the scent of flowers in the evening is more romantic than it is during the day, for as its cause is hidden, a semblance of mystery comes into being which produces festive sublimity along with the pleasing; the moon behind thunder clouds is more romantic than in a sky only slightly clouded; a blossoming garden on the sea shore is more romantic than on the banks of a brook; however, a brook surrounded by blossoms in a rocky valley is more romantic than rocky cliffs by the sea, which can be wild, awe-inspiring, sublime, but not romantic, without the admixture of something pleasant ...

Ein Frühlingstag kann schön sein, eine Frühlingsnacht ist romantisch; schon der abendliche Duft der Blumen ist romantischer, als derselbe am Tage, denn indem seine Ursache sich verbirgt, ensteht ein Schein des Mysteriösen, welcher neben dem Angenehmen das feierlich Erhabene hervorruft; der Mond hinter Gewitterwolken ist romantischer, als der, an leicht bewölktem Himmel; ein blühender Garten am Meerstrand ist romantischer, als an einem kleinen Fluß; hingegen ein umblühter Bach in einem Felsentale ist wieder romantischer, als das Felsengeklipp am Meere, welches wild, grausend, erhaben sein kann, aber nicht romantisch, ohne den Zusatz von etwas Angenehmem ...[95]

Haydn's instrumental music, Goethe's *Iphigenie*, peace, and classical enjoyment of sex are 'beautiful'; Mozart's symphonies, Goethe's *Tasso*, war, and chivalric erotic yearning are 'romantic.' These grotesque effusions were reprinted twice,[96] but even they were not the worst. One of the characters in Otto Heinrich Graf von Loeben's novel, *Guido*, which he published under the pseudonym, 'Isidorus Orientalis,' finds a 'particular charm' in the word *romantisch* and confesses:

Until now, I always felt ashamed to say how this word sways and moves me ... Often, when I am filled with nameless desire and want to cry with painful pleasure, and [wish to go] out, out into the bold and green, the blue and the grey – then I cry out: romantic, and then my breast feels free and true as if I now possessed it, as if I could grasp it for ever with both arms in the shape of a girl. Ah! everything looks like green air and golden earth when I pronounce that word.

Ich habe mich bisher immer geschämt, es zu sagen, wie mich dies Wort anfüllt und bewegt; nun ist es mir so lieb, daß Du dasselbe dabei fühlst. Ich weiß nicht – wenn ich oft keinen Namen für mein Verlangen habe und weinen möchte vor schmerzlichem Vergnügen und hinaus, hinaus ins Kühne und Grüne, ins Blaue und Graue – da ruf' ich: romantisch, nun wird die Brust mir frei und treu, als ob ich es nun besäße, als ob

*ichs in der Gestalt eines Mädchens mit beiden Armen auf ewig umschließen könnte.
Ach! es sieht aus wie grüne Luft und goldene Erde, wenn ich das Wort nenne.*[97]

If this sounds to us like a parody, it was taken quite seriously at least by one of Isidorus' readers; S. H. K. Michaelis, who had been Schiller's publisher at one time and lectured at the University of Heidelberg, concluded his essay 'Über klassische und romantische Poesie' with the following apostrophe to a group of romantics he did not like:

I do not know how those among my contemporaries who belong to Truth rather than to a faction will judge the works of the *new romantic poet*, who may not be a romanticist in your sense of the word; but I know that with him the problem: *What is romantic poetry?* is solved. With the works of this poet, its age must begin ... or the whole nature of this kind of poetry is a phantom, a phantasmagoria, a chimera of mere phrases and empty air. The first work that is destined to solve the problem is called – *Guido*; the poet – *Isidorus Orientalis.*

Ich weiß nicht, wie diejenigen unter meinen Zeitgenossen, die der Wahrheit, aber keiner Schule angehören, die Werke des neuen romantischen Dichters, *der kein Romantiker in eurem Sinne sein mag, beurteilen werden. Ich weiß aber, daß mit ihm die Lösung der Aufgabe:* was ist romantische Poesie? *gegeben ist. Mit den Werken dieses Dichters muß ihre Periode beginnen,* muß der [sic] Wachstum der Bibel *sichtbar werden – oder das ganze Wesen* dieser *Poesie ist Phantom, Schattenspiel, leeres Luft- und Wortgebilde. Das erste Werk, was die Aufgabe zu lösen bestimmt ist, heißt –* Guido; *der Dichter –* Isidorus Orientalis.[98]

It is hardly surprising that there were critics who felt that the word was a little overworked. Thus – and once again some very few illustrations must suffice – the review of Schink's *Romantische Erzählungen*, from which we have already quoted, contains the following expostulation:

The concept one is to associate with the word *romantisch* seems to be so utterly unclear to most authors who use it in the headings of their works that one may usually regard it as a warning to leave the work with such a title unread. Some believe themselves to have produced a romantic work when they have pieced together a lot of unlikely adventures and marvels; others, when they have treated subjects of real life with unbearably high-strung sentimentality. How so? Is the romantic not permitted to be *sensible?*

Der Begriff, den man mit dem Worte 'romantisch' zu verbinden hat, scheint den meisten Schriftstellern, die es ihren Arbeiten vorsetzen, noch so durchaus undeutlich zu sein, daß man es meistenteils als eine Warnung ansehen darf, das so getitelte Buch ungelesen zu lassen. Die Einen glauben etwas Romantisches geliefert zu haben, wenn sie recht viel Abenteuerlich-Wunderbares zusammenstoppelten; andre, wenn sie Gegenstände des wirklichen Lebens mit unerträglich überspannter Empfindelei behandelten. Wie? Darf denn das Romantische durchaus nicht vernünftig sein?[99]

In a similar vein, a reviewer in the *Zeitung für die elegante Welt* complains:

The meaning of the word *romantic* is becoming more and more diverse. Romantic poems are for the most part somewhat nonsensical, romantic plays display the world upside down, romantic girls flit about on the streets at night and join company with romantic men stimulated by the same romantic moods. Don't blame them for it. They are possessed by the romantic spirit.

Die Bedeutung des Wortes romantisch wird immer vielseitiger. Romantische Gedichte sind größtenteils etwas unsinnig, romantische Schauspiele spielen die verkehrte Welt, romantische Mädchen flattern abends auf den Straßen und gesellen sich zu ihren romantischen Männern, die von gleichen romantischen Stimmungen gestachelt werden. Man tadle nicht. Sie sind vom romantischen Geiste besessen.[100]

And Joseph Schreyvogel, a veteran among the opponents of romanticism, stated succinctly:

There are no romantic poems to which all or even just the majority of the characteristics of this concept apply, except for poems expressly modelled on it.

Es gibt keine romantischen Dichtungen, auf welche alle, oder auch nur die meisten Merkmale dieses Begriffes passen, paßten, diejenigen ausgenommen, die erst nach demselben gemodelt wurden.[101]

The word, however, was there to stay. Every protest that it was vague or meaningless merely provoked further attempts at defining it and thus added fuel to the fire. Literary critics seemed to be unable to do without it, and literary historians gave it the full weight of their authority. We have already quoted from Bouterwek's twelve-volume history of literature, where the word is used constantly, and more often in the later volumes than in the earlier ones; and although modern readers will find this vast compilation unreliable and tedious, Bouterwek's contemporaries had no equally detailed account to turn to. Last, but not least, the use of our word had the support of the leading literary critic and historian of the day, August Wilhelm Schlegel.

If we have only mentioned A. W. Schlegel in passing and have reserved him for special treatment, this is not because he was particularly original: a large part of his critical arsenal was borrowed from his younger brother. He was, however, less given to extremes; he had the greater gift for polished, lucid expression; he was a brilliant literary strategist, and thus it was his influence far more than that of any other romantic critic or theorist that mattered.

During the 1790s, A. W. Schlegel's usage of the word *romantisch* was fairly constant and quite conservative: he employed it either in the trivial sense of 'romance-like' or in the chronological sense popularized by Herder.[102] In the lectures on European literature he gave in Berlin in 1801–4,[103] he began to expound views long held by his brother; but, although he did so in a more lucid and persuasive fashion than did Friedrich and had a large and influential audience, these lectures (with the exception of some 90 pages in F. Schlegel's *Europa*) remained unpublished during his lifetime, and we shall deal with them very briefly, concentrating our attention on those parts of them that have a bearing on our subject. A. W. Schlegel explained – as Herder had done some 35 years previously – that it was wrong to judge modern poetry by standards abstracted from the ancients. He pointed out that the character of ancient poetry had been called 'klassisch,' that of the moderns 'romantisch,' and added that he approved of this terminology,[104] suggesting, however, that only classical poetry could be studied as a whole, whereas romantic poetry remained a fragment. (This is, of course, F. Schlegel's notion of the 'progressive' character of romantic poetry.) He explained very late in his lectures that *romantisch* is derived from *Romance* and *Roman*,* and at various points in the course of his lectures he defined the nature of the romantic in ways that are by now thoroughly familiar to us, but which were new to the majority of his listeners or were accepted gratefully as explanations of F. Schlegel's more obscure statements in the *Athenäum*. Among the major points are that the ancients in all their works of art incline to qualities that are particularly characteristic of scuplture, whereas the moderns tend towards the picturesque,[105] and that the Greeks practised the strict

---

*   'Ich will hier bemerken, daß der Name *romantische* Poesie auch in dieser historischen Rücksicht treffend gewählt sei. Denn Romanisch, *Romance*, nannte man die neuen aus der Vermischung des Lateinischen mit der Sprache der Eroberer entstandnen Dialekte; daher Romane, die darin geschriebnen Dichtungen, woher denn romantisch abgeleitet ist, und ist der Charakter dieser Poesie Verschmelzung des altdeutschen mit dem späteren, d.h. christlich gewordnen Römischen, so werden auch ihre Elemente schon durch den Namen angedeutet.' *DLD* xix: 17.

separation of the genres, whereas the romantic poets created an 'unresolvable mixture of all poetic elements,'[106] combining not merely the different genres, but earnestness and mirth, verse and prose, 'art' and 'nature.'[107] The canon of major poets presented by A. W. Schlegel is more or less the same as in F. Schlegel's 'Epochen der Dichtkunst,' except that Calderón is now added.

The period of A. W. Schlegel's Berlin lectures was followed by that of his close association with Mme de Staël, through whom and whose circle, as well as his own publications in French,[108] his views spread into France. The lectures on dramatic poetry he gave in Vienna in 1808 provided him with a still wider audience: published in the original German in 1809–11,[109] they were soon available also in French (1813), English (1815), and Italian (1817).* The major importance of these lectures is, of course, to be found in the field of practical criticism rather than in that of theory; the dichotomy of the classical and the romantic is, however, discussed significantly and at some length on two occasions, in the introductory lecture and again in Lecture xxv, in which he first turns to his favourite post-classical dramatists, Shakespeare and Calderón.

In the first lecture, A. W. Schlegel makes the point that ever since the rediscovery of the Greeks in the fourteenth century, scholars had made the grievous mistake of ascribing absolute authority to the ancients, while the truly great poets and artists had resolutely gone their own way and produced works that were diametrically opposed to those of the ancients. More recent thinkers, mainly in Germany, had realized that this opposition, which is merely one instance of the general rule that all basic forces in nature manifest themselves in polar opposites, may be the key to the whole history of the arts, both ancient and modern; and they had invented the name 'romantic' for the spirit of modern art in contradistinction to ancient or classical art. This name was suitable, for it was derived from *Romance*, the word used for the popular languages that had originated from the combination of Latin with old German vernaculars, just as the modern civilization itself had originated in the combination of Northern and ancient elements. It should be possible to show that one and the same contrast systematically pervaded the characteristic expressions of the ancients and the moderns in all the arts. Thus, Rousseau had shown that ancient music was dominated by rhythm and melody, modern music by harmony. Hemsterhuis had suggested

---

* Translations into Dutch (1810) and Polish (1830) remained incomplete. For details see Josef Körner, *Die Botschaft der deutschen Romantik an Europa* (Augsburg, 1929).

that the ancient painters had probably been too close to sculpture, whereas modern sculptors were too painterly, and had thus pointed to the basic distinction; for 'the spirit of the whole of ancient art and poetry is sculpturesque; that of the moderns is picturesque'/'*Der Geist der gesammten antiken Kunst und Poesie ist plastisch, so wie der modernen pittoresk.*'[110]

The civilization of the Greeks was a perfect product of nature; they had achieved everything possible to man within the limits of the finite; their whole art was an expression of their consciousness of complete harmony, and their poetics was a 'poetics of joy' (*Poetik der Freude*). In spite of all this, however, we could ascribe 'no higher character' to their civilization than that of a 'refined sensuality'/ '*Allein wie weit die Griechen auch im Schönen und selbst im Sittlichen gediehen, so können wir ihrer Bildung doch keinen höheren Charakter zugestehen, als den einer geläuterten, veredelten Sinnlichkeit.*'[111] After the decline of the ancient civilization, Europe had been revitalized and its spirit radically altered by the spread of a new religion and the influence of its Northern conquerors. In the union of the ethos of the Northerners and the sentiments of Christianity, the institution of knighthood had its origin, as had a new and purer spirit of love and a new concept of honour; and these new phenomena, knighthood, chivalric love, and honour, along with Christianity itself, were the subjects of medieval, romantic poetry. Moreover, Christianity had altered man's basic attitude to life. With the Greeks, human nature had been self-sufficient in its finitude. The Christian 'intuition of the infinite [*Anschauung des Unendlichen*] had destroyed the finite.'[112] This life had become a mere passing shadow preceding the dawn of the life eternal, and the modern spirit was dominated by the presentiment of the true happiness possible only in the beyond; hence, while

the poetry of the ancients was that of possession, ours is that of yearning; the former stands firmly rooted in the present, the latter hovers between recollection of the past and presentiment of the future.

... *die Poesie der Alten war die des Besitzes, die unsrige ist die der Sehnsucht; jene steht fest auf dem Boden der Gegenwart, diese wiegt sich zwischen Erinnerung und Ahnung.*[113]

Feeling has become more inward and intense (*inniger*), the imagination less concrete (*unkörperlicher*), thought more contemplative. In Greek art, there had been 'unconscious unity of form and subject';

in modern art, their opposition was realized and their interpenetration sought. Greek poetry had performed its task with complete perfection; modern poetry can never completely satisfy its infinite aspirations, and its semblance of imperfection exposes it to the danger of not being duly appreciated:

In der griechischen Kunst und Poesie ist ursprüngliche bewußtlose Einheit der Form und des Stoffes; in der neueren, sofern sie ihrem eigentümlichen Geiste treu geblieben, wird innigere Durchdringung beider als zweier Entgegengesetzten gesucht. Jene hat ihre Aufgabe bis zur Vollendung gelöset; diese kann ihrem Streben ins Unendliche hin nur durch Annäherung Genüge leisten, und ist wegen eines gewissen Scheins von Unvollendung um so eher in Gefahr, verkannt zu werden.[114]

In the twenty-fifth lecture, A. W. Schlegel claims that the 'similarity of the English and the Spanish theatre consists not only in the bold neglect of the unities of place and time and in the mixture of comic and tragic ingredients,' but above all in the 'spirit of romantic poetry, dramatically expressed' – a phrase which, because of the close connection of *romantisch* and *Roman*, has rather more piquancy in German than in English; and he follows this statement with the familiar generalizations:

Ancient art and poetry tend towards the strict separation of dissimilar things; romantic art and poetry delight in indissoluble mixtures: all contrarieties, nature and art, poetry and prose, seriousness and mirth, recollection and anticipation, spirituality and sensuality, the secular and the divine, life and death, are most intimately blended by it … The whole of ancient poetry and art is, as it were, a rythmic law [*nomos*], a harmonious promulgation of the permanently established legislation of a world beautifully ordered and reflecting in itself the eternal prototypes of all things. The romantic, on the other hand, is the expression of a secret attraction to a chaos hidden by the ordered creation … and forever striving after new and wonderful births: the animating spirit of original love hovers here anew above the waters. The former is simpler, clearer, and more like nature in the self-sufficient perfection of its separate works; the latter, notwithstanding its fragmentary appearance, is closer to the secret of the universe.

Die antike Kunst und Poesie geht auf strenge Sonderung des Ungleichartigen, die romantische gefällt sich in unauflöslichen Mischungen; alle Entgegengesetzten, Natur und Kunst, Poesie und Prosa, Ernst und Scherz, Erinnerung und Ahndung, Geistigkeit und Sinnlichkeit, das Irdische und Göttliche, Leben und Tod, verschmilzt sie auf das innigste miteinander. Wie die ältesten Gesetzgeber ihre ordnenden

Lehren und Vorschriften in abgemessenen Weisen erteilten, ... so ist die gesamte alte Poesie und Kunst gleichsam ein rhythmischer Nomos, eine harmonische Verkündigung der auf immer festgestellten Gesetzgebung einer schön geordneten und die ewigen Urbilder der Dinge in sich abspiegelnden Welt. Die romantische hingegen ist der Ausdruck des geheimen Zuges zu dem immerfort nach neuen und wundervollen Geburten ringenden Chaos, welches unter der geordneten Schöpfung, ja in ihrem Schoße sich verbirgt: der beseelende Geist der ursprünglichen Liebe schwebt hier von neuem über den Wassern. Jene ist einfacher, klarer, und der Natur in der selbständigen Vollendung ihrer einzelnen Werke ähnlicher; diese, ungeachtet ihres fragmentarischen Ansehens, ist dem Geheimnis des Weltalls näher.[115]

III

As we have seen, the adjective *romantisch* had established itself in the course of the first decade of the eighteenth century as a technical term in discussions of literature and had acquired a typological sense. Admittedly, 'romantic poetry' was primarily the characteristic poetry of post-classical Europe, but there was nothing absurd or paradoxical in applying the epithet to an ancient author.* Similarly, the word could be applied to contemporaries, but it did not specifically refer to what we now call German romanticism. Moreover, the word had become so familiar in the typological sense that it could not very easily acquire such a narrow and specific connotation. The next chapter in the history of our word and its cognates, which commenced in 1807–8, is therefore less concerned with the adjective than with the corresponding nouns, *Romantik* (romanticism) and *Romantiker* (romanticist). Before we can turn to the events of 1807–8, it will, however, be convenient to make a brief comment on some other words – the phrase *neue Schule* and the verb *romantisieren* – and to trace the history of the nouns *Romantik* and *Romantiker* prior to 1807.

The term *Schule* in its technical sense had been transferred from the field of painting to that of literature by Friedrich Schlegel, in his first published essay, 'Von den Schulen der griechischen Poesie' (1794). Within a few years of that date, it seems to have become quite usual, at least orally, to refer both to the followers of Fichte and to the Schlegels and their circle – two groups which overlapped to a very large extent – as the 'New School': this is how Henry

---

* Thus, F. Schlegel (Literary Notebooks, no. 1440) called the *Odyssey* romantic, and J. A. Apel (*Selene* I, i: 17) wrote that Euripides 'seemed to ... approximate the romantic.' With F. Schlegel, the tendency to find romantic traits in ancient writers went so far as to render the original dichotomy almost meaningless.

Crabb Robinson used the term in 1801.[116] Subsequently, we find the expressions 'die neuere Schule' in Jean Paul's preface to the first edition of his *Vorschule der Ästhetik* (1804),[117] 'die neueste Schule'[118] and 'die sogenannte neue Schule'[119] in reviews in the *Morgenblatt für gebildete Stände*, and 'die neue Schule' in a satirical pamphlet by Brentano and Görres;[120] but these phrases were not specific enough to catch on, and after 1808 they seem to have been used mainly in contexts where it is denied that a 'new school' exists at all.* Such terms as 'die Tiecksche Schule' or 'die Schlegelsche Schule' were even more short-lived.†

The verb *romantisieren* originally meant 'to write a novel (about something),' 'to convert into a novel,' just as *dramatisieren*, to dramatize, means 'to convert into a play.' Thus, a reviewer in the *Jenaische Allgemeine Literatur-Zeitung* wrote in 1797,

It is all the same to this author whether he dramatizes or romanticizes the story of Job or of Alexander, of Cleopatra, or Friedrich von Zollern,

Es gilt dem Verfasser gleich, den Hiob, *oder den* Alexander ... *die* Cleopatra *oder* Friedrich von Zollern *zu dramatisieren, und zu romantisieren,*[121]

and Friedrich Schlegel wrote about a year later that it was a 'bad mistake to write confessions,' that is, autobiographies in the manner of Rousseau, 'instead of modestly romanticizing one's life,' that is, writing a novel about it:

---

*   F. Schlegel used the phrase *die neue Schule* occasionally in his letters (e.g., 8 September and 26 October 1805, *Krisenjahre der Frühromantik*, ed. J. Körner, vol. 1, Brünn-Wien-Leipzig, 1936, pp. 230, 238), but subsequently denied that a 'new' or 'romantic' school existed at all. In his private notes, he wrote of 'die sogenannte neue Schule' (e.g., 'Zur Poesie und Litteratur. 1812,' fol. 27), and in his *Geschichte der alten und neuen Literatur* he declared: 'So wenig es ... in der deutschen Literatur ein goldnes Zeitalter gegeben hat; eben so wenig kann ich auch irgendwo etwas finden, was die Benennung einer neuen Schule rechtfertigen kann.' *KFSA* xi: 410. Cf. his comments in his review of Adam Müller's *Vorlesungen über die deutsche Wissenschaft und Literatur*, where he speaks of 'jene seltsame Erdichtung einer neuen Schule' (*Heidelbergische Jahrbücher für Philologie, Historie, Literatur und Kunst*, 1 (1808), 2. Heft, pp. 237, 239, 240.

†   Loeben speaks in a letter of 20 October 1814 of the 'Tiecksche Schule, von der Arnim und Brentano ausgegangen' and to which Eichendorff is supposed to belong (Eichendorff, *Werke*, ed. Kosch, Regensburg, 1908, xiii: 65). Franz Horn, in his *Umrisse zur Geschichte und Kritik der schönen Literatur Deutschlands während der Jahre 1790–1818* (Berlin, 1819), speaks of 'jene sogenannte Schule' and 'die Schlegelsche Schule,' but denies a few pages later that such a school exists 'in der wahren Bedeutung des Wortes' (pp. 130, 134, 145). More positively, Tieck reminisced in 1829: 'Es war damals [in 1800] meine Absicht, ein poetisches Journal ... herauszugeben, um ... die Kritik der neuen Schule in meinem Sinne fortzuführen.' (*Schriften*, Berlin, 1829, xi: lxiv.)

Arger Mißgriff Selbstbekenntnisse *zu schreiben, statt sein Leben bescheiden zu* romantisieren.[122]

Elsewhere – as in the passage from Novalis quoted on page 124 above – the word either meant 'to render romance-like,' 'to write in a romantic manner,' or hovered somewhere between these closely related meanings.[123] It soon died out again and is of interest only because it illustrates the strong tendency around 1800 to construe words based on the root *Roman* in analogy to the well-established words based on *Drama*. We have already discussed this tendency in the case of the adjective, *romantisch*; it remains for us to show it at work in the case of the nouns, *Romantik* and *Romantiker*.

The noun *Romantik* is widely held to have been coined by Novalis, but this is not correct. It occurs already in Part 1 of J. G. Müller von Itzehoe's novel *Herr Thomas* (1790), where it refers to the novels Thomas had tried to write as a young man:

He [Thomas] was unwilling to acquiesce without a murmur when Herr Bernd so inexorably panned his novels [*seine Romantik*]. He rejoined that in addition to that higher kind of novel [*des Romans*] which aimed particularly at character drawing and therefore admittedly required a knowledge of human nature, there were many other kinds that required no great knowledge of philosophy and other things ...

So ganz gutwillig wollte er denn doch das Gewehr nicht strecken, als Herr Bernd seine Romantik so unerbittlich in die Pfanne hieb. Er wandte ein, daß es außer jener höheren Gattung des Romans, welche eigentlich Menschendarstellung beziele, mithin allerdings Menschenkunde voraussetzte, manche andre Gattung gebe, die keinen Aufwand von Philosophie und anderen Kenntnissen erfodre ... *

Friedrich Schlegel used the noun in 1797, in a context that sheds no light on its meaning.[124] Shortly afterwards – in the winter of 1797–8 – it was used more significantly by Novalis, as the heading of several entries in an unpublished collection of notes known as 'das allgemeine Brouillon':

Romantik. *Absolutierung – Universalierung – Klassifikation des individuellen Moments, der individuellen Situation etc. ist das eigentliche Wesen des* Romantisierens. *Vide* Meister. Märchen ...

* J. G. Müller von Itzehoe, *Herr Thomas, eine komische Geschichte vom Verfasser des Siegfried von Lindenberg*, 4 vols. in 2 (Göttingen, 1790–1), 1: 66 *f*. Elsewhere in the same novel, the phrase *die besten romantischen und dramatischen Produkte* simply means 'the best novels and plays,' and 'romantische Süjets' are, for Müller, subjects suitable for use in a novel – a genre from which Müller expected the *'faithful portrayal of man as he is'* (ibid., 1: 49, 68). My attention was drawn to these passages by Professor Michael Hadley.

Romantik. *Sollte nicht der Roman alle Gattungen des Stils in einer durch den gemeinsamen Geist verschiedentlich gebundnen Folge begreifen?*[125]

As other headings in the immediate vicinity are 'Physik,' 'Numismatik', 'Politik' (physics, numismatics, politics), etc., it is evident that *Romantik* here means 'theory of the *Roman*,' just as *Dramatik* means 'theory of drama.'* Quite similarly, *Romantiker* was first used in the sense of 'novelist' by Novalis (*'Der Romantiker studiert das Leben, wie der Maler, Musiker, and Mechaniker Farbe, Ton und Kraft'*).[126] The same usage can be found with Jean Paul in 1800 (' *"Ein solcher Charakter"* (*schreibt Hafenreffer dabei*) *"wäre für Romanen-Kotzebues erwünscht ..."* *Mich dünkt, dieses ist, so viel ein Biograph von Romantikern urteilen kann, sehr treffend'*)[127] and occasionally in anonymous reviews.† These usages of *Romantik* and *Romantiker* were, however, soon forced out of circulation when the words acquired a typological meaning.

In this latter sense, *Romantik* seems to occur for the first time in the poem 'Hellenik und Romantik' by Mnioch and in an article on Polish women, probably also by Mnioch, which we have already mentioned.[128] In the *Zeitung für die elegante Welt* – the same paper in which the article on Polish women had been published – this new usage was ridiculed by a pseudonymous correspondent, who called himself 'Bonifazius Ehrlich' or 'honest Boniface' and who claimed that when, being rather old-fashioned, he had taken umbrage at F. Schlegel's novel, *Lucinde*, his son had put him at ease again by talking to him about Hellenism, romanticism, and – the coinage is

* In the sense of 'romanticism,' Novalis used 'Romantismus' (Novalis, *Schriften* II, ed. R. Samuel, H.-J. Mähl, and G. Schulz, Darmstadt, 1965, p. 635; not in the edition of 1928), but I have come across only two other occurrences of this word – in a letter of Brentano to Arnim of 12 October 1803 in Reinhold Steig, *Achim von Arnim und die ihm nahe standen* (Stuttgart, 1894), p. 102, where it is used as a term of abuse, and in Heinrich Laube's *Geschichte der deutschen Literatur* III (Stuttgart, 1840): 115. 'Romantizismus' was used by Goethe in a special context (see p. 293 below), by Ruge and Echtermeyer in 'Der Protestantismus und die Romantik,' *Hallische Jahrbücher*, 1839, no. 246, col. 1963, and by Thomas Mann, *Werke in zwölf Bänden* (Frankfurt a.M., 1960), X: 394, where it seems to be an Anglicism. Hermann Glaser used it pejoratively, on the analogy of *Klassizismus*, in his edition of Hebbel's *Agnes Bernauer* (Berlin, 1964), p. 149. Other cognates that are now obsolete are 'romanzisch' (first recorded in 1698 and frequently used by Herder; cf. Trübner, *Deutsches Wörterbuch* V, Berlin, 1954, p. 437) and 'romanesque' or 'romanesk' (*Der Freimütige*, 1804, no. 10, p. 38; *Hallische ALZ*, 1815, no. 89, col. 711).

† See, e.g., *Der Freimütige*, 1804, no. 66 (2 April), p. 264 *f.*, and no. 106 (28 May), p. 423, and *Morgenblatt*, 1808 (25 October), p. 1022, where the phrase 'unsere Romantiker von Profession' can best be rendered by 'our professional romancers.' In Joseph Görres, *Die teutschen Volksbücher* (Heidelberg, 1807), p. 134, 'die Romantiker' means 'authors of romances or chap-books.'

deliberately absurd – 'mysticity': *'Ich erinnere mich noch, wie ich anfangs so schwachköpfig war, an der* Lucinde *Ärgernis zu nehmen, da sprach mich mein Sohn mit* Hellenik, Romantik, Mystizität *ganz wieder zu gute.'*[129] The new noun was, however, there to stay. In 1804, Jean Paul used it repeatedly in his *Vorschule der Ästhetik*, where he, for instance, illustrated his views on romantic poetry in a subsection headed 'Beispiele der Romantik.'* In the same year, Goethe used the expression as the antonym of 'Hellenik' in a letter to Zelter.[130] In 1805, the word was used frequently in F. Ast's *System der Kunstlehre*[131] and at least once by Zacharias Werner:

Es bleibt uns kein Ausweg, als ein Mittelweg zwischen der für uns einmal verlorenen Griechheit und der total prosaischen Wirklichkeit, und das ist die Romantik und der mit ihr innigst verwandte Mythenglauben.[132]

In 1807, it was used repeatedly by Uhland in his essay, 'Über das Romantische,'[133] and so on. Evidently, by this time, *Romantik*, but not its derivative, *Romantiker*,† had become quite widely accepted among those belonging to or favourably inclined to the 'new school'. Neither word, however, had anything like the currency of the ubiquitous adjective, and they could therefore – the military metaphor seems appropriate – be conquered by the forces of the opposition and put to a new and warlike use. This is what happened in the rather silly but influential battle between Cotta's *Morgenblatt* and the Heidelberg romantics, to which we now must turn.[134]

In 1800, the *Athenäum* had ceased publication, and soon afterwards, the group of writers associated with it had lost its coherence. By 1805, a younger group of romantics began to emerge as a recognizable entity, partly because of joint publications and partly because of their (not very permanent) connection with a single city, Heidelberg. The first of this group to arrive was Brentano, who lived in Heidelberg from July 1804 to April 1807, and returned in April 1808. He was visited in 1805 by Achim von Arnim, who returned to spend most of 1808 in Heidelberg. In the fall of 1806, Joseph Görres moved there and stayed for two years, lecturing at the University on aesthetics. The three of them soon made friends

---

*   *Werke* v: 98; cf. pp. 62, 89, 91, 99, 100, 132, 422. It is worth noting that most of Jean Paul's examples are contemporary (Klopstock, Herder, Goethe, Klinger, Schiller, A. W. and F. Schlegel, Mnioch), although Shakespeare remains the 'genuine magician and master of the romantic spirit realm.' Why the compilers of Grimm's *Wörterbuch* (VIII: 1155) illustrate Jean Paul's usage with the one of the few passages where the word is used atypically – 'Die höhere Entzückung gehört der Lyra und der Romantik an' – is known only to themselves.

†   Cf., however, *Nachtwachen von Bonaventura*, ed. cit., p. 152; 'Goethe, der den Hans Sachs, die Romantiker und Griechen in sich vereinigt ...'

with Friedrich Creuzer, who had been appointed Professor of Classical Philology at Heidelberg in the Spring of 1804, but was a follower of Schelling and attempted to show in his *Symbolik und Mythengeschichte der alten Völker* (1810–12), much to the annoyance of the more narrow-minded among the classicists, that all myths and religions of the Western world were derived from a mono-theistic *Urreligion* that had its origin in India. Finally, in May 1807, Graf Loeben, or Isidorus Orientalis, as he called himself, moved to Heidelberg; he was barely acquainted with Brentano, Arnim, and Görres, but because of his ultra-romantic views was counted by their enemies as one of them.

It was in Heidelberg that Brentano and Arnim worked on their influential anthology, *Des Knaben Wunderhorn* (1805–8), that Brentano and Görres wrote their satirical pamphlet, the *Uhrmacher BOGS* (1807), that Görres produced his account of German chap-books, *Die teutschen Volksbücher*, as well as an obscure and long-forgotten tract, *Schriftproben* (1807), published under the pseudonym Peter Hammer, and that all three of them collaborated in the *Zeitung für Einsiedler*, 37 issues of which appeared from April through August 1808. Their publisher was a Heidelberg firm, Mohr & Zimmer.

Now it so happened that since July 1805, Heidelberg had also been the residence of an ardent and prominent classicist, J. H. Voß. In February 1807, he was joined by his like-minded son, Heinrich, and soon became the acknowledged leader of a group of minor writers of a conservative cast of mind, above all Alois Schreiber, S. H. K. Michaelis (who, however, admired Loeben), and Otto Martens. For a whole year, in spite of their totally different outlooks, Voß maintained quite friendly relations with the romantics, until a needless provocation on their part – out of pure mischief, Brentano made a bid on a house Voß wanted to buy from the university and substantially drove up the price – caused him to break off personal relations. Subsequently – whether rightly or wrongly is a matter for debate – Voß felt that some of the gibes at philistine anti-roman-tics in the *Uhrmacher BOGS* were personal attacks on him, and he now gave free vent to his hatred of most of what the romantics stood for: their love of Catholic art and poetry, of romance verse forms, of folksongs and ballads, of mystics like Jakob Böhme, and their dis-respect for many of the poets of the preceding (and Voß' own) generation, whom he admired.

Meanwhile, J. F. Cotta, the publisher, had founded a daily paper, the *Morgenblatt für gebildete Stände*, from which we have already quoted. It had been Cotta's intention that this paper, which was primarily devoted to cultural matters should be non-partisan, but its editorial office was from the beginning dominated by men – above all J. C. F. Haug and Friedrich Weißer – who had their roots in the Enlightenment and detested the new poetry and philosophy. The *Morgenblatt* was not yet a week old when Haug published in it an attack on the sonnet, which he condemned as totally unsuited to the German language.[135] Further attacks against romantic attitudes and practices followed, but they were neither particularly venomous nor specifically directed against the Heidelberg group until, in the winter of 1807–8, Voß and his faction began to harass the romantics, using the *Morgenblatt* as their preferred organ of publication and thus joining forces with Haug and Weißer.

It was in this campaign that the terms *Romantik* and *Romantiker* – and especially the latter – began to be used with specific reference to *contemporary* poets and writers.* Thus Voß, on 14 January 1808 (No. 12, pp. 47*f.*) published an article, 'Für die Romantiker,' in which he parodied A. W. Schlegel's translation of Thomas de Celano's 'Dies irae,' under the title 'Bußlied eines Romantikers.' Elsewhere in the article, he spoke of 'christkatholische Romantiker' and maintained that Schlegel himself could but feel disgust for the artificial ecstasies of those romantics who arouse themselves to states of mystical exaltation by reading Jakob Böhme. In November 1808, J. C. F. Haug ridiculed the nursery rhymes published by Arnim and Brentano as a supplementary volume of *Des Knaben Wunderhorn* in a poem which begins,

> *Heil dem Romantiker* NN,
> *Den wir leider nicht kennen!* –
> *Was Mägde, Kinder und Ammen*
> *Gefabelt und gestammelt,*
> *Hat er als olympische Flammen*
> *Großmütig gütig zusammen*
> *Für große Kinder gesammelt,*

Hail to the romanticist NN, whom we unfortunately do not know! –

* There are earlier, isolated instances, but they are quite rare, Thus, a sonnet, 'Der deutsche Romantiker,' possibly by Baggesen, in which the whole new trend in poetry, including Schiller, is rather indecisively parodied, was published in the monthly, *Apollon* (I, nos. 9–10, September/October 1803, p. 215; cited by *Ullmann*, p. 286); and in *Uhrmacher BOGS*, Brentano and Görres themselves referred ironically to the 'neue romatische Clique, die gegen die klassischen Uhrmacher einen Bund geschlossen' (Brentano, *Werke* II: 879).

What servant girls, children, and wet-nurses have fabled and stammered,
he generously and kindly collected for the benefit of big children
as if it were Olympic fire,

and which ends with the assertion that romanticists are children
and children romanticists:

> *Daß Romantiker wahre Kinder*
> *Und Kinder Romantiker sind.*[136]

In the same month, Voß wrote a long and vulgar attack on *Des
Knaben Wunderhorn*, which culminated in yet another parody, with
the title 'Lied der Romantiker an ihren Herrgott.'[137]

After 1808, the attacks on the romantics in the *Morgenblatt*
became less frequent, and we can pass over them in silence. Cotta's
daily was, however, not the only string to the bow of the classicists,
who vented their anger also in two long, separately published
lampoons, *Comoedia divina, mit drei Vorreden von Peter Hammer, Jean
Paul und dem Herausgeber* (without place or publisher, 1808), and *Der
Karfunkel oder Klingklingelalmanach*, with the sub-title 'Ein Taschenbuch für vollendete Romantiker und angehende Mystiker' (Tübingen, 1810). The former was published anonymously, two of the prefaces having been lifted, without the authors' consent, from the
pages of Jean Paul's *Vorschule der Ästhetik* and Görres' *Schriftproben*,
while the third is signed with a pseudonym, W. G. H. Gotthardt; as
we now know, it was written by Alois Schreiber, probably with the
assistance of the younger Voß and Otto Martens.[138] The latter
publication owes its existence to the arrival in Heidelberg, in the fall
of 1808, of the Danish poet Baggesen, whose name appears on the
title page of the *Klingklingelalmanach* as its editor. He seems to have
been persuaded by the elder Voß to write this lampoon, and did so in
collaboration with the authors of the *Comoedia divina*.[139]

The *Comoedia* and the *Klingklingelalmanach* contain some of the
wittiest satirical verse ever directed against the romantics, but
concern us here for a more sober reason. In both these works, the
terms *Romantiker* and *Romantik* were used with unmistakable reference to *contemporary* rather than historical or typological romanticism,
just as in the *Morgenblatt*; but they occurred far more frequently,
and the lampoons cast their net very much more widely than the
daily. In the *Morgenblatt* the attack was for the most part limited to
the Heidelberg group. The *Comoedia* directed its barbs against
A. W. and F. Schlegel, Novalis, Rostorf (Karl von Hardenberg),

Friedrich Ast, Loeben, Schütz, and some minor authors; and the *Klingklingelalmanach* provided a veritable roll-call of those who were held to belong to the new school:

DIE SIEBENUNDZWANZIG ROMANTIKER.
Erstes Sonett colla coda.

Horcht auf! Ich muß Euch hohe Dinge sagen:
Mit Eis die Brust umpanzert singt Ringseis.
Auf Friedrich Schlegel'sch durch romant'schen Steiß
Ihm applaudieren Chamisso, von Hagen.

Rottmanner, Giesebrecht, Bernhard jagen
Mit Kleist dem dritten um den Dichterpreis.
Arnim und Görres speisen Indus-Reis;
Lassaulx trägt bunte Jacken ohne Kragen.

Fromm singen Isidorus, Ast und Tieck;
Fromm klingen Rostorf, Loë, Loew und Brauser;
Fromm springen Florens, Lacrimas, Sylvester

Wie vor der Bundeslade König Pieck.
Auch Christian Schlosser, der romant'sche Sauser,
Und Pellegrin und Tiecks geistvolle Schwester

Erheben mit Brentano ihr Gequiek –
Dann baut noch Adam Müller, der Kalmauser,
Für alle diese Sänger Vogelnester.

Hark, I must speak to you of sublime things. His breast armoured with ice does [J. N.] Ringseis sing; [A. v] Chamisso and [F. H.] von [der] Hagen applaud him through their romantic backsides in Friedrich Schlegel's manner. [Karl] Rottmanner, [Karl] Giesebrecht and [A. F.] Bernhardi race with the third [i.e., Heinrich von] Kleist for the poet's crown. [Achim von] Arnim and [Joseph] Görres eat rice from the banks of the Indus; [Franz von] Lassaulx wears gaudy jackets without collars. Piously sing Isidorus [= O. H. von Loeben], [Friedrich] Ast, and [Ludwig] Tieck; piously ring Rostorf [= Karl von Hardenberg], Loë, Loew, and [E.R.] Brauser; piously spring Florens [=Joseph von Eichendorff]. Lacrimas [= C. W. von Schütz], Sylvester [= G. A. von Hardenberg], like King Pieck before the Ark of the Covenant. Also, romantically humming Christian Schlosser, Pellegrin [= Friedrich de la Motte-Fouqué] and Tieck's brilliant sister [Sophie Bernhardi] make quacking noises together with [Clemens] Brentano; and then there is Adam Müller, that pedant, who builds bird's nests for all these songsters.[140]

Evidently – as a footnote to the poem acknowledges – this roll-call of *Romantiker* is incomplete, but this hardly mattered; some of those omitted here were taken care of elsewhere. Nor does it matter to our purposes that the views of the Heidelberg classicists were rejected by the younger generation as outmoded and narrow. Their terminology, if not their views, served as obvious need. It had long been recognized – and Voß and his friends had made it even more obvious – that there was a large group of young writers opposed to most of the ways and attitudes of the earlier generation, and whose views resembled one another sufficiently for them to be regarded as a school. Until now, there had been no convenient collective name for them. Voß and his clique had found one, and convenience dictated that it be used.

If, nonetheless, the process of the general adoption of the terms *Romantik* and *Romantiker* with a contemporary reference was very gradual, there were good reasons for this. First of all, the terms had acquired this special reference in a context of vituperation, so that the romantics themselves, although they used them frequently during and with reference to the controversy of 1807–9,[141] were unlikely to adopt them permanently: it is quite characteristic, for instance, that Franz Horn, who favoured the romantics, almost went out of his way to avoid the terms in the account of the survey of recent German literature he published in 1819.[142] Secondly, the terms could be used in the historical rather than contemporary sense, an ambiguity which writers tried to avoid by using such terms as *neuromantisch*, *Neuromantik*, *Neuromantiker*, etc.* But as soon as it became possible to regard this 'new romanticism' in an historical perspective, these neologisms, which had in any case never gained a

---

* These terms are of course closely related to the expression 'neue Schule,' 'neuere Schule' etc. discussed on pp. 140 *f.* above. A transitional phrase is 'die neue romantische Clique' in the *Uhrmacher BOGS* (1807; see note p. 146). Subsequently, Molitor wrote of the 'großes Verdienst unserer neuen Romantiker,' who rediscovered the Middle Ages (*Zeitschrift für Wissenschaft und Kunst*, 1809, no. ii, pp. 11 *f.*), and we read in the *Morgenblatt* of the 'geheime Akademie der Neu-Romantik,' the 'Sonette der Neuromantiker, 'and the 'stolzen Jünger der Neoromantica' (4 May 1811 and 'Übersichten,' 1812, p. 16; cited by *Ullmann*, p. 316). In 1812, Wilhelm Grimm met 'neuromantische Studenten' in Göttingen (R. Steig and H. Grimm, *Achim von Arnim und die ihm nahe standen*, Stuttgart-Berlin, 1904, iii: 232). In 1809, Bouterwek (*Geschichte*, vii: 151) distinguished between the 'altromantische Poesie' in England before 1500 and the 'neuromantische Poesie' of the sixteenth century, but from 1812 on, he reserves such expressions as 'unsere neuen Romantiker,' 'neuromantisch' etc. for the contemporary school (e. g. *Geschichte* ix, ix; xi: 436, 450, 459, 472 etc.). See also Reinhold Grimm, 'Zur Vorgeschichte des Begriffs "Neuromantik," ' in Wolfgang Paulsen, ed., *Das Nachleben der Romantik in der modernen deutschen Literatur* (Heidelberg, 1969), pp. 32–50.

firm footing, gave way to the simpler terms, only to be revived again when a term was needed for the romantic revival of the 1890s.

IV

To trace the process of the gradual acceptance of *Romantik, Romantiker*, and, along with them, *romantische Schule** in detail would be a tedious undertaking; we shall content ourselves with commenting on a few authors who seem particularly representative.

In 1819, Bouterwek published the eleventh volume of his history of poetry – the volume in which he dealt with recent and near-contemporary German literature. He was bound, by the whole spirit of his undertaking, to adopt the neutral stance of the historian; he needed a term for the historical phenomenon he had to deal with, and it follows almost of necessity that we should find with him every possible variation of the terminology that had by now evolved, used purely descriptively, for purposes of identification, and implying in itself neither praise nor blame. Thus he speaks of *Romantik* and *Romantiker* without qualifying adjectives,[143] but also of the 'school of the new romanticism,' the 'new school, which for lack of another name might as well be called the romantic school', the 'new school of the so-called romanticists,' 'the new literary party of the so-called romanticists,' and so on.†

If Bouterwek here still betrayed a certain uneasiness about these terms, however often he used them, others soon used them with confidence. Thus Goethe, in his report of 1820 on 'Klassiker und Romantiker in Italien, sich heftig bekämpfend,' evidently felt sure that his readers would know to whom he referred in stating that 'our romantic poets and writers have the public on their side.'[144]

* One year after the remark about the 'neue romantische Clique' in the *Uhrmacher BOGS* quoted in the preceding footnote, we read of 'unsere romantisch-catholische Schule' in the *Comoedia divina* (ed. Franz Blei, Leipzig, 1907, p. 7). In a similar spirit, Friedrich Weißer, commenting on Kleist's suicide, called him one of the 'berüchtigsten Jünger der berüchtigten romantisch mystischen Schule' (*Morgenblatt*, 27 December 1811, no. 310, p. 1237; see *Höfle*, p. 147). The term gained wide currency through its repeated use in Bouterwek's *Geschichte* xi (1819).

† 'Auch aus der Schule der neuen Romantik ist manches treffliche Lied hervorgegangen,' x: 432; '... der *neuen Schule*, die nun einmal in Ermangelung eines anderen Namens die romantische heißen mag,' xi: 436; '[Werke] aus der neuen Schule der sogenannten Romantiker, die das griechische und römische Altertum kaum eines Seitenblicks würdigen,' xi: 368; 'gegen das Ende des achtzehnten Jahrhunderts, als die neue literarische Partei der sogenannten Romantiker sich zu regen anfing,' xi: 105 *f.*; 'Zu den glücklichen Wirkungen der neuen Romantik gehört eine neue Entwicklung des eigentlichen Epos im echt romantischen Sinne,' xi: 450; etc.

By 1835, Büchner could afford the anachronism of letting Camille Desmoulins, in the first scene of *Dantons Tod*, use the term *Guillotinen-romantik*. This does not mean, however, that the typological or the 'medieval' use of the word had died out. Goethe himself, while stressing that the 'contemporary' use of *romantisch* had become prevalent, still felt that the earlier usage had been more correct:

Wenn man z.B. [in Italien] anfängt, Inschriften statt wie bisher in lateinischer Sprache nunmehr in italienischer zu verfassen ... so glaubt man dieses auch dem Romantischen zu verdanken; woraus deutlich erhellt, daß unter diesem Namen alles begriffen sei, was in der Gegenwart lebt und lebendig auf den Augenblick wirkt. Zugleich ist uns ein Beispiel gegeben: daß ein Wort durch Gebrauchsfolge einen ganz entgegengesetzten Sinn annehmen kann, da das eigentlich Romantische unseren Sitten nicht näher liegt als Griechisches und Römisches.[145]

Heine, both in his short essay, 'Die Romantik' (1820), and in his book, *Die romantische Schule* (1835), used the term in both ways. Moreover, there was – and still is – room for doubt as to exactly who belonged to the romantic school. In 1820, Heine could still speak of Goethe and A. W. Schlegel as 'our two greatest romantics,'[146] thus including a poet who would now be excluded by any German literary historian; and in 1835, he excluded E. T. A. Hoffmann, whom everyone would want to include now. But if the expressions *romantische Schule*, *Romantik*, and *Romantiker* remained a little vague in their connotations, they were far more precise than any other term for the same thing, and this determined the issue. In virtually any history of German literature published after 1830, the chapter dealing with the writers named in the sonnet we have quoted from the *Klingklingelalmanach* had some such obvious title as 'Die romantische Schule,'[147] 'Romantische Dichtung,'[148] or, at worst, 'Die eigentliche Romantik,'* and no reader would have expected

---

* Wolfgang Menzel, *Die deutsche Literatur* (2nd ed., Stuttgart, 1836), IV: 131. In the first edition (Stuttgart, 1828), Menzel did not use chapter headings, but he reiterated the old complaint that 'man weiß nicht recht, was eigentlich unter dem Romantischen verstanden werden solle,' and he speaks of 'romantische Schulen' (1: 93 *ff*.) in the plural. In the second edition, he is far less hesitant, although he still occasionally uses such phrases as 'neue' or 'neuere Romantik.' That the qualifying adjective had become unnecessary is shown by numerous essay titles from the late 1830s, such as R. Kausler, 'Tieck und die deutsche Romantik,' *Freihafen* II (1839), nos. 3–4, or A. Ruge and T. Echtermayer, 'Der Protestantismus und die Romantik ... Ein Manifest,' *Hallische Jahrbücher für deutsche Wissenschaft und Kunst*, 1839, no. 245 – 1840, no. 64. The last-named essay is a particularly clear illustration of the stage that had been reached by the late 1830s: The authors state that 'no one will call, e.g., Schiller, Goethe, and Shakespeare, romanticists [*Romantiker*],' although 'everyone will, in many respects, call them romantic.' Ruge and Echtermayer, col. 1963. Cf. p. 513, n. 37 below.

that Dante or Shakespeare were to be discussed under this heading.

Of course, in a phrase like *romantische Schule* the meaning of our adjective is vastly narrowed down by its context, and in other contexts, it can still have most of the connotations it acquired in its long and chequered career. This has its disadvantages. There is hardly a better way to stop a conversation than to ask what it is that a romantic cottage, a romantic poem, and a romantic composer actually have in common. And as there is no short and simple answer to this question, there will always be scholars to suggest – like Wilhelm Dilthey[149] or Franz Schultz[150] – that a word that has caused so much confusion had better be dropped altogether. But even if this were really desirable, there is not the slightest chance that it will be done. The best we can hope for is that the future history of our word will be uneventful.

NOTES

1 Thomas Mann, *Buddenbrooks*, *Gesammelte Werke* (Frankfurt, 1960), 1: 350.
2 J. G. Herder, *Sämtliche Werke*, ed. Suphan (Berlin, 1877 ff.), 1: 266 (1767).
3 F. Schlegel, *Europa. Eine Zeitschrift hrsg. von Friedrich Schlegel* 1 (1803), ii: 58. See also ibid., p. 61, and his letter of 8 September 1805 in *Krisenjahre der Frühromantik*, ed. J. Körner, 1 (Brünn-Wien-Leipzig, 1936): 229 f., where he writes of 'romantic and old German metres.'
4 J. Görres, *Die teutschen Volksbücher* (Heidelberg, 1807), p. 128.
5 *Jenaische Allgemeine Literatur-Zeitung*, 2 June 1808; cited by Richard Ullmann and Helene Gotthard, *Geschichte des Begriffes 'Romantisch' in Deutschland* (Berlin, 1927), p. 293 (hereafter cited as *Ullmann*).
6 Samuel Richardson, *Pamela*, Everyman's Library (London, [1965]), 1: 77.
7 J. S. Eichhorn, *Literärgeschichte* 1 (Göttingen, 1799): 254; cited by *Ullmann*, p. 166.
8 *Jenaische Allgemeine Literatur-Zeitung*, 1801, no. 44, col. 351.
9 Review of J. C. F. Manso, *Vermischte Schriften*, in *Neue Bibliothek der schönen Wissenschaften und der freien Künste* LXVI (1802), i: 113.
10 Schiller, 'Brief eines reisenden Dänen' (1785), *Sämtliche Werke*, *Säkular-Ausgabe* (Stuttgart-Berlin, [1965]), XI: 102 f.
11 [Review of] *Hermann, der Sassen Herzog, Deutschlands Retter und Befreier. Ein romantisches Bild altdeutscher Freiheit und National-Größe*, 1 (Kopenhagen und Leipzig, 1804), in *Der Freimütige*, 1805, no. 95 (13 May), p. 377; signed 'G. M.'
12 *Hallische Allgemeine Literatur-Zeitung*, 1815, Ergänzungsblatt no. 8, col. 61.
13 Adelung, *Versuch eines vollständigen grammatisch-kritischen Wörterbuches der Hochdeutschen Mundart* (Leipzig, 1777), III: 1475 (hereafter cited as *Adelung*).
14 Cited by *Ullmann*, p . 23.
15 Schleiermacher, 'Über die Freiheit des Menschen,' in W. Dilthey, *Leben Schleiermachers* (Berlin, 1870), Appendix, p. 43.
16 *Berlinisches Archiv der Zeit und des Geschmacks*, 1800, p. 39.

17 *Friedrich Schlegels Briefe an seinen Bruder August Wilhelm*, ed. O. Walzel (Berlin, 1890), p. 311 (hereafter cited as *Friedrich Schlegels Briefe*).

18 *Kritische Friedrich-Schlegel-Ausgabe*, ed. E. Behler et al. (Paderborn, 1958 ff.), XVIII: 23 (hereafter cited as *KFSA*).

19 *Caroline. Briefe aus der Frühromantik*, ed. Erich Schmidt (Leipzig, 1931), I: 683 f.

20 *Die unsichtbare Loge*, preface to the 2nd ed., in Jean Paul, *Werke*, ed. N. Miller (Darmstadt, 1965), I: 14.

21 See *Ullmann*, pp. 83 ff., 93 ff.

22 F. Schlegel, *Prosaische Jugendschriften*, ed. J. Minor (Wien, 1906), I: 94, 98, 112, 128, etc.

23 Unavoidably, my remarks about Schlegel repeat what I have said elsewhere at greater length; see my article, 'F. Schlegel's Theory of Romantic Poetry,' *PMLA* LXXI (1956): 1018–41, the introductions to *KFSA* II and VI, and *Friedrich Schlegel* (New York, 1970).

24 F. Schlegel, *Prosaische Jugendschriften* I: 125.

25 Ibid., p. 22.

26 *Friedrich Schlegels Briefe*, p. 253.

27 F. Schlegel, 'Kritische Fragmente,' nos. 7, 84, 60, 91, 93; *KFSA* II: 147, 157, 154, 158.

28 *Friedrich Schlegels Briefe*, p. 318.

29 F. Schlegel, *Literary Notebooks 1797–1801*, ed. H. Eichner (London, 1957), no. 32.

30 'Athenäums-Fragmente,' no. 146; *KFSA* II: 188.

31 'Vorlesungen über die deutsche Sprache' (1807), fol. 47v of the unpublished MS.

32 See, e.g., *KFSA* XVIII: 24.

33 For a detailed interpretation, see *KFSA* II: lix ff.

34 *KFSA* II: 290–303.

35 *KFSA* II: 333.

36 *KFSA* II: 334.

37 F. Schlegel, *Literary Notebooks*, no. 1760. A definitive interpretation of Schlegel's concept of chaotic or fantastic form will be found in K. K. Polheim, *Die Arabeske. Ansichten und Ideen aus F. Schlegels Poetik* (Paderborn, 1966); for a brief account in English, see Eichner, *Friedrich Schlegel*, pp. 61 ff. It is worth noting that Adelung (n. 13 above) considered 'Verwirrungen' an essential feature of the *Roman*.

38 A. W. Schlegel, *Vorlesungen über schöne Literatur und Kunst*; first published posthumously by Jakob Minor in *Deutsche Literaturdenkmale des 18. und 19. Jahrhunderts* XVII–XIX (Stuttgart, 1884) (hereafter cited as *DLD*).

39 Brentano, *Godwi*, written in 1798–9 and published in 1801 in two volumes, dated 1801 and 1802.

40 See O. Fambach, *Ein Jahrhundert deutscher Literaturkritik*, II: *Schiller und sein Kreis in der Kritik ihrer Zeit* (Berlin, 1957).

41 *Musenalmanach für das Jahr 1802*, ed. A. W. Schlegel and L. Tieck (Tübingen, 1802), pp. 221–34.

42 'Über die polnischen Frauen,' *Zeitung für die elegante Welt*, 1802, no. 80 (6 July), col. 638 (unsigned; probably by Mnioch).

43 F. Kohlrausch, *Deutschlands Zukunft. In sechs Reden* (Elberfeld, 1814), pp. 35 f.

44 *KFSA* II: 348. For a very early assertion of his conviction that the synthesis was desirable, see his letter to his brother of 27 February 1794.

45 *KFSA* VII: 74.

46 F. Schlegel, Cologne lectures *Über deutsche Sprache*, pp. 54 ff. of the unpublished MS.

47 Ast, *System der Kunstlehre*, p. 301.

48 *Apollon*, ed. J. and A. Werden, August 1803, p. 93; see *Ullmann*, pp. 255 f.

49 'Briefe über William Shakespeare,' *Poetisches Journal*, ed. L. Tieck, I (1800), i: 45.

50   L. Tieck, *Minnelieder aus dem schwäbischen Zeitalter* (Berlin, 1803); cited by *Ullmann*, p. 194.

51   F. J. Molitor, 'Über die Tendenzen des jetzigen Zeitalters,' *Zeitschrift für Wissenschaft und Kunst* i (1808), ii: 10 *f.*

52   *Friedrich Schlegels Briefe*, p. 414.

53   F. Schlegel, *Prosaische Jugendschriften* i: 94.

54   *Jenaische Allgemeine Literatur-Zeitung*, 1806, no. 50, col. 396.

55   F. Bouterwek, *Geschichte der Poesie und Beredsamkeit* i (Göttingen, 1801): 3–40 (hereafter cited as *Geschichte*).

56   *Der Freimütige*, 1805, no. 135 (8 July), p. 23.

57   Ibid., no. 136 (9 July), p. 27.

58   Ibid.

59   *System der Kunstlehre*, p. 61.

60   Zacharias Werner, *Briefe*, ed. O. Floeck (München, 1914), i: 376, and ii: 61.

61   *Jenaische Allgemeine Literatur-Zeitung*, 1803, no. 259, cols. 570, 572.

62   Jean Paul, *Vorschule der Ästhetik* (1804), in *Werke* (1967), v: 93.

63   Ibid., 2nd ed. (1812) only, in *Werke* v: 92, 426.

64   Ibid., p. 89.

65   *Jenaische Allgemeine Literatur-Zeitung*, 1803, no. 259, col. 570 *f.*

66   Bouterwek, *Geschichte* i: 20, 21, 26.

67   *Neue Bibliothek der schönen Wissenschaften und der freien Künste* LXVI (1802), i: 140. According to Fambach (as in note 40), p. 515, the authors are Dyck and Manso.

68   *Zeitung für die elegante Welt* (5 January 1802); cited by *Ullmann*, p. 157.

69   'Neue Romane,' *Zeitung für die elegante Welt*, 1809, no. 98 (18 May), p. 782 (anon.).

70   G. Merkel, *Briefe an ein Frauenzimmer über die neuesten Produkte der schönen Literatur in Deutschland* i (Berlin, 1801): 585 *f.*; cited by *Ullmann*, p. 215.

71   J. J. Breitinger, *Critische Dichtkunst* (Zürich, 1740), i: 130 *f.*

72   Clemens Brentano, *Werke*, ed. Friedhelm Kemp, ii (München, 1963): 258 *f.*

73   See P. Requadt, *Die Bildersprache der deutschen Italiendichtung. Von Goethe bis Benn* (Bern, 1962).

74   See Ernst Behler, 'Das Indienbild der deutschen Romantik,' *GRM* XLIX (1968): 21–37, for a survey and bibliographical references.

75   Jean Paul, *Vorschule der Ästhetik*, 2nd ed. (1812) only, in *Werke* v: 89.

76   F. Schlegel, *Prosaische Jugendschriften* i: 88 *f.*

77   See p. 138 below.

78   Ast, *System der Kunstlehre*, pp. 37 *f.* Through Ast, some of the views expressed by Schelling in his lectures "Über die Philosophie der Kunst," held in 1802–3, repeated in 1804–5, and published posthumously, reached a wider public.

79   *Zeitung für die elegante Welt*, 1806, no. 70 (12 June), cols. 564–6.

80   E. T. A. Hoffmann, 'Beethovens Instrumentalmusik,' *Fantasie- und Nachtstücke*, ed. W. Müller-Seidel (Darmstadt, 1962), p. 41; see also p. 45.

81   Hemsterhuis, *Lettre sur la sculpture*, in *Oeuvres* (Paris, 1792), i: 46.

82   Jean Paul, *Vorschule der Ästhetik*, 2nd ed. (1812) only, in *Werke* v: 87.

83   F. Ast, *Zeitschrift für Wissenschaft und Kunst* i (1808), i: 54.

84   *Friedrich Schlegels Briefe*, p. 156.

85   Schiller, 'Über naive und sentimentalische Dichtung,' *Sämtliche Werke, Säkular-Ausgabe* (Stuttgart-Berlin, 1905), XII: 209.

86   *Der Freimütige*, 1804, no. 246 (10 December), p. 462.

87   Grillparzer, *Sämtliche Werke*, ed. Sauer, XIV (Wien [1925]): 27 *f.*

88   Schiller, *Säkular-Ausgabe* XII: 191.

89   Jean Paul, *Vorschule der Ästhetik*, in *Werke* v: 88.

90   F. Ast, 'Epochen der griechischen Philosophie,' *Europa* II, ii (1805): 65.

91   Uhland, 'Über das Romantische,' *Werke*, ed. L. Fränkel (Leipzig-Wien, n.d.), II: 348.

92   E. T. A. Hoffmann, *Fantasie- und Nachtstücke*, p. 41.

93   J. A. Eberhardt, *Handbuch der Ästhetik* II (Halle, 1805): 414; cited by *Ullmann*, p. 225.
94   *Zeitung für die elegante Welt*, 19 June 1807; cited by *Ullmann*, p. 269.
95   A. A[pel], 'Schön und romantisch,' *Selene* I (1807), i: 26 *f*.
96   See note p. 117 above.
97   O. H. von Loeben, *Guido* (Mannheim, 1808), p. 200 *f*.; cited by *Ullmann*, p. 285.
98   *Morgenblatt für gebildete Stände*, 1808, no. 55 (4 March), p. 219 (hereafter cited as *Morgenblatt*).
99   *Der Freimütige*, 1804, no. 106 (28 May), p. 421.
100 *Zeitung für die elegante Welt* (20 April 1809); cited by *Ullmann*, p. 311.
101 Schreyvogel, 'Über den Gebrauch des Ausdrucks: *romantisch* in der neueren Kunstkritik,' *Der Sammler* (21–6, February 1818); quoted from the partial reprint in Grillparzer, *Sämtliche Werke*, ed. Sauer, XIV (Wien [1925]): 237.
102 Cf. *Ullmann*, pp. 147–52.
103 *Vorlesungen über schöne Literatur und Kunst*, ed. J. Minor (Stuttgart, 1884), in *DLD* XVII–XIX. Some of the lectures were published in 1803 in F. Schlegel's *Europa* (I, ii: 72–87, and II, i: 3–95).
104 *DLD* XVII: 22.
105 *DLD* XVII: 156 *f*., 240; XVIII: 6 *f*.
106 *DLD* XVII: 356 *f*.; cf. *Europa* I (1803), ii: 74 *f*.
107 *DLD* XVIII: 25, 36, 385.
108 A. W. Schlegel, *Œuvres écrites en français*, ed. Böcking, 3 vols. (Leipzig, 1846); cf. C. Nagavajara, *A. W. Schlegel in Frankreich: Sein Anteil an der französischen Literaturkritik 1807–1835* (Tübingen, 1966).
109 A. W. Schlegel, *Über dramatische Kunst und Literatur*, 3 vols. (Heidelberg, 1809–11); quoted from the reprint (based on the revised second edition of 1816) in A. W. Schlegel, *Sämtliche Werke*, ed. Böcking (Leipzig, 1846), V–VI (hereafter cited as *Bocking*).
110 *Böcking* V: 10.
111 Ibid., p. 13.
112 Ibid., p. 16.
113 Ibid.
114 Ibid., p. 17
115 Ibid., VI: 161.
116 *Crabb Robinson in Germany 1800–1805. Extracts from his Correspondence*, ed. Edith J. Morley (Oxford-London, 1929), pp. 65, 72, 90.
117 Jean Paul, *Werke* V: 28. In the same year, the same usage occurs also in *Nachtwachen von Bonaventura*, ed. R. Riesneck (Frechen-Köln, 1955), p. 95; also p. 169.
118 'Übersicht über neue Taschenbücher,' *Morgenblatt*, 1807, no. 39 (signed 'Y.' = Friedrich Weißer); cited by Frieda Höfle, *Cottas Morgenblatt für gebildete Stände und seine Stellung zur Literatur und zur literarischen Kritik* (Berlin, 1937), p. 47 (hereafter cited as *Höfle*).
119 Review of *Romantische Wälder, vom Verfasser des Lakrimas* (= Wilhelm von Schütz), *Morgenblatt*, 1808, no. 212 (3 September), p. 847.
120 *Wunderbare Geschichte von BOGS, dem Uhrmacher* (Heidelberg, 1807), in Clemens Brentano, *Werke*, ed. Friedhelm Kemp (München, 1963), II: 878. The name 'BOGS' is made up of the name of the two authors, B[rentan]o + G[örre]s.
121 *Jenaische Allgemeine Literatur-Zeitung*, 1797, no. 240 (29 July), col. 270.
122 *KFSA* XVIII: 216, no. 266. Cf. Novalis' jotting, 'Romantisierung der Aline' (*Schriften* III: 97), which is evidently a reminder to himself to turn the story of Aline, the heroine of an opera by J. A. P. Schulz, into a novel or romance.
123 See e.g., F. Schlegel's *Athenäums-Fragment* 126 ('romantisierte Mimen') and his reference to the 'romantisierte Manier' of Shakespeare's mature plays in the 'Gespräch über die Poesie'; the latter phrase was changed by him in 1823 to 'romantisch blühende Manier' (*KFSA* II: 301).

124 F. Schlegel, *Literary Notebooks*, no. 455.
125 Novalis, *Schriften* III: 75, 88. See also p. 74, n. 85.
126 Novalis, *Schriften* III: 263; first published in 1802.
127 Jean Paul, 'Titan,' in *Werke* III: 381.
128 See pp. 117 *f.* and 153, n. 42 above.
129 'Patriotische Besorgnis, ' *Zeitung für die elegante Welt*, 1802, no. 122 (12 October), col. 978.
130 *Weimarer Ausgabe*, Abt. IV, vol. XVII, p. 222.
131 See *Ullmann*, pp. 235 *ff.*
132 Werner, *Briefe* I: 377; cited by *Ullmann*, p. 252.
133 Uhland, *Werke*, ed. Fränkel (Leipzig-Wien, n.d.), II: 347–51. See also, still in 1807, *Zeitung für die elegante Welt*, 1807, no. 3 (5 January), col. 18; ibid., 1807, no. 7 (9 January), cited by *Ullmann*, p. 162; Görres, *Die teutschen Volksbücher*, pp. 276, 277, 301 *f.*
134 For greater details on this quarrel than can be given here see Herbert Levin, *Die Heidelberger Romantik* (München, 1922), and *Höfle*.
135 *Morgenblatt*, 1807, no. 5 (5 January), pp. 15 *f.*
136 *Morgenblatt*, 1808, No. 268 (8 November), pp. 1071 *f.* Signed N. T. Görrasto. For the identification of the author, see Oscar Fambach, *Ein Jahrhundert deutscher Literaturkritik* V: *Der romantische Rückfall* (Berlin, 1963): 488, note 25. Haug's claim that he did not know who edited the *Wunderhorn* is, of course, mere pretense.
137 *Morgenblatt*, 1808, no. 283–4 (25 and 26 November), pp. 1129–30, 1133–4.
138 See *Höfle*, pp. 78 *f.*; 'Bulletin der Tagesbegebenheiten,' *Der Freimütige*, 1809, no. 106 (29 May), p. 424.
139 See *Höfle*, p. 101; Fambach, V: 321 *f.*
140 *Klingklingelalmanach*, p. 308. I have not been able to identify Loë and Loew; these names are probably parodistic references to Loeben.
141 Cf. *Ullmann*, pp. 292 *f.*, 318 *f.*
142 Franz Horn, *Umrisse zur Geschichte und Kritik der Schönen Literatur Deutschlands während der Jahre 1790 bis 1818* (Berlin, 1819).
143 Bouterwek, *Geschichte* XI (1819): 390, 435, 448, 532, etc.
144 Goethe, *Werke, Weimarar Ausgabe*, Abt. I, vol. XLI, pt. i, p. 133.
145 Ibid., p. 139.
146 Heine, 'Die Romantik,' *Tempel-Ausgabe* IX: 273.
147 E.g., Heinrich Laube, *Geschichte der deutschen Literatur* III (Stuttgart, 1840): 113; cf. Karl Rosenkranz, 'Ludwig Tieck and die romantische Schule,' *Studien* (Berlin, 1839), I: 277 *ff.*
148 E.g., G. G. Gervinus, *Geschichte der deutschen Dichtung* (4th ed., Leipzig, 1853), V: 518. The first edition – *Handbuch der Geschichte der poetischen National-Literatur der Deutschen* (Leipzig, 1842) – has no chapter headings, but uses the running titles 'Romantiker,' 'Romantische Lyrik,' 'Drama der Romantiker' (pp. 298, 302, 306).
149 Wilhelm Dilthey, *Das Erlebnis und die Dichtung* (5th ed., Leipizg, 1916), p. 269.
150 Franz Schultz, ' ''Romantik'' und ''romantisch'' als literarhistorische Terminologien und Begriffsbildungen,' *DVLG* II (1924): 358–66.

GEORGE WHALLEY

England /
Romantic – Romanticism

The word *romantic* glided unobtrusively into early nineteenth-century English usage. It was flexible enough to be accommodated to some serious uses, yet from implications accumulated in the previous century it was often used carelessly and voguishly enough to attract the amused scorn of superior intelligences. Too variable in meaning to serve as a rallying point for any artistic group – for we speak now of England – the word lacked the cutting edge that the malicious need when they attach a durable name to their enemies. To think of the first half of the nineteenth century in England, or the major poets of that period, as *romantic* was a comfortable aberration that canonized itself towards the end of the century. Certainly Wordsworth and Coleridge instituted a revolution: but was it *romantic*?

Thomas Warton's work on the history of English poetry and on Spenser, Edward Young's *Night Thoughts* (1742–5) and Thomas Gray's bardic odes (1757, 1761), Bishop Percy's *Reliques of Ancient English Poetry* (1765) and his translation of the *Northern Antiquities* (1770) represented and encouraged an imperfectly informed literary interest in medieval, 'primitive,' 'Northern,' and other exotic materials. This blended with the Gothic-sentimental strain that was partly architectural and partly an interest in 'inner goings-on' (to use Coleridge's phrase) seeded by Richardson, Sterne, and Rousseau; and it came to strange and specialized flowering in the Gothic romances of Horace Walpole's *Castle of Otranto* (1764: unique in being at once prototype and parody?), Mrs. Radcliffe's *Mysteries* *of Udolpho* (1794), and Matthew Gregory Lewis's *The Monk* (1797). William Taylor of Norwich (1765–1836), friend of Southey by 1798 and of Coleridge by 1799, was important as a translator from the German: his translation of Bürger's *Lenore* in July 1796 was crucial to Walter Scott, and was rhapsodically noticed by Coleridge, Lamb, and Wordsworth.[1] Tytler's translation of Schiller's *Die Räuber* (1792) made a strong impression on Coleridge in 1794,[2] and in 1800 Coleridge was to make a verse translation of Schiller's *Wallenstein*. The custom of interpolating ballads in Gothic romances gave wide currency to a new German enthusiasm and helped to bridge the gap between the acknowledged archaism of Percy's *Reliques* and the contemporary taste.* The contrived supernaturalism of the Gothic romances that Coleridge reviewed in 1797 did not impress him;† but his response to these converging literary fashions is to be seen in his Bristol reading and in some of his poems from 1794 to 1798.[3] These and other elements, crystallizing for literature a mood, tone, and method that in hindsight came to be called 'romanticism,' is much more clearly to be seen and traced in the work of minor writers and in the effusions of faceless contributors to periodicals and annuals. According to later literary historians – not always a clear guide to the incisive criticism of individual works and writers – a distinctive 'sensibility' was emerging, a growing awareness of the ambivalence

* Coleridge wrote to Wordsworth on 23 January 1798 referring to Lewis's *The Castle Spectre*: 'There is a pretty little Ballad-song introduced – and Lewis, I think, has great & peculiar excellence in these compositions. The simplicity & naturalness is his own, & not imitated; for it is made to subsist in congruity with a language perfectly modern –' (*Coleridge, Letters* 1: 379). For a less enthusiastic view of the quality of the interpolated ballads, see S. T. Coleridge, *Biographia Literaria*, ed. J. Shawcross (Oxford, 1907), 11: 24 (hereafter cited as *Biographia Literaria*). For Wordsworth on Percy's *Reliques*, see *Wordsworth, Poems* 11: 421, 425 (Preface of 1815). But it was Coleridge who drew upon the 'medieval' ballads; Wordsworth, although not unaffected by Percy's *Reliques*, was strongly influenced by the manner of the popular ballads and by Burns's popularised versions of older and current ballads.

† Part of the review of Lewis's *The Monk* is reprinted in *Inquiring Spirit*, ed. Kathleen Coburn (London, 1951), p. 192, from *Critical Review* (February 1797). Of the four reviews of Gothic romances assigned to Coleridge by Garland Greever in *A Wiltshire Parson and his Friends* (1926), only the review of *The Monk* now seems genuine. But one of the interpolated chapters of *Biographia Literaria* (ch. 23) is a long and contemptuous review (reprinted from the *Courier* of August-September 1816) of Maturin's gothic tragedy *Bertram* (1816); Coleridge refers to 'the whole breed of Kotzebues, whether dramatists or romantic writers [i.e., writers of romance], or writers of romantic dramas' (*Biographia Literaria* 11: 184). For Shakespeare's plays as 'romantic dramas, or dramatic romances,' different in degree from the plays of Sophocles and Aristophanes, see passage (*c*) on pp. 205–6 below.

of man's deepest emotions and impulses, that links the cult of sensibility, the Shandean world of Laurence Sterne, and the novels of Samuel Richardson with the writings of the divine marquis and the inevitability of Freudian psychology. But this development, if indeed it has been correctly traced and analyzed by historians, did not crystallize around the word *romantic*, although in the course of the century the words *romantic* and *romanticism*, not with entire inappropriateness, came to be used to describe certain widespread and elusive literary and artistic phenomena. I am not aware, for example, that any reviewer or admirer of Coleridge's *Ancient Mariner* ever in his own day referred to the poem as *romantic*, although later exponents of 'romanticism' find it an excellent instance of the procedures of exotic distancing, of the supernatural naturalized by pathological realism, and of the 'romantic' hero who wanders like the Jew bearing the mark of Cain and distinguished from his startled fellows by his glittering eye. When a writer in the *Critical Review* in 1816 referred to *Christabel* as 'a romantic fragment' and went on (sceptically) to speak of it as 'one of those dreamlike productions whose charm partly consisted in the undefined obscurity of the conclusion,' the word *romantic* probably looks back as much to the romance-world of the *Faerie Queen* as it looks forward to a later attempt to provide a general specification for *romanticism*.*

What concentrates our attention on the early nineteenth century when we think of the words *romantic* and *England* in the same breath is the way literary historians towards the end of the century use the word *romantic* to describe the major poetry of the first half of the century. The poets themselves never applied the term to themselves, nor did their enemies apply it to them. And the fact that the word was available for later reference turns on the historical accident that in 1813 Schlegel's distinction between classical and romantic, having received in the early years of the century a currency and interpretation that he himself had little intended, being then triumphantly established in Germany and in Europe generally, reached England with characteristic English delay. Coleridge's early advocacy of the distinction in his lectures from 1808 had not established it for serious critical consideration – it was after all a

---

* A review of *Christabel* in *The Times* 20 May 1816, recently identified as written by Charles Lamb (*Studies in Romanticism* IX, 1970, 114–19), observed that 'The scene, the personages, are those of old romantic superstition'; that the tale, though 'wild, and romantic, and visionary as it is has a truth of its own, which seizes on and masters the imagination' (p. 116); and that 'Another striking excellence of the poem is its *picturesqueness*' (p. 118).

German idea.* But after Madame de Staël's invasion of England in 1813, it slowly gained currency, apparently more in speech than in writing, until Pater in 1889 affirms the distinction as both new and axiomatic for the polarity of all literature. At the beginning of chapter 19 of *Middlemarch* (1871), George Eliot evidently expected her readers to follow her when she said: 'Romanticism, which has helped to fill some dull blanks with love and knowledge, has not yet [*c* 1830] penetrated the times with its leaven and entered into everybody's food; it was fermenting still ... in certain long-haired German artists at Rome, and the youth of other nations who worked or idled near them were sometimes caught in spreading the movement.'⁴ Dowden in 1878 refers to 'a leader of the Romantic movement'; and by the end of the century the phrases *romantic poets*, *romantic school*, *romantic movement*, and *romantic revival* had slid into respectable academic currency as affirmations of historical conclusions drawn from vaguely specified evidence and no better than casual analysis. Even if long before the end of the century death had not supervened upon the five major poets who are now so commodiously bundled under the single historical blanket term *romantic*, they would have protested that they never called themselves 'romantic,' that they had never formed a 'school', and that it was highly questionable whether they constituted a 'movement.' Their protest would have been very much to the point as things have turned out. Historical generalizations about the alleged uniformity of romanticism in the early nineteeth-century poets have established a complex and opaque set of conditioned critical reflexes which have – until less than 25 years ago – induced systematic distortion and misreading of the writings themselves. Thanks to those who were more interested in trends in the history of literature and the history of ideas than in the integrity of literature, the work of the five major poets has remained demurely withdrawn behind the historical presuppositions, waiting like a spirited child not only to be addressed in the right language, but to be spoken to in the right tone of voice.

The phrases *romantic poets* and *romantic movement* conceal a notable complication: the great 'romantic' poets – five in number – comprise two generations; and the younger generation was unaccommodating enough to die before the two masters who had

*   The part played by Percy's *Reliques* in early German romantic ballad-writing is illustrated by a curious coincidence. Wordsworth bought his copy of the *Reliques* in Hamburg immediately on arrival in Germany in September 1798, and Coleridge may have bought his copy there too.

given strong but not always salutary impulse to their work. William Wordsworth, the earliest born, lived the longest – 1770–1850; his contemporary and sometime friend, Samuel Taylor Coleridge, born in 1772, died in 1834. (Robert Southey, by all accounts a minor figure although Coleridge's brother-in-law and for years Wordsworth's neighbour, was born in 1774 and lived – though at the end not of sound mind – until 1843; and Charles Lamb, Coleridge's school-fellow and lifelong friend, born in 1775, died a few months after Coleridge and is a more significant figure for our study than Southey is.) The second generation falls comfortably even within Coleridge's lifetime, and they died in the reverse order of their births: George Gordon, Lord Byron, 1788–1824; Percy Bysshe Shelley, 1792–1822; John Keats 1795–1821. None of the second generation – not even the precocious Byron – would have read the first (1798), or even the second (1800), edition of *Lyrical Ballads* at publication, yet all lived to read Wordsworth's *Poems in Two Volumes* (1807), *The Excursion* (1814), and the *Poems* of 1815; and in addition to Coleridge's early collections of poems (1796, 1797) and the *Ancient Mariner* (1798), *Christabel*, and *Kubla Khan* (1816), they read the collection of poems entitled *Sibylline Leaves* (1817) and the *Biographia Literaria*. All of them one way and another had the rhythms and themes of Wordsworth's work in their minds and the tune and images of Coleridge's poems in their heads (and Shelley parodied some of both). But there was little or no coherence of sustained relationship between the members of the same generation or between the members of the different generations. Wordsworth and Coleridge came upon one of the most fruitful literary friendships we know of, but within little more than ten years it had suffered irremediable disruption. Shelley and Byron were close but not always comfortable friends for the last four years of Shelley's life. Keats avoided Shelley and Byron, met Coleridge only once by accident, and having missed Wordsworth on the only occasion he visited the Lakes saw 'a good deal' of him when he was in London from December 1817 to January 1818 and was at an 'immortal dinner' at Haydon's with Wordsworth, when Lamb addressed Wordsworth as 'you old lake poet, you rascally poet.'[5] Byron knew neither Wordsworth nor Coleridge; for a short time he admired Coleridge, used his influence to see the *Christabel* volume (1816) published, and tried to get it favourably reviewed; but he soon regretted this gesture of good poetic faith and in the end was unkind in verse to both Coleridge and Wordsworth and vituperative to Southey. Shelley knew neither Wordsworth nor Coleridge. The closest kinship of intelligence and poetic sensibility might have developed between Keats and Coleridge; Keats's witty, vivid, and affectionate account of Coleridge's conversation on the occasion of their one walk on Hampstead Heath suggests that, in spite of certain misgivings about Coleridge's discursive-encyclopedic tendencies in the later years, life and literature are impoverished by the circumstance of their never meeting again.*

Since word-usage and manner of speech were much clearer marks of class and locale in late eighteenth- and early nineteenth-century England than they are now, it is worth noting the social and educational differences among the five major poets.† Wordsworth and Coleridge came from similar backgrounds, although their way of speaking was as widely separate as Cumberland and Devon. Coleridge's father was a clergyman and polymath, and the family produced men of law, soldiers, clergymen, linguists, and schoolmasters; Wordsworth's father was an attorney and substantial estate manager, and the family ran to law, the church, and scholarship. Both Coleridge and Wordsworth had thorough orthodox schooling in the classical tradition – Wordsworth at Cockermouth Grammar School and Coleridge at Christ's Hospital. Coleridge was a brilliant, if erratic, undergraduate at Jesus College, Cambridge, but did not take a degree; Wordsworth, rendered morose by loneliness and lack of purpose, made less effort at St John's College, Cambridge, than he might have done, even in view of the debilitated condition of the universities at that time, but took his B.A. without honours. Neither can be seen on the pattern of the twentieth-century intellectual, and neither could have been an academic without taking Holy Orders. Byron (Harrow and Trinity College, Cambridge, after and during a stormy childhood and youth) was a good

---

*   *The Letters of John Keats*, ed. H. E. Rollins (Cambridge, Mass., 1958), II: 88–9 (hereafter cited as *Keats, Letters*); cf. 1: 193–4. Sir Walter Scott (1771–1832) is contemporary with all these, but is remembered as a novelist rather than as a poet. Although he was both a romancer and an exploiter of the sentimental medievalism that is one of the components of eighteenth century 'romanticism,' I have not included him in this study because he appears not to advance the uses of the word *romantic* beyond those current and recognized in the eighteenth century. Nevertheless, Stevenson said in 1882 that 'Walter Scott is out and away the King of the romantics' (*Longman's Magazine* 1: 77; cited in *OED*).

†   Cf. *Blackwood's*, October 1817. On the Cockney School, No. 1: 'All the great poets of our country have been men of some rank in society, and there is no vulgarity in any of their writings ...' Cf. Coleridge's *Table Talk* (Oxford, 1917, from Thomas Allsop's *Recollections*), p. 440: 'It is very singular that no *true poet* should have arisen from the lower classes, when it is considered that every peasant who can read knows more of books now than did Aeschylus, Sophocles, or Homer; yet if we except Burns, none such have been.'

scholar, widely read, and of highly cultivated intelligence and developed historical sense. Shelley, having survived Eton, was sent down from University College, Oxford; he came of a wealthy upper middle-class arriviste family – his father was a Member of Parliament and earned a Knighthood – and in his own way he managed to lay the foundations of a sound and curious learning, for he had a scholarly instinct that turned with almost equal intensity upon Gothic romances, chemistry, Italian, and the mastery of Greek that was to inform his poetry to the end of his life. Byron, as a peer of the realm, greeted Shelley as an equal and an intimate friend when both were exiles in Italy – even though Byron could never quite forgive Shelley his superiority as a pistol-shot. Keats, as the *Edinburgh Review* pointed out with unnecessary brutality, was a Cockney. His schooling was modest and limited but by no means ineffectual, and he developed a tough, original, and venturesome mind of his own, the force of which is undoubtedly heightened by his ignorance of most of the philosophical dross that clutters the instruction of the more fortunate. His friendships with Leigh Hunt, Hazlitt, and Haydon were for a time fertile, but his social self-consciousness seems to have been acute among strangers; he found Shelley's self-assured eccentricities of manner disconcerting, and in Shelley's company he could not preserve his own identity. All of them, with varying degrees of confidence and success, were able to enter the cultivated society of their time when occasion or need arose. But there is little reason for regarding them – even hypothetically – as a 'school.'

One outstanding anomaly remains. Byron, out of the five the one person who seriously and continuously sought to cultivate the virtues of Horace and the neoclassical manner of Dryden and Pope, is the one person who also cultivated – and at times to a ridiculous extreme of theatricality – the Wertherian dress, posture, stock responses, and fascinating omens of guilt and doom that were then considered distinctively 'romantic.' (Shelley could be catlike and bizarre in behaviour and was startlingly good-looking; but if that was to be 'romantic,' it was a different kind from Byron's.) Yet Byron's weakest major work, *Childe Harold's Pilgrimage*, is marred – particularly in the first two cantos – by an unconvincingly-assumed Wordsworthianism, and its immense popularity owed much to the thinly veiled 'romantic' figure of Byron himself at the centre of the poem. The *brio* and stride of the best parts are not so much 'romantic' as simply Byronic; and the unique manner first explored in *Beppo* and then established in *Don Juan* – founded on Italian models and informed by a most unromantic and un-English irreverence –

released and sustained a virtuosity of brilliant improvisation that declares an ironic and aristocratic intelligence of a very high order. In short, the specific differences that separate and define these five major poets are great enough to resist the most redoubtable generalist, and make the work of each of them a subject for close and individual inquiry each in its own right.

WORDSWORTH

The word *romantic* could hardly be regarded as a favourite of Wordsworth's: it occurs only ten times in poems that cover a span of more than forty years. Without engaging in any subtle classification, Wordsworth's uses can be seen to fall – with one exception – under three areas of reference: 1/the adjective of romance (tale) and the sentiments that are alleged to colour or arise from romance; 2/the colour of hope, joy, and lyrical impulse that accompanies the (perhaps undirected) sentiment of love; 3/a quality of landscape (he only once uses the word to refer directly to landscape, but some of the other uses – as might be expected of a 'nature-poet' – are related to a heightened awareness of landscape).

1   *Associated with romance (legend)*

1/1 *Prelude* I, 180 (1805) = I, 169 (1850):[6] speaking of his preparation for writing an epic poem, Wordsworth says that

> Sometimes, mistaking vainly, as I fear,
> Proud spring-time swellings for a regular sea,
> I settle on some British theme, some old
> Romantic tale, by Milton left unsung;
> More often resting at some gentle place
> Within the groves of Chivalry, I pipe
> Among the Shepherds ...

1/2 *The Excursion* VIII, 85:* composed 1809–12, published 1814. The Wanderer 'playfully draws a comparison between his

---

*   *Wordsworth, Poems* v: 268. Jeffrey, reviewing *The Excursion* in the *Edinburgh Review* (November 1814), suggested scornfully that the Wanderer was 'determined to embrace the more romantic occupation of a Pedlar.' For Coleridge's veiled objection to Wordsworth's plausible back-formation of the Pedlar's biography, see *Biographia Literaria* II: 106. Southey, in the *Quarterly Review* (October 1814), said that in *The Excursion* 'the dialogue throughout is carried on in the very heart of the most romantic scenery which the poet's native hills could supply' (p. 101).

itinerant profession and that of the Knight-errant,' and ends by
saying:

'... – By these Itinerants, as experienced men,
Counsel is given; contention they appease
With gentle language; in remotest wilds,
Tears wipe away, and pleasant tidings bring;
Could the proud quest of chivalry do more?'

'Happy,' rejoined the Wanderer, 'they who gain
A panegyric from your generous tongue!
But, if to these Wayfarers once pertained
Aught of romantic interest, it is gone ...'

Here the primary reference is clearly to the romance of the knights-
errant, given the context of the discussion at this point; but – is it
because of the peculiar verb *pertained*? – the word also encompasses
the heartsease that the Wanderer claims for the knight-errantry of
his 'poor brotherhood who walk the earth/Pitied, and, where they
are not known, despised.' Here the interfusion of meanings (1) and
(2) shows how fastidiously Wordsworth, being in fact no spontaneous overflow-er, has chosen the word *romantic* in this passage.
1/3 'Aix-la-Chapelle,' l. 3 [sonnet] in *Memorials of a Tour of the
Continent*,[7] composed 1820–1.

Was it to disenchant, and to undo,
That we approached the Seat of Charlemaine?
To sweep from many an old romantic strain
That faith which no devotion may renew!
Why does this puny Church present to view
Her feeble columns? and that scanty chair! ...

What has been lost by witnessing the actual place is faith in what had
been assumed on the evidence of legendary poems of Charlemagne
and Roland.
1/4 'The Armenian Lady's Love,' l. 86:[8] composed 1830, published
1835. A 'fair Armenian, / Daughter of the proud Soldàn,' falls in
love with a Christian slave, renounces her religion and her father's
house, and leaves her 'narrow world ... for evermore' informed by
the 'higher, holier' conviction that she must reject 'a sensual creed
that trampled/Woman's birthright into dust.'

Judge both Fugitives with knowledge:
    In those old romantic days
Mighty were the soul's commandments
    To support, restrain, or raise ...

The reference to romance (legend) is clear enough, because a head-note announces that 'the following poem is from the Orlandus of the author's friend, Kenelm Henry Digby.' Wordsworth first met Digby (1800–80) in November 1830 but was already acquainted with his *The Broad-Stone of Honour* (1822), a book of chivalry. Digby seems to have steered Wordsworth into a sentimental anachronism here.

1 / 5 'To Cordelia M————,' l. 5 [sonnet] in *Poems Composed or Suggested during a Tour, in the Summer of 1833*:[9] composed in 1833. The poem reflects upon Cordelia's necklace.

> Not in the mines beyond the western main,
> You say, Cordelia, was the metal sought,
> Which a fine skill, of Indian growth, has wrought
> Into this flexible yet faithful Chain;
> Nor is it silver of romantic Spain;
> But from our loved Helvellyn's depths was brought,
> Our own domestic mountain ...

Spain is here thought of, it seems, as 'Spain of legend,' not 'Spain that arouses "romantic" feelings.' Romantic Spain, for Coleridge, recalled Cervantes; and that may have been the case for Wordsworth.[10] Byron also thinks of Spain as 'romantic' more than once.[11]

1 /6 'Extempore Effusion upon the Death of James Hogg,' l. 41:[12] composed and published 1835. In this poem Wordsworth laments the death of James Hogg, but also the deaths, in the course of three years, of Sir Walter Scott, Coleridge, Lamb, George Crabbe, and Felicia Hemans. The last stanza of the poem reads:

> No more of old romantic sorrows,
> For slaughtered Youth or love-lorn Maid!
> With sharper grief is Yarrow smitten,
> And Ettrick mourns with her their Poet dead.

The 'romantic sorrows' feel literary – the abstract grief perhaps that Coleridge and Wordsworth had uttered when they thought of that talented but ill-tempered youth, Thomas Chatterton, as the emblem of poetic genius destroyed by insensate society. The 'love-lorn Maid' also feels like a perfunctory stock figure, lacking the primordial vitality and mysterious implication of Wordsworth's solitary reaper or Coleridge's 'woman wailing for her demon-lover.' The closing stanza does not make its point with the compelling force that an earlier passage demands:

Nor has the rolling year twice measured,
From sign to sign, its stedfast course,
Since every mortal power of Coleridge
Was frozen at its marvellous source;*

The rapt One, of the godlike forehead,
The heaven-eyed creature sleeps in earth:
And Lamb, the frolic and the gentle,
Has vanished from his lonely hearth.

In contrast to that mordant and personal grief, the 'old romantic sorrows' are indeed pale and insubstantial.

2   Associated with the sentiment of love (but with Wordsworth the association is at best oblique)

2/1 'Written with a Pencil upon a Stone in the Wall of the House, on the Island at Grasmere,' l. 30 (last line):[13] composed 1800, published 1800. Wordsworth tells how 'one Poet' sometimes rows his boat across to the island, laden with heath and fern, makes 'his summer couch' in the little house, and daydreams while the sheep 'Lie round him, even as if they were a part/Of his own Household' –

> nor, while from his bed
> He looks, through the open door-place, toward the lake
> And to the stirring breezes, does he want
> Creations lovely as the work of sleep –
> Fair sights, and visions of romantic joy!

Despite the landscape setting, the emphasis may be amorous or erotic,† but in the absence of firm control of context, the visions may be simply of a romance-world.

---

*   The use of 'marvellous source' in referring to Coleridge echoes the phrase 'the marvellous Boy' used of Chatterton in 'Resolution and Independence' (*Wordsworth, Poems* II: 236). Coleridge had written a 'Monody on the Death of Chatterton' at Christ's Hospital and revised it extensively in 1795. Of the last 18 lines of the revised version he said in July 1797 that 'tho' deficient in chasteness & severity of diction, [they] breathe a pleasing spirit of romantic feeling ...' As for the rest of the poem, he said, there was nothing 'which might not have been written [by a drunken pauper?].' In a marginal note in a copy of the *Statesman's Manual* (1816) presented to Southey, Coleridge said: 'I myself feel that this introduction is too romantic and (if I may dare whisper my own thoughts) too good for the semi-real, semi-verbal Allegory, or Metaphorage, that follows ...' (*Coleridge, Letters* I: 333).

†   But *romantic* could also refer to an unreal or superficial attitude to love. Wordsworth, for example, spoke of Mrs Hemans's 'long separation from an unfeeling husband, whom she had been led to marry from the romantic notions of in-

2/2 *The Recluse*, pt. 1, book 1, 'Home at Grasmere,' l. 311:[14] composed early 1800, not published by Wordsworth. In this poem Wordsworth celebrates his taking up residence in Dove Cottage, Grasmere, late in December 1799, with his sister Dorothy. The poem is charged with intense affection both for his sister and for the place, but *romantic* here may mean 'other worldly' – that is, not consonant with reasonable expectation.

> But not betrayed by tenderness of mind
> That feared, or wholly overlook'd the truth,
> Did we come hither, with romantic hope
> To find, in midst of so much loveliness,
> Love, perfect love; of so much majesty
> A like majestic frame of mind in those
> Who here abide, the persons like the place.

2/3 *Prelude* VII, 474 (1805) = 442 (1850): composed 1804; 1805 version quoted. This is a much more complex passage that needs to be quoted at length because of the eventual connection with the word *romance*. Wordsworth is speaking of his first desolate spell in London (1793–5) and how the theatres were his consolation, not as escape but for the activity of mind that they generated. He wishes 'To shew what thoughts must often have been mine/At theatres, which then were my delight,/A yearning made more strong by obstacles/Which slender funds imposed.' He gives a vigorous and amusing sketch of the stock figures on the stage (including an anticipation of Yeats's 'tattered coat upon a stick' in the 'scare-crow pattern of old Age, patch'd up/Of all the tatters of infirmity').

> Through the night,
> Between the show, and many-headed mass
> Of the Spectators, and each little nook
> That had its fray or brawl, how eagerly,

experienced youth' (*Wordsworth, Poems* IV: 461–2). When Coleridge wrote for the *Morning Post* in October–November 1802 three notes on the alleged marriage between Alexander Augustus Hope, MP, and 'The Beauty of Buttermere,' and entitled the first two 'Romantic Marriage' and the third 'Fraudulent Marriage,' it is difficult to tell whether 'Romantic' was much less derogatory than 'Fraudulent' (*Essays on his Own Times*, ed. Sara Coleridge, 1850, II: 585–92). Cf. *Coleridge, Notebooks* III: 3562: '... Love in its highest sense ... is yet an act of the will – ... This most important [&] practicable – for if it were not true, either Love itself is all a romantic Hum, a mere connection of Desire with a form appropriated to that form by accident or the mere repetition of a Day-dream ...' In a marginal note on Beaumont and Fletcher he speaks of Spanish drama introducing to the English stage 'romantic Loyalty to the greatest Monsters.'

And with what flashes, as it were, the mind
Turn'd this way, that way! sportive and alert
And watchful, as a Kitten when at play,
While winds are blowing round her, among grass
And rustling leaves. Enchanting age and sweet!
Romantic almost, looked at through a space,
How small of intervening years! For then,
Though surely no mean progress had been made
In meditation holy and sublime,
Yet something of a girlish child-like gloss
Of novelty surviv'd for scenes like these;
Pleasure that had been handed down from times
When, at a Country-Playhouse, having caught,
In summer, through the fractur'd wall, a glimpse
Of daylight, at the thought of where I was
I gladden'd more than if I had beheld
Before me some bright Cavern of Romance,
Or than we do, when on our beds we lie
At night, in warmth, when rains are beating hard.

The 1850 revision refurbishes the last eight lines into a more consciously literary mode, thereby destroying the direct and personal connection with the Grasmere island poem. The earlier and more trenchant version points towards a 'spot of time' otherwise unrecorded – another instance of the distinctive Wordsworthian concentration of all his faculties in a still moment of symbolic vision, the symbol eluding him. In his case the word *romantic* points, not to something exotic, but to something as homely as the sources of Shakespeare's comedies and as common to the English social landscape as 'what has been and may be again.' Wordsworth could not have carried the word *romantic* closer to the mainsprings of his curious and intractable art than he does in this passage; but he never returned to it.

3   Associated with landscape of awesome grandeur, whether real or contrived

3/1 *Descriptive Sketches ... taken during a pedestrian Tour in the Italian, Grison, Swiss, and Savoyard Alps.* l. 283 (1793) = 226 (1849) :[15] the key line is identical in both versions, except for punctuation; the 1793 version is quoted. The section preceding the key line is an account of

Sckellened-thal; in his note dictated to Isabella Fenwick in 1843 Wordsworth said: 'I will only notice that the description of the valley filled with mist, beginning – "In solemn shapes," was taken from that beautiful region of which the principal features are Lungarn and Sarnen. Nothing that I ever saw in nature left a more delightful impression on my mind than that which I have attempted, alas, how feebly! to convey to others in these lines. These two lakes have always interested me especially, from bearing, in their size and other feature, a resemblance to those of the North of England ... '[16] The word *romantic* therefore lies at a key position, referring to a scene of memorable beauty (but not, apparently, wildness) which is also linked in Wordsworth's mind to his native Lakes.

> On as we move, a softer prospect opes,
> Calm huts, and lawns between, and sylvan slopes.
> While mists, suspended on th' expiring gale,
> Moveless o'er-hang the deep secluded vale,
> The beams of evening, slipping soft between,
> Light up of tranquil joy a sober scene; –
> Winding it's dark-green wood and emerald glade,
> The still vale lengthens underneath the shade;
> While in soft gloom the scattering bowers recede,
> Green dewy lights adorn the freshen'd mead,
> Where solitary forms illumin'd stray
> Turning with quiet touch the valley's hay,
> On the low brown wood-huts delighted sleep
> Along the brighten'd gloom reposing deep.
> While pastoral pipes and streams the landscape lull.
> And bells of passing mules that tinkle dull,
> In solemn shapes before th' admiring eye
> Dilated hang the misty pines on high,
> Huge covent domes with pinnacles and tow'rs,
> And antique castles seen thro' drizzling show'rs.
>   From such romantic dreams my soul awake,
> Lo! Fear looks silent down on Uri's lake ...

Although in the end there are the 'pinnacles and tow'rs,/And antique castles' that the generalized romantic formula would lead us to expect, the scene is actually one of gentleness, greenery – for all its steepness – reminiscent of home; and the word *romantic* refers less to the awesome grandeur of the scene (if that is what it was) than to the reminiscent – but not noticeably nostalgic – feelings aroused by the scene.

3/2 *Prelude* VI, 193 (1850 only): composed ? after 1824.

> In summer, making quest for works of art,
> Or scenes renowned for beauty, I explored
> That streamlet whose blue current works its way
> Between romantic Dovedale's spiry rocks;
> Pried into Yorkshire dales, or hidden tracts
> Of my own native region, and was blest
> Between these sundry wanderings with a joy
> Above all joys ...

The 1805 version is more condensed, relies upon the evocative power of the names, needs no reinforcement of the rhetorical word *romantic*, and does not fall back upon an adjective coined in the standard eighteenth-century special-poetic manner – *spiry*.

> In summer among distant nooks I rov'd
> Dovedale, or Yorkshire Dales, or through bye-tracts
> Of my own native region, and was blest ...

Here the object of the search is not self-consciously designated as 'making quest for works of art,/Or scenes renowned for beauty.' This late diffuse instance is the only case that I find in Wordsworth's poems of the word *romantic* used as a weak *cliché*.

In the Isabella Fenwick note on the 'Extempore Effusion upon the Death of James Hogg,' Wordsworth remembers a conversation with Hogg in which Wordsworth said he wished Hogg were as 'zealous and diligent [a] labourer' as a poet as he was as a Minister of the Gospel. 'I happened once to speak of pains as necessary to produce merit of a certain kind which I highly valued: his observation was – "It is not worthwhile." You are quite right, thought I, if the labour encroaches upon the time due to teach truth as a steward of the mysteries of God: if there be cause to fear that, write less: but, if poetry is to be produced at all, make what you do produce as good as you can.'[17] Poetry well made does not declare the difficulty of the making; but Dorothy Wordsworth's journals and letters, even at a glance, give ample evidence of the obsessive concentration that Wordsworth brought to bear on the writing and revision of his poems. It is not surprising then that his uses of *romantic* – a word with fashionable currency in his day – should be few, fastidious, and – with the one exception above in the *Prelude* 3/2 – complex and sharply controlled by the context. Even in *Descriptive Sketches*, a youthful poem recording what memorable landscapes he had seen in walking through the Alps – at that time the romantic setting *par excellence* – the word *romantic* occurs only once and then with un-expected and complex implications. This is only one piece of evidence that within the Wordsworth-Coleridge circle *romantic* was a tiresome vogue-word: outsiders used the word uncritically, but here where language was respected the word was used seldom, and if it was used at all it would be with contempt or merriment. The one careless or perfunctory use (3/2) is in reference to landscape. 'Romantic' landscape, in the standard view, was generally awe-inspiring, steep, dark, savage; specifically it referred to such effects deliberately produced or cultivated in landscape gardening, by cross-fertilization with the literary-archaeological cult of sentimental medievalism called 'Gothic.' If the landscape that is 'romantic' in its own natural right is also provided with an isolated tower or castle the romantic quality is reinforced by 'Gothic' implication; and this is to be seen to some extent in *Descriptive Sketches* (3/1).

I have not searched the Wordsworth letters for uses of the word *romantic*, but I have searched Dorothy Wordsworth's journals with interesting results. Although the account of the Scotch Tour of 1803 is full of highly detailed descriptions of what we would recognise as 'romantic' settings and scenes, she never uses the word *romantic* to describe them or to reinforce her description. The Alfoxden and Grasmere journals also include many descriptions that say to *us* 'romantic,' but she does not use the word. Although the restraint in Somerset may be unexpected, it is easy to understand why she did not use the word in reference to the Lakeland scenery: the Lakes were not 'strange' to her or to William – that was their 'native region.'* This makes the slip about 'romantic Dovedale's spiry rocks' particularly striking, and the late date of the slip makes it all the more interesting. There *is*, however, one place where Dorothy uses *romantic*; and that is in a specific, even technical, reference to a Gothic garden.

April 15th [1798]. Set forward after breakfast to Crookham, and return to dinner at three o'clock. A fine cloudy morning. Walked about the squire's grounds. Quaint waterfalls about, about which Nature was very successfully striving to make beautiful what art had deformed – ruins,

* Cf. *Wordsworth, Letters: Middle Years* (2nd ed., Oxford, 1969), 1: 271–2 of October 1808: declining to venture on 'a theme so boundless as this sublime and beautiful region,' Wordsworth adds: 'you can easily conceive that objects may be too familiar to a Man, to leave him the power of describing them. This is the case with me in regard to these Lakes and mountains, which are my native Country ...' But his correspondent must have been an importunate bore; Wordsworth had in fact been writing what was later called his *Guide to the Lakes*, and it was published in 1810.

hermitages, etc. etc. In spite of all these things, the dell romantic and beautiful, though everywhere planted with unnaturalised trees. Happily we cannot shape the huge hills, or carve out the valleys according to our fancy.[18]

If William and Dorothy rejected the word *romantic* as a cult word, it seems to have been not because it implied a 'literary' response to landscape but because it involved a cultish expectation about the intensity and kind of response that should be registered in the presence of a hypothetically romantic scene. On 21 August 1803, as Dorothy records, when Dorothy, William, and Coleridge were at Cora Linn waterfall sitting on a bench placed there to enjoy the view, they were joined by 'A lady and gentleman, more expeditious tourists than we.' The strangers moved on, but then joined them again 'at another station above the Falls.'

C[oleridge], who is always good-natured enough to enter into conversation with anybody whom he meets in his way, began to talk with the gentleman, who observed that it was a '*majestic* waterfall.' Coleridge was delighted with the accuracy of the epithet, particularly as he had been settling in his own mind the precise meaning of the words grand, majestic, sublime, etc., and had discussed the subject with Wm. at some length the day before. 'Yes, sir,' says Coleridge, 'it *is* a majestic waterfall.' 'Sublime and beautiful,' replied his friend. Poor C. could make no answer, and, not very desirous to continue the conversation, came to us and related the story, laughing heartily.[19]

In fact, Dorothy herself associated the landscape sense of *romantic* very closely with 'romance (legend)' and so kept sharp control on the definition of her response without using the word *romantic*. On her visit to Calais in 1802 she saw the fort in the evening twilight – 'we could not see anything of the building but its shape, which was far more distinct than in perfect daylight, seemed to be reared upon pillars of ebony, between which pillars the sea has seen in the most beautiful colour that can be conceived' – and adds: 'Nothing in romance was ever half so beautiful.'[20] The next year, near the Scottish border, at a turn of the road they saw 'at the distance of less than a mile, a tall upright building of grey stone, with several men standing upon the roof, as if they were looking over battlements. It stood beyond the village, upon higher ground, as if presiding over it, – a kind of enchanter's castle, which it might have been, a place which Don Quixote would have gloried in.'[21] Later, reflecting on the different effects of brooks and of open water, she concludes that 'The beauties of a brook or a river must be sought. and the pleasure is in going in search of them; those of a lake or of the sea come to you of themselves.' They were on the Clyde, looking at Bothwell Castle, a fortress where English nobility had been imprisoned after the Battle of Bannockburn; and she continues: 'These rude warriors cared little perhaps about either [river or sea]; and yet if one may judge from the writings of Chaucer and from the old romances, more interesting passions were connected with natural objects in the days of chivalry than now, though going in search of scenery, as it is called, had not then been thought of.'[22] Later again, sheltered from a night of rain in a lonely hut near Loch Ketterinə, she lay awake listening to the rain, the sound of the lake-water, and a beck running nearby. 'I was less occupied by remembrance of the Trossachs, beautiful as they were, than the vision of the Highland hut, which I could not get out of my head. I thought of the Fairyland of Spenser, and what I had read in romance at other times, and then, what a feast would it be for a London pantomime-maker, could he but transplant it to Drury Lane, with all its beautiful colours!'[23] Dorothy's reactions to the word 'romance' give depth and clarity to William's use of *romantic* in sense 1 / and reinforce the impression that his own reference is neither vague nor approximate. But it is complex and personal, calling to mind at once their own reading of romances as visionary, and their sense of the primordial continuity of deep feeling in people who live a 'natural' life. This second point of emphasis is made clear by discussion between Dorothy and William after an unexpected encounter in the rain near Tarbet in twilight, when 'all was solitary and huge – sky, water, and mountains mingled together.'

While we were walking forward, the road leading us over the top of a brow, we stopped suddenly at the sound of a half-articulate Gaelic hooting from a field close to us; it came from a little boy, whom we could see on the hill between us and the lake, wrapped up in a grey plaid; he was probably calling home the cattle for the night. His appearance was in the highest degree moving to the imagination: mists were on the hillsides, darkness shutting in upon the huge avenue of mountains, torrents roaring, no house in sight to which the child might belong; his dress, cry, and appearance all different from anything we had been accustomed to. It was a text, as Wm. has since observed to me, containing in itself the whole history of the Highlander's life – his melancholy, his simplicity, his poverty, his superstition, and above all, that visionariness which results from a communion with the unworldliness of nature.[24]

On 8 November 1805 Dorothy Wordsworth noted in her journal: 'Mrs Luff's large white dog lay in the moonshine upon the round knoll under the old yew-tree, a beautiful and romantic image – the dark tree with its dark shadow, & the elegant creature as fair as a Spirit.' This recalls the painterly image Coleridge had used in a poem of 1796 ('To a Young Friend ...,' example 1/1 on p. 178 below), and the pictorial-romantic sense of the stunted thorn that seems to have been the starting-point for Wordsworth's poem *The Thorn*. It also has the tactile feeling of *Christabel* and, perhaps even more strongly, of Wordsworth's *White Doe of Rylstone*, which was not to be written until 1807–8.

There is one more use of the word *romantic* by Wordsworth in the Preface to the *Poems* of 1815. This Preface, given over mostly to an explanation for the peculiar arrangement of his poems that was to persist to the end of his life, was one of the things that propelled Coleridge in writing *Biographia Literaria*, for it includes a partial – and in Coleridge's view incorrect – account of the distinction between imagination and fancy. Compared with the sustained but confused rhetorical impetuosity and grand phrasing of the Preface to the *Lyrical Ballads*, the 1815 Preface is a dry, tightly controlled, even Augustan performance. Near the end, just before his account of fancy and imagination, Wordsworth seems to be aware of the by-then-current and fashionable distinction between classical and romantic (which also has Coleridgean connections); but the gesture of recognition is no more than the flicker of an eye, and has the ironic allusiveness that T. S. Eliot was inclined to adopt when noticing a tricky matter that he preferred not to discuss in public.

All Poets, except the dramatic, have been in the practice of feigning that their works were composed to the music of the harp or lyre: with what degree of affectation this has been done in modern times, I leave to the judicious to determine. For my own part, I have not been disposed to violate probability so far, or to make such a large demand upon the Reader's charity. Some of these pieces are essentially lyrical; and, therefore, cannot have their due force without a supposed musical accompaniment; but, in much the greatest part, as a substitute for the classic lyre or romantic harp, I require nothing more than an animated or impassioned recitation, adapted to the subject.[25]

The distinction may be a standard metonymic distinction between the epic and the lyric manner, but the terms do not sit comfortably here in specifying the middle ground that Wordsworth requires for speaking some of his verse; and the phrase may be a distant though confused echo of the German distinction. As will be seen, the classical-romantic distinction had suddenly entered England in 1813. Wordsworth had been in London, and had seen Coleridge; but if this matter ever came up for discussion between them, the effect on Wordsworth cannot be regarded as volcanic.

LAMB

Charles Lamb, incorrigible Londoner, never tired of making Rabelaisian lists of the delights of 'London with-the-many-sins'; he was not easily to be infected with his friends' enthusiasm for rocks and woods and waterfalls. His salty observations, varying a little in acerbity depending on his correspondent, provide valuable comment from close range – comment not only on the general currency of the sentimental-romantic response to landscape but also on Wordsworth and Coleridge as praisers of sublime landscape. To Thomas Manning, November 1800, he said: 'Consider Grasmere! Ambleside! Wordsworth! Coleridge! I hope you will. Hills, woods, lakes, and mountains, to the eternal devil. I will eat snipes with thee, Thomas Manning ... For my part, with reference to my friends northward, I must confess that I am not romance-bit about *Nature*. The earth, and sea, and sky (when all is said) is but as a house to dwell in ...' As he goes on to rehearse and celebrate the 'furniture of my world,' the letter becomes a feat of affectionate virtuosity.[26] In January 1801, when Wordsworth actually invited Lamb to Grasmere, Lamb replied:

Separate from the pleasure of your company, I don't much care if I never see a mountain in my life. I have passed all my days in London, until I have formed as many and intense local attachments, as any of you mountaineers have done with dead nature ... I have no passion (or have had none since I was in love, and then it was the spurious engendering of poetry & books) to groves and vallies ... Have I not enough, without your mountains? I do not envy you. I should pity you, did I not know, that the Mind will make friends of any thing. Your sun & moon and skys and hills & lakes affect me no more, or scarcely come to me in more venerable characters, than as a gilded room with tapestry and tapers. where I might live with handsome visible objects ...[27]

In February 1801 he wrote to Charles Lloyd, who was not yet installed at Old Brathay: 'Let them talk of lakes and mountains and romantic dales – all that fantastic stuff; give me a ramble by night, in the winter nights in London – ...'[28] Again, he wrote to John Rickman, in July 1803, from Cowes: 'In short nothing in this house goes right till after supper, then a gentle circumambience of the weed [tobacco] serves to shut out Isle of Wight impertinent scenery and brings us back in fancy to Mutton Lane and the romantic alleys ever green of nether-Holborn, green that owes nothing to grass, but the simple effect of cabbage-water, tripe-cauls, children's st[oo]ls, etc.'[29] But in the summer of 1802 Charles and Mary Lamb did go to the Lakes and reached Coleridge's house in Keswick unannounced. They spent some time there, missed the Wordsworths but saw the Clarksons at Ullswater. What he wrote to Coleridge afterwards was probably genuine enough: 'I feel that I shall remember your mountains to the last day I live. They haunt me perpetually. I am like a man who has been falling in love unknown to himself, which he finds out when he leaves the Lady. I do not remember any very strong impression while they were present; but, being gone, their mementos are shelved in my brain.'[30]

A few days later he wrote to Thomas Manning, a little chastened, giving a brilliant account of his visit, and the only detailed picture of Coleridge's study in Greta Hall we have.

We thought we had got into Fairy Land ... we entered Coleridge's comfortable study just in the dusk, when the mountains were all dark with clouds upon their heads. Such an impression I never received from objects of sight before, nor do I suppose I can ever again. Glorious creatures, fine old fellows, Skiddaw, &c. I never shall forget ye, how ye lay about that night, like an intrenchment ... In fine, I have satisfied myself, that there is such a thing as that which tourists call *romantic*, which I very much suspected before: they make such a spluttering about it, and toss their splendid epithets around them, till they give as dim a light as at four o'clock next morning the lamps do after an illumination ... Besides, after all, Fleet-Street and the Strand are better places to live in for good and all than among Skiddaw. Still, I turn back to those great places where I wandered about, participating in their greatness ...'[31]

I am reasonably sure that a thorough search of Lamb's letters would provide a number of occurrences of the word *romantic*, but I doubt whether their uses would go beyond what these few passages convey by jocular and inverted emphasis.

COLERIDGE

The 'deep romantic chasm' of *Kubla Khan* must surely be the most widely known use of the word *romantic* in the whole corpus of English poetry; yet Coleridge used *romantic* only four other times in the whole of his poems, and in senses of less poetic complexity than most of the uses made by Wordsworth. Coleridge's use of the word, however, can be expected to be of peculiar interest, not only because of his eminence as poet and philosopher, and not only because he was the earliest exponent of the classical-romantic distinction in England, but also because he was a word-maker of exceptional and ingenious fertility and a man who insistently 'desynonymized' pairs of approximately identical terms whenever he encountered them – fancy–imagination, reason–understanding, imitation–copy, genius–talent, and the like.

All Coleridge's uses of *romantic* in his poems fall within the last five years of the eighteenth century; and only one of these occurs in a major poem. Four refer to landscape (although one is used perhaps in a painterly sense), the other is mock-amorous. (The notation used for Wordsworth is continued for Coleridge.)

I   *Associated with romance (legend)*

I / I 'To a Young Friend on his proposing to domesticate with the Author,' l. 32:[32] composed 1796, published 1797. This poem falls within the *annus mirabilis*; it imagines 'A mount, not wearisome and bare and steep,/But a green mountain variously up-piled' – 'The Hill of Knowledge' that Coleridge as master and Charles Lloyd as pupil will climb together. The allegoric sketch is provided with much minute detail taken from the Somerset landscape. He imagines how one of them might drop musing behind, while the other, going ahead, would shout eagerly 'from the forehead of the topmost crag' –

> for haply *there* uprears
> That shadowing Pine its old romantic limbs,
>   Which latest shall detain the enamour'd sight
> Seen from below, when eve the valley dims,
>   Tinged yellow with the rich departing light ...

The pinetree, caught up into 'allegoric lore,' seems not to be directly observed or remembered, although it may be a painter's image in the manner of Salvator Rosa; for why not windswept and thereby more 'romantic' for its frozen declaration of force than for its

langorous shelter?* Unfortunately Coleridge's poem is paratactic
and not very clear as it unfolds. What at first sight looks like an un-
focussed landscape use of *romantic* seems more probably, on reflection, to refer to 'romance' (legend): the tree assumes the aspect of
some huge figure from romance, perhaps human or bestial but not
clearly discernible, and portentous – a little like the figure of the
leech-gatherer in 'Resolution and Independence' that lies on the
margin between terrestrial and human, between living and dead,
between monster and man; the tree may be a huge indistinct figure
from primordial myth or from the less awe-inspiring contrivances of
romance. That the poem is admittedly allegoric rather than descriptive reinforces the conjecture.

2   *Associated with love*

2/1 'Lines written in the Album at Elbingerode, in the Hartz
Forest,' l. 14:[33] composed 17 May 1799, published September 1799.

> And the Gale murmuring indivisibly,
> Preserv'd it's solemn murmur most distinct
> From many a Note of many a Waterbreak,
> And the Brook's *Chatter*; on whose islet stones
> The dingy Kidling with it's tinkling Bell
> Leapt frolicsome, or old romantic Goat
> Sat, his white Beard slow-waving! ...

On this occasion Coleridge had walked to the top of the Brocken
with certain irreverent undergraduates and had looked upon scenes
that were unquestionably 'romantic.' The transferred epithet from
the scenery to the well-known amorous propensities of the goat is a
more eloquent comment on the tone of the conversation between
the walkers than evidence for a scrupulous poetic practice.

*   Only five days after Dorothy visited the Gothic garden at Crookhom, and the
     day after Coleridge had left Alfoxden, she and William 'walked in the evening
     up the hill dividing the Coombes. Came home the Crookham way, by the
     thorn, and the "little muddy pool" ' (*Dorothy Wordsworth's Journals* 1: 15–16).
     This refers to 'The Thorn' which Wordsworth wrote on 19 March 1798. In the
     Isabella Fenwick note, Wordsworth said that the poem 'Arose out of my
     observing, on the ridge of Quantock Hill, on a stormy day, a thorn which I had
     often passed in calm and bright weather without noticing it.' Sir George
     Beaumont 'painted a picture from it [i.e., the poem], which Wilkie thought his
     best' (*Wordsworth, Poems* 11: 513). It is in a long note to this poem (1798) that
     Wordsworth said that 'poetry is passion: it is the history or science of feelings'
     (ibid., 11: 513). For Coleridge on Salvator Rosa, see pp. 197–8 below.

3 Associated with landscape of awesome grandeur, whether natural or man-made

3/1 'To the Rev. W. J. Hort while teaching a young Lady some Song-tunes on his Flute,' l. 18:[34] composed 1795, published 1796. Coleridge says that when, according to the scheme of Pantisocracy, he and his friends (and their several wives) have taken themselves to the idyllic banks of the Susquehanna River, he will still remember this occasion.

> In Freedom's UNDIVIDED dell,
> Where *Toil* and *Health* with mellow'd *Love* shall dwell,
>   Far from folly, far from men,
>   In the rude romantic glen,
>   Up the cliff, and thro' the glade,
>   Wandering with the dear-lov'd maid,
>   I shall listen to the lay,
>   And ponder on thee far away ...

This is not one of Coleridge's ablest poems. From what Coleridge knew of the Susquehanna, the place he was going to was not particularly savage. Yet the phrase 'rude romantic glen' seems to be reaching out toward 'that deep romantic Chasm' of *Kubla Khan* by way of a cancelled passage in *This Lime-Tree Bower*, two lines of which poem, as sent to Southey in a letter of 17 July 1797, read: 'Wander delighted, and look down, perchance, / On that same rifted Dell ...' Coleridge has added in a footnote:

> Wand'ring well-pleas'd, look down on grange or dell
> Or [that deep gloomy *cancelled*] deep fantastic Rift ...

As first published in 1800, by which time *Kubla Khan* had been written, the thread is lost in 'that still roaring dell ... The roaring dell, o'erwooded, narrow, deep ...'

3/2 *Religious Musings*, l. 250:[35] composed late 1794?, published 1796. Coleridge declares how, at the apocalyptic change of society to perfection, the philosophers and bards will 'tame the outrageous mass' –

> Moulding Confusion to such perfect forms.
> As erst were wont, – bright visions of the day! –
> To float before them, when, the summer noon,
> Beneath some arched romantic rock reclined
> They felt the sea-breeze lift their youthful locks ...

This image of visionary day-dreaming recalls Wordsworth's 'Written with a Pencil ...' (p. 167 above, 2/1); but although late enough to fall within the newly discovered manner of 'Shurton Bars' and 'The Eolian Harp,' it is evidently informed less by an actual occasion than by some recollection of oracular literature. Yet the words 'arched romantic rock' by anticipation partake of the world of *Kubla Khan* in two senses.

3/3 *Kubla Khan*, l. 11:[36] composed 1798, published 1816; Crewe MS quoted.

In Xannadù did Cubla Khan
A stately Pleasure Dome decree;
Where Alph, the sacred River, ran
Thro' Caverns measureless to Man
Down to a sunless Sea.
So twice six miles of fertile ground
With Walls and Towers were compass'd round:
And here were Gardens bright with sinuous Rills
Where blossom'd many an incense-bearing Tree,
And here were Forests ancient as the Hills
Enfolding sunny Spots of Greenery.
But o! that deep romantic Chasm, that slanted
Down a green Hill athwart a cedarn Cover,
A savage Place, as holy and inchanted
As e'er beneath a waning Moon was haunted
By Woman wailing for her Daemon-Lover:
From forth this Chasm with hideous Turmoil seething,
As if this Earth in fast thick Pants were breathing,
A mighty Fountain momently was forc'd,
Amid whose swift half-intermitted Burst
Huge Fragments vaulted like rebounding Hail,
Or chaffy Grain beneath the Thresher's Flail:
And mid these dancing Rocks at once & ever
It flung up momently the sacred River.
Five miles meandering with a mazy Motion
Thro' Wood and Dale the sacred River ran,
Then reach'd the Caverns measureless to Man,
And sank in Tumult to a lifeless Ocean; ...

If there is any source for this landscape it may be found in 'Some wilderness-plot, green & fountainous & unviolated by Man' of an early opium vision,[37] perhaps in the walking tour with Hucks in North Wales in the summer of 1794,[38] perhaps (as Geoffrey

Grigson has suggested[39]) in a visit to the Gothic garden at Haford on that walking tour, perhaps even in a visit to the Gothic garden at Crookham or an account of it.[40] But such sources account for rather less than everything, for the passage is a spell-binding trans-figuration of the romantic landscape and its Gothic literary evoca-tions – called forth and crystallizing upon (as we know well) a passage in *Purchas His Pilgrimage* (1626). It is worth noticing the origin in literature, the exotic setting and names, the Gothic theme of the 'Woman wailing for her Daemon-Lover,' the primordial – even menacing – sense of power. But its origin is also to be seen in the direct links with actual places, and with actual instants of heightened observation and vivid feeling, which impart force and momentum of a kind that is not to be found in what Coleridge was later to distinguish in *Biographia Literaria* as fanciful constructions of 'fixities and definites.'

In all five occurrences of the word *romantic* in his poems, Cole-ridge had placed the word in exactly the same verbal and metrical structure: a phrase of three words – monosyllabic adjective + *romantic* + monosyllabic noun. This pattern (and Wordsworth uses it four times, in all of them choosing 'old' for his anacrustic word, although once ending with the disyllabic 'sorrows') inevitably throws the main emphasis off the word *romantic*. It may be a trick of careless versifying that makes Coleridge choose 'old' as the introduc-tory adjective twice, and Wordsworth four times; but it is more likely that that adjective recurs because *romantic* – whatever else it may imply – is strongly connected in their minds with 'romance' and the fact of distance in time, whether historical, psychic, linguis-tic, or imaginative. It is presumably in the sense of distance, in the word *old*, that *romantic* refers simultaneously to 'romance' and to the Gothic elements of the medieval, the dark, and the psychologically unaccountable. At least for Coleridge, two of the three occurrences of 'romance' in his poems call in the word *old*, and the third implies a context historically distant.

'Lines in the Manner of Spenser,'[41] 1795:

(No fairer deck'd the flowers of old Romance)

'The Silver Thimble,'[42] 1795:

As oft mine eye with careless glance
Has gallop'd thro' some old romance ...

– allegedly written by Mrs Coleridge, but one can well believe her later statement that 'she wrote but little of these verses.'

'The Garden of Boccaccio,'[43] 1828:

Mid gods of Greece, and warriors of romance.

These uses are standard enough: but in prose writings Coleridge clarifies and locates his meaning of 'romance' and in doing so brings them recognizably close to the uses of Dorothy and – by implication – of William Wordsworth.

In the second of the essays 'On the Principles of Genial Criticism,' published in *Felix Farley's Bristol Journal* in August and September 1814, Coleridge allows us to go a little behind the tantalizing scrap of conversation that (according to Dorothy) he had with the unnamed tourists in 1803 in Scotland. 'There are few mental exertions more instructive, or which are capable of being rendered more entertaining, than the attempt to establish and exemplify the distinct meaning of terms, often confounded in common use, and considered as mere synonyms. Such are the words Agreeable, Beautiful, Picturesque, Grand, Sublime.'[44] He evolves the terms *agreeable* and *beautiful* at considerable length but leaves the series incomplete. In a letter to Thomas Allsop [in 1825?] he gives a brief account of a more extended list in terms of the relation of the whole to the parts: shapely, beautiful, formal, grand, majestic, picturesque, sublime. No account of the romantic is found in any such formal or reflective context.

Most of Coleridge's uses of the word *romantic* in his Notebooks and letters refer to landscape. The earliest record was written from the walking tour in North Wales in the summer 1794 that may have laid the seeds for the 'deep romantic Chasm.' Writing to Southey while both were still undergraduates, his use of the word *romantic* is some indication of its vogue currency. He found Llangunnog 'a Village more romantically situated'; the mountains thence to Bala were 'most sublimely terrible'; and at Bala 'The rugged and stony Clefts are stupendous – and in winter must form Cataracts most astonishing.' (The crescendo of adjectives is probably facetious.) Then he and his companion made their way from Llangollen to Wrexham to Ruthin to Denbigh.

At Denbigh is a ruined Castle – it surpasses every thing I could have conceived – I wandered there an hour and a half last evening ... Two well drest young men were walking there – Come – says one – I'll play my flute – 'twill be romantic! Bless thee for the thought, Man of Genius & Sensibility! I exclaimed – and pre-attuned my heartstring to tremulous emotion. He sat adown (the moon just peering) amid the most awful part of the Ruins – and – romantic Youth! struck up the affecting Tune of *Mrs Casey*! – 'Tis fact upon my Honor!*

In May 1799 when he climbed the Brocken, Coleridge's only poetical record of the grandeur of the scene is in the 'Lines written in the Album at Elbingerode' – in which he had turned the actual belled cattle into kids and goats so that he could make a mildly indelicate jest on the word *romantic*. There is record of this same walk both in a Notebook and in a letter. The Notebook entry is particularly interesting for his repeated use of the word 'coombs'† (one of his favourite features of the Somerset landscape), for the repetition of the word *greenery* (a year after composing *Kubla Khan*) and the prominence of the word *green* (although admittedly the landscape forced that on him); and 'In short the scene extremely resembles some parts of the River Wye/& still more the Coombes about Porlock &c.' As they climbed up from one valley to another they suddenly found 'all the verdure gone, the Trees leafless, & low down & close along the Banks of the River the Concial Fir Trees, in great multitudes/a melancholy & romantic Scene that was quite new to me. –'[45] Later, when they came to the foot of the great Brocken, climbed to the top, and visited 'the Blocksberg, a sort of Bowling Green inclosed by huge Stones, something like those at Stonehenge' – the 'place where the Witches dance' – they saw 'nothing particularly wild or romantic.'‡

In August 1802, walking by himself, Coleridge made note of 'Ponsonby Hall & Calder Bridge Village & romantic Mill just on the line at the opposite end.'[46] A few days later he 'passed over a common, wild, & dreary, and descending a hill came down upon Ulpha Kirk, with a sweet view up the River, with a large mirror over a rapid/Ulpa Kirk is a most romantic vale, the mountains

*   *Coleridge, Letters* 1: 89–90. Coleridge repeats much of this account almost word for word several days later, but says that when he was walking by the castle he was 'feeding on melancholy' (ibid., pp. 91–2), and also clarifies the point about 'Mrs Casey' by quoting the first two lines of the song. The sentimental flautists may well have been – like Coleridge – undergraduates, indulging in a grave and elaborate lark.

†   Yet he only once used the word *coomb* in a poem (*Coleridge, Poems* 1: 94); it appears also in the title of that poem in a place-name.

‡   *Coleridge, Letters* 1: 504; *Coleridge, Notebooks* 1: 412. For the argument that these descriptions were noted down *before* the composition of *Kubla Khan*, and that *Kubla Khan* was composed in 1800 rather than 1798, see Elisabeth Schneider, *Coleridge, Opium, and 'Kubla Khan'* (Chicago, 1953), particularly pp. 174–8. For Coleridge's abrupt rejection of 'sentimental associations,' especially of the literary kind, see *Coleridge, Notebooks* II: 2026 and 2169. In the second note he says: 'Childish minds alone, I am more than ever convinced, can attach themselves to (so called) antiquities.'

that embosom it, low & of a remarkably wild outline / and higher mountains looking in from behind.'[47] In Sicily in October 1805, near Giardini, he saw 'a Church Tower (*white*) most romantically placed on [the slope] of one [Hill], just before the rise of another';[48] and near Naples that December he saw 'Romantic round Tower at projecting Battlements of Fondi.'[49] Then in May 1806, after leaving Rome, he took

a *sweet* ride to Nepi, the most romantic place I have seen, both when first its then round ruined Tower & extinguisher-steeple peeped thro' the Trees – & it continues improving to the very last / Its walls, ivy, double Gate, picturesque & novel waterfalls between the 1st & second / ... indeed from this place even to Terni thro' Borchetto, is a continued scene of beauty chiefly in the style of the River Wye – only the clefts are deeper, more romantic, & more wooded – but the river, is very inferior/ ...[50]

Through these few notes two strains run through the word *romantic*: one is the Gothic sense of menacing force concentrated into the *Kubla Khan* image, with darkness and 'melancholy'; the other is is more domestic, gentler, reminding him of the Wye Valley. Tower, mill, church are important, it would seem, because of the sense of lives lived there long ago, or lives obscurely lived still that cannot be known, or simply the sense of human life imprinted upon the landscape (as one may sense the immanence of Saracens in the Provençal hills); even the recollection of Stonehenge is less powerful than that. Particularly noticeable is the absence of literary reference and the restraint from any expected or formulated response of feeling. The notebook entries themselves need to be read carefully to see with what painstaking precision the detail is rendered into words, even when the notes are terse, broken, and elliptical. There is no air of fine writing, but rather the patient fidelity of the poet obsessed with affectionate accuracy, as Gerard Manley Hopkins was when he set down the look of broken water, or the texture of leaves, or 'a lovely damasking in the sky.' In this, being what he was, Coleridge uses even the word *romantic* with fastidious meaningfulness in his prose rendering of landscape.

In March 1805 Coleridge made note of an uncongenial conversation with an unknown person in Malta.

Of country – Great Britain for me – none of your romantics! – and what then do you mean? If my feelings are romantic, upon what are yours founded? Why should you love your country at all? It is an axiom. Be it so! But still an Axiom implies definition, & is preceded by it. What do you mean by country? The clod under your feet? or where you were born? What if I had been born in a Sicilian Vessel, my mother an English-woman being there brought to bed? No, where my Parents were born. – What then if my Father had been so born, &c &c.[51]

The note is clearer if expanded a little and repunctuated.

Of Country

[*Coleridge*] 'Great Britain for me.' [*Interlocutor*] 'None of your romantics!' 'And what then do *you* mean? If my feelings are *romantic*, upon what are yours founded? Why should you love your country at all?' 'It is an axiom [that I should love my country].' 'Be it so! But still an Axiom implies definition, & is preceded by it. What do you mean by *country*? The clod under your feet? or where you were born? What if I had been born in a Sicilian Vessel, my mother an Englishwoman being there brought to bed?' 'No, where my Parents were born.' 'What then if my Father had been born [in a Sicilian Vessel], &c &c?'

The charge of indulging in 'romantics' evidently implies 'roman-cing,' placing an imaginative gloss over the thought of (a disreputable) Great Britain, imparting a colour that no 'realist' would recognize as proper to the state of the nation; it also implies that Coleridge is responding sentimentally – in the order of an inappropriate trigger-response – to the thought of his country. Coleridge, in replying, reads 'romantic feelings' as allegedly feelings that are not shaped and controlled by the object which has aroused them. But he sees the word *romantic* as pointing not simply to an assumed distinction between the actual and the imagined, but also to the question whether the object of affection is worthy to arouse the affection expressed. 'Why should you *love* your country at all?' Coleridge asks, and the argument has been turned from a simple question of actualities and appropriateness to a question of values and the source of values. The remark 'None of your romantics!' is clearly a contemptuous dismissal. Coleridge, without examining the term, accepts the basis of the dismissal, thereby acknowledging a current pejorative usage.

John Foster, in his tiresomely diffuse and sententious essay 'On the Application of the Epithet Romantic,' written in 1805, confirms this use.

A thoughtful judge of sentiments, books, and men, will often find reason to regret that the language of censure is so easy and so undefined. It costs no labour, and needs no intellect, to pronounce the words, foolish, stupid, dull, odious, absurd, ridiculous. The weakest or most uncultivated mind may therefore gratify its vanity, laziness, and malice, all at once, by a prompt application of vague condemnatory words, where a wise and liberal man would not feel himself warranted to pronounce without the most deliberate consideration, and where such consideration might perhaps terminate in applause ...

These vague epithets describe nothing, discriminate nothing; they express no species, are as applicable to ten thousand things as to this one and he has before employed them on a numberless diversity of subjects. But he can perceive that censure or contempt has the smartest effect, when its expressions have an appropriate peculiarity, which adapts them more precisely to the present subject than to another ...

He despatches *puritan*, *methodist*, and *Jacobin* briefly, then turns to *romantic*.

For having partly quitted the rank of plain epithets, it has become a convenient exploding word, of more special deriding significance than the other words of its order, such as wild, extravagant, visionary. It is a standard expression of contemptuous dispatch, which you have often heard pronounced with a very self-complacent air, that said, 'How much wiser I am than some people,' by the indolent and inanimate on what they deemed impracticable, by the apes of prudence on what they accounted foolishly adventurous, and by the slaves of custom on what startled them as singular. The class of absurdities which it denominates, is left so undefined, that all the views and sentiments which a narrow cold mind could not like or understand in an ample and fervid one, might be referred hither; and yet the word *seems* to discriminate their character so conclusively as to put them out of argument. With this cast of significance and vacancy of sense, it is allowed to depreciate without being accountable; it has the license of a parrot, to call names without being taxed with insolence. And when any sentiments are decisively stigmatized with this denomination, it would require considerable courage to rescue and defend them; for as the epithet *romantic* is always understood to deny sound reason to whatever it is fixed upon, the advocate may expect to be himself enrolled among the heroes of whom Don Quixote is the time immemorial commander-in-chief. At least he may be assigned to that class which occupies a dubious frontier space between the rational and the insane.

Not without labour, Foster then extricates at considerable length the various aspects of the notion: a) it refers to the ascendancy of imagination over judgment; b) 'The extravagance of imagination in romance has very much consisted in the display of a destiny and

course of life totally unlike the common condition of mankind';
_c_/'If this excessive imagination is combined with tendencies to
affection, it makes a person *sentimentally* romantic'; _d_/'an exclusive
taste for what is *grand*'; _e_/'an utter violation of all the relations
between ends and means' (he remarks particularly upon novels that
are 'full of these lucky incidents and adventures, which are introduced as the chief means toward the ultimate success').[52] If anything is clear from Foster's lucubrations, it is that the word *romantic*
in its contemptuous and condemnatory sense in the early nineteenth
century had not moved very far from the notion of *romance* and that it
preserves a strong literary connection simultaneously with the 'old
romances' and with 'that class of fictitious works called *novels*.'

Inasmuch as the word *romantic* is related primarily to 'romance'
it might be taken to mean 'other-worldly,' referring to a world not
ours, distant in time and space yet coherent in terms recognizably
acceptable to us. Romance is a dream-world; but dreams are part
of our experience and we tend to assume that dreams, in the act of
dreaming, 'make sense' even though they do not structure themselves
much under the 'light of common day'; and we recognize – as
Coleridge did – that there are different kinds of dreams, and that
even the crudest classification of dreams would draw a line between
the dreams that are projections of our desires and the dreams that
are visions 'given' to us. 'Every thing, that lives, has its moment of
self-exposition,' Coleridge noted.[53] The non-logical structuring of
poems can be seen as dream-working or dream-making: the elements, otherwise unrelated, put themselves together in a structure
that convinces us of this coherence – if we grasp them in an appropriate mode.

At the beginning of Chapter 14 of the *Biographia Literaria* – the
section on the 'Occasion of the Lyrical Ballads,' which is the most
commonly known part of the book – Coleridge says that in one of the
two sorts of poems he and Wordsworth had agreed to write

the incidents and agents were to be, in part at least, supernatural; and the
excellence aimed at was to consist in the interesting of the affections by
the dramatic truth of such emotions, as would naturally accompany such
situations, supposing them real. And real in *this* sense they have been to
every human being who, from whatever source of delusion, has at any
time believed himself under supernatural agency ... [I]t was agreed, that
my endeavours should be directed to persons and characters supernatural,
or at least romantic; yet so as to transfer from our inward nature a human
interest and a semblance of truth sufficient to procure for these shadows

of imagination that willing suspension of disbelief for the moment, which constitutes poetic faith.*

The word *romantic* here means primarily 'in or from romance,' but it gathers to itself complex and important relations. It is associated with the supernatural, with the 'dramatic truth of emotions,' with an implied distinction between delusion and illusion (the second being in Coleridge's view the working basis of imaginative 'truth'), and with an implied tension between truth and reality. Furthermore 'a semblance of truth' can be secured for these 'shadows of imagination' only by a function exerted by the poem itself: not by a collusive pact of make-believe on the reader's part, but by the poem commanding in the reader a sudden transposition into belief in the poem as poetic-imaginative and in the drama of the poem as imaginative-real. The 'willing suspension of disbelief for the moment' is a compulsive or charmed stepping over the threshold into the 'self-expository' world of the poem, the poem being self-expository in the way a dream is. To be able to take the decisive step over the threshold into a state of *faith* (which is not quite the same as mere 'belief') depends upon the power of the poem to command our whole attention so that we refrain for the moment from saying No; we then pay attention to the poem in the same way that we watch a dream gravely unfolding. Like the Wedding-guest we 'cannot choose but hear.' Although *romantic* in this passage at first sight looks like the simple adjective of 'romance,' I know of no other place in Coleridge's writing where *romantic* lies so firmly and reverberantly within the nucleus of his theory of poetic imagination. On this basis, I suggest, and on no basis less complex and paradoxical, could Coleridge be regarded as 'romantic' in terms that he himself would recognize as valid.

Accounts of literary 'romanticism' make much of exoticism – in manners, setting, colour, states of mind – as though the introduction of such *materials* were enough to secure a specific quality in the poem. Coleridge knew better, from his early reviewing of Gothic romances and from watching Southey make 'cold-blooded carpentry' of spectacularly exotic materials. What matters in a poem, however, is not the materials used, or even the 'colour' of the materials used, but the functioning and interaction of all the materials within the

---

*   *Biographia Literaria* II: 5–6. Cf. II: 107: 'That *illusion*, contra-distinguished from *delusion*, that *negative* faith, which simply permits the images presented to work by their own force, without either denial or affirmation of their real existence by the judgement ...' – a passage that may have helped Keats arrive at his 'doctrine' of negative capability.

poem: if they function well the poem has 'its moment of *self-exposition*.' When Coleridge made extensive revision of *The Rime of the Ancient Mariner* in 1800 (first published 1798), he removed a quantity of Gothic and charnel material, and most of the elements of archaic vocabulary,[54] because he recognized that they were of the order of emotional rhetoric, that they were gratuitous stage-effects that clogged rather than catalyzed the functions of the poem, and that they had arisen from, and appealed too obviously to, a widespread literary fashion of the day. The revisions clarify the inner functioning of the poem, and particularly the modes of 'distancing' that allow the poem to construct its own universe. The theme of the poem is extremely complex, the cognitive intensity of a very high order: these demand resources of an extraordinary kind, the functioning of exceptional forces in a suitably complex and intricate manner. It is clear that for Coleridge, on the evidence of this poem, there is no common-sense distinction between 'natural' and 'supernatural' – that whatever in the poem is 'supernatural' is 'natural' because the two words refer merely to the two poles of a continuous order.[55] For example, the 'supernatural' visions and events can as well be explained as the eidetic fantasies (or hallucinations) of a mind driven to extremity by deprivation and loneliness as they can be ascribed to the use of 'supernatural machinery' (for which Coleridge had the utmost contempt). The poem is not a fairy-tale that we may condescendingly accept if we wish, but an affirmation of a world we all recognize (although sometimes with horror) as our world, 'supernatural' perhaps inasmuch as it is not of the order of common experience, but 'natural' inasmuch as it delineates an area in which our haunted and desperate attempts to understand our lives are engaged. That Coleridge never wrote the prefatory essay on the supernatural that he promised for the *Ancient Mariner* is greatly to be lamented.

Coleridge discovered – or more properly rediscovered – that 'distancing' was an outstanding means of securing both intensity and concentration in poetry. The discovery is the more remarkable when we consider that the resources for 'distancing' that he chose were the very same materials that were commonly and fashionably used as a narcotic stimulus to induce 'sentiment,' horror, melancholy, *frisson*. Mario Praz in *The Romantic Agony* tells us a great deal about the application of these sensational materials through the nineteenth century; but his account includes suspiciously little of the work of any major writer. That is, he tells us how the *materials* were applied; he does not tell us how – in the hands of a major artist

– they were made to function poetically. Yet Wordsworth's 'The Solitary Reaper' and Keats's 'Ode to a Nightingale' are brilliant examples of the way 'distancing' can trace out the exact movement of mind; and in both cases the movement is defined in psychic space in terms of literary exoticism.

From the parish clerk of Grasmere, and no way connected with the Scotch Tour of 1803, Wordsworth heard an eye-witness story of a blind Scottish boy whose most fervent desire was to go to sea as the men of his village did; and how he set out on Loch Leven, to his great peril, in an improvised vessel, and was with difficulty and against his wish rescued by the fishermen. Wordsworth wrote a poem on this story in December 1806 and called it 'The Blind Highland Boy.' To the delight of his ill-wishers Wordsworth sent the boy to sea in

> A Household Tub, like one of those
> Which women use to wash their clothes –

and so the text ran when it was published in *Poems in Two Volumes* in 1807.[56] Coleridge was at Coleorton when Wordsworth wrote the poem; whether he protested at that time we cannot say. But in January 1808 he made the following note.

I almost fear, that the alteration would excite surprize and uneasy contempt in Verbidegno's [Wordsworth's] mind – towards one less loved, at least: – but had I written the sweet Tale of the Blind Highland Boy, I would have substituted for the washing Tub, and the awkward Stanza in which it is specified the image suggested in the following lines from Dampier's Travels ... : 'I heard of a monstrous green Turtle once taken at the Port Royal in the Bay of Campeachy, that was four feet deep from the back to the belly, and the belly six feet broad. Captn Roch's Son, of about 9 or 10 years of age, went in it as in a boat, on board his Father's Ship, about a quarter of a mile from the Shore.' ... Why might not some Mariners have left this Shell on the shore of Loch Levin for a while, about to have it transported inland for a curiosity; & the blind boy have found it. Would not the incident be in equal keeping with that of the child, as well as the image & *tone* of romantic uncommonness –[57]

Coleridge's advice prevailed. In the *Poems* of 1815 the wash-tub was turned into a turtle-shell; and Wordsworth added a note referring to Dampier, and acknowledging his 'deference to the opinion of a Friend' but attesting his authority for 'the less elegant vessel in which my blind Voyager did actually entrust himself to the danger-ous current of Loch Leven, as was related to me by an eye-witness.'

Jeffrey in the *Edinburgh Review*, and the anonymous author of *The Simpliciad* (1808), made merry about the wash-tub; but Charles Lamb, as soon as he saw the turtle-revision in 1815, defended the original to Wordsworth. '... that substitution of a shell (a flat falsification of history) ... The tub was a good honest tub in its place, and nothing could fairly be said against it. You say you made the alteration for the friendly reader, but the malicious will take it to himself.'[58] Barron Field in 1828 endorsed Lamb's view, and Wordsworth replied testily: 'greatly as I respect your opinion and Lamb's, I cannot now bring myself to undo my work; though if I had been aware before-hand that such judges would have objected, I should not have troubled myself with making the alteration.'[59]

Coleridge may have misjudged Wordsworth's capacity to make effective use of 'romantic uncommonness'; neither in 'The Blind Highland Boy' nor in the introduction to 'Peter Bell' does this sort of 'imaginative' material lie any more easily than the Gothic material Wordsworth tried unsuccessfully to introduce into a few juvenile poems. But Coleridge, with his own particular cast of poetic mind, could see how the 'romantic uncommonness' of the turtle shell (which after all on Dampier's evidence was by no means impossible or implausible) could resonate to the strangeness of the world of desire the boy's imagination had constructed in his blindness. In this particular case everything in Wordsworth's nature was inhospitable to such a resonance: the actuality of the story, the eyewitness account, the fact that he himself had seen Loch Leven, all called forth that '*matter-of-factness*' which Coleridge saw as both a defect and a strength in Wordsworth's work – as a defect it involved 'a laborious minuteness and fidelity in the representation of objects and their positions as they appeared to the poet himself.'[60]

Wordsworth's poem is better – more consistent, more Wordsworthian – as Lamb could see, if the tub is used instead of the turtle. But Coleridge was also correct in his own terms. For him, 'romantic uncommonness' was not so much a property of the thing perceived as the mode in which the perception was cast. In that mode of perception even the commonest thing could have the sudden strangeness of a familiar word heard as pristine, original, and new – and it is the business of poets to make words so. Both Wordsworth and Coleridge, if the *Biographia* account of the origin of *Lyrical Ballads* is to be taken for literal truth (as I think it is), saw 'the poetry of nature' as 'The sudden charm which accidents of light and shade, which moonlight or sunset diffused over a known and familiar landscape':[61] this poetry of nature argued to them that it was possible to combine 'a faithful adherence to the truth of nature' and 'the interest of novelty' in one poem.[62]

The mode of perception that sees the 'romantic uncommonness' of a thing commands a state of feeling that is at once intense and sharply – often obsessively if dreamily – concentrated; this is the source of poetic symbolism, and in the ambience of this activity anything whatsoever may become symbolic. For Coleridge in the matter of the tub and the turtle there is no evasion of 'the truth,' no blurring of precision either in perception or response. His notebooks, particularly in the earlier years, attest to the recurrence of images actually apprehended in this mode, that command fixed attention and prolonged and wondering attention, that hint at a symbolic language that alphabets the world, clamouring for '*self-exposition*.' For Coleridge, as far as an image is precise, it is symbolic; as far as it is symbolic, it is definitive; as far as it is definitive, it is inexhaustible to reflection. At the end of a letter describing the Harzreise, Coleridge adds a curious observation made at Oder Teich. 'Here & else where we found large rocks of violet Stone which when rubbed or when the Sun shines strong on them, emit a scent which I could not [have] distinguished from violet. It is yellow-red in colou[r].'[63] Some such recollection was in his mind perhaps when, in the *Biographia Literaria*, he considered the 'characteristic excellence' in Wordsworth that was the counterpart to the defect of his '*matter-of-factness.*'

Fourth: the perfect truth of nature in his images and descriptions as taken immediately from nature, and proving a long and genial intimacy with the very spirit which gives the physiognomic expression to all the works of nature. Like a green field reflected in a calm and perfectly transparent lake, the image is distinguished from the reality only by its greater softness and lustre. Like the moisture or the polish on a pebble, genius neither distorts nor false-colours its objects; but on the contrary brings out many a vein and many a tint which escape the eye of common observation, thus raising to the rank of gems what had been often kicked away by the hurrying foot of the traveller on the dusty highroad of custom.[64]

When the best poems of Wordsworth and Coleridge are seen, not as descriptive, but as symbolic, the phrase 'romantic uncommonness' refers to a process, a function, and a quality that is not confined to any period, although the word *romantic* perhaps properly is: it refers to whatever is radical to the power and process of poetry, whether we think of poetry as a distinctive way of putting words together or as an integrative-imaginative resource which is our common birthright and radical to our human nature. How the more specifically literary trappings of the word *romantic* come in – the Gothic colour, the melancholy and sentimentality, the intimations of guilt and spiritual disease – is another matter, being a study of the sources and applications of certain *materials*; a matter that belongs more properly in the field of literary history. When we study the function of certain materials in particular poems, however, it is a matter for poetics, and for considerations that lie at a more philosophical level than criticism. Confronted by the work of Coleridge and Wordsworth, Tolstoy's proposition that 'Romanticism comes from the fear of looking straight into the eyes of truth' seems rather wide of the mark.

KEATS, BYRON, AND OTHERS

John Keats used the word *romantic* only four times: twice in letters and twice in poems, the poems being of early date. In the letters and one poem he uses the word jocularly; in the other poem he uses it in a Spenserian context. In 'Imitation of Spenser' (1812?) he writes:

> For sure so fair a place was never seen
> Of all that ever charm'd romantic eye ...

In the 'Epistle to George Felton Mathew' (1816) –

> Should e'er the fine-eyed maid to me be kind,
> Ah! surely it must be whene'er I find
> Some flowery spot, sequester'd, wild, romantic,
> That often must have seen a poet frantic ...

From Inverness he wrote in August 1818: 'But I must leave joking & seriously aver, that I have been *werry* romantic indeed, among these Mountains & Lakes.'[65] And from the Isle of Wight in July 1819 to his sister Fanny: 'Bonchurch too is a very delightful place – as I can see by the Cottages all romantic – covered with creepers and honey sickles [*sic*] with roses and eglantines peeping in at the windows. Fit abodes, for the People I guess live in them, romantic old maids fond of novels or soldiers widows with a pretty jointure – or any body's widows or aunts or any things given to Poetry and a Piano forte –'[66]

Keats knew painters and painting, sometimes wrote his poetry with particular paintings in mind, and learned in the end how to 'paint pictures of his own' in his poems – 'By allowing his imagination to work in the way in which a painter's works, he could produce a passage of which we cannot say whether it is based on a particular work of art or not.'[67] In his mind's eye were the paintings of those masters of the picturesque, Claude, Poussin, and Titian; Salvator Rosa, an early enthusiasm, faded early.[68] And after March 1817, when Haydon took him to see the Elgin Marbles recently acquired for the nation and installed in the British Museum, Keats's imagination was fired with the reality of a Greek art that he had earlier glimpsed only dimly from literary and blurred impressions – from the conversation of painters, from engraved representations, and from Tassie's gems.* Byron thought that Keats 'took the wrong line as a poet, and was spoilt by Cockneyfying, and Suburbing, and versifying Tooke's Pantheon and Lempriere's Dictionary';[69] but De Quincey, who found *Endymion* an example of 'fantastic effeminacy,' also recognized that *Hyperion* 'presents the majesty, the austere beauty, and the simplicity of Grecian temples enriched with Grecian sculpture.'[70] Keats's *Endymion*-manner, carried through Tennyson and Rossetti to the early Hopkins and early Yeats, became vague, dreamy, and allusive; but the painterly manner of *The Eve of St Agnes* and *La Belle Dame sans Merci* continued into the paintings of the Pre-Raphaelite Brotherhood where posture and conception may have been languid but the outline was never vague. The word *romantic* seems not to have travelled with Keats's name (although 'Beauty' did); perhaps because his mature poems were seen as sculptural or statuesque, and therefore 'classical'; perhaps also because the word *classical* did not yet in England call up as polar opposite the word *romantic*.

Byron uses the word *romantic* fifteen times in his poems. None of these refers to landscape, unless 'renown'd, romantic Spain' (in 'The Age of Bronze'), 'lovely Spain! renown'd romantic land' (in *Childe Harold* I, xxxv), and the 'romantic hills' of Spain (in *Childe Harold* I, xxx) can be regarded as landscape references when their first meaning is 'Spain of romance.'

In *Hours of Idleness* (1807) there are four occurrences. 'On a distant View ... of Harrow' uses the phrase 'friendships ... too romantic to last' – which is matched in *Marino Faliero* (349) by 'love, romantic love, which in my youth/ I knew to be illusion.' In 'To a Lady' he asks 'Then wherefore souls we sigh and whine .../Merely to make

---

* Haydon was privileged to study the Elgin Marbles – sometimes by lantern light – when they were still temporarily stored in a shed behind Burlington House. For Haydon this was a turning-point in his life; he communicated that conviction to Keats, and Keats (whether or not correctly) regarded Haydon as having taken heroic initiative in securing the Elgin Marbles for the nation.

our love romantic?' – here rhyming *romantic* with *frantic*, as he does again in *Don Juan* (IV, xviii; XII, lxviii), and as Keats did in the 'Epistle to George Felton Mathew.' In 'The Tear,' 'The soldier braves death for a fanciful wreath/In Glory's romantic career'; and in 'Childish Recollections,' 'My soul to Fancy's fond suggestion yields,/And roams romantic o'er her airy fields.'

Considering the tone and purpose of *Don Juan*, the occurrences of *romantic* are surprisingly few in number (seven), and unevenly distributed (two in Canto IV, one in XI, and four in XII). In IV, xviii, he speaks of 'Young innate feelings ... what we mortals call romantic,' and in IV, iii, he says that 'sad truth ... Turns what was once romantic to burlesque.' All the other uses are flippant or ironic comment on the love relation: in XII, lxv, preliminary love-making is called 'romantic homages,' and in XII, xxii, the comment on the expected duty of providing subsistence for wife and child is 'That's noble! That's romantic!' In XI, xxxiii, rumours of Don Juan's 'wars and loves' have gone before him, 'And as romantic heads are pretty painters ... He found himself extremely in the fashion;' so also, in XII, xxvii, Leila's 'charming figure and romantic history/Became a kind of fashionable mystery'; and in XII, lxviii, Juan is noted as 'coming young from lands and scenes romantic,/Where lives, not lawsuits, must be risk'd for Passion.' Byron had already made clear in his 1813 addition to the Preface to *Childe Harold* I and II, that he was not unaware of the connection between romantic sentiment (although he does not use the phrase) and the romances of chivalry. We note with admiration that the man who has long been recognized in Europe as the supreme figure of the romantic man has left us – it may be out of aristocratic fastidiousness and a genuine classical sense – no notable uses of the word *romantic*.

Ian Jack has brought together Leigh Hunt's uses of the word in the first version of his autobiography, *Lord Byron and some of his Contemporaries* (1828).[71] 'The centre from which the different shades of meaning radiate,' he says, 'is of course "like something in a story."' Hunt described Byron as listening to music 'with an air of romantic regret,' and says that Byron discovered 'that the romantic character was not necessary to fame.' When Hunt refers to the 'classical and romantic' associations of Italy and the Mediterranean, however, he evidently does not touch upon the nerve of Schlegel's distinction.

Hazlitt's uses are different again and rather more fluid than in any other writer we have studied, and on the whole less specific than some.[72] He refuses to 'pamper [his] natural aversion to affectation or pretence, by romantic and artificial means' (1821; p. 46); the imaginary figure in the essay 'On going a Journey' is 'Our romantic and itinerant character ... not to be domesticated' (1822, p. 82); at the point of death 'the extreme points [of life] close and meet with none of that romantic interval stretching out between them that we had reckoned upon' (1821, p. 164). He speaks of the 'feelings excited by a long walk in some romantic situation' (1826, p. 254); and when he hears a 'chapel-bell with its simple tinkling sound' it has – as Keats said of the Isle of Wight cottages – 'a romantic and charming effect' (1827, p. 343). When Hazlitt calls Ben Jonson's visit to Drummond of Hawthornden a 'romantic visit' (1826, p. 534), the word *romantic* seems a synonym of *sentimental* in Sterne's sense. Although Hazlitt found Coleridge 'too romantic for the herd of vulgar politicians' (1825, p. 733), his account of their first meeting puts Coleridge in a less contemptuous context: 'A poet and a philosopher getting up into a Unitarian pulpit to preach the gospel, was a romance in these degenerate days, a sort of revival of the primitive spirit of Christianity, which was not to be resisted' (1823, p. 502).[73] Poets in general he accused of being 'As romantic [?Quixotic] in their servility as in their independence'; and he happily says that Sir Walter Scott is 'like a man who had got a romantic spinning-jenny, which he has only to set a going, and it does his work for him much better and faster than he can do it for himself.'[74]

In the Nonesuch selection studied, there are few landscape references for the word *romantic*; more interesting connections turn up for the word in landscape painting, and so make a link with Keats and Coleridge. For Coleridge, for Keats, and for Hazlitt himself, the landscape painters that came most readily to mind in their day were Poussin, Claude Lorraine, and Salvator Rosa. Although Coleridge and Wordsworth are known to have used at times the 'Lorraine glass' to enhance the picturesque quality of landscape,[75] Poussin and Claude were too much a neoclassical vogue to appeal much to either. Salvator Rosa was a different matter. Rosa (1615–73) – painter, engraver, poet (Coleridge knew his poetry), musician, and actor – developed a flamboyant and dramatic style of landscape painting ('the sinister romantic' is one name for it) in opposition to the 'classical' manner of Poussin and Claude. Although the fashion for his work had passed its peak by about 1805, Coleridge was very much aware of it, as he was also aware of the contemporary vogue for Henry Fuseli without sharing in it. Hazlitt, who at times wrote with admiration of Coleridge in his reminiscences never hesitated to deal roughly with him in anonymous reviews. In his essay 'On a Portrait of an English Lady, by Vandyke' (?1826) he notes that 'Mr. Coleridge used to say, that what gave the romantic and mysterious interest to Salvator's landscapes was their containing some implicit analogy to human or other living forms. His rocks had a latent resemblance to the outline of a human face;* his trees had the distorted jagged shape of a satyr's horns and grotesque features. I do not think this is the case; but it may serve to supply us with an illustration of the present question.'[76] Elsewhere, in his *Edinburgh Review* essay on Lady Morgan's *Life of Salvator* (July 1824) Hazlitt enlarges upon the theme of Salvator as a romantic landscape painter.†

Salvator was the victim of a too morbid sensibility, or of early difficulty and disappointment ... Landscape painting is the obvious resource of misanthropy. Our artist, escaping from the herd of knaves and fools, sought out some rude solitude, and found repose there ... In the coolness, in the silence, in the untamed wildness of mountain scenery, in the lawless manners of its inhabitants, he would forget the fever and the anguish, and the artificial restraints of society. We accordingly do not find in Salvator's rural scenes either natural beauty or fertility, or even the simply grand; but whatever seizes attention by presenting a barrier to the will, or scorning the power of mankind, or snapping asunder the chain that binds us to the kind – the barren, the abrupt, wild steril regions, the steep rock, the mountain torrent, the bandit's cave, the hermit's cell, – all these, while they released him from more harassing and painful reflections, soothed his moody spirit with congenial gloom, and found a sanctuary and a home there ... There is not in Salvator's scenes the luxuriant beauty and divine harmony of Claude, not the amplitude of Nicolas Poussin, nor the gorgeous richness of Titian – but there is a deeper seclusion, a more abrupt and total escape from society, more savage wildness and grotesqueness of form, a more earthy texture, a fresher atmosphere, and a more obstinate resistance to all the effeminate refinements of art. Salvator Rosa then is, beyond all question, the most *romantic* of landscape painters; because the very violence of his temper

---

*   Cf. *Coleridge, Notebooks* II: 1899 (23); of a painting by Sir George Beaumont: 'A Mad Yew-tree alone, with a grand S. Rosa-Eye more than half way up its rifted Trunk/ ...' Cf. *Coleridge, Notebooks* III: 3526: 'I found an admirable illustration of my theory of obscure Hieroglyphics of human or animal life being the foundation of the *pathos* of natural Scenery, in Rock, Woods, & Waters – in an emblem of Daphne's metamorphosis.' Beaumont made a painting based on Wordsworth's 'The Thorn'; see note, p. 179 above, and *Wordsworth, Poems* II: 511–12.

†   Joseph Warton had said in his *Essay on Pope* (1756) that Thomson's scenes are 'as wild and romantic as those of Salvator Rosa.'

threw him with instinctive force upon those objects in nature which would be most likely to sooth and disarm it ...*

Hazlitt, himself a moody and misanthropic man, greatly admired Titian's work and copied some of it. His treatment of Salvator, whether or not psychologically correct, suggests that the term *romantic* does not for him necessarily signify praise or self-identification.†

THE ROMANTIC-CLASSICAL DISTINCTION

In February 1818, when Coleridge was on the point of beginning a series of lectures on Shakespeare, he wrote to thank James Perry for defending him against a charge that in his earlier lectures on Shakespeare he had drawn upon Schlegel, without acknowledgment, for his leading ideas.

The close resemblance in the general principles of my Lectures given on the same subject at the present Lecture-Room, to those of Schlegel, since then translated but of which the first Copy that arrived in England was presented to me in the Room by a German Gentleman just arrived from Germany, was so very striking that the utter improbability of my having read the work would scarcely have borne me out in the assertion, it was wholly the effect of concidence and the study of the same philosophy – had not these very Lectures, in all the substance of their contents, been delivered to crowded audiences of the highest respectability at the Royal Institution three years before Schlegel had given his Lectures at Vienna – nay, Mr Hazlitt in answer to the charge that I had borrowed my opinions from Schlegel had openly said – 'That must be a Lie: for I myself heard

---

*   *Hazlitt, Works* xvi: 289–90; cf. x, 24. I wonder whether Hazlitt recognised the force of Thomas Bewick's wood-engraved vignettes in the *General History of Quadrupeds*; these appealed strongly to Wordsworth's sense of the grotesque, and somewhat match Wordsworth's poetic temper. The *Excursion* reminded Hazlitt that 'His poems bear a distant resemblance to some of Rembrandt's landscapes, whom more than any other painter, created the medium through which he saw Nature, and out of the stump of an old tree, a break in the sky, and a bit of water, could produce an effect almost miraculous' (xix: 19). For Hazlitt on Keats's *The Eve of St Agnes*, see xii: 225. For Keats on a book of engravings of Italian paintings 'Grotesque to a curious pitch,' see *Keats, Letters* ii: 19.

†   I have not yet searched Hazlitt's works for the word *romantic* as thoronghly as they deserve; the otherwise excellent index volume has no entry for *romantic*. For Hazlitt on the romantic-classical distinction, see Herbert Weisinger, 'English Treatment of the Classical-Romantic Problem,' *MLQ* vii (1946): 477–88, especially pp. 482–5 (hereafter cited as *Weisinger*). In at least one place Hazlitt speaks of 'the Gothic or romantic' (*Hazlitt, Works* vi: 347–8).

Coleridge give the very same theory before he went to Germany and when he did not even understand a word of German –' ...[77]

The story, and the wrangling that went with it, is not easy to sort out. The point at issue is whether Coleridge was independent of Schlegel in defending Shakespeare as a man of conscious artistic judgement, against the received view that Shakespeare was a wild genius who always put his feet right without knowing what he was doing.* Coleridge claimed that he had declared such a view before he had read anything of Schlegel's; and the claim can be plausibly supported by a note as early as October 1802.[78] As a few contemporaries were quick to point out, and as Sara Coleridge, John Shawcross, T. M. Raysor, René Wellek, and G. N. G. Orsini (to mention only a few) have since traced in closer detail, Coleridge did at times in his lectures virtually translate from the text of Schlegel's *Vorlesungen über dramatische Kunst und Litteratur.*† This is no concern of ours at present except as far as it helps to trace the introduction into English usage of the distinction between romantic and classical literature.

There can be no doubt that the exposition of this distinction as given by Coleridge in his literary lectures from 1809 onward owes a great deal in substance and wording to Schlegel. It should be stated, however, that although Coleridge was admittedly careless at times in making direct and unacknowledged use of the work of others –

---

*   *Biographia Literaria* II: 19–20: 'What then shall we say? even this: that Shakespeare, no mere child of nature; no automaton of genius; no passive vehicle of inspiration possessed by the spirit, not possessing it; first studied patiently, meditated deeply, understood minutely, till knowledge became habitual and intuitive wedded itself to his habitual feelings, and at length gave birth to that stupendous power, by which he stands alone, with no equal or second in his own class ...'

†   Coleridge owned a copy of the 1809–11 Heidelberg edition, said to have been annotated, but it has disappeared without any record of the notes. He describes the volumes in a letter of October 1813, and remarks: 'Besides, you will remember that I used to take them to the Surrey Institution' – that is, to the lectures of 1812–13 (*Coleridge, Letters* III: 446). Baron von Humboldt had lent him the first volume of Schlegel's 'translations from Spanish poetry' – *Spanisches Theater* (1803) – in Rome in 1806 (ibid., III: 359). Coleridge also knew, and apparently owned a copy of, Schiller's *Über naive und sentimentalische Dichtung.*

     For recent accounts of Coleridge's 'borrowings' from Schlegel, see René Wellek, *A History of Modern Criticism: 1750–1950* (New Haven, 1955), II: 155–6; and G. N. G. Orsini, 'Coleridge and Schlegel Reconsidered,' *Comparative Literature* XVI (1964): 97–118 (the evidence displayed in parallel columns). The question of Coleridge's 'plagiarisms' and the history of his acquaintance with Schlegel's work is considered in detail by Thomas McFarland, *Coleridge and the Pantheist Tradition* (Oxford, 1969); his Excursus Note I, 'Coleridge's Indebtedness to A. W. Schlegel' (pp. 256–61), supersedes everything previously written on the subject.

---

usually for convenience but never with plagiaristic intent – he used only materials that were harmonious with views and positions that he already held himself.* Widely read, with 'a memory capacious and systematising,' and thoroughly familiar with the landscape of his own mind and memory, Coleridge generously supposed that others would assume good faith in such instances. He had noted in April 1805: 'What is the right, the virtuous Feeling, and consequent action, when a man having long meditated & perceived a certain Truth finds another, a foreign Writer, who has handled the same with an approximation to the Truth, as he had previously conceived it? – Joy! – Let Truth make her Voice *audible!*'[79] In December 1811, Coleridge gave a detailed account of how Bernard Krusve gave him his copy of the *Vorlesungen* after a lecture that seemed to owe much to Schlegel;† and Henry Crabb Robinson, not an easy man to fool, although a friend of Coleridge's, read the *Vorlesungen* after hearing Coleridge's lectures and noted: 'Coleridge, I find, did not disdain to borrow observations from Schlegel, tho' the coincidences between the two lectures are for the greater part coincidences merely and not the one caused by the other.'[80] Nevertheless, the fragmentary records of his lectures show that Coleridge *did* make very effective use of Schlegel's text.

René Wellek has said that 'The distinction of classical-romantic occurs for the first time in Coleridge's lectures, given in 1811, and is there clearly derived from Schlegel ... But these lectures were not published at that time, and thus the distinction was popularized in England only through Madame de Staël.'[81] The lectures Coleridge gave between 1808 and 1813, it is true, were not published until long afterward, and then only in fragmentary form.[82] For that reason it is worth going back to trace Coleridge's use of the distinction. Perhaps he had glimpsed it independently for himself, and certainly

---

* See, for example, *Biographia Literaria* i: 95: 'While I in part translate the following observations from a contemporary writer of the Continent [i.e. Schelling], let me be permitted to premise, that I might have transcribed the substance from memoranda of my own, which were written many years before his pamphlet was given to the world; and that I prefer another's words to my own, partly as a tribute due to priority of publication? but still more from the pleasure of sympathy in a case where *coincidence* only was possible.' Cf. i: 102: in certain works of Schelling 'I first found a genial coincidence with much that I had toiled out for myself, and a powerful assistance in what I had yet to do.' The rationale (or 'psychology') of Coleridge's literary borrowings is patiently and brilliantly discussed by Thomas McFarland in Ch. 1 of *Coleridge and the Pantheist Tradition*.

† *Coleridge, Letters* iii: 359–60. Wellek denies Coleridge's claim (see *History of Modern Criticism*) and so does Griggs, at least implicitly, in his note to the letter cited. Orsini reviews the evidence at p. 105, n. 15 (see note, p. 200).

it was reinforced and clarified by his reading of Schiller and Schlegel.

As for Madame de Staël, we know that her *De l'Allemagne*, originally suppressed by Napoleon on the point of publication, was finally published in London in 1813, and almost simultaneously (also in London) in English translation. That the book contained much repetition and exposition of Schlegel's work was well known. The book was favourably and extensively reviewed by Sir James Mackintosh (whom Coleridge had known for fifteen years and distrusted) in the *Edinburgh Review* in October 1813, and by William Taylor of Norwich in the *Monthly Review*; both reviews drew attention to the romantic-classical distinction, and we know that Madame de Staël approved of the Taylor review (at least).[83] Madame de Staël may no doubt have been responsible for spreading throughout England Schlegel's romantic-classical distinction, with other Schlegelian doctrine, but evidently not to Coleridge. With an introduction from Southey, Coleridge paid a call on Madame de Staël in October 1813. It is unlikely in any case that he expected to get from her an exposition of Schlegel's theories; for five years he himself in his lectures had been drawing a distinction between antique and modern, classical and romantic, had already read a good deal of Schlegel in the original and was beginning – according to Henry Crabb Robinson's evidence – to express sharp reservations both in detail and in principle.[84] The meeting would make a good subject for an imaginary conversation: Coleridge, as Wilson noted drily, was 'justly admired for his extraordinary loquacity,' and as for Madame de Staël's prowess we have Byron's evidence that 'really her society is overwhelming – an avalanche that buries one in glittering nonsense – all snow and sophistry.' Coleridge seems to have got the better of the encounter. He tells us nothing about the meeting except that de Staël had made a disparaging comment on *Faust*. As for Madame de Staël, she told Southey that 'Pourtant, pour M. Coleridge, il est tout à fait un *monologue*!'* Crabb Robinson heard the same from her: 'Think of him? Why, that he is very great

*   *Letters of Robert Southey* II: 332n. Byron's comment is from a journal of 1813–14; the entry begins – 'More notes from Madame de Staël unanswered – and so they shall remain. I admire her abilities, but really ...' Nevertheless there is a copy of *De l'Allemagne* with a long note by Byron in the Harvard Library (*Wellek, Concepts*, 148n). Goethe was more patient, although he found her equally exasperating: he praised her as 'a mighty implement' that had broken the Chinese wall of European literary ignorance: see Thomas Carlyle, *Critical and Miscellaneous Essays* ('The Edinburgh Edition,' London, 1869), II: 298 (hereafter cited as *Carlyle, Essays*).

in monologue, but that he has no idea of dialogue'; and so the remark found its way into the *Quarterly Review*.[85]

It is worth noticing in passing that Coleridge owned a copy of the *Athenaeum* (1798–1800) and annotated the first of the three volumes. The date of the notes has not been accurately determined; many of the notes are quizzical. What Wellek calls 'the famous fragment, No. 116 ... by Friedrich Schlegel, which defines "romantic poetry" as "progressive Universalpoesie," ' has no note by Coleridge; but Fragments 99 and 119 do. Whenever Coleridge made his notes, whether before or after the dispersal of Schlegel's doctrine in England, his silence on Fragment 116 suggests that his heart did not exactly leap up when he read it.*

Taken in chronological order – as far as the order can be determined from the fragmentary remains – Coleridge's awareness of a classical-romantic distinction moves from a distinction between antique and modern to a more qualitative distinction between classical and romantic, and comes in the end to a statement about the romantic that is both earlier and more substantial than the textbooks assign to any English writer.†

* In September 1814 Coleridge, in discussing John Murray's proposal to write a verse translation of *Faust*, suggested that an 'introductory critical essay' would be essential: 'In my Essay I meant to have given a full tho' comprest critical account of the 4 Stages of German Poetry from Hans Sachs to Tie[c]k and Schlegel, who with Goethe are the living Stars, that are now culminant on the German Parnassus –' (*Coleridge, Letters* III: 528). Coleridge had met Tieck in Rome in 1806, and Tieck on his visit to England in 1817 made his way to Highgate to talk Shakespeare with Coleridge. Coleridge busied himself for a time trying to form a sort of club called 'Friends of German Literature,' partly in Tieck's honour, but the proposal came to nothing. Crabb Robinson first met Tieck on 13 June 1817 at a dinner given by J. H. Green, Coleridge's philosophical collaborator and a keen Germanist. Though Robinson did not think Tieck looked much like 'a romantic poet,' he leaves no hint that German romanticism was a subject of discussion (*Robinson, Books* 1: 207). Seven years later, at a large party at Green's, Robinson was 'displeased' because 'Coleridge spoke bitterly of Schlegel in general, and of Tieck's *Vorschule von Shakespeare*, with a hint that Tieck ought to have noticed *him*. Coleridge thinks German philosophy in a state of rapid deterioration' (ibid., 1: 307). After Tieck's visit, however, Coleridge's host James Gillman sent Tieck a copy of Burton's *Anatomy of Melancholy* with Coleridge's marginalia in it; it happened to belong to Lamb. Although a number of Tieck's books are now in the British Museum the annotated Burton is not one of them.

† Herbert Weisinger (see note, p. 199) deals particularly with the effect of the romantic-classical and antique-modern distinctions upon the criticism of Elizabethan drama. Although the discussion was confined in England to a surprisingly limited group – Coleridge and De Quincey particularly, but also Hazlitt, Scott, Crabb Robinson – the outcome was to include the Middle Ages in the modern era, thereby leaving only two European periods – classical and romantic. For illustrative quotations from Coleridge, not using the word *romantic*, see *Weisinger*, pp. 479–82.

a   British Museum Add. MS 34225, fol. 167: associated by Raysor with notes for the 1808 lectures, but surely somewhat later than the publication of Schlegel's Vienna lectures.*

Ancients, statuesque; moderns, picturesque. Ancients, rhythm and melody; moderns, harmony. Ancients, the finite, and, therefore, grace, elegance, proportion, fancy, dignity, majesty, – whatever is capable of being definitely conveyed by defined forms or thoughts. The moderns, the infinite and indefinite as the vehicle of the infinite; hence more [? devoted] to the passions, the obscure hopes and fears – the wandering thro' [the] infinite, grander moral feelings, more austere conceptions of man as man, the future rather than the present – sublimity.

Raysor notes that Coleridge is here condensing Schlegel's first lecture, 'with some possible reminiscence in the second sentence of Schiller's essay ...' Coleridge had known Schiller's *Über naïve und sentimentalische Dichtung* since – at latest – December 1803.[86]

b   British Museum MS Egerton 2800, fol. 46;[87] watermark 1810, apparently a note for a lecture. The original is heavily revised; a plain text, neglecting cancellations, is here given.

To perceive and feel the Beautiful, the Pathetic, and the Sublime in Nature, in Thought, or in Action – this combined with the power of conveying such Perceptions and Feelings to the minds and hearts of others under the most pleasurable Forms of Eye and Ear – this is poetic Genius. A gift of Heaven confined to no one Race or Period, a ray which penetrates to the Savage in the depth of Wildernesses, and throws a nobler Light, a glory beyond its own, on the splendor of the Palaces. If then Poetry itself be a free and vital power which never wholly deserts any

---

*   *Coleridge: Shakespearean Criticism*, ed. T. M. Raysor (Everyman ed., London, 1960), I: 195–6 (hereafter cited as *Raysor*); *variatim* in *Literary Remains of S. T. Coleridge*, ed. H. N. Coleridge (1836–9), II: 23 (hereafter cited as *Literary Remains*); also quoted by *Weisinger*, p. 480, n. 8. Raysor was concerned to show that certain lecture notes in Notebook 25 were used by Coleridge in his 1808 lectures, and that some material that *looks* Schlegelian was being uttered by Coleridge at the some time that Schlegel was giving his first Vienna lectures (*Raysor* II: 18–19n). To one of the notes from Notebook 25, used in a lecture in 1808 but written earlier, Raysor has attached from another MS the note quoted above; his implicit dating of the second fragment as 1808 must be an oversight. (In *Literary Remains* this fragment was printed at the end of remarks on Greek drama as though from the 1818 lectures, but H. N. Coleridge is not infallible in dating.) Coleridge's claim for independence of Schlegel in 1808 was primarily for his assertion of the regularity of Shakespeare's poetic judgement. When the verbal coincidences with Schlegel are as detailed as Raysor shows them to be in this fragment, we must conclude that the note derives from the 1809–11 edition of Schlegel's Vienna lectures.

age or Nation unless it have previously deserted itself, that Criticism, which would bind it down to any one Model, and bid it grow in a mould is a mere Despotism of False Taste, and would reduce all modern Genius to a state which (if it were not too ludicrous) might be justly compared to that of the Soldier Crabs on the Tropical Islands, which wander naked and imperfect till they creep into the cast off Shells of a nobler Race.

To counteract this Disease of long-civilized Societies, and to establish not only the identity of the Essence under the greatest variety of Forms, but the congruity and even the necessity of that variety, is the common end and aim of the present Course [of lectures].

... Beauty, Majesty, Grace and Perspicuity, and before the Harmony we have described came to its perfection, Vehemence and Impetuosity – these are the constituents of the Greek Drama – and the great Rule was the separation, or the removal, of the Heterogeneous – even as the Spirit of the Romantic Poetry, is modification, or the blending of the Heterogeneous into an Whole by the Unity of the Effect. Such were the deeper and essential contra-distinctions – and to these we must add the more accidental circumstances, from the origin of the Drama, and the size, arrangement, and object of the Theatres.

c   British Museum MS Egerton 2800, fols. 19–20;[88] watermarked 1810: according to Raysor, with 'evidence of indebtedness to Schlegel.'

I have before spoken of the Romance, or the language formed out of the decayed Roman and the northern tongues; and comparing it with the Latin we found it less perfect in simplicity and relation, the privileges of a language formed by the simple attraction of homogeneous parts, but yet more rich, more expressive and various, as one formed out of a chaos by more obscure affinities of atoms apparently heterogeneous. As more than a metaphor, as an analogy of this, I have named the true genuine modern poetry the romantic; and the works of Shakespeare are romantic poetry revealing itself in the drama ... They are in the ancient sense neither tragedies nor comedies, nor both in one, but a different genus, diverse in kind, not merely different in degree, – romantic dramas, or dramatic romances. And even a recurrence to my recent explanation of Romance would awake a presentiment that the deviation from the simple forms and unities of the ancient stage is an essential principle and, of course, an appropriate excellence, of the romantic; that these unities are to a great extent the natural form of that which in its elements was homogeneous, and its representation addressed eminently to the outward senses; and tho' both fable, language, and characters appealed to the reason rather than the mere understanding, inasmuch as they supposed an ideal state rather than referred to an existing reality, yet it was a reason which must strictly accommodate itself to the senses, and so far became a sort of more elevated understanding. On the other [hand], the romantic poetry, the Shakespearian drama, appealed to the imagination rather than to the senses, and to the reason as contemplating our inward nature, the workings of the passions in their most retired recesses ...

The appeal in the closing sentence to what he elsewhere calls 'inward goings-on' is pure Coleridge.

d 'Syllabus of a Course of Lectures on the Belles Lettres ... [November] 1812 [to January 1813].'[89]

Lecture IV. On Poetry *in genere*, and as common to antient Greece and to Christendom. On the Poetry of the Antients as contradistinguished from that of the Moderns; or, the differences of the *Classical* from the *Romantic* poetry, – exemplified in the Athenian Dramatic Poets.

Raysor comments: 'Evidently Schlegel's first lecture, with illustrations from the succeeding lectures on Greek drama.'

Lecture VI. ... The Deluge of Nations ... and the formation of mixed languages, in which the decomposed Latin became amalgamated, in different proportions, with the Gothic or Celtic. These, collectively, were called the *Romance*, and in this sense of the *mixed*, as opposed to the *simple* or homogeneous the word *Romantic* is used, – and not exclusively with reference to what we now call Romances.

This is clearly parallel to *c*.

Something of the sort was also given in May-June 1812; Henry Crabb Robinson heard about a quarter of an hour of the first lecture: 'I perceived only that he was in a digressing vein. He spoke of religion, the spirit of chivalry, the Gothic reverence for the female sex, and a classification of poetry into the ancient and romantic.' The second lecture was 'a beautiful dissertation on the Greek drama.' The fourth lecture was 'on the nature of comedy, about Aristophanes, etc. The mode of treating the subject very German, and, of course, much too abstract for his audience, which was but thin.' [90] Robinson recognized that these lectures were a refurbishing of the series given at Fetter Lane. Similar matter, similarly treated, found a place in the lectures given in Bristol in 1813–14,[91] and the underpinning of Schlegel is no less strong.

Coleridge gave lectures on literature in 1808, 1811–12, 1812, (twice), 1812–13, 1813 (Bristol), January-February 1818, and

1818–19. Little record remains of either of the last two courses, but the prospectuses show a thorough recasting of the elements. Lecture xi of the first 1818 series has as its announced topic: 'On the Arabian Nights Entertainments, and on the *romantic* Use of the Supernatural in Poetry, and in Work of Fiction not poetical.'[92] A fragment of Lecture xi connects with what has already been said about dreaming:

The Asiatic supernatural beings are all produced by imagining an excessive magnitude, or an excessive smallness combined with great power; and the broken associations, which must have given rise to such conceptions, are the sources of the interest which they inspire, as exhibiting, through the working of the imagination, the idea of power in the will. This is delightfully exemplified in the Arabian Nights' Entertainments and indeed, more or less, in other works of the same kind. In all these there is the same activity of mind as in dreaming, that is – an exertion of the fancy in combination and recombination of familiar objects so as to produce novel and wonderful imagery ...[93]

As far back as 1797, in a review of Lewis's *The Monk*, he had said: 'The romance writer possesses an unlimited power over situations; but he must scrupulously make his characters act in congruity with them. Let him work *physical* wonders only, and we will be content to *dream* with him for a while; but the first *moral* miracle which he attempts he disgusts and awakens us.'[94]

The first lecture of the second series was announced as being on '*The Tempest*, as a specimen of the Romantic or Poetical Drama of Shakespeare.'[95] This does not look new, but there is no record of what was said. At the same time that he was giving these literary lectures, he was also giving a series of philosophical lectures. Here, in Lecture x, something seems to have overflowed from his earlier discussion of the romantic and classical. In tracing the development of the European philosophical mind, he explains first how the scholastic philosophy introduced into all the languages of Europe 'the power and force of Greek and Roman connexion,' and (through the Nominalist-Realist controversy) introduced 'the true engine of all speculation' – the ability to distinguish between universals and the words that refer to 'forms of the mind' as 'forms ... truly correspondent to connexions in nature.' The other component in the European mind was the Gothic – 'an antidote, which was to grow as the scholastic philosophy was losing more and more its utility, and finally to take its place when it was superannuated.' He continues:

e   *Philosophical Lectures*, pp. 291–2.

This was the other part, the Gothic mind – the inward, the striking, the romantic character, in short the genius, but genius marked according to its birthplace; for it grew in rude forests amid the inclemencies of outward nature where man saw nothing around him but what must owe its charms mainly to the imaginary powers with which it was surveyed. There nothing outward marked the hands of man. Woods, rocks and streams, huge morasses, nothing wore externally the face of human intellect; and yet man cannot look but intellect must be either found or placed ... They had nothing but what was to be inward and sullenly refuse[d] to disclose itself otherwise than in terrors. So powerfully was this held, so strongly did the inwardness of the Gothic nature work, that the first great children of genius...never could in the least degree approach near to the centre. They believed themselves imitators. They professed to follow the ancients as guides. They sometimes actually copied ... but [they were] imitators only as nature imitates herself, when the same energies are excited under other circumstances, and on different materials through which she is to diffuse her creative and shaping mind.*

There is no sign that Coleridge was particularly interested in the romantic-classical distinction as matter for sustained reflection or emphatic public declaration. He makes no mention of it (as far as written record shows) when he refers to A. W. Schlegel or to Madame de Staël, and there is no mention of it in *Biographia Literaria* (written in 1815, published with later additions in 1817). By 1815, his mind had in any case largely turned away from what we would now call questions of literary criticism: in place of the distinction between fancy and imagination he was preoccupied with the distinction between reason and understanding, of which imagination and fancy was a special instance. Writing to William Mudford early in 1818 (he was then 46), he said of his earliest lectures (1808): 'three fourths ... appeared at that time startling Paradoxes ... [and] have since been adopted even by men who at the time made use of them as proofs of my flighty and paradoxical turn of mind.' He goes on to speak of his distinction between judgment and genius, particularly as seen in Shakespeare, and says that he anticipated Schlegel in this view;[96] but there is no mention of the romantic-classical distinction, although that too had played its part in the lectures. How much his listeners were struck by the distinction, how much he – or they –

*   In the source, there is the word *of* after *part* in the opening sentence. See also *Philosophical Lectures*, ed. Kathleen Coburn (London, 1949), p. 442, n. 6.

singled it out as a daring new thought, is not clear; perhaps not much. Coleridge's influence was, then and later, largely subterranean and unacknowledged, even in matters of importance, so that we are unlikely to be able to trace his influence in this small but vexatious (and not uninteresting) detail. That Coleridge himself was aware of the historical development in which he himself had played no insignificant part is shown by a note written in 1820 or a little later.

The revived attention to our elder Poets, which Percy and Garrick had perhaps equal share in awakening, the revulsion against the French Taste which was so far successful as to confine the Usurper within the natural limits of the French Language; the re-establishment of the Romantic and Italian School in Germany and G. Britain by the genius of Wieland, Goethe, Tieck, Southey, Scott, and Byron among the poets, and the Lectures of Coleridge, Schlegel, Campbell and others among the Critics; these, at once aided and corrected by the increased ardor with which the study of ancient literature, and especially the Greek Poets and Dramatists, is pursued, esteemed and encouraged by the Gentry of the Country, and men of the highest rank and office, have given a spread and a fashion to predilections of higher hope and (what is still better) to principles of Preference at once more general and more just.*

In view of Coleridge's importance as an intelligent introducer and disseminator of German literature and thought in England, at a time when Englishmen knew little German and did not much like what little they knew, it is ironic that the very German distinction between romantic and classical, which he had repeatedly disclosed to the public in his lectures, should have been given currency and impetus by a French expositor of a triumphant German literary vogue when it was already passing its peak. Even then, the English

---

*   *Inquiring Spirit*, pp. 158–9, from British Museum MS Egerton 2800, fols. 54–5, watermark 1820. The reference to Campbell is puzzling, since in 1805 Coleridge regarded Campbell as one of the 'pseudo-poets ... [who] both by their writings & moral characters tend to bring poetry into disgrace' (*Coleridge, Notebooks* II: 2601) and he never altered that view. Between 1812 and 1818 Campbell gave and repeated lectures that some auditors thought superior to Coleridge's (see, e.g., *Robinson, Books* I: 88). After Murray had decided not to publish the lectures – he had published Campbell's *Specimens of the British Poets* with an 'Essay on British Poetry' in 1819 – Campbell printed them serially in his *New Monthly Magazine* 1820–6 (vol. I-XVII). Of the twelve lectures all but the introductory lecture and one on Hebrew poetry were on Greek poetry and Greek drama. What we know of Campbell's acquaintance with Schlegel and Mme de Staël does not encourage the view that he had anything interesting to say about romantic poetry or about the romantic-classical distinction. In the spring of 1813 he read some of his lectures of Mme de Staël – 'one of them [the introductory lecture] against her own doctrine of poetry. She battled hard with me; but was very good-natured and complimentary.'

were not instantly captivated. Coleridge, on the continental tour with Wordsworth in 1828, finally met A. W. Schlegel at a literary gathering in Bonn. They talked in English, and praised each other's work on that occasion; but afterwards Coleridge told Colley Grattan that Schlegel was a 'consummate coxcomb.' Coleridge may not have lived to see part IV of the *Transactions of the Royal Society of Literature*; if he did, he may not have rejoiced to find his own essay on the *Prometheus* of Aeschylus followed by a paper of Schlegel's.[97]

The early reviews of *De l'Allemagne* in England were favourable, copious, and respectful; but there was no landslide. The anonymous review of the French translation of Schlegel's *Vorlesungen* in the *Quarterly Review* for October 1814 drew attention to the German source of the romantic classical distinction.

The comparative merit of the ancients and moderns has long afforded abundant matter for dispute. Latterly, however, men of literary reputa- tion, particularly in Germany, have endeavoured to simplify the question. Without detracting from the excellence of their precursors, they were desirous of establishing the claims of their contemporaries upon a sure and solid foundation. This investigation led them to distinguish the productions of antiquity by the appellation of *classic*, those of modern times by that of *romantic*; a name intended to designate the popular idioms that have been formed by a mixture of the Latin tongue with the ancient dialects of Germany (p. 113.)

A footnote adds: 'Madame de Staël had made the British public familiar with these expressions'; but in the course of the 34-page review there is no further mention of the distinction. Hazlitt's review of John Black's translation of the *Vorlesungen*, in *Edinburgh Review* for February 1816, is more to the point. Here is found what must be the most coherent English review of the romantic-classical dis- tinction – unless Coleridge made a better fist of it in the lectures for which we have only fragmentary record.

The author ... proceeds to unfold that which is the *nucleus* of the prevailing system of German criticism, and the foundation of this whole work, namely, the essential distinction between the peculiar spirit of the modern or *romantic* style of art, and the antique or *classical*. There is in this part of the work a singular mixture of learning, acuteness and mysticism. We have certain profound suggestions and distant openings to the light; but, every now and then, we are suddenly left in the dark, and obliged to grope our way by ourselves. We cannot promise to find a clue out of the labyrinth; but we will at least attempt it. The most obvious distinction between the two styles, the classical and the romantic, is, that the one is conversant with objects that are grand and beautiful in themselves, or in consequence of obvious and universal associations; the other, with those that are interesting only by the force of circumstances and imagination. A Grecian temple, for instance, is a classical object: it is beautiful in itself, and excites immediate admiration. But the ruins of a Gothic castle have no beauty or symmetry to attract the eye; and yet they excite a more powerful and romantic interest from the ideas with which they are habitually associated. If, in addition to this, we are told that this is Macbeth's castle, the scene of the murder of Duncan, the interest will be instantly heightened to a sort of pleasing horror. The classical idea or form of any thing, it may also be observed, remains always the same, and suggests nearly the same impressions; but the associations of ideas belonging to the romantic character, may vary infinitely, and take in the whole range of nature and accident ... Even Lear is not classical: for he is a poor crazy old man, who has nothing sublime about him but his afflictions, and who dies of a broken heart ...

The great difference, then, which we find between the classical and the romantic style, between ancient and modern poetry, is, that the one more frequently describes things as they are interesting in themselves, – the other for the sake of the associations of ideas connected with them; that the one dwells more on the immediate impressions of objects of the senses – the other on the ideas which they suggest to the imagination. The one is poetry of form, the other of effect. The one gives only what is necessarily implied in the subject; the other all that can possibly arise out of it. The one seeks to identify the imitation with an external object, – clings to it, – is inseparable from it, – is either that or nothing; the other seeks to identify the original impression with whatever else, within the range of thought or feeling, can strengthen, relieve, adorn or elevate it. Hence the severity and simplicity of the Greek tragedy, which excluded every thing foreign or unnecessary to the subject ... Hence the perfection of their execution; which consisted in giving the utmost harmony, delicacy, and refinement to the details of a given subject. Now, the characteristic excellence of the moderns is the reverse of all this. As, according to our author, the poetry of the Greeks is the same as their sculpture; so, he says, our own more nearly resembles painting, – where the artist can relieve and throw back his figures at pleasure, – use a greater variety of contrasts, – and where light and shade, like the colours of fancy, are reflected on the different objects. The Muse of classical poetry should be represented as a beautiful naked figure: the Muse of modern poetry should be represented clothed, and with wings. The first has the advantage in point of form; the last in colour and motion ...[98]

The leading virtue of Christianity – self-denial and generosity – produced 'the spirit of chivalry, of romantic love, and honour.'

The mythology of the romantic poetry differed from the received religion: both differed essentially from the classical. The religion, or mythology of the Greeks, was nearly allied to their poetry: it was material and definite. The Pagan system reduced the Gods to the human form, and elevated the powers of inanimate nature of the same standard. Statues carved out of the finest marble, represented the objects of their religious worship in airy porticos, in solemn temples and consecrated groves ... All was subjected to the senses. The Christian religion, on the contrary, is essentially spiritual and abstract; it is 'the evidence of things unseen.' In the Heathen mythology, form is everywhere predominant; in the Christian, we find only unlimited, undefined power. The imagination alone 'broods over the immense abyss, and makes it pregnant.' There is, in the habitual belief of an universal, invisible Principle of all things, a vastness and obscurity which confounds our perceptions, while it exalts our piety. A mysterious awe surrounds the doctrines of the Christian faith: the Infinite is everywhere before us, whether we turn to reflect on what is revealed to us of the Divine nature or our own (pp. 70, 72–3, 74–5).

Whether Hazlitt hoped to be (anonymously) influential we cannot say. His faithful and painstaking account of Schlegel's distinction, however, is to a great extent negated by the 'unmeaning sneer' that opens his essay.

... we will explain at once what appears to us to be the weak side of German literature. In all that they do, it is evident that they are much more influenced by a desire of distinction than by any impulse of the imagination, or the consciousness of extraordinary qualifications. They write, not because they are full of a subject, but because they think it is a subject upon which, with due pains and labour, something striking may be written. So they read and meditate, – and having, at length, devised some strange and paradoxical view of the matter, they set about establishing it with all their might and main. The consequence is, that they have no shades of opinion, but are always straining at a grand systematic conclusion. They have done a great deal, no doubt, and in various departments; but their pretensions have always much exceeded their performance (p. 67).

Hazlitt's hostility towards the Germans was as ungracious and un-intelligent as his contemporaries' reflex assumption that all things

German were nurtured in what Coleridge called 'the holy jungle of transcendental metaphysics.' Hazlitt's critical authority in such matters is further diminished – in a butcherly review of the *Biographia Literaria*, a book now acknowledged as probably the most fertile book of critical theory and practice published in the century – when he says that the system of 'the great German oracle Kant' is 'the most wilful and monstrous absurdity that ever was invented.'[99]

De Quincey's evidence, although set down later, is earlier than, or at most contemporary with, Hazlitt's. In his autobiography (*Tait's Magazine*, 1833–41) he was reminiscing, and even though he noticed the romantic-classical distinction many times in his writing he speaks as though it were in the historic past and no longer a live issue. As an undergraduate and even before he could read German, he says in his autobiography, he had formed in his own mind, from his reading of Greek and Elizabethan tragedy, 'the elementary grounds of difference between the Pagan and Christian forms of poetry.' His distinction was between 'the Christian and the Antique'; but he found 'Schiller and Goethe applauding the better taste of the ancients' as against the Christians in certain points of symbolism, and was 'much surprised to hear Mr. Coleridge approving of the German sentiment.'

These speculations, at that time, I pursued earnestly; and I then believed myself, as I yet do, to have ascertained the two great and opposite laws under which the Grecian and the English tragedy has each separately developed itself. Whether wrong or right in that belief, sure I am that those in Germany who have treated the case of Classical and Romantic are not entitled to credit for any discovery at all. The Schlegels, who were the hollowest of men, the windiest and wordiest (at least, Frederick was so), pointed to the distinction; barely indicated it; and that was already some service done, because a presumption arose that the antique and the modern literatures, having clearly some essential differences, might, perhaps, rest on foundations originally distinct, and obey different laws. And hence it occurred that many disputes, as about the unities, etc., might originate in a confusion of these laws. This checks the presumption of the shallow criticism, and points to deeper investigations. Beyond this, neither the German nor the French disputers on the subject have talked to any profitable purpose.[100]

Unaffected, clearly, by the German arguments, De Quincey continued to reiterate his own view (which was in fact more derivative than he seems to have thought), sometimes making the conventional distinction between the picturesque and the statuesque (as Coleridge had) and in 1838 adding the refinement that 'life' was the mark of English drama and 'death' the mark of classical drama.[101]

So it seemed (at least to some knowledgeable persons) that the distinction established by Schlegel and others in Germany, and expounded by Coleridge, Madame de Staël, Bowles, and others in England, had soon gone underground again. On 14 October 1820 Byron wrote to Goethe:

I perceive that in Germany, as well as in Italy, there is a great struggle about what they call '*Classical*' and '*Romantic*' – terms which were not subjects of classification in England, at least when I left it four or five years ago [*i.e.*, 1816]. Some of the English Scribblers, it is true, abused Pope and Swift, but the reason was that they themselves did not know how to write either prose or verse; but nobody thought them worth making a sect of. Perhaps there may be something of the kind strung up lately, but I have not heard much about it, and it would be such bad taste that I shall be sorry to believe it.[102]

The following year, when Bowles had written strictures on Pope by discoursing on 'the Invariable Principles of Poetry,' Byron noticed that 'Schlegel and Madame de Staël had endeavoured ... to reduce poetry to *two* systems, classical and romantic – the effect is only beginning.'[103] In 1831, Thomas Carlyle said – a little ruefully – that 'we are troubled with no controversies on romanticism and classicism – the Bowles controversy having long since evaporated without results'; and Emerson in 1841 thought that 'The vaunted distinction between ... Classic and Romantic Schools, seems superficial and pedantic.'*

It is clear that Coleridge worked out for himself in his lectures before 1811 convincing arguments to support his view that Shakespeare was a conscious and gifted craftsman of clear judgment rather than a lucky *lusus naturae*; it is also clear that Coleridge became acquainted with Schlegel's *Vorlesungen* almost as soon as they were published, that he found Schlegel's position strongly consonant with his own, and that in subsequent lectures he used Schlegel to illuminate and support his own critical attitude to

---

*   *Essays in History*; quoted in *OED*. Wellek records a small scattering of other uses of *romantic* in England in the first half of the nineteenth century: Thomas Campbell in *Essay on Poetry* (1819) finds Schlegel's defence of Shakespeare's irregularities on 'romantic principles' 'too romantic for his conception'; Samuel Singer in the introduction to his edition of Marlowe's *Hero and Leander* (1821) writes that 'Musaeus is more classical, Hunt more romantic' (*Wellek, Concepts*, pp. 147, 149).

Shakespeare. For the distinction between antique and modern, classical and romantic, he seems not to have claimed priority – indeed it was a distinction that he showed little interest in. In criticism, as in politics, he was repelled by the half-truths of partisanship; his desire was not to carry a position or even to establish one, but rather to arrive at certain central recognitions about Shakespeare's art in particular and about poetry altogether. His habit of mind was comprehensive, not divisive; unitary, not categorical; his distinctions were intended to clarify the centre and direction of inquiry, to enlarge understanding, to strengthen the reflective and heuristic powers of the mind; in this 'method' a category is a means, not an end, and for him the end is always implicit in the means. His interest at the time of his literary lectures was in the nature of poetry and its status as a dynamic way of knowing that was potentially declarative of truth. In his lectures, his criticism was primarily concentrated upon Shakespeare, in the *Biographia Literaria* it was centred upon Wordsworth; his intention was not to make definitive declarations upon either (though he did in fact make some) but to make discoveries – and declarations – about the nature, function, and uses of poetry. His own experience of making poetry, particularly *The Ancient Mariner*, provided him with a centre of reference of a kind that few 'critics' have had direct access to, and it imparted a commanding impulse to his desire to explore the nature of poetry. In choosing Shakespeare as his centre of inquiry in the lectures he was no more sentimental than he was nepotistic in choosing Wordsworth as the centre for the *Biographia*: each in his own way provided him with inexhaustible evidence of the way poetry worked and of the demands that such poetry made on a reader.

Coleridge's lectures on Shakespeare made an impression when they were delivered, but the tradition, being oral, was evanescent. The lectures were not published until 1836, and then only as a fragmentary patchwork that gives us only part of what he intended to say and only part of what a few other people thought he had said. *Biographia Literaria* has not – until recent years – been an influential book, and despite the presence of some Schelling in it it does not overtly reinforce the Schlegelian position. Whatever Coleridge contributed to the general currency of Schlegel's notion of romanticism, the *Biographia* did not have the effect either of giving wider currency to *romantic* as a cult term (either of praise or abuse), nor did Coleridge apply it as a label for 'modern' poetry – neither Wordsworth's nor his own. His sense of the continuity of human thought and of imaginative endeavour was too compelling for him to see the history of literature as a simple oscillation of actions and reactions from one set of literary 'values' (or fashions) to another; he saw the history of literature – like the history of philosophy – as the variable self-discovery and self-affirmation of the human mind and psyche, as a declaration of the life of the human spirit irrespective of time and place. In so far as 'romantic' and 'classic' represented two 'positions' for poetry, he saw them not as critical categories or orders of literary accomplishment, but as poles of imaginative activity. What he found 'romantic' in Shakespeare was his proliferating variety and his mixed forms, his breadth of human apprehension, his power of securing unity in multeity. Coleridge knew the Greek language too well, and the monuments of Greek literature, ever to call eighteenth century poetry 'classical'; and he revered the power of intellect, judgment, and discrimination far too highly ever to suppose that the dream-world of 'romance' represented more than a part – though an essential part – in the total imaginative activity of the human mind. He might well feel aggrieved that his name had found no place in Tieck's history of Shakespeare criticism: he had said things that were radical in his own time, and what he had said was by no means always identical with what the proponents of 'romanticism' were saying. In evolving his position, the concept 'romantic' served some purposes, but it is only one among many factors that brought him to his view of Shakespeare, of dramatic art, and of poetry altogether.

'THE ROMANTIC POETS'

How the five major English poets of the early nineteenth century came to be called the 'Romantic Poets' is not easy to trace; the title is a late invention. Any attempt there might have been in the first thirty years of the century to arrive at an accurate general specification for five poets so markedly individual and distinct was frustrated by the critics' persistent concentration upon the doctrine of the Preface to *Lyrical Ballads* and their treating it primarily as a political issue. This, in the public mind, threw Coleridge into uneasy identification with Wordsworth, and isolated Wordsworth and Coleridge (in the critical view) as much from Scott, Campbell, Moore, and Southey as from Byron, Shelley, and Keats. In a climate of political tumult, national danger, and social suspicion springing out of the French Revolution, it was perhaps inevitable that a revolution – even one as detachedly poetic as Wordsworth's – should be associated with other kinds of revolution. Coleridge and

Southey had been labelled Jacobins in the late nineties, and the names of 'L[loy]d, and L[am]be and Co' had been linked with theirs in the *Anti-Jacobin*; but the label could not be made to stick. Wordsworth was even more elusive.

That Wordsworth and Coleridge had actually instituted a revolution in poetry with the publication of *Lyrical Ballads* was not openly acknowledged by the critics until long after the forces were engaged and the revolutionaries apparently discredited. In October 1817 John Wilson ('Christopher North'), trying to repair the damage done to Wordsworth by Francis Jeffrey, wrote in *Blackwood's*: 'Mr Wordsworth is a man of too much original power not to have very often written ill; and it is incredible that, 'mid all his gigantic efforts to establish a system (even allowing that system to be a right one), he has never violated the principles of taste or reason. He has brought about a *revolution* in Poetry; and a revolution can no more be brought about in Poetry than in the Constitution, without the destruction or injury of many excellent and time-hallowed establishments. I have no doubt that ... Posterity will hail him as a regenerator and a creator.'[104]

Four years later, the brilliant young barrister Henry Nelson Coleridge wrote: 'That to Coleridge and Wordsworth the poetry, the philosophy, and the criticism of the present day does actually owe its peculiar character, and its distinguishing excellence over that of the last century, those who would trace the origin of the present opinions back for thirty years would find no difficulty in believing.'[105] But for the twenty years after the first publication of the Preface in 1800, the policies of the great new quarterlies encouraged critics to think according to a political analogy, even in the literary field, and to cast each individual writer as a member of some party or 'school' which in turn was to be seen as in conflict with other parties or schools in the prevailing social ferment precipitated by the American and French revolutions.* If there was ever any justice in seeing the work of the five great English poets as the triumph of 'romanticism' in England, and on that account any reason for attaching the epithet 'romantic' indifferently to all of them as though they were of one 'school' or party, that was not what

---

* *Blackwood's* notice of Hazlitt's seventh lecture On English Poetry, April 1818, reported that 'Mr Hazlitt here entered at some length into the origin of what has been called the *Lake School of Poetry*, and endeavoured to trace it to the events of the French Revolution.' See *An Estimate of William Wordsworth by his Contemporaries 1793–1822*, ed. Elsie Smith (Oxford, 1932), p. 257 (hereafter cited as *E. Smith*).

their contemporaries (literary or political) wished to see or acknowledge. If their world could be seen as 'romantic,' it would be revolutionary; and revolution was a topical threat not to be encouraged. The critics – absent-mindedly perhaps, but no less positively – tried to disarm the revolution by saying that it was uncivilized and silly, dissenting rather than revolutionary. The reviewers, with tedious insistence, singled out the 'mawkish affectations of childish simplicity and nursery stammering,'[106] and chose that one characteristic as butt for merriment, lampoon, parody, amused contempt, patronizing sarcasm, and even vicious personal attack. In this there was no conspiracy; it was a sign of the times. Since neither Wordsworth nor Coleridge was partisan enough to be open to direct political attack, the violence and extent of the reaction to their work shows how mercilessly they had blown cold air on the exposed nerves of the *Zeitgeist*.

Wordsworth had indeed trailed his coat; and Coleridge, whether he wanted to or not, could not escape from the bond of their first collaboration. The very title *Lyrical Ballads* was itself a paradox if not an open scandal (if lyrical, not ballads; if ballads, not lyrical – that would be the contemporary assumption); and it was difficult not to see the Preface as anything but a deliberate outrage. For better or worse, the Preface announced itself as 'a systematic defence of the theory upon which the poems were written' – the poems, that is, that were written experimentally 'to ascertain, how far, by fitting to metrical arrangement a selection of the real language of men in a state of vivid sensation, that sort of pleasure and that quantity of pleasure may be imparted, which a Poet may rationally endeavour to impart.' This involved an attack not only on the 'inane phraseology' inherited from an inert neoclassicism, but also on the sentimental-romantic-Gothic writing that had recently seized upon public taste – 'frantic novels, sickly and stupid German Tragedies, and deluges of idle and extravagant stories in verse.' In choosing 'incidents and situations from common life' – from 'humble and rustic life' – and claiming that 'in that condition, the essential passions of the heart find a better soil in which they can attain their maturity,' he was not only reviving the debate between town and country, urban and rural, cultivated and naïve; he was also talking darkly in the language of the French revolution. By insisting that he would write about a real 'country' populated with real people, he would join 'the company of flesh and blood,' turning his back on those stylized landscapes-with-figures which Thomson and even

Goldsmith saw through the Lorraine-glass of an urbane and condescending sophistication. Without political or parabolic intent, Wordsworth might seem to threaten his readers with glimpses of the world as it existed – a world of grotesque human suffering and injustice, of brutal penal laws, and a corrupt governmental system, a world in which slavery was not a romantic theme but a squalid and lucrative reality. Even if these issues never came to the surface either in his poems or in the reviews of them, the poems that were not identifiably lyrical ballads were strange and perplexing, demanding more than usual critical steadiness. 'In all perplexity,' Coleridge noted in *Biographia Literaria*, 'there is a portion of fear, which predisposes the mind to anger.'[107] It is well known that anger, whatever its source, does not clear a critic's perception. Well might the *Blackwood's* reviewer of *The River Duddon* in May 1820 say, 'The age has unquestionably produced a noble band of British Poets ... Scott, Byron, Wordsworth, Southey, and Coleridge ... Yet, when a man asks of himself, what has really been said ... concerning any one of these poets – how lamentably must we feel the worthlessness of all the criticism of the most critical age the world produced.'[108]

In the *Biographia Literaria* (1817) Coleridge tried to set the record straight and to establish the possibility of just and philosophical criticism; he rehearsed the history of the origins of *Lyrical Ballads*, examined 'Mr Wordsworth's doctrine' with a sensitive justice that his own circumstances could scarcely account for, attacked 'the present mode of conducting critical journals,' and confronted the critics with some genuine criticism; and he crowned the work, which had Wordsworth as its starting-point, provocation, and theme, with a long chapter (ch. 22) which must stand as one of the glories of English literary criticism. This performance of Coleridge's was unpardonable as well a perplexing. When Jeffrey had opened his review of *The Excursion* in 1814 with the words 'This will never do!' he had referred to much beyond *The Excursion* and had spoken for more than himself.

The critics could not stem the slowly rising tide of public approval for Wordsworth's poems. After the slow reception of the 1815 collection, another followed in 1820, the first American edition in 1824, and thereafter collective editions appeared at regular intervals steadily accumulating the canon. From 1820 onwards the reviewers spoke of him more often with respect. After 1822, except for *Yarrow Revisited* (1835), he published no other substantial single work; *The Prelude* had to wait for his death in 1850. There seems to be a note of relief or exhaustion in the *Edinburgh Review* notice of *Memorials of a Tour* in November 1822: the battle was over and the sting of the outrage of *Lyrical Ballads* had been drawn.

The Lake School of Poetry, we think, is now pretty nearly extinct. Coleridge, who had by far the most original genius among its founders, has long ceased to labour for the fraternity, and gave their reputation a most unkind cut at parting, by the publication of *Christabel* [in 1816], which they had all been lauding, while it remained unprinted, as the crowning glory of their sect. The laurel seems to have proved mortal to the vivacious Muse of Southey – and the flame of his aspirations, after waxing woefully dim in various songs of triumph and loyalty, at last fairly went out in his hexameter *Vision of Judgment*. The contact of the Stamp-office appears to have had nearly as bad an effect on Mr. Wordsworth. His *Peter Bell* and his *Waggoner* put his admirers, we believe, a little to their shifts; but since he has openly taken to the office of a publican, and exchanged the company of leech-gatherers for that of tax-gatherers, he has fallen into a way of writing which is equally distasteful to his old friends and his old monitors – a sort of prosy, solemn, obscure, feeble kind of mouthing ...*

As long as Wordsworth and Coleridge could be held as the central figures for attack, the younger poets – although profoundly influenced by their two great predecessors – were not included much in the general assault. Keats, for example, was much more fairly reviewed than either Wordsworth or Coleridge; the one or two allegedly murderous reviews were precisely those that made him, through his acquaintance with Leigh Hunt, a political target. Once 'the Lake school' seemed to be extinct, even Coleridge drifted out into the clear. His collective editions of 1828, 1829, and 1834 (the year of his death) drew some perceptive reviews; and even *Sibylline Leaves* had an outstandingly favourable review in the *Edinburgh*. It was around Coleridge's name – not Wordsworth's – that the word 'romantic' begins tentatively to crystallize, particularly in two reviews by his nephew Henry Nelson Coleridge. And in July 1833 William Maginn referred to Coleridge as 'the founder of the romantic school of poetry.'[109]

How Wordsworth, Coleridge, and Southey came to be called 'the Lake School' or 'the Lake Poets,' and how – singly and as a group – they eluded critical definition in a single qualitative name, is

* E. *Smith*, pp. 352–3. Cf. Coleridge's *Table Talk* (23 October 1833): 'he [Wordsworth] has won the battle now, ay! and will wear the crown, whilst English is English.' Cf. also *Blackwood's*, May 1855: 'the name of Wordsworth has become a household word on the banks of the Mississippi and the Ganges ... Now Wordsworth is studied all Scotland over.'

virtually a special study; but it can be briefly outlined. As early as October 1800 Coleridge was noticed as the founder of 'a distinct school in poetry,'[110] but that was a 'school' identified with Coleridge's two early volumes of poems and with the pantisocratic name of Southey (and marginally with Lamb, Lloyd, and Lovell), and guyed by the *Anti-Jacobin* since 1797.* Francis Jeffrey, reviewing Southey's *Thalaba* in October 1802, gives what must be one of the earliest extended general accounts of the 'new school of poetry,' later to be called 'the Lake school' (although Lamb's name is still connected here with Coleridge's).

The author who is now before us [*i.e.*, Southey], belongs to a *sect* of poets, that has established itself in this country within these ten or twelve years, and is looked upon, we believe, as one of its chief champions and apostles. The peculiar doctrines of this sect, it would not, perhaps, be very easy to explain; but, that they are *dissenters* from the established systems in poetry and criticism, is admitted, and proved indeed, by the whole tenor of their compositions. Though they lay claim, we believe, to a creed and a revelation of their own, there can be little doubt, that their doctrines are of *German* origin, and have been derived from some of the great modern reformers in that country. Some of their leading principles, indeed, are probably of an earlier date, and seem to have been borrowed from the great apostle of Geneva ...

The disciples of this school boast much of its originality, and seem to value themselves very highly, for having broken loose from the bondage of ancient authority, and reasserted the independence of genius ... The productions of this school, we conceive, are so far from being entitled to the praise of originality, that they cannot be better characterized, than by an enumeration of the sources from which their materials have been

---

*   The 'Jacobin Art of Poetry' is outlined in the number for 20 November 1797, and afterwards the products of the 'school' were repeatedly parodied, often very wittily: see *The Poetry of the Anti-Jacobin* (1799). Both Coleridge and Southey were charged with silliness as well as Jacobinism. Lamb, Lloyd, and Lovell were taken for members of the school because they had published in Coleridge's *Poems* of 1797; all were Pantisocrats. Southey was seriously embarrassed by the unauthorized publication of his youthful *Wat Tyler* in 1817. In August 1803 Coleridge told the Beaumonts: 'I do seriously believe, that the chief cause of Wordsworth's & Southey's having been classed with me, as a *School*, originates entirely in our not hating or envying each other / it is so unusual, that three professional Poets, in every respect unlike each other, should nevertheless take pleasure in each other's welfare – & reputation' (*Coleridge, Letters* II: 965). In 1808 he wrote more bitterly: 'Of me and of my scanty juvenile writings people know nothing; but it has been discovered, that I had the destiny of marrying the Sister of Mrs Southey, that I am intimate with Mr Southey, & that I am in a more special manner the Friend and Admirer of Mr Wordsworth ...' – but the MS ends so (ibid., III: 84).

derived. The greater part of them, we apprehend, will be found to be composed of the following elements: 1/The antisocial principles, and distempered sensibility of Rousseau – his discontent with the present constitution of society – his paradoxical morality, and his perpetual hankerings after some unattainable state of voluptuous virtue and perfection. 2/The simplicity and energy (*horresco referens*) of Kotzebue and Schiller. 3/The homeliness and harshness of some of Cowper's language and versification, interchanged occasionally with the *innocence* of Ambrose Philips, or the quaintness of Quarles and Dr Donne. From the diligent study of these few originals, we have no doubt that an entire art of poetry may be collected, by the assistance of which, the very *gentlest* of our readers may soon be qualified to compose a poem as correctly versified as Thalaba, and to deal out sentiment and description, with all the sweetness of Lambe, and all the magnificence of Coleridge (pp. 63–4).

Jeffrey is taking the strong neo-classical line here: he objects to most of the features in *Thalaba* that later historians of literature would single out as signs of literary 'romanticism,' and he accuses the new 'school' of breaking with 'antient authority' and of deriving their doctrines from German models. While he notes with strong disapproval Southey's deviation from the neo-classical norms, he does not put a name to what Southey is doing – the romantic-classical distinction has not yet reached him; and he declares that strong English prejudice (which Hazlitt held in extreme form) against things German, representing them as obscure, 'metaphysical,' or gratuitously terrible.*

*   Jeffrey, however, in March 1799 had expressed his admiration for *The Ancient Mariner* and understood that it was by Coleridge (*Jackson*, p. 60). Jeffrey joined in forming the *Edinburgh Review* in 1802 (first issue, October 1802), and was editor 1803–29. Southey – who had described *The Ancient Mariner* as 'a Dutch attempt at German sublimity' – had had only intermittent poetical association with Coleridge to this date, and virtually none with Wordsworth. Jeffrey's adverse review of *Thalaba* enhanced Southey's hitherto obscure reputation as a poet by joining his name with Wordsworth and Coleridge. Even after establishing at Keswick in 1803, it was fifteen years or more before Southey felt anything but uneasy in Wordsworth's company. For Wordsworth's contemptuous reaction to Jeffrey's identification of a new 'school' in this review, see *The Letters of William and Dorothy Wordsworth: The Early Years*, ed. E. de Selincourt (2nd ed., rev. C. L. Shaver, Oxford, 1967), pp. 433–4.
    In 1808 Mrs. Piozzi thought, like Jeffrey in 1802, that the poetry of Scott and Southey would be a flash in the pan. 'The fashionable poetry of Southey and Scott will fall into decay – it will never be classical. It leaves too little behind it. Handel and Milton must be for ever felt; Bach's Lessons and Pope's Moral Essays must be for ever *recollected*; Madoc and Thalaba, Teviot Dale and Marmion depend too much on their *colouring*. In a hundred years people will wonder why they were so much admired' (*Thraliana*, ed. K. C. Balderston, 1942, p. 1096).

In October 1807, in a review of Wordsworth's *Poems in Two Volumes*, the 'new school' is associated with the Lake District: 'The author is known to belong to a certain brotherhood of poets, who have haunted for some years about the Lakes of Cumberland.'[111] After a few tentative variants, the phrase 'Lake poets' seems first to have been used in a review of John Wilson's *The Isle of Palms* in February 1812;* and in 1814 John Taylor Coleridge, writing in the *Quarterly Review*, mentions 'a colloquial title, the Lake Poets.'† The identity of the 'Westmoreland triumvirate of Bards' had long been established – Wordsworth, Coleridge, and Southey.‡

*   *Edinburgh Review* (February 1812): *E. Smith*, p. 127; and cf. p. 191 (1815). The review declares Wilson 'a new recruit to the company of Lake Poets' because 'he wears openly the badge of their peculiarities, and professes the most humble devotion to their great captain, Mr. Wordsworth.' *The Isle of Palms* has indeed a strong Wordsworthian tone. In March 1808, when Wilson was building his house Elleray on Windermere, Dorothy described him as 'a very amiable young man, a Friend and *adorer* of William and his verses' (*Wordsworth, Letters: Middle Years*, 2nd ed., 1: 206).

†   *Quarterly Review* (April 1814): *Jackson*, p. 175, and cf. p. 178. Thereafter, scornful references to 'the Lake Poets' under various styles are too numerous to record. For 'Bards of the Lake(s),' see ibid., p. 30 '1809), p. 390 (1817); for 'scribblers of the Lake School,' see ibid., p. 377 (1819), p. 393 (1817). Jeffrey could not resist the metaphorical temptations of the name 'Laker' and wondered whether Wordsworth 'has dashed his Hippocrene with too large an infusion of lake water' (1815: *Wain*, p. 60); the *Monthly Review* in January 1819 linked the Lake Poets with the absurd simplicity of John Taylor (1580–1653) by calling them 'Water-Poets' (*Jackson*, p. 399); in 1820 we read of 'Lakish ditties' (*E. Smith*, p. 319); and it is said of Wordsworth in the *River Duddon* sonnets that 'Here and there, a little metaphysical mud, a Lakish tincture, mingles with the stream, and it occasionally runs somewhat shallow' (*E. Smith*, p. 325).

‡   *Eclectic Review*, July 1809: *E. Smith*, p. 115. By then the local title was, for the time being, accurate. Wordsworth, born in the Lakes, had lived in Grasmere since the turn of the century and was to live in the Lakes for the rest of his life. Coleridge lived in Greta Hall, Keswick, from 1800 until at the end of 1803 he set out for the Mediterranean; after his return he separated from his wife, but took up residence with the Wordsworths in Grasmere from September 1808 until in May 1810 he moved back to Greta Hall for five months. Southey, a West-countryman, came to Greta Hall in September 1803 not intending to stay but lived there for the rest of his life, incidentally taking charge of the Coleridge family in Coleridge's absence. For about two years all three were in the Lakes; and it happened that Francis Jeffrey's one visit to Coleridge was to Greta Hall in autumn 1810 where he also met Southey. Coleridge accused Jeffrey later of breach of hospitality in writing about 'the School of whining and hypochondriacal poets that haunt the Lakes' (see *Biographia Literaria* 1: 36–7n; and for Jeffrey's stiff rejoinder, attached to Hazlitt's savage review of the *Biographia*, see *Jackson*, pp. 314–18n). The poems in *Lyrical Ballads* (1798) were composed in the West Country; the Preface and Wordsworth's new poems in the 1800 edition were composed in the Lakes. Southey was estranged from Coleridge during the *annus mirabilis*. H. N. Coleridge was correct in his later comment: 'the Lake School – as two or three poets, essentially unlike to each other, were foolishly called –' (*Jackson*, p. 629). On 18 June 1847 Crabb Robinson said: 'Coleridge and Wordsworth ought never to have been coupled in a class as Lake-poets.

The task of finding an appropriate designation for the distinctive style and quality of three writers as 'essentially unlike to each other' as these was too much for the critics. They settled for a local label and proceeded to spin around it selective descriptions that purported to be comprehensive. When Jeffrey reviewed George Crabbe's *Poems* in the *Edinburgh Review* of April 1808, he made a luxurious digression to attack 'The gentlemen of the new school' – in contrast to Crabbe – because they 'invent for themselves certain whimsical and unheard of beings, to whom they impute some fantastical combination of feelings, and then labour to excite our sympathy for them, either by placing them in incredible situations, or by some strained and exaggerated moralisation of a vague and tragical description.' Wordsworth, he says, 'represents his grey-haired rustic pedagogue [Matthew] as a sort of half crazy, sentimental person, overrun with fine feelings, constitutional merriment, and a most humorous melancholy'; but even in so promising a context Jeffrey does not use the word *romantic*. Again, in January 1809 the *Edinburgh Review* used Burns as pretext to say that 'These gentlemen [of "the new school of poetry"] are outrageous for simplicity.'[112]

In November 1814 Wordsworth's *Excursion* fell into Jeffrey's hands. 'This will never do!' he cried indignantly. 'It bears no doubt the stamp of the author's heart and fancy: but unfortunately not half so visible as that of his peculiar system ... We have imitations of Cowper, and even of Milton here; engrafted on the natural drawl of the Lakers – and all diluted into harmony by that profuse and irrepressible wordiness which deluges all the blank verse of this school of poetry ...' Next year Jeffrey found that *The White Doe of Rylstone* consisted of 'a happy union of all the faults, without any of the beauties, which belong to his school of poetry. It is just such a work, in short, as some wicked enemy of that school might be supposed to have devised, on purpose to make it ridiculous.'[113]

In Thomas Moore's review of the *Christabel* volume in 1816 – contemptuous in spite of Byron's urgent request that Moore give Coleridge some encouragement – Coleridge is identified with 'the Lake School.'[114] An anonymous contributor to *Blackwood's* in October 1817 published, as the first of a series 'On the Cockney School of Poetry,' a scurrilous attack on Leigh Hunt. After Hunt, John Keats was to be the next victim. The opening words run: 'While the whole critical world is occupied with balancing the merits,

They are great poets of a very distinct & even opposite character. Southey is a poet far below them both. Lamb had more genius than Southey' (MS letter in Dr. Williams's Library.)

whether in theory or in execution, of what is commonly called *The Lake School*, it is strange that no one seems to think it at all necessary to say a single word about another new school of poetry which has of late sprung up among us ... *The Cockney School*.' [115]

In the same number of *Blackwood's*, John Wilson, in a scathing condemnation of *Biographia Literaria*, recognized that Wordsworth had 'brought about a *revolution* in Poetry.'[116] And in the following year, coming to Wordsworth's defence in the first of a series of 'Essays on the Lake School of Poetry,' he claimed that 'scarcely one syllable of truth – that is, of knowledge – has ever appeared in the *Edinburgh Review* on the general principles of Wordsworth's poetry, or, as it has been somewhat vaguely, and not very philosophically, called, the Lake School of Poetry.'[117] As for the poetical revolution, Byron, who had anointed with vitriolic contempt the names of Wordsworth, Coleridge, and Southey (as well as many others) in *English Bards and Scotch Reviewers* (1809) and yet was deeply influenced by both Wordsworth and Coleridge, was not certain about his own place in the revolution. In 1817 he wrote to John Murray:

I am convinced, the more I think of it, that ... *all of* us – Scott, Southey, Wordsworth, Moore, Campbell, I – are ... in the wrong, one as much as another: that we are upon a wrong revolutionary poetical system, or systems, not worth a damn in itself, and from which none but Rogers and Crabbe are free; and that the present and next generations will finally be of this opinion. I am the more convinced in this by having lately gone over some of our classics, particularly Pope ... I took Moore's poems and my own and some others, and went over them side by side with Pope's, and I was really astonished ... and mortified at the ineffable distance in point of sense, harmony, effect, and even, *Imagination*, passion and *Invention*, between the little Queen Anne's man, and us of the lower Empire. Depend upon it, it is all Horace then, and Claudian now ... and if I had to begin again, I would model myself accordingly.*

---

*   *Byron, Works: Letters* IV: 169 (15 September 1817); cf. p. 489. On Claudian, see Coleridge, *Table Talk*, 18 August 1833. Byron does not refer to 'the Lakers' until his opening cannonade on Southey in *Don Juan* (1819). Jeffrey had written of Byron in December 1816:' ... in his general notion of the end and the means of poetry, we have sometimes thought that his views fell more in with those of the Lake poets, than of any other existing party in the poetical commonwealth: and, in some of his later productions, especially, it is impossible not to be struck with his occasional approaches to the style and manner of this class of writers' (*Wain*, p. 143). Wilson replied: 'If Byron be altogether unlike Scott, Wordsworth is yet more unlike Byron' (ibid., p. 127). Byron's hierarchy of poets, drawn up in November 1813, had Scott at the top, then Samuel Rogers, then Moore and Campbell, then Southey, Wordsworth, and Coleridge, and below them 'the many'.

That there was a revolution in progress – whenever and wherever it started – Byron did not doubt. The hostile and scathing notices of 'the Lake Poets' all in their various way adopted or assumed a 'classical' position; but the obvious consequence does not follow – they do not use the word *romantic* as term of identification, praise, or contempt. Byron did not name a leader of the Revolution, but others did not hesitate to name the leader – Wordsworth. This had serious consequences.

When *Lyrical Ballads* was first published anonymously in 1798, Coleridge had a wider reputation than Wordsworth and was thought to offer greater poetic promise. Rumour in literary circles quickly established the identity of the two authors, and correctly assigned *The Ancient Mariner* to Coleridge. In the second edition (1800) Wordsworth's name appeared alone on the title page, the proportion of his poems was greatly increased by the addition of a second volume, and the emphasis on Coleridge's poems was reduced by moving *The Ancient Mariner* from the place of honour at the beginning to the end of Volume I (where 'Tintern Abbey' had originally been). Wordsworth identified Coleridge's poems in the Preface, but he did not give Coleridge's name. The note made it clear that the book was really Wordsworth's and that Coleridge had been invited to 'assist' because Wordsworth 'believed that the poems of my Friend would in a great measure have the same tendency as my own, and that, though there would be found a difference, there would be found no discordance in the colours of our style; as our opinions on the subject of poetry do almost entirely coincide.'[118] Although Coleridge had made a brilliant revision of *The Ancient Mariner* for the 1800 edition, Wordsworth drafted a long and ungracious section of the Preface pointing out 'the defects of the poem'; Lamb seems to have been responsible for persuading Wordsworth not to print these comments. Wordsworth felt that *The Ancient Mariner* had damaged the sales of *Lyrical Ballads* and at first intended to omit it from the second edition – 'I shall probably add some others in Lieu.'[119] Also, Part I of *Christabel* was actually set in type for this edition and Coleridge was hard at work on the completion when Wordsworth peremptorily cancelled the proofs and rejected the poem.[120] *Lyrical Ballads* was not really a two-handed engine.

From 1800 to 1814 Wordsworth's publication was persistent rather than prolific; during those years Coleridge's reputation as a poet-of-promise suffered as the silence stretched out from the perfunctory edition of his poems in 1803. There were reports – and later, imitations and parodies – of a marvellous poem in manuscript called *Christabel*; but reviewers felt entitled to express their disapproval of his 'strange and unworthy indolence.' When the *Christabel* volume came out in 1816, the critics were outraged at 'one of the most notable pieces of impertinence of which the press had lately been guilty' (Moore) – even though, or because, it was known to have been published with Byron's encouragement. What Wordsworth had said publicly in 1800 about the coincidence of 'our opinions on the subject of poetry' was at that time endorsed in private by Coleridge: 'The Preface contains our joint opinions on Poetry'; but less than two years later Coleridge had told Southey that 'altho'' Wordsworth's Preface is half a child of my own Brain ... I rather suspect that some where or other there is a radical Difference in our theoretical opinions respecting Poetry.'[121] Coleridge had been increasingly irritated at the way his name was linked with Wordsworth's and with 'Mr. Wordsworth's theory.' But he had no way of stating his own position and of unravelling the subtle difference until the *Biographia* (written mostly in 1815) was published in 1817. By then it was much too late to reverse a convenient and reiterated half-truth.

In the critics' minds Wordsworth was the 'leader' and 'most prominent ornament' of the 'school,' and Coleridge 'the inner priest of the temple.'[122] Critics who saw Coleridge as of the same 'school' as Wordsworth, and mocked him (as they did Wordsworth) for the 'babbling imbecility' induced by the principles of the Preface, were obliged to overlook the important difference between Wordsworth's lyrical ballads and *The Ancient Mariner*, and paid little or no systematic attention to the searching critical questions raised by the 'Conversation poems' and 'Tintern Abbey,' the Immortality Ode and the Dejection Ode, 'The Solitary Reaper,' the Lucy poems, and *Kubla Khan* – questions that could not be much illuminated by concentrating on the Preface. Certainly the chances of accurately defining the 'revolution in poetry' were not enhanced by this crucial oversight.

The title 'Lake Poets,' however, provided a centre around which certain stylistic generalizations could cluster – some of them just and perceptive – and to which the work of other poets could be referred. But as long as Wordsworth was seen as the 'leader of the school' his powerful individuality defied accurate critical definition and at the same time interfered with the construction of a broader basis for generalization. There had been a 'revolution' certainly; it was one revolution, not several; an appropriate name was needed, and none came to hand. Why 'romantic' was not chosen can be seen in two remarks made in 1817 and 1818. Hazlitt, in his savage review of the *Biographia* in August 1817 says that Coleridge had acknowledged that there were 'silly and puerile passages' in *Lyrical Ballads*, and he adds that they were 'equally unworthy of the poet's [Wordsworth's] genius and *classical* taste.'[123] Then in 1818 in the fourth of the essays on 'The Cockney School of Poetry,' the anonymous author abuses Keats for putting together the names of 'Wordsworth and Hunt! What a juxta-position! The purest, the loftiest, and, we do not fear to say, the most *classical* of living English poets, joined together in the same compliment with the meanest, the filthiest, and the most vulgar of Cockney poetasters.'* If classical, how conceivably – since Coleridge's lectures and Mme de Staël's invasion of England – *romantic*?

Had those critics who admired 'Tintern Abbey' and the Immortality Ode decided to write off the 'childish simplicity' as a venial aberration, and call Wordsworth a 'classical' poet? Even that manoeuvre was not easy. Wordsworth was a strong child of the eighteenth century; Charles James Fox, 'master of all the best of the ancient and modern poets,' who took Vergil and Pope as his favourites, particularly admired 'Goody Blake and Harry Gill.' Perhaps in

---

*   *Blackwood's* (August 1818): *Wain*, p. 190; my italics. Cf. *Quarterly Review* (December 1841): 'But what some persons would consider the poetic or romantic view of things never shuts out from Mr. Wordsworth's mind the contemplation of the whole truth.' The *Eclectic Review*, November 1842, however, quotes with approval an unidentified critique: 'to him [Wordsworth] the high reputation is due, of having been the first of the poets of this century to emancipate himself from the bondage of the classical school.'

   Hazlitt, reviewing *Marino Faliero* in the *London Magazine*, May 1814, found Byron 'romantic,' using the term as the adjective of 'romance' but also with the pejorative overtone of 'non-classical': 'The characters and situations there [in *Manfred*] were of a romantic and poetical cast, mere creatures of the imagination; and the sentiments such as the author might easily conjure up by fancying himself on enchanted ground ... Lord Byron can gaze with swimming eyes upon any of the great lights of Italy, and view them through the misty, widespread glory of lengthening centuries: that is, he can take a high and romantic interest in them, as they appear to us and to him; but he cannot take an historical event ...' (*Hazlitt, Works* XIX: 44). Others, however, could see Byron as 'classical.' The *Edinburgh Review* on *Childe Harold* IV, in June 1818 (p. 99) noticed that 'certain regions of Europe of late years have induced a sort of romantic pleasure,' and adds: 'This fanciful and romantic feeling was common to those who went to see those countries, and to those who remained at home to hear the narration of the adventurers.' This effect was not brought about by Byron's *Childe Harold*, the reviewer continues, 'but was there already in great force and activity.' Yet 'we think the genius of Byron is, more than any other modern poet, akin to that peculiar genius, which seems to have been diffused among all powers and artists of ancient Greece ... singleness, simplicity, and unity' (p. 103); and the *Quarterly Review* of April 1818 (p. 230) notices that the 'general structure [of *Childe Harold*] is bold, severe, and as it were Doric, admitting few ornaments ...'

time the 'simplicity' might be ignored, but then *The Excursion* (1841) administered another bitter drench: this was not 'simple' surely – it was (the critics said) 'metaphysical,' or a 'fantastical oddity,' 'not always so intelligible as ... might fairly be expected.'[124] Then, as *The White Doe of Rylstone* (1815) and *Peter Bell* and *The Waggoner* (both 1819) followed, attention was drawn again to the alleged silliness and puerility. The reaction was a trigger-response; for, as Coleridge said, 'In the critical remarks ... prefixed and annexed to the "Lyrical Ballads," I believe that we may safely rest, as the true origin of the unexampled opposition which Mr. Wordsworth's writings have been since doomed to encounter.'[125]

The reaction could be very violent. Coleridge's poem 'To a Gentleman, composed on the night after his recitation of a poem on the growth of an individual mind' was first published in *Sibylline Leaves* (1817); a reviewer concluded correctly that the 'Gentleman' was Wordsworth and assumed that the poem – which happened to be *The Prelude* – was 'some nonsensical piece of mysticism, spouted forth by that solemn but flimsy author.'[126] In 1819 a review of *The Waggoner* says, less contemptuously: 'Shakespeare had exquisite taste. Milton's taste was still more refined. But Mr. Wordsworth's system pours contempt on all those finer rules which his predecessors have worked by: he is for bringing in a Gothic horde of potters and pedlars and waggoners upon the classic regions of poetry: he has attempted to set up a new reign of taste, and he has sacrificed his genius in the adventure.'[127]

In 1820, an essay in the *New Monthly Magazine* on 'Lake School of Poetry. – Mr. Wordsworth' repeated the Gothic theme with perhaps greater accuracy than the writer knew.

Unless the true and general maxim 'the proper study of mankind is man' be *now* disputed, and must *now* be superseded, we cannot approve of that part of the system of the Lake Minstrels, that neglects rational exalted man, [to] lavish his powers upon naturals, idiots, and madmen – that transfers poetical agency from rational to irrational creatures, from animated to inanimate nature ... It seems to be a kind of poetical materialism too, to subject mind to matter, to bind down the imperishable spirit in the trammels of perishable objects, which is a system uniformly preserved in the entire range of the Lake poesy ... The Lakers seem to have ridiculed the purity, simplicity, and philosophy of their admired models – Cowper and Akenside, by German exaggeration. For the same morbid sensibility manifested in the creation of character and sentiment and action in the one class of writers, is transferred to the feelings derived from the visible creation, by the other. So that the Lake poetry is a sort of mongrel minstrelsy, made up of English truth and simplicity, and German exaggeration and eccentricity; of English meaning and German mystery, so blended, that it takes the air of something *novel*, sometimes beautiful, sometimes ridiculous, and always so in exact proportion to the predominant likeness it bears to one or the other of the ill-mated partners of its parentage.

As the writer continues, he ascribes to Wordsworth a mind 'meditative, mild, and philosophical, and a heart delicately sensitive to all the impulses from visible nature.' His peculiar quality arises from 'a communion of sense and soul.'

In the happier effects of this mental process, his poetry is like a mild autumn day, with quick and fleeting successive alternations of sun and shadow – or rather like a soft moonlight night, where objects are not less lovely for being less defined, where those that can be seen, are seen more accurately than in the glare of day, and where the distant scenes, though obscured by an impervious shadow, undefined and undefinable to the most piercing ken, yet the mysterious veil that envelops them is so glowing, so mild, and so mellow, that though we cannot admire them selves, we admire the painted mist that wraps them from our grosser sense with its rich and delicate texture.[128]

This recalls a passage in the *Biographia Literaria*, and ascribes 'romanticism' of a sort with a vengeance. But it must have been a cheating glimpse; for the writer goes on – 'we can never read many pages before we are disgusted, with silliness, rudeness, meanness, affectation, eccentric thinking and false simplicity, which when it is not merely babyism, degenerates into perfect folly ...'

I find the word *romantic* used with reference to Wordsworth up to 1822 only three times. Two of these refer to landscape: the 'wild, romantic scenes of Switzerland' in the *Descriptive Sketches* (1793) and the 'beautiful and romantic scenery' of the *White Doe* (1816).[129] The third is rather more to our point – in a fulsome review of *The Excursion* in 1815: 'Some ineffable spell Mr. Wordsworth possesses, the meanest circumstance he raises into dignity; to the homeliest feature he communicates grace; whatever, in "Nature, Man, or Society," was indifferent to us before, becomes interesting and romantic, when it comes under his notice.'* But in the eyes of one or

---

*   *Eclectic Review* (January 1815): *E. Smith*, p. 181. A review of Wordsworth's *Poetical Works* in *Quarterly* November 1834– a spiritless performance compared with H. N. Coleridge's essay in the previous number – agrees to ignore what is 'vapid and laborious' and to overlook the 'occasional aberrations and lapses,'

two critics at least, the word *romantic* had a different ambience and a sharper specification when it referred to Coleridge. In October 1819, J. G. Lockhart in reviewing *The Friend* wrote:

The whole essence of his [Coleridge's] poetry is more akin to music than that of any other poetry we have ever met with ... The love he describes the best is a romantic and spiritual movement of wonder, blended and exalted with an ineffable suffusion of the powers of sense. There is more of aerial romance, than of genuine tenderness, even in the peerless love of his Genevieve. Her silent emotions are an unknown world which her minstrel watches with fear and hope, and yet there is exquisite propriety in calling that poem 'Love,' for it truly represents the extent of that passion—where the power acquired over the human soul depends so much upon the awakening, for a time, of the idea of infinitude, and the bathing of the universal spirit in one interminable sea of thoughts undefineable. We are aware that this inimitable poem is better known than any of its author's productions – and doubt not that many hundreds of our readers have got it by heart long ago, without knowing by whom it was written.[130]

A much clearer focus is achieved by Henry Nelson Coleridge – Coleridge's nephew, born in the year of *Lyrical Ballads* and named for Lord Nelson– in a remarkable essay published in the *Etonian* in 1821, when he was 23 years old. In the course of a sustained contrast with Wordsworth, he writes: 'From the natural bent of his genius there is a tendency to the strange, the wild, and mysterious; which, though intolerable in the cool pursuit of Truth, is yet oftentimes the fruitful parent of the very highest Poetry. To this he adds a power of language truly wonderful, more romantically splendid than Wordsworth's, and more flexible and melodious than that of Southey.'* In 1834 Henry Nelson Coleridge published in the *Quarterly Review* what may be regarded as the first entirely sympathetic and judicious general critical evaluation of Coleridge's poetry. He knew what he was writing about: he had been recording Coleridge's conversation for ten or twelve years and had just finished editing, under Coleridge's

and finds in the narrative poems 'nothing romantic.' This review gives an interesting account of the growth of Wordsworth's reputation.

* *Jackson*, p. 463: 'On Coleridge's Poetry,' written under the pseudonym of 'Gerard Montgomery.' Coleridge first met HNC as a boy on 11 May 1811. When HNC visited Coleridge at Highgate late in 1822, he fell in love with Coleridge's daughter Sara, whom he finally married in September 1829. In 1822 he made the first notes of Coleridge's conversation towards the *Table Talk* (1835). In his *Quarterly Review* essay of 1834, he said of Coleridge's *Remorse* that 'its character is romantic and pastoral in a high degree' (*Jackson* p. 641).

eye, the last collective edition to be published in Coleridge's lifetime. This review was published in August 1834, the month after Coleridge's death, but Coleridge himself had almost certainly read the review in proof. Here the word *romantic* turns up in a readily recognizable reference, but the extreme difficulty of ready definition is made clear.

The volumes before us contain so many integral efforts of imagination, that a distinct notice of each is indispensable, if we would form a just conclusion upon the total powers of the man. Wordsworth, Scott, Moore, Byron, Southey, are incomparably more uniform in the direction of their poetic mind. But if you look over these volumes for indications of their author's specific powers, you find him appearing in at least half a dozen shapes, so different from each other, that it is in vain to attempt to mass them together. It cannot indeed be said, that he has ever composed what is popularly termed a *great* poem; but he is great in several lines, and the union of such powers is an essential term in a fair estimate of his genius. The romantic witchery of the 'Christabel' and 'Ancient Mariner,' the subtle passion of the love-strains, the lyrical splendour of the three great odes, the affectionate dignity, thoughtfulness, and delicacy of the blank verse poems – especially the 'Lover's Resolution,' 'Frost at Midnight,' and that most noble and interesting 'Address to Mr. Wordsworth' – the dramas, the satires, the epigrams – these are so distinct and so whole in themselves, that they might seem to proceed from different authors, were it not for that same individualizing power, that 'shaping spirit of imagination' which more or less sensibly runs through them all.*

Here, however, the term *romantic* refers especially to *Christabel, The Ancient Mariner*, and *Zapolya*; in the 1821 essay it had also referred to *Love*. In Henry Nelson Coleridge's usage the word has lost its pejorative overtones, but he does not use it to cover either the whole of Coleridge's poetry or 'the Lake School.' It is worth recalling that

*   *Jackson*, p. 647. Cf. p. 642 where he speaks of *Zapolya* as 'a mixture of the pastoral and the romantic,' and p. 645 where he says: 'The thing attempted in "Christabel" is the most difficult of execution in the whole field of romance – witchery by daylight; and the success is complete.' Noticeably he does not call *Kubla Khan* 'romantic' – the one poem in which Coleridge had used the word *romantic* with peculiar emphasis. Hazlitt's review of *Christabel* (*Examiner*, 2 June 1816) reads almost like an anticipatory parody of what HNC was to write. 'It is more like a dream than a reality. The mind, in reading it, is spellbound ... There is something disgusting at the bottom of his subject, which is but ill glossed over by a veil of Della Cruscan sentiment and fine writing – like moon-beams playing on a charnel-house, or flowers strewed on a dead body' (*Jackson*, p. 207). Hazlitt had heard or read the poem before from manuscript; in this review he recalls(?) a line not otherwise recorded among the variants of *Christabel*: 'Behold her bosom and half her side – | *Hideous, deformed, and pale of hue.*'

Wordsworth's reason for excluding *Christabel* from *Lyrical Ballads* (1800) was that 'the poem was in direct opposition to the very purpose for which the Lyrical Ballads were published – viz – an experiment to see how far those passions, which alone give any value to extraordinary Incidents, were capable of interesting, in & for themselves, in the incidents of common Life.'[131]

When Shelley's *Laon and Cythna* and *The Revolt of Islam* were reviewed in the *Quarterly* in April 1819, Shelley was drawn into the field of the 'Lake Poets'; *The Revolt of Islam* 'resembles the latter productions of Mr Southey, though the tone is less subdued, and the copy altogether more luxuriant and ornate than the original. Mr Shelley indeed is an unsparing imitator; and he draws largely on the rich stores of another mountain poet, to whose religious mind it must be matter, we think, of perpetual sorrow to see the philosophy which comes pure and holy from his pen, degraded and perverted ... by this miserable crew of atheists or pantheists ...'* In the previous August, *Blackwood's* had sneered at Keats for his defective classical learning. The shifting pattern was disturbed further when Macaulay discoursed upon Byron in the *Edinburgh Review* of June 1831 with the full force of his precocious, opinionated, and quarrelsome talent. Byron's lot, he said, 'was cast in the time of a great literary revolution ... The real nature of this revolution has not, we think, been comprehended by the great majority of those who concurred in it.' He mentions Scott, Wordsworth, Coleridge, Shelley; but his thesis is a curious one.

The forerunner of the great restoration of our literature was Cowper ...

---

* Wain, pp. 157 f. Shelley used *romantic* thrice in his prefaces. (*a*) to *The Cenci* (*Complete Poetical Works*, ed. T. Hutchinson, Oxford, 1934, p. 276). Shelley found that whenever the story of the Cenci was mentioned in Italian society 'the feelings of the company never failed to incline to a romantic pity for the wrongs, and a passionate exculpation of the horrible deed to which they urged her ...' (*b*) Advertisement to *Epipsychidion* (p. 411): 'His life was singular; less on account of the romantic vicissitudes which diversified it [he had bought and "fitted up the ruins of an old building" on "one of the wildest of the Sporades"], than the ideal tinge which it received from his own character and feelings.' The sentence had already received final form in Draft III (p. 425); but in Draft II the 'old building' was 'a Saracenic castle.' In Draft I this sentence occurs in germinal form, and *romantic* is drawn into the context: 'The circumstances to which the poem allude[s], may easily be understood by those to whom [the] spirit of the poem is intelligible: a detail of facts, sufficiently romantic in their combinations.' (*c*) Preface to *Adonais* (pp. 430–1): 'John Keats died at Rome ... and was buried in the romantic and lonely cemetery of the Protestants in that city, under the pyramid which is the tomb of Cestius, and the massy walls and towers, now mouldering and desolate, which formed the circuit of ancient Rome ... It might make one in love with death, to think that one should be buried in so sweet a place.'

During the twenty years which followed the death of Cowper [1800], the revolution in English poetry was fully consummated. None of the writers of this period, not even Sir Walter Scott, contributed so much to the consummation as Lord Byron. Yet he, Lord Byron, contributed to it unwillingly, and with constant self-reproach and shame ... He now and then praised Mr Wordsworth and Mr Coleridge; but ungraciously, and without cordiality ... Lord Byron was ... the mediator between two generations – between two hostile poetical sects. Though always sneering at Mr Wordsworth and the multitude ... Lord Byron founded what may be called an exoteric* Lake School of poetry; and all the readers of poetry in England, we might say in Europe, hastened to sit at his feet. What Mr Wordsworth had said like a recluse, Lord Byron said like a man of the world, – with less rofonnpd feeling, but with more perspicuity, energy, and conciseness. We would refer our readers to the last two cantos of Childe Harold and to Manfred, in proof of these observations.†

How influential Macaulay's essay was, it is difficult to say; but it had performed the feat of congering the two generations (but excluding Keats) into a single revolution, and with perverse ingenuity had placed them both under the uneasy title of 'the Lake School.' If Macaulay's essay points towards the comfortable phrase 'the Romantic Poets,' it is to be remarked that Macaulay was an historian, and that his verses do not argue that he was anything else.

In July 1833 William Maginn contributed to the 'Gallery of Literary Characters' in *Fraser's Magazine* a sketch of Coleridge:

> Sorry are we to present
> > The noticeable man with large grey eyes –
> the worthy old Platonist – the founder of the romantic school of poetry ... the good honest old thoroughgoing Tory – even Samuel Taylor Coleridge himself – in an attitude of suffering ...[132]

The portrait is written without affection, compassion, or admiration. Whether Maginn's patronizing coinage of 'the romantic school' had any precedent, or any currency thereafter, I cannot say. It seems not to have been taken up directly. If what H. N. Coleridge meant by 'romantic' was what Maginn meant by 'romantic,'

---

*   'Esoteric' in *Edinburgh Review*, but 'exoteric' must be intended, the wrong word having been carried over from the earlier phrase 'a few esoteric disciples.'
†   *Edinburgh Review* (June 1831), pp. 553, 560, 562–3, 565. That Byron was 'touched by' the Lake Poets is noticed in the *Edinburgh Review* (December 1816) pp. 277–8, 304–5 (influenced by Wordsworth and Southey); and in *Quarterly Review* (October 1816), pp. 203–4 (influenced by Coleridge).

Maginn was not far adrift in seeing Coleridge as 'the founder of the romantic school' in England. But the quality that H. N. Coleridge had defined at least tentatively was much harder to find in Wordsworth; and it was on Wordsworth that the critics had concentrated their attention when they wrote about 'the Lake School.'

LATER HISTORY

The last part of the history of the word *romantic* in nineteenth-century England is indistinct and has to be inferred, largely from negative evidence. It is clear that when Southey's *Thalaba* was reviewed in October 1802 the German distinction between romantic and classical had not effectively reached England; Warton and Gray, as much as Wordsworth and Coleridge, could have been identified as asserting 'the independence of genius' and advocating a break from 'the bondage of ancient authority'–that is, the neoclassical tradition in England. One of the outstanding differences between the English and German literary traditions in the early nineteenth century was that English 'classicism' was almost exclusively Latin and Horatian, whereas the German classical enthusiasts were consumed with Greek. Coleridge himself, in the *Biographia Literaria*, seems to repudiate the notion of literary revolution: 'At present it will be sufficient for my purpose, if I have proved, that Mr. Southey's writings no more than my own, furnished the original occasion to this fiction of a *new school* of poetry, and to the clamors against its supposed founders and proselytes.'[133] Coleridge's view of his own work, and of Wordsworth's, was shaped by a powerful sense of continuity, of the immanence of the literary past in the present; in spite of all the revolutionary talk – social, political, and literary – that had filled the air in his youth, he did not see himself as a revolutionary breaking out of a benighted past, although he did seek to purge his work of the flaccid habits of poetification that he had inherited from his immediate predecessors. He could admire Pope and Dryden, as Wordsworth did, although somewhat short of idolatry, and could find fruitful resources in such different second-raters as Akenside, Cowper, and Bowles. But his eye was on poetic excellence wherever he could find it; his rage against Samuel Johnson was against a man of authoritarian temper who seemed to reduce poetry to didactic common sense and to advocate a sort of everyman's egalitarianism that looked too much like the current trend of enclosed 'rationalism.' He rightly saw Wordsworth as a modern Milton – a *modern* Milton

– and meant this specifically; for he knew Wordsworth well enough to know that his powerful egotism had produced in his best work a bleak intransigence of manner that was without parallel in the language.*

The notion that a poetical revolution had started with *Lyrical Ballads* was a commonplace of the reviews by 1814. But it was Southey, not one of the enemies of the Lakers, who (reviewing Chalmers's *English Poets* in 1814 in the same number of the *Quarterly* that ran Hazlitt's review of Schlegel) said: 'To borrow a phrase from the Methodists, there has been a *great revival* in our days – a pouring out of the spirit. The publication of Percy's Reliques led the way.'[134] Coleridge could not reverse the conviction that 'a new school' had arisen; even the most vicious assailants of that school accepted the proposition, having initiated it. But no name lay comfortably to hand, and as late as 1831 Macaulay was trying to see at least four of the 'Big Five' as members of 'the Lake School.'

We have already put forward one reason why the term *romantic* did not suggest itself, either for self-commendation or for purposes of abuse. Perhaps, also, the word had become so eroded by the late twenties that it could serve none of the exact or suggestive meanings that it had had earlier in Germany. If it had, we should expect to find it in the reviews. Reviewers, unlike scholars or critics, deal with books not yet familiar to themselves or to anybody else; and a scholar or critic can find himself in the position of a reviewer. The craft of reviewing, even when anonymous, being a form of journalism, encourages cleverness and superiority; when anonymous, it encourages brutality and secret vanity. If the romantic-classical distinction had been current in whatever was the middle nineteenth-century equivalent of the literary cocktail party, the anonymous reviewers could be expected to have used it. But they did not. The evidence of the reviews is not conclusive; but it suggests that 'romantic' was not an exciting word and that the romantic-classical distinction was not a lively issue in the twenties in England – if it ever was. Those who saw the influence of Keats on Tennyson, or of Wordsworth on Arnold, seem to have preferred not to connect the later poets with the earlier 'schools.' *Romantic* was not a favourite or

---

* Macaulay in his 1831 essay on Byron said: 'We cannot conceive him, like Milton or Wordsworth, defying the criticism of his contemporaries, retorting their scorn, and labouring on a poem in the full assurance that it would be unpopular, and in the full assurance that it would be immortal' (pp. 563–4). Coleridge's critique of Wordsworth's poetry in Chapter 22 of *Biographia Literaria* is unsurpassed for its directness, precision, and rightness.

even special word with any of the 'romantics', and none of the new poets set it in currency. Tennyson, the most direct poetic link with the poets of the early nineteenth century, did not use *romantic* in his poems at all; it occurs twice in Browning's poems, only once in Arnold's;* it does not seem to have been a word current among the pre-Raphaelites; and Gerard Manley Hopkins never once used it in a poem.

Certain tenuous threads, however, may be picked up in the writing of Thomas Carlyle (1795–1818) – a man born in the same year as Keats and who was to live to within seven years of Matthew Arnold's death. Though in Arnold's view, Carlyle was 'the living writer who has done most to make England acquainted with German authors,'[135] he was remarkably wary of the word *romantic*. In a notebook of 1827 he observed that 'Grossi is a Romantic and Manzoni a romanticist';[136] he can imagine the terrific assault of 'those new Paper Goths' (led by Schiller and Kotzebue) upon the discreet

---

* Browning, *Colombe's Birthday* (1844), Act v:
  MELCHIOR   Yet, all the same, proceed my way,
  Though to your ends; so shall you prosper best!
  The lady, – to be won for selfish ends, –
  Will be won easier my unselfish ... call it,
  Romantic way.
  Melchior's 'romantic way' is that Prince Berthold should gain the duchy by wooing the Duchess Colombe, although he insists that 'I am past that now'. As the Duchess enters, Melchior tries to reinforce Berthold's resolution by saying: 'You'll keep, then, to the lover, to the man?' In *Red Cotton Night-Cap Country* (1873) Browning uses *romantic* with the same generally erotic reference:
  As to the womankind – renounce from those
  The hope of getting a companion-tinge
  First faint touch promising romantic fault!
  (*The Complete Poetical Works of Robert Browning* (New York, 1907), p. 327, ll. 59–63; p. 977, ll. 49–51). Cf. Arnold's use in note, p. 239 below.
  The following extract from Hallam Tennyson's *Memoir* (1897, II: 222) for the years 1875–82, printed in *TLS* for 16 October 1969, shows a more pertinent usage. On an occasion when Ruskin came to lunch, and he and Tennyson agreed that 'Everything bad is to be found in London and other large cities' and both 'deprecated in the strongest possible language the proposed Channel Tunnel,' Tennyson said to Ruskin as he was leaving: ' "Do you know that most romantic of lyrics?
  He turn'd his charger as he spake,
  Upon the river shore,
  He gave his bridle-reins a shake,
  Said Adieu for evermore,
  My love!
  And adieu for evermore."
  "Do I not?" said Ruskin, "I am so glad you like it, Tennyson; I place it among the best things ever done by anyone." ' (David Daiches identifies this as Scott's version, in *Rokeby*, of the third stanza of Burns's reworking of an old Chapbook ballad 'Mally Stewart.')

sensibilities of the English;[137] and only a Scotsman (one imagines) could have written of the Age of Romance as Carlyle did:

Roland of Roncevalles too ... found rainy weather as well as sunny; knew what it was to have hose need darning; got tough beef to chew, or even went dinnerless; was saddle-sick, calumniated, constipated (as his madness too clearly indicates); and oftenest felt, I doubt not, that this was a very Devil's world, and he, Roland himself, one of the sorriest caitiffs there. Only in long subsequent days, when the tough beef, the constipation and the calumny had clean vanished, did it all begin to seem Romantic ...'[138]

He rises joyously to the bait of the sub-title to Goethe's *Helena – a classico-romantic Phantasmagoria*: 'In fact, the style of *Helena* is altogether new ... passing by a short gradation from Classic dignity into Romantic pomp.' His concluding comment shows that he is alert to such a distinction: 'It is wonderful with what fidelity the Classical style is maintained throughout the earlier part of the Poem; how skilfully it is at once united to the Romantic style of the latter part, and made to reappear, at intervals, to the end.'[139] In the 'State of German Literature' (1827) he hailed the dawn of a new quality of criticism, which Tieck and the two Schlegels had 'laboured so meritoriously' to impress and diffuse 'first in their own country, and now also in several others.' However,

we should err widely if we thought that this new tendency of critical science pertains to Germany alone. It is a European tendency, and springs from the general condition of intellect in Europe. We ourselves have all, for the last thirty years, more or less distinctly felt the necessity of such a science ... our increased and increasing admiration not only of Shakespeare, but of all his contemporaries, and of all who breathe any portion of his spirit; our controversy whether Pope was a poet; and so much vague effort on the part of our best critics everywhere to express some still unexpressed idea concerning the nature of true poetry; as if they felt in their hearts that a pure glory, nay a divineness, belonged to it, for which they had as yet no name and no intellectual form. But in Italy too, in France itself, the same thing is visible. Their grand controversy, so hotly urged, between the *Classicists* and *Romanticists*, in which the Schlegels are assumed, much too loosely, on all hands, as the patrons and generalissimos of the latter, shows us sufficiently what spirit is at work in that long-stagnant literature. Doubtless this turbid fermentation of the elements will at length settle into clearness, both there and here, as in Germany it has already in a great measure done; and perhaps a more serene and genial poetic day is everywhere to be expected with some confidence. How much the example of the Germans may have to teach us in this particular, needs no farther exposition.

The authors and first promulgators of this new critical doctrine were at one time contemptuously named the *New School*; nor was it till after a war of all the few good heads in the nation with all the many bad ones had ended as such wars must ever do, that these critical principles were generally adopted; and their assertors found to be no *School*, or new heretical sect, but the ancient primitive Catholic Communion, of which all sects that had any living light in them were but members and subordinate models.*

Carlyle had no doubt that 'a new era in the spiritual intercourse of Europe is approaching';[140] he wrote essays on Goethe, Schiller, Novalis, Tieck, Hoffmann, Fouqué, Jean Paul (to choose only central names); he added a revealing footnote to his translation of Jean Paul's review of Madame de Staël's *De l'Allemagne* (1830): '*Romantisch*, "romantic," it will be observed, is here used in a scientific sense, and has no concern with the writing or reading (or acting) of "romances." '[141] Yet he fought shy of both the term and the title *romantic*, referring carefully in preference to the 'New School' – 'which has been the subject of much unwise talk, and of much not very wise writings.'[142] He had his own views upon the history of the movement he celebrated, but declined to correct 'colloquial literary history' except by implication;[143] it remained for Matthew Arnold to rebuke him for ignoring Heine.† How much influence Carlyle exerted in spreading the gospel of romanticism in Britain does not appear, and he himself eventually lost heart; in any case we are concerned with the word *romantic*, not primarily with the history of 'romanticism.' That Carlyle was not ignorant is clear;

---

*   *Carlyle Essays*, 1: 45–6. At 'as such wars must ever do,' Carlyle adds a footnote stating that the movement 'began in Schiller's *Musenalmanach* for 1797' with the 'series of philosophic epigrams jointly by Schiller and Goethe.' 'The agitation,' he continues, 'was extreme; scarcely since the age of Luther has there been such a stir and strife in the intellect of Germany; indeed, scarcely since that age has there been a controversy, if we consider its ultimate bearings on the best and noblest interests of mankind, so important as this, which, for the time, seemed only to turn on metaphysical subtleties, and matters of mere elegance. Its farther applications became apparent by degrees.'

†   *Arnold, Essays* III: 107: 'Heinrich Heine' (1863). 'Mr Carlyle attaches ... too much importance to the romantic school of Germany – Tieck, Novalis, Jean Paul Richter ... Far more in Heine's work flows this main current.' But, Arnold adds, Carlyle '– man of genius as he is ... has, for the functions of the critic, a little too much of the self-will and eccentricity of a genuine son of Great Britain.' Was Arnold perhaps irritated that the 'Heyne' Carlyle wrote an essay on in 1828 was Christian Gottlob Heyne, the classical scholar?

that he was not indifferent is equally clear. In his 'Schiller' essay (1831) he said: 'we [*i.e.*, people in Britain] are troubled with no controversies on Romanticism and Classicism, the Bowles controversy on Pope having long since evaporated without result.'[143] I cannot agree with Wellek that this represents a 'complacent' attitude; to the contrary, in this passage, and in many others, Carlyle shows that he was ashamed how little the English had recognized the importance of this 'turbid fermentation of the elements,' and how trifling a part they seemed to have played in it.*

In 1831 Carlyle wondered whether 'instead of isolated, mutually repulsive National Literatures, a World Literature may one day be looked for?'[144] Matthew Arnold (1822–88), born in the year of Shelley's death, wished to see the best ideas prevail and sought to obliterate national boundaries of time and language in the country of criticism. As something like the next critical commissar after Johnson, he adopted the position of the stern classicist, chose to declare the modernity of ancient art, and to develop a distinction between Hellenism and Hebraism. Being a dyed-in-the-wool Wordsworthian and – like T. S. Eliot – an inverted 'romantic,' he is germane to this study, in spite of his exclusiveness of manner. He recognized the word *romantic* as a technical term in Heine's phrase *Die romantische Schule* and used the phrase 'romantic school' in his essays on Maurice de Guérin (1862) and Heine (1863).† In 1863 he delivered at Oxford a lecture entitled 'The Modern Element in Romanticism,' but it was not published, and a valuable piece of evidence has thereby been lost.‡ He seems not to have been inter-

---

*   *Wellek, Concepts,* p. 149. See, for example, *Carlyle, Essays* I: 30, 189, 222; III: 217–21. Taine thought so too: '... two currents from France and Germany at this moment swept into England. The dykes there were so strong, they could hardly force their way, entering more slowly than elsewhere, but entering nevertheless. They made themselves a new course between the ancient barriers, and widened without bursting them, by a peaceful and slow transformation which continues till this day' (Tr. H. van Laun, Edinburgh, 1871, II: 227–8).

†   Heine's *Die romantische Schule* was published in German in 1836, but had previously appeared in French as *De l'Allemagne* in 1835; it seems to have had no currency in English until almost the end of the century, if then. Arnold praises Guérin's incisive (and rancorous) criticism of the immaturity of 'the romantic school' (*Arnold, Essays,* p. 21) and of 'the French romantic school' (p. 29). In the Heine essay he rebukes Carlyle for ignoring Heine (pp. 107–8; and see note, p. 239 above). The whole 'Heine' essay is of peculiar interest; and see p. 119 – 'the mystic and romantic school of Germany lost itself in the Middle Ages.'

‡   One of the matters to be discussed was 'the origin of what is called the "romantic" sentiments about women, which the Germans quite falsely are fond of giving themselves the credit of originating' (letter of December 1860, in *Arnold, Essays,* p. 491). He was then reading Renan in preparation for the Celtic lectures.

ested in refining the romantic-classical distinction, and his single poetical use of the word *romantic* (in an elegiac poem of 1864) is not much other than the simple adjective of 'romance' – if that adjective can ever be simple.* In 1866, when he tried to delineate the quality that 'suddenly magicalized by a romance touch,' he called it not 'romantic' but 'Celtic': 'If I were asked where English poetry got these three things, its turn for style, its turn for melancholy, and its turn for natural magic, for catching and rendering the charm of nature in a wonderfully near and vivid way, – I should answer, with some doubt, that it got much of its turn for style from a Celtic source, with less doubt, that it got much of its melancholy from a Celtic source; with no doubt at all, that from a Celtic source it got nearly all its natural magic.'[145] He finds the 'romance touch' in Celtic romance itself, of course, but also in 'Shakespeare's touch in his daffodil, Wordsworth's in his cuckoo, Keats's in his Autumn, Obermann's in his mountain birchtree, or his Easter-daisy among the Swiss farms.' 'The gift for natural magic,' he decides after due examination, is properly Celtic rather than Germanic, although not totally absent in German poetry.† 'Only the power of natural magic Goethe does not, I think, give; whereas Keats passes at will from the Greek power to that power which is, as I say, Celtic; from his "What little town, by river or seashore – "to his "White hawthorn and the pastoral eglantine,/Fast-fading violets cover'd up in leaves –" or his "... magic casements, opening on the foam/Of perilous seas, in fairy lands forlorn –.' " For such a fine specification, Arnold seems to have found the word *romantic*, as adjective of *romance*, too broad a term, too intricately reverberating with overtones and presuppositions that he preferred to exclude; yet it is in his own 'Celtic' sense that he draws the 'romantic' figures in 'A Southern Night.' With something

*   'A Southern Night,' written on the French Mediterranean coast in 1861 in memory of his brother, who had died at Gibraltar in April 1859 on his way home from India.
> But *you* – a grave for Girl or Sage,
>   Romantic, solitary, still,
> Oh, spent ones of a work-day age!
>   Befits you ill.

The figures elliptically recalled through the 'Girl or Sage' appear earlier in the poem: Sage, Knight, Troubadour, the Pirate-Lover's Girl. All are imagined to have come to their deaths 'by these Waters of Romance.'

†   In his first annual report as school inspector (1 January 1853), Arnold said that 'the difference between Wales and England will probably be effaced' and added: 'they are not the true friends of the Welsh people, who, from a romantic interest in their manners and traditions, would impede an event which is socially and politically so desirable for them' – by insisting upon the study of the Welsh language. I wonder whether Charles Prince of Wales has come upon this observation of Arnold's.

of the perverse insularity of British spirit that he accuses Carlyle of, Arnold himself avoids the word *romantic* and transfers into an un-localized 'Celtic' quality many of the characteristics, historical and emotional, that the European theorists and poets had attached to the word *romantic*. There can be no question of the immense in-fluence of Arnold's work upon the next half-century of English letters. It may be that the pervasive (and in this respect evasive) effect of his writing – so much less austere and classical in tone than he seems to have wanted – did much to establish for the late nine-teenth and early twentieth centuries certain unexamined and happy English generalizations about the quality of the 'romantic' poets that dominates Palgrave's selective view* and which through second-hand and derivative books of instruction has perverted direct criticism of the 'romantic' poets. It is difficult to avoid the conclusion that in the second half of the nineteenth century and for some time thereafter, the English use of *romantic* and *romanticism* has secured for itself an insular existence, largely unpurified either by historical sense or by the careful thinking that had gone into European theories of romanticism.†

Yet the word *romantic* must have had some currency in England in the thirty years after the Great Exhibition, and so must the ro-mantic-classical distinction, eroded no doubt, but not so stale as to be no longer worth discussing. Although the world of classical scholarship may not be expected to be in nervous resonance at that date with currents of English literary-critical speculation, the pre-face to the Butcher and Lang translation of the *Odyssey* (1879) is not without interest; for it was a commonplace of the time that the *Iliad* was 'classical' and the *Odyssey* 'romantic.' 'After the belief in the ballad manner follows the recognition of the romantic vein in Homer,

*   F. T. Palgrave's *The Golden Treasury of the Best Songs and Lyrical Poems in the English Language* was first published in London in 1861. Arnold did not find Palgrave's critical judgment impeccable, and considered the inclusion of 22 Shelley poems – outnumbered only by Wordsworth and Shakespeare – strange (*Arnold, Essays* III: 34, 252–5).

†   As late as 1886, writing his *Encyclopaedia Britannica* article on Sainte-Beuve, Arnold again avoided general discussion of the literary-critical upheaval in which Sainte-Beuve had played a powerful if not decisive role. Arnold, who regarded Sainte-Beuve as 'a perfect critic – a critic of measure, not exuberant; of the centre, not provincial,' knew Sainte-Beuve's early deliberately Words-worthian poems and his championing of romanticism; yet he will venture no farther than the technical phrase 'the romantic school in France.' See *Five Uncollected Essays of Matthew Arnold*, ed. K. Allott (Liverpool, 1953), pp. 74, 72. The *Encyclopaedia Britannica* article, written for the 9th ed., still survives, un-identified and in savagely butchered form, in the current (14th) ed. For another Arnold essay on Sainte-Beuve, see *Essays, Letters, and Reviews of Matthew Arnold*, ed. F. Neiman (Cambridge, Mass., 1960), pp. 164–8.

and, as a result, came Mr. Worsley's admirable Odyssey. This masterly translation does all that can be done for the Odyssey in the romatic style.'* Pope, Worsley, and Hawtrey, the preface continues, '*must* be adding to Homer'; yet 'it would be impertinent indeed to blame any of these translations in their place. They give that which the romantic reader of poetry, or the student of the age of Anne, looks for in verse ...' Butcher and Lang sought a style that was 'old and plain,' and settled into a manner that was more Ossianic than biblical.

And the tone of Walter Pater's 'Postscript' to his *Appreciations* (1889) is some indication that the romantic spirit was not utterly moribund in England. After an essay on style, separate essays on Wordsworth, Coleridge, and Lamb, three on Shakespeare, and one on Dante Gabriel Rossetti, the 'Postscript' begins:

> The words, *classical* and *romantic*, although like many other critical expressions, sometimes abused by those who have understood them too vaguely or too absolutely, yet define two real tendencies in the history of art and literature. Used in an exaggerated sense, to express a greater opposition between those tendencies than really exists, they have at times tended to divide poeple of taste into opposite camps. But in that *House Beautiful*, which the creative minds of all generations – the artists and those who have treated life in the spirit of art – are always building together, for the refreshment of the human spirit, these oppositions cease; and the *Interpreter* of the *House Beautiful*, the true aesthetic critic, uses these divisions, only so far as they enable him to enter into the peculiarities of the objects with which he has to do.

The term *romantic*, he says, 'has been used much too vaguely, in various accidental senses ... But the romantic spirit is, in reality, an ever-present, and enduring principle, in the artistic temperament; and the qualities of thought and style which that, and other similar uses of the word *romantic* really indicate, are indeed but symptoms of a very continuous and widely working influence.' He studies a little the history of the emergence and use of the term; his general conclusion is that 'the essential elements ... of the romantic spirit are curiosity and the love of beauty; and it is only as an illustration of these qualities, that it seeks the Middle Age, because, in the overcharged atmosphere of the Middle Age, there are unworked sources

* Philip Stanhope Worsley (1835–66) published his translation of the *Odyssey* in 1861. His translation of *Iliad* I–XII appeared in 1865. Chap. 32 of Andrew Lang's *History of English Literature* (1912) opens: 'The Romantic Movement begins with Coleridge'; it includes Coleridge, Wordsworth, Southey, Shelley, Byron, Keats, Landor.

of romantic effect, of a strange beauty, to be won, by strong imagination, out of things unlikely or remote.' The essay now seems at once unduly emphatic and unduly soothing. Was the distinction current at Oxford? Was it debated between tutor and undergraduate, as forty years later there was still debate about Faith and Reason? Oxford – as Arnold had reflected nearly twenty-five years earlier in his Preface to *Essays in Criticism* –

Beautiful city! so venerable, so lovely, so unravaged by the fierce intellectual life of our century, so serene!
    'There are our young barbarians, all at play!'
And yet, steeped in sentiment as she lies, spreading her gardens to the moonlight, and whispering from her towers the last enchantments of the Middle Age, who will deny that Oxford, by her ineffable charm, keeps ever calling us nearer to the true goal of all of us, to the ideal, to perfection, – to beauty, in a word, which is only truth seen from another side? – nearer, perhaps, than all the science of Tübingen. Adorable dreamer, whose heart was been so romantic! who hast given thyself so prodigally, given thyself to sides and to heroes not mine, only never to the Philistines! home of lost causes, and forsaken beliefs, and unpopular names, and impossible loyalties! ...[146]

In this dead zone where navigation is difficult we make an unexpected landfall in a letter of Gerard Manley Hopkins dated 1 December 1881. There may be a connection with Pater, for Hopkins as an undergraduate could have heard Pater lecture, and he had certainly worked under Pater for a time between 1866 and 1868. But if there is any connection with an elder master in these matters it might as well be with Matthew Arnold; for Hopkins referred to the 'Joubert' essay and 'The Function of Criticism' in January 1865, and a month or so later made note to read 'Arnold's Essays.' On 26 May 1866 he heard Arnold give the last of his four lectures on Celtic Poetry and so heard uttered (although he does not comment upon it) the passage at the opening, which is quoted on p. 238 above.[147] In September 1878 he recommended the 'Guérin' essay and suggested that, to correspond to the subtitle of the 'Joubert' essay – 'A French Coleridge' – the 'Guérin' might be called 'The Keats of France';* and five years later he objected to Bridges' name

---

* *The Letters of Gerard Manley Hopkins* (vol. I, to Robert Bridges: vol. II, to Richard Watson Dixon), ed. C. C. Abbott (Oxford, 1935), II: 11–12 (hereafter cited as *Hopkins, Letters*) – thereby anticipating by more than sixty years George H. Ford in *Keats and the Victorians* (New Haven, 1944).

for Arnold – 'Mr. Kidglove Cocksure' – declaring that Arnold was 'a rare genius and a great critic.'[148] The letter to Dixon in 1881 is as interesting for its use of the idea of 'schools' as for its use of the term *romantic*.

I must hold that you and Morris belong to one school, and that though you should neither of you have read a line of the other's. I suppose the same masters, the same models, the same tastes, the same keepings, above all, make the school. It will always be possible to find differences, marked differences, between original minds; it will be necessarily so. So the species in nature are essentially distinct, nevertheless they are grouped into genera: they have one form in common, mounted on that they have a form that differences them. I used to call it the school of Rossetti: it is in literature the school of he Prae-raphaelites. Of course that phase is in part past, neither do these things admit of hard and fast lines; still consider yourself, that you know Rossetti and Burne Jones, Rossetti through his sympathy for you and Burne Jones – was it the same or your sympathy for him? This modern medieval school is descended from the Romantic school (Romantic is a bad word) of Keats, Leigh Hunt, Hood, indeed of Scott early in the century. That was one school; another was that of the Lake poets and also of Shelley and Landor; the third was the sentimental school, of Byron, Moore, Mrs. Hemans, and Haynes Bailey. Schools are very difficult to class: the best guide, I think, are keepings. Keats' school chooses medieval keepings, not pure nor drawn from the middle ages direct but as brought down through the Elizabethan tradition of Shakspere and his contemporaries which died out in such men as Herbert and Herrick. They were also realists and observers of nature. The Lake poets and all that school represent, as it seems to me, the mean or standard of English style and diction, which culminated in Milton but was never very continuous or vigorously transmitted, and in fact none of these men unless perhaps Landor were great masters of style, though their diction is generally pure, lucid, and unarchaic. They were faithful but not rich observers of nature. Their keepings are their weak point, a sort of colourless classical keepings: when Wordsworth wants to describe a city or a cloudscape which reminds him of city it is some ordinary rhetorical stage-effect of domes, palaces, and temples. Byron's school had a deep feeling but the most untrustworthy and barbarous eye, for nature; a diction markedly modern; and their keepings any gaud or a lot of Oriental rubbish. I suppose Crabbe to have been in form a descendant of the school of Pope with a strong and modern realistic eye; Rogers something between Pope's school and that of Wordsworth and Landor; and Campbell between this last and Byron's, with a good deal of Popery too, and a perfect master of style. Now since this time Tennyson and his school seem to me to have struck a mean or compromise between Keats and the medievalists on the one hand and Wordsworth and the Lake School on the other (Tennyson has some jarring notes of Byron ...). The Lake School expires in Keble and Faber and Cardinal Newman. The Brownings may be reckoned to the Romantics. Swinburne is a strange phenomenon: his poetry seems a powerful effort at establishing a new standard of poetical diction, of the rhetoric of poetry; but to waive every other objection it is essentially archaic, biblical a good deal, and so on: now that is a thing that can never last; a perfect style must be of its age. In virtue of this archaism and on other grounds he must rank with the medievalists.[149]

René Wellek has noted that David Macbeth Moir (1798–1851) in his *Sketches of the Poetical Literature of the past half Century* (1852) reckoned Matthew Gregory Lewis to be the leader of the 'purely romantic school,' with Scott, Coleridge, Southey, and Hogg–but not Wordsworth – as disciples; and that W. Rushton of University College, London, in his *Afternoon Lectures on English Literature* (1863, delivered in Dublin) discussed the 'Classical and Romantic School of English literature as represented by Spenser, Dryden, Pope, Scott and Wordsworth' – which suggests a somewhat more comprehensive and continental approach.[150] But it appears that, from whatever usage Hopkins picked out the word *romantic* in 1881, the habit of referring to the English poets of the early nineteenth century, collectively, singly, or generically, as 'the Romantic Poets' and 'the Romantic School' came from literary historians rather than from critics, and that it was reinforced by – if not actually initiated by – European ideas. Wellek suggests that the turning-point came with Lady Eastlake's translation of Alois Brandl's *Coleridge und die romantische Schule in England* (1887), the 'School' comprising Wordsworth, Coleridge, Southey, and Scott, but not Keats, Byron, or Shelley – in effect, one version of the 'Lake Poets.' But the picture is both more complex and more elusive than that. Indeed it is by no means clear that there was any 'turning-point.' As we search back towards the date of Wordsworth's death in 1850, we find *romantic* used as an historical label much earlier than Brandl; we find also that at least two attempts to clarify the definition for English poetry (and Hopkins's letter, although late, is also of this kind) were not influential enough to prevent deepening confusion.

Hippolyte Taine used the phrase 'English Romantic school'

almost twenty years before Lady Eastlake's translation was published; in the *Histoire de la littérature anglaise* (first published in 5 volumes, 1864–9, translated into English in 2 volumes, 1871–2) he shows Burns as a precursor, groups Lamb, Coleridge, Southey, Moore, and Scott together, and treats both Wordsworth and Byron separately on a large scale.*

Other evidence in a less illustrious source shows *romantic* being used in an historical application at about the time that Matthew Arnold wrote his essays on Guérin and Heine – and possibly almost twenty years earlier. *A History of English Literature* by Thomas Budd Shaw (1813–62), enlarged and revised by William Smith, was published by John Murray in 1864 as 'The Student's Manual of English Literature.' The original form of this book – *Outlines of English Literature* – was written and published by Shaw in 1846 at the request of the Imperial Alexander Lyceum in St. Petersburg for the use of its pupils, Shaw having been professor of English literature there since 1842 (and tutor to the grand dukes of Russia from 1853). The book was not nearly so obscure as this sounds: the first (? St. Petersburg) edition was 'speedily sold'; it was immediately reprinted in Philadelphia, and in 1849 John Murray issued an edition in London; after Shaw's death Murray commissioned Smith to prepare for the press the extensive revision of the *Outlines* that Shaw had been working on at the time of his death.† Chapter 19 is entitled 'The Dawn of

---

* Book IV is entitled *L'Age Moderne*; within that book, ch. 1, Sect. 4 opens: 'Now appeared the English romantic school.' Sect. 5, mostly on Wordsworth, opens: 'Side by side with this development there was another, and with history philosophy entered into literature, in order to widen and modify it.' 'The philosophical spirit,' represented in Europe by Goethe, Schiller, Heine, Beethoven, Victor Hugo, Lamartine, de Musset, was 'constrained to transform itself and become Anglican, or to deform itself and become revolutionary; and, in place of a Schiller and Goethe, to produce a Wordsworth, a Byron, a Shelley' (tr. van Laun, II: 259–60). The whole of ch. II is devoted to Byron – 'One alone, Byron, attains the summt' – and Shelley receives short shrift in the middle of Sect. 5. For Dowden on Taine, see pp. 252–3 below.

† Smith's edition of Shaw, perhaps because it was alone in the field as a book 'with a special view to the requirements of Students,' was very widely used (1st ed., 1864; 2nd ed., 1865; 4th ed., 1868; 13th ed., 1881; 16th ed., 1887). There were also several American editions; the New York 1868 copy held by Queen's University (original price $1.75) has an added 'Sketch of American Literature' by H. T. Tuckerman.

Shaw, son of an eminent architect, was born in London, spent part of his childhood in the West Indies, was 'a favourite pupil' of Samuel Butler at Shrewsbury, took his degree at St. John's College, Cambridge in 1836, went to Russia in 1840 after working as a tutor, and settled in St. Petersburg in 1841. He translated much Greek and Latin verse and at least one novel from the Russian.

Whether Shaw or his editor Smith was responsible for the uses of the word

Romantic Poetry,' and section 1 opens: 'The great revolution in popular taste and sentiment which substituted what is called the romantic type of literature for the cold and clear-cut artificial spirit of that classicism which is exhibited in its highest form in the writings of Pope was, like all powerful and durable movements, whether in politics or in letters, gradual.'* Chapter 20 is entitled 'Walter Scott' and the opening sentence of section 1, 'Romantic School,' reads 'The great revolution in taste, substituting romantic for classical sentiment and subjects, which culminated in the poems and novels of Walter Scott, is traceable to the labours of Bishop Percy'; Chapter 21 is devoted to Byron, Moore, Shelley, Keats, and Campbell; Chapter 22, on Wordsworth, Coleridge, and Southey, begins with 'William Wordsworth ... the founder of the so-called

romantic that follow cannot be established without reference to the posthumous Shaw MS that Smith was working from. Differences between the *Outlines* and the *History* suggest that Smith, not Shaw, was responsible for the emphasis on the word *romantic*, and that the pervasiveness of the term was not established by Shaw in Russia, where (he admits) he 'could have no access to an English library of reference.' In his preface to the *Outlines*, Shaw mentions 'the romantic school of fiction' and 'Byronism.' In ch. 16 (p. 356) he asks: 'What is the distinction between the tone of the eighteenth and that of the nineteenth century? ... The full and complete daylight of this new era is to be found in Scott, in Byron, in Shelley, in Wordsworth.' He speaks of Scott's *Minstrelsy* as the best preparation for 'the future triumphs of the romantic poet and novelist of Scotland' – the romancer, that is (p. 390). He was acute enough to find in Southey's poems 'a most painful air of *laxity* and want of intellectual *bone and muscle*' (p. 418) – a phrase that happily survives in Smith's version. He speaks of Scott as 'the type, sign or measure of the first step in literature towards romanticism, or rather of the first step made in modern times *from* classicism – from the regular, the correct, the established' (p. 423). Byron he considered 'the most extraordinary man of his age, and perhaps the most extraordinary person in the modern history of Europe' (p. 431); a shoulder-note marks a group of Byron's 'Romantic Poems' (p. 434) and Shaw refers to *Childe Harold*, in comparison with Spenser, as 'a tale of romantic chivalrous adventure.' Under the heading of 'Modern Romantic Drama' he discusses principally Joanna Baillie, Sheridan Knowles, T. N. Talfourd, and Henry Taylor (p. 503). Then in his closing chapter (21), Shaw makes a very curious observation on 'Wordsworth, Coleridge, and the New Poetry': 'The throne of English poetry, left vacant by the early death of Byron, is now unquestionably filled by Wordsworth'; the current that had set from 'the old classicism ... has carried us insensibly, but irresistibly, first through Romanticism, and has now brought us to a species of metaphysical quietism' (p. 518). In Smith's version all these passages are reworked (except the comment on Southey), the dominant admiration for Byron is diminished, and the account of the 'Romantic Poets' is thrown into the entirely different pattern outlined in the text following.

* The text then discusses Beattie, Blair, Thomson, Collins, Gray, the Wartons, Cowper, Falconer, Erasmus Darwin; the Ossian, Chatterton, and Ireland forgeries; Crabbe, Burns, 'Peter Pindar,' and the comic drama of the eighteenth century.

Lake School of poetry.' Shaw does not use the word *romantic* other-wise in this chapter; and in singling out (as Henry Nelson Coleridge had done) *The Ancient Mariner, Christabel, Kubla Khan,* and *Love,* he tries to specify their character without recourse to any single generic term. '... *The Ancient Mariner,* a wild, mystical, phantasmagoric narrative ... is a splendid dream, filling the ear with the strange and floating melodies of sleep, and the eye with a shifting, vaporous succession of fantastic images, gloomy or radiant. The poem of *Christabel,* and the fragment called *Kubla Khan,* are of the same mystic, unreal character ...' (p. 453).

He uses the phrases 'Romantic Poetry,' 'romantic literature,' 'romantic sentiment and subjects' as referential labels; he does not examine the term *romantic* by itself, nor does he try to evolve a general view of 'the romantics' out of a general account of 'roman-ticism.' He writes as though he were merely repeating current literary-historical axioms.

Walter Bagehot (1826–77), with less *panache* than Hazlitt and more of the steady intellectual drive of Leavis, takes a very English position: 'For the English, after all, the best literature is the English.' In his essay on Shelley (1856) he attempts, on the evidence of English poetry, a correct distinction between classic and roman-tic. Picking up Macaulay's suggestion that Shelley has 'many of the qualities of the great old masters,' he writes:

... his imagination is classical rather than romantic, – we should, perhaps, apologise for using words which have been used so often, but which hardly convey even yet a clear and distinct meaning; yet they seem to the best for conveying a distinction of this sort ... When we speak of this distinction [between the classical and romantic imagination], we seem almost to be speaking of the distinction between ancient and modern literature. The characteristic of the classical literature is the simplicity with which the imagination appears in it; that of modern literature is the profusion with which the most varied adornments of the accessory fancy are thrown and lavished upon it ... Ancient poetry is like a Grecian temple, with pure form and rising columns, – created, one fancies, by a single effort of a creative nature: modern literature seems to have sprung from the involved brain of a Gothic architect, and resembles a huge cathedral – the work of the perpetual industry of centuries – complicated and infinite in details; but by their choice and elaboration producing an effect of unity which is not inferior to that of the other, and is heightened by the multiplicity through which it is conveyed. And it is this warmth of circumstance –

this profusion of interesting detail – which has caused the name 'romantic' to be perseveringly applied to modern literature.*

Again, in an essay on Wordsworth, Tennyson, and Browning (1864) he proposes a scheme rather more complex than the classical-romantic polarity.

The great divisions of poetry, and of all other literary art, arise from the different modes in which these *types* – these characteristic men, these characteristic feelings – may be variously described. There are three principal modes which we shall attempt to describe – the *pure*, which is sometimes, but not very wisely, called the classical; the *ornate*, which is also unwisely called romantic; and the *grotesque*, which might be called the mediaeval ... The essence of pure art consists in its describing what is as it is, and this is very well for what can bear it, but there are many inferior things which will not bear it, and which nevertheless ought to be described in books. A certain kind of literature deals with illusions, and this kind of literature has given a colouring to the name romantic ... Ornate art is within the limits as legitimate as pure art. It does what pure art could not do ... Illusion, half belief, unpleasant types, imperfect types, are as much the proper sphere of ornate art, as an inferior landscape is the proper sphere for the true efficacy of moonlight. A really great landscape needs sunlight and bears sunlight; but moonlight is an equaliser of beauties; it gives a romantic unreality to what will not stand the bare truth. And just so does romantic art.[151]

In this essay, Bagehot was not trying to set up absolute critical canons; he was reviewing Tennyson's *Enoch Arden* and Browning's *Dramatis Personae*, and wanted to prepare the ground for his conclusion that Tennyson is an instance of the *ornate* and Browning of the *grotesque* (the *pure* being represented, in passing, by Wordsworth and some others). Bagehot was a man of affairs, an economist, banker, and businessman; but he took his task as a critic seriously and, having a somewhat Arnoldian European sense, set about his criticism in a semi-Coleridgean way: 'though no complete theory of the poetic art as yet be possible for us ... yet something of some certainty

* Walter Bagehot, *Literary Studies* (Everyman, 1911, 1916), II: 227 (1856); I: 103–6. (These 'Studies' were all reviews.) At the second elision, Bagehot quotes the opening stanza of the 'Ode to a Grecian Urn,' remarking without disapproval: 'No ancient poet would have dreamed of writing thus' (I: 104–5). Keats, he says, is 'the most essentially modern of recent poets'; and after quoting from 'Ode to a Nightingale' and from Shelley's 'Skylark,' he concludes: 'We can hear that the poetry of Keats is a rich, composite, voluptuous harmony: that of Shelley a clear single ring of penetrating melody' (I: 104 108).

may be stated on the easier elements, and something that will throw light on these two new books.'*

With Edward Dowden (1843–1913) we move into an academic setting, for he was professor of English literature at Trinity College, Dublin, from 1867. In his 1878 collection of essays he had referred to Byron as 'A leader of the Romantic movement, yet a worshipper of the poetry of Pope.'[152] In his essay on Coleridge (1889) he again shows himself disinclined to lapse into enervating generalities; he is seeking, for the distinctive quality of Coleridge's poetry, a more exact specification than what 'the critics tell us of the romantic strangeness of his work ... its wealth of fantastic incident, its dream-like inconsequence, its cloud-like and rainbow-like splendours.'† Looking back through the eighteenth century, he finds that 'In the literature of the time thare were two powerful tendencies, each of which was liable to excess when it operated alone, each of which needed to work in harmony with the other. A little before the death of Johnson English poetry had almost reached the lowest ebb. It has often been said that its revival was due to the excitement and enthusiasm caused by the Revolution in France; but this is certainly untrue.' He cites Cowper's *The Task*, Burns, and Crabbe as representing the one tendency, and as the second tendency, confusing and 'also strong,' 'the tendency towards romance, which gave their popularity to the *Mysteries of Udolpho* and *The Italian, ...*'; 'The Gothic revival which in our own century became learned and antiquarian was then sentimental and imaginative.'

Here then were two movements in our literature, each operating apart from the other and each prone to excess – naturalism, tending to a hard, dry, literal manner, unilluminated by the light of imagination; romance, tending to become a coarse revel in material horrors. English poetry needed first that romance should be saved and ennobled by the presence and the power of truth, and, secondly, that naturalism, without losing any of its fidelity to fact, should be saved and ennobled by the presence and the power of imagination. And this was precisely what Coleridge and Wordsworth contributed to English poetry in their joint volume of

*   Ibid., ii: 307. Cf. 317: 'elementary criticism, if an evil, is a necessary evil; a little while spent among the simple principles of art is the first condition, the absolute pre-requisite, for surely apprehending and wisely judging the complete embodiments and miscellaneous forms of actual literature.'
†   *Fortnightly* (September 1889), in Edward Dowden, *New Studies in Literature* (1895), pp. 313–14. Swinburne had 'admirably compared' Coleridge to a footless bird of paradise, plucking the image out of 'The Eolian Harp.'

Lyrical Ballads,' which in consequence may justly be described as marking if not making an epoch in the history of our literature.[153]

From an examination of English poetry itself, Dowden – like Bagehot – was trying to define the nature and contribution of the early nineteenth-century English poets. Like Bagehot, he was fully aware of European literary currents, but he was not being carried along on any European wave of theoretical generalization. His Taylorian Lecture of 20 November 1889 – 'Literary Criticism in France' – makes this clear: 'No wonder that such a critic [as Nisard] was not popular with young and ardent spirits in the first fervours of the Romantic movement [in France] ... His view was determined by a deeper and a truer insight than that of M. Taine or of the romantic critics of an earlier date. The revolt of the [French] Romantic school itself testifies to the strength in France of the classical tradition, and no critic of French literature can be a sure guide who does not recognise the force and value of that tradition.'[154] 'Two debts we certainly owe to M. Taine,' Dowden says: 'first, he has helped us to feel the close kinship between the literature of each epoch and the various other manifestations of the mind of the time; and secondly, he has helped to moderate the passion for pronouncing judgments of good and evil founded on the narrow aesthetics of the taste of our own day.'

But there are two things which as they express themselves in literature he has failed to enable us to comprehend – the individual genius of an artist, that unique power of seeing, feeling, imagining, what he and he alone possesses; and again, the universal mind of humanity, that which is not bounded by an epoch nor contained by a race, but which lives alike in the pillars of the Parthenon and in the vault of the Gothic cathedral, which equally inspires the noblest scenes of Sophocles and of Shakespeare ... The critic [Taine] does not possess the delicate tact which would enable him to discover the individuality of each writer; it suits his thesis rather to view the individual as one member of a group. Nor does he possess that higher philosophical power which would enable him to see in each great work of art the laws of the universal mind of man ... M. Taine's critical writings have tended to reduce the importance of the individual, have operated together with the scientific tendencies of our time in antagonism to the lyrical, personal character of the Romantic school ... A play of Shakespeare's, a group of Victor Hugo's odes or elegies, is for M. Taine not so much the work of its individual author as the creation of the race, the *milieu*, and the moment – a document in the history and the psychology of a people.*

Edward Dowden, we take it, is not to be reckoned among the English fathers of the History of Ideas.

By such means, and no doubt by many other means more un-assuming, the term *romantic* was handed on to the eighties and nineties in England – the word that Macaulay seemed to be reaching for, the term that Carlyle and Arnold avoided, and that Hopkins with a poet's fastidious discrimination hesitated to use (distrusting it perhaps for some uncritical currency that I have not been able to trace). As an ill-defined historical category it was cross-fertilized by the shimmering echoes of early German romanticism in Walter Pater's essay, and by the Celtic qualities that Arnold celebrated and that the early Yeats turned into twilight.† Before the end of the century the word had quietly taken root as a referential term that cast iridescent colours, irritating for its vagueness yet scarcely arousing resolute definition. In 1893 William Lyon Phelps published his doctoral dissertation, *The Beginning of the Romantic Movement*, and Henry A. Beers's *History of English Romanticism* followed in 1903: both American, both writing about the eighteenth century prelude to 'The Romantics' and both thereby assuming or evading the central term. Other combinations follow: *The Romantic Triumph* (T. S. Omond, 1900), *The Romantic Revolt* (C. E. Vaughan, 1907); and 'The Romantic Revival' – Southey's phrase grafted on to the

---

* Edward Dowden, *New Studies in Literature* (1895), pp. 410, 411, 414. Dowden felt that 'the Romantic movement' had speedily exhausted itself because 'it consisted of an endless series of confessions,' and that 'that movement of our own day which has assumed the title of naturalism or realism' arose from its search for the inexhaustible riches to be found in 'the study of outward things and of social life' (p. 414). Dowden ascribes to Brunetière a laudable unwilling-ness to accept 'the ingenious paradox that every classic was in his own day a romantic' (p. 406).

† Yeats's *Celtic Twilight* was published in 1893. In his essay 'The Celtic Element in Literature' (1897) he discusses Arnold's essays on this subject and their source in Renan: see W. B. Yeats, *Essays and Introductions* (London, 1961), pp. 173–88. He singles out the passage quoted at p. 241 above and reaches a conclusion rather different from Arnold's (pp. 177–8). 'Certainly the descriptions of nature made in what Matthew Arnold calls "the faithful way," or in what he calls "the Greek way," would have lost nothing if all the meadow fountains or paved fountains were but what they seemed. When Keats wrote, in the Greek way, which adds lightness and brightness to nature ... when Shakespeare wrote in the Greek way ... when Virgil wrote in the Greek way ... they looked at nature without ecstasy ... in the modern way, the way of people who are poetical, but are more interested in one another than in a nature which has faded to be but friendly and pleasant, the way of people who have forgotten the ancient religion.'

architects' 'Gothic Revival' – provides an evocative rallying-point by suggesting renaissance, new birth through 'romanticism.'* Yet in some quarters *romantic* was distinct and abusive enough in 1897 for Jowett to say that he disliked Carlyle and Froude 'as romantics, if not charlatans'[155] – some indication of the counter-currents of 'rational' scientism that sorely afflicted some of the Victorians.

Whatever Bagehot and Dowden had achieved in scrupulous if limited definition was not a permanent heritage. The English concentration on things English seems to have encouraged many to react adversely to any study of the English 'romantics' in the context of European 'romanticism.' Sir Walter Raleigh (1861–1922), appointed in 1904 as first holder of the chair of English literature at Oxford, is an interesting case in point – even if he carries us outside the nineteenth century: he shows into what a sad state of confusion, in the mind of an eminent professor, the word *romantic* could fall by the time of the First World War. In his essay, 'On the Decline and Fall of Romanticism in 19th-century Poetry' (1913), the tags spring into being like warriors from a scattering of dragon's teeth: 'the early Romantics,' 'the Romantic Revival,' 'the new Romantic school,' 'the Romantic poets' ('rebels and exiles,' 'Revivalists, resuscitators of the past, they attain ... only to make-believe'), 'the Romantic era,' 'the Romantic age,' 'Romantic poetry,' 'the romantic apotheosis of individual feeling,' 'a modern Romantic,' 'the Romantic attitude.' The 'Romantic poets' were (in his book) Wordsworth, Coleridge, and Southey; Shelley, Byron, Landor, Keats. Then there were 'the later Romantics' – Tennyson, Morris, Rossetti, Swinburne, Browning ('the most triumphant and assured of the Romantics') – and there is mention of 'ultra-romantic poets,' 'decadent Romantic art,' 'the melancholy of the Romantic,' 'the full-blown Romantics,' 'the older Romantics.' The source of the hysteria peeps out, perhaps, when he speaks of Meredith as 'a poet whose inspiration comes from order, measure, law – from all that the Romantic poets, or most of them, made war on.'† In May 1915

*   C. L. Eastlake, author of *A History of the Gothic Revival* (1891), considered that the Gothic Revival in architecture had been finally established by the laying of the foundation of the new Parliament Houses in 1840. The revival however had become self-conscious with Horace Walpole's reconstruction of Strawberry Hill beginning in 1747. The phrase 'Romantic Revival' is curiously ambivalent through confusion of the (implied) subjective and objective genitive. (*a*) = revival of romance (romantic values); (*b*) = revival by way of (*or* through) the romantick (*or* romanticism).

†   Walter Raleigh, *On Writing and Writers, being extracts from his notebooks*, ed. George Gordon (London, 1926), pp. 187–214. Gordon writes in his Preface: 'Of the two courses on nineteenth century topics here anthologised, the earlier, on

he gave two lectures at Princeton on the theme of romance – that is, near enough, romanticism. This time he does not compound the word *romantic* with such catholic abandon as before; unlike Bagehot and Dowden he makes no attempt at clear definition; his own position is ambiguous, belligerent, desperate. But he had some inkling that all was not well in the way *romantic* was being used in literary-critical circles.

Between these two dates [1783 and 1832] a great company of English writers produced a literature of immense bulk, and of almost endless diversity of character. Yet one dominant strain in that literature has commonly been allowed to give a name to the whole period, and it is often called the Age of the Romantic Revival. We do not name other notable periods of our literature in this fashion. The name itself contains a theory, and so marks the rise of a new philosophical and aesthetic criticism. It attempts to describe as well as to name, and attaches significance not to kings, or great authors, but to the kind of writing which flourished conspicuously in that age ... Scientific names, for all their air of learned universality, are merely fossilized impressions, stereotyped portraits of a single aspect ... Mammal, amphibian, coleoptera, dicotyledon, cryptogam, – all these terms, which ... would be seen to record very simple observations, yet do lend a kind of formal majesty to ignorance.

So it is with the vocabulary of literary criticism: the first use of a name, because the name was coined by someone who felt the need of it, is often striking and instructive; the impression is fresh and new. Then the freshness wears off it, and the name becomes an outworn print, a label that serves only to recall the memory of past travel. What was created for the needs of thought becomes a thrifty device, useful only to save thinking. The best way to restore the habit of thinking is to do away with the names.

Romanticism, dates from the summer and late autumn of 1904. "The thesis," he then wrote, "is that the seeds of subsequent extravagance and decay were in the early poets – indeed, the purpose is mainly anti-Romantic." These lectures were to contain his "real creed, up-to-date ... the Classic creed, with trimmings." This, and the other course on Lamb, Hazlitt, and the rest, were combined for delivery at Cambridge in 1910–11, and were offered as alternatives when he was invited [by Emile Legouis], in 1913, to lecture at the Sorbonne.' In 'A Note on Criticism' (ibid. [1910–11], p. 216) Raleigh attacks a Crocean lecture of Spingarn's entitled 'The New Criticism,' saying: 'This new freedom and antinomianism has been produced, without doubt, by the Romantic Revival.' In his *History of Criticism* (1903) George Saintsbury decided to use the term *Modern* rather than *Romantic* in referring to the early nineteenth century: 'Some would call this criticism "Romantic"; but that term, in addition to a certain vagueness, has the drawback both of question-begging and of provocation' (III: 3). For his account of the romantic-classical debate, see Interchapter VIII, 'Summary of the Revolt' (III: 408–28).

The word Romantic loses almost all its meaning and value when it is used to characterize whole periods of our literature ... It is not needful, nor indeed is it possible, to define Romance ... The word Romance supplies no very valuable instrument of criticism even in regard to the great writers of the early nineteenth century ...*

Eventually the word *romantic* itself began to come under historical and critical investigation, with all the hazards of trying to define one complex term by reference to an equally complex and ill-defined countervailing term, in Quiller-Couch's not very strenuous essay, 'On the Terms "Classic" and "Romantic" ' (1918), and more minutely in Logan Pearsall Smith's monograph, *Four Words: Romantic, Originality, Creative, Genius* (1924), which is pretty much where this paper started on its backward exploration.

The collective terms *romantic* and *romantic poets*, and even *romanticism*, remain historians' terms. Beset as the terms were with a variety of conflicting definitions, they were for too long – and still too often are – offered as skeleton keys to a poetry and criticism of strong individuality and of definition subtle enough to demand an approach less diffuse than an historical generalization. In practice the poetry resists many of the fashionable techniques of exposition, being perfectly capable of declaring itself in its own right. Every careful reader of Wordsworth, for example, knows for how long stock generalizations about 'romantic poets' have distracted attention from the incisive, direct, and forthright criticism that Coleridge devoted to Wordsworth's art in *Biographia Literaria* – a book written in 1815 by the earliest intelligent proponent in England of romantic theory, at the time when the currents of German romantic theory were beginning tentatively to pluck at the ironbound coasts of Britain.

The term *romantic* has been clarified somewhat by critical examination in recent years, but it remains a convenient historical abstraction that at best serves a critical purpose by its divergences from particular poems and poets rather than by its coincidence. The most recent sense of *romantic* reached by back-formation from historical generalisation – a parody of what Schlegel intended – has done widespread (but probably not irreversible) damage to the precise apprehension of the early nineteenth-century poets and their

* Walter Raleigh, *Romance* (Princeton & Oxford, 1916), pp. 1–3, 8, 33. Cf. p. 36: 'If I had to choose a single characteristic of Romance as the most noteworthy, I think I should choose Distance, and should call Romance the magic of Distance.'

work. 'For,' as Wordsworth said in his Essay, supplementary to the 1815 Preface, 'to be mistaught is worse than to be untaught; and no perverseness equals that which is supported by systems, no errors are so difficult to root out as those which the understanding has pledged its credit to uphold.' Now perhaps the term *romantic poets* can without harm be used as a neutral indicator, devoid of much specific implication, meaning simply 'the major English poets of the early nineteenth century.' The rest can be left to the scholars who know how to navigate warily around and through the historical categories and make – as is the critic's way – opportunist use of what happens to be handy and happens to suit their purpose, criticism not being a science.

And yet we find a poet, who had used the word *romantic* only once before in a poem (to lament that 'Romantic Ireland's dead and gone') – a greater poet it may be than any of them – writing in 1931:

> We were the last romantics – chose for theme
> Traditional sanctity and loveliness;
> Whatever's written in what poets name
> The book of the people; whatever most can bless
> The mind of man or elevate a rhyme;
> But all is changed, that high horse riderless,
> Though mounted in that saddle Homer rode
> Where the swan drifts upon a darkening flood.

NOTES

1 See *The Letters of Charles and Mary Lamb*, ed. E. V. Lucas (London, 1935), 1: 37 (hereafter cited as *Lamb, Letters*); *Collected Letters of Samuel Taylor Coleridge*, ed. E. L. Griggs (Oxford, 1956, 1959), 1; 438, 565–6 (hereafter cited as *Coleridge, Letters*); *The Notebooks of Samuel Taylor Coleridge*, ed. Kathleen Coburn (London and New York, 1957, 1961), 1: 340 and n. (hereafter cited as *Coleridge, Notebooks*). For Wordsworth on Bürger, see *The Poetical Works of William Wordsworth*, ed. E. de Selincourt and Helen Darbishire (Oxford, 1940–49), 11; 422 (hereafter cited as *Wordsworth, Poems*). William Taylor also published translations of Lessing's *Nathan der Weise* (1791) and of Goethe's *Iphigenie auf Tauris* (1793). In 1829–30 he collected his various publications on German literary topics into a 3-volume *Historic Survey of German Poetry*, but by then his views were seriously out of date, and Carlyle handled this 'General Jail-delivery of all Publications and Manuscripts, original or translated, composed or borrowed, on the Subject of German Poetry' very roughly indeed in the *Edinburgh Review*.

2 See *The Complete Poetical Works of Samuel Taylor Coleridge*, ed. E. H. Coleridge (Oxford, 1912), 1: 72 (hereafter cited as *Coleridge, Poems*); and *Coleridge, Letters* 1: 122.

3 See my 'Bristol Library Borrowings of Southey and Coleridge, 1795–98,' *The*

Library, 5th series, IV (1949); and 'Coleridge and Southey in Bristol, 1795,' *Review of English Studies* I (1950).

4 I am grateful to Dr. Hans Eichner for drawing this passage to my attention.
5 Haydon's account is reprinted in *Lamb, Letters* II: 222–3n. Haydon was at the time working on 'Christ's Triumphal Entry into Jerusalem,' which includes the faces of Keats and Wordsworth.
6 W. Wordsworth, *The Prelude*, ed. E. de Selincourt, revised by Helen Darbishire (Oxford, 1959) (hereafter cited as *Prelude*) prints the 1805–6 and 1850 texts on facing pages.
7 *Wordsworth, Poems* III: 168.
8 Ibid., II: 99.
9 Ibid., IV: 54.
10 *Prelude*, pp. 12, 13; cf. *Wordsworth, Poems* III: 168; IV: 54.
11 For Byron on 'romantic Spain,' see p. 195 below.
12 *Wordsworth, Poems* IV: 278.
13 Ibid., IV: 198.
14 Ibid., V: 324.
15 Ibid., I: 58.
16 Ibid., I: 324.
17 Ibid., IV: 460.
18 *Journals of Dorothy Wordsworth*, ed. E. de Selincourt (London 1952) (hereafter cited as *Dorothy Wordsworth's Journals*) I: 15.
19 Ibid., I: 223–4. This episode is discussed further at p. 183 below.
20 *Dorothy Wordsworth's Journals* I: 174–5.
21 Ibid., I: 207.
22 Ibid., I: 234.
23 Ibid., I: 278.
24 Ibid., I: 286.
25 *Wordsworth, Poems* II: 435. Coleridge wrote in July 1816 that he had on his shelves 'long original poems, epic, and romantic, full of images and incidents and *mother-and-child* Sentiments and sensibilities' none of which impressed him, as Frere's poems did, with 'that sense of inventive and constructive power' (*Coleridge, Letters* IV: 647).
26 *Lamb, Letters* I: 223–4.
27 Ibid., I: 241.
28 Ibid., I: 244; cf. 251.
29 Ibid., I: 357.
30 Ibid., I: 312.
31 Ibid., I: 315–16.
32 *Coleridge, Poems* I: 156.
33 *Coleridge, Poems* I: 315; cf. *Coleridge, Letters* I: 501, 504–5, and *Coleridge, Notebooks* I: 411, 412. The kidling and goats seem to have been 'cattle' in actual life. See also p. 184 below.
34 *Coleridge, Poems* I: 92.
35 Ibid., I: 118.
36 For the 1816 version, see *Coleridge, Poems* I: 297–8. The Crewe manuscript, now British Museum Add MS 50847, is reproduced in full in *British Museum Quarterly* XXVI (1963), plates XXX, XXXI.
37 *Coleridge, Notebooks* I: 220; see also *Coleridge, Letters* I: 394, 737; and J. L. Lowes, *The Road to Xanadu* (Boston, 1930), 364–70.
38 Joseph Hucks, Coleridge's companion, published an account of the walk: *A Pedestrian Tour through North Wales in a series of Letters* (1795). On the 'shocking' quality of the North Wales landscape, perhaps because of its human emptiness, see *Inquiring Spirit*, p. 193.
39 Geoffrey Grigson, *Cornhill* (Spring 1947).
40 See note p. 179 above, and my letter to *TLS* (21 June 1947).

41 *Coleridge, Poems* I: 95.
42 Ibid., I: 104.
43 Ibid., I: 480.
44 *Biographia Literaria* II: 226.
45 *Coleridge, Notebooks* I: 411.
46 *Coleridge, Notebooks* I: 1211.
47 Ibid., I: 1225.
48 Ibid., II: 2691.
49 Ibid., II: 2757.
50 Ibid., II: 2848. Wordsworth in 'Tintern Abbey' noticed 'these steep and lofty cliffs' and the 'wild secluded scene' of the Wye Valley (*Wordsworth, Poems* II: 259).
51 Ibid., II: 2515. Cf. Coleridge, *Friend*, ed. B. Rooke (London & Princeton, 1969), I: 439: 'The restless spirit of republican ambition, engendered by their [*i.e.*, the Athenians'] success in a just war, and by the romantic character of that success, had already formed a close alliance with luxury in its early and most vigorous state, when it acts as an appetite to enkindle, and before it has exhausted and dulled the vital energies by the habit of enjoyment.'
52 The essay was first published in 1805, issued twice again in 1806, 9th ed., 1830. The passage quoted here is from the 1813 ed., pp. 167–245.
53 *Coleridge, Notebooks* III: 4397, *f.* 53 (10 March 1818); *variatim* in *Literary Remains* I: 225, and *Biographia Literaria* II: 259.
54 *The Rime of the Ancient Mariner*, first published in *Lyrical Ballads* (1798), was extensively revised for *Lyrical Ballads* (1800). The 1798 version can be found in *Coleridge, Poems* II: 1030–48, and is printed facing the last version in the Nonesuch edition, ed. Stephen Potter. The marginal gloss was added – not quite complete in all details – in *Sibylline Leaves* (1817).
55 See, for example, *Inquiring Spirit*, pp. 190–1.
56 *Wordsworth, Poems* III: 91n.
57 *Coleridge, Notebooks* III: 3240. Cf. Hopkins' use of *keeping*, p. 245 below.
58 *Lamb, Letters* II: 153.
59 *The Letters of William and Dorothy Wordsworth: The Later Years*, ed. E. de Selincourt (Oxford, 1939) I: 308 (hereafter cited as *Letters of Wordsworth: Later Years*). A telescoped account of these proceedings is given in *Wordsworth, Poems* III: 447–8.
60 *Biographia Literaria* II: 101.
61 Cf. Wordsworth on the twisted thorn tree which, long familiar, suddenly became compelling and symbolic (note, p. 179 above).
62 *Biographia Literaria* II: 5.
63 Ibid., II: 303.
64 Ibid., II: 121.
65 *Keats, Letters* I: 360.
66 Ibid., II: 125.
67 Ian Jack, *Keats and the Mirror of Art* (Oxford, 1967), p. 141.
68 The *London Magazine* for April 1820 recognizes all four of these painters in *Endymion*.
69 *The Works of Lord Byron*, ed. R. E. Prothero and E. H. Coleridge (London, 1898–1904), XVI: 123 (hereafter cited as *Byron, Works*).
70 *Tait's Edinburgh Magazine* (1846).
71 Ian Jack, *English Literature 1815–1832* (Oxford, 1963), pp. 408–10.
72 The following group of references to Hazlitt is to the Nonesuch edition, ed. Geoffrey Keynes (1930), giving date of composition followed by page reference. Corresponding references to *The Complete Works of William Hazlitt*, ed. P. P. Howe (London, 1933) (hereafter cited as *Hazlitt, Works*) are given in n. 73.
73 Nonesuch, p. 46 = *Hazlitt, Works* XII: 224; 82 = VIII: 189; 164 = VIII: 325; 254 = XII: 135; 343 = XVII: 243; 534 = XVII: 130; 733 = XI: 34; 502 = XVII: 108.
74 *Hazlitt, Works* XVI: 27; XII: 343.

75 See, for example, *Coleridge, Notebooks* I: 452, 1412. Cf. ibid., II: 1973: 'A complex Ship to Vandervelt was completely *one* Thing, one abstract, as an Egg or one of its ropes to an ordinary Artist. Sir G. Beaumont found great advantage in learning to draw from Nature thro' Gause Spectacles.'

76 *Hazlitt, Works* XII: 289' See also XX: 217, for his statement that Coleridge preferred Salvator Rosa to Claude.

77 *Coleridge, Letters* IV: 831.

78 *Coleridge, Notebooks* I: 1255.

79 *Coleridge, Notebooks* II: 2546.

80 *Henry Crabb Robinson on Books and Their Writers*, ed. E. J. Morley (London, 1938): I: 63, 11 February 1811 (hereafter cited as *Robinson, Books*); cf. entries for 29 January and 6 November 1811.

81 René Wellek, 'The Concept of "Romanticism" in Literary History,' in his *Concepts of Criticism* (New Haven, 1963), pp. 128–98 (hereafter cited as *Wellek, Concepts*). See especially pp. 145–6. This article was first published in *Comparative Literature* I (1949).

82 In *Literary Remains*, ed. H. N. Coleridge, I, II (1836); and in *Coleridge's Shakespearean Criticism*, ed. T. M. Raysor (1930), the 2nd ('Everyman') ed. of which in 1960 was the occasion of Orsini's article on Coleridge and Schlegel.

83 *Robinson, Books* I: 135; but cf. p. 178. Henry Nelson Coleridge draws an incisive contrast between Coleridge and Mackintosh in the essay quoted on p. 232 below. (*Jackson*, p. 623).

84 For example, *Robinson, Books* I: 21, 123, 200, 208, 307. Edith J. Morley (H. C. Robinson, *Blake, Coleridge, Wordsworth, Lamb, &c*, London, 1922, p. xiv) states that Robinson, 'who, as a student at Jena, had been introduced to Goethe, had heard Schelling lecture upon Methodology, and had successfully impersonated Fichte, ... never forgot to sing the praises of Kant, to magnify the Schlegels, and to spread the gospel of transcendentalism,' also provided Mme de Staël with 'most of the information which resulted in her *De l'Allemagne*: she summoned him to Berlin in 1804 ... that he might help her to acquire some notion of German philosophy.' For Schlegel's confirmation of this statement, see *Robinson, Books* I: 298–9; and for a meeting of Robinson, Mme de Staël, and A. W. Schlegel in 1814, ibid., I: 149.

85 *Robinson, Books* I: 132; cf. p. 17.

86 See *Coleridge, Notebooks* I: 1705 and n.

87 Printed in *Inquiring Spirit*, ed. Kathleen Coburn (London, 1951), pp. 151–2. See also *Raysor* I: 5: 'Whence the harmony that strikes us in the wildest natural landscapes, – in the relative shapes of rocks, the harmony of colors in the heath ferns, and lichens, the leaves of the beech and oak, the stems and ripe choc[ol]ate branches of the birch and other mountain trees, varying from verging autumn to returning spring ... The [landscapes] are effected by a single energy, modified *ab intra* in each component part.'

88 Printed in *Raysor* I: 175–6; *variatim* in *Literary Remains* II: 32–6.

89 Printed in *Raysor* II: 199–200; a more discursive version by Coleridge in *Coleridge, Letters* III: 418–19.

90 *Robinson, Books* I: 84, 85, 88.

91 See, for example, *Raysor* II: 216.

92 Ibid., II: 242.

93 *Literary Remains* I: 188.

94 *Inquiring Spirit*, p. 192. For a parody of Gothick romance-writing, see Coleridge's letter on Scott's *Lady of the Lake* (*Coleridge, Letters* III: 291–5).

95 *Raysor* II: 255. Cf. II: 252, 257.

96 *Coleridge, Letters* IV: 839. The claim to have anticipated Schlegel in the distinction between judgment and genius is also found in *Biographia Literaria* I: 22n and 102–3.

97 A. W. Schlegel was appointed an Honorary Fellow of the Royal Society of

Literature and read a three-part paper on 4 and 18 December 1833 and 23 April 1834.

98   *Hazlitt, Works* XVI: 61–6: also quoted in *Weisinger*.
99   *Hazlitt, Works* XVI: 123.
100   De Quincey, *Collected Writings*, ed. D. Masson (Edinburgh, 1889–90), II: 72–4; also quoted more fully in *Weisinger*.
101   See *Weisinger*, pp. 485–7.
102   *Byron, Works* V: 104. For other comments by Byron, see *Wellek, Concepts*, p. 148, n. 58.
103   Ibid., V: 554n.
104   *Contemporary Reviews of Romantic Poetry*, ed. John Wain (London, 1953), p. 84. (hereafter cited as *Wain*). This collection offers an interesting small group of reviews of Wordsworth, Coleridge, Byron, Shelley, Keats, and Tennyson; the text in some cases is abbreviated. For a comprehensive group of reviews of Coleridge, see *Coleridge: The Critical Heritage*, ed. J. R. de J. Jackson (London an New York, 1960) (hereafter cited as *Jackson*). Thomas Love Peacock, in *The Four Ages of Poetry* (1820), saw Wordsworth as leader of a school of poets in 'The Age of Brass.' James Montgomery, *Lectures on General Literature* (1833), described the age since Cowper as the third era of modern literature, and called Southey, Wordsworth, and Coleridge the 'three pioneers, if not the absolute founders, of the existing style of English literature' (*Wellek, Concepts*, p. 155).
105   *Jackson*, p. 469. HNC was writing in the *Etonian*; see p. 231 and note.
106   *Edinburgh Review* (November 1812), noticing a parody of *Lyrical Ballads* in James and Horace Smith's anonymous *Rejected Addresses*: *E. Smith*, p. 128.
107   *Biographia Literaria* I: 52.
108   *Blackwoods*,' May 1820: *E. Smith*, p. 318.
109   See p. 234 below.
110   *Critical Review* on Coleridge's *Wallenstein* translation: *Jackson* p. 64.
111   *Edinburgh Review* (October 1807): *E. Smith*, p. 76.
112   *Wain*, pp. 54–5, 53.
113   *Edinburgh Review* (November 1814, October 1815): *Wain*, pp. 71, 60.
114   *Edinburgh Review* (September 1816): *Jackson*, pp. 234–5.
115   *Blackwood's* (October 1817): *Wain*, p. 183.
116   Quoted on p. 217 above; see n. 104. For a sustained contrast wih 'all the other great living Poets' to Coleridge's discredit, see *Jackson*, pp. 330–3.
117   *Blackwood's* (July 1818): *Wain*, p. 64.
118   *Wordsworth, Poems* II: 385.
119   *Coleridge, Letters* I: 602; *Wordsworth, Letters: Early Years* (2nd ed.), p. 263.
120   *Coleridge, Letters* I: 123, 631; cf. *Dorothy Wordsworth Journal* I: 63–4 (4–6 October 1800).
121   Ibid., I: 627: II: 830.
122   Leigh Hunt, *Foliage* (1818): *E. Smith*, pp. 276–7. See also ibid., p. 127, 'great captain'; p. 216, 'founder'; p. 273, 'head'.
123   *Edinburgh Review* (August 1817): *Jackson*, p. 302. My italics. Cf. Hazlitt (Nonesuch ed.), p. 744: 'His [Wordsworth's] later philosophic productions ... are classical and courtly.'
124   See, e.g., *E. Smith*, pp. 99, 163, 187–9, 262, 333, 336, 360, and *Jackson*, p. 386. Hazlitt referred to *The Excursion* as 'a scholastic romance' (*London Magazine* (May 1814): *Hazlitt, Works* XIX: 44).
125   *Biographia Literaria* I: 50–1. Cf. Coleridge, *Letters* III: 433.
126   *Monthly Review* (January 1819): *Jackson*, p. 411.
127   July 1819: *E. Smith*, p. 310.
128   *New Monthly Magazine* (October 1820), ? by T. N. Talfourd: *E. Smith*, pp. 359–60, 360–1.
129   *E. Smith*, pp. 6, 237.
130   *Blackwood's* (October 1819): *Jackson*, pp. 450–1. At p. 447 he praises particularly

Love, The Ancient Mariner, and *Christabel,* and thought that if *Christabel* were completed it would be 'the most splendid of the three.'

131   *Coleridge, Letters* I: 631.
132   *Jackson,* p. 606.
133   *Biographia Literaria* I; 50.
134   *Quarterly Review* (October 1814), p. 90.
135   Matthew Arnold, *Lectures and Essays in Criticism,* ed. R. H. Super (Ann Arbor, 1962), III: 107: 'Heinrich Heine' (1863) (hereafter cited as *Arnold, Essays*).
136   *Two Notebooks of Thomas Carlyle,* ed. C. E. Norton (New York, 1898), p. 111; cited in *Wellek, Concepts.*
137   *Carlyle, Essays* III: 218: 'Historic Survey of German Poetry' (1831), for which see also n. 144 below.
138   Ibid., v: 134 (1837).
139   Ibid., I: 141, 170 (1828).
140   Ibid., vI: 249: 'Ludwig Tieck' (1827).
141   Ibid., II: 276.
142   Ibid., I: 246. Cf., for example, I: 46, 101; II: 197; III: 235.
143   Ibid., III: 71.
144   Ibid., III: 249. Carlyle had the concept from Goethe.
145   *Arnold, Essays* III: 361. Originally delivered in four lectures at Oxford, 'On the Study of Celtic Literature' was later provided with an introduction and later again divided into six sections. The 4th lecture opened at the beginning of what was later section vi. For Coleridge's notice of Celtic influence, see p. 206 above.
146   *Arnold, Essays,* III: 290. Ruskin, in *Modern Painters* (1843) and *The Stones of Venice* (1853), finds the 'essence of modern romance' in Scott, notes its weaknesses, and decides that Romance 'depends for its force on the existence of ruins and traditions ... The instinct to which it appeals can hardly be felt in America' ('Library Ed.,' 1906, xI: 224, v: 335–7, 369). In 1854 he declares that 'this [romantic] feeling ... is one of the holiest parts of your being ... true affection is romantic – true religion is romantic' (ibid., xII: 53 *ff.*). In 1873 he says that the work of 'Romantic writers and painters ... however brilliant or lovely, remains imperfect, and without authority' (ibid., xxIII: 122; cf. 119, 124). In 1883 (Oxford lectures) he says: 'I use the word "romantic" always in a noble sense; meaning the habit of regarding the external and real world as a singer of Romaunts would have regarded it in the Mid Ages, and as Scott, Burns, Byron, and Tennyson have regarded it'; and 'I do not use the word Romantic as opposed to Classic, but as opposed to the prosaic characters of selfishness and stupidity, in all times, and among all nations' (ibid., xxxIII: 269, 374; cf. 291–2).
147   *The Journals and Papers of Gerard Manley Hopkins,* ed. Humphry House and Graham Storey (Oxford, 1959), pp. 54, 56, 137.
148   *Hopkins, Letters* I: 172.
149   Ibid., II: 98–9.
150   *Wellek, Concepts,* p. 150. Although I have not considered *romantic* as a musical-critical term in England, I note its frequency in the translation of Schumann's 2-vol. *Music and Musicians* by the American Fanny R. Ritter (London, [?1876, 1880]. In 1853 Schumann collected his periodical writings for 1831–44.
151   Walter Bagehot, *Literary Studies* (Everyman, 1911, 1916), II: 317, 332, 337.
152   Edward Dowden, *Studies in Literature 1789–1877* (1878), p. 25.
153   Ibid., pp. 336–8.
154   Ibid., p. 405.
155   Leslie Stephen, *Studies of a Biographer* (London, 1898–1902), II: 142: cited in *OED.*

MAURICE Z. SHRODER

France /
Roman – Romanesque –
Romantique – Romantisme

Romantique has been, from the eighteenth century to the twentieth, one of the most emotion-laden words in the French language; it has also been one of the most difficult to define with any precision. The grotesque efforts of Musset's comic provincials, Dupuis and Cotonet, have given way, it is true, to the more serious investigations of such scholars as Alexis François, André Monglond, and Charles Bruneau;[1] but modern lexicographers often seem no more sure of themselves when they confront *romantique* and *romantisme* than did their predecessors of the 1820s.[2] Those earlier lexicographers were justified, of course, in that they had witnessed a radical change in the meaning of the words. The confusion of Dupuis and Cotonet in 1836 merely echoes that voiced twenty years before by Auguste, vicomte de Saint-Chamans, in his critique of Schlegel, Sismondi, and Mme de Staël, *L'Anti-romantique* (1816): 'Et que dirai-je du mot romantique? *que de peines n'ai-je pas prises, que de lignes n'ai-je pas lues pour en découvrir le sens juste, et l'apprendre à mes compatriotes! peines superflues! lectures infructueuses! quand je crois le saisir, il change de masque, et s'offre sous un nouveau sens.*'[3] That same year, the satirist, Joseph-Etienne Jouy, had noted the transformation of meaning that was just occurring: 'Romantique. *Terme de jargon sentimental, dont quelques écrivains se sont servis pour caractériser une nouvelle école de littérature sous la direction du professeur Schlegel ... Ce mot envahisseur n'a d'abord été admis qu'à la suite et dans le sens de* pittoresque, *dont on aurait peut-être dû se contenter; mais il a passé tout à coup du domaine descriptif, qui lui était assigné, dans les espaces de l'imagination.*'[4] Jouy's distinction is clear, but it is too absolute. Even in the eighteenth century, '*les espaces de l'imagination*' coloured the use of *romantique*. On the other hand, it was indeed first and foremost a descriptive term, and the most important early instances of its use occur in connection with landscape – a use which followed not merely that of *pittoresque* but also that of the much older *romanesque*.[5] To understand Jouy's mock anger or the mock confusion of Saint-Chamans, we must look back to the eighteenth century, to the gradual emergence of *romantique* and the gradual discrediting of *romanesque*.

The *locus classicus* of the word *romantique* in the eighteenth century is undoubtedly Jean-Jacques Rousseau's *Rêveries du promeneur solitaire*. When Rousseau wrote, near the beginning of the 'Cinquième promenade,' that '*les rives du lac de Bienne sont plus sauvages et romantiques que celles du lac de Genève,*' he conferred on the word an authority it had never before possessed, the authority concomitant with its use by a major writer. Yet Rousseau himself hesitated in his use of this neologism, which his host at Ermenonville, René de Girardin, had just explained and defended in his *De la composition des paysages* (1777). The '*rives romantiques*' have, by the end of the 'Cinquième promenade,' become merely '*les romanesques rivages,*' a phrase that could have disturbed no eighteenth-century reader.

Curiously enough, the year that saw the posthumous appearance of the *Rêveries*, 1782, witnessed the publication of another text important to the history of *romantique* – *Les Jardins, ou l'art d'embellir les paysages*, a versified manual on the art of gardening by the academic poet, Jacques Delille. In accord with the taste of his century, Delille expresses his preference for 'English gardens' – those which emphasize and even exaggerate the picturesque effects of nature, those which recall the tormented landscapes of Salvator Rosa. In an apostrophe to Thomas Whately, the author of one of his sources, *Observations on Modern Gardening* (1770), Delille declares:

> *Loin de ces froids essais qu'un vain effort étale,*
> *Aux champs de Midleton, aux monts de Dovedale,*
> *Whateli, je te suis ; viens, j'y monte avec toi.*
> *Que je m'y sens saisi d'un agréable effroi !*
> *Tous ces rocs variant leurs gigantesques cimes,*
> *Vers le ciel élancés, roulés dans des abîmes,*
> *L'un par l'autre appuyés, l'un sur l'autre étendus,*
> *Quelquefois dans les airs hardiment suspendus,*

Les uns taillés en tours, en arcades rustiques,
Quelques-uns à travers leurs noirâtres portiques
Du ciel dans le lointain laissant percer l'azur,
Des sources, des ruisseaux le cours brillant & pur,
Tout rappelle à l'esprit ces magiques retraites,
Ces romanesques lieux qu'ont chantés les poètes.[6]

In the revised edition of *Les Jardins* published twenty years later, having emigrated to England during the Terror, Delille altered the final line of this apostrophe and used the word which Rousseau (and, for that matter, Whately) had used before him: '*Ces romantiques lieux qu'ont chantés les poëtes.*'[7] By this time, *romantique* had more than Rousseau's authority behind it, since the Académie Française had admitted it to the fifth edition of its dictionary (1798): '*Il se dit ordinairement Des lieux, des paysages, qui rappellent à l'imagination les descriptions des poëmes et des romans.*'

As the Académie's definition and the texts from Rousseau and Delille indicate, *romantique* had entered the French language as a vaguely exotic, anglicized doublet for the authentically French word *romanesque*. Pierre Letourneur, in the *Discours* which serves as preface to his translation of Shakespeare (1776), had defended the anglicism on the grounds that '*le mot Anglois est plus heureux & plus énergique*' than either *romanesque* or *pittoresque*.[8] By 1791, with the examples of Letourneur, Girardin, and Rousseau as justification, the authors of the volumes on the fine-arts in Panckoucke's *Encyclopédie méthodique* can write: '*Le mot* romantique *appartient à la langue Angloise: plusieurs écrivains françois en ont fait usage, & comme il n'a point d'équivalent dans notre langue, il mérite d'y être adopté.*'* The *t* which betrays the English origin of *romantique*, its derivation from the medieval *romaunt* rather than from *roman*, bothered even the grammarian Domergue, who noted (also in 1791): '*Il me semble qu'on devrait dire romanique. Un pays romantique,*' he continued, nevertheless, '*est un pays propre aux idées que réveillent les romans.*'[9] Like the Académie, he drains the word of all emotional connotation, reducing it merely to a derivative adjective. Emotion was, however, what *romantique* was designed to convey, as Letourneur had already written. Like *romanesque*, it derived its meaning from the word *roman* – and in the eighteenth century, in spite of the development of

* A. Millin, in his *Dictionnaire des beaux-arts* (1806), revises this passage in such a way as to indicate an increased knowledge about the word and an increased use of it: 'Le mot romantique appartient aux langues anglaise et allemande; plusieurs écrivains français en ont fait usage, et comme il n'a point d'équivalent dans notre langue, il a mérité d' être adopté en peinture comme en littérature.'

the French novel from Marivaux to Laclos, *roman* still carried the weight of that tradition which had flourished in Honoré d'Urfé's *Astrée* and in the works of the precious novelists of the mid-seventeenth century. A *roman* – a romance rather than a novel – was, according to the Académie, an '*ouvrage ordinairement en prose, contenant des fictions qui représentent des aventures rares dans la vie, et le développement entier des passions humaines.*' One has only to think of Rousseau's *Confessions* in order to understand the effect of romance on a reader:'*Ces émotions confuses, que j'éprouvois coup sur coup, n'altéroient point la raison que je n'avois pas encore; mais elles m'en formèrent une d'une autre trempe, et me donnèrent de la vie humaine des notions bizarres et romanesques, dont l'expérience et la réflexion n'ont jamais bien pu me guérir.*'[10] Extraordinary adventures, the revelation of passion, the bizarre and the fabulous – one understands why Balzac, defending the *Scènes de la vie privée* as accurate representations of nineteenth-century life, should prize the veracity of details more than the variety of situations in such '*ouvrages improprement appelés* Romans.'[11] As he so often does when discussing the theory of the novel, Diderot had anticipated Balzac's argument (and had provided an unwitting gloss on Rousseau's analysis of his own reactions) in his *Eloge de Richardson* (1762): '*Par un roman, on a entendu jusqu'à ce jour un tissu d'événements chimériques et frivoles, dont la lecture était dangereuse pour le goût et pour les mœurs. Je voudrais bien qu'on trouvât un autre nom pour les ouvrages de Richardson, qui élèvent l'esprit, qui touchent l'âme, qui respirent partout l'amour du bien, et qu'on appelle aussi des romans.*'[12] Such objections were rare; the Académie recorded common usage in noting that '*On dit d'Un récit destitué de vraisemblance et de preuves,* Cela a tout l'air d'un roman.' In their root meanings, then, *romanesque* and *romantique* conveyed notions of a reason which reason knows not, of the fabulous, the bizarre, the sentimental – and, although the novel has changed, such meanings endure even today. (*Roman* itself remains ambiguous, a fact that has forced some critics to designate prose romances by the monstrous tautology, *roman romanesque.*)

Instances of these root meanings of *romantique* – the adjective which suggests the atmosphere of the *roman*, if not its actual form – are not common even in the later eighteenth century. Two, however, occur in a single work, Chateaubriand's *Essai sur les révolutions* (1797) – written, significantly enough, in London. As he reviews the peoples of the ancient world and arrives at the Celts, Chateaubriand contemplates the literary possibilities which he himself will realize in *Les Martyrs:* '*Le tableau des nations barbares offre je ne sais quoi de roman-*

tique qui nous attire. Nous aimons qu'on nous retrace des usages différents des nôtres, surtout si les siècles y ont imprimé cette grandeur qui règne dans les choses antiques, comme ces colonnes qui paroissent plus belles lorsque la mousse des temps s'y est attachée.'[13] His examples, 'le Gaulois à la chevelure bouclée, aux larges bracca' and 'la jeune fille, à l'air sauvage et aux yeux bleus,' recall the picturesque qualities which were generally associated with the *romantique*. His reflections on the tragic episodes of the *Helvetiorum Respublica*, on the other hand, announce the romanticized history that will form the basis of nineteenth-century melodrama: 'L'aventure du vieux Henri, auquel le gouverneur de Landeberg fit arracher les yeux, celle du gentilhomme Wolffenschiesz avec la femme du paysan Conrad, la surprise des divers châteaux des ducs d'Autriche par les paysans, portent avec elles un air romantique qui, se mariant aux grandes scènes naturelles des Alpes, cause un plaisir bien vif au lecteur.'[14] In the end we return to the vistas of nature and to the customary use of *romantique* in the eighteenth century.

When applied to landscapes or to decor in general, *romanesque* and *romantique* recalled the elaborate descriptions, poetic and picturesque, which Furetière had ridiculed, in *Le Roman bourgeois*, as early as 1666. The poetaster, Evariste-Désiré de Parny, could satirize this 'vrai nouveau, / Qui ne veut rien de la nature, / Un vrai dont la raison murmure,' in 'Radotage,' a short poem addressed to novelists (1810):

O combien de pensers profonds,
Combien de sentiments féconds,
Dans un clair de lune ou d'étoiles !
Un précipice? avidement
J'écoute sa voix sympathique.
Un désert? quel tressaillement
A cette voix si romantique !
Dans les ruines, dans les bois,
Sous les rochers, par-tout des voix.[15]

But Parny was incidentally noting the new popularity of the word he chose to ridicule. It was a popularity that did not come without question. An anonymous reviewer of Charles-François-Philibert Masson's *La Nouvelle Astrée, ou les aventures romantiques du temps passé* (1805), in criticizing the style of the work, made this passing reflection: '...je le prie de me dire ce qu'il entend par aventures romantiques. Il seroit fâcheux pour un membre de l'Institut d'avoir mis sur le titre même de son ouvrage un mot qui n'est pas français.'[16] And yet French it had become.

Louis-Sébastien Mercier celebrated it in his *Néologie* (1801): '*Je salue tout ce qui est Romantique avec une sorte d'enthousiasme.*' He continued, anticipating the difficulties of later lexicographers: '*On sent le Romantique, on ne le définit point; le romanesque, dans les arts, est faux et bizarre auprès de lui.*' The emphasis on emotion is constant; and, as Mercier's final sentence reveals, a curious separation of functions was taking place. *Romanesque* retains its negative connotations, whereas *romantique* benefits from more positive associations. The contrast was, in fact, apparent as early as the 1770s, in Letourneur's *Discours* and Girardin's essay on gardening. Panckoucke's authorities on the fine arts are following Girardin when they make their largely neutral distinction between the two words: '*Le* romanesque *est ce qui appartient au roman, le* romantique *est ce qui lui convient ou qui a l'air de lui appartenir. Le sujet d'un tableau peut être tiré d'un roman, & par conséquent être* romanesque, *sans être traité d'une manière qui ait rien de* romantique.' A romantic manner, they add, depends on '*d'agréables bizarreries dans les ajustemens, des parures fantasques, d'ingénieuses singularités dans le site, dans la disposition de la scène*'; their major example is, surprisingly enough, Watteau. When Senancour considers the words in the curiously titled fragment of *Obermann*, '*De l'expression romantique et du* ranz des vaches,' he emulates Letourneur by casting the distinction in more emotional terms: '*Le romanesque séduit les imaginations vives et fleuries; le romantique seul suffit aux âmes profondes, à la véritable sensibilité.*'[17] And by 1846, the Bescherelle brothers' *Dictionnaire national* makes the distinction perhaps even more absolute than a modern lexicographer would admit:

Ce qui est romanesque *est étrange, et à ce mot s'attache toujours une idée plus ou moins marquée d'ironie, d'invraisemblance et d'incrédulité; il fait songer à une suite ou à un tissu d'aventures surnaturelles, ou il marque le goût qu'on a pour ces sortes de faits.* Romantique *est une qualification sérieuse et en bonne part, qui n'annonce rien de bizarre, de fantastique, d'extravagant, mais une ressemblance plus ou moins grande, sous le rapport de la beauté, entre un site réel et ceux qui sont décrits dans les romans.*

The *Dictionnaire national* still makes the distinction in terms of landscape. Ten years earlier, Musset's Dupuis and Cotonet, pursuing their investigations of *romantique* and *romantisme*, had been astonished to hear a young lady use the word in that sense: '... *elle se retourna du côté du moulin à eau qui est près du gué, où il y avait des sacs de farine, des oies et un bœuf attaché: "Voilà un site romantique,*" dit-elle à sa gouvernante. *A ce mot, nous nous sentîmes saisis de notre curiosité première. Eh, ventrebleu, dis-je, que veut-elle dire? ne saurons-nous pas à quoi nous en tenir?*'[18] What is more surprising is that the eighth (and most recent) edition of the Académie's dictionary (1935) retains the eighteenth-century meaning: '*Il s'est dit des Lieux, des paysages qui rappellent à l'imagination les descriptions des poèmes et des romans.*' Only the tense of the verb suggests what Paul Robert finally makes explicit, that this use of the word is obsolete.

The use of *romantique* as a qualification of landscapes was, as I have said, its real entry into the French language; and it is necessary to examine that use in more detail. When the abbé Le Blanc reported on the state of English gardens in 1745, he remarked '*un air, qu'ils appellent en leur Langue*, Romantic, *c'est-à-dire, à peu près*, Pittoresque'; the particulars he observed were the construction of artificial ruins, ridiculous obelisks, pathetic arches of triumph.[19] His emphasis, as his translation of the English *romantic* indicates, is purely pictorial, although he does evoke the notion of ambience. That notion is clarified by Letourneur. Rejecting *romanesque* as too suggestive of the fabulous and the unnatural, Letourneur goes on to reduce *pittoresque* to a mere effect of pictorial inspiration: '*Si ce vallon n'est que* pittoresque, *c'est un point de l'étendue qui prête au Peintre & qui mérite d'être distingué & saisi par l'art. Mais s'il est* Romantique; *on desire* [sic] *de s'y reposer, l'œil se plaît à le regarder & bientôt l'imagination attendrie le peuple de scènes intéressantes: elle oublie le vallon pour se complaire dans les idées, dans les images qu'il lui a inspirées.*'[20] The romantic landscape, in other words, is one which may become a springboard for the poetic imagination; the word *romantique* suggests less about the landscape itself than it does about the state of mind of the observer. We do not read the 'Cinquième promenade,' after all, for what it has to say about *l'île Saint-Pierre* and the *lac de Bienne*; it is Rousseau's emotions and reflections that give a meaning to his surroundings.

What the state of the observer is, and what kind of landscape will provoke or stimulate it, is a much more complex question. Rousseau's coupling of the adjectives *romantiques* and *sauvages* recalls Letourneur's evocation of dense forests, mountains, the expanse of the sea and the cloudy sky. Girardin, on the other hand, seems to negate these associations: '... *sans être farouche ni sauvage, la situation* Romantique *doit être tranquille et solitaire.*'[21] Yet the landscape he goes on to describe is an Alpine panorama, uncivilized and untrammeled, where man himself may be free from the constricting effects of civilization. This is the connotation which Senancour will recall in *Obermann*: '*Les effets romantiques sont les accens d'une langue que les hommes ne connaissent pas tous, et qui devient étrangère à plusieurs contrées. On cesse bientôt de les entendre quand on ne vit plus avec eux; et cependant cette harmonie romantique est la seule qui conserve à nos cœurs les couleurs de la jeunesse et la fraîcheur de la vie. L'homme de la société ne sent plus ces effets trop éloignés de ses habitudes.'*[22] *Romantique*, then, goes beyond the simply imaginative and conveys that paradoxical love for the simple and the uncivilized that developed during the age of enlightenment: the *paysage* (or *situation*) *romantique* provides an alternative to the rationalism and the elegant artifice of civilization. It is not quite nature in the raw, as the very derivation of *romantique* implies; it is, like the landscape of the pastoral, a natural perspective idealized and dignified by literary associations.[23]

Delille, in *Les Jardins*, all but defines the nature of that poetic colouration of the landscape when he describes his reactions to the English countryside: '*Que je m'y sens saisi d'un agréable effroi!*' The oxymoron, while it may have been inspired by Boileau's reflections on tragedy (*Art poétique* III, 17–20) –

> Si d'un beau mouvement l'agréable fureur
> Souvent ne nous remplit d'une douce 'terreur,'
> Ou n'excite en notre âme une 'pitié' charmante,
> En vain vous étalez une scène savante ...

– recalls at the same time the definition of the sublime, of which (according to both Boileau and Burke) terror is always the ruling principle. The notions occur side by side in another descriptive poem by Delille, *L'Homme des champs* (1800):

> Reprenons notre course autour de vos domaines,
> Et du palais magique où se rendent les eaux
> Ensemble remontons aux lieux de leurs berceaux,
> Vers ces monts, de vos champs dominateurs antiques.
> Quels sublimes aspects, quels tableaux romantiques![24]

The awe that one feels in the presence of untamed nature is the emotion conveyed by the word *romantique*.

The landscape becomes, then, any one that can inspire that awe. Parny may have mocked the 'déserts' and the 'précipices'; a long line of writers found themselves drawn to what Senancour epitomized as the *romantisme* of the Alps.[25] Rousseau's happiness during his last days at Ermenonville, according to a letter written by René de Girardin, was provoked by the resemblance of his surroundings to Switzerland:

Le plus souvent, et surtout dans les ardeurs du jour, il s'enfonçait dans la profondeur de la forêt; d'autrefois [sic] il se promenait en rêvant sur le bord des eaux, ou bien *gravissait sur les montagnes couvertes de bois et qui dominent le village. Le pays le plus sauvage avait pour lui des charmes d'autant plus intéressants qu'il y retrouvait mieux la touche originale et franche de la nature. Les rochers, les sapins, les genévriers tortueux y rappelaient de plus près à sa féconde imagination les situations* romantiques *du pays bien-aimé de son enfance, et lui remettaient sous les yeux les heureux rivages de* Vevai *et les rochers amoureux de* Meillerie.**

The emphasis on emotion and memory recalls the 'Cinquième promenade' itself; but *romantique* crops up even in the more arid context of the Swiss geologist Horace-Bénédict de Saussure's *Voyages dans les Alpes* (1796):

On voit dans cette gorge que les montagnes qui forment cette enceinte sont d'une serpentine demi-dure. En sortant de la gorge, on voit une belle chute & un engouffrement du torrent du Mont-Cervin, qui se perd ensuite sous des rocs. On entre de là dans une autre petite enceinte, dont le fond plat est une belle prairie que traverse le ruisseau du Mont-Cervin, avec un chalet & des troupeaux sur ses bords, & une chapelle dans le haut, situation vraiment romantique.[26]

The context is, in general, more poetically realized; Saussure's use of *romantique* indicates how automatically the word arises in descriptions of Switzerland – or of landscapes which recall the topography of that country. Delille's England, with its mountains and distant panoramas, could easily pass for the Swiss Alps; the same might be said about Chateaubriand's America. By a coincidence that James Joyce would have appreciated, Chateaubriand, like Rousseau, was forced to pass some time on an *île Saint-Pierre,* this one off the coast of Newfoundland:

Durant les quinze jours que nous passâmes à terre, T. et moi nous allions courir dans les montagnes de cette île affreuse; nous nous perdions au milieu des brouillards dont elle est sans cesse couverte. L'imagination sensible de mon ami se plaisoit à ces scènes sombres et romantiques *: quelquefois, errant au milieu des nuages et des bouffées de vent, en entendant les mugissements d'une mer que nous ne pouvions découvrir, égarés sur une bruyère laineuse et morte, au bord d'un torrent rouge qui rouloit entre des rochers, T. s'imaginoit être le barde de Cona; et, en sa qualité de demi-Ecossois, il se mettoit à déclamer des passages d'*Ossian, *pour lesquels il improvisoit des airs sauvages.*[27]

---

*   René-Louis de Girardin, 'Lettre à Sophie, comtesse de ***' (July 1778), in [Stanislas de Girardin], *Lettre de Stanislas Girardin, à M. Musset-Pathay, auteur de l'ouvrage intitulé Histoire de la vie et des ouvrages de J. J. Rousseau* (Paris, 1824), pp. 34–5. Compare Rousseau's evocation of the Alpine landscape: 'Il me faut des torrens, des rochers, des sapins, des bois noirs, des montagnes, des chemins raboteux à monter et à descendre, des précipices à mes côtés qui me fassent bien peur' (*Confessions* I: 277).

For those of us who know the New Jersey Palisades as they are to-day, encumbered by factories and amusement parks, the other instance of *romantique* in the *Essai sur les révolutions* is a little more surprising. Traveling by boat from New York to Albany, Chateaubriand passed not far from Tappan, where Major John André, the young English Adjutant General who conspired with Benedict Arnold for the surrender of West Point, had been hanged in 1780, 'lamented,' according to his sarcophagus in Westminster Abbey, 'even by his foes.' As an American girl sang a ballad inspired by the execution, Chateaubriand contemplated his surroundings:

*Le soleil se couchoit; nous étions alors entre de hautes montagnes. On apercevoit çà et là, suspendues sur des abîmes, des cabanes rares qui disparoissoient et reparoissoient tour à tour entre des nuages mi-parties blancs et roses, qui filoient horizontalement à la hauteur de ces habitations. Lorsque au dessus de ces mêmes nuages on découvroit la cime des rochers et les sommets chevelus des sapins, on eût cru voir de petites îles flottantes dans les airs. La rivière majestueuse, tantôt coulant nord et sud, s'étendoit en ligne droite devant nous; puis tout à coup, tournant à l'aspect du couchant, elle courboit ses flots d'or autour de quelque mont qui, s'avançant dans le fleuve avec toutes ses plantes, ressembloit à un gros bouquet de verdure noué au pied d'une zone bleue et aurore ... L'idée de ce jeune homme [major André], amant, poëte, brave et infortuné, qui, regretté de ses concitoyens et honoré des larmes de Washington, mourut dans la fleur de l'âge pour son pays, répandoit sur cette scène romantique une teinte encore plus attendrissante.**

The *airs sauvages* of the first passage and the folk ballad that accompanies the second announce not only the nineteenth-century predilection for music, but the opinion of Senancour: '*C'est dans les sons que la nature a placé la plus forte expression du caractère romantique; c'est surtout au sens de l'ouïe que l'on peut rendre sensibles, en peu de traits et d'une manière énergique, les lieux et les choses extraordinaires.*'[28] Obermann is writing of the melancholy *ranz des vaches*, the song of the Alpine cowherd; what colours Chateaubriand's two texts is the element of Ossianic melancholy, also a part of the complex of emotions conveyed by *romantique*.

As we consider the nature of these emotions, other texts become

---

* Chateaubriand, *Essai sur les revolutions*, pp. 540–1. For a discussion of the songs and verses connected with André's execution, see Winthrop Sargent, *The Life and Career of Major John André* (New York, 1902), pp. 524–30. Among other witnesses to the popularity of such ballads, Sargent cites Brillat-Savarin, who heard 'la complainte du major André' while on a turkey-hunt in Connecticut in 1794 (*Physiologie du goût*, 3rd ed., Paris, 1829, 1: 171–2). George Washington's evaluation of André, 'more unfortunate than criminal,' occurs in a letter to J.B.D. de Vimeur, comte de Rochambeau, dated 10 October 1780 (in *Writings*, ed. John C. Fitzpatrick, Washington, 1931–44. XX: 151).

suggestive. A note in the *Gazette de France* (20 July 1804) describes a transformation of coach-lights at the dawn of the nineteenth century: '*Il y a une mode pour tout, même pour les lanternes de voiture ; et dans ce moment, un équipage du bon genre ne saurait être éclairé que par des lanternes à foyer, fond rose ou orange, qui éclairent le cocher sans l'éblouir, et qui jettent un jour plus doux ou plus mélancolique dans l'intérieur de la voiture. Tout est aujourd'hui romantique, jusqu'aux lanternes de carosse.*'[29] *Romantique* could even be used for effects beyond melancholy and beyond that terror which informs the sublime. Addressing the Convention Nationale in 1793, Joseph Lakanal described his search for the hidden wealth of the *ci-devant prince de Condé* in the isolated, forest-girt château at Chantilly: '*Les ouvertures qu'on a faites dans les murs pour faciliter les fouilles, ont offert à nos regards surpris des tours entièrement ignorées, des trappes secrettes sur des caveaux profonds, des escaliers mouvans, et tout ce que la féerie présente de plus romantique pour épouvanter les esprits crédules et timides.*'[30] *Romantique* becomes the very adjective for that particular horror inspired by Gothic romances.

Lakanal's conjunction of *le romantique* and *la féerie* should remind us that even when used to describe landscapes and decor, the adjective *romantique* recalls its derivation, its association with novels and romances. Marmontel tells us, in 'Les Solitaires de Murcie,' of the letters he received from the count de Creutz, the Swedish ambassador to the Spanish court, which described Spain as '*un pays romantique.*'[31] A few sentences later, he clarifies his meaning when he speaks of '*l'air poétique et fabuleux qu'il donnait aux descriptions de la Grenade et de la Murcie.*' The point of the passage is, however, not the description of Spain, but the presentation of the count's character. It takes such a man, melancholic and *sensible*, to see the world in such a way, through the veil of poems and works of fiction. Stendhal also suggests as much in a long descriptive letter to his sister Pauline, written from Italy in 1800:

Après trois heures de marche, nous aperçumes au milieu de ce lac divin une montagne verte et à droite une plage et une petite maison blanche. L'île à gauche est Isola Bella, celle à droite Isola Madre. Mais je m'aperçois que je bavarde ; n'importe, puisque tu commences à voir cette situation romantique, tu en parcourras les détours enchanteurs. Surtout ne montre cette lettre à personne, par l'idée qui m'en reste elle est pleine de ridicule pour les âmes froides.[32]

On the one hand the *âmes froides*, on the other those who perceive the nature of the *romantique* – those men of feeling and of imagination who respond to the poetry of nature and who appreciate beauty.

What should not be surprising, therefore, is that in the last years of the eighteenth century, *romantique* was already being used to describe people as well as things. Marmontel, in speaking of Mlle Gaucher, the mistress of the English ambassador, Lord Albemarle, writes in his *Mémoires*: '*Le caractère de mademoiselle Gaucher était naïvement exprimé dans toute sa personne. Il y avait dans sa beauté je ne sais quoi de romantique et de fabuleux, qu'on n'avait vu jusque-là qu'en idée.*'[33] Here, of course, as in connection with the description of landscape, *romantique* may convey only the vague feelings aroused by descriptions of female beauty in works of literature. But the meaning is altered by a later passage from the *Mémoires*: '*L'âme ardente et l'imagination romantique de Mlle l'Espinasse lui firent concevoir le projet de sortir de l'étroite médiocrité où elle craignait de vieillir.*'[34] In this instance, Marmontel clearly uses *romantique* in reference to character and not appearance, although the character is surely still that of the adventurous and imaginative figures who people romances and novels. This meaning of *romantique* (almost synonymous with *romanesque*) has endured to this day: it is equivalent to imaginative, or sensitive, or, at its worst, to *chimérique*. Baudelaire apostrophizes the self-created Balzac as '*le plus héroïque, le plus singulier, le plus romantique parmi tous les personnages que vous avez tirés de votre sein!*'[35] Renan notes, in a journal he kept in 1845–6: '*Je suis né romantique. Non, jamais je ne me contenterai d'un système intellectuel qui s'en tienne à la forme, et ne fasse que charmer par l'harmonie, système tel que Boileau, par exemple, le dessine dans son Epître au marquis de Seignelay. Non, il me faut l'âme, quelque chose qui me mette au bord de l'abîme.*'* By that time, it is true, something had happened to the word which was both to extend and to delimit its meaning.

If *romantique* could be applied to character as well as to landscape, the French reader of 1807 might have been able to understand the following passage from A. W. Schlegel's *Comparaison entre la Phèdre de Racine et celle d'Euripide*:

... *les poëtes tragiques grecs des deux premières époques paraissent avoir exclu entièrement l'amour de leurs compositions, ou tout au plus l'y avoir introduit d'une manière subordonnée et épisodique. La raison en est claire: la tragédie étant principalement destinée à faire ressortir la dignité de la nature humaine, ne pouvait guère se servir de l'amour, parce qu'il tient aux sens que l'homme a en commun avec les animaux. L'antiquité, franche en tout, déguisait beaucoup moins cette partie de l'amour que les nations modernes, chez qui la galanterie chevaleresque*

---

*   Ernest Renan, *Cahiers de jeunesse* (*1845–1846*) (Paris, 1906), pp. 326–7. Renan refers to Boileau's 'Epître IX,' of which the most famous (and representative) line is: 'Rien n'est beau que le vrai: le vrai seul est aimable.'

et les mœurs du Nord en général ont introduit un culte plus respectueux pour les femmes, et chez qui l'enthousiasme du sentiment s'efforce, ou de subjuguer les sens, ou de les purifier par sa mystérieuse alliance. C'est pourquoi l'amour devenu romantique peut et doit jouer un beaucoup plus grand rôle dans nos compositions sérieuses et mélancoliques, que dans celles des anciens, où cette passion se montre avec des caractères purement naturels, tels que les produit le Midi.[36]

That love could be *romantique* would probably have come as no surprise to the reader; but the implied antithesis *romantique-ancien* (and its parallel *Nord-Midi*) could have had no conceivable meaning for a Frenchman who had not followed the literary affairs of Germany. Schlegel's use of the word heralds the transformation of its significance in France, one that is derived from German rather than from English, and one that belongs rather to the history of literature than to the history of taste and of sensitivity. When one confronts a text from the period of that transformation, it is often difficult to decide which meaning is intended, that of the eighteenth century, which had gone beyond the merely picturesque almost from the beginning, or the more specifically literary meaning of the nineteenth century. The nineteen-year-old Charles de Rémusat writes to his mother, in 1816: '*Savez-vous que me voilà vieux, et d'âge et d'expérience? Hélas! je sais bien peu de choses pour mon âge, et puis, cependant, je sais trop, j'ai tout deviné, ou tout découvert. Il n'y a plus de mystère, plus d'inconnu pour moi. Voilà une phrase un peu romantique, mais tant pis, il faut un peu de tout.*'[37] Rémusat may be using the word just as Marmontel had used it in speaking of Julie de Lespinasse; he may, on the other hand, have been thinking of the literary modes which *romantique* had recently come to designate.

The semantic problem for the early French participants in the debate about those new literary phenomena was the lack of a general word, specifically a noun, that enjoyed wide acceptance. *Le romantique* was merely a substantive adjective and designated (in Mercier's *Néologie*, for example) the cluster of associations evoked by the adjective alone. Usage varied, therefore, between 1810 and 1824, when *le romantisme* finally triumphed over other less viable forms. Charles de Villers (to whom, given the suppression of the 1810 edition of *De l'Allemagne*, must go the honour of having been the first to reveal German poetic theory to his compatriots) spoke both of *la poésie romantique* and of *la Romantique* – a literal translation of the German substantive, *die Romantik*, a feminine form, which never gained recognition in France.[38] *La poésie romantique* is the phrase that occurs in the introduction by Villers's friend Philippe-

Albert Stapfer to the French translation of the volumes on Spain from Friedrich Bouterwek's *Geschichte der Poesie und Beredsamkeit seit dem Ende des dreizehnten Jahrhunderts*, as it does in *De l'Allemagne*.[39] *La littérature romantique* and *le genre romantique* (which has special connotations to which I shall return) both occur frequently throughout the early years of the Restoration.[40] Senancour had used the otherwise unknown word *romantisme* (in the sense of *caractère* or *ambiance romantique*) in *Obermann*; but it was probably Charles Brifaut, in his review of Saint-Chamans's *L'Anti-romantique* (in the *Gazette de France* of 6 April 1816) who gave the word its modern meaning, in denouncing '*les phrases obscures des apôtres du* romantisme.'[41] *Le romantique*, still a substantive adjective, pressed by necessity into new linguistic service, continues to be more common than *le romantisme*. Apparently no one besides Stendhal used the Italianate form, which occurs for the first time in a letter from Beyle to his friend Adolphe de Mareste, written from Milan in 1818: '*Lisez-vous le* Conciliatore? *Non, car* 1° *il est bête;* 2° *il est libéral. Cependant s'il paraît chez Galignani lisez dans les six derniers numéros, des articles signés* E.V., *c'est-à-dire Ermès Visconti (le marquis). C'est sur le romanticisme; c'est-à-dire sur cette question: Voulons-nous la tragédie à la* Xipharès *ou la tragédie à la* Richard III?'* What is curious is that Visconti, in his *Idee elementari sulla poesia romantica* (1818), speaks rather of *il romantismo* than of *il romanticismo*, although Stendhal must certainly have formed his neologism on an Italian model.[42] *Le romanticisme* is the subject of the first *Racine et Shakespeare* (1823); by the time the second appeared, in 1825, Stendhal had adopted the more durable *romantisme*. It seems, ironically enough, to have been the members of the Académie Française who popularized the latter term, in their very efforts to discredit the literature it designated. The younger Lacretelle, in a speech to the Société Royale des Bonnes-Lettres (4 December 1823), raged against '*l'autorité de Schlegel, ce Quintilien du romantisme, ce déplorable contempteur de Racine, de Molière, de Boileau, de La Fontaine!*'[43] And when Louis-Simon Auger pronounced the Académie's official anathema upon the new movement (24 April, 1824), it was under the title *Discours sur le romantisme* (Stendhal was incorrect, although more expressive, in calling Auger's discourse *Manifeste contre le romantisme*). When Hugo writes the *Préface de 'Cromwell'* in 1827, he can speak of *le romantisme* with no fear of being

---

* Stendhal, *Correspondance* I: 951. Since Xipharès is one of the tyrant's sons in Racine's *Mithridate*, the opposition is already that of Racine and Shakespeare. Littré (in the *Supplément* to his dictionary) makes the erroneous statement that *romanticisme* was as common as *romantisme*, at least until 1824.

misunderstood. By this time *le romantique* (and *les romantiques*) had generally been limited to a single one of its meanings and designated a man rather than a mode, a proponent of the new school of literature.

The eighteenth century had explained *romantique*, like *romanesque*, as an adjective derived from the substantive *roman*. In his 'Lettre ... sur un Recueil d'anciennes poésies allemandes' (1810), Villers follows his German sources and suggests another derivation when he says of medieval poetry that '*on peut* [*l'*]*appeler la* poésie romantique, *à cause de la langue* romane *dans laquelle elle s'exprimoit le plus souvent.*'[44] The same explanation occurs in the works of Sismondi and in a significant article on German literature by the playwright and historian, Etienne Aignan (1818): '*Lorsque ensuite, du débris de la langue latine, il naquit dans l'Europe un idiome commun, germe principal de nos langues actuelles, on le nomma* roman, *d'abord pour rappeler la langue à laquelle il devait son origine ; ensuite, par opposition à cette langue elle-même ; et la littérature de la langue romane ainsi que de celles qui en sont dérivées, est la littérature* romantique, *c'est-à-dire, indigène, par opposition à la littérature exotique, ou des écoles.*'[45] The confusion in these definitions is a double one. First, *le roman*, or *la langue romane* (or occasionally *la langue romance*)* seems to designate Vulgar Latin, Provençal, and even Old French; *la littérature romantique* is variously that written in Vulgar Latin (whatever that may be!), in Provençal, in Old French – and Aignan seems to suggest that it includes all literatures in all the Romance languages, medieval or modern.

The association with the Middle Ages was nevertheless the dominant one in the early years of the debate; in the absence of the term *moyen âge* (which would not become current until the 1820s), *romantique* even became a purely historical and ethnographical qualification. Villers speaks of '*une foule de poésies manuscrites de l'époque* romantique' recently discovered in various libraries; Sismondi defines *les mœurs romantiques* as those '*composées des habitudes des peuples du Nord, et des restes de la civilisation romaine,*' and *la race romantique* as that '*formée du mélange des Germains et des Latins.*'[46] Finally Charles Nodier, with a cavalier disregard for comprehensibility, is able to write: '*Homère marque le passage des siècles héroïques aux siècles*

---

* *Le roman*, in this linguistic sense, dates from the sixteenth century and has proved to be the most durable of the three terms. *La langue romane* was the common usage in the early nineteenth century. Paul Robert attests the use of *la langue romance* in Antoine Furetière's *Dictionnaire universel* (1690) and in Voltaire's *Dictionnaire philosophique* (1764), s.v. *Français*. It occurs as well in August Wilhelm Schlegel, *Cours de littérature dramatique* [trans. Albertine Necker de Saussure] (Paris, Geneva, 1814), 1: 16, but it is a rare form and one that has not endured.

classiques. Le Dante a marqué celui des siècles romanesques aux siècles romantiques et à la restauration des lettres.'[47] The quadripartite division of history is not perhaps as clear as it might be; but at least two of Nodier's terms stood in clear opposition to each other.

As late as 1842, Alfred Michiels would feel forced to justify his use of the antithesis *classique-romantique*: '*Je me suis fréquemment servi de* classique *et de* romantique ... *On les a ridiculisés chez nous avant de les comprendre, selon l'habitude de la nation. Mais j'aurais regardé comme une sottise et une faiblesse de mettre à l'écart des termes si nécessaires. Je les ai donc employés toutes les fois que je l'ai jugé convenable.'*[48] Yet by 1820, Jean-Charles-Thibault de Laveaux had admitted the new definition of *romantique* to his *Nouveau Dictionnaire de la langue française*: '*On dit, en littérature*, genre romantique, style romantique. *En ce sens, il est opposé à* classique.' The simple opposition gives no sense of the emotional weight the two words carried, nor of the battle that had already raged about them for several years. Schlegel, in his *Comparaison*, and Villers, in his 'Lettre' of 1810, had suggested the full import of the antithesis; but it was Mme de Staël who first explained it with any clarity, in *De l'Allemagne*: '*On prend quelquefois le mot classique comme synonyme de perfection. Je m'en sers ici dans une autre acception, en considérant la poésie classique comme celle des anciens, et la poésie romantique comme celle qui tient de quelque manière aux traditions chevaleresques.'*[49] She had already defined *la poésie romantique*, a few lines earlier, as '*la poésie dont les chants des troubadours ont été l'origine, celle qui est née de la chevalerie et du christianisme.'* The simplest form of the opposition is, therefore, an historical one, the ancient *versus* the medieval – although Mme de Staël has indeed suggested the moral and religious opposition on which Schlegel had founded his contrast of *Phèdre* and the *Hippolytus*.

The absence of such a general term as *le romantisme* led, however, to a peculiar interpretation of the relationship between *le classique* and *le romantique*. In his review of the French translation of Schlegel's *Vorlesungen über dramatische Kunst und Literatur*, Charles Nodier asked, '*Qu'est-ce donc que le genre* romantique, *ou si l'on veut, qu'est-ce donc qu'un beau qui n'est pas classique et qui ne peut pas l'être?'*[50] All beauty, he had written, is '*essentiellement* classique'; the terms *classique* and *beau* are synonymous. If the equation is true, then *le romantique* becomes simply a true *genre* – one form, or mode, or style, whereas *le classique* embraces the whole of literature. The Académie de Toulouse, for example, proposed the following subject for a dissertation in 1820 (and doubled its prize from 450 to 900 francs, in order to attract contestants): '*Quels sont les caractères distinctifs de la littérature à laquelle on a donné le nom de romantique, et quelles ressources pourrait-elle offrir à la littérature classique?*'[51] Aignan had already suggested an answer, in 1818, when he defined romantic literature as national literature: '*Le caractère propre de la littérature romantique est donc d'exprimer l'ordre nouveau d'idées et de sentimens né des nouvelles combinaisons sociales; il tient tout entier à la substance, et nullement aux formes, dont il est tellement loin d'exclure la pureté, que c'est d'elle seule qu'il peut recevoir tout son éclat.*'[52] The *romantique* was thus reduced to a simple matter of the choice of subject.[53] All modern literatures, Aignan had continued, would have to be a mixture of the *classique* and the *romantique*, the eternally beautiful forms expressing novel ideas and emotions. As Lamartine wrote to Adolphe de Mareste, after reading Stendhal's *Racine et Shakespeare* of 1823: '*Classique pour l'expression, romantique dans la pensée; à mon avis, c'est ce qu'il faut être.*'[54] The echo of Chénier's dictum – '*Sur des pensers nouveaux, faisons des vers antiques*' – is obvious. Victor Hugo had predicted the confluence of minds when he noted, in a parallel of Chénier and Lamartine: '*... si je comprends bien des distinctions, du reste assez insignifiantes, le premier est* romantique *parmi les* classiques, *le second est* classique *parmi les* romantiques.'[55]

Only one of the responses to the question posed by the Académie de Toulouse seems to have been published, and its anonymous author (since identified as Julien Castelnau) had to wait until 1825 to see his essay in print. By that time, he was able to distinguish a progression in the notion of *le romantique*: '*... ce qui n'étoit d'abord qu'un* genre de style, *qu'une* manière d'écrire, *est devenue l'expression générale de la civilisation particulière des modernes.*'[56] This opposition of two systems of literature was of course first expressed in France by Schlegel, by Sismondi, by Mme de Staël; and the more perceptive reviewers of their books had looked beyond the moral and religious distinctions in subject matter to the aesthetic distinctions which they necessitated. Reviewing *De l'Allemagne* in 1814, the Danish geographer and publicist, Konrad Malte-Brun, could speak of '*le caractère soi-disant* romantique, *ou opposé aux règles classiques*'[57] – and it was, of course, in terms of the rules that the battle was finally pitched. Definitions of *le romantique* in these terms tend to be overwhelmingly negative, in that the opponents of the new theory possessed a confidence that its proponents lacked. Saint-Chamans reduces the question to its simplest form in writing that '*Les ouvrages réguliers, où l'on suit les lois établies, voilà ce qu'ils nomment* le genre classique. *Les ouvrages irréguliers, où l'on ne reconnaît aucune loi, voilà* le genre romantique.'[58] His tone is somewhat more representative of the attacks on romanticism when he says that '*La* *littérature romantique, c'est celle qui a secoué toute espèce de frein, où le génie s'abandonne au hasard à tous ses caprices, où quelques éclairs brillent à travers un fatras obscur, où les perles sont ensevelies dans le fumier.*'[59] An anonymous writer for the *Lettres champenoises* (1820) compounds the comparison with political overtones and impartially curses both houses:

Si j'osais hasarder une comparaison, je dirais que les classiques *sont les* ultras *de la littérature: appuyés sur leurs vieilles traditions, ils craindraient de faire un pas hors du terrain de l'antiquité … De leur côté, les* romantiques *sont les* libéraux *de la littérature. Abandonnés sans frein et sans règle au dévergondage de leur imagination, ils renversent toutes les bornes, se précipitent dans les exagérations et finissent trop souvent par arriver à l'absurde.**

It is not long before the defenders of romanticism in *Le Globe* take up the cudgel in the same terms. Prosper Duvergier de Hauranne sketches a programme for the romantics in 1825: '*En un mot, asservissement aux règles de la langue, indépendance pour tout le reste: telle doit être au moins la devise des romantiques; tel est le drapeau qu'ils opposent à celui qui porte en grosses lettres les mots* intolérance *et* routine: *l'avenir dira lequel est le meilleur.*'[60] Another writer for *Le Globe* simply equates classicism and romanticism with the political doctrines of authority and liberty.[61] Finally Victor Hugo gives the simile its lapidary form in 1830 in the preface to *Hernani*: '*Le romantisme, tant de fois mal défini, n'est, à tout prendre, et c'est là sa définition réelle, si l'on ne l'envisage que sous son côté militant, que le* libéralisme *en littérature.*'[62]

It is in terms of the rejection of classic rules (although freed from the political analogy) that *romantique*, in its new meaning, finally gains admission to the dictionary of the Académie Française (1835): '*ROMANTIQUE, se dit encore De certains écrivains qui affectent de s'affranchir des règles de composition et de style établies par l'exemple des auteurs classiques.*' The verb *affectent* still conveys the Académie's negative bias, an emotional colouration which is little by little reduced. The latest edition of the Académie's dictionary offers this definition: '*Il se dit aujourd'hui de l'Ecole qui, au début du dix-neuvième siècle, dans les diverses branches de l'art, s'est affranchie des formules et des disciplines classiques.*' From the point of view of the lexicographer, the definition's neutrality is more than balanced by the extension of *romantique* to other arts than literature – an extension that occurred in the 1820s, in terms, again, of liberation from rules and established

---

* Quoted in Ch.-M. Des Granges, *La Presse littéraire sous la Restauration (1815– 1830)* (Paris, 1907), p. 321 (hereafter cited as *Des Granges*). Nodier had already suggested the parallel of liberalism and the new modes of literature in his first article provoked by the 1818 edition of *De l'Allemagne* (*Mélanges* II: 328).

practices. Schlegel had suggested the possibility of that extension; Stendhal, in a treatise addressed to Romain Colomb, had discussed the nature of *le romanticisme* in painting and music – although both authors agree that sculpture is, of necessity, classical.[63] Reviewing the evolution of French painting, which had accompanied that of French literature, Auguste Jal wrote in 1826: '*On crie au romantisme chez M. de Quatremère de Quincy comme chez M. Auger. On parle, dans l'atelier de M. Garnier comme dans le cabinet de M. Baour-Lormian, des usurpations du* laid *sur l'empire du* beau.'* The painter and art-critic Etienne Jean Delécluze might hesitate a year later: '*On ne sait pas encore au juste ce qu'on entend à présent par peinture romantique*'; but the critic of the Salon of 1827 for the *Revue française* tells us that the term had become as current in painting as in poetry: '*Géricault est le chef de cette nouvelle école qui se propose pour but la représentation fidèle des émotions fortes et touchantes, et qu'à tort ou à raison on appelle* école romantique.'[64] He returns to the question of the rules when he says of '*la réforme* romantique' that '*elle aspirait ... à l'affranchissement de l'art de peindre, entravé par un système de lois et de restrictions arbitraires.*'[65] It is in the same terms, although without the same sympathy, that the Belgian musicologist, François-Joseph Fétis, extends the use of the word to music, returning, as he does so, to the German writers who embodied the new aesthetic conception:

Le système de la transcendance des idées *que la philosophie de Kant avait mis en vogue, la direction nouvelle que les travaux de Lessing, de Schiller et de Goethe avaient imprimée aux esprits, tout concourait à faire adopter avec enthousiasme des compositions où l'on affectait de s'affranchir des règles communes. Les succès de Beethoven tracèrent la route aux jeunes musiciens; chacun s'empressa de la suivre, et comme il n'est pas facile de s'arrêter dans ce romantisme de la musique, on finit par trouver le modèle trop simple, et par dépasser les bornes dans lesquelles il était resté.*[66]

To define *le romantisme* in terms of *l'affranchissement des règles* is, whatever one's position in the debate, to define it negatively (for that matter, according to critics as diverse as Ferdinand Brunetière and Paul Valéry, this is the only way it can be defined).[67] When it came to positive assertions in the 1820s, the situation was somewhat more difficult. Given the rapid transformations of French literature

---

*   Auguste Jal, 'De la nouvelle école de peinture,' *Le Mercure du dix-neuvième siècle* XIII (1826): 548. Antoine Chrysostome Quatremère de Quincy, author of an *Essai sur l'idéal* (1805), appears here as the champion of imitation; Etienne-Barthélemy Garnier, member of the Institut, had three enormous paintings, neoclassic in style and historical in subject, in the Salon of 1827; Marie-François Baour-Lormian was the author of an anti-romantic satire sanctioned by the Académie, *Le Classique et le romantique* (1825).

between 1820 and 1830, the radical shift in the political and philosophical bias of the new school from the *Méditations poétiques* to *Hernani*, Musset's Dupuis and Cotonet have good reason to become confused in their quest for even a minimal certainty. Whether they define their subject as the imitation of German, English, and Spanish models, as the *genre historique* or the *genre intime*, as a system of political economy or the refusal to shave, the two citizens of La Ferté-sous-Jouarre never really get beyond their original reflection that '*en province, le mot* romantique *a, en général, une signification facile à retenir, il est synonyme d'absurde, et on ne s'en inquiète pas autrement.*'[68]

Yet there was one positive meaning of *le romantique* and *le romantisme* that did predominate, at least during the 1820s – a meaning that was derived from the early contrast of medieval and ancient literatures, from the rejection of classical rules. As early as 1814, Charles Nodier, in his review of Schlegel's *Cours de littérature dramatique*, suggested the extended meanings: '*Le* classique *est* [*le genre*] *dont les anciens ont donné l'exemple et les règles, le* romantique *est propre à toutes les nations modernes qui n'ont pas adopté la poétique des anciens.*'[69] The doctrine of imitation, to which Nodier indirectly refers, had of course dominated classicism from its inception, when Du Bellay recommended it in the *Défense et illustration de la langue française*. The rejection of that doctrine was a basic tenet of romanticism; as Hugo put it in his preface to the 1826 edition of *Odes et ballades*, '*celui qui imite un poète* romantique *devient nécessairement* classique, *puisqu'il imite.*'[70] This is still largely a negative way of phrasing things; but Duvergier de Hauranne had already clarified the question when he wrote of the young French poets of the Restoration: '*Ainsi leur hardiesse va-t-elle jusqu'à croire qu'il convient toujours mieux de copier la nature que des copies de la nature, de recevoir l'impulsion de son temps que celle d'un autre, de créer que de reproduire.*'[71] The alernative to imitation is a doctrine that preaches both originality of inspiration and fidelity to nature. Looking back from the vantage point of 1860, Hugo will be able to say: '*Ce qu'on a appelé il y a trente ans la dispute des classiques et des romantiques n'était pas autre chose qu'un rappel à la nature. Traduire l'homme de l'homme même, et non de tel ou tel livre.*'[72] He had written, more than thirty years before, that '*le poète ne doit avoir qu'un modèle, la nature ; qu'un guide, la vérité.*'[73] This is equivalent to saying that *romantique* means more or less what we mean by 'realistic' – and the *Globe* journalist Ludovic Vitet came close to saying it when he wrote: '*Le romantisme, c'est l'imitation des choses telles qu'elles sont ; le classicisme se plaît dans l'idéal, le romantisme dans le réel.*'[74] This was one of the major points Stendhal had tried to make in both versions of *Racine et Shakespeare*. In the first, he had written that the question of *le romanticisme*, reduced to its most basic terms, was the question of those '*moments d'illusion parfaite*' that made Shakespeare's theatre superior to that of Racine.[75] (This definition explains Stendhal's remarkable reference to Samuel Johnson as the '*père du romanticisme*': his notion of theatrical realism was inspired by Johnson's preface to Shakespeare.)[76] Two years later, when he outlines a play, *Lanfranc ou le poète*, he can say that it is '*une comédie romantique, parce que les événements* ressemblent *à ce qui se passe tous les jours sous nos yeux*.'[77] Realism is, however, more than a mere question of subject matter; it depends upon the audience's acceptance of what it sees or what it reads. With his Italian sources as inspiration, Stendhal offers his famous definition of romanticism as '*l'art de présenter aux peuples les œuvres littéraires qui, dans l'état actuel de leurs habitudes et de leurs croyances, sont susceptibles de leur donner le plus de plaisir possible*.'[78] Romanticism, which less than ten years before had been synonymous with medievalism, now became synonymous with modernity. Hugo jokingly reduces the opposition to romanticism to the following argument: '– *Nous condamnons la littérature du dix-neuvième siècle, parce qu'elle est* romantique ... – *Et pourquoi est-elle romantique ? – Parce qu'elle est la littérature du dix-neuvième siècle*.'[79] Not many years later, Emile Deschamps comes to the obvious conclusion: '*il n'y a réellement pas de romantisme, mais bien une littérature du dix-neuvième siècle*.'[80] And Hugo, in exile, will recall the political analogies of the 1820s, in noting that 'Romantisme, Socialisme, *ce sont les pseudonymes du dix-neuvième siècle. Ce sont, en littérature et en politique, ses deux noms*.'[81]

No one in the 1820s seems, however, to have understood the real aesthetic implications of this identification of *le romantique* and the modern. Stendhal comes closest, when he associates romanticism and the pleasure experienced by an audience; but, as his response to Lamartine's objections to *Racine et Shakespeare* indicate, he, like his contemporaries, was at least able to conceive of *le classique* as the eternal form of beauty, and *le romantique* as a mere mode of expression or choice of subject.[82] One must wait for Baudelaire to see the question in its most profound form, to define romanticism in terms of the relativity of what we consider beautiful: '*Chaque siècle, chaque peuple ayant possédé l'expression de sa beauté et de sa morale, – si l'on veut entendre par romantisme l'expression la plus récente et la plus moderne de la beauté, – le grand artiste sera donc, – pour le critique raisonnable et passionné, – celui qui unira à la condition demandée ci-dessus, la naïveté, – le plus de romantisme possible*.'[83] He is still more precise in his equation when he writes:

'*Qui dit romantisme dit art moderne, – c'est-à-dire intimité, spiritualisme, couleur, aspiration vers l'infini, exprimées par tous les moyens que contiennent les arts.*'[84]

The association of romanticism with spirituality, with feeling, derives from its earliest definitions in France, its dependence on Christianity – if not from the late eighteenth-century opposition of the *âmes froides* and those *âmes sensibles* who could appreciate the romantic elements in nature. *Le Globe*'s Desprès defines *le romantisme*, in 1825, as '*le transport du spiritualisme dans la littérature*'; and many early texts emphasize the associations of the Romantic and the poetic – as Nodier puts it in 1818, '*des aspects encore inaperçus des choses, un ordre de perception assez neuf pour être souvent bizarre, je ne sais quels secrets du cœur humain dont il a souvent joui en lui-même sans être tenté de les révéler aux autres, et qui produisent sur nous, quand nous les rencontrons dans les livres, un plaisir analogue à celui que fait la vue d'un ancien ami.*'[85] Emile Deschamps simply reduces the war between the *classiques* and the *romantiques* to '*l'éternelle guerre des esprits prosaïques et des âmes poétiques.*'[86] Musset has a field day with this notion of romanticism, limiting the 'poetic' to its most extravagant forms:

Le romantisme, c'est l'étoile qui pleure, c'est le vent qui vagit, c'est la nuit qui frissonne, la fleur qui vole et l'oiseau qui embaume; c'est le jet inespéré, l'extase alanguie, la citerne sous les palmiers, et l'espoir vermeil et ses mille amours, l'ange et la perle, la robe blanche des saules ... ! C'est l'infini et l'étoilé, le chaud, le rompu, le désenivré, et pourtant en même temps le plein et le rond, le diamétral, le pyramidal, l'oriental, le nu à vif, l'étreint, l'embrassé, le tourbillonnant ...[87]

Lest one think he was exaggerating, one has only to turn to the young Victor Hugo: '*La poésie romantique, par ses formes vagues et indécises, échappe à la critique: semblable à ces hôtes fantastiques de l'Elysée païen, qui frappaient la vue et se dérobaient à la main qui les voulait saisir.*'[88] ('*Et tout le reste,*' one is tempted to say with Verlaine, '*est littérature.*') These connotations of *romantique* and *romantisme* fortify the applications of the adjective to human beings current since the eighteenth century. *Romantique*, according to the volume of the *Grand Larousse encyclopédique* published in 1964, '*se dit des personnes chez qui la sensibilité l'emporte sur la sagesse raisonnable*'; whereas *le romantisme* is equivalent to '*rêverie poétique.*' Still more recently, the *Dictionnaire du français contemporain* (1966) associates *romantique* with '*la sensibilité, la rêverie,*' and notes that in such instances, it is once more synonymous with *romanesque*. The antonym to *romantique* in this sense is the equally problematic *réaliste*.

The antithesis *romantique-réaliste* which takes its place beside the older *classique-romantique* reflects one of the ironies of nineteenth-century literary history. For Stendhal, Deschamps, and Hugo, romanticism was the literature of the nineteenth century, adapted to a modern public and reflecting accurately the world that public knew. But romanticism had in reality spawned another aesthetic, and a division of functions was to occur. As the nineteenth century progresses, *romantique* comes to designate the poetic and imaginative tendencies of modern literature, whereas *réaliste* (and later *naturaliste*) suggests fidelity to nature and (in Vitet's phrase) *'l'imitation des choses telles qu'elles sont.'* A characteristic statement of the opposition is to be found in the first number of Philippe Duranty's review, *Réalisme*, in an article by Jules Assézat: *'Pour les romantiques, le but de la littérature était une chose fantastique; pour nous, c'est une chose réelle, existante, compréhensible, visible, palpable: l'imitation scrupuleuse de la nature.'*[89] (Given certain of the statements made about romanticism in the 1820s, one can understand why Victor Hugo should consider realism as simply a parasitical movement, the mistletoe that had grown on the oak of the older school.) In an article on Zola, Emile Faguet identifies romanticism with the active rejection of the real: *'Les romantiques vivent dans l'imagination comme le poisson dans l'eau et ont la crainte de la réalité comme le poisson de la paille. Elle les gêne, parce qu'elle les limite, les réprime, les refoule et les étouffe … C'est leur vocation, leur prédestination et leur office propre d'écarter la vérité … Le romantisme est un appel à la liberté du rêve et une insurrection contre le réel.'*[90] Zola, in turn, writing about Victor Hugo, had compounded the irony by equating romanticism and classicism: *'Remarquez d'ailleurs que la formule classique et la formule romantique sont identiques, sauf le décor; elles reposent toutes les deux sur la conception idéaliste et réglementée de l'art. La formule naturaliste est l'autre face de la question; elle base une œuvre sur la nature, et explique les déviations du vrai par le tempérament de l'artiste.'*[91] What is surely important to notice is that Zola used the words *romantique* and *romantisme* far more than Victor Hugo ever had. Hugo was exaggerating when he wrote in 1864:

Ce mot, romantisme, a, comme tous les mots de combat, l'avantage de résumer vivement un groupe d'idées; il va vite, ce qui plaît dans la mêlée; mais il a, selon nous, par sa signification militante, l'inconvénient de paraître borner le mouvement qu'il représente à un fait de guerre; or ce mouvement est un fait d'intelligence, un fait de civilisation, un fait d'âme; et c'est pourquoi celui qui écrit ces lignes n'a amais employé les mots romantisme ou romantique. On ne les trouvera acceptés dans aucune des pages de critique qu'il a pu avoir occasion d'écrire.[92]

Yet the exaggeration is not very great: outside the *Préface de*

'Cromwell' and one or two similar texts, the word occurs rarely in Hugo's criticism – and when it does, it is usually hedged about by hesitations and apologies. By 1830, Hugo seemed delighted to be rid of it: '*Les misérables mots à querelle,* classique *et* romantique, *sont tombés dans l'abîme de 1830, comme* gluckiste *et* picciniste *dans le gouffre de 1789. L'art seul est resté.*'[93] The major romantics no more called themselves *romantiques* than the authors of the seventeenth century had called themselves *classiques*. It was the journalists of the 1820s, and the minor poets like Deschamps, who most often used the word. The farther a writer was, or the farther he drifted, from the 'school' or the *cénacle,* the more unhappy he became with the label. Vigny, for example, having withdrawn to his ivory tower, wrote to the Prince Royal of Bavaria: '*L'élégie, l'ode, le poème naquirent ensemble sous de nouvelles formes, et leurs voix séparées, bien distinctes, n'eurent point de sons pareils, presque aucune ressemblance. Ce fut là ce qu'on prit pour une école, et ce qu'on nomma* Romantique *à tout hasard.*'[94] From a certain point of view, Hugo was correct when he noted in a journal he kept on Guernsey: '*On n'a jamais plus parlé du romantisme que depuis qu'on dit:* le romantisme est mort.'[95] It was the brothers Goncourt who blamed their humiliation at the hands of the police, and the trial of Flaubert, on the imperial powers which wanted '*la mort du romantisme, devenu un crime d'Etat*'; it was Flaubert who called himself *un vieux romantique,* '*débris d'un monde disparu, vieux fossile du romantisme.*'[96] Catulle Mendès would have preferred the term *néo-romantiques* for the poets who contributed to the *Parnasse contemporain*; Rimbaud refers to Leconte de Lisle and to Banville, as well as to Gautier, as '*les seconds romantiques.*'[97] Even Zola has to admit that, in poetry, his contemporaries had arrived at '*la troisième période du romantisme*'; his mouthpiece in *L'Œuvre,* Pierre Sandoz, makes a similar statement about the novelists and the painters of the period.[98]

In the mouths of these authors of the mid- and late nineteenth century, *romantique* and *romantisme* refer specifically to the movement that had flowered in the 1820s and '30s. One of the problems in that earlier period (which perhaps explains, at least in part, the reluctance of major writers to use the words) was voiced in 1821 by Charles Nodier: '*Le fait est qu'il n'y a point de genre romantique en France, tant qu'il ne s'est pas élevé dans ce genre un talent qui nous en fasse comprendre la puissance.*'[99] It was not until after the writers we ordinarily think of as the great romantics had produced their works – and had for the most part fallen silent – that the movement could be defined. Yet it is important to note that *romantique* and *romantisme,* even in their literary senses, remain as emotionally charged as ever – whether positively, as when Pierre Trahard defines romanticism as '*un renouvellement de la sensibilité humaine*,' or negatively, as in Pierre Lasserre's echo of Goethe: '*Le Romantisme est primitivement maladie.*'*

Both of these definitions suggest the broadening of the concept of romanticism that has occurred in the twentieth century. Modern criticism is, more often than not, loath to accept either 1843 or 1848 – the failure of *Les Burgraves* or the fall of the bourgeois monarchy – as the *terminus ad quem* of the romantic movement in France. As early as 1846, Baudelaire had suggested the direction of this re-evaluation when he wrote: '*Le romantisme n'est précisément ni dans le choix des sujets ni dans la vérité exacte, mais dans la manière de sentir. Ils l'ont cherché en dehors, et c'est en dedans qu'il était seulement possible de le trouver.*'[100] Time has ratified the judgments of Flaubert, of Rimbaud, of Zola: Parnassianism and realism, naturalism and symbolism have come to seem more like extensions or developments of romanticism than like outright alternatives to the school of the 1820s and '30s. To speak of the nineteenth century as a whole as *le siècle romantique* is to recognize the persistence of certain modes of emotion and of perception, in spite of the changes in subject matter, in form, and in specific aesthetic aims.

There has even been a tendency in the twentieth century to divorce the word *romantisme* from any specifically historical context, to see it as an eternal principle of the human mind. '*Tout classicisme suppose un romantisme antérieur*,' declares Paul Valéry; and André Gide's opposition of classicism and romanticism in couched in the same general terms: '*Il importe de considérer que la lutte entre classicisme et romantisme existe aussi bien à l'intérieur de chaque esprit. Et c'est de cette lutte même que doit naître l'œuvre; l'œuvre d'art classique raconte le triomphe de l'ordre et de la mesure sur le romantisme intérieur. L'œuvre est d'autant plus belle que la chose soumise était d'abord plus révoltée.*'[101] The notion of control surely derives from the aesthetic debate of the 1820s; but the

* Pierre Trahard, *Les Maîtres de la sensibilité française au XVIIIe siècle (1715–1789)* (Paris, 1931–33), 1: 7; Pierre Lasserre, *Le Romantisme français* (Paris, 1907), p. 18. Cf. J. P. Eckermann, *Gespräche mit Goethe* (21st ed., Leipzig, 1925, pp. 263 f.), 2 April 1829: 'Mir ist ein neuer Ausdruck eingefallen, sagte Goethe, der das Verhältnis nicht übel bezeichnet. Das Klassische nenne ich das Gesunde, und das Romantische das Kranke. Und da sind die *Nibelungen* klassisch wie der *Homer*, denn beide sind gesund und tüchtig. Das meiste Neuere ist nicht romantisch, weil es neu, sondern weil es schwach, kränklich und krank ist, und das Alte ist nicht klassisch, weil es alt, sondern weil es stark, frisch, froh und gesund ist. Wenn wir nach solchen Qualitäten Klassisches und Romantisches unterscheiden, so werden wir bald im Reinen sein.' *Maximen und Reflexionen* (*Goethes Werke*, ed. Trunz, xii, Hamburg, 1953, p. 487): 'Klassisch ist das Gesunde, romantisch das Kranke.'

terms are as applicable to Valéry and to Gide as to a nineteenth- or a seventeenth-century author. When one can speak of *le romantisme des classiques*, one has moved beyond the categories of debate established by Mme de Staël and Charles Nodier. The same could be said of such a phrase as *le romantisme des réalistes* – a dichotomy that recurs in Albert Camus's *L'Homme révolté*: '*Loin d'être un romantisme, la révolte, au contraire, prend le parti du vrai réalisme. Si elle veut une révolution, elle la veut en faveur de la vie, non contre elle.*'[102] Once again, the words recall the literary arguments of the nineteenth century, the Realists' or Naturalists' contention that romanticism had failed because it had turned its back on life; but Camus's use of the indefinite article gives a far more catholic significance to the words.*

Romantique-classique, romantique-réaliste – the antitheses are still with us, in both literary and non-literary contexts. But there is still another irony in the history of *romantique* and its cognates, still another antithesis to consider. *Romantique* entered the French language as a doublet for *romanesque*; the distinctions between the two words made in the later eighteenth century are invariably in favour of the neologism. In certain cases, however, in reference to human character, the two have continued to be synonymous to this day: *un esprit romantique, un esprit romanesque* – the nuance of difference is almost imperceptible. And yet René Girard is able to entitle his fine theoretical work on the novel *Mensonge romantique et vérité romanesque* (the neat antithesis is lost in the English translation). Although the first part of the title would have been perfectly comprehensible to any eighteenth- or nineteenth-century Frenchman, it has not been long that the second half has been anything but an outrageous oxymoron. As the novel has developed, as the theory of the novel has joined older literary theories, *romanesque* has lost its original negative connotations and has regained the meaning implied by its etymology: *le genre romanesque, les techniques romanesques* designate merely the form and the techniques of the modern novel, with no emotional charge whatsoever. As for the *mensonges romantiques*, they are Quixoticism, Bovarysm – all the chivalric and sentimental illusions originally designated by *romanesque*, before *romantique*, with its enduring emotional weight, drained them away. In the context of

---

*   Cf. the *Dictionnaire de l'Académie Française* (8th ed., 1935): '[*Romantique*] se dit encore, par analogie, des Œuvres ou des personnes chez qui l'imagination l'emporte sur le sens des réalités. *Une politique romantique.* Substantivement, *Cet homme d'Etat est un grand romantique.*' The *Grand Larousse encyclopédique* (1964) returns to the quarrels of the 1820s, but applies the old terms in more general ways, in defining *romantisme* as a 'système qui prétend s'affranchir des règles établies: *Romantisme économique.*'

Professor Girard's title, the excesses of romanticism fortify the etymological associations of *romantique*; the ambiguity that results creates the peculiar flavour that the word possesses in modern usage.

NOTES

1 Alexis François, 'Romantique,' *Annales de la société Jean-Jacques Rousseau* V (1909): 199–236, and 'Où en est "Romantique," ' in *Mélanges d'histoire littéraire générale et comparée offerts à Fernand Baldensperger* (Paris, 1930), I: 321–31; André Monglond, *Le Préromantisme français* (Grenoble, 1930), I: 111–18; Charles Bruneau, *L' Epoque romantique* (vol. XII of Ferdinand Brunot, *Histoire de la langue française des origines à 1900*) (Paris, 1948), pp. 116–31.

2 I have consulted the following dictionaries and encyclopediae, s.v. *roman, romanesque, romantique, romantisme*: the 5th, 6th, 7th, and 8th eds. of the *Dictionnaire de l'Académie Française* (Paris, 1798, 1835, 1884, 1935), and the *Complément du Dictionnaire de l'Académie Française* (Paris, 1847); [C. H. Watelet et al.], *Beaux-Arts* (in Panckoucke's *Encyclopédie méthodique*) (Paris, 1791); William Dupré, *Lexicographia-Neologica Gallica* (London, 1801); Louis-Sébastien Mercier, *Néologie, ou Vocabulaire de mots nouveaux, à renouveler, ou pris dans des acceptions nouvelles* (Paris, 1801); John Garner, *Le Nouveau Dictionnaire universel, françois-anglois, et anglois-françois* (Rouen, 1802); A. Millin, *Dictionnaire des beaux-arts* (Paris, 1806); Jean-Charles-Thibault de Laveaux, *Nouveau Dictionnaire de la langue française* (Paris, 1820), and 2nd ed. (Paris, 1843); François-Joseph-Michel Noël and Charles Pierre Chapsal, *Nouveau Dictionnaire de la langue française* (Paris, 1828); Jean-Baptiste Bonaventure de Roquefort, *Dictionnaire étymologique de la langue françoise* (Paris, 1829); Pierre-Claude Victoire Boiste, *Dictionnaire universel*, rev. Charles Nodier (Brussels, 1835); Louis-Nicolas and Albert Bescherelle, *Dictionnaire national ou dictionnaire universel de la langue française* (Paris, 1846); Pierre-Benjamin Lafaye, *Dictionnaire des synonymes de la langue française* (Paris, 1857); M. A. Mazure, *Dictionnaire étymologique de la langue française* (Paris, 1863); Pierre Larousse, *Grand Dictionnaire universel du XIXe siècle* (Paris, 1865–76); Emile Littré, *Dictionnaire de la langue française* (Paris, 1873–4), and *Supplément* (Paris, 1897); Jules Adeline, *Lexique des termes d'art* (Paris, 1884); Adolphe Hatzfeld and Arsène Darmesteter, *Dictionnaire général de la langue française* (Paris, 1895–1900); Henri Bénac, *Dictionnaire des synonymes* (Paris, 1956); *Grand Larousse encyclopédique* (Paris, 1960–4); Paul Robert, *Dictionnaire alphabétique et analogique de la langue française* (Paris, 1960–4); Hector Dupuis, *Dictionnaire des synonymes et des antonymes* (Montreal, 1961); Jean Dubois et al., *Dictionnaire du français contemporain* (Paris, 1966).

3 [Auguste de Saint-Chamans], *L'Anti-romantique, ou examen de quelques ouvrages nouveaux* (Paris, 1816), p. 3 (hereafter cited as *Saint-Chamans*).

4 Joseph-Etienne Jouy, 'L'Hermite de la Guyane. Miroir des mœurs. *Dictionnaire des gens du grand monde*,' *Gazette de France* (21 October 1816), in Edmond Eggli, *Le Débat romantique en France* (Paris, 1933), p. 492 (hereafter cited as *Eggli*).

5 Excellent discussions of the recognition of the *je ne sais quoi* in nature and the subsequent use of *pittoresque, romanesque*, and *romantique* are to be found in François, 'Romantique,' pp. 206–7, and in Logan Pearsall Smith, 'Four Romantic Words,' in *Words and Idioms* (5th ed., London, 1943), pp. 66–134, especially pp. 67–87.

6 Jacques Delille, *Les Jardins, ou l'art d'embellir les paysages* (5th ed., Paris, Rheims, 1782), pp. 62–3. Whately's volume had been translated into French by François de Paul Latapie in 1771, under the title *L'Art de former les jardins modernes*.

7 Jacques Delille, *Les Jardins, poème* (Paris, 1801), p. 89.
8 Pierre Letourneur, 'Discours extrait des différentes préfaces que les éditeurs de Shakespeare ont mises à la tête de leurs éditions' (hereafter cited as *Letourneur*), in William Shakespeare, *Œuvres* (Paris, 1776), I: cxxiii.
9 Urbain Domergue, article in *Journal de la langue française* (24 September, 1791), in Fernand Baldensperger, ' "Romantique," ses analogues et ses équivalents: tableau synoptique de 1650 à 1810,' *Harvard Studies and Notes in Philology and Literature* XIX (1937): 88.
10 Jean-Jacques Rousseau, *Confessions*, ed. Francis Bouvet (Paris, 1961), I: 65.
11 Honoré de Balzac, preface to *Scènes de la vie privée* (1st ed., 1830), in *La Comédie humaine* XI, ed. Roger Pierrot (Paris, 1959), p. 165.
12 Denis Diderot, *Eloge de Richardson*, in *Œuvres esthétiques*, ed. Paul Vernière (Paris, n.d.), p. 30.
13 François-René de Chateaubriand, *Essai sur les révolutions* (Paris, 1859), p. 381 (hereafter cited as *Chateaubriand*).
14 Ibid., p. 397.
15 Evariste-Désiré de Parny, 'Radotage,' *Almanach des Muses* (1810), pp. 3, 5.
16 In *Journal de l'Empire* (13 September, 1805).
17 Etienne Pivert de Senancour, *Obermann* (Paris, 1840), p. 158 (hereafter cited as *Senancour*). First published 1804.
18 Alfred de Musset, 'Lettres de Dupuis et Cotonet' (1836), in *Œuvres complètes en prose*, ed. Maurice Allem and Paul Courant (Paris, 1960), p. 826 (hereafter cited as *Musset*).
19 Jean-Bernard Le Blanc, *Lettres* (5th ed., Lyons, 1758), II: 293–4.
20 *Letourneur*, p. cxxiii.
21 R. L. Gérardin [René-Louis de Girardin], *De la composition des paysages, ou des moyens d'embellir la nature autour des habitations, en joignant l'agréable à l'utile* (Geneva, Paris, 1777), p. 128.
22 *Senancour*, pp. 158–9.
23 Cf. Smith, *Words and Idioms*, p. 82.
24 Jacques Delille, *L'Homme des champs, ou les Géorgiques français* (Paris, 1800), p. 111.
25 *Senancour*, p. 480.
26 Horace-Bénédict de Saussure, *Voyages dans les Alpes* (Neuchâtel, 1796), IV: 408.
27 *Chateaubriand*, pp. 604–5.
28 *Senancour*, p. 161.
29 Quoted in A. Aulard, *Paris sous le premier Empire* (Paris, 1912), I: 121.
30 Quoted in *Le Moniteur* (26 March, 1793), p. 380.
31 Jean-François Marmontel, 'Les Solitaires de Murcie,' in *Nouveaux Contes moraux* (Paris, 1818), p. 36.
32 Stendhal, *Correspondance*, ed. Henri Martineau and V. Del Litto (Paris, 1962), I: 9.
33 Jean-François Marmontel, *Mémoires* (Paris, 1818), I: 241. Written in the early 1790s.
34 Ibid., I: 478.
35 Charles Baudelaire, 'Salon de 1846,' in *Œuvres complètes*, ed. Y.-G. Le Dantec (Paris, 1951), p. 672.
36 August Wilhelm Schlegel, *Comparaison entre la Phèdre de Racine et celle d'Euripide* (Paris, 1807, reprinted and redistributed by A. L. Pollard, Old Marston, Oxford, 1962), pp. 11–12.
37 Charles de Rémusat, *Correspondance*, ed. Paul de Rémusat (Paris, 1883–6), I: 308.
38 [Charles de Villers], 'Lettre de M. Charles Villers, correspondant de l'Institut de France, à M. Millin, membre de l'Institut et de la Légion d'honneur, sur un Recueil d'anciennes poésies allemandes,' *Magasin encyclopédique* V (1810): 5–24, passim (hereafter cited as *Villers*).
39 Philippe-Albert Stapfer, 'Préface' (1812), in *Eggli*, pp. 34–5; Mme la baronne

de Staël-Holstein, *De l'Allemagne* (5th ed., Paris 1818), 1: 260–6, passim (here-after cited as *Mme de Staël*).

40 For both terms, and a variety of others (e.g., *le théâtre romantique, les romantiques*), see Léonard Simonde de Sismondi, *De la littérature du Midi de l'Europe* (Paris, Strasbourg, 1813), II: 156–60, passim, and (2nd ed., Paris, 1819), III: 468–84, passim (hereafter cited as *Sismondi*).

41 Quoted in *Eggli*, p. 445.

42 Ermès Visconti, *Idee elementari sulla poesia romantica* (Milan, 1818), p. 3.

43 Quoted in *Annales de la littérature et des arts* XIII (1823): 421.

44 *Villers*, p. 7.

45 *Sismondi* (1813), II: 156; Etienne Aignan, 'Sur la littérature allemande,' *Minerve française* IV (1819): 55 (hereafter cited as *Aignan*).

46 *Villers*, p. 14; *Sismondi* (1813), II: 156, 160.

47 Charles Nodier, *Mélanges de littérature et de critique*, ed. Alexandre Barginet (Paris, 1820), I: 231.

48 Alfred Michiels, *Histoire des idées littéraires en France* (Paris, 1842), I: xiv-xv.

49 *Mme de Staël* I: 260.

50 Charles Nodier, review of A. W. Schlegel, *Cours de littérature dramatique* (*Journal de l'Empire*, 4 March 1814), in *Eggli*, p. 113.

51 Announcement in *Le Conservateur littéraire* (June 1820), ed. Jules Marsan (Paris, 1922–38), II, 1: 155.

52 *Aignan*, p. 55.

53 Cf. René Bray, *Chronologie du romantisme* (Paris, 1963), pp. 1–37, passim.

54 Quoted in Stendhal, *Racine et Shakespeare*, ed. Georges Eudes (Paris, 1954), pp. 234–5.

55 Victor Hugo, review of Lamartine, *Méditations poétiques*, in *Le Conservateur littéraire* (April 1820), I, 2: 195.

56 [Julien Castelnau], *Essai sur la littérature romantique* (Paris, 1825), p. 4.

57 Quoted in *Eggli*, p. 153.

58 *Saint-Chamans*, p. 33.

59 Ibid., p. 34.

60 Prosper Duvergier de Hauranne, 'Du romantique' (1825), in Pierre Trahard, *Le Romantisme défini par 'Le Globe'* (Paris, n.d.), p. 13 (hereafter cited as *Trahard*).

61 'Situation du romantisme au 1er novembre 1825,' in *Trahard*, p. 88.

62 Victor Hugo, preface to *Hernani*, in *Théâtre complet*, ed. J.-J. Thierry and Josette Mélèze (Paris, 1963), I: 1147.

63 Schlegel, *Cours* I: 17–20, 31; Stendhal, *Correspondance inédite* (Paris, 1855), I: 106–11, and *Racine et Shakespeare*, pp. 147–56.

64 Etienne-Jean Delécluze, *Traité de peinture* (Paris, 1827), p. 250, quoted in Louis Hautecœur et al., *Le Romantisme et l'art* (Paris, 1928), p. 1; 'Salon de 1827,' *Revue française* (1828), p. 196.

65 Ibid., p. 200.

66 François-Joseph Fétis, 'Examen de l'état actuel de la musique en Italie, en Allemagne, en Angleterre et en France,' Septième article: 'Allemagne,' *Revue musicale* I (1827): 352–3.

67 Ferdinand Brunetière, *L'Evolution de la poésie lyrique en France au dix-neuvième siècle* (4th ed., Paris, 1905), I: 172–9; Paul Valéry, 'Situation de Baudelaire' (1924), in *Œuvres*, ed. Jean Hytier (Paris, 1957–60), I: 599–601 (hereafter cited as *Valéry*).

68 *Musset*, p. 822.

69 Quoted in *Eggli*, p. 113.

70 Victor Hugo, preface to *Odes et ballades* (1826), in *Œuvres poétiques*, ed. Pierre Albouy (Paris, 1964), I: 282.

71 Duvergier de Hauranne, 'Du romantique,' in *Trahard*, p. 13.

72 Victor Hugo, *William Shakespeare* (Paris, 1937), p. 364.

73 Hugo, preface to *Odes et ballades*, in *Œuvres poétiques* I: 283.
74 Ludovic Vitet, 'De l'indépendance en matière de goût' (1825), in *Trahard*, pp. 22–3.
75 Stendhal, *Racine et Shakespeare*, p. 17.
76 Stendhal, *Correspondance inédite*, I: 108.
77 Stendhal, *Racine et Shakespeare*, p. 52. This is, according to Stendhal, why Molière was a romantic playwright: Alcestes and Orontes abounded in the seventeenth century (p. 55).
78 Ibid., p. 27.
79 Hugo, preface to *Odes* (1824), in *Œuvres poétiques* I: 272.
80 Emile Deschamps, *Un Manifeste du romantisme. La Préface des Etudes françaises et étrangères* (1828), ed. Henri Girard (Paris, n.d.), p. 6 (hereafter cited as *Deschamps*).
81 Victor Hugo, *Océan, Tas de pierres* (Paris, 1942), p. 354.
82 Stendhal, 'Réponse à quelques objections,' in *Racine et Shakespeare*, pp. 25–6.
83 Baudelaire, 'Salon de 1846,' in *Œuvres complètes*, p. 601.
84 Ibid., pp. 602–3.
85 Desprès, 'Du romantisme considéré historiquement' (1825), in *Trahard*, p. 81; Nodier, *Mélanges* II: 344–5.
86 *Deschamps*, p. 81.
87 *Musset*, p. 830.
88 Hugo, review of Thomas Moore, *Lalla Roukh*, in *Le Conservateur littéraire* (June, 1820), II, 1: 261.
89 Quoted in Bernard Weinberg, *French Realism: the Critical Reaction (1830–1870)*, private edition, distributed by the University of Chicago Libraries (Chicago, Ill.). Reprint of Modern Language Association of America, General Series (1937), p. 122.
90 Emile Faguet, 'Emile Zola,' in *Propos littéraires*, 3rd series (Paris, 1905), pp. 257–8.
91 Emile Zola, 'Victor Hugo,' in *Documents littéraires*, ed. Maurice Le Blond (Paris, n.d.), p. 50.
92 Hugo, *William Shakespeare*, p. 208.
93 Hugo, preface to *Marion de Lorme* (1830), in *Théâtre complet* I: 958.
94 Alfred de Vigny, letter to Prince Royal of Bavaria (17 September 1839), in *Œuvres complètes*, ed. Fernand Baldensperger (Paris, 1950), I: 587.
95 Hugo, *Océan, Tas de pierres*, p. 349.
96 Edmond and Jules de Goncourt, *Journal* (Paris, 1904), I: 168; Gustave Flaubert, *Correspondance*, ed. René Dumesnil et al. (Paris, 1926–33), V: 242, and *Correspondance (Supplément)* (Paris, 1954), II: 284.
97 Catulle Mendès, *Légende du Parnasse contemporain* (Brussels, 1884), pp. 11–13; Arthur Rimbaud, letter to Paul Demeny ('Lettre du voyant,' 15 May 1871), in *Œuvres complètes*, ed. Rolland de Renéville and Jules Mouquet (Paris, 1951), p. 257.
98 Zola, 'Les Poëtes contemporains,' in *Documents littéraires*, p. 134.
99 Nodier, preface to translation of Maturin's *Bertram* (1821), in *Des Granges*, p. 218.
100 Baudelaire, *Œuvres complètes*, p. 602.
101 *Valéry*, p. 604; André Gide, 'Réponse à une enquête de la Renaissance sur le classicisme,' in *Incidences* (Paris, 1924), p. 217.
102 Albert Camus, *L'Homme révolté* (Paris, 1951), p. 368.

OLGA RAGUSA

Italy /
Romantico – Romanticismo

I

Romantico! This word, uncommon for Italians, still unknown in Naples
and the happy Campania, current at most among German artists in
Rome, has for some time been causing a great uproar in Lombardy and
especially in Milan. The public is divided into two factions that stand
facing each other ready for battle. And whereas we Germans when the
occasion arises use the adjective romantic quite peacefully, in Milan the
two expressions romanticism and classicism designate two irreconcilable
sects.

Romantico! *den Italienern ein seltsames Wort, in Neapel und dem glücklichen
Kampanien noch unbekannt, in Rom unter deutschen Künstlern allenfalls üblich,
macht in der Lombardei, besonders in Mailand, seit einiger Zeit großes Aufsehen.
Das Publikum teilt sich in zwei Parteien, sie stehen schlagfertig gegeneinander,
und wenn wir Deutschen uns ganz geruhig des Adjektivum* romantisch *bei
Gelegenheit bedienen, so werden dort durch die Ausdrücke* Romantizismus *und*
Kritizismus [sic] *zwei unversöhnliche Sekten bezeichnet.**

With these words, written in 1818, Goethe took cognizance of the
heated debate which had been raging in Milan since 1816. In

---

*   *Goethes Werke*, ed. Karl Heinemann (Leipzig und Wien, n.d.), xxv: 320. All the
editions of Goethe's works that I have been able to consult, including the
Sophien-Ausgabe (XLI, 1 : 133), give *Kritizismus* without benefit of correction or
annotation. The Italian translator of the article, however, which appeared in
Antologia xx (December 1825), substituted *classicismo* for *Kritizismus*, as the
meaning would seem to demand. Cf. Egidio Bellorini, ed., *Discussioni e
polemiche sul romanticismo* (Bari, 1943), II: 476 (hereafter cited as *Bellorini*).

January of that year the new periodical *Biblioteca italiana* had begun publication with its great journalistic coup, Mme de Staël's article 'De l'esprit des traductions.'[1] In it she urged Italians to turn to the translation of recent English and German poetry in order to renew and enrich their literary tradition. But the advice was taken as an affront, and the translator of the article himself voiced the opinion of the vast majority of Italian men of letters when in a later article of his own he defended the poetic perfection first achieved by the Greeks and Romans and later continued by their legitimate descendants, the Italians.* Overnight Mme de Staël's name became the rallying point for both attack and defense in a new version of the *querelle des anciens et des modernes*.

By the time the battle of romanticism was concluded and won ten years later, the Italian language was the richer by a word: the 1825 edition of D'Alberti di Villanova's *Dizionario universale critico*, significantly identified on the title page as the first Milanese edition,[2] lists both *romanticismo* and *romantico*. The words are designated as neologisms and the reader is referred back to *classico*, which 'is said of a Thing excellent and perfect, as of the first class' / '*si dice di Cosa eccellente e perfetta, quasi di prima classe.*' The definition reveals strong awareness of the etymology of the word: from Latin *classicus*, applied to the civic classes of the Roman people and especially to the first class created by Servius Tullius.[3] Furthermore, D'Alberti di Villanova illustrates the usage of *classico* with the expression *Autore classico*, 'ancient, approved author, who is considered an authority in certain subjects. Homer, Plato, Cicero, Virgil are called classical authors' / '*Autore antico, approvato, che fa autorità in certe materie. Omero, Platone, Cicerone, Virgilio sono detti Autori classici.*' Compared to the broader range of meaning in other languages, where *romantic* referred to 'romance-like,' 'extravagant,' 'absurd,' and 'picturesque' alike, it is striking that Italian *romantico* came into existence as a strictly literary term.

Italy, according to Wellek, 'was the first Latin country to have a romantic movement which was aware of its being romantic.'[4] Entering the language at a later stage in the development and definition of the concept, the Italian *romantico*, however fluctuating and

---

* [Pietro Giordani], 'Un italiano risponde al discorso della Staël,' *Biblioteca italiana* (April 1816). The article is erroneously attributed to Giovanni Gherardini in *Bellorini* 1: 16. Mario Marcazzan, *Le origini lombarde nel romanticismo italiano* (Milan, 1967), p. 163 (hereafter cited as *Marcazzan*), describes the article as 'la formulazione di un'estetica classicistica in anticipo sui tempi di un'estetica romantica ancora *in fieri.*'

emotion-laden in meaning throughout the period of the romantic polemic, began as a technical term of restricted connotation. Only later was its meaning extended to apply to the description of sentiment and character, and of landscape. *Il piccolo Alberti*, a school dictionary based on the original D'Alberti di Villanova and supplemented by the contributions of later dictionaries, gives in its 1888 edition a very conservative, that is, a negative, definition of *romanticismo*: 'the doctrine of those who in literature and in the arts do not adhere rigorously to the example of the classics' / '*dottrina di quelli che nelle lettere e nelle arti non s'attengono con rigore agli esempi de' classici.*'[5] But it has *romantico*, both as adjective and noun, with the meaning of 'eccentric' as well as with the by then conventional meaning of 'follower of romanticism' / '*Romantico a. e sm. seguace del romanticismo – Fantastico.*' *Il piccolo Alberti* also includes the expression *Luogo romantico* ('romantic spot'), 'pleasant, secluded' / '*ameno, solitario,*' thus regaining the meaning of English *romantick* given by Baretti's *Dizionario delle Lingue italiana ed inglese* as 'Scenic, secluded, solitary, wild, fanciful; and it is said for the most part of a place which is charmingly rural' / '*Scenico, solitario, romitico, selvaggio, capriccioso; e dicesi per lo più d'un luogo vagamente campestre,*'* and by Letourneur in that *locus classicus* of his translation of the Shakespeare Prefaces where he felt it necessary to insert a discussion of the same word, ending with the famous summary in which the three key concepts – romance-like, picturesque, and romantic or emotionally moving – are brought together in exemplary fashion:

The paintings of Salvator Rosa, some spots in the Alps, a number of gardens and country places in England are not at all fanciful (*romanesques*); but one can say that they are more than picturesque, that is, that they are touching and romantic.

Les tableaux de Salvator Rosa, quelques sites des Alpes, plusieurs jardins et campagnes de l'Angleterre ne sont point romanesques; mais on peut dire qu'ils sont plus que pittoresques, c'est-à-dire, touchans et romantiques.[6]

* Giuseppe Baretti, *Dizionario delle Lingue italiana ed inglese*. Nuova edizione, corretta e migliorata, da F. Damiani (Londra, 1798). Baretti also includes *romitano* (hermitic) in his list of translations. See also 1816 edition (prima edizione fiorentina, Firenze): '*Romantick*, adj. (belonging to romance) favoloso, vano, chimerico. Romantick (improbable, false) improbabile, inverisimile, falso. Romantick (fanciful, full of wild scenery) scenico, solitario, romitico, romitano, selvaggio, capriccioso; e dicesi per lo più d'un luogo vagamente campestre.' C. Apollonio, *Romantico: Storia e fortuna di una parola* (Firenze, 1958), p. 77 (hereafter cited as *Apollonio*), gives the same adjective from a Venice edition of Baretti, 1787.

Baretti and Letourneur are both quoted by Giovanni Gherardini in his translation of Schlegel's *Vorlesungen über dramatische Kunst und Literatur*.[7] It is significant that their authority is appealed to, not the first time the word *romantic* occurs, but the only time that it is used in connection with landscape instead of literature. Gherardini, that is, felt no compunction in translating '*Esprit de la poésie classique et de la poésie romantique*' (chapter subheading of Lesson I) as '*Spirito della poesia classica e della poesia romantica*,' but he did feel that the expression 'romantic forest' used by Schlegel in connection with *As You Like It* needed to be justified.* In other words, in accordance with what we have just pointed out, the translator was quite willing to use the neologism in the context of literature, but did not feel equally at ease when the word appeared with a different meaning, a meaning which in England, France, and Germany had preceded its strictly literary one.

By his own admission, Gherardini based his translation not on Schlegel's German original but on the French translation of the work by Mme Necker de Saussure, a cousin of Mme de Staël.† This fact dramatizes the direct dependence of Italian romanticism, at least as a self-conscious movement, upon suggestions that came from France. Enrico Maier, the translator of Goethe's 'Klassiker und Romantiker in Italien, sich heftig bekämpfend,' assessed the interplay of German and French influences on the discussions in Italy quite correctly, when he commented upon the surprise felt by the Germans at seeing romanticism rejected in Italy while they themselves considered such Italian masterpieces as the *Orlando furioso*, the *Divina Commedia*, and even the *Gerusalemme liberata* as romantic. Maier attributed the difference in reaction in Germany and Italy to the fact that the romantic debate came to Italy from France and not from Germany, and that it was actually simply a prolongation of the older dispute concerning 'the dramatic unities and the external forms of poetry':

Or io considerando tanta diversità d'opinione in Germania e in Italia sul medesimo

---

* The note is appended to the sentence, 'Se ad alcuno spiacesse di non vedere osservato il ceremoniale da teatro in questa romantica selva ...'

† A. W. Schlegel, *Cours de littérature dramatique* (Genève, 1813). This translation is by declaration of Schlegel himself the only authentic one and represents a revised and corrected edition of the original. There is therefore some justification for Gherardini's choice of it as his basic text. In a translator's note, Gherardini, who later turned his interests to lexicography, warns the reader that he has used a number of words in their French rather than Italian meaning. The list (*genio, sviluppo, originale, vista, influenza*, etc.) does not include *romantico*.

*punto, sospetto che più dai francesi, che dai tedeschi abbiamo ereditato una tal di-
puta, e che questa si riduca in ultima analisi a quella più antica e già tante volte
discussa sulle* unità nell'arte drammatica, *e sulle forme esterne della poesia.**

Thus, Italian romanticism would originally appear to be not a totally new kind of art resulting from a new sensibility, but a new trend in poetics – interest in new rules of rhetoric which were by and large defended by the same appeal to reason that had dominated classical aesthetics.

The derivation of Italian romanticism from the French – or to be more precise, of rationalistic Lombard romanticism from the milieu of Coppet[8] – was to leave its mark on the movement. It finds an echo in Manzoni's distinction between two kinds of romanticism and in his rejection of the second kind, which he describes as

... I know not what muddle of witches and ghosts, a systematic disorder, a search for the eccentric, a renunciation of common sense; a romanticism, in brief, which it would have been reasonable to refute and to forget, if indeed anyone had proposed it.

*... non so qual guazzabuglio di streghe, di spettri, un disordine sistematico, una ricerca
stravagante, una abiura in termini del senso comune ; un romanticismo insomma, che
si sarebbe avuta molta ragione di rifiutare e di dimenticare, se fosse stato proposto da
alcuno.†*

And it finds a later, more confused echo in De Sanctis's expression of relief that romanticism 'in its German and French exaggeration did not take root in Italy,' that its scattered appearance only 'accentuated the repugnance felt for it by the Italian spirit,' and that the romantics themselves 'were happy when they were able to rid themselves of that borrowed name, origin of so many misunderstandings and squabbles, and take instead a name acceptable to all':

*Il romanticismo, in questa sua esagerazione tedesca e francese, non attecchì in
Italia ... I pochi tentativi non valsero che a meglio accentuare la ripugnanza del genio*

---

*   Enrico Maier, 'Goethe e i romantici italiani,' *Antologia* xx (December 1825):
      24–9. Also in *Bellorini* ii: 475–80. Note that Bellorini erroneously encloses the
      last paragraph in quotation marks, thus attributing to Goethe what is Maier's.
      The Goethe passage ends with the words '... che il greco e il romano.'

†   A. Manzoni, *Lettera sul romanticismo*, written in 1823, first published in 1846.
      Now in *Opere* (Milano, 1943), ii: 620. Rereading the whole passage from the
      beginning of the paragraph, in the light of what we have said regarding the
      initial meaning of *romantico* and *romanticismo* in Italy, makes it perfectly clear
      that Manzoni's distinction between two kinds of romanticism is firmly rooted in
      his awareness of the chronological sequence in the development of the meaning
      of the term.

italiano. E i romantici furono lieti quando poterono gittar via quel nome d'imprestito, fonte di tanti equivoci e litigi, e prendere un nome accettato da tutti.[9]

That name, De Sanctis says, was 'modern national literature,' seeming to forget in the flow of his eloquence that this was after all one of the original meanings of the term as it had first emerged in German discussions of the subject.*

But if Italian literary historians have encountered difficulty with romanticism, they have done no less so with pre-romanticism. Italy had of course its own pre-romantic movement, whether in an inclination towards the melancholy and graveyard poetry of Gray, Hervey, Young, and Thomson, or in the widespread admiration for Ossian, or in the popularity of *La nouvelle Héloïse* and *Werther*, or in the *Sturm und Drang* of Alfieri's passion for liberty and the untrammeled rights of genius, or in the 'romantic personality' and poetic intensity of Foscolo, persistently mislabelled as a neoclassicist. These aspects of the late eighteenth century, however, were revalued only much later, when the long distrust of romanticism, which characterizes so much Italian criticism and literary history down through the First World War, had finally been muted if not completely destroyed.[10] It was only then that the phenomenon of Italian romanticism was viewed without nationalistic or moralistic overtones and its relation to other romantic movements in Europe as well as its origin in the literary tradition of Italy itself studied objectively and dispassionately.† In 1816, however – and later, as we have already seen with De Sanctis – it was the 'foreignness' of the movement that stood out, leading to such outbursts as Carlo Botta's,

Oh! All poor Italy needed was to chase after German nonsense after having already wasted her time with French foolishness! The fogs of the Caledonian and Hercynian marshes will have greater sway on Italian minds than the light of Greece and Rome, and of Italy herself!

* There is obviously some chronological confusion in De Sanctis on this point. He seems to postulate a kind of historical transcendence between an inferior kind of romanticism and a superior kind, which I do not think can be argued from historical evidence: 'Anche in Germania il romanticismo fu presto attirato nelle alte regioni della filosofia e, spogliatosi di quelle forme fantastiche e quel contenuto reazionario, riuscì sotto nome di "letteratura moderna" nell'ecletismo (*sic*), nella conciliazione di tutti gli elementi e di tutte le forme sotto i princípi superiori dell'estetica o della filosofia dell'arte' (p. 450). See also pp. 326–9 below.

† J. G. Robertson, *Studies in the Genesis of Romantic Theory in the Eighteenth Century* (Cambridge, 1923), attributes great importance in the formation of the doctrine of European romanticism to Italian critics and aestheticians of the eighteenth century.

Oh non mancava altro alla misera Italia, che andar dietro alle tedescherie dopo d'aver corso dietro alle franceserie! Le nebbie delle maremme caledoniche ed erciniche avran più forza nelle menti italiane della luce greca, latina, e della luce italiana stessa![11]

– or to spoofs such as the 'Parodia dello statuto d'una immaginaria accademia romantica,' in which everything concerning the romantics was lampooned, from their love of the medieval and the picturesquely decaying to their praise of the modern literatures at the expense of the ancient, their extolling of sentiment and nature, and even their disordered dress and abstracted, introspective look.[12]

This violent anti-romanticism, in which customs and attitudes rather than literature were the object of attention, was to influence not only the historiography of Italian literature but also Italian lexicography. Niccolò Tommaseo, in many respects a romantic himself and a close friend and admirer of Manzoni, lists a new adverb, *romanticamente* (romantically), and two new nouns, *romanticheria* (romantic notion) and *romanticume* (romantic nonsense), in his *Dizionario della lingua italiana.** Tommaseo's definition of all three words implies censure: *romanticamente*, in *descrivere romanticamente* (to describe in a romantic way), is explained as 'with exaggerated colours, or with too great indulgence in minutiae,' and in *vivere, amare romanticamente* (to live, to love romantically) as 'affecting a feeling one does not really have'; *romanticheria* is explained as 'affecting a feeling, or a way of doing, or a way of writing that is romance-like or romantic,' and its synonym *romanticume* as 'even worse, as the form indicates':

Descrivere romanticamente, con colori esagerati, o compiacendosi troppo nelle minuziosità. Vivere, amare romanticamente, con affettazione di sentimento che sul serio non si ha.

Romanticheria. Affettazione di sentire e di fare e di scrivere romanzesco o romantico.

Romanticume, peggio; come la forma dice.

The stress in all three definitions is on unnaturalness and affectation, on a kind of psychological dishonesty.

*   Niccolò Tommaseo and Bernardo Bellini, *Dizionaria della Lingua italiana* (Torino-Napoli, 1872). The compilation of the dictionary was begun in 1857; publication was started in 1858, interrupted, and resumed in 1862. The work was completed by Giuseppe Meini. Tommaseo's *Dizionario estetico* (Firenze, 1867) speaks disparagingly of the romantic debate, discounting the idea of a literary school and attributing originality to talent and spontaneity rather than to a programmatic rejection of one set of rhetorical rules in favour of another (p. 795).

Tommaseo's bias appears also in his definition of *luogo romantico*, 'of exceptional pleasantness, and such as is described in romances,' and especially in his definition of *gita, passeggiata romantica* (romantic excursion or walk) –

either because of the nature of the places visited, or because of its pleasures, or because of what happened during it, which was either unusual or which one wishes to make seem unusual

Luogo romantico. D'amenità singolare, e qual suole descriversi ne' romanzi. – Gita, Passeggiata romantica, o per la qualità de' luoghi visitati, o per il diletto avutone, o per i casi incontrati che tengano, o vogliasi far parere che tengano del singolare

– where again we encounter distrust of the motives behind the quality of the feeling which the adjective designates. Naturally, Tommaseo includes *romanticismo*, 'the doctrine of those who in the arts and in literature would wish that nature be imitated as it is, and that the example and the doctrines of the ancient masters be abandoned':

Romanticismo. La dottrina di coloro che nelle arti e lettere vorrebbero che s'imitasse la natura tale quale è, e si abbandonassero le tracce e le dottrine poste dagli antichi maestri.

This definition still bears traces of the word's origin as a neologism for the opposite of classicism, but now gives primary importance to the principle of mimesis, thus pointing to the eventual identification of romanticism with realism. Tommaseo does not overlook the literary meaning of the adjective *romantico*, 'what is made in accordance with the doctrine of romanticism,' and he adds the expressions *autori romantici; scuola, biblioteca romantica* (obviously patterned on D'Alberti di Villanova's *autore classico*), to which again he gives more than a purely descriptive definition, 'said of authors who called themselves romantic, or who were considered such,' thus continuing to underline his disapproval: '*Romantico. Che è fatto secondo la dottrina del romanticismo. Autori romantici; Scuola, Biblioteca romantica, D'autori che si sono intitolati romantici, o che furono presi per tali.*'

The usage of *romanticismo* and *romantico*, both noun and adjective, is abundantly illustrated by Tommaseo with quotations taken for the most part from Monti's *Opere inedite e rare*.[13] This work had also been one of the sources for Giovanni Gherardini, Tommaseo's predecessor, in his *Supplimento a' Vocabolarj italiani*.[14] In the romantic debate Monti had started out in a rather neutral position; he was the leading man of letters in Milan and it was natural that what were to become the opposing factions both sought the prestige of his support. He ended, however, by espousing the cause of the classicists. Monti's statements, as quoted by Tommaseo, reinforce the impression of disparagement created by the latter's whole treatment of *romantico* and its cognates. The same is not true for Gherardini's use of the identical references. Thus, for instance, Monti's observation –

As far as the romantics are concerned, who can help saying that they are raving mad when they expect to banish mythology from poetry? And not only to banish it, but to see it entirely dead? And to see dead with it the source of all ideal beauty in the arts?

In quanto ai romantici chi può mai rimanersi dal dire che delirano allorchè pretendono di sbandirla [la mitologia] affatto dalla poesia? ; e non solo sbandirla, ma volerla spenta del tutto? ; e spenta con essa la fonte del bello ideale nelle belle arti?[15]

– is cited in its entirety by Gherardini in his definition of the noun *romantico*;[16] but it is abbreviated by Tommaseo in such a way that it ends after '... banish mythology,' thus throwing the idea of 'raving mad' into stronger relief. Tommaseo's own normative comment, 'It [mythology] should be neither proclaimed nor banished, but left alone and mentioned only as an historical subject or a symbolic image'/'*Né bandirla né sbandirla; lasciarla ire: e accennarne come di soggetto storico o di simbolica immagine,*'* further underlines his estrangement from the initial romantic position.

The tone of Tommaseo's definitions is a direct result of the expansion in meaning which *romantico* had undergone; by losing its restricted literary meaning, it came to be even as a literary term at the mercies of its (in Italy) non-literary meaning. Gherardini's definition of *romantico*,

Said of places, villages, etc., which recall to the imagination the descriptions read in romances; used now to refer to what is imagined or composed in accordance with the religion, the customs, and the spirit of modern times; refers to the opposite of classical, that is, composed and imagined without rules and as it comes from nature,

Dicesi de' Luoghi, de' Paesetti, ec., che risvegliano nell'imaginativa le descrizioni che si leggono ne' poemi romanzeschi; si dice oggi di Ciò che è imaginato o dettato conformemente alla religione, a' costumi ed al genio de' tempi moderni; si usa per

* The play on words is naturally lost in translation.

chiamare Ciò che è l'opposto del classico, cioè dettato, imaginato senza regole e come viene da natura,

as we have shown, has been both simplified and subtly deformed in Tommaseo. The reason for the shift is that Tommaseo, born in 1802, joined the romantic debate only at the end, when the doctrine itself was no longer *in fieri* and its separate elements no longer as clear and distinct as they were to Gherardini, who had been deeply involved in the development and definition of the concept from the beginning.*

We shall now turn to look more closely at the terms and the history of the debate, for it is from *romantico* in a literary context that we must move back to the older *romanzesco*, which – like *romanesque* in France and *romantic* in England – had contributed to the choice of the word to name the movement.

II

Mme de Staël's article in *Biblioteca italiana* was not the first appearance of her name in the Italian press. The controversy to which her recommendations gave rise is in some respects but a continuation of earlier discussions sparked by her not always fair-minded remarks on Italy and the Italians. Animosity had already been released by the translation of her *De la littérature considérée dans ses rapports avec les institutions sociales.*[17] Although this work preceded the romantic debate by more than a decade, it stated with great clarity what was to become one of the basic controversial points. At the time of writing it, Mme de Staël had not yet come under the influence of the German romantics, and there is therefore no mention of romanticism in the work. But although she continued to subscribe to the classical criterion of an absolute standard for taste and beauty 'at

---

*   In addition to Schlegel's *Vorlesungen*, Gherardini also translated the part of Sismondi's *De la littérature du midi de l'Europe* that deals with Italy: *Della letteratura italiana del secolo XIV fino al principio del XIX* (Milano, 1820). Gherardini was also the author of a manual used in schools in Lombardy, *Elementi di poesia italiana* (Milano, 1820). *Bellorini* II: 135–65 brings passages from ch. IX to XII of the work. In defining classic and romantic, Gherardini follows the chronological and cultural division of poetry of the ancients and poetry of the moderns. He has an interesting observation on the use of *classico* as a genre designation, noting that it is the 'new school', i.e., the romantics, who have given that name to the 'system' of the Greeks. On the relationship between Italian neo-classicism and romanticism, see Mario Puppo, 'Le poetiche del romanticismo dal Foscolo al Carducci,' in *Momenti e problemi di storia dell'estetica* (Milano, 1959–61), pp. 981–1066. Puppo states pithily that 'il neo-classicismo italiano è il *riflesso* del romanticismo,' whereas 'il neo-classicismo europeo è un *aspetto* del romanticismo' (p. 982, italics mine).

least in its general principles,' she introduced at the same time a relativistic view of literature, which took into consideration as determining factors such variables as historical and political circumstances, as well as climate and customs. Moreover, she characterized the literatures of the South and of the North comparatively, defining the former as brilliant, sensual, and lively, whereas the latter 'reaches beyond this world,' 'shakes' the imagination, and carries the soul 'toward the future and toward a different world.'[18] In *De l'Allemagne*, written after a number of works by other critics had repeated this differentiation[19] – particularly relevant to discussions of French tragedy as against romantic drama and Shakespeare* – Mme de Staël substituted for the geographical designations of literature of the North and literature of the South the expressions 'poésie romantique' and 'poésie classique.'

The Italian translation of *De l'Allemagne*† appeared almost simultaneously with the Paris edition, and notice of the work in Italy was first taken in the Milanese periodical *Lo spettatore*, which was at that time simply the Italian version of the homonymic Paris publication, *Le Spectateur*.‡ In 1814 *Lo spettatore* published in Italian translation both Conrad Malte-Brun's long, favourable review of *De l'Allemagne* and Antoine Jay's anti-romantic 'Discours sur le genre romantique en littérature.'[20] In both texts there are occurrences of *romantique*, which the translation (unlike that of *De l'Allemagne*) renders simply as *romantico*. It is true that the translator of Jay's piece reveals a certain degree of uneasiness in making use of a word that is not part of the Italian lexicon.§ On the other hand,

---

* Discussions of the theatre accompanied and in part preceded discussons of the classical-romantic polarity. We have already mentioned Maier's comment (note p. 296) above. We could add Gherardini's long footnote at the end of Schlegel, Lesson IX (cf. *Bellorini* 1: 201–5), in which the situation of the Italian theatre is discussed within the context of the generalized contrast between two aesthetic ideals.

† Davide Bertolotti, tr. (Milano, 1814). The Paris edition of *De l'Allemagne* (1814) is the so-called third edition. The first French edition was destroyed in 1810; the second edition was published in London in 1813. Bertolotti renders *romantique* by *romanzesco*, not by *romantico*.

‡ *Lo spettatore ovvero Mescolanze di viaggi, di storia, di statistica, di politica, di letteratura e di filosofia* was published by Antonio Stella from 1814 to 1818. It became independent after Conrad Malte-Brun's *Le Spectateur ou Variétés historiques, littéraires, critiques, politiques et morales* ceased publication with the 20 May 1815 number.

§ Jay had written apropos *The Tempest*: '... et comme tout, dans cet ouvrage, est hors des limites de la nature et de la vraisemblance, *nous dirons qu'il appartient au genre romantique.*' The translation reads: '... appunto una di quelle composizioni che interamente oltrepassando i confini della natura e del verosimile, *si dicono appartenenti al genere ... chiamato romantico*' (italics mine).

Malte-Brun exhibits the same perplexity for French when he has recourse to such expressions as 'The so-called romantic characteristic, opposed to the classical rules ...' or 'This modern taste, which Mme de Staël and the Germans call romantic ...'/'*Le caractère soi-disant romantique, ou opposé aux règles classiques* ...' and '*Ce goût moderne que madame de Staël et les Allemands appellent romantique* ...' which show that he feels that he must accompany the word by its definition or by mention of an authority for its usage. In 1814, in other words, neither in Italy nor generally in France do we have that unself-conscious reliance on the word that we find in Bouterwek's *Geschichte der Poesie und Beredsamkeit seit dem Ende des dreizehnten Jahrhunderts,*[21] in Schlegel's *Vorlesungen,*[22] in Sismondi's *De la Littérature du midi de l'Europe,** and in *De l'Allemagne.*

The citing of these titles emphasizes that interdependence of European cultural movements in the early nineteenth century that makes romanticism a subject *par excellence* for comparative studies, and it shows the central importance of works of dissemination and of translations to document the passing of the romantic aesthetic, and with it the word *romantic*, from Germany to France to Italy, in that order. In 1816 an unidentified correspondent wrote to *Lo spettatore*, now an independent Italian publication, asking for the exact meaning of *romantico*, especially with reference to the French expressions *genre romantique*, *site romantique*, and *cœur romantique*. The writer, whose communication was printed under the title, 'Ricerca di un nuovo vocabolo da introdursi nella lingua italiana,' said that whenever he was on the point of grasping the sense of the word, 'a sentence all peppered with *vague de la pensée*, *poésie de l'âme*, and *prose du cœur* would be the result'/'... *scappava fuori un periodo tutto cosperso di* vague de la pensée, *di* poésie de l'âme, *di* prose du cœur.' To which the editors replied, 'The French word *romantique* and also the English *romantic* derive from the German *romantisch*, which, according to Konig's dictionary, in Italian means picturesque, that is,

---

* Delivered as a lecture course in Geneva in 1812, published in Paris and Strasbourg, 1813. Ch. xxx, 'Du Théâtre dans la poésie romantique,' which Sismondi had completely redrafted for the 1819 edition of his work, was translated into Italian and published under the title, *Vera definizione del romanticismo ove sono svolti i diversi sistemi relativi delle principali nazioni.* Traduzione dal francese del D. M. (Milano, 1819). The translation was based on an extract of the *Biblioteca universale ginevrina* and can now be read in *Bellorini* II: 464–74. Wellek (*Concepts of Criticism*, New Haven and London, 1963, p. 143) notes that the translator, whose name he cites as D. M. Dalla (?), uses the noun *romanticismo*, although the equivalent word does not appear in the French original. This is true insofar as Sismondi used the adjective *romantique*, whereas the translator used the noun *romanticismo* to render *poésie romantique.*

after the manner of painters.' And further, voicing that fear of contamination which united classicists and conservatives in the Risorgimento,

The word [*sic*] *genre romantique*, in speaking of literature ... has a crooked meaning from which God preserve us Italians, inasmuch as we hold dear our individuality, which makes it possible for us to be recognized and distinguished from among the inhabitants of the five parts of the globe.

E noi diremo che la parola francese romantique, *come pure l'inglese* romantick, *sono derivate dalla tedesca* romantisch, *la quale, secondo il dizionario del Konig, suona in italiano* pittoresco, *cioè alla maniera di pittore ... La parola* genre romantique, *parlando di letteratura ... ha uno storto significato da cui Dio ci scampi noi Italiani, per quanto ci è caro di conservare la nostra fisonomia, onde essere conosciuti e distinti in mezzo agli abitanti delle cinque parti del mondo.**

And this explanation surely makes clear why the word should create such difficulties in spite of its being freely used: it was heavy with emotional connotations, and dictionaries – in this case bilingual English-Italian and German-Italian dictionaries – did not yet include the literary meaning which it had come to assume in the critical and theoretical writings of the period.†

*   *Lo spettatore* VI (1816), no. 56, pp. 128–30. I have been unable to identify the dictionary referred to and its author, Konig, König, or Koenig. Professor Renzo Negri of Milan, who very kindly engaged in further research in the libraries of the city to which he refers as 'the Bologna of the first half of the nineteenth century as far as dictionaries were concerned,' suggests that the name is either a misprint or a conventional name, such as 'royal' or the like. Professor Negri was able to consult a number of the bilingual dictionaries listed in the preface to F. Valentini, *Gran dizionario grammatico-pratico tedesco-italiano, italiano-tedesco*, 4 vols. (Leipzig, 1831–6): Kramer, Castelli, Veneroni, Flathe, Jagemann, Filippi. The first four precede the romantic period. C. M. Jagemann, *Italienisch-Deutsches und Deutsch-Italienisches Wörterbuch* (Leipzig, 1803), new edition by G. De Vogtberg and E. Kapher (Wien, 1816), gives '*Romantisch*, adj. romanzesco, strano, che ha del romanzesco; adv. in modo romanzesco'; '*Romanzesco*, romantisch, romanhaft'; but understandably enough does not have *romantico*. D. A. Filippi, *Dizionario Italiano-Tedesco e Tedesco-Italiano* (Wien, 1817) gives '*Romanmäßig, Romantisch*, adj. romanzesco, che ha del romanzesco; adv. in modo romanzesco.' The anonymous *Grande dizionario Italiano-Tedesco, Tedesco-Italiano compilato sui più accreditati vocabolari delle due lingue ed arricchito di molte migliaja di voci e di frasi* (Milano, 1937) lists '*Romantico*, agg. romantisch,' '*Romanticismo*, m. die Romantik,' '*Romanhaft*, agg. e avv., romanzesco, da romanzo, *eine romanhafte Geschichte*, storia da romanzo, romanzesca,' '*Romantisch*, agg. *eine romantische Gegend*, contrada d'incanto, un incantesimo.' The word *Romantik* is missing, and, as Professor Negri points out, *Romantisch* itself is not translated, but its use is illustrated in the meaning of 'incantevole.' There is, in other words, in none of the early sources any effort to give the *literary* meaning that the Italian word had.

†   Italian-English dictionaries have yielded the following results: for Baretti, see note p. 295, above; F. Altieri, *Dizionario Italiano ed Inglese* (London, 1749) lists '*Romantick*, adj. belonging to romance, favoloso, vano, chimerico'; Comelati and

In the wake of Mme de Staël's article, *romantico* began to appear with increasing frequency in pamphlets, articles, and reviews written directly in Italian, not only in translations from the French, as we have observed up to now. The most important discussions of romanticism in 1816, referred to as 'the triptych of romantic manifestoes' by Marcazzan,[23] were Ludovico Di Breme's *Intorno all'ingiustizia di alcuni giudizi letterari italiani*, Pietro Borsieri's *Avventure letterarie di un giorno, o consigli di un galantuomo a vari scrittori*, and Giovanni Berchet's *Sul 'Cacciatore feroce' e sulla 'Eleonora' di Goffredo Augusto Bürger. Lettera semiseria di Grisostomo al suo figlinolo.*[24] Although Berchet's pamphlet was the last to be published, it was by far the most successful, so that Berchet's name has remained next to Manzoni's as that of one of the two representative authors of the Italian romantic movement. The *Dizionario etimologico italiano* of

Davenport, *A New Dictionary of the Italian and English Languages* (London, 1854) has '*Romantic*, romantico, romanzesco; improbabile; solitario, romitico.' Comelati and Davenport have no entry for *romanticism*, but there is '*Romanticismo*, the romantic school as opposed to the classical'; *romantico, romanzesco*, and *romanzevole* are all translated into English as *romantic*. For German-Italian dictionaries, in addition to what is cited in the previous note, I have seen F. Valentini, *Dizionario portatile italiano-tedesco* (Leipzig, 1888), which does not list *romantico*; and F. A. Weber, *Nuovo dizionario Italiano-Tedesco e Tedesco-Italiano* (Leipzig, 1907?), which gives *Romantisch, romanzesco, Romanmäßig*, but does not list *romantico*. O. Bulle and G. Rigutini, *Nuovo dizionario italiano-tedesco e tedesco-italiano* (Leipzig, Tauchnitz, and Milano, Hoepli, 1907), on the other hand, has a complete coverage: of special interest to us is the translation of '*Romanticismo* m. Romantik, f. (als litterarische u. künstlerische Schule u. Richtung),' and of '*Romantico* agg. zur Schule der Romantiker gehörig; romantisch // fam. gefühlselig; schwärmerisch; phantastisch; romantisch ... // *sost.* m. Romantiker; Schriftsteller, Dichter, Künstler der romantischen Schule, m. // fam. romantische angelegte Persönlichkeit; Phantast; Schwärmer; Romantiker, m.'

It is interesting to note some of the solutions found by Italian translators from the German and English when faced by the difficult word for which there was no Italian equivalent. G. Grassi, for instance, in his 1782 translation of *Werther* renders the sentence 'Ich will sterben, und das schreibe ich dir ohne romantische Überspannung' from the letter dated 20 December 1772, with the circumlocution, 'Non v'è più ripiego, Carlotta: voglio morire, e te lo dico con l'animo quieto, e nulla punto alterato.' Michele Leoni in his 1818 translation of Thomson's *The Seasons* avoids the word *romantic* every time: *Spring*, v. 1025, *Summer*, v. 458 and v. 1372 (see *Apollonio*, pp. 114–16, for quotations in full). All this is further evidence for the fact that Italian *romantico* was initially applied only to the literary movement.

With regard to the semantic confusion caused by the passing of romanticism from one country to another, the remarks made by Mme Necker de Saussure in her preface to the translation of Schlegel's *Vorlesungen* are particularly significant. She explains that for a subject treated in a novel manner she could not avoid using 'quelques termes, peut-être inusités, mais dont les analogues sont devenus techniques en Allemagne.' Thus, for instance, she mentions specifically that 'l'épithète de classique dans l'ouvrage [est] une simple désignation de genre, indépendante du degré de perfection avec laquelle ce genre est traité.'

Battisti and Alessio gives Berchet as the authority and 1816 as the date for *romantico*; Manzoni and 1823, for *romanticismo*.* But even apart from the appearance of *romantico* in the periodical literature of 1814, a great many other instances of the word before Berchet can be cited. Thus, for instance, Silvio Pellico in a letter to his brother, dated 11 December 1815,[25] makes a distinction between the two genres 'called classical and romantic' which is obviously patterned on A. W. Schlegel's use of the terms. Pellico emphasizes the opposition between ancient and modern literatures and classifies the major Italian writers as romantic, by virtue of their belonging to the modern category even though they occasionally observed the classical rules and the principle of imitation:

It is not the observance or violation of the unities of time and place that constitutes the genres called classical and romantic. To the first belong all the ideas derived or adapted from the old Greek civilization and then adopted as models of poetry; to the second the ideas that bear the imprint of modern civilization. Thus, if the correct limits are established, the masterpieces of Italian literature are seen to belong to the romantic genre; Dante, Petrarch, and (in spite of the rules he observed and of some instances of imitation) Tasso, and without any doubt Ariosto.

Non è l'osservanza o la violazione dell'unità di tempo e di luogo che costituisce i generi chiamati classico e romantico. Al primo appartengono tutte le idee derivate o modificate secondo l'antica civilizzazione greca, adottate poi come modello poetico: alla seconda quelle che portano l'impronta della civilizzazione moderna, di maniera che a chi stabilisce i giusti limiti appartengono al genere romantico appunto i capi d'opera della letteratura italiana, Dante, Petrarca, e (malgrado le osservate regole e qualche imitazione) Tasso, e senza contesa l'Ariosto.†

* Carlo Battisti and Giovanni Alessio, *Dizionario etimologico italiano* (Firenze, 1950–7). The historical background of *romantico* as given by Battisti and Alessio is only in part more reliable than the one of the editors of *Lo spettatore* quoted earlier (p. 304 above): '*Romantico*, m. e agg. appartenente al movimento letterario ed artistico di rinnovamento diffuso in Italia coll'articolo di Mme de Staël nel 1816 e d'origine tedesca, dove per Wieland ed Herder *romantisch* indicava la poesia cavalleresca medioevale nelle lingue romanze. In fr., dove già esisteva *romantique* (a. 1694) nel senso di "romanesco" e di "pittoresco" (anglicismo), la v. passò nello Schlegel (*Cours de littér. dram.*, a. 1813) e ancora prima con Mme de Staël (a. 1810) a tradurre il ted. *romantisch* in opposizione a *classique*.' It is to be noted that Schlegel's lectures, with their terminology, were delivered in Vienna in 1808 and that Mme de Staël took the term from him; the Italian translation of Schlegel, which attests to the use of *romantico*, appeared in 1817; the 1813 French translation can at most be cited as an authority for the new literary sense of Fr. *romantique*.

† This passage illustrates perfectly Maier's contention (p. 296 above) that the Italian debate took its terms from the French and therefore initially emphasized the question of the dramatic unities and of the rhetorical rules rather than

In contrast to as informed a statement as Pellico's are the remarks of Count Trussardo Caleppio, police commissioner and aspiring *littérateur*, in two articles of protest against Mme de Staël and her Italian champions, which appeared in the Milanese *Corriere delle dame*. 'Imitate the English and the Germans, we are told by *madama* and by a number of modern intellects as well as by all those who are partisans of romantic poetry' / '*Imitate gl'inglesi e i tedeschi, ci diranno con madama alcuni cervelli moderni, non che tutti i partigiani della poesia romantica ...*'[26] he writes, thereby showing that militant anti-romantic circles cared little for the general acceptance of the term and were content to use it – differing in this from the French – to refer to anyone who was suspected of being an admirer of foreign literatures.

Ludovico Di Breme, on the other hand, who had met Mme de Staël during her visit to Milan in the winter of 1815 and who was later to be a welcome guest at Coppet, is fully conversant with the different meanings of the term as used by the French and reveals, moreover, exceptional insight into the civic and national dimension of the literary debate, into the eighteenth-century origins of its poetics, and into the very essence of romanticism, which he understands as the rejection of the traditional view of art as imitation of nature in favour of an expressive theory in which man himself becomes the rival of nature, the source of creative activity.* In the

following the German use of *romantic* with reference to the literature of the Middle Ages. The emphasis on chivalric poetry as an aspect of romanticism and the consequent importance of Ariosto, 'il poeta del fantastico svagare e del poetico errare' (*Apollonio*, p. 135), therefore take us back to the German rather than the French origin of the Italian polemic. Both origins naturally coexisted in the consciousness of contemporaries and contributed in no little way to the confusion.

On the identification of romantic poetry with modern poetry, see also C. G. Londonio, *Cenni critici sulla poesia romantica* (Milano, 1817), who tries, however, to save the classical tradition as well: '... se per poesia *romantica* quella si dee intendere che deriva il soggetto dalla moderna civilizzazione, che si veste di affetti e di opinioni moderne, che mette in iscena i costumi, i caratteri, le passioni de' nostri tempi, noi siamo ben lungi dal volerla escludere dall'Italia, e ci facciam anzi gloria di averla professata prima che gli stranieri venissero ad apprendercela ...' (*Bellorini* 1: 231)and '... Romantici vogliamo esserlo anche noi italiani ... romantici nelle idee, nelle opinioni, negli affetti, ma fedeli all'esempio e ai precetti dei classici nell'applicazione delle forme e nelle regole dell'arte '(*Bellorini* 1: 233).

* A re-evaluation of the central importance of Di Breme in the initial phase of Italian romanticism can be found in *Marcazzan*, pp. 135–40 and 147–91. The significant passage in *Intorno all'ingiustizia* ... reads: 'Quegli spurî greci che determinarono l'andatura degli studi nostri, non seppero intendere (e volesse Iddio che lo intendessero daddovero i nostri precettisti) siccome nella natura, in ogni età e per prima cosa, rispetto all'uomo, v'ha l'uomo. Perchè la natura non ti ha già composto nella mira che tu imitassi lei in quel solo modo che intendi;

strict context of terminology, Di Breme exhibits some degree of perplexity. He confuses the adjective *romantico* with *romanzo* (pertaining to the early period in the development of the Romance languages), uses *romantico* as an equivalent of *meridionale*, and defines romantic poetry as the poetry pertaining to the *modern* period.

Di Breme's confusion of *romantico* and *romanzo* occurs in connection with a long quotation from Gravina, in which the latter was concerned with the epic poem and the romance, and not, as Di Breme thought, with the definition of a poetics of romanticism.* His identification of *romantico* and *meridionale* is illustrated by his statement, '*... noi di robusta e di gentile e di sublime schiatta italiana; e la chiamino coi più generici titoli di schiatta Meridionale o Romantica, come loro talenta.*' As for the correspondence of *romantico* and *moderno*, it can be deduced from his description of the perfect romantic lyric as one

that, leaving aside all mythology and ancient allegories, derives its effectiveness from the customs, the influence, and I would almost say the flavour of modern times, those times which have in them so much of the majestic, the pathetic, and the splendid.

... quella poesia, che, prescindendo da ogni ragione mitologica e di antica allegoria, deriva tutta la sua efficienza dai costumi, dagli affetti e oserei quasi dire dal sapore di quelle moderne età, che han pur tanto in sè di grandioso, di patetico e di risplendente.[27]

chè anche tu sei la natura, e sei per di più il suo interprete, il suo rivale nell'ordine morale, sensitivo e imaginoso; e ciò in tutti i tempi del mondo; e se non vorrai cantare mai sempre se non gli armenti della Sicilia e lo stretto d'Abido e gli occhi cervieri e Progne e Filomela e i polmoni di Stentore e le stalle di Augia, invece di dipingere con efficacia, nudi e vivaci quei fenomeni che si producono in te dagli oggetti di che ella ti ha circondato, e l'armonia loro, non potrai già dire che tu la imiti, e molto meno potrai dire che tu imiti, che tu *traduca* te stesso nelle opere tue. In vista dunque d'imitarla, innalziamoci a gareggiare con lei nella stessa creazione ...' *Calcaterra*, pp. 109–10.

* Di Breme's quotation from Gravina includes the following two statements: 'Onde io ... nemmeno il romanzo dal poema so distinguere ... le quali narrazioni per nome aggettivo chiamavano romanzi, sottintendendovi il nome sustantivo di poemi ...' and 'Noi nell'epico genere anche abbracceremo que' poemi eroici, che per essere di varie fila tessute, comunemente s'appellano *Romanzi* ...' *Calcaterra*, p. 105. For a unique use of *romanzo* as an adjective with the meaning of *romantico* (of character), see Foscolo's 1801 letter to Antonietta Fagnani Arese: 'Chiamami *romanzo*, ed hai forse ragione; ma non lo sono per elezione ... io devo alla natura questa ardente imaginazione e questo cuore che mi hanno fatto soffrire tanti tormenti, ma che non sono mai stati domati, né dall'esperienza, né dalle sventure.' P. Carli, ed., *Epistolario* (Firenze, 1949), 1: 225.

† *Calcaterra*, p. 107. In a note Calcaterra observes, 'In questo punto il Di Breme adopera la frase "schiatta meridionale o romantica" nel senso di "schiatta romanza," come molti intendevano in quel tempo.' The derivation from Sismondi's *De la Littérature du midi de l'Europe* is obvious.

Di Breme also uses the noun *romantico* (synonymous with *autore romantico*) in the expression 'the northern romantics' / *'Questo carattere dell'unità di soggetto, combinato colla varietà di personaggi principali ... lo hanno comune cogli Epici nostri* i Romantici settentrionali Shakespeare e Schiller *nella tragedia,'** a juxtaposition that would occasion a strange clash of meanings if the reader were not as ready as the author to pass from *romantico* as a geographical term equivalent to *meridionale* to *romantico* as a literary term descriptive of a certain kind of writing. Finally we must note Di Breme's use of the feminine noun *la Romantica*, probably patterned on the German *die Romantik*: '*Che la* Romantica *sia per sè un solenne genere di letteratura, non è più da porsi in dubbio ...*'

Borsieri's pamphlet is less austerely ethical and less concerned with aesthetic theory than Di Breme's. Within the narrative framework of the imaginary but quite credible comings and goings of a Milanese gentleman with more than an amateur's interest in literature, Borsieri discusses with wit and liveliness such problems as the Italian language, the role of dialects, and the need to supply Italy with novels, comedies, and newspapers comparable to those of other European countries. Referring directly to Di Breme, Borsieri repeats his defence of Mme de Staël, reminding the reader that she had in *Corinne* given ample praise to such great Italians as Dante, Petrarch, Michelangelo, Raphael, Pergolesi, Galileo, and others, thus correcting the unfavourable impression made earlier by statements critical of Italy in *De la littérature*. Apropos of the term *romantic*, Borsieri speaks of Di Breme's inclusion of the *Divina Commedia*, the *Canzoniere*, and the *Orlando furioso* within the category of '*letteratura così detta romantica*,' describing the genre as 'completely infused by the ideas of philosophic spiritualism, of Christianity, and of chivalric idealism ... the three principal elements of romanticism':

[*Di Breme*] *ha pure assunto a provare che la* letteratura *così detta* romantica *non è frutto esclusivamente proprio del Nord; poichè la* Divina Commedia, *il* Canzoniere *del Petrarca e il* Furioso *appartengono a tal genere di poesia che non ha verun modello nell'antichità greca e latina; e che essendo tutto animato dalle idee dello* spiritualismo, *del* cristianesimo, *e del* genio cavalleresco, *racchiude appunto in se stesso i tre principali elementi della* Romantica.[28]

Borsieri's use of *la Romantica* instead of *romanticismo*, a word which

*   *Calcaterra*, p. 105, italics mine. The context in which the expression appears illustrates once again the initial preponderance of the questions of the rules in Italian romanticism. Di Breme also uses the noun *romantico* apropos Ariosto: 'Ariosto lussureggiante romantico,' *Calcaterra*, p. 108.

had not yet come into the language, parallels exactly what we have already seen in the case of Di Breme. In a note, Borsieri refers with scorn to the dialogue, *La romanticomania*, which had appeared in the Florentine *Giornale di letteratura e belle arti*, and accuses its author, Francesco Benedetti da Cortona, of complete ignorance of the meaning of *romantico*, an ignorance made patent by Benedetti's indiscriminate lumping together of contemporary English and German literature with 'the literatures of the Thracians, the Carthaginians, the Persians, the Egyptians, and the flowing-haired, breeched, and toga-wearing Gauls':

Lo [il Giornalista] *preghiamo anche di riflettere che la letteratura dei presenti Inglesi e Tedeschi non va confusa con quella 'dei Traci, de' Cartaginesi, de' Persiani, degli Egizj, e de' Galli chiomati, bracati e togati'*.[29]

To correct this preposterous confusion, Borsieri advises the reading of Jean-Joseph Dussault's articles in the *Journal des débats* and of Saint-Chamans' *L'antiromantique*.

Whereas Di Breme and Borsieri drew their documentation preponderantly from French sources, Berchet's command of German permitted him direct access to the basic German texts, among them Goethe, Lessing, Schiller, Herder, Bürger, and Bouterwek. His familiarity with German is reflected not only in his translations but also in a lexical choice: he uses the word *romanzi*, modelled on the German *Romanzen*,* to refer to Bürger's ballads. The word as used by him had no success in Italy, for it already existed to designate a type of narrative literature, in verse or prose, whose subject matter was either completely fictional or a mixture of fiction and history.† *Werther, Jacopo Ortis*, and the novels of Scott were the best known *romanzi* of early romanticism, in that more current meaning. Berchet's defence of his *romanzi*, lyrical narratives known more frequently as *ballate romantiche, ballate romanze*, or

---

*   *Calcaterra*, p. 267n, states explicitly that Berchet translated the word directly from the German. See also Berchet's use of *romanzieri* (*Calcaterra*, p. 316) to refer to the authors of romantic ballads. Bulle and Rigutini, *Nuovo dizionario Italiano-Tedesco e Tedesco-Italiano* (Leipzig, 1907), give the word *romanzista*, marking it as obsolete, and translating it as *Romanzendichter* (composer of ballads). G. Devoto, *Avviamento alla etimologia italiana* (Firenze, 1967) gives both the masculine Spanish *romance* and the feminine French *romance* as predecessors of the feminine Italian *romanza*. Berchet's use of the masculine would appear to go back to the original Spanish rather than to the German, which was itself derived from Spanish.

†   *Calcaterra*, p. 267n, gives as the definition of *romanzi* in the more usual sense, 'narrazioni atte a trattenere piacevolmente in prosa o in versi con fatti e soggetti d' invenzione o misti di storia e d'invenzione,' without citing the source of his quotation.

simply *romanze*,[30] leads him to consider Herder's theory of the folk origins of poetry and to support the view of the universality of art:

All men, from Adam down to the shoemaker who makes our handsome boots, have in the depths of their souls a tendency to poetry.

Tutti gli uomini, da Adamo in giù fino al calzolaio che ci fa i begli stivali, hanno nel fondo dell'anima tendenza alla poesia.[31]

The republic of letters is one, and all poets, without exceptions, are its citizens.

La repubblica delle lettere non è che una, e i poeti ne sono concittadini tutti indistintamente.[32]

Berchet devotes considerable space to the classical-romantic polarity, suggesting that it is contemporaneity above all else that determines the distinction:

I feel that I can call the former (i.e., classical poetry) the poetry of the dead, and the latter the poetry of the living. Nor do I fear to be greatly mistaken if I maintain that Homer, Pindar, Sophocles, Euripides, etc., were for their own time in a certain sense romantic, for they wrote not about what mattered to the Egyptians and the Chaldeans but about what mattered to them, the Greeks.

Però io stimo di poter nominare con tutta ragione poesia de' morti la prima, e poesia de' vivi la seconda. Nè temo d'ingannarmi dicendo che Omero, Pindaro, Sofocle, Euripide, ec.ec., al tempo loro furono in certo modo romantici, perchè non cantarono le cose degli Egizj o de' Caldei, ma quelle dei loro Greci.[33]

Although Berchet recognizes that the debate is more than a question of terminology, his strong anti-purism (the latter part of the *Lettera* is a sarcastic attack on the cultural narrowness of the pedants of the *Crusca*) makes him rejoice at the thought that the quarrel is also a semantic one and that the classicists are as annoyed by the new word as they are by the new ideas:

... irritated by the novelty of the word *romantico*, our pedants raise a racket that resounds from Dan to Beersheba, swearing up and down, and confounding one another as though they were in Babylon ... the division by which they are tormented is for them more mystical than the most mystical of the doctrines of the Talmud ...

...irritati dalla novità del vocabolo romantico, da Dan fino a Bersabea si levano a fracasso i pedanti nostri, e fanno a rabbuffarsi l'un l'altro, e a contumeliarsi, e a

sagramentare, e a non intendersi tra di loro, come a Babilonia ... la divisione, per cui si arrovellano, è per loro più mistica della più mistica dottrina del Talmud ...[34]

Among the defenders of romanticism *avant la lettre* with whom we have been dealing, there existed, in spite of rebelliousness against the tyranny of lexicographers and grammarians, a deep respect for language as a means for communicating ideas and an honest effort, therefore, to clarify linguistic difficulties that might stand in the way of correct and rapid understanding. The many definitions and discussions of *romantico* are part of this effort, an effort related to the ideal of social usefulness, which the Lombard romantics had inherited from their predecessors of the Enlightenment. It is surprising to note how cautious these writers were in their language – the prime example being, of course, Manzoni, whose prose is an unparalleled model of limpidity and precision – while they at the same time spoke with vigour and passion of unconventional, indeed uncomfortable, ideas. Among the classicists, instead, we find a degree of what might be called linguistic intemperance. In their anti-romantic parodies, if nowhere else, they called upon the full resources of the language, compounding words and forming derivatives with gusto.

We have already spoken of Francesco Benedetti's *La romantico-mania*, an imaginary dialogue between *Madonna* (Mme de Staël), *Messer lo Giornalista* (the author), and *il Cavaliere* (Di Breme).* A similar title, *La romanticomachia*, was chosen by Ottavio A. Falletti di Barolo for a supposedly true account of the battle between classicists and romanticists. Berchet, in reviewing the pamphlet for *Il conciliatore*, described it as an allegorical novel whose key remains a mystery for most readers and whose language is characterized by the rhetorical figure of amplification.[35] Among the characters and personifications that appear in the work are 'subversive Democracy,' 'frenzied Metaphysics,' 'unbridled Romanticism,' 'romanticized Heroes,' and 'the Promoters of the new Romanticism' / '*sovvertitrice Democrazia*,' '*delirante Metafisica*,' '*sfrenato Romanticismo*,' '*inromantescati Eroi*,' '*Promotori della nuova Romanticità*.'[36] Falletti attempts to distinguish

---

*   *Calcaterra*, p. 225n, confuses this work with the 'Parodia dello statuto d'una immaginaria accademia romantica' (see p. 299 above), which also appeared in *Giornale di letteratura e belle arti*. *La romanticomania*, however, appeared in September 1816, the 'Parodia' in 1817. In the latter there are also some examples of verbal inventiveness (for instance, the name *Fanfaluconia* for the ancient castle where the academy of romanticists is meeting), but none that involves the root of *romantico*.

between *genere romantico* and *romanticismo*, but, according to Berchet, he fails miserably – an outcome hardly surprising, given the obviously impossible undertaking. A third title of those years, again a satirical attack, is *La romantea*, a work by G. A. Maggi, not further identified but directed against Berchet's *Lettera*.[37]

The 'semi-heroic, tragi-comic drama,' *I romanticisti*, later set to music and presented as *Marsia*,[38] also falls into the category of parody. In giving notice of it in the *Gazzetta di Milano*, Francesco Pezzi, another police commissioner turned man of letters, starts out by referring to 'today's romanticists [*romantichieri*], romantomaniacs [*romanticomani*], or romantographers [*romanticografi*],' who are convinced that all attacks against their 'transcendentalism' are the result of ignorance and envy, since there can be no question that they are the 'wisest, most civilized, most amiable and beautiful of the animal species':

Uno dei tratti caratteristici degli odierni nostri romantichieri, o romanticomani, o romanticografi, è l'intimo convincimento in cui sono, che tutti gli attacchi diretti contro il loro transcendentalismo, *sieno lo sfogo dell'ignoranza o dell'invidia, mentre si suppongono, in buona fede, i più dotti, i più inciviliti i più amabili e i più belli della specie animale.*[39]

In the course of the article, Pezzi also speaks of ultra-romanticism (*ultra-romanticismo*) and of ultra-romanticists (*ultra-romanticisti*) – apparently making use of expressions that occur in the 'drama'–and he mentions one of the allegorical characters, a certain *Romanticomano*. Finally, still in the area of parody, there is the short-lived *L'Accattabrighe, ossia Classicoromanticomachia*, the 'pink sheet' founded by Trussardo Caleppio for the purpose of harassing the 'blue sheet,' *Il conciliatore*. In its issue of 20 December, 1818, *L'Accattabrighe* announced the publication of *Il grande Almanacco romantico, o sia l'Almanacco più che transcendentalissimo* printed in the mythical but not unrecognizable city of *Romanticopoli*.[40]

Of all the 'learned' derivatives and compounds that we have been able to document, only *romanticismo* and for a time *romanticista* appear to have gained general currency.* *Romanticismo* seems to have been used for the first time in a review of Byron's *Giaour* written by Francesco Pezzi for the *Gazzetta di Milano*:

*   None of the dictionaries I have been able to consult gives *romanticista*. The *Dizionario enciclopedico italiano* (Roma, 1959) has *romantichiere*, 's.m. non comune spreg. Chi scrive in modo esageratamente romantico, sentimentalistico, smanceroso.' The word appears also in H. Charrel, G. Lagorio, and V. Ferrari, *Vocabolario italiano-francese e francese-italiano* (1st ed., Torino, n.d.): '*romantichiere*, sm. écrivain de choses romanesques.'

A bitter war is raging between romanticists and classicists ... while on one hand there is the attempt to prove the preponderance of *Romanticism*, on the other hand, one notices the powerlessness to produce anything classical.

Arde aspra guerra tra i romantici *e i* classici ... *mentre si vuol provare da un lato la preponderanza del* romanticismo, *si prova dall'altro l'impotenza di riprodurre qualche cosa di classico.*[41]

The word also occurs in an ironic verse epistle with accompanying notes, *Epistola di Camillo Piciarelli all'amico F.M. per la più estesa propagazione del divino romantico gusto, con alcune osservazioni,*[42] which tells of a poet's efforts to convert a painter friend to the new fashion in art:

> *Prendila come vuoi per buona o trista*
> *La nuova che ti do; ma sappi, amico,*
> *Che divenuto io son* romanticista.

Take the news I give you as good or as bad, as it pleases you; but know, my friend, that I have become a romanticist,

the poet begins, using (for the first time?) the noun *romanticista*, possibly coined on the spur of the moment to rhyme with *trista*. Although the poet urges the painter to join the ranks of the *romanticisti,* he confesses that he has difficulty trying to understand 'the new and strange name.' There follows a long note in which the author discounts the definition of romanticism as 'a type of poetry that rejects mythology and deals only with historical and religious events, or with human passions as produced by new customs.' This kind of poetry, he says, has always existed, it has always been recognized as poetry, indeed as classical poetry whenever it had classical beauty. The romantics, therefore, have invented 'a monstrous name' to distinguish two things that are not distinguishable, for all poetry, if it is beautiful, is, by definition classical. Piciarelli, however, knows of the existence of another kind of poetry, 'similar to a dream of Hell and having no unity of subject, time, or place.' To give such poetry any name at all is 'a perversion of common sense':

Se pretendesi dare il nome di romanticismo *ad un genere di poesia che rigetti ogni idea mitologica o si occupi soltanto di fatti storici e religiosi, o tratti di umane passioni giusta i nuovi costumi, un tal nome è vano, perchè noi sempre abbiamo avuto questo genere di poesia, la quale si è fatta sempre chiamare poesia, e classica poesia se aveva classiche bellezze, senza verun bisogno che i* romantici *la distinguessero con un nome mostruoso da un'altra poesia ugualmente classica, se bella, la quale ammetta la favola ad imitazione dei greci. È più che vano poi questo nome, anzi pervertitore del buon senso, se esprime un genere di poesia che, simile ad un sogno d'inferno, non conosce legge veruna d'unità di soggetto, di tempo e di loco.*[43]

Of special interest is a passage in which the poet tells the painter in concrete terms what his becoming a romanticist will mean: instead of painting Venus on Paphos or Cnidus he will paint a pretty English girl with her parasol, a black bodice, and a yellow skirt; instead of painting the Council of the Gods, he will show Henry VIII in the act of repudiating his wife; and contrary to Horace's injunctions against monsters, he will choose as subject the mermaid represented on the print that illustrates the pamphlet.[44]

Of greater significance than the ephemeral and trivial anti-romantic tracts of which we have been speaking is Ermes Visconti's *Idee elementari sulla poesia romantica*.[45] It is a methodical exposition, divided into articles and paragraphs, of the differences between classicism and romanticism, especially insofar as subject matter is concerned. Visconti was highly regarded by his contemporaries – Fauriel, Goethe, and Stendhal – and he was a close friend of Manzoni, whom he advised in great detail on the first draft of *I promessi sposi*.[46] Literary historians no longer recognize his work as distinguished, but consider him 'a superficial popularizer' whose *Idee* are by no means essential to an understanding of Italian romanticism.[47] It is, however, in the *Idee* that we find for the first time a clear awareness of the fact that discussions of romanticism, especially among the anti-romantics, were being muddied by a confusion between two distinct meanings of *romantico*:

The romanticism (*il romantico*) recently invented by the Germans must not be mistaken for the old English word *romantick*, which corresponds to *romanesque*; to do so would be like confusing the three Graces with the grace granted by sovereigns when they pardon criminals.

Non si confonda il romantico recentemente ideato dai Tedeschi colla vecchia parola inglese romantick, *la quale corrisponde a* romanzesco: *sarebbe un confondere le tre Grazie colle grazie che fanno i sovrani quando assolvono un reo.**

*   *Calcaterra*, p. 379. A letter written by Clarina Mosconi from Verona on 14 February 1820 throws amusing light on this confusion: 'La malattia del *romanticismo* non ha qui fatto strage,' she wrote to Monti, 'tranne in alcune Damine che forse senza approfondire la materia si sono abbandonate a questa per loro seducentissima setta che a lor sembra sinonimo di *romanzesca*.' Quoted in A. Manzoni, *Le tragedie secondo i manoscritti e le prime stampe* (Firenze, 1958), II, I: lxvi (italics mine).

The statement is particularly meaningful because it occurs at the end of the first paragraph of the article entitled 'Rettificazione di alcuni falsi supposti,' in which Visconti rapidly reviewed the notions of romanticism contrary to the system as conceived by the German aesthetic philosophers and by some of Visconti's own compatriots:

Romanticism does not consist in constantly telling tales of witches or hobgoblins ... or in moaning and shaking with terror in cemeteries ... Romanticism does not consist in the gloomy and the melancholy ... The romantic genre does not aim at blindly exalting feudal times, nor at regretting them with senseless nostalgia ... The theories of the so-called innovators are not an expedient for escaping from rules; they only exempt one from the nuisance of pedantry ...

Il romanticismo adunque non consiste nel favoleggiare continuamente di streghe e folletti ... o nel gemere e raccapricciarsi ne' cimiteri ... Il romanticismo non consiste nel lugubre e nel malinconico ... Il genere romantico non tende ad esaltare ciecamente i tempi feudali, nè ad invidiarli con desiderio insensato ... Le teorie de' così detti novatori non sono un mezzo termine per sottrarsi alle regole; dispensano soltanto dagl'impicci della pedanteria.[48]

Though Visconti's categories differ from those that Manzoni in his *Lettera sul romanticismo* will list as the negative part of the doctrine – that is, its interdictions – the method of exposition is the same, as is also the surer view that emerges of what romanticism is *not* as against what it is. From a linguistic point of view, it is interesting to note the use of a masculine substantive adjective, *il romantico*, paralleling the feminine *la romantica*, which we saw in Di Breme and Borsieri.[49]

More important, of course, is the introduction of the word and even more so of the concept *romanzesco* (romance-like), which takes us back through the identification of one of the aspects of the romantic aesthetic (actually for Visconti this is not one of the aspects but an erroneous notion to be avoided), to the adjective *romanzo* (pertaining to the early period in the development of the Romance languages). At the very beginning of the *Idee*, Visconti had already written:

The expression *romantic poetry* was invented in Germany to distinguish the characteristics of the art of the modern poets from the characteristics pertaining exclusively to the ancient classical poets ...

La frase Poesia Romantica *fu inventata in Germania per distinguere i caratteri proprj dell'arte de' poeti moderni dalle qualità esclusivamente spettanti ai classic antichi.*[50]

And he had concluded his initial summary of the characteristics in question by mentioning the origin and etymology of the hated word:

It was suggested to the Germans by courtesy and frankness toward our country and toward other Latin nations. Romantic poetry is one of the most splendid ornaments of present-day culture, and this culture began to develop in the provinces where the so-called *Romance* or *Roman* tongues arose, formed by a mixture of Latin and the idioms of the North. Among these tongues were Italian, Provençal, and the Old French of the region beyond the Loire. This is the fact to which the inventors of the new word wished to allude; whoever objects, is complaining about an act of courtesy.

Fu suggerito ai Tedeschi da gentilezza e sincerità verso la patria nostra e verso le altre nazioni latine. La poesia romantica è uno dei più splendidi ornamenti della presente coltura, e la coltura cominciò a svilupparsi nelle provincie ove sorsero le così dette lingue romanze, o romane formate dal miscuglio del latino cogl'idiomi del Nord: fra le quali appunto l'Italiano, la Provenzale, e l'antico francese al di là della Loira. A ciò vollero alludere gl'inventori del nuovo vocabolo; chi ne è malcontento si lagna d'un atto cortese.[51]

The German origin of the romantic movement is reflected here in a theory of the origin of Romance tongues, which was later to be proved erroneous. As is well known, the Romance languages were not formed by a mixture of Latin and Germanic, but evolved naturally from the Latin spoken by the uneducated classes of a wide-flung Empire. Through this philological error, however, Visconti and his fellow theorists and polemicists were drawn in their discussion of the more distant historical premises of romanticism to the early Middle Ages and to the *romances*, the repositories of the cultural and social life of those times.

In the article headed 'Definizione della poesia romantica,' Visconti, in speaking of the 'chivalric heroism' which grew out of the political, religious, and national conditions of the Middle Ages, incidentally traces a remarkable history of the romance leading up to and into the modern novel. The sense of continuity, which twentieth-century research in the area of the novel has done much to restore, was almost completely obliterated in the later nineteenth century, when the 'realistic' novel was conceived of as in antithesis to the 'romantic' novel, or, to use an Italian expression, when, already with Manzoni, the whole question of the *romanzo non-romanzesco* began to come to the fore.* Since Italian makes no distinction in terms between romance and novel, *romanzo* being both 'a book written in a Romance language, that is, in the vernacular, an imaginative tale of medieval knights,' and 'a fictional story,'† Visconti found no difficulty in connecting 'various ancient *romances* in praise of the champions of King Arthur' / '... *varj antichi* romanzi

*   '*Romanzo non-romanzesco*' (un-novel–like novel) is the expression used by Renato Bertacchini (*Il romanzo italiano dell'Ottocento*, Roma, 1964, p. 61) with reference to *I promessi sposi*. The *locus classicus* of the question in Manzoni occurs in his letter of 29 May 1822 to Fauriel where he describes his method of composition in the novel. The contrast between a *roman romanesque* and a realistic kind of novel, one that reflects 'la vie réelle,' is stated quite clearly, although Manzoni's contemporaneous concern with the unities gives a different slant to the question than it will have in later discussions of the novel as a work of realism: 'Quant à la marche des événements, et à l'intrigue, je crois que le meilleur moyen de ne pas faire comme les autres [i.e., other novelists], est de s'attacher à considérer dans la réalité la manière d'agir des hommes, et de la considérer surtout dans ce qu'elle a d'opposé à l'*esprit romanesque*. Dans tous les romans que j'ai lus il me semble de voir un travail pour établir des rapports intéressants et inattendus entre les différens personnages, pour les ramener sur la scène de compagnie, pour trouver des événements, qui influent à la fois et en différentes manières sur la destinée de tous, enfin une *unité artificielle*, que l'on ne trouve pas dans la *vie réelle*.' Alessandro Manzoni, *Carteggio* (Milano, 1921), II: 27 (italics mine).

†   '*Romanzo*: come sm. era libro scritto in lingua romanza, cioè in volgare, racconto fantastico de' cavalieri del medio evo: ora è racconto d'invenzione.' Francesco Zambaldi, *Dizionario etimologico italiano* (Città di Castello, 1889). It is impossible to undertake here a study of the word *romanzo* to parallel our study of *romantico*. The subject would deserve investigation inasmuch as there is no comprehensive treatment of it. Among the dictionaries I have consulted, the following contain interesting material; *Bolza*: '*Romanzo*, favolosa narrazione di accidenti straordinari tanto questo vocabolo che il precedente, i.e., *Romanza*, nella significazione moderna, emersero da ciò che tali componimenti erano scritti originariamente e cantati dai Trovatori in lingua romanza.' Battisti and Alessio, *Dizionario etimologico italiano* (Firenze, 1950–7): '*romanzo* m. XIII sec., storia favolosa; (XIV sec.) anche cronaca in volgare; a. fr. e a. prov. *romanz, romans*; dal lat. **romanice (loqui)*.' Ottorino Pianigiani, *Vocabolario etimologico della lingua italiana* (Milano, 1937): '*Romanzo*, a. fr. *romanz, romans*; prov. e mod fr. *roman*. Narrazione vera o finta, scritta in versi o in prosa, nell'antico rustico o *volgare*, sul quale vennero formandosi le nuove lingue neo-latine. Poi con questo nome s'intese qualunque storia finta, scritta in prosa, nella quale l'autore cerca di eccitare interesse colla pittura delle passioni, dei costumi, o per la singolarità delle avventure narrate.' N. Tommaseo, *Nuovo dizionario de' sinonimi della lingua italiana* (rev. ed., Napoli, 1906): see nos. 3226–34 for the relationships between *storia, cronaca, romanzo, novella*, and derivatives. Pietro Fanfani, *Vocabolario della lingua italiana* (Firenze, 1880): '*Romanzo*, s.m. storia favolosa propriamente in versi; ma ve ne sono anche in prosa. *Romanzo*, fu detto anche per *Romanismo* (così furono dette le lingue volgari di Europa che nacquero all'alterazione della Latina; dette anche *romanze*.) Ora chiamansi *romanzi* tutti i racconti più o meno coloriti ed esagerati, di cose amorose, intrecciate con molti avvenimenti. Romanzo storico è quello che racconta fatti simili, ma presi veramente dalla storia; dove gli altri sono di pura invenzione.'

che lodano i campioni d'Artù ...' with 'the sentimentalism, the amorous intrigues, the conjugal love combined with the quasi equality of husband and wife, and the exaggerations and profound truths' found in 'recent *novels*':

... il sentimentalismo, la galanteria, l'amor coniugale combinato con l'eguaglianza quasi perfetta dei coniugi, le esagerazioni e le verità profonde dei romanzi recenti; insomma il bene ed il male di questa passione immensa, e fra i vizi anche quelli che sembrano procedere da principj virtuosi nell'atto stesso che offendono la moralità.[52]

With no evidence of forcing, he passes from 'chivalric heroism,' the ideal of a society that admires power and 'recognizes individual worth only in things that are likely to gain positive advantages for the individual':

... è un ideale nascente in gran parte da una pretta ammirazione della potenza da un egoismo che riconosce perfezione individuale soltanto nelle cose atte a procacciare vantaggi positivi all'individuo[53]

to 'romantic love,' a feeling, which – nourished by the 'veneration in which the northern peoples held women,' by the 'mysticism of the Asiatics,' and by the 'contemplative tendencies of Christianity' – differs deeply from love as experienced in Greece and Rome.*

Just as the chivalric ideal found its narrative outlet in the adventures of the Knights of the Round Table, the paladins of Charlemagne, and the story of *Amadis de Gaule* and its imitations, prolonging its echoes into the *Gerusalemme liberata*, Goethe's *Egmont*, and even to such modern heroes as Lafayette fighting by the side of Washington,[54] so the analysis of love as practised by the troubadours in the courts of love, expressed by Petrarch in the ceaseless alternation of his hope and regret, his abandonment and his resistance, sharpened by the Cartesian spirit of the seventeenth century, led eventually to such works as Mme de Staël's *Delphine* and Laclos' *Liaisons dangereuses*. 'It would have been impossible for the ancients,' Visconti says in conclusion,

to describe even one in a hundred of the many accidents described by the lyric, epic, and dramatic poetry of the romantics. To the ancients, *Delphine* would have seemed a book of riddles, *Les Liaisons* the fanciful satire of what are perhaps impossible vices.

Era impossibile che gli antichi descrivessero uno in cento de' tanti accidenti descritti dalla poesia lirica, epica e drammatica dei romantici. La Delfina *di*

---

*   *Calcaterra*, pp. 371–2. By 'Asiatici' Visconti no doubt means 'Arabi' (cf. p. 369), i.e., the Moslems.

Madame de Staël sarebbe parsa loro un libro d'enimmi, le Liaisons dangereuses *una satira capricciosa di vizi forse impossibili.*[55]

Visconti's discussion of the modern novel is thus firmly set within the familiar context of a definition of romanticism through the distinction of contraries. No one seems to have been struck at the time or later by Visconti's contribution in this passage to the emergence of an embryonic concept of a theory (in some ways reminiscent of the views of F. Schlegel) of a comprehensive narrative genre embracing the epic, the romance, and the novel.*

III

The question of the novel during the romantic period in Italy is not tangential to our concern with the history of the changing meanings of the word *romantico*. Indeed, it becomes at this point quite central, and it is surprising that so little attention should have been devoted to it. There is general agreement that the novel turned out to be in the long run the distinctive genre of the nineteenth century. Not only was there a steady increase in the production of novels throughout the century, but theoretical and critical discussion reached a high level of technical refinement and expectations. In the 1820s and '30s, however, insofar as there was a question of the novel in Italy, that question concerned the historical novel exclusively.†

---

*   Folco Portinari, 'Un aspetto della polemica romantica: il romanzo,' in *Problemi critici di ieri e di oggi* (Milano, 1959), is to my knowledge the first author to have examined the writings of the romantic polemicists for traces of interest in the novel. He makes much of Chapter VII of Borsieri's *Avventure letterarie*, but overlooks Visconti completely. His essay contains interesting material not only on reviews of novels that appeared in the periodical literature of the time, but also on efforts to theorize the two complementary narrative genres, the *novella* and the novel. (On this point, Monti's reference to *I promessi sposi* as 'la vostra Novella' in a letter to Manzoni, dated June 1827, is not without significance. V. Monti, *Opere*, Milano-Napoli, 1953, p. 1244.). Renato Bertacchini, *Il romanzo, italiano dell' Ottocento,* follows Portinari in the importance attributed to Borsieri, and so does A. Leone De Castris, *La polemica del romanzo storico* (Bari, 1959). Perplexity as to terminology was also felt by Foscolo in his 1796 *Piano di studi* where he broke the heading *Romanzi* into two groups: '*Romanzi I* – Ariosto, la novella della *Botte* di Swift, Cervantes, Pignotti. *Romanzi II* – Telemaco, Amalie, Nouvelle Heloise [sic]' (U. Foscolo, *Prose*, Bari, 1912, 1: 4). Before leaving Visconti's *Idee*, the single appearance in it of the word *romantismo* in lieu of *romanticismo* (*Calcaterra*, p. 376) should be mentioned. I feel that undue importance has been given to this isolated departure of Visconti's from the conventional form. It is interesting to note, however, that Visconti formed the word *classicisticheria* (*Calcaterra*, p. 387), with its pejorative connotation, on the model of *romanticheria*.

†   See A. Leone De Castris, *La polemica del romanzo storico*. The discussion, which

Attention focussed on the relationship between historical truth and fiction and on the didactic aspect of a type of literature that had also high entertainment value and therefore provided a means for '*insegnar dilettando*.' Moreover, since the first adherents of romanticism were dominated so strongly by the desire to modernize literature, to break with their classical past, the Italian novel was of necessity seen and continued to be seen throughout the century against the backdrop of developments in the more advanced nations, England and France.* Both the problems raised by the historical novel and those connected with the social and political function of the novel in general tended to discourage the synthetic view suggested by Visconti when he pointed to the internal continuity between early romance narrative and the contemporary novel. As far as the private emotions were concerned, they were quite naturally pushed into the background. And principal among the private emotions is of course love, to which Visconti gave so prominent a place in *romanzi* both medieval and m odern, and which is commonly thought of as so much the dominant theme of the novel that Bulle and Rigutini, for instance, in their *Nuovo Dizionario Italiano-Tedesco e Tedesco-Italiano* give *Liebesgeschichte* (love story) as one of the translations of *romanzo*.[56]

On the evidence we have, the early romantics – at least those who led the fight and whose writings we have noted as important in the development of the concept of *romantico* – by and large ignored the subject of love in the novel. Manzoni's famous digression at the beginning of Book II of *Fermo e Lucia* (as the first draft of *I promessi sposi* is known), although far from typical, expresses in the very context that concerns us here that sense of deep moral commitment to society as a whole – to the individual *in* society – which was characteristic of Lombard romanticism. In deciding to omit the more passionate details of the love story of his two protagonists, Manzoni weighs the different human sentiments against one another and comes to the conclusion that the novelist fulfils a more useful function if he writes of compassion, altruism, sympathy, and sacrifice of self, than if he writes of sexual love, of which, says Manzoni, there

began in the wake of the introduction of the novels of Scott, led through Tommaseo's *Del romanzo storico* (1830) and was concluded by the time Manzoni published his *Del romanzo storico, e, in genere de' componimeti misti di storia e d'invenzione* (1845).

* For the romantic novel the terms of comparison are *Werther* and *La nouvelle Héloïse*; for the historical novel it is Scott; from Balzac to the end of the century, it is always France that offers the model and the ideal. Comprehensive treatments of the Italian novel of the nineteenth century, such as Gino Raya's *Il romanzo* (Milano, 1950) or the relevant passages in Guido Mazzoni's *L'Ottocento* (Milano, 1956), follow this pattern.

is at a rough estimate six hundred times more in the world than is necessary for the preservation of 'our esteemed species':

... dell'amore come vi diceva, ve n'ha, facendo un calcolo moderato, seicento volte più di quello che sia necessario alla conservazione della nostra riverita specie.[57]

But Manzoni's statement must be complemented and in a sense corrected by Mme de Staël's earlier observation on the absence of novels in Italy, an absence which she very significantly attributes to the national attitude towards love:

In this nation where one thinks of nothing but love, there are no novels, for love here is so rapid and public that it does not lend itself to any elaboration. In order to describe truthfully the general customs in this regard, one would have to begin and end with the first page.

*Dans cette nation où l'on ne pense qu'à l'amour, il n'y a pas un seul roman, parce que l'amour y est si rapide, si public, qu'il ne prête à aucun développement, et que pour peindre véritablement les mœurs générales à cet égard, il faudrait commencer et finir dans la première page.**

Neither Manzoni's reserve, however, nor Mme de Staël's discovery of a paradox must be taken to mean that there was no literature or sub-literature at the beginning of the century in Italy that dealt with the tender feeling which has popularly been the single concept most strongly identified with the romantic sensibility.†

---

*   Mme de Staël, *Corinne ou l'Italie*, Livre VI, Chap. 1. Stendhal also remarked on the absence of novels in Italy: 'D'autres avantages de l'Italie,' he wrote in chapter XLIII of *De l'amour*, 'c'est le loisir profond sous un ciel admirable et qui porte à être sensible à la beauté sous toutes les formes ... C'est le manque de la lecture des romans et presque de toute lecture qui laisse encore plus à l'inspiration du moment ...' In one of the early drafts of the Introduction to *I promessi sposi*, Manzoni humorously defended himself against the accusation of having written a novel, 'genere proscritto nella letteratura moderna, la quale ha la gloria di non averne o pochissimi. E benchè questa non sia la sola gloria negativa di questa nostra letteratura, pure bisogna conservarla gelosamente intatta, al che ben provvedono quelle migliaja di lettori e di non lettori i quali per opporsi a ogni sorta d' invasioni letterarie si occupano a dar se non altro molti disgusti a coloro che tentano d' introdurre qualche novità. Oltre di che questo genere, quand'anche non sia altro che una esposizione di costumi veri e reali per mezzo di fatti inventati, è altrettanto falso e frivolo, quanto vero e importante era ed è il poema epico e il romanzo cavalleresco in versi.' *Tutte le opere di Alessandro Manzoni*, a cura di Alberto Chiari e Fausto Ghisalberti (Milano, 1964), vol. II, t. III, p. 5.

†   In a popularized account of Italian literature in the nineteenth century, Umberto Bosco writes: 'Le parole *Romanticismo* e *romantico* le usiamo spesso, direi quasi ogni giorno, anche se non ci occupiamo di letteratura. Se dobbiamo definire, per es., una ragazza sentimentale, che ama sognare, fabbricare castelli in aria; che non tien conto di necessità o opportunità pratiche e magari del buon senso; *che pensa che la cosa più importante e più potente del mondo sia l'amore*, anzi

But this literature, which consisted of verse novellas or *poemetti*, composed very often in the traditional narrative verse form, the *ottava*, was obviously not categorizable as *romanzi*, that is, as prose works falling within the area of the social concerns of the innovators. What the concept of romanticism in the second half of the century owed to this genre has never been brought into full relief.* But the fact is that verse narratives continued to be written throughout the century, and Fogazzaro, for instance, whose name is more readily associated with regionalism and realism, made his debut in 1874 with just such a composition in hendecasyllables, *Miranda*.

In the early part of the century, Manzoni's friend, Tommaso Grossi, composed not only an historical novel in verse, the famous *I Lombardi alla prima crociata* (1826), reputedly modelled on *Ivanhoe*, but a verse novella in Milanese dialect, *La fuggitiva* (1815), and another one in standard Italian, *Ildegonda* (1820), before he finally turned to the conventional prose novel with *Marco Visconti* (1834). *I Lombardi* is of particular interest here, because its publication was accompanied by a minor literary scandal. Felice Romani, journalist, reviewer, and partisan of Monti, took issue with Grossi for having described his work with the simple subtitle 'Canti quindici' (Fifteen Cantos), rather than attempting a more precise designation in terms of the accepted genres.[58] '*Un pasticcio*' (a mess), Romani called *I Lombardi*, in an outburst vividly reminiscent of Voltaire's caustic comments on the *Divina Commedia*† and he concluded triumphantly that, after all, Grossi had written 'only a novel.' To which Marcazzan, writing from the perspective of history, rejoins,

A novel *sui generis* ... but the novelty of *I Lombardi* lies precisely in this: it

la passione; che è sempre pronta a intenererirsi e ad esaltarsi: noi diciamo comunemente che ella è una ragazza *romantica*' (*Letteratura italiana dell'800*, Torino, 1959, p. 7; italics mine).

*   In his important analysis of Prati's *poemetto*, *Edmenegarda*, Umberto Bosco (*Realismo romantico*, Caltanisetta-Roma, 1959, pp. 79–90) considers its realistic rather than its romantic tendencies. This critical orientation is in keeping with the teleological view of literary developments: since the nineteenth century ended up with realistic fiction, the trend towards realism appears as the one most worthy of attention. A different view of the nineteenth century determines the exposition of romantic literature found in Mario Praz's *La carne, la morte e il diavolo nella letteratura romantica* (Firenze, 1948): here the ultimate end is seen in terms of decadence. What is missing for Italian romantic narrative literature is a work comparable to Karl Kroeber's *Romantic Narrative Art* (University of Wisconsin Press, 1966), in which genre rather than literary movement is the organizing principle.

†   In the *Dictionnaire philosophique* Voltaire describes the *Divina Commedia* as a 'salmagundi' and calls its style 'bizarre' because it does not belong to any of the accepted genres.

carries us, without any evasions and respecting and maintaining a connection ... from the world of the epic to that of the novel.

Un romanzo sui generis, *se vogliamo, ma la novità dei* Lombardi *è proprio questa: di trasportarci, rispettando e salvando una connessione e senza evadere ... dal mondo dell'epopea in quello del romanzo.*[59]

This connection between epic (or romance) and novel, felt more strongly, *et pour cause*, in the case of the verse narrative than in that of the prose novel, accounts to some extent for such a muddled definition of romanticism as that given by Ilario Casarotti in 1829, in which the ideals of the liberal, Catholic, and ethical romanticism of the Lombards merge in ludicrous fashion with the familiar figures and *topoi* of a quite different kind of romanticism, whose ascendancy goes back not only to Berchet's predilection for Germanic myths and fairy tales, but also to the influence of that other participant in the early romantic debate, Lord Byron.* In an open letter to a certain Professor A. Antogina of Monza, Casarotti summarized the tenets of romanticism thus:

To scorn the pedagogical rules of the ancients taught us at school. To abandon deceptive fictions and adhere to the pure and simple truth. To imitate nature faithfully, exactly as it is. To substitute for mythological gods, in whom it is sinful to believe, demons and angels as some would have it, or, as others would have it, fairies and witches and other superstitions, as long as they be alive in the faith of the people. To try in every way to make life more gentle, to promote virtue, to perfect humanity. And for this purpose to stir cold and stupid hearts by representing graveyards, skeletons, and ghosts, by writing about highwaymen and ruffians, about hunting and love, always seeking to add variety by speaking of hypocritical hermits, of feasts and prisons, of stakes and gallows. To mix the scared and the profane, pleasures and horrors, the trivial and the noble, the profound and the sublime. To consider Christianity the best source for subjects, strumming principally of religious matters, or if not religious then at least matters pertaining to modern history and in harmony with current practices in religion and philosophy. To unbind and lay bare the sores of the Catholic Church, the violence of the crusades, the atrocities of the Inquisition, the lusts of ecclesiastics, in order, I believe, to cure

* Byron visited Italy in 1816. His *Giaour* received extensive attention: Ludovico Di Breme, for instance, wrote on it at length in *Lo spettatore*, and included passages translated by Silvio Pellico (see *Bellorini* 1: 254–313). On Byron in Italy, see Mario Praz, 'Rapporti tra la letteratura italiana e la letteratura inglese,' in A. Momigliano, ed., *Letterature comparate*, vol. IV of *Problemi ed orientamenti critici di lingua e di letteratura italiana* (Milano, 1948).

those evils. To extol women, advising men to love them as a spur to art, urging that they be worshipped and venerated as was done in the good old days of chivalry and as is proper, given their innate excellence ...

Disprezzare le regole pedagogiche degli antichi, dettate a noi nelle scuole; abban- donar finzioni ingannevoli ed attenersi alla pura e semplice verità; imitar fedelmente, e tal qual'è la natura; agli dei mitologici, ai quali è colpa dar fede, surrogar, chi dice i demoni e gli angeli, chi le fate e le streghe, ed altri superstizioni, quando sian vive, taluno aggiunge nella credenza del popolo; procurare per ogni verso di dar gentilezza ai costumi, di promuovere la virtù, di perfezionare l'umanità e perciò scuoter le anime fredde e stupide, rappresentando cimiteri, scheletri, larve, e di ladroni cantando e di sgherri, di cacce e d'amori, di eremiti ipocriti, di feste, di carceri, di roghi, di forche cercar l'utile varietà: mescere col sacro il profano, coi raccapricci i piaceri, il nobile col triviale, col sublime il profondo; il Cristianesimo dover essere la fonte su cui meglio che ad altri attingere gli argomenti; materie di religione doversi principalmente por sulla cetra, e le non sacre dover essere almanco di storia moderna e non dalla religione o dalla corrente filosofia dissonanti; sfasciare e mettere in vista le piaghe della chiesa cattolica, i furori delle crociate, le atrocità del Santo Ufficio, le libidini degli ecclesiastici a fine, cred'io, di sanar questi mali; portar in alto le donne, consigliarne l'amore seme dell'estro ed esortarne alle venerazioni e al culto, come faceasi al buon tempo della cavalleria, e com'è dovuto alla loro innata eccellenza ...[60]

IV

In Casarotti's statement there is only the slightest echo of the terms of the discussion as it had become familiar during the romantic debate. Gone is the whole historico-cultural view of two types of literature opposed to one another either chronologically or environ- mentally, or both chronologically *and* environmentally, according to the method favoured by the 'philosophical' literary historians of the first quarter of the century.[61] Gone is the feeling of romanticism as an avant-garde movement. We are, instead, well on the way towards the formulation of romanticism as a school, or, as De Sanctis put it, as a manner.

In his *Storia della letteratura italiana nel secolo XIX*, a series of lectures delivered in Naples in the 1870s, the great Italian critic discussed at length what he calls the 'degeneration' of romanticism. Writing from a socio-political perspective that idealized the national literature of Italy – roughly characterized as realistic, democratic, and secular – De Sanctis saw in romanticism not only a non-indigenous, imported movement, but one that was no longer in its prime when it came to Italy. German romanticism, he says, had behind it already more than a half century of development:

It fell on Italy ... when its stage had become the Middle Ages, which had supplanted the modern world; when the idealism of Fichte, with which it had many connections, had become mysticism and scholasticism; when the freedom from rules, which it championed, had fallen into the gravest errors of the imagination, leading to the extravagantly imaginary and fantastic, and to a new machinery: Nordic mythology.

Piovve in Italia ... quando il suo teatro era divenuto il Medio Evo, sopprimendo il mondo moderno, quando l'idealismo di Fichte con cui aveva tante attinenze, era divenuto misticismo e scolasticismo, quando la libertà delle regole che propugnava era caduta ne' più ampi trascorsi dell'immaginazione, producendo il fantastico ed un nuovo macchinismo, la mitologia nordica.[62]

This romanticism could, of course, have little in common with the romanticism of Manzoni, and De Sanctis – whose romantic background was not Lombardic but Neapolitan, and who therefore had little acquaintance with the rational romanticism of the group of *Il conciliatore* – took pains to dissociate Manzoni from the movement to which he actually belonged:

Alessandro Manzoni fu tirato per le falde nel romanticismo; i seguaci lo battezzarono romantico e forse egli stesso vi credette; ma era uno di quegli ingegni stampati in Italia, la cui natura, le cui facoltà di uomo e di artista ripugnavano al corrotto romanticismo francese e tedesco.[63]

For De Sanctis, Italian romanticism was characterized by belief in 'art for art's sake' and by the 'spiritualization of form,' that is, absolute freedom of the imagination, sentimentality, and musicality. Such a view of romanticism would appear to us to be more appropriate to symbolism – a fact not too surprising when we bear in mind that Italian literary historians have postulated a second and third romantic movement covering the whole nineteenth century and including the period more commonly referred to as symbolist or decadent.[64] Essentially, De Sanctis is simply telescoping the second and third stages of this later view of a continuing romanticism, projecting what to him are their characteristics, globally conceived, backward upon the first stage, to which, as we have seen, he in a certain sense denies Italian citizenship.

Instead of taking Manzoni as the representative of the first stage of Italian romanticism, he takes Grossi, and it then becomes easy to attribute to the movement an anti-rational, 'phantastic' aesthetics:

Romantic form ... is not rooted in reality, but rather in the imagination left at its own mercy, in the realm of spirits, witches, and fairies, in miracles and saints as in the Middle Ages ... Based on 'curved lines,' it produces hard, harsh contrasts which at first sight strike one as contrary to reality, contrary to normal proportions. Thus, as in painting so in literature we had the 'grotesque.'

Questa forma non ha base nella realtà; ma piuttosto nell'immaginazione lasciata in balìa di se stessa, nel regno degli spiriti, delle streghe, delle fate, dei miracoli e dei santi come nel Medio Evo ... Fondata su 'linee curve,' produce contrasti duri, crudi, che a prima vista fanno effetto contrario alla realtà, alle proporzioni normali, e come nella pittura così nella letteratura si ebbe il 'grottesco.'

In addition to this general medieval background, De Sanctis found in Grossi a sentimental writer whose female protagonists succeeded in wringing tears from the reader, and who, belonging to 'a world of consumptive women,' introduced that long line of doomed heroines whose most striking example was to be *la dame aux camélias*. Finally, in Grossi's predilection for the verse novella, De Sanctis could cite evidence of that preference for the musical and the lyrical as against the plastic that was for him a further characteristic of romanticism. It is interesting to note in this connection that De Sanctis was very much aware of the relationship between the narrative genre chosen by Grossi and the ballad. As he put it, in a synthesis which loses much in translation, 'Grossi's novel is in essence a tale, and the tale is in essence a ballad'/'*Il romanzo del Grossi, in fondo, è una novella, e la novella, in fondo, è una romanza.*'[65]

In concluding the chapter on Grossi, De Sanctis has further harsh words on romanticism:

It took classicism several centuries to become empty form; romanticism in Italy lasted only fifteen years. It was something vague and indefinite, corresponding to the state of depression in which Italy found itself. Outside of Italy there were V. Hugo, the Schlegels, Chateaubriand, and others who made a deep impression. In Italy romanticism turned at once into 'manner.' And what is 'manner'? It is to take content and form and to turn them into simple colour ... Read the gift numbers that were

---

*   *De Sanctis*, II: 14. The passage has many points reminiscent of what will later be a common characterization of the baroque.

published at the beginning of each year at that time, and you will find no *canzone* or sonnet without its mixture of convents, graveyards, crosses, angels, and visions. Then came the academies. Under despotism those who lacked the strength to fight introduced a new Arcadia; the degenerated school of Manzoni's followers became empty sound ...

Il classicismo impiegò parecchi secoli per divenir vuota forma; il romanticismo in Italia durò appena un quindici anni. Era qualcosa di vago, d'indefinito, corrispondente allo stato d'accasciamento in cui si trovavano gli Italiani. Fuori erano V. Hugo, gli Schlegel, Chateaubriand, ed altri che fecero grande impressione. In Italia il romanticismo si trasformò subito in 'maniera.' E cosa è la 'maniera'? È pigliare il contenuto e la forma e mutarli in semplice colorito ... Leggete le strenne che si pubblicavano allora al principio di ogni anno, e non vi sarà canzone o sonetto in cui non troviate quel miscuglio di conventi, cimiteri, croci, angeli, visioni. Poi vennero le accademie. Sotto il dispotismo quelli che non aveano forza di combattere, introdussero una nuova Arcadia; la scuola di Manzoni tralignata diventò vuota sonorità ... [66]

What Guido Muoni calls the morbid sentimentalism of the minor romantics[67] had in the long run little survival power. The writers discussed by De Sanctis in the series of lectures published under the title *La scuola cattolico-liberale* and the *scapigliati*, the *bohème* writers of the second generation, in conjunction with one of whom Carducci used the expression 'romantic scrofula,'[68] are remembered only by specialists. But the negative views of De Sanctis and even more so of the decidedly anti-Catholic, pro-Risorgimento militants, such as Luigi Settembrini, contributed significantly to the distrust of romanticism which we have already noted as characteristic of Italian literary historiography. By cutting Manzoni off from the movement, De Sanctis had exempted him from condemnation, indeed attributing to him the great merit of having achieved 'the measure of the ideal,' of having expelled, that is, rhetorical abstractions and empty generalities from the field of art, in favour of 'truth,' defined as life in its concrete reality.[69]

From Mazzini – an almost perfect contemporary of Tommaseo – there derived, however, a different formula for the assessment of contemporary Italian literature: not 'truth' and realism as the ultimate purpose of art, but political action. As early as 1829, in his *Saggio sopra alcune tendenze della letteratura europea nel XIX secolo,* Mazzini, echoing Pellico's statement of 1819 that 'to call someone a romantic is equivalent to calling him a liberal'[70] found in the literature of the early romantics 'a daring, fiery, generous and sublime thought which spoke of country, rebirth, and glory.'* In 1832, however, Mazzini considered this first heroic, 'individualistic' period already concluded and a new period opened, '*l'epoca dei popoli.*'[71] The second stage of romanticism, which De Sanctis saw vitiated by sentimentalism, musicality, and empty formalism – all terms applicable to aesthetic considerations – Mazzini saw vitiated by an innate weakness, which made it unable to stir men to positive action:

The doctrine of romanticism is a doctrine of individualism; therefore, it is powerful in the destruction of old literary tyrannies, but powerless to institute a new literature.

*La dottrina romantica è dottrina d'*individualità *: quindi, potente a distruggere le vecchie tirannidi letterarie, impotente a fondare una nuova letteratura.*[72]

Moreover, this second stage was marked for Mazzini by the presence of the surviving followers of the Byrons and the Goethes, men who in comparison with their masters were 'pygmies without a name, without a faith, without a banner, without strength of intellect or heart ... a crowd of insignificant plebeian writers'/'... *una gente pigmea, una gente senza nome, senza fede, senza bandiera, senza potenza d'intelletto o di core ... una turba di scrittorelli plebei ...*'[73]

It is essentially this view of the 'degeneration' of romanticism in the second period that enabled P. Emiliani Giudici in his *Storia della letteratura italiana* to accuse the 'inspired romantic hymnists' of having preached 'resignation, peace, and tranquillity,'[74] and that enabled Settembrini in his *Lezioni di letteratura italiana* to discover 'the Catholic reaction' in Italian romanticism, 'an old idea appearing in new forms: the Middle Ages with pope, friars, and barons all candied over with modern sugar'/'...*la reazione cattolica, idea vecchia in forme nuove, il Medio Evo col Papa i frati i baroni confettati nelle dolcezze moderne ...*'[75] In Settembrini's colourful negative formulation of romanticism, in which the bric-a-brac of minor romantic literature becomes symbolic of ideology, even Manzoni, whom De Sanctis saw as heir to the great liberal or national tradition started by Parini, is overridden. *I promessi sposi* becomes 'the book of reaction, of religious reaction,' and in its extolling of 'patience, submission, and forgiveness,' it is seen as representing at the time of its publication – against Manzoni's intention, Settembrini concedes – acceptance of Austrian domination in Lombardy and Venetia, of papal

*   G. Mazzini, *Opere* (Imola, 1906), 1: 234. In a footnote Mazzini gives the meaning and origin of *romanticismo*, and although he does not consider the word 'di cattivo augurio,' he suggests that it be abolished.

rule in Rome, and of Bourbon tyranny in Naples. From an artistic point of view Settembrini is more sympathetic, although there too the religious imagery which has become associated with romanticism colours his expression tendentiously:

Manzoni's novel, considered simply as a work of art, seems like a devout little country church to me, of chastened Italian architecture, new, clean, shiny, with finely embroidered vestments … Walter Scott's novels remind me of the great Gothic church of Westminster, where are buried the kings, queens, Isaac Newton, and so many national heroes …

*Il romanzo del Manzoni a riguardarlo soltanto come opera d'arte mi ha tutta l'aria d'una divota chiesetta di villa, di casta architettura italiana, nuova, pulita, lucente, con arredi di fino lavoro … I romanzi di Walter Scott mi ricordano il gran tempio gotico di Westminster, dove sono i sepolcri dei re, e delle regine, e di Isacco Newton, e tante glorie nazionali … ***

Of fundamental importance in the history of the changing meanings of *romantico* and *romanticismo* is the introduction toward the end of the century of the view of romanticism as a state of mind or sensibility. 'Classicism and romanticism are not only two literary schools, but two states of mind and almost two different qualities of soul,' wrote Federico De Roberto in 1898.[76] We have already seen how in the very midst of the romantic debate questions of behaviour and of psychological attitudes intruded into the discussion of literary choices and programmes. In that earlier stage, characterizations of romanticism in non-literary terms were for the most part the work of classicists retrenched behind a defensive position that used ridicule of the opposition as one of its weapons. By the end of the century there were no longer any barricades, yet the effects of the previous division persisted.

Among the effects, sharpened by the political tensions which eventually led to Italy's entry into the War against Germany and Austria, were a number of works in which more subtle means than ridicule were used to discredit and reject romanticism. Borgese's important *Storia della critica romantica in Italia*,[77] the first work to examine comprehensively the shift from classical to romantic

---

*   *Settembrini* II: 1076–7. Settembrini's analysis would appear to be patterned on Giovita Scalvini's famous remark on *I promessi sposi*: '… non ti senti spaziare libero per entro la gran varietà del mondo morale: t'accorgi spesso di non essere sotto la gran volta del firmamento che cuopre tutte le multiformi esistenze, ma bensí d'essere sotto quella del tempio che cuopre i fedeli e l'altare.' Written in 1831, now in G. Scalvini, *Foscolo, Manzoni, Goethe* (Torino, 1948), p. 221. Notice, however, that Settembrini has radicalized and politicized the observation.

aesthetics and criticism, presented Milanese romanticism as an adaptation of classicist positions rather than as an introduction of truly new ideas. Only with Pascoli's theory of the *fanciullino*, which posits the child-like, instinctive nature of poetry, does Borgese recognize the presence of a fully romantic aesthetics in Italy. In historical terms, he sees Italian romanticism as no more than 'the failure of an attempt of the German intellectual movement to invade Italy'/'*un tentativo fallito d'invasione intellettuale germanica ...*'[78] Even more radical was the thesis of Gina Martegiani, which she announced in the very title of her book, *Il romanticismo italiano non esiste*.[79] Basing her argument on a comparison of German and Italian romantic texts, she arrived at the conclusion that the Italian ones, in their sentimentalism and with their moralistic, socialistic, and patriotic tendencies, had little in common with the German ones, in which mysticism, philosophical idealism, and individualism predominate. Galletti in his edition of Berchet's *Lettera semiseria*[80] reiterates the notion of a fundamental opposition between the 'common-sense and balanced' romanticism of Italy and what he calls the imperialistic 'Teutonicism' of the Germans.[81] The Italians misunderstood German romanticism, he claims, and adopted it in their effort to renew their literary tradition only because they failed to recognize it as an attempt to 'combat the civilisation of Rome.'* Thus their effort was doomed to failure from the beginning.

Although it developed almost contemporaneously with the anti-romanticism of which we have just spoken, the view of romanticism as a state of mind or a sensibility was derived from a diametrically-opposed apprehension of the facts. According to this view, the different romanticisms which had been apparent from the beginning of the movement could be traced back not to ethnic or

---

* Galletti describes German romanticism as 'un raccogliersi, ripiegarsi e raggricchiarsi dello spirito tedesco intorno a ciò che di più intimo, di più etnico e incomunicabile vi era nel suo passato storico, nei suoi istinti originari, nelle sue passioni profonde, per attingervi nuova forza a combattere la civiltà di Roma' (*Grisostomo*, p. 27). The notion that Italian romanticism was a betrayal of the Roman heritage recurs in the literature of anti-romanticism. V. Gioberti, for instance, wrote: 'Ora siamo divenuti romantici, il che nella lingua moderna, osservantissima (come ognun sa) delle etimologie e del vero valore delle parole, vuol dire nemici del genio romano, e teneri delle cose angliche e tedesche' (*Del primato morale e civile degli italiani*, Torino, 1920, III: 42). *Calcaterra*, p. 14, connects romanticism with *romanicità*, 'cioè quella immensa temperie entro cui molti secoli prima si erano formati i popoli moderni d'Europa, allorchè gli elementi superstiti della civiltà romana, il sentimento religioso cristiano, tutto rivolto all'interiorità, e lo spirito giovine delle popolazioni barbariche, sopraggiunte nella storia, così si erano fusi da destare nuovi sensi di vita.' Etymological dictionaries tend to confuse the Roman and the Romance worlds, thus contributing to the misunderstanding which Gioberti's statement underlines.

historical determinants but to psychological and philosophical attitudes and systems. Guido Muoni's *La fama del Byron e il byronismo in Italia* and his *Note per una poetica storica del romanticismo*[82] presented the idea of a wide-spread romantic ideology underlying the self-indulgent melancholy which had resulted from the awareness of an irreconcilable clash between reality and aspirations to an ideal.[83] In his review of the second of Muoni's works,[84] Croce broadened Muoni's categories by recognizing the co-existence of three kinds of romanticism: 'moral romanticism' (the pathological state of mind known as *mal du siècle*, which Muoni's analysis emphasized), 'romanticism as an aesthetic concept' (exemplified in the works of the romantic school), and 'philosophical romanticism' (the postulation of intuition and imagination rather than reason as the touchstone of art).* Later, in the fuller analysis of the phenomenon in his *Storia d'Europa nel secolo decimonono*, Croce reduced the three categories to two: romanticism as a philosophy and romanticism as a pathological state of mind, two things which are 'different and even opposite.'[85] Historically and intellectually, the first phase of romanticism marked for Croce the rejection of the rationalistic philosophy and the literary academicism of the Enlightenment. It laid the basis for aesthetics, 'the new science of the imagination'; for an ethics in which spontaneity, passion, and individual responsibility loomed large; and for modern historiography, in which the past is no longer viewed with derision but as preparation for the present and the future. In its emphasis on the individual, this first phase of romanticism, according to Croce, opened the way to the liberal trends of the later nineteenth century and, in the context of Italian history, to the Risorgimento.[86] The other kind of romanticism represented the negative aspect of the age. It followed upon the religious crisis that grew out of the new philosophy, and Croce defines it as 'lack of faith, tormented by the anxiety of creating a faith and by the incapacity of doing so',/'una mancanza di fede, travagliata dall'ansia di foggiarsene una, e con l'impotenza di ciò fare.'[87] Thus in conclusion, historicism turned into sentimental nostalgia for the past, nationalism into fanaticism, liberty into anarchy, and the importance of poetry for life into the decadent confusion of art and life:

...falsificando la storicità nel sentimentalismo del passato e nella nostalgia restauratrice, la nazionalità nel fanatismo della stirpe e della razza, la libertà nell'egoarchia

---

* Because of the difficulties presented by translating Croce's terminology into English, compare with the summary given by G. N. G. Orsini, *Benedetto Croce: Philosopher of Art and Literary Critic* (Carbondale, Ill., 1961), p. 192.

e nell'anarchismo, e il valore della poesia per la vita nella poesia-vita e nella vita-poesia.[88]

Croce's position on romanticism, however, cannot be fully understood without reference to his theory of art as the *a priori* synthesis of content and form, of sentiment and image. This theory actually led him to deny the usefulness of the distinction between romanticism and classicism, since he maintained that they could have no meaning except in a synthesis, which would surpass both while preserving both:

.. i due termini non hanno verità se non nella loro sintesi, la quale non può essere data da uno dei due astratti che scacci via l'altro, ma dalla risoluzione dell'uno nell'altro che lo superi e conservi ...[89]

It is for this reason, Croce continues, that the concept of *classicità* must be revived. The word has been criticized for being without meaning, but this is precisely its merit, he says. For inasmuch as it does not postulate any specific content or form, *classicità* can be used to mean simply 'excellence or perfection of expression, beauty,' and it thus allows for the basic value judgment of art as good or bad regardless of whether it is romantic or classical:

... onde al classicismo e al romanticismo si è contrapposta la classicità, *parola alla quale si è dato il demerito, che è invece suo merito, di 'non significare niente,' e che in effetto non pone nessuna determinazione contenutistica o astratta, perchè significa semplicemente l'espressione eccellente, l'espressione perfetta, la bellezza.*[90]

What this means in terms of the dictionary definitions we examined earlier is that D'Alberti di Villanova's definition of *Autore classico* – 'ancient, approved Author, who is considered an authority on certain subjects. Homer, Plato, Cicero, Virgil are called classical Authors' – could now be brought up to date by omitting the word *ancient* and by adding to the authors cited some that do not belong to classical antiquity: all of them would be 'classics.'* Indeed this

---

* An examination of dictionaries for *classicità* has yielded the following results: *Dizionario enciclopedico italiano* lists *classicità*, 'Carattere classico, spirito classico; limpidezza, serenità, castigatezza nell'espressione artistica: *la castità della forma, che si suole chiamare "classicità"* (Croce).' *Dizionario Garzanti della lingua italiana* (Milano, 1965) lists the word with the definitions, '1. carattere, spirito classico: *la classicità del Canova* 2. l'antichità classica.' Battisti and Alessio date the word for the twentieth century. S. Battaglia, *Grande dizionario della lingua italiana* (Torino, 1964) gives three definitions, '1. valore esemplare (di un'opera d'arte, per cui essa è giudicata "classica") 2. eleganza misurata, compostezza, equilibrio 3. antichità classica, mondo classico'; the illustrations are taken not only from Croce but also from Pavese and Panzini. On the adjective *classico*, as in *autore classico, Dizionario enciclopedico* includes as an extended meaning, 'i più grandi

is what Croce himself does when he designates as *classici* both Sophocles and Shakespeare, Racine and Goethe, Dante and the other medieval poets, and even Villon, Baudelaire, and Maupassant 'when they are good.'[91]

We have seen how the first German literary historians of the romantic period used the adjective *romantisch* to describe the pastoral dramas of the Italian Renaissance and the tragedies of Shakespeare as well as the writings of their contemporaries. Similarly transcending the concepts of romanticism or classicism as 'schools,' Croce now finds in the terms *classical* and *classicism*, which were at one time almost discredited, the root for a word that once again calls to mind 'what belongs to the first class.' But if art is for Croce by definition the perfect synthesis of form and content (*classico* being but a synonym for *perfetto* or *esemplare*), then the romantic period, in splitting the perfect whole (i.e., art) into two different kinds of art and considering only the second kind (*'quella conforme ai tempi moderni'*) exemplary, was no more than a moment of crisis, a period of transition on the way to a new synthesis.[92] The artistic production of the romantic period must therefore be subjected to the test of *classicità*, so that the permanent works of art can be distinguished from the transitory though characteristic examples of contemporary taste and programmatic intentions. This is what Croce himself did in essays such as the one on Foscolo, in which he writes: 'Foscolo's classicism resides in this honesty of feeling and not at all in his exquisite Graeco-Latin culture and in his longing for ancient mythology':

In questa integralità del sentire, e non punto nella sua squisita cultura greco-latina e nel suo vagheggiare l'antica mitologia, è la classicità del Foscolo.[93]

Similarly, Cesare De Lollis says of Manzoni that he is 'more classical than any classic ... because of his moderateness, his balance, his orderliness' / '... *classico più di qualsiasi classico ... per via della qualità della misura, dell'equilibrio, della compostezza,*'[94] while at the same time criticizing Berchet, Manzoni's contemporary and fellow-romantic, for lacking these qualities.[93] In synthesizing the result of his dichotomous view of romanticism as a general aesthetic category and an historical trend or school, Croce arrived at the conclusion that the term *romanticism* 'can have only a negative value in the theory of poetic form, as of a varied imperfection' / '... *non può avere nella teoria*

autori delle letterature moderne'; *Garzanti* says, 'si dice di scrittore, di artista o di opera, che, per la loro eccellenza, sono ritenuti degni di essere imitati.' A collection of works under the general title, *I classici del romanticismo*, is therefore not unthinkable, although I know of none that is actually in print.

della forma poetica se non un senso negativo, come di varia imperfezione,[95] and that 'the present problem of Aesthetics is the restoration and defence of classicism against romanticism, of the synthetic, formal, and theoretical moment – which is the essence of art – against the emotional one':

Il problema attuale dell'Estetica è la restaurazione e difesa della classicità contro il romanticismo, del momento sintetico e formale e teoretico, in cui è il proprio dell'arte, contro quello affettivo ... [96]

In the final analysis, then, Croce joins the critics of the later nineteenth century who expressed strong reservations about romanticism, but he does so from a philosophical rather than an historical point of view.

In his introduction to *La carne la morte il diavolo nella letteratura romantica*, Mario Praz recognized that 'the epithet *romantico* and the antithetical terms *classico* and *romantico* are approximate labels ... elusive, tiresome, indispensable,' which neither the 'exorcisms' of the philosopher nor the efforts of the grammarian have succeeded in eliminating.* He favours the retention of these 'serviceable makeshifts,' for they allow the critic to speak meaningfully of a 'definite,' that is, historically localized, revolution in sensibility. Praz's work is but one of a number of studies which, beginning with the post-World War I period, passed beyond the long tradition of Italian suspicion of romanticism to a more dispassionate view of the total phenomenon. As the effect of the anti-romantic French critics wore off and as German romanticism began to be investigated with greater sympathy and understanding,† both romanticism on a European scale and the romantic movement in Italy became the object of scholarly investigation rather than partisan passion.

An important step toward the greater knowledge of romanticism in Italy was the publication in 1943 of the Bellorini anthology to which we have often had occasion to refer. This was followed by many partial studies, including Carla Apollonio's '*Romantico*': *Storia e fortuna di una parola*, of which we have likewise made use. Apollonio's work covers not only the romantic polemic and its sequel through 1846, but – what is of greater interest from a comparative point of

---

* The quotation is taken from the translation of Praz's book, *The Romantic Agony* (Cleveland and New York, 1963), p. 1. The 'philosopher' referred to is, of course, Croce; the word 'grammarian' should perhaps more properly be 'lexicographer.'

† P. Lasserre, *Le Romantisme français* (Paris, 1907) and E. A. Seillière, *Le Mal romantique, essai sur l'impérialisme irrationnel* (Paris, 1908) are the basic French anti-romantic works.

view – the pre-history of the word, which we have intentionally omitted from this essay. Her analysis of the pre-romantic movement in Italy differs from other such studies in that it is focussed lexically on the three terms *patetico*, *pittoresco*, and *romanzesco*, words which appeared variously in other languages as synonyms for *romantico*. Thus, she is able to conclude that *romantico* was in essence no more that 'a new word for a theory that was not new' / '*la parola nuova di una teoria non nuova.*'[97] As such it has had a truly extraordinary fortune, for it continues to exist today with the different meanings that it has accumulated in its relatively short history. While there is no question in the minds of literary and cultural historians that the basic meaning of *romanticismo* can be defined as 'a complex cultural movement which arose at the end of the eighteenth century and which became established especially in the nineteenth,' with all the further qualifications that a specific study of the period and its personalities might suggest, the word has at the same time become strongly identified in a negative sense with 'excessive sentimentality,' egocentricity, and passion.* It is this dual aspect which promises to insure continued robust life to it in a tension between the literary phenomenon itself and its evaluation.

* *Dizionario Garzanti della lingua italiana*: '*romanticismo*, 1. complesso movimento culturale, sorto alla fine del sec. xix, che, opponendosi all'illuminismo in filosofia e al classicismo nel campo letterario e artistico, ripudiava ciò che è schematico, astratto e formale per esaltare la spontaneità e l'originalità della creazione individuale, la libera fantasia, il sentimento e le forze istintive della vita, e difendeva le tradizioni e il patrimonio spirituale dei singoli popoli ... . 3. eccessiva sentimentalità, sentimentalismo.'

NOTES

1 Translated by Pietro Giordani as *Sulla maniera e sulla utilità delle traduzioni*.
2 *Dizionario universale critico-enciclopedico della lingua italiana* dell'Abate D'Alberti di Villanova (Lucca, 1804; 2nd ed., Milano, 1825).
3 Eric Partridge, *Origins. A Short Etymological Dictionary of English* (New York, 1959). Also G. Bolza, *Vocabolario genetico-etimologico della Lingua Italiana* (Vienna, n.d.) (hereafter cited as *Bolza*).
4 René Wellek, *Concepts of Criticism* (New Haven and London, 1963), p. 141.
5 Ignazio Cantù, ed., *Il piccolo Alberti. Vocabolario della Lingua Italiana ad uso delle Scuole*. Quinta edizione aumentata de' più moderni vocaboli per cura di O. Ferrario (Milano, 1888).
6 Pierre Letourneur, 'Discours extrait des différentes préfaces que les éditeurs de Shakespeare ont mises à la tête de leurs éditions,' in William Shakespeare, *Œuvres* (Paris, 1776), 1: cxviii.
7 A. W. Schlegel, *Corso di letteratura drammatica* (Milano, 1817), iii: 205–7.
8 For an excellent discussion of the intellectual components of Milanese romanticism and of the importance of the Coppet group, see *Marcazzan*, especially pp. 103–36.

9 F. De Sanctis, *Storia della letteratura italiana*, first published 1870–1. See the edition of Luigi Russo (Milano, 1960), II: 449–50.

10 For a comprehensive view of Italian criticism on romanticism, see Ferdinando Giannessi, 'Breve storia del problema romantico in Italia,' in *Orientamenti culturali. Le correnti* (Milano, 1956), II: 643–62; and Domenico Consoli, 'Gli studi del romanticismo dopo il De Sanctis,' *Cultura e scuola* III, 11 (1964): 33–4.

11 Carlo Botta, 'Al signor Lodovico di Breme figlio' (Letter dated Paris, 19 September 1816), *Antologia* XXII (April 1826): 74–81. Also in *Bellorini* I: 185–200.

12 Arnaldo, 'Lettera ai Signori compilatori del *Giornale di letteratura e belle arti* e verbale di seduta d'una immaginaria Accademia,' *Giornale di letteratura e di belle arti* (Florence, 1817), pp. 7–11. Also in *Bellorini* I: 208–11.

13 Vincenzo Monti, *Opere inedite e rare*, 5 vols. (Milano, 1832–4) (hereafter cited as *Monti*).

14 *Supplimento a' Vocabolarj italiani*, proposto da Giovanni Gherardini (Milano, 1857). Giovanni Gherardini, *Voci e maniere di dire italiane additate a' futuri vocabolaristi* (Milano, n.d.).

15 *Monti* V: 259.

16 *Supplimento a' Vocabolarj italiani*.

17 On Mme de Staël's reputation in Italy prior to the *Biblioteca italiana* article, see *Marcazzan*, pp. 108–11; specifically on *De la littérature* and *Corinne*, see Geneviève Gennari, *Le premier voyage de Mme de Staël en Italie et la genèse de Corinne* (Paris, 1947), pp. 198–222. On the whole question of the French background of the romantic debate prior to *De l'Allemagne*, see E. Eggli and P. Martino, *Le débat romantique en France* (Paris, 1933), pp. 11–37 (hereafter cited as *Eggli and Martino*). On Mme de Staël's contribution to romantic literary historiography, see F. Simone, 'Un aspetto fondamentale del contributo di Madame de Staël alla storiografia letteraria,' *Studi francesi* XXXV (1968): 208–28.

18 Quoted in *Eggli and Martino*, pp. 18–19.

19 *Ibid.*, p. 140n.

20 *Eggli and Martino*, pp. 149–54, 243–56.

21 Bouterwek, *Geschichte der Poesie und Beredsamkeit seit dem Ende des dreizehnten Jahrhunderts*, 12 vols. (Göttingen, 1801–19). There is no evidence that Bouterwek was translated into Italian, but Berchet devoted a number of articles to his work in *Il conciliatore* (1 October 1818, 15 October 1818 and 12 November 1818). Cf. pp. 119, 123, 135, and 150 above.

22 Schlegel, *Vorlesungen*, delivered in Vienna in 1808, published in Heidelberg, 1809–11. Cf. pp. 137–40 and, for the Italian translation, p. 296 above.

23 *Marcazzan*, p. 100.

24 All three were published as pamphlets in Milan, the first two by G. P. Giegler (note misspelling in *Bellorini* II: 486 and 487), the latter by Gio. Bernardoni. Now in Carlo Calcaterra, ed., *I manifesti romantici del 1816* (Torino, 1951) (hereafter cited as *Calcaterra*).

25 I. Rinieri, *Della vita e delle opere di Silvio Pellico* (Torino, 1899), I: 146.

26 T. C. [Trussardo Caleppio], 'Secondo articolo italiano,' *Il corriere delle dame*, May-June 1816. Now in *Bellorini* I: 62.

27 *Calcaterra*, p. 120.

28 *Calcaterra*, p. 226.

29 *Calcaterra*, p. 224. Bellorini confuses the two works, *Della romanticomachia* and *La romanticomania*, throughout; cf. *Bellorini* I: 150 n. and II: 487 with *Calcaterra*, pp. 410–15 and 224–5.

30 *Calcaterra*, p. 273, n. 3.

31 *Ibid.*, p. 276.

32 *Ibid.*, p. 277.

33 *Ibid.*, p. 283.

34 *Ibid.*, pp. 285–6.

35 *Calcaterra*, pp. 410–15, gives Berchet's review, which appeared in *Il conciliatore*, 29 October 1818. *Bellorini* I: 362–86 summarizes and anthologizes the review.

36 *Calcaterra*, pp. 410–11.

37 Mentioned in *Apollonio*, p. 158.

38 My information is derived from G. Pezzi, 'I romanticisti, melodramma di X. Y. Z.,' *Gazzetta di Milano* (16 and 19 May 1819) (now in *Bellorini* II: 73–81), and G. A., 'Marsia, melodramma di X. Y. Z. messo in musica dal maestro Gambarana,' *Gazzetta di Milano* (4 December 1819) (now in *Bellorini* II: 107–8). X. Y. Z. is identified as dott. Pagani by V. Branca, ed., *Il Conciliatore* (Firenze, 1965), I: xxx n.

39 *Bellorini* II: 73.

40 See F. Allevi, *Testi di poetica romantica* (Milano, 1960), pp. 161 and 231; *Calcaterra*, p. 178n, and *Bellorini* I: 427–8.

41 *Gazzetta di Milano* (31 January 1818). Now in *Bellorini* I: 252.

42 Bellorini was unable to locate a copy of the pamphlet but reprints the review of it that Pezzi wrote for the *Gazzetta di Milano* (24 May 1818) (*Bellorini* I: 358–61). My information is derived from this review. Note the error in Bellorini's citing of the title (p. 358) where he substitutes *esatta* for *estesa* (cf. also p. 489).

43 *Bellorini* I: 359.

44 Ibid., I: 361.

45 Ermes Visconti, 'Idee elementari sulla poesia romantica,' *Il conciliatore* (19 November through 6 December 1818). In *Bellorini* I: 435–69; *Calcaterra*, pp. 349–91.

46 Vincenzo Paladino, *La revisione del romanzo manzoniano e le postille del Visconti* (Firenze, 1964).

47 *Calcaterra*, pp. 13 and 349. Cf. *Marcazzan*, pp. 354–9.

48 *Calcaterra*, pp. 378–9.

49 See pp. 310 f. above.

50 *Calcaterra*, p. 351.

51 Ibid., p. 353.

52 *Calcaterra*, pp. 367 and 371 f., emphasis mine.

53 Ibid., p. 367.

54 Ibid., p. 370.

55 Ibid., p. 372.

56 Oscar Bulle and Giuseppe Rigutini, *Nuovo Dizionario Italiano-Tedesco e Tedesco-Italiano* (Leipzig, 1907).

57 A. Manzoni, *Tutte le opere* (Milano, 1959), II, iii: 145.

58 M. Marcazzan, 'Tommaso Grossi,' in *Orientamenti culturali. Letteratura italiana. I minori* (Milano, 1961), III: 2418–19.

59 *Marcazzan*, p. 379.

60 Ilario Casarotti, 'Lettera al prof. A. Antogina di Monza,' quoted in *Apollonio*, pp. 218–9.

61 On the 'philosophical' character of literary historiography at the beginning of the nineteenth century, see G. Getto, *Storia delle storie letterarie* (Firenze, 1946), pp. 137-47.

62 F. De Sanctis, *Storia della letteratura italiana nel secolo XIX* (Milano, 1958), II: 5 (hereafter cited as *De Sanctis*).

63 Ibid., II: 5–6.

64 M. Marcazzan, 'Dal romanticismo al decadentismo,' in *Letteratura italiana. Le correnti* (Milano, 1956), II: 663–896, is a comprehensive discussion of the whole development of romanticism.

65 *De Sanctis* II: 44.

66 Ibid., II: 39.

67 Guido Muoni, *Note per una poetica storica del romanticismo* (Milano, 1906), p. 96 (hereafter cited as *Muoni, Poetica*).

68 G. Carducci, 'Dieci anni a dietro,' 22 February 1880; now in *Opere* (Bologna, 1939), XXIII: 248.
69 This statement of De Sanctis is referred to in Mario Puppo, 'Le poetiche del romanticismo dal Foscolo al Carducci,' *Momenti e Problemi di Storia dell'Estetica* (Milano, 1961), p. 1047.
70 Pellico in a letter to L. Porro, 8 August 1819, quoted in C. Cantù, *Il Conciliatore e i carbonari* (Milano, 1878), p. 86.
71 Mazzini, *Opere* (Imola, 1906), I: 353–4.
72 Ibid., VIII: 94.
73 Ibid., VIII: 9.
74 P. Emiliani Giudici, *Storia della letteratura italiana* (Firenze, 1855), II: 489.
75 L. Settembrini, *Lezioni di letteratura italiana*, first published 1866–72. See the Sansoni edition (Firenze, 1964), II: 1067 (hereafter cited as *Settembrini*).
76 F. De Roberto, *Leopardi* (Milano, 1898). Quoted in *Muoni, Poetica*, p. 100.
77 G. A. Borgese, *Storia della critica romantica in Italia* (Milano, 1905).
78 Ibid., 1920 ed., p. x.
79 G. Martegiani, *Il romanticismo italiano non esiste* (Firenze, 1908). The work has recently been attributed to Giovanni Papini. See Mario Puppo, 'La "scoperta" del Romanticismo tedesco,' *Lettere italiane* XX (1968): 330n.
80 A. Galletti, ed., *Lettera semiseria di Grisostomo* (Lanciano, 1913) (hereafter cited as *Grisostomo*).
81 Ibid., p. 18.
82 G. Muoni, *La fama del Byron e il byronismo in Italia* (Milano, 1903); *Muoni, Poetica*.
83 *Muoni, Poetica*, pp. 86–90, contains the essence of his thought on romanticism.
84 B. Croce, 'Le definizioni del romanticismo,' *La critica* IV (1906): 241–5. Now in *Problemi di estetica* (Bari, 1923), pp. 289–95.
85 B. Croce, *Storia d'Europa nel secolo decimonono* (Bari, 1938), p. 47.
86 Ibid., p. 48.
87 Ibid., p. 50.
88 Ibid., p. 56.
89 B. Croce, *La poesia* (Bari, 1936), p. 118.
90 Ibid.
91 B. Croce, *Terze pagine sparse* (Bari, 1955), II: 6.
92 B. Croce, 'Aesthetica in nuce,' *Encyclopaedia Brittanica* (1928). Now in *Ultimi saggi* (Bari, 1935), especially pp. 26–8.
93 B. Croce, 'Foscolo,' in *Poesia e non poesia* (Bari, 1923), p. 87.
94 Cesare De Lollis, *Saggi sulla forma poetica dell'Ottocento* (Bari, 1929), p. 52.
95 Croce, *La poesia*, p. 296.
96 Croce, *Ultimi saggi*, p. 28.
97 *Apollonio*, p. 23.

DONALD L. SHAW

Spain /
Romántico – Romanticismo –
Romancesco –
Romanesco – Romancista –
Románico

Almost from the outset, the word *romántico* and its various cognates, *romanesco, romancesco, romancista,* and *románico,* had two closely related but separate connotations. The first of these was literary and was related to the fact that the romantics rejected certain attitudes, forms, and standards of judgment that had been current at an earlier period. The second connotation was moral. It arose from the fact that the romantics were seen by certain critics as subversive, not merely of literary standards and traditions, but also of ideas and beliefs, particularly in the political and religious spheres, on which the stability of society was thought to depend. Although the existence of these two connotations has not been overlooked, no attempt has been made so far to study them together. It is hoped that by making good this deficiency in the present paper, a truer perspective for the history of the word *romántico* in Spain will be achieved.

For the sake of easier orientation, it may be well to begin by distinguishing the following four periods in the history of our word:

1 *1764–1814.* In this period, *romanesco* and some of its cognates (but not *romántico* itself) began to gain acceptance, but as yet had no very well-defined meaning.

2 *1814–34*: the period of the 'Fernandine critics.' The word *romántico* (introduced in 1818) now came rapidly into general use. Its meaning began to be defined, but in isolation from any Spanish context, since no romantic works – in the modern sense of the word –

had as yet been written. The word was applied indiscriminately to medieval and later European literature of Christian inspiration, in contrast to classical and neoclassical literature. With specific regard to Spanish literature, the term was considered by some critics to be especially applicable to that of the Golden Age.

1834–77. This was the period of the Spanish romantic movement itself and of the post-romantic reaction. As Spanish romantic works appeared and others were translated, it became increasingly clear that the Fernandine definition of *romántico* was inadequate to describe them, but it was not abandoned. Instead, there was a tendency to distinguish between romanticism as seen by the Fernandine critics (now usually referred to as 'historical romanticism') and 'contemporary romanticism.' Although a few critics saw in this latter an expression of the changing sensibility and outlook of the times, the majority stigmatized it as subversive of religion and morality.

4   *1877 to the present.* It was only after 1877 that more detached and scholarly criticism became possible and that a systematic study of romantic techniques of versification, imagery, symbolism, narrative and dramatic structure, etc. was undertaken. Two schools of thought emerged. The one eventually headed by E. A. Peers, while accepting the fact that the word *romántico* has a narrower range of application than the one suggested by the Fernandine critics, defined its meaning in terms of a strictly literary movement, indigenous to the Spanish temperament and characterized by emphasis on freedom, passion, patriotism, Christianity, and medievalism. As such, romanticism represented for them a constant in Spanish literature which, after the Golden Age, revived gradually during the eighteenth century and burst forth with special vigour in the 1830s and '40s. The other school, represented by H. Juretschke, J. Casalduero, A. del Río, and others, approached the definition of the word *romántico* from the angle of the history of ideas. They attempted to penetrate its meaning basically from the starting point of its associated *Weltanschauung* and related it to the ideological and spiritual crisis of the late eighteenth and early nineteenth centuries.

EARLY OCCURRENCES

Among the various words that came to be used in connection with romanticism in Spain, *romántico* itself was a comparatively late arrival. Peers' patient researches have revealed that among the earliest pieces of evidence we possess is a phrase from Nipho's *La* *nación española defendida de los insultos del 'Pensador' y sus secuaces* (Madrid, 1764), in which the author states that the gravity of Spanish habits produced in the drama *'una grandeza romanesca o de novela'*[1] – a romantic or novelistic grandeur. Twelve years later, in 1776, we find the more properly Spanish *romancesco* being used by Antonio Ponz, who speaks in his *Viaje de España* of *'sucesos maravillosos, romancescos, y raros'*[2] – events so marvellous that one might associate them with the world of romance rather than with reality. This form was used again in 1789, when Llampillas called *Don Quixote* a *'poema épico romancesco'* fraught with *'aventuras romancescas,'* and in 1799, when Arrieta referred to *'el gusto romancesco de los españoles.'*[3] Significantly, when in 1798 J. L. Munárriz translated Blair's *Lectures on Rhetoric and Belles Lettres* (London, 1783) into Spanish, he rendered the phrase 'which give to the performance a romantic and unnatural appearance' with the words *'dan a la obra un ayre romancesco.'*[4] By 1805, a third word had appeared on the scene: the *Variedades de Ciencia, Literatura y Artes* (Madrid, 1805, II, no. 4, p. 427) refers to the *romancistas of* Germany.[5] But this term – like *románico*, which appeared in the *Crónica científica y literaria* (Madrid) in 1818* – was not destined to survive. Thus, when in 1814, the controversy between J. N. Böhl von Faber and J. J. de Mora – the first landmark in the study of Spanish romanticism – broke out, the word that was gaining acceptance was *romancesco*. Böhl himself complained in 1818 that the other words in general use, *romanesco, románico,* and *romántico,* were quite improper, and Mora continued to use *romancesco* until as late as 1847.† By then it has acquired a more specific meaning, but a scrutiny of the cases where the term was used prior to 1814 reveals that it meant little more than what we should mean today by 'novelistic' in the sense of 'exaggerated and far-fetched.'

THE FERNANDINE CRITICS

It was the controversy between Böhl von Faber and Mora that first narrowed down the meaning of *romancesco*.[6] Before we can deal with this debate, it is, however, necessary to make two important reservations.

First, there were in Spain at this time neither works nor doctrines that we should call in any strict sense romantic. The debate

---

*   *Becher,* p. 31. A number of other examples of *romanesco, romancesco, romántico* etc., mostly from the year 1818, are listed by Peers in 'The Term "Romanticism" in Spain,' *RH* LXXXI (1933): 411–18.

†   *Peers, History,* II: 32. Becher also records the use of *romancesco* in a Barcelona periodical of 1835.

took place in the void. Its terms of reference were either abstract and theoretical or referred to foreign productions and works of the Spanish Golden Age. Second, Böhl was a very recent convert to Roman Catholicism and an ultra-conservative monarchist in politics; his home was a meeting place for the so-called *servil* party in Cadiz. The clash which took place was political and ideological as well as literary. In defending Calderón, Böhl was defending what Calderón stood for: the Spanish Catholic and monarchical tradition, so recently reinstated. In attacking French classicism, he was attacking, as he saw it, semi-pagan rationalism. Hence his remark: 'It is not Calderón whom the Myrtles [i.e., Mora and those like him] hate; it is the spiritual system, which is linked and united to poetic enthusiasm, the importance it attributes to faith, the limits it sets to reason' *('No es Calderón a quien odian los Mirtilos; es el sistema espiritual que está unido y enlazado al entusiasmo poético, la importancia que da a la fe, los límites que pone al raciocinio.'* In his turn, Mora, in defending the classical ideal, was indirectly defending opinions that were speedily to send him, along with some of the major romantics, into exile.

Following A. W. Schlegel, Böhl made a sharp distinction between the ancient, classical literature of Greece and Rome and the 'modern' (i.e., medieval and subsequent) literatures in the various European languages. It was to these latter that the term *romancesco*, in the broadest sense, applied. Modern critics, Böhl asserts,

have invented, to designate the spirit peculiar to modern art, in contra-distinction to ancient classical art, the name *romanesco*; and not without good cause, since this word derives from romance or the vulgar tongue born of the mixing of Latin with the Gothic languages, just as modern culture proceeds from the mingling of the Gothic styles with the fragments of antiquity which were found engrafted into the nations of southern Europe.

han inventado, para designar el espíritu peculiar del arte moderno, en contra-posición del antiguo o clásico, el nombre de romanesco; y no sin fundamento, pues esta palabra se deriva de romance o lengua vulgar, nacida de la mezcla del latín con los idiomas góticos, lo mismo que la cultura moderna procede de la baraja de los estilos góticos con los fragmentos de la antigüedad, injertos en las naciones meridion-ales de Europa.[7]

***

*   Cited by *Herrero*, p. 79. The political context of this polemic is very heavily underlined by J. F. Montesinos in a long review of Llorens Castillo's *Liberales y románticos* in *NRFH* IX (1955): 283–92.

Since these various literatures in the vulgar tongues spontaneously express the special character of the people in whose language they are written, they tend to differ from each other; but at the outset, they had certain features in common, which can be brought under the broad heading of 'the Christian and chivalric spirit.' The Christian aspect of this especially continues to condition their development and is the fundamental cause of their being different in essence from classical literature.

Thus, beneath Böhl's initial distinction lies another: that between pre-Christian (clásica) and Christian (romancesca) literature. The former, according to Böhl, rests on a pagan, naturalistic view of life – this life; it has a serene outlook, satisfied with life's possibilities and basically rationalistic. Modern, Christian, romancesca literature, on the other hand, is spiritually orientated. It is conscious of this life as a separation from the next, towards which it constantly aspires, seeking through the imagination for indications and symbols of the eternal; 'it always contains more or less clearly the sublime ideas of eternity, infinity, love, detachment, union; all of which are born of Christianity' / 'Encierra siempre con más o menos claridad las ideas sublimes de eternidad, inmensidad, amor, desprendimiento, unión; todas, hijas del cristianismo.'[8]

To these two types of literature belong wholly different techniques. The classical, which is self-imitative, uniform, and rational, can be subjected to rules; the romancesco, which strives towards its spiritual ideal as best it can through the medium of images and symbols, and which reflects the multiplicity of the racial characters that it expresses, cannot be so constrained and must find its own forms and manner. To attempt to subject romancesco literature to rationally conceived, uniform rules is to endanger its spiritual essence and to ignore its relationship to its particular mother-culture. This had been the error (fortunately short-lived) of the Spanish neoclassical writers in the eighteenth century. The next phase of Spanish literature, Böhl confidently predicted, would see a conscious return to the great old tradition, with literature once more reflecting the popular, heroic, monarchical, and Christian ideals of the Golden Age. Thus, it would take its stand alongside the church and the restored absolute monarchy in combating the subversive principles of the Encyclopédie and the French Revolution.

The importance of Böhl's views cannot be overemphasized. Two features of them in particular, both as a result of Böhl's reading of A. W. Schlegel, were destined to bedevil criticism for decades to come: the attempt to link romanticism (although still not called by that name) with Christianity and the failure to recognize in romanticism a rigorously *contemporary* movement. At the same time, the tendency made its appearance to see an evil and dangerous influence in all literature that failed to reflect a Christian and monarchical view of society.

Meanwhile, in the course of the controversy, the word *romántico* had begun to be employed. On 26 June 1818, we find the *Crónica científica y literaria* using it for the first time, and three days later Böhl protested against the use of the word to describe 'what does not smell French [i.e., neoclassical].'[9] For him, it was quite obviously a pejorative expression. But this was not the case for long. In December 1818, the *Diario Mercantil* of Cádiz used *romántico* with no more than a fine shade of irony, and by 1821, Quintana could write quite straightforwardly of '*dos géneros, clásico y romántico o romancesco.*'[10] Thereafter, *romántico* displaced its several rivals and became universal. Credit for this triumph is generally ascribed to Luigi Monteggia's article 'Romanticismo' in *El Europeo*, 25 October 1823.

Monteggia's explanation of *romántico* is similar to Böhl's:

The Romance language [he writes] (which is the one spoken in Europe while Latin was falling out of use and the modern languages were in process of formation) was the language which gave their name to the poems which were called romantic.

La lengua romanza (que es la que se hablaba en Europa mientras se iba perdiendo el uso de la latina, y formándose las modernas) fue la que dió nombre a las poesías que s llamaron románticas.[11]

Like Böhl, he emphasizes the fertile fusion of the old classical cultures of southern Europe with those of the north and of the Moors (to whom he attributes the importation of the chivalric ideal), the result being the poetry of the troubadours. Passing on nimbly to the dispute between classicists and romantics, he adduces the familiar argument that, just as the classical writers reflected the age in which they lived, so the romantics wish to do likewise. Indeed, any writers who reflect 'the colour of the epochs in which they lived' are in that sense romantics: Homer, Pindar, and Virgil just as much as Dante, Camoens, Shakespeare, Calderón, Schiller, and Byron. The last two, in fact, together with Manzoni and Chateaubriand, are cited as the modern romantics. The important thing, Monteggia goes on to imply, is that the subjects (although he really means the characters) should be portrayed in such a way that the modern reader can perceive immediately their relevance to his own experience and be able to identify with them. Respect for the unities of time and place, Monteggia argues, militates just as much against the illusion of reality which it is supposed to preserve as neglect of them; the only unity he recognizes is that of interest.

For Monteggia, therefore, *romántico* meant relevant to and reflecting the outlook of its time and place so far as content is concerned, and free from subjection to the unities in what relates to manner. On other aspects of technique he is, like his fellow critics, vague. Only one, in retrospect significant, reservation is made in the article: 'unduly terrible and fantastic, *sad* ideas' such as those of Byron's *Manfred* are to be avoided as mere 'wordplay,' interesting neither the heart nor the mind.

Among the more interesting features of Monteggia's article are its conciliatory tone and its restriction of the discussion to the purely literary field. There is only a passing reference to 'the establishment of Christianity' and no mention at all of the monarchical system. What Monteggia opposes is the neoclassicists' assumption that only by exploring the changeless human situation that lies beneath the surface of appearances can a writer create a work of lasting quality. He takes the view instead that what confers immortality on a work of literature is the author's ability to interpret and express memorably for posterity the world-view of his own time. We are thus brought appreciably nearer to the view that recognized in romanticism a strictly contemporary phenomenon.

A few months later, in November 1823, Monteggia's fellow editor of *El Europeo*, López Soler, took up the issue afresh in two articles, which largely re-state his colleague's views on classicism and romanticism. He too insists on the gulf that separates medieval and modern man from the world-view of the classical writers and coins a romantic slogan, which sums up this aspect of the debate: 'New causes,' he writes, 'demand a new style.'[12] Where López Soler differs from Monteggia is in his adherence to the Schlegelian idea of a close relationship between literature and religion. For López Soler as for Böhl von Faber, it was the advent of Christianity that dug the gulf between the old world and the modern one. 'Who is unaware,' he asks, 'of the notable change that was brought about by the appearance of Christianity in human society? ... This is the origin of romanticism'/'*Quién ignora la notable mudanza que ocasionó la aparición*

*del cristianismo en la sociedad humana? ... He aquí el origen del roman-
ticismo.*'[13] But like his fellow editor, López Soler ends on a conciliatory note, admitting that

Romanticists and classicists alike, although by different means, are able to
interest the heart and have found the secret of pleasing and instructing at
the same time, which is the object of all good poetry, there being in the
former more imagination and in the latter more regularity.

*Románticos y clásicistas, bien que con distintos medios, saben interesar el corazón y
han hallado el secreto de deleitar enseñando, que es el objeto de toda buena poesía,
habiendo en los unos más imaginación y en los otros más regularidad.* [14]

We may note in passing that some years later López Soler modified
his ideas somewhat and became a more exalted romantic.

All that was now needed to complete the view of romanticism
adumbrated by Böhl von Faber and developed by Monteggia and
López Soler – the primitive or 'historical' view, as it has been called
by Juretschke – was the appearance of a strongly nationalistic
approach put forward by a native-born Spaniard. This took place
with the publication of Agustín Durán's *Discurso* of 1828.[15] Durán's
views, except in one particular, are not very different from those of
the earlier writers. Like them, he identifies romanticism with the
literature of modern times and Christian inspiration, a literature
which stretches back (with a deplorable, but fortunately short,
interruption by the neo-classicists) to the Middle Ages. What distinguishes him from Monteggia and López Soler (though less from
Böhl, to whose ideas he was much indebted) is his insistence on the
view that the country to which pride of place belonged in this period
was Spain. What matters to him is not so much that 'the seed of the
sublime beauties which romantic creations contain' is to be found in
the 'heroic centuries of the Middle Ages,' but that this seed was
Spanish. The flowering of this seed, and hence the peak of post-
classical literary production in Europe, was for Durán beyond all
question the Spanish Golden Age. Since his *Discurso* was primarily
concerned with drama, he made no bones about calling the drama
of the Spanish Golden Age simply *romántico*, in the same way that
the medieval Spanish ballads he collected were to him 'truly romantic poetry.' For Durán, just as France was naturally the home of
modern classicism, Spain was the natural fatherland of romanticism. Romanticism, in a word, was the instinctive mode of self-
expression of the Spanish temperament.

With the publication of Durán's *Discurso*, the first phase of critical discussion of romanticism in Spain came to an end. Little real progress had been made towards a working definition of the word *romántico*, and ideas had been put into circulation which were to mislead students and critics for more than a century. Still, the word *romántico*, albeit with far too comprehensive a meaning, was now in general use.

In retrospect, the major shortcoming of the Fernandine critics was their failure to associate romanticism with a specifically contemporary *Weltanschauung*. From this failure sprang their inability to distinguish between the old romantics such as Shakespeare and Calderón and the new romantics such as Byron. This in turn precluded serious discussion of romantic innovations in literary technique and restricted reference to themes and outlook. Inseparable from these defects is the Fernandine critics' excessive dependence on the ideas of A. W. Schlegel, which led them to exaggerate the relationship between romanticism and Christianity. In the circumstances of Spain at the time, this meant identifying romanticism with Catholicism and reactionary absolutism. Durán, in particular, glorifies the Habsburg period of Spanish history and vilifies the French Revolution, accusing France of breaking with its Catholic and monarchical past to embrace subversive doctrines in all the major aspects of thought and culture. Böhl's views are no less extreme; but, as V. Llorens Castillo shrewdly observes. 'to identify the new trend in literature with absolutism just when the overwhelming majority of Spanish writers were liberals and reformers and were suffering harsh oppression as a result, could only serve in the end to discredit the cause which he [Böhl] defended.'[16]

A second misleading conception, which grew out of A. W. Schlegel's admiration of Calderón, is that which purports to see in romanticism something indigenous to Spain and pre-eminently Spanish. Quite apart from the fact that critics, having adopted a suitable definition of romanticism, have claimed it as native to nearly every major European country, A. del Río has amply demonstrated in an important article that, if anything, his country has probably the least claim to an indigenous romantic literature.[17] In fact, if we are to take seriously the views of the writers so far mentioned, we are driven to conclude either that all literature in the Christian era is romantic or that, at least, all Spanish literature (except for a brief period in the eighteenth century) is romantic. Both these views, although surviving in the work of Peers and Tarr in a modified form,[18] render the definition of romanticism so vague as to be virtually meaningless.

Between 1828 and the publication in 1834 of Alcalá Galiano's famous preface to Rivas' long narrative poem *El moro expósito*,[19] little modification of the views hitherto described took place. Romanticism continued to be seen as Christian in inspiration, medieval or Golden Age in setting, and anti-classical in spirit and technique. Thus, a correspondent to the Madrid periodical, *Cartas Españolas*, in 1833 could still make the familiar point that

Modern German critics applied the name of Romantic [*Romántico o Romanesco*] to every kind of composition that drew its thoughts and forms from the writings that illustrate the new direction taken by poetry, faith, and customs in the Middle Ages. Thus, then, having analysed the etymological question, we come to the conclusion that the word *Romance* indicated in each respective country first a language, than a certain type of writings of entertainment and poetic fiction, and finally the word *Romántico* or *Romanesco* now expresses the kind of literature and poetry which has as its basis the ways of being and thinking, both political and religious, of the Middle Ages or the chivalric centuries.

Los críticos alemanes modernos aplicaron el nombre de Romántico *o* Romancesco *a todo género de composición que tomaba sus pensamientos y formas en los escritos donde se halla la nueva marcha que tomó la poesía, la fe y las costumbres en los siglos medios. Así, pues, analizada la cuestión etimológica, venimos a parar en que la palabra* Romance *indicó primero en cada país respectivo una lengua, después cierta clase de escritos de recreo y ficción poética, y últimamente la voz* Romántico *o* Romancesco *expresa el género de literatura y poesía que tiene su base en el modo de existir y pensar político y religioso de la edad media o siglos caballerescos.*[20]

Similarly, two years later, E. de Ochoa in *El Artista* (Madrid, 1835) could still define the romantic writer as one who 'wishes to see reproduced in our century the sacred beliefs, the virtues, and the poetry of chivalric times' / *'... quisiera ver reproducidas en nuestro siglo las santas creencias, las virtudes, la poesía de los tiempos caballerescos.'*[21]

CONTEMPORARY ROMANTICISM

Alcalá Galiano's preface to *El moro expósito*, the first genuine romantic manifesto, opens with a refreshingly sensible criticism of Durán and those who share his ideas (although no names are mentioned). Galiano points out that to lump together Golden Age drama and what he calls 'contemporary romanticism' – *'el romanticismo actual'* – is to ignore much of the evidence. He goes on to assert crushingly that if romantic poetry is indigenous anywhere, it is in

Germany, not Spain, that we must seek its origins. He next disposes of the belief that the classical French drama, because of its imitation of the Greek, can be regarded as anachronistic and irrelevant to modern culture, thereby demolishing a favourite argument of those who identified modern Christian culture exclusively with romanticism old and new. Having underlined implacably the classical elements in Dante, Ariosto, and Trissino (all by Monteggia's standards of romantic), he then carried his attack back onto home ground, pointing to similar elements in the major Golden Age Spanish poets.

In the middle of the preface, Galiano takes issue with those who would rally romanticism, through its supposedly essential links with the medieval to Golden Age period and with Christianity to the defence of traditional Catholic and absolutist political ideas. Like Böhl von Faber's antagonist, Mora, Galiano was a liberal. He surveyed the Golden Age from the standpoint of one who was suffering under the reactionary absolutism of Ferdinand vii. He saw in it a period characterized less by chivalric ideals and Christian virtues than by fanatical obscurantism resulting from the double tyranny, religious and political, which prevailed throughout its length.

Government, laws, and religion [he wrote audaciously, though from the safety of exile in France] were not matters of free examination and daring controversy, but objects of violent resignation, precise obedience, and frightened veneration. Such being the state of things, it was inevitable that people should occupy themselves merely with bringing fresh refinements to trivial thoughts and with padding out commonplace ideas.

*No eran el gobierno, las leyes y la religión materia de examen libre y de atrevida controversia, sino objeto de resignación violenta, de obediencia precisa y de veneración medrosa. En tal estado forzoso era que se entretuviese en refinar pensamientos triviales y en abultar ideas comunes.**

After a rapid consideration of romanticism in various European countries, notable for its hostility to the French movement, and after having duly observed that Spain in 1833 still remained completely in the grip of pre-romantic canons of art, Galiano turns finally to the task of describing, not the vague, allegedly centuries-

---

*   Rivas, *Obras completas* ii: xiii. In a lecture at the University of London 15 November 1828, Mora also rejected Durán's contention that the Spanish Middle Ages were the real romantic period: 'The Spanish authors who flourished before the sixteenth century,' he declared, 'are generally judicious and timid, not, as some have thought, bold and romantic.' Cited by H. Juretschke, *Origen doctrinal y génesis del romantismo español* (Madrid, 1954), p. 29 (hereafter cited as *Juretschke, Origen doctrinal*).

old 'romanticism' against which his critique had been directed, but the new contemporary romanticism that he saw in the work of Hugo, Byron, and Scott, Inevitably, at so early a date, his synthesis is deficient. Notwithstanding his earlier defence of Racine, he still considers classical stories and settings to be 'inappropriate to our society' and suggests that writers should turn instead to the chivalric Middle Ages. But he breaks fresh ground by advocating exotic settings such as the Americas, Greece, India, and Persia. Literary precepts, he goes on, are no longer accepted passively, but are subjected to rational examination. Romantic works arise from the nature and disposition of the country in which they are written instead of being forced into molds borrowed from abroad. Their characters combine the natural and the idealized. Their themes range from flights of fancy illustrating 'all that is vague, indefinable and inexplicable to the mind of man' to patriotism, metaphysical speculation, and above all the exploration and expression of familiar human emotions. Their appropriate tone is passionate and sincere; their aim is to move, to surprise, to soften.

There can be no doubt that Alcalá Galiano's preface introduces a new and original note into Spanish writings about romanticism. The influence of Schlegel, the broad 'historical' approach, have disappeared, and as mention of Shakespeare, Dante, and Calderón is at least replaced by informed reference to contemporary romantic writers, the word *romántico* begins for the first time to acquire a concrete and recognizable meaning.

In the light of future developments, what is strikingly novel in Galiano's approach is his double reference to 'metaphysical' poetry i.e., that which expresses what he calls our 'internal commotions.' It is this, together with his critique of Golden Age obscurantism and insistence on 'the crucible of reason,' that cuts him off from the Fernandine critics and announces the current of spiritual unrest that was now about to flow into Spain from abroad.

The return of the exiled writers took place in 1834, the year in which Galiano's preface was published. The result has been trenchantly described by H. Juretschke in his *Origen doctrinal y génesis del romanticismo español* (Madrid, 1954). After quoting Sainte-Beuve's article in *Le Globe* of 11 October 1830, which records the French romantics' shift away from reactionary ideas towards liberalism after 1824, he continues:

If a Spaniard had taken in 1840 a general look at literary life in Madrid, he would have been able to draw a similar conclusion, merely by writing 1834 instead of 1824. The French pattern had repeated itself in Spain in similar terms after the death of Ferdinand VII. Here too, Dumas and Hugo, together with their Spanish disciples, Pacheco, García Gutiérrez, Larra, Gil y Zárate and others, had given literature, and above all the theatre, an entirely new look. The rending passions and self-destruction characteristic of romanticism, anti-social tendencies and open, violent anti-clericalism are the hallmarks of this theatre and of most of literary life, which after the death of Ferdinand was subject to strong pressure from revolutionary political groups. Pacheco's *Alfredo* Larra's *Macías*, García Gutiérrez's *El rey monje* corresponded to *Antony* and other similar works of Dumas. The younger generation had rapidly forgotten the doctrines of Durán and Lista,[22] however much both of them may have protested from the beginning against 'bad romanticism.'

Si un español hubiese lanzado en 1840 una mirada de conjunto a la vida literaria de Madrid, le hubiera sido posible un juicio parecido, con sólo escribir 1834 en lugar de 1824. El proceso francés se había repetido en España en términos semejantes después de la muerte de Fernando VII. También aquí, Dumas y Hugo, junto con sus discípulos españoles, Pacheco, García Gutiérrez, Larra, Gil y Zárate y otros, habían dado a la literatura y, sobre todo, al teatro un aspecto totalmente nuevo. El desgarramiento y la autodestrucción románticos, tendencias antisociales y un declarado y violento anti-clericalismo, caracterizan este teatro y la mayor parte de la vida literaria, que después de la muerte de Fernando, recibió fuertes impulsos de los grupos políticos revolucionarios. El Alfredo, *de Pacheco; el* Macías, *de Larra;* El rey monje, *de García Gutiérrez; correspondían al* Antony *y a otras obras semejantes de Dumas. La juventud se había olvidado rápidamente de las doctrinas de Durán y Lista por más que ambos protestaran desde el principio contra el 'romanticismo malo.'*[23]

What, in fact, had happened? The standard answer is that of E. A. Peers and Courtney Tarr. Viewing romanticism in narrowly literary terms, they seek to minimize the importance of the exiles' return and see the period which then opened as merely the culmination of a process of reviving interest in the Golden Age which extends far back into the eighteenth century. Yet, curiously enough, both admit a difference. For Peers it is the difference between the romantic 'revival' and the romantic 'revolt'; for Tarr the difference between 'real' romanticism and 'external traditional' romanticism. In both cases the distinction is unaccountably divorced from reference to the all-important ideological issues. (It is only in passing that Tarr dates the end of the old absolutist and theocratic order from the triumph of 'real' romanticism, and he carries the argument no further.) A second answer is implied by Llorens and Montesinos, who, accepting that a definite change took place, attempt to distinguish between the extreme and virulent form of romanticism characteristic of works translated from the French and the more moderate form adopted by the Spanish writers themselves. Works of the latter that fail to fit the pattern are explained as conforming reluctantly to a fashion that had already conquered the stage while the exiles were returning.

The third answer is that which underlies the work of del Río, Juretschke, Casalduero, and other writers including the present one.[24] It asserts that the problem of the origin and definition of romanticism can best be solved by reference to the climate of ideas of the times and, specifically, to the collapse in the minds of the intellectual minority of the traditional world-view and its replacement by another, with consequent changes in many major categories of value.

This is, for the present writer, the heart of the matter: the origins of romanticism, in Spain and elsewhere, are to be sought not in national character or in literary conditions, but in the spiritual and philosophic crisis of the end of the eighteenth century. Without attempting to describe this crisis in detail, it will be sufficient to stress here, with Peckham, Lovejoy, and others,[25] its all-embracing nature. It involved the apparent collapse of previously established absolute values, whether these rested on religion or rationalism. It represented the great watershed of modern thought. With its emergence, a new age of doubt, anxiety, and even anguish came into being – the age in which we still live. The first to become seriously aware of this great change were the romantics. That this was so in Spain it is hoped to show by reference to the philosophic and critical reaction that followed the decline of the movement itself.

It follows that only from an investigation of the ideological aspect of the movement can we hope to achieve a better understanding of the meaning of the word *romántico* after 1834. Peckham's invaluable article, with its division of romanticism into a positive and a negative wing complementary to each other and produced by the same crisis, offers a starting point for such an investigation; but the student of Spanish romanticism would be wise to examine the evidence carefully before applying Peckham's conclusions wholesale to his own field. In particular, he will need to look critically at Peckham's definition of negative romanticism and his heavy emphasis on its positive counterpart.

A substantial measure of agreement exists among scholars who have studied the ideology of romanticism that, in the face of the crisis of traditional ideals and beliefs, many of the European romantics achieved some form of positive response. Opinions naturally differ as to the kind and validity of this response and descriptions of it range from 'integration with the group' to 'belief in the dominance of the intuitive and spiritual element of mentality over sense-perception' with a bewildering variety of definitions in between.[26] But it is crucial to observe that, whether these more positive individual responses amounted to an entirely new cosmic explanation or merely a shift of emphasis, the fact remains that their acceptance seems greater in proportion as we look to Britain and Germany, with their relatively liberal ideological atmosphere, and less as we look to France and above all to Spain.

Here, such attempts to solve the dilemma met with tenacious opposition from a body of traditionalist Catholic opinion already alarmed by encyclopedic ideas and fervently hostile to any innovations in thought that might prove subversive. In Spain, certainly, there was not the least possibility of an emergence of that fusion of orthodoxy and 'the desire to bring God, man and nature, finite and infinite, real and ideal, familiar and strange, into a thrilling unity of diverse elements through the shaping power of the imagination,' which Fairchild[27] perceives in Germany. Far more evident, on the contrary, was 'the impossibility that the new ideas, the new interpretation of the world, the new revolutionary and unorthodox philosophy of romanticism, could take root in the orthodox and Catholic soil of Spain.'[28] For the Spanish writer who had become conscious of the collapse of the old world-view among the intellectual minority, there was no possibility of compromise and little hope of working out his own solution in peace. The choice for him was between orthodoxy and the void.

We are now very far from the picture of Spanish romanticism presented either by the Fernandine critics or in our own times by Peers and Tarr. Peers, indeed, so far from being able to trace any coherent response to the crisis, is quite unconscious of it and blandly asserts that 'the major Spanish romantics got on quite well with the world!'[29] More in line with the opinions expressed here are those of the French critic Aynard, who declared that romanticism '*est né avec la désillusion ... Ce qui est commun a tous les romantiques, c'est l'inquiétude morale, religieuse ou métaphysique, c'est une manque de foi et non une foi.*' These views, as well as Aynard's tentative definition, '*nous appellerons romantiques ceux qui ... ont fait voir une sensibilité douloureuse excitée par le sentiment de la fin d'un monde,*'[30] have been accepted by other influential scholars. How far the assertion that they are valid for Spain can be supported by references to the works of the major Spanish romantics necessarily depends to some extent on the examples chosen and on the presuppositions that govern the critical interpretation of them. Without wishing to suggest that the arguments about to be brought forward are conclusive, it is hoped that they will cast some degree of doubt on the assertion of Peers mentioned above.

By any objective test, the leaders of the Spanish romantic movement were Larra and Espronceda. Such a test is provided by E. Carrilla's fully-documented account of the impact of the movement on Latin-American writers in his *El romanticismo en la América Hispánica* (2nd ed., Madrid, 1967), which shows beyond a doubt that these two were the outstanding influences. A consideration of the meaning of the word *romántico* based on the writings of the romantics themselves must clearly begin from an analysis of the works of these two figures. Relevant also even to a study as short as this are such acknowledged masterpieces of the romantic theatre as continue to be frequently studied; these include Martínez de la Rosa's *La conjuración de Venecia*, Rivas' *Don Álvaro*, García Gutiérrez's *El trovador* and Hartzenbusch's *Los amantes de Teruel*. Less relevant probably are the work of Zorrilla and the poetry of Rivas, including the *Romances históricos*. If it is objected that this statement deliberately excludes the main body of evidence in favour of a Christian, chivalric, and medieval interpretation of romanticism, it can only be replied that even if the latter works are given equal weight with the former, the most that can be shown is that Spanish romanticism did in fact have aspects which accord with the traditional interpretation. But numerically and qualitatively these latter works are inferior and have clearly withstood the test of time less well. The romanticism that has survived is negative romanticism.

We may begin with a glance at a famous work of transition, Martínez de la Rosa's *La conjuración de Venecia* (1834). Martínez de la Rosa (b. 1787), like Rivas (b. 1791), was among the older romantics, whose links with neoclassicism were especially strong. In the preface to his *Poesías* (1833), he still adopts a strikingly conservative note, censuring 'the longing for novelty' as leading directly to 'licence and extravagance,' but his best-known play (first performed in 1834) exhibits a number of novel characteristics. Three of these deserve special mention. The first is the melancholy displayed by the hero of *La conjuración de Venecia*, Rugiero. It will not escape the attentive reader of the earlier-mentioned documents on Spanish romanticism that the word melancholy recurs with a certain regularity, usually along with references to Christianity, although the connection is not obvious. Nor is melancholy a purely Spanish phenomenon; we find it just as much in evidence at this time in France and Germany. A. Wayne Wicherly explains that it is the mood which accompanies a shift of sensibility, the forerunner of romantic despair and *mal du siècle*.[31] It is clear that Martínez de la Rosa had realized, albeit vaguely, that melancholy was part of the make-up of the typical romantic hero, but he had no deeper understanding of its significance. Thus, Rugiero, who is young, handsome, surrounded with loyal friends, and outstandingly successful in love and arms, is presented as deeply unhappy on no better grounds than that he is illegitimate. Even this misfortune is more symbolic than real, being simply a dramatic device to provide a recognition-scene in the last act, with the added advantage of underlining Rugiero's sense of isolation from his fellow-men. There is really no objective justification for his melodramatic remark in Act III, Scene iii to the heroine, Laura: 'It is enough for you to be mine, for you to be unhappy.'

His relationship with Laura is conceived in equally romantic terms. The romantics' response to their growing awareness of the precarious basis on which traditional ideals and beliefs had rested was to convert human love, divorced from emotional and sexual fulfilment, into the main prop and support of existence. So Rugiero, in terms rapidly to become familiar, exclaims to Laura, 'Heaven sent you in order to make me carry on with life' (II, iii), after she herself had declared: 'I was born for you, Rugiero, to console you in your afflictions, to make you forget your orphaned state, and to fill the emptiness of your heart.'

The third important characteristic of the play is the role played in it by fate. In spite of the fact that unjust fate is possibly the major dramatic force in the Spanish romantic theatre, little critical attention has been devoted to it. 'It derives,' remarks N. González Ruiz in the only book on the subject, 'from certain ideas, certain criteria connected with existence';[32] but what these ideas and criteria are he neglects, or perhaps prefers not, to say. We do not need to look far to find them. Adverse fate is the symbol of divine injustice, or, since this is a contradiction in terms, of inability to conciliate earthly experience with belief in a divinely-ordained and hence benevolent pattern of existence.

The recurrence in later romantic works of these three characteristics – a negative view of life, love as the only real existential prop, and regular reference to adverse fate – underlines the similar outlook of the Spanish romantics after their return from exile in 1834.

That year also saw the first performance of Larra's *Macías*. It was written with all the intensity of a man whose life literally came to depend on the realization of the love-ideal. Almost the last words spoken by Macías stress the indissoluble link between love and existence: 'The bonds which bound us to the world are broken.' The survival of their love having become impossible, the lovers' grip on life is lost. Again and again Macías insists that life without love is meaningless misery. In the lyrical climax of Act III he declares:

> Los amantes son solos los esposos
> Su lazo es el amor. ¿ Cuál hay más santo?
> ... ¿ Qué otro asilo
> pretendes más seguro que mis brazos?
> Los tuyos bastaránme, y si en la tierra
> asilo no encontramos, juntos ambos
> moriremos de amor. ¡ Quién más dichoso
> que aquel que amando vive y muere amado!

Lovers alone are truly married – their bond is love. Which other is more sacred? ... What other refuge can you hope for than my arms? Yours suffice for me, and if we can find no refuge on earth, we will both together die of love. Who can be more happy than he who lives loving and dies beloved!

The audacity of these words, spoken to a married woman in nineteenth-century Spain, is striking, even when the effect is attenuated by Elvira's reply.

A feature of Macías' character-presentation is the fact that Larra does not trouble to symbolize in orphanhood or illegitimacy that essential deprivation of confidence in life which is at the root of his total dependence on emotion for vital support. Equally we notice again the role of adverse fate in preventing Macías (like Mansilla in Hartzenbusch's *Los amantes de Teruel*) from keeping the tryst on which love and life depend.

It is fate also which, from the sub-title – *The Force of Destiny* – on, dominates Rivas' *Don Álvaro*, the key play of the Spanish romantic movement. What we perceive more clearly in this work than in any other Spanish romantic production except Espronceda's *El diablo mundo* is the clash between love and insight, the positive and the negative vital principles. When this conflict is translated into dramatic terms, the adverse principle can be incarnated in a man (such as Fernán Núñez in *Macías*), or in a duty to another ideal (such as liberty in *La conjuración de Venecia*); but the most effective way of portraying it is by using the symbol of fate: in this way, the dramatist brings into play not merely the temporary hostility of men and current ideals but the eternal hostility of an unchanging principle. This is why all the major Spanish romantic dramas introduce the idea of fate, and why Rivas here exploits it systematically. The deliberate fortuitousness of the events of the play, which has called forth so much thoughtless derision, points to the conclusion that they are chosen not for what they are but for what they represent: arbitrary blows of malign destiny falling successively on the hero until, unable to bear any longer an existence so obviously indicative of the absence of a benign providence, his is driven to take his own life. As Casalduero puts it, 'the romantic's dead body bears witness to life's lack of meaning.'

The centre of the play is don Álvaro's first soliloquy (III, iii):

¡ Qué carga tan insufrible
es el ambiente vital
para el mezquino mortal
que nace en sino terrible!
¡ Qué eternidad tan horrible
la breve vida! ¡ Este mundo,
qué calabozo profundo
para el hombre desdichado! ...
... risueño un día
uno solo, nada más,
me dio el destino; quizás
con intención más impía.
Así en la cárcel sombría
mete una luz el sayón,
con la tirana intención
de que un punto el preso vea
el horror que lo rodea
en su espantosa mansión.

What an unbearable burden life is for the unhappy mortal born with so terrible a destiny! What a horrible eternity is this brief life! This world, how deep a dungeon for the man bereft of happiness! ... One single day of smiling fortune, no more, did destiny allow me; perhaps with the cruellest of intentions. For so in the darkest prison the jailor places a light, with the tyrannous intention that the prisoner may see for a brief moment the horror which surrounds him in his frightful abode.

The prison image recurs regularly in Spanish romantic literature, as it does in that of the rest of Europe. The implication of a humanity trapped within an existence presided over by a God of wrathful injustice (Espronceda's 'God of vengeance, [who] ... metes out anguish, pain and death to the deluded mortal, who implores him in vain')* cannot be easily ignored in assessing the outlook of a poet who uses this or similar images. But what the soliloquy really tells us is that the melancholy noticed by the Fernandine critics, now deepened into despair, is the result of a new insight into the human situation.

Hardly less typical in Rivas' play is the precariousness of the love-ideal as a vital support. The reference to it as a mere ray of light serving only to reveal the full horror of existence reminds us that the romantics, while desperately seeking to absolutize human love, were haunted with the sense of its ephemerality. In the event, every major romantic work stresses its inevitable failure: the final confirmation of the vanity of human hopes. Thirdly, we must note the intervention for the first time of religion into the symbolic pattern, represented by don Álvaro's retreat into the monastery of Los Ángeles. Its significance, as we shall see from *El trovador*, is not to be underestimated. Don Álvaro and the heroine Leonor both seek refuge in the monastery and embrace the religious life, symbolizing the romantics' nostalgia for the traditional solution to the enigma of life, which is supplied by faith. But the gesture is in vain; the peace of the cloister is shattered successively by the duel of don Álvaro and the vengeful don Alfonso, the death of the latter after murdering his sister, and the suicide of don Álvaro himself.

The symbolism here visible is more explicit in García Gutiérrez's *El trovador* (1836). The heroine, who is again named Leonor, also seeks refuge in a religious house and takes the veil. But the ultimate irrelevance of the religious solution for her is never in doubt. Even before entering the convent, she admits, referring to the hero, Manrique:

> ... *Todavía*
> *delante de mí le tengo*
> *y Dios, y el altar, y el mundo*
> *olvido cuando le veo* (ii, iii).

* *El diablo mundo*: prólogo. Cf. Larra, 'Luego que estuvo el mundo formado / Y cayó de tu mano omnipotente, / Tu con el pie empujándole indignado / "Rueda," dijiste y sufre eternamente.' Cited by C. de Burgos, *Fígaro* (Madrid, 1919), p. 61.

Yet I still behold him before me, and God, the altar, and the world are forgotten when I see him.

In the next act, she specifically subordinates the power of grace to that of love:

Cuando en el ara fatal
eterna fe te juraba,
mi mente, ¡ Ay Dios!, se extasiaba
en la imagen de un mortal ...
No; tu poder no es bastante
a separarla de aquí ... (III, iv).

When I vowed thee eternal faithfulness before the fatal altar, my mind, O God! adored with ecstasy the image of a mortal man ... No, thy power is not sufficient to blot it from my mind.

Like don Álvaro, she abandons her refuge without hesitation, in the full knowledge of the spiritual consequences; and when even the sacrifice of her hope of salvation proves vain, she too, in true romantic style, dies by her own hand.

In Hartzenbusch's *Los amantes de Teruel* (1837), the 'existential' conception of love as the only life-principle achieves its maximum expression. In each of the plays so far mentioned, the frustration of love is inevitably followed by the death of the lovers. What we have not hitherto seen is a direct connection. Here it is. Neither Mansilla nor Isabel dies from any external cause. There is no recourse either to violence or to suicide. When the lovers find themselves deprived of their last hope of love-fulfilment they die, as simply and inevitably as a watch stops when its main-spring breaks.

Where the world-view illustrated from different angles in the works so far mentioned finds its most coherent expression is in the work of Espronceda. His return from exile seems to have been accompanied by growing intellectual preoccupation. Beside the patriotic poet and revolutionary dreaming of love and glory, a new figure appears: the seeker after truth. But as he attempts to comfort himself for the loss of the earlier illusions by making sure that the underlying metaphysical position is still secure, we see his efforts fail. In Espronceda's *Hymn to the Sun*, for example, the sun is identified with the idea of eternal duration, with all that is reliably time-defying, including by implication those ideals, beliefs, and absolutes which like the sun illuminate the world. But the climax of the whole poem is a simple negation:

¿ Y habrás de ser eterno, inextinguible,
Sin que nunca jamás tu inmensa hoguera
Pierda su resplandor, siempre incansable
Audaz siguiendo tu inmortal carrera,
Hundirse las edades contemplando
Y solo, eterno, perenal, sublime,
Monarca poderoso, dominando?
No ...

And shalt thou be eternal, inextinguishable, so that thy immense conflagration shall never lose its splendour, forever tireless, boldly following thy immortal course, contemplating the ages as they sink behind, and alone, eternal, ageless, sublime, like a monarch in his power, dominating all? No ...

Thus, nothing is secure, The poem ends with a vision of the world exploding and falling shattered from the hands of a God apparently unable to prevent it from slipping finally into the eternal night.

Espronceda's last work, the narrative poem *El diablo mundo* (1841), was intended as an allegory of life in general. Although unfinished, its meaning is clear. Adam, symbol of the poet and mankind, is granted the choice between death (and the solution of life's enigma) and eternal life. Disregarding the grim warning of the Spirit of Life, he eagerly embraces immortality and illusion, coming naked and guileless into the world. There he finds himself immured (literally and figuratively) in the prison-house, and though at the touch of love his shackles are broken, happiness and fulfilment are short-lived. Having become progressively aware of ignobility, suffering, cruelty, oppression, and crime, Adam, in the audacious brothel scene, comes face to face at length with divine injustice, the death of the innocent at the hands of an implacable and arbitrary divinity. It is only to this point that the poem is worked out in detail, but the main lines of the rest are obvious enough. Adam was destined to discover that the immortality he unwisely chose was to prove merely an endless sequence of pain and disillusionment. The pleasures of the Devil World are the fruit of self-deception, and ultimate finality is a mere dream: 'We bend our steps onward, knowing not whither'/'*Vamos andando sin saber adónde*' (*El diablo mundo*, v. 2184).

It must surely be clear from this all-too brief survey of a few major Spanish romantic texts that no definition of the word *romántico* in the terms proposed by Peers, Tarr, and their followers can do justice to the profound spiritual disquiet which underlies the major creative work of the movement and which is its principal legacy to our time.

Outside the field of creative literature, the romantics' own statements are disappointing. In an early article,[33] Espronceda defends a conception of romanticism indistinguishable from that of Fernandine critics. Hartzenbusch's article 'Sobre la tragedia española,' although reproduced in *BSS* VIII (1931), with other romantic documents, is irrelevant. Enrique Gil will be mentioned presently. The only other romantic of note whose opinions are worth discussion is Larra, but his ideas are contradictory and present considerable difficulties of interpretation. Although in his famous manifesto, 'Literatura' (*El Español*, 18 January 1836), and elsewhere, he repeatedly demands truth and relevance to modern thought at whatever cost and calls for 'a literature that is the daughter of experience and history... analytic, philosophic, profound, thinking everything and saying everything, ... teaching truths ...'[34] it appears from his equally famous critique of Dumas' *Antony*, written only a few months later, that there were some truths which were to be withheld. The revealing feature is that Larra never for an instant denies the truth of what he holds to be the premise of Dumas' play: the absence of any ultimate finality in human life. On the contrary, he presents it as the inevitable discovery of the future. He simply asserts that Spanish audiences are not yet ready for such revelations.

Equally confused is the reaction of Donoso Cortés. Unlike Larra, who, although a sceptic, recoiled before the exposition in dramatic form of the extreme consequences of his own ideas, Donoso was an ultra-Catholic propagandist. While voicing his repugnance for

those who, without understanding romanticism, write their name on its banner ... because they have seen appear before them a delirious sleepwalker, dagger in hand, whose mouth utters nothing save blasphemies ... who seeks a still beating breast from whose blood to slake her thirst, and who bears written on her brow the words *incest, profanation,*

los que, sin comprender el romanticismo, escriben su nombre en su bandera ... porque han visto aparecer en su presencia una somnámbula delirante, cuyo brazo esta armado de un puñal, cuya boca sólo profiere blasfemias ... que busca un seno que aun palpite para saciar su sed con su sangre y que lleva escrito en su frente incesto, profanación,[35]

he nevertheless praised such a playwright in his review of J. F. Pacheco's *Alfredo* (*La Abeja*, 25 May 1835). Three years later, in the essay 'El clasicismo y el romanticismo,' he attempted to resolve the contradiction by reverting to the old 'historic' view of romanticism as the literature of medieval and modern societies, while at the same time distinguishing between such 'romantics' as Dante, Shakespeare, and Calderón, on the one hand, and, on the other, those contemporaries of his own for whom

the world is a horrible desert without verdure and vegetation; in the midst of its solitude stands a scaffold and at the foot of this there is usually a threatening headsman and a groaning victim.

el mundo es un horrible desierto sin vegetación y sin verdura; en medio de su soledad se levanta un cadalso, y al pie de ese cadalso suele haber un verdugo que amenaza y una víctima que gime.[36]

The dramatists of our day, he goes on, sing only of the horrors of this world.

Both Larra and Donoso clearly sensed that they were in the presence of a new and profoundly disturbing literary phenomenon and that beneath the extravagances of *Antony* and *Alfredo* lay deeper issues. Thus, Donoso unhesitatingly affirms that 'the issue that is being argued between classicism and romanticism is not only a literary issue, but also a philosophic, political, and social issue,'[37] and sees in Byron, for example, the personification of 'a crisis.' Similarly Larra's *volte-face* on the question of truth in literature cannot be dissociated from his consciousness of 'the ruin of former beliefs' and of the 'dreadful uneasiness' hovering over Europe as a result.

THE ANTI-ROMANTIC REACTION

There were others, however, who saw the matter in far simpler terms. Failing to recognize that the appearance of new ideas in literature usually indicates a wider shift of ideology, they saw in romantic writings simply the arbitrary exaltation of vice and crime. From here, it was but a step to accusing the romantics of threatening the very foundations of society and of religious confidence. Thus, in the late 1830s, the word *romántico* rapidly began to acquire a moral connotation already foreshadowed in the writings of Böhl von Faber and in Monteggia's warning against the 'terrible ideas' of Byron. As the tide of romanticism began to ebb, there emerged in the work of a number of writers a growing concern for what seemed to them the increasing ideological confusion and religious scepticism that the movement had engendered. An early example is the article 'El Artista' by A. Fontcubierta in his Catalan periodical *El Vapor* (February 1837), in which hostility to rules and precepts in art is directly associated with 'an epoch in social life in which beliefs of all kinds are being weakened and snuffed out.* Shortly afterwards, Enrique Gil complained à propos of Zorrilla's poem *To a Skull* of 'this bitter and disconsolate genre of poetry which strips from the soul even the pleasure of melancholy [!] and shrouds from our eyes the sweetest of futures, the future of religion'; and in reviewing Espronceda's *To Jarifa*, Gil lamented 'this sceptical, tenebrous, faith-bereft poetry, stripped of all hope and rich only in disillusion and pain,' attributing it to 'an epoch in which mankind sees the future enveloped in clouds.' Such a literature, he asserts, though it must be accepted as expressing 'the present disquiet and unrest,' can only lead to moral anarchy.

Este género desconsolado y amargo, que despoja al alma hasta del placer de la melancolía y anubla a nuestros ojos el porvenir más dulce, el porvenir de la religión ... esa poesía escéptica, tenebrosa, falta de fe, desnuda de esperanza y rica de desengaño y de dolores ... la de una época en que el hombre divisa el porvenir cubierto de nieblas ... la inquietud y desasosiego presente ...†

The statements of these two writers are confirmed by the weightier testimony of Balmes, who now emerged as the leader of the philosophic-religious counter-movement against romanticism that was slowly coming into being. In 1841, he opened his first important work, *Cartas a un escéptico en materia de religión*, with a clear diagnosis of what he agreed with Fontcubierta and Gil was 'one of the plagues characteristic of the epoch': scepticism. It is defined in the opening letter as 'that emptiness of the soul which torments and disquiets it, that frightful absence of all faith, of all hope, that incertitude about God, about nature, about the origin and destiny of

---

*   'Una época en la vida social en que todas las creencias se apagan y se debilitan.' Cited by R. Silva, 'Two Barcelona Periodicals,' *Liverpool Studies in Spanish Literature*, ed. Peers, I (Liverpool, 1940): 86. In the same year, R. de Mesonero Romanos, reviewing García Gutièrrez's *El paje*, refers to the conversion of Genius by the romantics into an 'arma ponzoñosa de seducción y maldades, que prestan a la nueva escuela literaria un carácter inmoral,' *El Semanario Pintoresco* III (1837): 166.

†   *Obras completas* (Madrid, 1954), pp. 484 and 549. Similarly, A. Gil y Zárate, 'Teatro antiguo y teatro moderno,' *Revista de Madrid* (1841), pp. 112–14 (reproduced in *BSS* VII, 1930), while insisting that the new drama must contain 'más filosofía,' goes on to complain that 'Es un mal ... para los ingenios a quienes desgraciadamente ha tocado escribir en estos tiempos. De aquí resulta que sus composiciones han de participar forzosamente de ese carácter de incertidumbre y exageración que es propio de la época ... [sin] ... ideas fijas y dominantes.'

mankind.' 'Emptiness of soul' was already a stock ingredient of caricatures of the romantics.[38] But Balmes was not a man to rest content with veiled allusions.

This emptiness [he goes on] is more deeply felt in proportion as it oppresses souls all of whose mental faculties have been excited by a mad literature whose soul aim is to produce strong effects.

Una de las plagas características de la época ... ese vacío del alma que la desasosiega y atormenta, esa ausencia espantosa de toda fe, de toda esperanza, esa incertidumbre sobre Dios, sobre la naturaleza, sobre el origen y destino del hombre ... vacío tanto más sensible cuanto recae en almas excitadas en todas sus facultades mentales por una literatura loca que sólo se propone producir efecto.[39]

If any doubt remained about the movement of 'mad literature' that Balmes had in mind, it was speedily removed by his violent attack on the romantics in *El criterio* (1845).

Those men [he wrote] complain of everything, blaspheme against God, calumniate the whole of humanity, and when they rise to philosophic considerations carry off the soul through a region of darkness, where they find nothing but despairing chaos.

Esos hombres se quejan de todo, blasfeman de Dios, calumnian a la humanidad entera y cuando se elevan a consideraciones filosóficas llevan el alma por una región de tinieblas, donde no encuentran más que un caos desesperante.[40]

Stigmatizing romantic writings as nothing short of a public calamity, he advocated in their place a literature based exclusively on a return to the soundest principles of religion and morality.

Between the publication of the *Cartas a un escéptico* and that of *El criterio*, the chorus of attack on the romantics' supposed immoral influence was swelled by the voices of two other eminent writers: Alberto Lista and his pupil Ventura de la Vega. Lista derived the word *romántico* from *roman*, and declared that 'if we limit ourselves to its etymology, it seems that its meaning applies only to those things which are related to, or belong to, or are similar to, the novel' /'*Limitándonos a su etimología parece que no puede extenderse su significación a más que a las cosas relativas, pertenecientes o semejantes a la novela.*'[41] He lamented the fact that the more Spanish *novelesco* had not been adopted instead. Later, however, we find him accepting the familiar Schlegelian distinction between classical pagan literature, on the one hand, and medieval and Golden Age literature, with its Christian moral values, on the other. This latter he was willing to call romantic, asserting that

In consequence, romantic poetry, if it is to be true and genuine, should depict man living with himself, examining himself constantly, struggling against the emotional impulses which incline him towards evil and ever aspiring to the perfection of his being.

Por consiguiente, la poesía romántica si ha de ser verdadera y genuina, nos ha de pintar al hombre viviendo consigo mismo, examinándose continuamente, luchando con los afectos que lo inclinan al mal y aspirando siempre a la perfección de su ser.[42]

This view is hardly compatible with such representative works as *Don Álvaro* and *El diablo mundo*, and it is not surprising that we presently find Lista distinguishing, this time like Alcalá Galiano, between this old 'historical' romanticism and 'contemporary romanticism,' which, of course, he detested.

Decency and morality trodden underfoot [he thundered] in descriptions of adulterous amours and of villains whom the author attempts to render interesting; furious language; nature, in a word, changed out of all recognition – this is what is now called romanticism.

La decencia y la moral holladas en las descripciones de amores adúlteros y de malvados que se esfuerza el autor en hacer interesantes; el lenguaje furibundo; la naturaleza, en fin, sacada de su quicio, esto es lo que ahora se llama romanticismo.[43]

Lista fully recognized that the literature of any age was and should be 'a faithful picture of its ideas'; what he did not recognize were the new ideas which were beginning to prevail, and he continued to insist that 'contemporary' romanticism was quite out of touch with the times. It has been argued in his justification that what he really had in mind was imported French romantic drama; but when his pupil, Ventura de la Vega, in his speech on entering the Spanish Academy in 1842, delivered another scathing attack on the romantics, it was directed specifically against the Spanish group: 'Their tendencies,' Ventura roundly asserts, 'were to pervert society; their plan of destruction was complete; their shots were aimed both at head and heart, at intelligence and morality'/'*Sus tendencias eran a pervertir la sociedad; su plan de destrucción era completo; los tiros se atestaban a la cabeza y al corazón, a la inteligencia y a la moral.*'[44]

Thus, by the early 1840s, a reaction against romanticism was already well under way, and for another twenty years or more neo-catholic critics struggled to limit the effects of the romantic revolt against established ideas. Their efforts have been carefully studied and analyzed by Professor Eoff in an illuminating article,[45] which after a full review of the evidence sums up the situation as follows:

'A reactionary spirit both in politics and religion comes into evidence in the criticism of the 1840s, but the reaction does not appear to be very pronounced ... This reaction, which is noticeable from 1840 at least, becomes intensified in the 1850s.' During this latter decade, the two most notable contributions to the interpretations of romanticism, such as they were, came from the novelist J. Valera and the critic J. Borao. Valera's article, 'Del romanticismo en España y de Espronceda,'[46] first published in 1854, although bringing out once more Durán's idea that there is no more romantic country than Spain, has the merit of dealing exclusively with 'the romanticism which appeared twenty years ago.' Avoiding any attempt to define it, Valera lists rather superciliously what seemed to him its main characteristics: rejection of neoclassical precepts; admiration for Byron and Scott; use of local colour; preoccupation with the deformed and ugly, with vice and crime, and with unrequited love and despair; emphasis on poetic mission and inspiration; and intolerable verbosity and insincerity.

The main part of Valera's essay, however, is an attack on *El diablo mundo*, the gist of which is that in an age when the collapse of belief made great religious epic poetry impossible, it ought not to be attempted at all. Valera's whole outlook can be summed up in his assertion here that literature should be written to please, not to teach, and in his expansion of this idea when he asks the revealing questions, 'What profit is there in portraying the truth, when the truth is always vile? Would it not be better to lie for the sake of consolation?' With so unworthy an outlook it is hardly surprising that he should attempt to cast a veil over Espronceda's 'bitter truth.' But his essay is useful for the way in which it reveals once more the widespread recognition that involved with the word *romántico* was a threat to settled comfortable beliefs, be they literary, religious, or philosophic.

J. Borao, also writing in the *Revista española de ambos mundos* (II, 1854), dismisses many of the criticisms of romantic literary innovations as exaggerated or of secondary importance and, like the majority of the critics mentioned here, places the emphasis squarely on content. Unfortunately, his discussion of content merely brings us back to the old triad of Christianity, nationalism, and liberty.

The articles of Valera and Borao mark a point of transition in criticism of Spanish romanticism and were followed by a period of declining interest in the subject. Twenty-three years were to pass before another significant contribution to the debate appeared, but with F. M. Tubino's 'Introducción al romanticismo en España,'[47] modern criticism of Spanish romanticism may be said to begin. For the first time the movement was related broadly to its period, and the word *romántico* was now seen to denote a genuine shift of sensibility, nourished by French encyclopedic thought that was 'anti-catholic, anti-latin, and revolutionary in form and content.'

Henceforth, the divergence of attitude about Spanish romanticism mirrored that which was visible beneath the chaos of conflicting statements about European romanticism generally. There is a clear line of continuity from Durán and Borao, through Piñeyro's *El romaticismo en España* (Paris, 1904), which was translated by Peers in 1934, to the latter's own work and his interpretation of Spanish romanticism in terms of freedom, patriotism, Christianity, and medievalism in chapter 7 of his history. This interpretation Courtney Tarr and many other critics broadly supported. Meanwhile, however, Tubino was followed in 1908 by A. Bonilla y San Martín's essay on Espronceda's thought in *La España moderna* (Madrid, año xx, no. 234, June 1908, pp. 69–101), by E. Ospina in his *El romanticismo* (Madrid, 1937), by Casalduero, Cossío, and by del Río, all of whom associate the word *romántico* with the origins of the crisis of belief that is characteristic of our time. Although this view has not wholly displaced the superbly documented and closely argued views of Peers and his followers, it is probably destined to gain adherents until the arrival in Spain of a sociologico-Marxist definition of *romántico*, which – if the present writer reads the signs aright – is already a foreseeable event.

NOTES

1 E. A. Peers, *A History of the Romantic Movement in Spain* i: (Cambridge, 1940), 37 (hereafter cited as *Peers, History*).
2 Cited by W. Brüggemann, 'Apologie der spanischen Kultur ...,' in *Homenaje a Johannes Vincke* (Madrid, 1962–3), ii: 711.
3 Ibid.
4 Ibid.
5 H. Becher, 'Nota histórica sobre el origen de la palabra "romántico," ' *BBMP* xiii (1931): 31 (hereafter cited as *Becher*).
6 The early articles by Böhl von Faber, Mora, and other critics involved in this controversy published in the *Mercurio Gaditano* (Cadiz) in 1814 and later in the *Crónica científica y literaria* (Madrid) and the *Diario Mercantil* (Cadiz) in 1817–20, as well as many of the *folletos* and books arising out of them, are now very difficult of access. They have been carefully studied by C. Pitollet in *La Querelle Calderónienne de J. N. Böhl von Faber et J. J. de Mora* (Paris, 1909) – itself a most inaccessible book, in passing in *Peers, History* i: 115–19, and especially by J. Herrero in the first two chapters if his indispensable *Fernán Caballero: un nuevo planteamento* (Madrid, 1963) (hereafter cited as *Herrero*).
7 Böhl, *Pasatiempo crítico* ii: 78, cited by *Herrero*, p. 108.

8   Böhl, *Donde las dan, las toman*, p. 14; cited by *Herrero*, p. 112.
9   Cited by *Becher*, p. 31.
10 *Becher*, p. 32.
11 Quoted from the reprint of Monteggia's article in *BSS* VIII (1931): 144–9. Cf. A. W. Schlegel's similar statements referred to above, pp. 136 and 137.
12 López Soler, *BSS* VIII: 202.
13 Ibid., p. 198.
14 Ibid., p. 204. For the influence of Böhl on López Soler, see B. J. Dendle, 'Two Sources of López Soler's Articles in *El Europeo*,' *Studies in Romanticism* V (1965): 44–51. Cf. also E. A. Peers, 'Some Spanish Conceptions of Romanticism,' *MLR* XVI (1921): 281–96, M. J. Cattaneo, 'Gli esordi del romanticismo in Ispagna e *El Europeo*,' *Tre studi sulla cultura spagnola* (Milano-Varese, 1967), 75–137, and E. Caldera, *Primi manifesti del romanticismo spagnolo* (Pisa, 1962).
15 Agustín Durán, *Discurso sobre el influjo que ha tenido la crítica moderna en la decadencia del teatro antiguo español, y sobre el modo con que debe ser considerado para juzgar convenientemente de su mérito peculiar* (Madrid, 1828); reprinted in *Memorias de la Academia Española* II (Madrid, 1870): 282–318.
16 V. Llorens Castillo, *Liberales y Románticos* (Mexico, 1954), p. 354.
17 A. del Río, 'Present Trends in the Conception and Criticism of Spanish Romanticism,' *RR* XXXIX (1948): 229–48 (hereafter cited as *Río*).
18 *Peers, History* I: 37; F. Courtney Tarr, 'Romanticism in Spain and Spanish Romanticism,' *BSS* XVI (1939): 313–37, and 'Romanticism in Spain,' *PMLA* LV (1940): 35–46. Cf. also H. Díaz-Plaja, *Introducción al estudio del romanticismo español* (Madrid, 1936), J. García Mercadal, *Historia del romanticismo en España* (Barcelona, 1943), and the series of articles by F. Caravaca, 'Romanticismo y románticos españoles,' in *Langues Neolatines* LI–LIII, LV–LVII, LIX–LX (1957–66).
19 Reprinted in Angel de Saavedra, Duque de Rivas, *Obras Completas* II (Madrid, 1854).
20 Cited by Peers, 'Some Spanish Concepts of Romanticism,' *MLR* XVI (1921): 292.
21 Ibid., p. 293.
22 Cf. A. Lista, 'Del Romanticismo,' *La Estrella* (25 January 1834), his later essays in *Ensayos literarios y críticos* (Seville, 1844), J. C. J. Metford's 'Alberto Lista and the Romantic Movement in Spain' in *Liverpool Studies in Spanish Romanticism*, ed. E. A. Peers (Liverpool, 1940), I: 19–43, and H. Juretschke, *Vida, obra y pensamiento de A. Lista* (Madrid, 1951).
23 *Juretschke, Origen doctrinal*, p. 30.
24 J. Casalduero, *Forma y visión del Diablo Mundo* (Madrid, 1951). D. L. Shaw, 'Towards the Understanding of Spanish Romanticism,' *MLR* LVIII (1963): 190–5, and 'The Anti-Romantic Reaction in Spain,' *MLR* LXIII (1968): 606–11.
25 Morse Peckham, 'Towards a Theory of Romanticism,' *PMLA* LXVI (1951): 5–23. A. O. Lovejoy, 'The Meaning of Romanticism for the Historian of Ideas,' *JHI* II (1941): 257–78.
26 See, e.g., M. Bowra, *The Romantic Imagination* (London, 1950), especially pp. 271 *ff.*; E. N. Anderson, 'German Romanticism as an Ideology of Crisis,' *JHI* II (1941): 301–18; F. L. Saulnier, *La Littérature du siècle romantique* (Paris, 1948), especially pp. 40 *ff.*, and, in general, R. Wellek, 'The Concept of Romanticism in Literary History,' in Wellek, *Concepts of Criticism* (New Haven [1963]), pp. 128–98.
27 H. N. Fairchild, in 'Romanticism: A Symposium,' *PMLA* LV (1940): 22.
28 *Río*, p. 239.
29 *Peers, History* II: 281.
30 J. Aynard, 'Comment définir le romantisme,' *RLC* V (1925): 650 and 652.
31 A. Wayne Wicherly, 'Melancholy in German Literature,' *PQ* XXX (1951): 186–93.

32 N. Gonzáles Ruiz, *El Duque de Rivas o la fuerza del sino* (Madrid, 1944), p. 13.
33 Espronceda, 'Poesía,' *El Siglo* (24 January 1834).
34 Larra, *Artículos completos* (Madrid, 1961), p. 983.
35 Donoso Cortés, '*Alfredo* de J. F. Pacheco,' *Obras completas* (Madrid, 1956), I: 173.
36 Ibid., I: 407
37 Ibid., I: 385.
38 See *Peers, History* II: 9.
39 Balmes, *Cartas a un escéptico en materia de religión.* Carta primera (Buenos Aires, 1948), p. 20.
40 Balmes, *El criterio* (Buenos Aires, 1946), ch. 19, sect. iii, p. 243.
41 Alberto Lista, *Ensayos literarios y críticos* II (Seville, 1844); 34.
42 Alberto Lista, 'Del Romanticismo,' *La Estrella* (Madrid, 25 January 1834).
43 Ibid.
44 Ventura de la Vega, *Memorias de la Academia Española*, año I (Madrid, 1870), II: 12.
45 S. H. Eoff, 'The Spanish Novel of Ideas: Critical Opinion,' *PMLA* LV (1940): 531-58.
46 Valera, 'Del romanticismo en España y de Espronceda,' *Obras completas* II (Madrid, 1949): 7-19.
47 F. M. Tubino, 'Introducción al romanticismo en España,' *Revista contemporánea* VII (Madrid, 1877): 77-98 and 184-98.

P. M. MITCHELL

Scandinavia /
Romantisk – Romantik –
Romantiker

I

In 1868 Denmark's great middle-class novelist of the nineteenth century, Meir Goldschmidt (who is known abroad primarily as an antagonist of Søren Kierkegaard) drafted a letter to the perceptive young Danish critic Clemens Petersen which contains the following remarks:

What do you understand by romanticism? You once said to me that I was the only romantic poet who had appeared in Denmark since Oehlenschläger. You added that there was something petit bourgeois about the Danish people and their literature and that even Heiberg was petit bourgeois. I thought therefore that you were trying to pay me a compliment? but now I learn that you elsewhere have spoken with ridicule about romanticism, and in 'Fædrelandet' [a newspaper] you have also intimated that there is something undependable about it. What do you understand by romanticism and why do you call me a romantic?

Hvad forstaaer De ved Romantik? De sagde engang til mig, at jeg var den eneste romantiske Digter, der havde viist sig i Danmark siden Oehlenschläger. De tilføiede, at der var noget Spidsborgerligt ved det danske Folk og dets Poesi, og selv Heiberg var spidsborgerlig. Jeg troede altsaa, at De havde villet sige mig en Compliment; men saa erfarer jeg, at De andensteds har udtalt Dem med Haan om Romantiken, og i 'Fædrelandet' har De ogsaa hentydet til, at det er noget Upaalideligt. Hvad forstaaer De da ved Romantik og hvorfor kalder De mig Romantiker?[1]

The querulousness and uncertainty in Goldschmidt's mind is exemplary of the inexactness of the term *Romantik* from the time it was first widely used in Scandinavia at the beginning of the nineteenth century until the present day. We should like to have Clemens Petersen's reply to Goldschmidt's enquiry, but we do not even know for sure that Petersen received the letter.

The currency that the noun *Romantik* and the adjective *romantisk* gained in Scandinavia in the early nineteenth century is primarily a reflex of the importance of the same words in Germany from the last decade of the eighteenth century on. The origins of a traditionally 'romantic' literature in Scandinavia are regularly assumed to be sought at least in part in the writings of Friedrich and August Wilhelm Schlegel and a few other figures of the new literary movement in Germany around 1800. Despite the association of Shakespeare with literature identified as 'romantic,' there seems to have been little awareness of England's role in projecting the term *romantic* into aesthetic criticism.

The word *romantisk* is rare in the Scandinavian languages prior to 1800. The Norwegian poet, Edvard Storm, spoke of a 'romantic pen'/'romantisk Pen' in his *Samlede Digte* ('Poems,' Copenhagen, 1785, p. 59). Although a definition of the term even in context is guesswork, the associations are with natural beauty:

> Will the power of evil be broken and virtue be strengthened
> When, though guided by truth, a romantic pen describes
> The mound where I lie, the reed-grown island
> Which swims before my eyes in the mirror-smooth lake?

> *Mon Lastens Vælde brudt, og Dydens styrket bliver*
> *Naar (skiønt af Sandhed ført) romantisk Pen beskriver*
> *Den Høi jeg hviler paa, den sivbegroede Øe*
> *Som svømmer for mit Syn i spejleblanke Søe?*

Still earlier, the Danish naturalist, O. F. Müller, in describing a journey in Norway (*Reise igiennem Ovre Tillemarken*, Copenhagen, 1778, p. 78) commented that Telemark was 'seen romantically'/ '*bliver set romantisk*'. There are other examples of the term being applied to landscapes, notably by Friedrich Sneedorff who, writing from Switzerland in 1791, found the view from an inn in Zurich 'charmingly romantic'/'*fortryllende romantisk.*' His subsequent description of the landscape suggests certain connotations for the word *romantisk*:

The river Limmat flows down below and washes against the house; from here the view extends over Zurich and the Lake of Zurich to the snow-covered Alps; indeed, here in Switzerland there is endless life in nature, but I find less of it among the people than I had expected.

Floden Linmat [sic] *flyder neden under, og beskyller Huset; fra det gaaer Udsigten over Zürich og Zürchs Søe, hen til de sneebedækkede Alper; ja her er uendelig meget Liv i Naturen i Schweitz, men jeg finder mindre deraf hos Menneskene end jeg havde troet.*[2]

In the spirit of Albrecht von Haller, Sneedorff seems here to subsume the idyllic and the grandeur of nature under the term *romantisk*.

In G. A. Silfverstolpe's periodical, *Literatur-Tidning* (Uppsala, 1796), the following passage occurs in a review:

In boldly surprising juxtaposition and with great contrasts, marvelous, dreadful, and even frightening scenes unite in the romantic landscape with lively ones to become an harmonious whole ...

I det romantiska landskapet förena sig underbara, rysliga, och äfven förskräckliga scener med ljufva och likande i en dristig öfverraskende sammanställning, under starka afbrott, til en harmonisk totalbild ... (p. 367).

Here as elsewhere there is a double connotation – grandeur and harmony.

There are many examples of this use of the word during the nineteenth century. In discussing a book on the Scottish highlands, for example, a reviewer in *Swensk Literatur-Tidning* in 1819 mentioned 'romantic valleys in which thundering mountain streams fling themselves to form waterfalls of the most exquisite beauty in the world' / '*romantiska dålder, i hwilka dånande bergströmmar kasta sig og bilda wattenfall af den utmärktaste skönhet i werlden ...*' (no. 6, col. 97).

Jumping ahead three decades, we find one of Meir Goldschmidt's correspondents, Charlotte Munch, using the phrase 'no romantic hut, for it does not lie in a woods or by a lake but on a rather bald hill ...' / '*ingen romantisk Hytte, thi den ligger ikke i en Skov, eller ved en Søe, men paa en temmelig bar Bakke ...*'[3]

Romantisk seems scarcely to have been employed in Sweden prior to its acceptance in Denmark and Norway. To be sure, the word was used several times in 1784 by Thomas Thorild in such phrases as '*romantisk Kärlekshistorie*' ('romantic love-story') in his *Lyckan*, 1784. The combination of words suggests the connotations of *romantisk* in this and similar instances. In a letter written from Scarborough four years later, Thorild employed the word again.

but now in a broader context: 'I had to laugh at this place, for everything is strange here; romantic, fantastic, original, antique in ruins ... *ˡ'Jag måste le åt detta ställe, så är all ting besynnerligt här; romantiskt, fantastiskt, originalt, antikt i ruiner ...'*⁴ We note, however, that Thorild was engaged in translating works from the English at the time; his isolated use of *romantisk* is explained by his English orientation.

In an essay on the terms *romanesk, romantisk,* and *romantik* in Swedish until the year 1810 (written prior to the publication of volume XXI of the historical *Ordbog över svenska språket*), Gunnar Reinhard demonstrated that around 1800 *romantisk* generally meant picturesque; he quotes, for example, from the *Journal för swensk literatur* II (Stockholm, 1798): 255, 'a romantic countryside through which a swift-running river [flows]'*/'en romantisk landsbyggd, genom hvilken en strid ström ...'*⁵ Reinhard points out that the term *romanesk* (which does not appear in the oldest Swedish dictionaries) was used as early as 1778 with the meaning 'öfverdriven' ('exaggerated'), 'romanaktig' ('as in a novel, novelistic'), and is a form parallel to *romantisk.*

Ordbog över svenska språket records the use of *romanesk* clearly in the sense of 'novelistic'; 'En...romanesque död' ('a novelistic death') from *Swenska Mercurius* in 1764 (p. 581) – and even a recent example from the year 1929. There is a still earlier record of the word – from 1754 – but in a slightly different sense: 'all our cavalier [*Romanesque*] ideas about helping the Academy to some glory'*/'alla våra Romanesque idéer om Academiens uphjelpande til någon glans'* – and the dictionary lists a recent example from the year 1950. Incidentally, Reinhard notes that 'romantisk' was defined as 'romantisch, romanenmäßig, romanenhaft' in Carl Heinrich's *Svenskt och Tysk Lexikon,* 1814.

Swedish used *romanesk* and *romansk* interchangeably, whereas Danish and Norwegian had only the form *romansk.* Early in the eighteenth century, *romansk/romanesk* suggested the extravagances of the romance or the novel. Thus, in the comedy, *Ulysses von Ithacia* (1725), the Dano-Norwegian historian and playwright, Ludvig Holberg, lets one of his characters say, with regard to the suicide which she had threatened, 'When I reflect, it does seem rather novelistic [*romansk*]'*/'Naar jeg ogsaa betænker mig, saa lader det noget romansk'* (act IV, scene 14). Twenty years later, in the first volume of his *Heltinde-Historier* (1745), p. 346, he describes a princess who 'had been rather novelistic [*romansk*] and had wanted to make love after the fashion that is found in novels, in the reading of which she was well versed'/'*haver været noget Romansk og haver villet giøre Amour efter den Plan, som findes i Romaner, udi hvis Læsning hun haver været verseret.*' The association of *romansk* with *amour* occurs again in the title of F. C. Hjort's novel of the year 1782: *Gunders mærkværdige Reise ... til Amors Rige. En romansk Drøm.* Whether the subtitle should be translated as 'a novelistic dream' is a matter of conjecture.

The first time that both Reinhard and the editors of *Ordbok över svenska språket* record the noun *romantik* is striking in its implications. P. D. Atterbom – traditionally one of the leading poets identified as 'romantic' by Scandinavian literary historians – writes in a letter dated 29 February 1808 that he is looking forward to living

romantically ... Then I shall read Homer and the erotic singers of Rome; there I shall be with Tieck's *Romantische Dichtungen* in hand ... There my mother, Romanticism, will take me up in her motherly arms again for a filial kiss.

romantiskt ... Der skall jag läsa Homeros och Romas erotiska sångare; der skall jag med Tiecks Romantische Dichtungen *i handen ... Der skall min moder, Romantiken, åter till en sonlig kyss lyfta mig i sina moderliga armar ...*[6]

The sporadic occurrence of the term *romantisk* before about 1812 attests that the word was not widely used in the Scandinavian languages and was not an integral part of the living vocabulary. The situation changed rather rapidly by about 1812, however, as the use of *romantisk* and *Romantik* multiplied in direct proportion to the awareness of a new German literature that was often identified as *romantisch*, and which used the term in a vigorous and positive – if not a particularly lucid and restrictive – manner.

When in 1802–3 the Norwegian-born Henrik Steffens brought the gospel of the new German literature and philosophy with him to Copenhagen and preached it to receptive and enthusiastic audiences, the word *romantisk* was essential to his vocabulary.

The subsequent popularity of the word in Scandinavia, as well as an awareness of the new German literary school, can be attributed in no small part to Steffens' impact on young critical and creative minds. From the very start, Steffens had espoused the dialectical contrast, 'classical *vs* romantic,' a phrase which has clung tenaciously to life in Scandinavia as elsewhere – and is an insuperable oversimplification even today. Steffens had declared: 'The romantic signifies the life, poetry, and art of that time [i.e., during Catholic Christianity] and also gives us a clear contrast to the classical'/'*Det*

Romantiske betegner den Tids Liv, dens Poesie og dens Kunst og giver os tillige tydelig nok Modsætningen mod det antike.[7] There are echoes everywhere of the 'classical-romantic' phrase in Steffens' sense despite Atterbom's association of the romantic with the literature of classical Rome in the quotation above.

Literature that was *romantisk* was for early nineteenth-century Scandinavia often either medieval (and not modern) or a reworking of medieval subject matter. This attitude is clearly implied in 1802 in the title of a work by one Salomon Soldin published in Copenhagen: *Marsk Stig, et romantisk Skilderi af det 13de Aarhundrede* ('M.S., a romantic portrayal of the thirteenth century'). The work was *romantisk* because it dealt with the thirteenth century. When Esaias Tegnér said in his lectures on poetics that 'The flowers of modern poetry grow in romantic soil ...'/'*Den nyare poesiens blomma växer på romantisk grund ...*'[8] he meant in medieval literature – which, he went on to remark, in turn needed to be schooled (*uppdragas*) in Greek culture. There is an interesting passage in a letter written about three years later by Tegnér to the Swedish historian, Erik Gustaf Geijer, in which Tegnér calls it absurd 'to want to introduce Greek, romantic, Scandinavian, or whichever obsolete forms into poetry'/'*... att vilja införa Grekiska, romantiska, Nordiska eller hvad föråldrade former som helst i Poësien ...*'[9] Could not one equally well defend writing verse in 'Greek, *lingua romana*, or Gothic ...' he asks, in objecting to the revival of 'cast-off forms.'

The references to medieval or Renaissance literature as *romantisk* are legion. The Swedish periodical, *Polyfem*, for example, in a note about the German Parnassus, stated (rather ambiguously) that the brothers Schlegel had agitated for a popular knowledge of 'the true poetry of antiquity or romanticism'/'*... Antikens eller Romantikens sanna poesi ...*';[10] and S. Meisling, writing in the Danish periodical, *Athene* (I, 1813, p. 279), mentioned the 'Italian romantic epopees' of Pulci, Boiardo, Ariosto, Cieco, and Tasso. In 1814 one could read in *Swensk Literatur-Tidning* formulations such as, 'There was a time, a chivalric, romantic time ...'; 'three great eras: the antique, the romantic, and the modern'; and – in discussing Goethe – 'He has employed ... eternal patterns, which the deep feeling and endless associations of the romantic era fixed in classical regularity.'

Det gafs en tid, en ridderlig, romantisk tid ... (col. 64).

Trenne werldsåldrar: den antika, *den* romantiska *och den* moderna (col. 240).

Han har anwändt ... ewiga mönster, der den romantiska tidens djupa känsla och

oändliga syftning fixerat sig i organisationer af en clasisk regelbundenhet ...
(col. 253).

In column 607 of *Swensk Literatur-Tidning* there is reference to A. S.
Vedel's edition of 'a hundred old romantic national songs' / *'hundra
stycken gamla romantiska nationalsånger.'* The Danish critic, Christian
Molbech, was specifically to label the late medieval Danish ballads
as 'romantic folksongs' / *'de romantiske Folkeviser'*[11] some years later. A
review in *Swensk Literatur-Tidning* in 1819 identifies the foremost
products of 'the art of romanticism, such as the lay of the Nibelungen...' / *'Romantikens konst, såsom Niebelungerqwädet ...'* (Col. 10), which
are then contrasted with *Moderniteten.* After mentioning examples of
Gothic architecture as 'products of romanticism,' the reviewer
identifies 'the perfectly romantic' / *'det rent fulländada Romantiska,' viz.*
works by 'Correggio, Bramante, Raphael ...' In another review two
years later, the same Swedish periodical defined *det romantiska
Tidehwarfwet* ('the romantic era') as Europe's flowering.[12]

P. L. Møller, one of Denmark's leading critics, writing in 1840,
spoke of 'a difference between the romantic Middle Ages and our
time ...' / *'En Forskjel mellem den romantiske Middelalder og vor Tid ...'*[13]
In N. M. Petersen's history of Danish literature – the standard work
on the subject until well into the second half of the nineteenth century – the term *romantisk* was employed sparingly and then only for
certain works of medieval literature; in the second edition of N. M.
Petersen's work, edited by C. E. Seeler in 1867, one finds only these
categories under *romantisk*: '*Romantiske Krönikker og rimede Æventyr:
Karl Magnus, Griseldis, Jan Præst, Eufemiaviserna, Laurins Krönikker ...'*
(1: 106) and '*Episk-romantiske Digtninger: Flores og Blanseflor; Holger
Danske; Personober'* (1: 209). There is otherwise no application or
descriptive explanation of the word *romantisk.*

Not all critics applied *romantisk* only to medieval literature or
the literature which took its inspiration from the Middle Ages. The
'romantic' was for them fundamentally the non-classical. A footnote in volume II of the Swedish journal, *Polyfem*, in 1810, for
example, stated that 'the poetry which is called modern is the same
as the romantic' / *'den egentligen så kallade moderna poesien, som är den-
samme som den romantiska.'*[14] A more emphatic view, expressed by the
Swedish critic C. A .Ehrenswärd, was reported in *Swensk Literatur-
Tidning* in 1814: 'He views classical antiquity and romanticism as
phenomena of the two end-points of a straight line. / *'Han betraktar
Antiken och Romantiken såsom phenomener af de twenne polerna i den absoluta*

enhets-linien ...'[15] This sort of argument was spun out upon a hundred verbal wheels.

The Swedish journal, *Iduna*, which had scarcely made use of the term *romantisk* since publication began in 1811, was in 1817 to use the 'classical-romantic' antithesis with broad connotations:

... the contrast between centuries ... the struggle between republicanism and feudalism ... everywhere ... recognizable ... under various names, such as the contrast between the ancient and the modern, the classical and the romantic, the southern and the northern.

motsatsen emellan århundraden ... striden mellan Republikanism och Feudalism ... öfwerallt ... kännbar ... under åtskilliga namn, såsom motsatsen emellan det Antika och Moderna, det Klassiska och Romantiska, det Sydlige och Nordliga (p. 101).

Swensk Literatur-Tidning commented on the popularity of the contrast between 'classical' and 'romantic' in 1820:

Mme de Staël-Holstein, in her brilliant book about Germany, rather carelessly chose the epithet *classical* as a general term for the culture of antiquity in contrast to that of modern Europe, or that which she and her friends call the romantic.

Fru Stael-Holstein, i sin genialiska bok öfwer Tyskland, mindre wälbetänkt walde epithetet classisk *till allmän slägtbenämning för den antika witterhäten i motsats till den nyare Europas, eller den af henne och hennes wänner såkallade romantiska* (no. 52, col. 821).

In 1822 the Swedish poet, Erik Johan Stagnelius, formulated his opinion using the 'classical-romantic' contrast (in a posthumously published essay) as follows:

The classical tragedy directs its efforts to create an effect, to move – not persons but a people; quite the contrary, the romantic tragedy ... has to do only with individual interests ...

Den klassiska tragedien riktar sitt bemödande att göra effekt, att röra, icke åt personer, utan åt ett folk; tvärtom den romantiska ... endast har att göra med individuella intressen ...[16]

Complementary to this position is a remark about Stagnelius made by the Danish critic, Christian Molbech, in 1827 in *Nordisk Tidsskrift for Historie, Literatur og Kunst I* to the effect that 'with a classical training in language, he was in spirit a romantic' / '... *med en classisk Dannelse i Sproget, var han i Aanden Romantiker*.'[17]

When Esaias Tegnér, traditionally the foremost romantic in Swedish literature, lectured in 1822-4 'om det Romantiska i Grekiska Poesien' ('On the Romantic in Greek Poetry'), he explained,

The great difference, which one easily discovers, between the old and modern literature has in recent times caused both these kinds of poetry to be viewed as opposed to one another and consequently for all literature to be divided into two main categories, ancient and romantic. This difference has been expressed in various ways. Objective and subjective literature, plastic and musical, naïve and sentimental, classical and modern, ancient and romantic, are all more or less fitting terms to express substantially the same idea.

Den stora skiljaktighet som man lätteligen upptäcker mellan den gamla och moderna Poësien har i sednare tider gifvit anledning att betrakta dessa begge skaldearter såsom hvarandra motsatta, och till följe derutaf indela all poësie i tvenne hufvudarter, antik och romantisk. Man har på mångfaldigt sätt uttryckt denna skiljaktighet. Objectif och subjectif poësie, plastisk och musikalisk, naif och sentimental, klassisk och modern, antik och romantisk, äro allt mer eller mindre passande benämninger för att uttrycka väsendtligen samma begrepp.[18]

Unlike several of the critics already quoted, Tegnér declared that 'Romantiska Poesien' should not be equated with 'den moderna,' since the former has

much that suggests the qualities which characterize the classical ... On the other hand, however, features are found not only in Roman but even in Greek poetry itself which, according to general usage, must be called romantic.

mycket som påminner om de egenheter hvilka caracterisera den antika ... På andra sidan åter förekomma icke blott i Romerska utan äfven i sjelfva Grekiska Poësien drag som efter allmänna språkbruket måsta kallas romantiska.[19]

In an unsystematic manner he gratuitously provided several definitions, or attempts at definition: The romantic, he wrote, must be but a modification of the beautiful. 'Were it otherwise, there could not be a romantic literature' / '*Vore det annorlunda så kunde det ej gifvas en Romantisk poësie*,'[20] he added, rather enigmatically. Furthermore,

The romantic ... is, rather, beauty for the imagination which exists in complexity and to whose adventurous combinations it gives freer play.

Precisely through this striving for the unlimited and the infinite the romantic is related to and often united with the sublime ...

On the other hand, the romantic is similar to the marvelous ...

Thus precisely romanticism degenerates into the fantastic and marvelous through the misuse of freedom.

det romantiska ... är snarare en skönhet för phantasien som lefver i det mångfaldiga och för hvars äfventyrliga sammanställningar det öppnar ett friare spelrum.[21]

Just genom detta sträfvande till det obegränsade och oändliga är äfven det romantiska beslägtadt och ofta förenadt med det sublima ...[22]

På en annan sida åter är det romantiska likartadt med det underbara ...[23]

... så urartar äfven det romantiska genom frihetens missbruk till det phantastiska och vidunderliga.[24]

By 1827, Johan Ludvig Heiberg – who was to become the high priest of a new literary school in Denmark – could write in a review of Esaias Tegnér's *Frithiofs Saga*:

... romantic poetry is speculative and could therefore be called the poetry of the spirit, for it is to classical poetry as the spirit is to nature ...

'*Endelig er den romantiske Poesie speculativ, og kunde derfor kaldes Aandens Poesie, thi den forholder sig til den classiske som Aanden til Naturen ...*'[25]

Moreover, Heiberg had an imaginative new explanation for the contrast:

The new romantic style is to the old classical style as the interpretation of the sacrament at the altar by the Lutheran church is to that by the Reformed church. The former says, '*This is*'; the latter says, '*This means.*'

Den nye romantiske Stiil forholder sig til den gamle classiske ganske som den lutherske Kirkes Formular ved Alterens Sacrament forholder sig til den reformeertes: Den første siger: 'Dette er'; den anden siger: 'Dette betyder.'[26]

As early as 1820 the *Swensk Literatur-Tidning* had questioned the validity of the black-and-white distinction between the 'classical and the romantic' and had deplored the

incredible blindness, not to see that in general the Greeks and Romans had many characteristics of what in later times has been called romantic and sentimental and has been assumed to belong exclusively to *us* – and similarly not to observe how frequently idealistic and romantic literature evinces realistic naïveté and a happy enjoyment of nature. Even the

Iliad can furnish us with a goodly store of sentimental and romantic passages ...

utomordentlig blindhet, att icke i allmänhet hos Grekerne och Romarne urskonja de många förekommande drag af hwad man i senare tider under namn af Romantiskt och Sentimentalt welat göra till wår *uteslutande tillhörighet, som att icke finna huru ofta den idealistiska och romantiska poesien yppar den realistiskas naivetet och glada naturbehag. Redan Iliaden lemnar oβ ett godt förråd på sentimentala och romantiska ställen* ... (col. 827).

The 'classical-romantic' dialectic nevertheless remained in constant use. In 1841, P. L. Møller declared that Tegnér himself embodied a disharmonic struggle between classical and romantic elements 'which appear in his later poems, especially in "Frithiof"' / '*som fremtræder i hans senere Digte især i "Frithiof."* '[27] In the same year Møller reviewed the first part of Frederik Paludan-Müller's monumental Danish epic, *Adam Homo*, and concluded that it expressed 'the temporal and eternal contrast between sensual and spiritual love, as a symbolic expression of the classical and the romantic principles of life ...' / '*den timelige og evige Modsætning imellem den sandselige og aandelige Kjærlighed, som symbolsk Udtryk for det klassiske og det romantiske Livs-Princip* ...'[28] Møller's negative attitude toward Paludan-Müller's shorter epic, *Tithon*, was a corollary of his observation that this writer had incorporated 'both classical and romantic forms in one and the same poem, or a classical idea and a romantic treatment ...' / '*saavel antike som romantiske Former i eet og samme Digt, eller en antik Idee og romantisk Behandling* ...'[29] He reiterated one of Tegnér's arguments when he complained that 'the poem thus becomes neither classic, romantic, nor modern, since it wants to be something of all three genres' / '*Digtet bliver saaledes hverken antikt, romantisk eller modernt, fordi det vilde være noget af alle tre Genrer.*'[30]

The identification of the concept *romantisk* with the Middle Ages or with modernity represents two of several usages. The word had begun to be more frequently employed after the first decade of the nineteenth century, but without much precision and without a focus. Around the year 1815 a vague need to define the term was already widely felt – and literary publications of the time soon contained many attempts, not a few of which seem aggressively conceived, to limit the meaning of *romantisk*.

In *Swensk Literatur-Tidning* in 1813 there is found a definition of the novel which accords with the older view that *romantisk* pertains in the first instance to the *roman*, i.e., the novel; this explanation attests the awareness of (or even dependency on) German critical thought regarding the term: 'A novel is in the true sense of the word a romantic book or the presentation of a romantic life'/'*En Roman i ordets äkta mening, är en romantisk bok, eller främstillningen af ett romantisk lif.*'[31] To the query, what is a romantic life, the reviewer answered, paraphrasing Jean Paul's *Vorschule der Ästhetik* (1. Abt., 5. Programm), that

Romantic is the inward, fresh and almost unconscious striving for the infinitely highest in religion, in courage, in love: in a word, in everything noble and great.

Romantisk är det innerliga friska och nästan omedwetna sträfwandet efter det oändligen högsta i religion, i tapperhet, i kärlek, med ett ord: i allt ädelt och stort.[32]

The reviewer continued that the difference between the romantic and the sentimental had yet to be defined and noted that the sentimental was 'nothing but a sickly longing, a pointless and destructive self-contemplation'/'*intet annat än en sjuklig längtan, en orkeslös och sig förtärande sjelf-contemplation*'(col. 355). When Adam and Eve were in paradise, said the reviewer, their condition was romantic; thereafter, it was sentimental.

Oehlenschläger, traditionally identified as the great romantic of Danish literature, turned the matter of a definition over in his own mind in 1813; in writing about Johannes Ewald in the periodical *Athene*, he made a statement which is worth recording because of its diffuseness, but also because of its national orientation:

... the romantic combines more than strength, amiability, and that which is heathen, the worldly and the heavenly, and is therefore the more beautiful territory of poetry. Our entire history is associated with this poetry ...

... det Romantiske forener meer end det Hedenske, Kraft og Elskværdighed, det Jordiske og Himmelske; og er derfor Poesiens skjønnere Grund. Hele vor Historie forbinder sig med denne Poesie ...[33]

The romantic was for Oehlenschläger not merely medieval, then, but an element of the past that was an integral part of the national heritage.

The Swedish writer, Fredric Cederborgh, let the main character of his novel, *Ottar Trallings Lefnads-Målning* (1814), discuss 'romantic' art, which he felt revealed its realism in 'the plasticity of modern literature' and in 'Romanticism's principle of the picturesque,' and which possessed 'absolute idealism'/'*... moderna Poesiens plastik ... Romantikens pittoreska princip ...*'[34] His association of realism as well as the picturesque principle and absolute idealism with 'romanticism' suggests that the concept he was trying to delineate must have been very unclear in his own mind, although one should perhaps add that the words 'realism,' 'picturesque,' and 'idealism' may have had rather different connotations for him than they have for us today. In any case, he gives no definition capable of being applied effectively as a literary criterion.

Very different is another Swedish definition from the same year (1814) in a review of L. Hammersköld's *Poetiske Studier* in the *Swensk Literatur-Tidning*, to the effect that 'the character of true romantic poetry does not lie in something sick, unclear, and confused, but in the energetic and clear symbolization of conscious perfect harmony'/'... *den* sant *romantiska poesiens charakter icke ligger i det sjuka, töckniga och förwirrade, utan i energisk och ljus symbolisering af medwetandets fulländade harmoni*' (col. 168).

The longing for harmony was expressed many times from the beginning of the century onward, and the new literature generated a hope that it might itself incorporate an ideal of harmony. In a letter to Erik Gustaf Geijer on 10 June 1813, Tegnér had asked,

Is not all our modern poetry from Dante down to Schiller an angel in mourning, a long sigh over the lost pleasure of life? Harmony between nature and men has once and for all been done away with because of the direction our education has taken.

Är icke all vår moderna Poësie, ifrån Dante ner till Schiller, en sorgklädd Engel, en lång suck öfver lifvets förlorade glädje? Harmonien mellan natur och menniska är nu en gång för alla genom hela riktningen af vår bildning upphäfven.[35]

While a reviewer in *Swensk Literatur-Tidning* in 1816 (col. 14) could speak of '*romantiska enkelhet*' ('romantic simplicity') and Christian Molbech, writing in the Danish journal, *Athene*, in 1817, saw fit to quote A. W. Schlegel that 'everything that the art of poetry is able to do unites in a romantic whole'/'*Alt, hvad Digtekonsten er i Stand til at udrette, samler sig til et romantisk Heelt,*'[36] Molbech himself in the same year complained in a review of Søetoft's *Romantiske Digte* of 'the disharmony which the romantic adaption brought forth'/'... *den Disharmonie, som den romantiske Bearbeidelse frembragte* ...'[37] Harmony, then, was desirable; but the 'romantic' might either augment or diminish it.

A Danish critic, Axel Garde, has remarked pointedly that

in the history of Danish romanticism there are two men who perhaps most intensely recreate the temper of romantic feeling, the natural scientist, Hans Christian Ørsted, and the poet, Schack Staffeldt – however different the two were from each other, antitheses to each other, the one perfecting the harmony in which he lived, the other lonely and despairing, always seeking a harmony which he never found.

I den danske Romantiks Historie er der to Mænd, der maaske inderligst genskaber den romantiske Følelses Sindelag, Naturforskeren H. C. Ørsted og Digteren Schack Staffeldt, hvor forskellige de saa var, hinandens Modpoler, den ene fuldendende den Harmoni han levede i, den anden ensom og fortvivlet, altid søgende en Harmoni, han aldrig fandt.[38]

Molbech found that the admixture of 'romantic mysticism with Scandinavian subjects' in Søetoft was 'against nature'/'*Men denne Indblanding af en romantisk Mysticisme i nordiske Emner er imod Naturen*'[39] and warned that 'the fantastic and ... even the significant and symbolic' should not be confused with 'the purely romantic'/ '*Man vogte sig overalt vel for at sammenblande det Phantasiefulde og Kiærlige, ja selv det Betydningsfulde og Symboliske med det reen romantiske.*'[40] In the same year – 1817 – however, Johan Ludvig Heiberg equated the symbolic and the romantic in his dissertation on Calderón. A decade later, he discussed Tegnérs' *Frithiofs Saga* as symbolic in the sense of romantic. The association of the symbolic and the romantic was continued to be made occasionally, thus by the Dane, Vilhelm Andersen, in his *Bacchustoget i Norden* ('Bacchus' Procession in Scandinavia,' Copenhagen, 1904) and by the Swede, Oscar Levertin, in his review of Andersen's book.[41]

Also in 1817, Molbech contrasted everyday life with that of 'a higher romantic sphere'/'... *Hverdagslivet, eller en høiere, romantisk Sphære* ...'[42] and found proof in the Danish folk tales that romantic imagination had Scandinavia as its home/'*Den vil være et Beviis mere for, at Norden er det egentlige Hiem for slige den romantiske Phantasies og den grublende Eftertankes Frembringelser* ...'[43] Molbech took considerable pains to describe the history and meaning of the term *romantisk* in his – negatively critical – review of Søetoft's *Romantiske Digte*:

By romantic literature [he wrote], we understand all that literature that was fostered in the romantic age, when chivalry, great political unrest, the Christian religion, and the dogma of the church and of scholasticism developed their own spirit in history ... Romantic poems are therefore now written either in an attempt to capture the spirit and style in which those [of the Middle Ages] were written ... or insofar as our time rests upon that romantic [age] ... But essentially all poems become equally romantic ....

... forstaae vi derimod ved romantisk Poesie, al den Poesie, som fostredes i den romantiske Tidsalder, da Ridderlivet, de store politiske Giæringer, den christelige Religion og Kirkens og Scholastikens Lærdomme udviklede en egen Aand i Historien ... Romantiske Digte skrives derfor nu enten som Forsøg i den Aand og Stiil, hvori hine digtedes ... eller ogsaa forsaavidt som vor nuværende Tid hviler paa hiin romantiske ... Men da blive alle Digte i det Væsentlige lige romantiske.[44]

Four further definitive statements, two each from the years 1815 and 1816, are worth citing here, in order to accentuate the lack of agreement among critics regarding the denotations of *romantisk* at that time. In an article about the Danish poet and novelist, B. S. Ingemann, Peder Hjort stated that imagination and feeling evoked the incomprehensible – and just therein lay 'the romantic' / *'Phantasie og Følelse kalder det [det Ubegribelige] blot frem, og deri ligger just det romantiske.'*[45] In *Swensk Literatur-Tidning*, the reviewer of a novel entitled *Aurora, eller den Norrska Flickan* (I-II, 1815), applauded the author of *Aurora* for wanting to create something 'romantic,' but declared:

The romantic does not become romantic in that one accidentally disengages one's self from the everyday, but by creating a more beautiful world, more noble conditions and deeds than does common and practical life.

... det Romantiska blir icke derigenom Romantiskt, att man på winst och förlust lössliper sig från det alldagliga, utan derigenom, att man skapar en skönare werld, ädlare förhållanden och handlingar än det wanliga praktiska lifwets.[46]

Yet another view of the 'romantic element' was presented by another reviewer, who, also in writing in *Swensk Literatur-Tidning* in 1816 (p. 171), identified it with '*äfwentyret, tapperheten, galanteriet*' (adventure, courage, gallantry). It seems difficult to find the common denominator for these several ideas about the term *romantisk*, all put to paper between about 1813 and 1816, and it is quite impossible to bring them into agreement with the many other occurrences of the word in critical journals. A fourth example, with yet another connotation, may be quoted here, if only because of the humorous parellelism with a common use of the term *romantic* in present-day English parlance:

As far as the *romantic* in the present travel book is concerned, it is of the following nature: The author is in love with a Miss Feodorowna of Archangel; 'a beautiful, soulful girl' whom he must abandon because he has been falsely accused by a French emigré ...

Hvad det romantiska *i närwarande Resebeskrifning beträffar, är det af följande beskaffenhet. Förf. är i Archangel förälskad i en fröken Feodorowna;* 'en skön, *själfull flicka,' från hwilken han, falskt angifwen af en fransysk emigrant, måste rymma* ...[47]

The Swedish reviewer seems here to be using *romantisk* almost sarcastically, as his citing of a hackneyed phrase indicates.

The connotation of the adventurous and the exotic became more widespread as the direct identification of the 'romantic' with the medieval decreased. Evidence of the predominance of this connotation may be found frequently from about 1815. Thus, a review of a work by C. A. Buchholz in Swedish entitled *Romantiska Scener utur Romerska Historien* is outspoken:

By *romantic* he understands *piquant, interesting* ... and selects preferably those scenes which can be *romanticized,* so that they could to advantage be included in a modern bandit-novel ...

... *Med* Romantiskt *förstår han* pikant, intereßant ... *och utwäljer då helst sådanna scener, som kunna så* romantiseras, *att de med fördel skulle kunnat få rum i en modern bandit-roman* ...[48]

In discussing Atterbom's *Poetisk Kalendar 1814,* a reviewer remarks that Swedish life 'in its sober monotony offers so few romantic contours'/'*i sin allwarsamma enformighet, erbjuder så få romantiska contourer*'[49] and that the poet Palmblad drew on India, Greece, Spain, and Norway for the 'romantic' qualities in his writing. The desire to delineate *hwardagscharakterer* ('everyday characters') was castigated two years later in the same periodical as 'low and un-romantic'/'*låga och oromantiska.*'[50]

In 1817, Christian Molbech paired the terms '*Eventyrlige og Romantiske*' ('the adventurous and romantic') in speaking of Spanish literature (in a review of J. L. Heiberg's *Dristig vovet, Athene* VIII: 90) and went on to mention 'romantic mysticism'/'*den romantiske Mystik*' (p. 91). Spanish drama, declared Molbech, was quite romantic, and not to be compared with the dramatic works of the ancients'/'*aldeles romantisk, og uden al Efterligning af de Gamles dramatiske Værker.*'[51] The association of the 'romantic' with the mystic was reiterated by the Danish poet, novelist, and aesthetician, Carsten Hauch, in the same volume of *Athene.* He found Oehlenschläger had 'not only chiselled out of Scandinavia's pale marble with sharp lines, but also surrounded it by a romantic veil ...'/'*... ikke blot udhygget Nordens blege Marmor i faste Omrids, men ogsaa omslynget det med et romantisk Slør ...*' (*Om Digtet Helge af Oehlenschläger.*)[52]

Everything that the mermaid says in *Helge* by Adam Oehlenschläger, Hauch found to contain a 'romantic, more picturesque, and almost oriental poetry ...'/'*en romantisk, mere billedrig og ligesom orientalsk Poesie ...*'[53] In 1818, *Swensk Literatur-Tidning* suggested that the authoress of a contemporary novel should 'better familiarize herself with the marvelous and half-hidden elements of true romanticism, in order another time to give the public proof of a purer and truer romantic talent'/'*... göra sig något mere förtrogen med den egentliga Romantikens underbara och halfdunkla elementer, för att en annan gång kunna lämna allmänheten prof på en renare och sannare Romantisk talang.*'[54]

A mosaic of brief quotations illustrating the use of *romantisk* in the first half of the nineteenth century with the connotation of 'fantastic' or 'exotic' is easy to assemble. For example,

The romantic, which comprises the major part of the Eddic myths, gives to this epic world a wild, fantastic nature ...

... a series of enthusiastic thoughts, which are reflected in a romantic element.

... beyond the border of the romantic, the mystic and marvelous, or whatever one wants to call that which lies beyond the natural precincts of reason ...

a romantic tale, embellished with erotic adventures, magic scenes, and marvelous happenings.

the clever composition of the romantic events [in Cervantes' *Don Quixote*].

... enthusiastic, romantic love ...

Det Romantiska, som utgör hufwud-elementet i Edda-mytherne, ger denne episka werld en wild phantastisk natur ...[55]

... en kedja af swärmiska tankar, hwilka spegla sig i ett romantiskt element.[56]

... over Grændsen af det Romantiske, det Mystiske og Vidunderlige, eller hvad man vil kalde det, der ligger uden for Forstandens naturlige Enemærker ...[57]

... en romantisk, med Kiærlighedseventyr, Trolddomsscener og vidunderlige Tildragelser udsmykket Fortælling.[58]

... den sindrige Composition af de romantiske Begivenheder ... [59]

... en sværmerisk, romantisk Kjærlighed ...[60]

In contrast to the widespread and long-lived association of

romantisk with the fantastic, some Swedish critics, at least, brought *romantisk* in association with the adjective *Christian*. A number of examples may be found in *Swensk Literatur-Tidning* between 1813 and 1820. In 1813 a reviewer points out that 'to be sure, a purely Christian and romantic mind – which both Lessing and Winckelmann lacked – is needed in order to understand this Christian-romantic art ...'/'... *wißerligen behöfwes det ett rent christligt och romantiskt sinne – hwilket saknades så hos Lessing som Winkelmann – för att förstå denna christligt-romantiska konst ...*'[61] A review in 1814 was more specific: 'The character which Christianity has given to art and which some of our most careful aesthetic writers call by the name romantic ...'/'*Den charakter, som Christendomen gifwit åt konsten, och som af wåra grundligaste ästhetiska författere betecknats med namnet romantisk...*'[62] A review in 1816 differentiated between '*den gammel-christligt romantiska Poesien*' ('the old-Christian romantic poetry') and '*den gammel-nordiska Romantiska Poesien*' ('the old-Scandinavian romantic poetry'). Catholicism was found to be 'sensual, mystic, clothed in a romantic twilight'/'... *sinlig, mystisk, höljd [sic] i en romantisk skymning ...*'[63] unlike Protestantism. In 1820, the editor of *Poetiska Kalender* is criticized for having wanted to translate '*det Romantiska*' with '*det christligt Sköne*' ('Christian beauty'), but the critic would not deny 'that Christianity let the romantic principle *prevail* in the entire area of the arts'/'... *att Christendomen gjorde den romantiska principen herrskande i hela de sköna kunstnernas område ...*'[64] Elsewhere, in the same periodical and in the same year (1820, col. 831), occurs the phrase '... *den* christna (*eller* europeiska) *romantiken ...*' ('Christian, or European romanticism'). On this point Tegnér raised a sharp dissenting voice. In his lectures, 'Om det Romantiske i Grekiska Poesien,' in 1822–4, he argued that Christian and romantic poetry were not basically the same and asked, 'if Christianity were a necessary prerequisite for romantic poetry, how would we then explain the several kinds of heathen romanticism with which the history of literature is familiar?'/'... *vore Christendomen ett nödvändigt villkor för Romantisk poësie, huru vilja vi då förklara oss de flere arter af hednisk romantik som Poësiens historia känner?*'[65]

As a further contrast to the widespread association of the fantastic with *romantisk* may be quoted a passage from a review of the journal, *Iduna*, in *Swensk Literatur-Tidning*, 'the foremost demand and goal of romantic poetry: that the ideal of beauty must be the ideal of morality'/'*den romantiska poesiens högsta fordran och syftemål: att idealet af Skönhet skall wara idealet af Sedlighet ...*'[66]

As the word *romantisk* gained more and more currency in the

Scandinavian languages, we observe, it became less rather than more specific. In the second decade of the nineteenth century, the word was applied loosely, as an *à la mode* term, and with multiple meanings.

In his lectures on Greek poetry, referred to above, the author of *Frithiofs Saga* struggled to identify and describe the romantic. His attempts at explanation are worth brief mention as evidence of the many facets the problem of defining the word *romantisk* had acquired before 1825. After stating that the romantic was the fulfilment of the highest ideal of beauty and deploring that the romantic degenerated into the fantastic and marvelous through the 'misuse of freedom,' Tegnér provides a series of examples:

General usage often confuses the regular or plastically beautiful with the beautiful in general; but it separates this again from the romantic. A palm tree, for example, with its straight pillarlike trunk and its regular crown is called beautiful, but an oak that stretches its irregular form over a cliff or a waterfall is called romantic. A Greek temple with its fixed symmetrical relationships is beautiful; but a landscape with alternating hills and dales, trees and water, is romantic. A summer day in all its clearness is beautiful; but a summer night where moonlight shines down upon dark masses, is romantic. The rising sun is beautiful, but the setting sun that sinks into the unfathomable ocean and leaves room for shadows and for night, is romantic. In the first of each of these cases our feeling discovers an aesthetic unity, something which more or less points to a rule: but in the second of each of these cases there is a greater variety of parts and their interconnection more or less escapes our awareness.

Allmänna Språkbruket förblandar vanligtvis det regelbundet eller plastiskt sköna med det sköna i allmänhet; men det skiljer det samma bestämdt från det romantiska. Ett palmträd t. ex. med sin raka pelarestam och sin regelbundna krona i toppen kallas skönt: men en ek som lutar sina oregelbundna former öfver en klippa eller ett vatten-fall, nämnes romantisk. Ett Grekiskt tempel med sina bestämda symmetriska förhållanden, är skönt: men ett landskap omvexlande af dålar och berg, af träd och vatten, är romantiskt. En sommardag med sin klarhet är skön, men en sommarnatt, när månskenet faller öfver de dunkla massorna, är romantisk. Skön är den uppgående solen, men den nedgående som sjunker i det outgrundliga hafvet och lemnar rum för skuggorna och natten, är romantisk. I de förstnämnda af dessa föremål upptäcker alltid känslan en esthetisk enhet, ett mer eller mindre bestämdt hänförande till en regel: men i de sistnämnda råder en större mångfaldighet af delar och sambandet dem emellan undandrar sig mer eller mindre uppmärksamheten.[67]

While efforts were being made to produce an acceptable definition of the words *romantisk* and *Romantik* between about 1815 and 1820, numerous books appeared that identified themselves in title or sub-title as *romantisk*, thus calling forth appraisals by critics who took it upon themselves to differentiate between the romantic and the non-romantic. The Danish critic, Peder Hjort, for example, declared that Søetoft's *Romantiske Digte* (1815) 'are absolutely not romantic'/'... *slet ikke ere romantiske* ...'[68]: the poems lacked 'inward, spiritual substance, in contrast to a sometimes striking imagination that has demonstrated its ability to create many picturesque, original images ...'/'... *indvortes, sialelig Gehalt, ved Siden af en, undertiden endog, eminent Phantasie, der har viist sin Evne til at danne flere maleriske, originale Billeder* ...'[69] 'Without being in possession of the spirit of romance,' Søetoft's poems have 'assumed one of the artificial masks formed by a misused imagination'/'... *uden at være i Besiddelse af Romanzias Aand, have ... paataget en af den misbrugte Phantasie forfærdiget konstig Maske* ...'[70] Hjort was equally unqualified in his dismissal of B. S. Ingemann's 'Varners poetiske Vandringer, et romantisk Digt' as unromantic. He complained that 'the poem is not romantic unless one might apply the same description to all poems written since the birth of Christ'/'... *Digtet ikke er mere romantisk, end forsaavidt som man kunde tillægge alle Digte, forfattede efter Christi Fødsel, dette Prædicat*.'[71] Hjort expatiated on the term *romantisk* as employed by Ingemann:

That the word is not to be taken in its true meaning is clear from the content, which is simply romanesque or novelistic; and since the poet has used the word correctly pertaining to *The Black Knights*, one must view this use of the word as a slip of the pen or assume that the poet did not discover the correct interpretation (of the word) until later. Surely, the mixed form is not supposed to make it romantic.

At Ordet ikke er taget i den sande Betydning, sees klarligen af Indholdet, der simpelt hen er romanesk eller romanagtigt; og da Digteren desuden har brugt det rigtigen ved de sorte Riddere, saa maae vi ansee denne Brug af Ordet som en Skrivefeil, eller ogsaa antage, at Digteren først siden efter er kommen i Besiddelse af den rette Udtydning. Den blandede Form giør det dog vel ikke romantisk?[72]

In the next volume of *Athene* (VI, 1816), Hjort reviewed Ingemann's *De sorte Riddere. Et romantisk Epos i ni Sange* ('The Black Knights. A romantic epic in nine cantos,' Copenhagen, 1814) and contradicted his earlier judgment: 'then we must *absolutely deny* that the poem,

The Black Knights, can rightfully be called a *romantic epic'* / '... *saa maa vi dog aldeles benegte, at Diglet, de sorte Riddere, med Rette kan kaldes et romantisk Epos.'*[73] Later in the same review, Hjort indicated what his own concept of the romantic was. He called love *'Romantikens Grundidee'* ('the basic idea of romanticism,' p. 159). He considered essential to a romantic poem 'the romantic fullness which flowering strength and courage and a tender, faithful love produce ...' / *'Den romantiske Fylde, som blomstrende Kraft og Heltemod og en øm, trofast Kiærlighed frembringe ...'*[74] and he felt that this quality was absent in Ingemann. A few pages later he italicized a principle that he felt to be basic to romantic poetry: *'The limitations of time and space are as nothing for the imagination'* / 'Tidens og Rummets endelige Skranker ere Intet for Phantasien ...'[75] In the same year, *Swensk Literatur-Tidning* printed two reviews that similarly disputed the romantic quality of ostensibly romantic works. The reviewer of *Herdinnan wid Hagalund. Romantisk Berättelse,* I–II (Stockholm, 1816), stated bluntly: 'She [the heroine] is the daughter of cottage inspector Albin Stök, born in 1702. This is not romantic' / *'Hon är dotter af HytteInspektören Albin Stök, född anno 1702. Dette är icke romantiskt.'*[76] In the same volume of *Swensk Literatur-Tidning,* Wieland's *Oberon* in Swedish translation, which bore the sub-title 'Romantisk Hjeltdigt' (Stockholm, 1816) received equally brusque treatment: 'the content of this poem ... certainly is not romantic' / '... *innehållet af dette poem ... wißerligen icke är romantiskt.'*[77] In the reviewer's opinion, 'there is nothing which contradicts more the real and true romanticism than the relaxed and insolent opinion of female virtue which is expressed throughout' / '... *är det ingenting som mer motstrider den äkta och sanna romantiken, än den slappa och fräcka åsigten af qwinlig dygd, hvilken här öfwerallt uttaler sig...'*[78] Another reviewer found Baggesen's *Emma,* with its new sub-title, 'Et romantisk Eventyr,' 'as unromantic as one can imagine' / '... *saa uromantisk som man kan tænke sig ...'*[79]

How difficult it was to produce a work that would be accepted as fulfilling the imaginary ideal of the romantic is suggested by the categorical statement:

'we do not yet possess a single novel worth mentioning ... the reason [is] that we completely lack the concept of the *romantic,* the basic element in a novel. Most efforts ... consist in a more or less successful representation of everyday events.'

... wi ännu icke äga en enda roman, som förtjenar nämnas ... orsaken i att man hos oß alldeles saknat allt begrepp om det romantiska, om sjelfwa elementet i en

roman. De fleste forsök ... bestått i en mer eller mindre lycklig framställning af hwardags händelser ...[80]

A final example may suffice to illuminate the deadlock regarding the meaning and application of the word *romantisk*. Of the stories contained in the anthology *Romantisk Tidsfördrif 1819* (Stockholm, 1818), the reviewer stated: 'None of these stories is romantic in the slightest; quite the opposite, they confine themselves to the small sphere of the everyday' / '*Ingendera af deßa berättelser är på minsta sätt romantisk; twertom hålla sig alla inom den trånga hwardaglighetens krets ...*'[81]

From these many quotations a preliminary conclusion may now be drawn: *romantisk* was on the whole a desirable epithet, even though the word could not be defined with precision and could not be used in a way acceptable to the leading critics of the day, whose own definitions, partial definitions, and implications refused to amalgamate. As the *Swensk Literatur-Tidning* put it in 1820:

It still remains for somebody to clarify our view of *that* which we view as the *essential being* of the romantic; this is a subject the treatment of which by the best of our contemporary aestheticians leaves much to be desired.

Det återstår alltså, att nogare göra redo för wår åsigt af det, som wi anse för det Romantiskas egentliga wäsende; ett ämne hwars behandling äfwen hos de bäste af samtidens ästhetiska författare lemnar mycket öfrigt att önska.[82]

A few pages later there is, nevertheless, an attempt at a characterization of romanticism:

The romantic is the beautiful *represented with a marvelous infinity as background* ... for which reason all romanticism is *picturesque* and all true painting is *romantic* – just as all music must be so too ...

Romantiskt *är det sköna* framställdt med en underbar oändlighet såsom bakgrund ... *hwarföre all sann Romantik är* pittoresk *och allt sannt Måleri är* romantiskt – *liksom att Musiken måste wara det ...*[83]

Although the words *romantisk* and *Romantiker* seemed to have had many a desirable attribute in the early part of the nineteenth century, the terms were sometimes used deprecatingly. In a spirit of parody, Jens Baggesen had used *Romantiker* in the sub-title of the notorious *Karfunkel oder Klingklingel-Almanach*, 'Ein Taschenbuch für vollendete Romantiker und angehende Mystiker,' which he edited for Cotta in Tübingen in 1809.[84] Christian Molbech employed the word with a negative cast several times in the 1820s. He was most outspoken in 1827 in a discussion of B. S. Ingemann's

Valdemar Sejr in which he declared that 'a romantic story ... is a bad product, to be rejected: we feel both the connoisseurs of history and poetry will agree ...'/'*Men at en* romantisk Historie ... *er et slet og forkasteligt Product: troe vi, baade Historiens og Poesiens Kiendere ville være enige om* ...'[85] The story in question, Molbech felt, could better be called a '*romanticizing* story, a novelistic version of King Valdemar's life ...'/'... *en romantiserede Historie, en romanaktig Indklædning af Kong Valdemars Levnets-Historie* ...'[86] Writing of Walter Scott, Molbech deplored his wanting to '*make history romantic* ... for what is romanticism, even in the most imaginative writing, compared with the infinitely romantic lives and grandeur [recorded] in history?'/ 'giøre Historien romantisk – *et overflødigt og vanmægtigt Foretagende; thi hvad er Romantiken i den meest phantasierige Digtning imot Historiens uendelig romantiske Liv og Storhed?*'[87] In a more clearly pejorative sense, J. L. Heiberg spoke in 1830 of 'a strange, romantic mixture of the sentimental and the pathetic ...'/'... *en forunderlig, romantisk Blanding af det Sentimentale og det Pathetiske* ...'[88] although a page or two later, in referring to Spain, he spoke in another vein of Cervantes' 'romantic fatherland.' In 1837, Carsten Hauch let one of the figures in a dialogue call Victor Hugo's *Han d'Islande*, '... a misdirected monstrosity like a comic parody of the entire new French romantic nuisance,' after mentioning the 'convulsive works' of the French romantics/'... *et forfeilet Uhyre, som en comisk Parodie paa det hele nyfranske, romantiske Uvæsen.*'[89] About the same time, in discussing Calderón, P. L. Møller spoke of 'a mixture of Arabic-romantic sentimentalism and heroism'/'*Maureren, en Blanding af arabisk-romantisk Sentimentalitet og Heroisme* ...'[90] Although Møller (who rarely used the term *romantisk* except in referring to literary schools) more than once deplored the excesses of the German 'romantic school,'[91] the so-called 'romantic' literature coming from France began to give Scandinavian critics second thoughts about the desirability of 'the romantic.' In an aphorism from about the year 1841, Esaias Tegnér stated,

Although the French waited for a long time before they came to romanticism, they are now again getting the worst of it. The shocking, the tasteless, the disgusting, and the cannibalistic they seem to view as the principal constituent of romanticism. They are giving us cannibalistic poetry ...

Om Fransoserna dröjt länge innan de kommit in i Romantiken, så taga de också nu sin skada igen. Det rysliga, det osmakliga, det otäcka och kannibaliska tyckas de anse för Romantikens hufvudelement. De ge oss en kannibalisk poesi ...[92]

The pejorative use of *romantisk* and *Romantik* has continued down to the present day, sometimes even by writers that critics tend to identify as 'romantic.' If we glance through the letters of the Norwegian, Bjørnstjerne Bjørnson, to Danish correspondents in the 1880s and 90s, we find such formulations as

See in the Schleswig question romanticism from first to last, doctrinaire, stubborn emotionalism instead of a practical, healthy treatment of a sick question.

Se i den Slesvigske sak fra først til sist romantik, doktriner, halstarrigt føleri istedetfor praktisk sund behandling af et sykt spørsmaal.[93]

What is this about 'the right of the king' other than romanticism ... just as uselessly romantic as the hussars ... the single class's selfishness hides damned conveniently behind all this romanticism ...

Hvad er dette med 'Kongens ræt' annet æn romantik ... like sa unyttig romantisk som hæst-garden? ... den enkelte stans egennytte bor forbannet bekvæmt bak al denne romantik ...[94]

Your reasoning is romantic, old-fashioned...

Dit ræsonnement er romantisk, gammeldags ...[95]

The idea of 'romanticizing' was at first ambiguous, but came more and more to be a term of reproach. *Swensk Literatur-Tidning* could write in 1819 of a translation that 'this romanticized treatment is certainly brilliant'/*'Denna romantiserade behandling är wißerligen genialisk ...'*[96] and approvingly call *Örvar-Odds saga* a 'romanticized saga'/*'den romantiserade Sagan.'*[97] But Oscar Levertin was not being complimentary to Paul Bourget when in 1900 he said of one of his works, 'All this is romanticized journalism'/*'Allt detta är romantiserad journalistik,'*[98] or to a biographer of Henri Beyle when, two years later, he said *en passant*, 'But when all the romanticized retouching is removed ...'/*'Men när all romantiserad retuschering aflägsnats ...'*[99]

During the 1830s and 40s the concepts of a 'romantic' literature identified with the beginning of the nineteenth century and recognizable as a school became fixed, despite the terminological conservatism of an N. M. Petersen, mentioned above. As early as 1821, in an article about the current state of Swedish literature, *Swensk Literatur-Tidning* had explained that there were two parties in

Swedish literature, the 'Gothic' or 'Phosphorist' and the 'German' or 'Romantic.' The author of the article pointed out that, except for personalities, the two parties resembled one another strongly.[100] The partisan terminology of early nineteenth-century Swedish literature has been preserved down to our own day, but both the 'Gothic and the 'Phosphorist' writers are subsumed under the label 'romantic.' Viewing the early 1830s in retrospect, it is hard to distinguish between the abstract use of *romantisk* and its use as an appellation identifying a certain group of writers. The Norwegian poet, Henrik Wergeland, who himself used the word *romantisk* rarely, mentioned 'the spirit of romanticism'/'*Romantikens Aand*' in a poem alluding to Tegnér's *Frithiofs Saga* in 1832.[101] The same year, Molbech wrote of 'a newly arisen school' in France, the members of which 'also there were called romantics ...'/'*en nylig opkommen Skole, hvilken man ogsaa der tillægger Navn af Romantikernes ...*'[102] Wergeland, in his dramatic piece 'Stockholmsfareren' in 1837, had one of his characters say, 'He ... wanted to explain how in the first decade of the century an epoch began in our romantic poetry'/'*Han ... vilde docere over hvorlunde i det første Decennium af Aarhundret en Epoke indtraadte i vor romantiske Poesi.*'[103] Soon the identifications were accepted. Thus P. L. Møller wrote in 1841 about Atterbom as the leader of the romantic school of writers (the 'Phosphorists')[104] and reiterated that the 'Phosphorists' were the Stockholm branch of the German romantic school.[105]

In Sweden the identification of specifically medieval literature as 'romantic' seems to have been stronger than in Denmark and Norway, for the term *nyromantisk* (neoromantic) came to be used to characterize the literature and writers that elsewhere were categorized simply as 'the romantic school.' Erik Gustaf Geijer, in a review of Atterbom's *Samlade Skrifter* in 1838, called Atterbom 'the neoromantic poetry's foremost representative'/'*... den ny-romantiska poesiens förnämsta representant ...*' and associated him with 'the neoromantic school, the fatherland of which was Germany and the leaders of which were the brothers Schlegel and Tieck'/'*... den ny-romantiska skolan, vars fädernesland var Tyskland och vars koryféer voro bröderna Schlegel och Tieck.*'[106] The term *nyromantisk* has continued to be used in Swedish literary history, although in the twentieth century the prefix *ny-* has recently tended to be dropped and there has occasionally been some slight confusion with the German term *Neuromantik*, which was rendered in Swedish as *nyromantik* by Fredrik Böök.[107] The equivalent of neoromantic in the sense of 'romantic' is not used in Danish,* although in his doctoral dissertation in 1921, Paul V. Rubow did employ *Nyromantik* in discussing Jens Baggesen around the year 1807.[108] A Danish critic might, however, speak of 'a tone of "modern" romanticism,' as P. L. Møller did in a review of Emil Aarestrup's *Digte* (1838) – '... *en tone af "modern" Romantik ... af den "romantiske Skole" i strengere Forstand.*'[109] The Icelandic poet and critic, Benedikt Gröndal, whose non-Icelandic literary orientation certainly was Danish in the first instance, mentioned the term *neoromanticism* in a lecture given in 1888. In the same lecture he spoke of 'older romanticism' as applicable to medieval literature 'conjoined with the Church and knighthood':

... menn sneru sér aftur til miðaldanna með öllu þeirra andalífi, álfum og forynjum, og þannig kom upp hin svonefnda 'nýja rómantík.' ... Hin eldri rómantík, sem var á miðöldunum ... er samvaxin kirkjunni og riddaraskapnum.†

II

If by mid-century the proliferation of meanings of *Romantik* and *romantisk* was not complete, the words had nevertheless undergone such a remarkable and complete exfoliation that they already defied literary taxonomists. Confronted by a plethora of meanings and attempted definitions, we note ironically that one of Meir Goldschmidt's correspondents admonished him on 20 February 1851: 'You complain that the romantics have disappeared; seek the thread in your own heart ...'/'*De klager over at Romantiker er forsvunden og borte; søg Traaden i Deres eget Hjerte ...*'[110] Goldschmidt still thought he could identify romanticism, however: eight years later he wrote to F. C. Sibbern that the 'great romantics' 'satisfy and nevertheless leave one full of longing, which I believe to a certain extent can be a definition of "romanticism" ...'/'*store Romantikere ... de tilfredsstille og dog lade En længselsfuld, hvilket jeg tror i visse Maader kan være en Definition af 'Romantik' ...*'[111]

Compared to the new life given to the words *romantisk* and

---

*   There is no entry for 'Nyromantik' or 'nyromantisk' in Dahlerup's *Ordbog over det danske Sprog.*

†   Benedict Gröndal, *Ritsafn* IV (Reykjavik, 1953): 230, 228. Incidentally, the first occurrence of the terms *rómantíska* and *rómantík* in Icelandic are from 1866, in the introduction to Matthías Jochumsson's translation of Tegnér's *Frithiofs Saga*, according to the records of the Icelandic dictionary currently being compiled in Reykjavik under the direction of Dr. Jakob Benediktsson.

Romantik in Scandinavia through the lectures and books of Scandinavia's most influential critic, Georg Brandes, from about 1870 onward, the words are not of high frequency in the 1850s and '60s. Their diversity of meaning, however, is suggested by glancing on the one hand at the earlier work of Henrik Ibsen, and, on the other, at an annual 'calendar' or anthology, the *Folkekalender for Danmark*, addressed to a broad public. The (incomplete) glossary appended to the great memorial edition ('Hundreårsutgave') of Ibsen's work cites only six significant passages in which Ibsen used the words *romantisk* and *Romantik* – earliest in 1850 and latest in 1883. The passages are worth recording here. In a sketch, 'Fangen paa Agershuus' ('The Captive at Agershuus') from the year 1850, is found the sentence, 'We had stepped into the cemetery because he wanted there to show me ... where a person in suspended animation had awakened under highly romantic circumstances which were still more romanticized by him'/ *'Vi vare traadte ind paa Kirkegaarden fordi han der vilde vise mig ... hvori engang en Skindød under højst romantiske og af ham endmere romantiserede Omstændigheder var opvaagnet.'*[112] Here, romantic suggests the fantastic, and 'to romanticize' connotes exaggeration. In 1859 Ibsen wrote but did not publish 'Fjeldfuglen. Romantisk Opera i tre Akter' ('The Mountain Bird. Romantic Opera in three Acts'). In *Love's Comedy* (1862) Miss Skjære says about another character, who mentions that he has written some verse, 'He is romantic by nature' / *'Han er romantisk af sig.'* The remark is countered by Falk's observation, 'Varnish and romanticism wear off with time'/ *'Fernis og Romantik gaar af med Tiden.'*[113] The juxtaposition of attitudes here is similar to that of the year 1850. Later in the same act, *romantisk* is clearly used in the sense of novelistic – although overtones of other meanings cannot be excluded: 'His life's novel.' 'Novel?' 'Novel. I call that novelistic [*romantisk*], which cannot be evaluated by everyday people'/*"... hans Livs Roman.'* '*Roman?*' '*Roman. Jeg kalder Sligt romantisk, Som ej af Hverdagsfolk vurderes kan.'*[114] In Act v of *The League of Youth* (1869), Daniel Hejre states that affairs of the heart 'must be kept secret; that is what one calls romanticism'/*'Det skal holdes hemmeligt; det er det man kalder Romantik.'*[115] Ibsen's final use of the concept reverted to an older, critical meaning of the term *romantik* when in the preface of the second edition of *The Feast at Solhaug* in 1883 he mentioned 'the literary romanticism of the Middle Ages'/ *'... middelalderens literære romantik ...'*[116]

The *Folkekalender for Danmark* for 1853 contains a description of a West Jutland marriage celebration where there is mention of a 'romantic love story ...'[117] whereas in the volume for the year 1857, Danish castle ruins are described in a way suggesting the earliest uses of *romantisk* in the Scandinavian languages:

Castle ruins ... have a highly interesting, not to say romantic location ... our castles, although they do not have in their history the blinding colours of romanticism ...

Borgruiner ... ere af en høist interessant, for ikke at sige romantisk, Beliggenhed ... vore Borge, om de end ikke have i deres Historie Romantikens blændende Farver... [118]

Finally, in 1858, in a story by B. S. Ingemann entitled 'Den Fremmede'('The Stranger'), there is found the clause, '... an impression, which through several conversations with him had been heightened to become a romantic, passionate attraction'/'... *et Indtryk, der ved flere Samtaler med ham var steget til en romantisk, lidenskabelig Hendragelse.*'[119]

When the strong new voice of the young critic, Georg Brandes, was heard in Scandinavia in the early 1870s, the concept and the word *Romantik* became more frequently applied than before, especially in connection with particular eras in the literature of the recent past. In the long series of lectures subsequently published under the general heading 'Main Currents in Nineteenth Century Literature,' Brandes devoted one sequence to 'the romantic school in Germany' and one to the 'romantic school in France.' As far as Scandinavia is concerned, Brandes' lectures mark the fixing of the literary-historical concept of 'romantic school.' Brandes' contemporaries and successors accepted the term without question and have continued to use the adjective *romantisk* freely and ambiguously.

For Georg Brandes, *Romantik* meant reaction. In his lectures on the romantic school in Germany (1873), he said, for example, 'in romanticism there was hidden a reactionary principle from the first ...'/'... *i Romantiken fra først af var dulgt et reaktionært Princip* ...'[120] In making a reference to Kierkegaard, Brandes maintained that the Danish thinker had failed throughout his life to draw any practical or social conclusions from his own teaching – 'and this trait is truly romantic'/'... *undgaar imidlertid hele sit Liv igennem – og dette Træk er ægte romantisk – at drage nogensomhelst ydre eller social Følgeslutning af sin Lære* ...'[121] Two pages later he could nevertheless speak in quite a different tone of 'the fire of romanticism,' which Henrik Steffens had brought to Copenhagen in 1802.[122] Further along in the lectures on the German romantic school, Brandes was more specific:

The whole history of romanticism [he wrote] confirms the definition which Ruge gave in his time.[123] A romantic is a writer who, with our cultural means, opposes the era of enlightenment and revolution, and who rejects and combats the principle of pure humanity in the areas of science, art, morals, and politics.

Romantikens hele Historie stadfæster den Definition som Ruge i sin Tid gav: En Romantiker er en Skribent, som med vor Dannelses Midler træder fjendligt op mod Oplysningens og Revolutionens Tidsalder, og som forkaster og bekæmper den rene Humanitets Princip paa Videnskabens, Kunstens, Moralens og Politikens Omraader.[124]

Needless to say, this attitude differs markedly from earlier identifications of the 'romantic' as radical, advanced, and exotic. Romanticism was for Brandes an interesting but an undesirable phenomenon: 'Poetically the romantics have enriched their nation's emotional life, although they more frequently gave expression to sick than to healthy expressions of feeling' / *'Poetisk har Romantikerne beriget deres Folks Stemningsliv, om de end hyppigere har givet sygelige end sunde Stemninger Udtryk.'*[125]

In his lectures on 'Den romantiske Skole i Frankrig' ('The Romantic School in France,' 1879, published in 1882), Brandes commented on the history of the word *romantisk*. When originally introduced into Germany, he declared, it signified *romansk*, i.e., Roman, romanesque:

it meant romanesque swirls and puns, sonnets and canzoni; the romantics were smitten with Roman [*romansk*] Catholicism and with the great Romance [*romansk*] poet Calderon, whose works they discovered, translated, and praised. When romanticism reached France a generation later, the word meant … just the opposite: the German-English cultural current in contrast with the Greek-Latin-Romance … This was simply because that which was strange seemed romantic. A people with an homogeneous culture like the old Hellenes achieve a classic art and poetry; but as soon as a people, proceeding from their own culture, discover another which seems strange and adventurous, then that culture seems to it to be romantic, i.e., it is like a landscape viewed through a coloured glass.

… det betegnede romanske Snirkler og Ordspil, Sonetter og Canzoner; Romantikerne sværmede for romansk Katolicism og for den store romanske Digter Calderon, hvis Værker de opdagede og oversatte og priste. Da Romantismen en Menneskealder senere naaede Frankrig, betød Ordet efter Sprogbrugen det stik Modsatte, den tysk-engelske Aandsretning i Modsætning til den græsk-latinsk-romanske … Det beroede

simpelthen paa, at det Fremmede overhovedet virker romantisk. Et Folk med ensartet Kultur som de gamle Hellenere faar en klassisk Kunst og Poesi; men saasnart et Folk ud fra sin egen Kultur opdager en anden, der forekommer det fremmed og æventyrlig, saa synes denne Kultur det romantisk: den virker som en igennem et farvet Glas betragtet Egn.[126]

While Brandes himself usually alluded to the 'romantic' schools when he used *romantisk* and *Romantik*, these words were also part of his vocabulary in a more general way. They could indicate a certain kind of literature, as, for example, when he spoke of 'romantic tales for children'/'... *romantiske Børneeventyr ...*' or said of Paul Heyse, 'he is far too much a child of the sun to have remained in romantic twilight'/'*... han er i altfor høj Grad et Solbarn til at han kunde være bleven stikkende i det romantiske Tusmørke.*'[127]

The same denotations *romantisk* had for Brandes are found in the works of his Norwegian contemporary, the critic, Henrik Jæger. Writing in 1878, for example, Jæger labelled an expression by Wergeland 'unrevolutionary, romantic-reactionary'/'*... urevolutionær, romantisk-reaktionær Udtalelse ...*' and called Steffens 'a distinct reactionary, a full-blooded romantic and Schelling-disciple of the first water'/'*en udpræget reaktionær Person, en Fuldblods-Romantiker og Schellingianer af det reneste Vand ...*'[128] In Jæger we meet with one of the early uses of the concept 'national-romanticism' – which subsequently has become a standard term referring especially to Norwegian literature of the first half of the nineteenth century. The term was coined by retrospective critics; it was not used by the generation now identified as national-romantic. In discussing Jørgen Moe, for example, Jæger italicized a definition of the new direction in Norwegian literature which Moe represented: 'a necessary stage in the national development ... offshoot of a general European movement, romanticism /'*Den nye Retning ... et nødvendigt Led i den nationale Udvikling ... Udløber af en almindelig europæisk Bevægelse, Romantiken.*'[129] Several times he used the phrase *romantisk-national* in referring to Norwegian literature of the early decades of the century. Also, like Brandes, Jæger spoke of 'unhealthy aesthetic-romantic elements'/'*usunde æsthetisk-romantiske Elementer.*'[130] In an early critical work, the Danish novelist, Herman Bang, nominally contrasted romantics and realists: Men 'ceased being romantics and by turning to life became realists'/'*man ... holdt op med at være Romantiker og ved at vende sig mod Livet overhovedet blev Realist ...*'[131] In practice, however, he found it difficult to separate romantics from realists. Thus, two of his best-known contemporaries on the Danish parnassus, Jens Peter Jacobsen and Holger Drach-mann, were, respectively, 'in all his realism a great romantic,' and 'realism's romantic.'[132] Zola was similarly characterized: 'The standard-bearer of naturalism not only began as a romantic; he has never ceased being one'/'*Naturalismens Bannerfører er ikke blot begyndt som Romantiker, han er aldrig holdt op med at være det.*'[133] 'His materialism,' Bang continued, in an obviously disapproving tone, 'turns into a romantic mysticism.'[134]

In two books, *Guldalderen* ('The Golden Age,' 1890) and *Svensk Romantik* ('Swedish Romanticism,' 1894), the Danish critic and academician, Valdemar Vedel, described the romanticisms of Danish and Swedish literature. His thesis in *Guldalderen* was that 'romanticism' in Germany and Denmark was a revolt against culture and therewith 'a continuation of the revolutionary subjecti-vism of the "Sturm und Drang" '/'*... en Fortsættelse af 'Storm-og-Trængsels' tidens oprørske Subjektivisme.*'[135] The romantic poet, he felt, was in the first instance a writer who moved 'often rather superficially in the direction of the picturesque'/'*... ofte lidt overfladisk Retning mod det Pittoreske.*'[136] The picturesque element he found in Hans Christian Andersen, Henrik Hertz, and Emil Aarestrup. 'Blicher represents in his poorer short stories the romantic, awful-beautiful madness ...'/'*Blicher giver i de daarligere Noveller det romantiske, frygtelig-skjønne Vanvid ...*'[137] he added. After a long series of pejora-tive statements pertaining directly to German, but indirectly to Danish romanticism, Vedel expanded his first characterization by declaring that 'romanticism seeks the unusual, the peculiar, and the variegated'/'*Romantiken søger det Sjældne, Ejendommelige og Brogede.*'[138] In speaking of the Danish novelist and poet, Carsten Hauch, he distinguished between 'the curvilinear, romantic spirit in contrast with the French, rectilinear'/'*den krogliniede, romantiske Aand i Modsætning til den franske, retliniede.*'[139] It is noteworthy that Vedel at so early a date attempted to distinguish between different move-ments which ordinarily were identified by the same term. In *Svensk Romantik* he wrote in a similar vein (in referring to Tegnér, Geijer, Atterbom, and the 'Phosphorists'), that 'Swedish romanticism ... [is] a special Swedish form of what in the vaguest and broadest sense can be called romantic'/'*Svensk Romantik ... en særlig svensk Form af, hvad der i vageste og videste Forstand kan kaldes romantisk.*'[140]

With Nordic enthusiasm, Vedel declared of King Charles XII:

How Swedish-romantic are not all the features of his heroic figure! Tall, straight, and slender, blue-eyed, with fine blond hair, beardless ... his entire being was simple and straightforward.

Hvor svensk-romantiske er ikke ogsaa alle Træk i denne Helteskikkelse! Høj, rank og slank, blaaøjet, med fint blondt Haar, skægløs ... hele hans Væsen var enkelt og ligefremt.[141]

This description seems hardly compatible with the 'romantic' as Vedel had described it in *Guldalderen*. Also, despite the many reservations that are implied in his use of the word *romantisk* throughout *Guldalderen*, Vedel concluded this book by prophesying that 'the truly romantic tones can never fail to find a response in men ...'/'*Heller ikke de egentlig romantiske Toner kan nogensinde miste Sangbund i Menneskene...*'[142] This conciliatory and euphonic note has been struck by several Scandinavian writers in the course of time. Thus, the Norwegian writer, Hans E. Kinck, wrote in 1920, 'Literature does not exist without romanticism'/'*Der eksisterer ikke digtning uten "romantik."*'[143]

Until the turn of the century neither Norway nor Sweden had a critic whose impact was comparable to that of Brandes. In seeking an important example beyond Denmark's borders, we may, however, ask how the many-sided genius, August Strindberg, used *romantisk* and *Romantik*. As a matter of fact, Strindberg used the words very little. In his earliest essays he seems to have used *romantisk* only once, and here in direct contrast to *realistik* in describing an art exhibit in 1877.[144] In *Giftas* ('Married,' 1885) *romantisk* is employed only sarcastically. Strindberg ridicules Nora in Ibsen's *A Doll's House* as 'a romantic miracle, a product of the beautiful philosophy of life which is called idealism ...'/'*... ett romantiskt vidunder, en produkt av den sköna världsåskådning som kallas idealism...*'[145] and declares that her mention of 'the miraculous' (i.e., that Helmer might assume her guilt) 'is so romantic-idiotic that it doesn't deserve mention'/'*Hennes joller om det "vidunderliga" att Helmer skulle ange sig för hennes brott är så romantiskt-fånigt, att det icke förtjänar ett ord.*'[146] The entire play he dismissed as 'old-fashioned romantic gallantry'/ '*... ett gammalmodigt romantiskt galanteri ...*'[147] but at the same time turned a humorous phrase in suggesting that 'a romantic hound ... bit me in the leg and wanted to prove to me that I was a romantic just when I attacked and ridiculed romanticism'/'*En romantisk dogg ... bet mig i benet och ville bevisa mig att jag var romantikus, just då jag angrep och förlöjligade romantiken ...*'* Strindberg was not alone in

* Strindberg in *Samlade Skrifter* xiv: 35. The allusion is to Hugo Nisbeth.

seeing the romantic in Ibsen's later plays: the Swedish critic and poet, Carl David af Wirsén, in a review of *The Wild Duck* (1884), spoke, unlike Strindberg, in a spirit of admiration of 'Hedvig's romantic figure'/*'Hedvigs romantiska bild.*'[148]

In reviews and essays by Oscar Levertin, who, although not an international luminary or a pan-Scandinavian figure like Georg Brandes, was probably the most important Swedish critic around 1900, there are several fairly distinct uses of the word *romantisk*. The meanings span from a description of nature in the spirit of the primary eighteenth-century use of *romantisk* (for example, 'the well-known, romantic trip from "tra los montes" over to Spain'[149]) to a compound word frequently used in discussing a certain type of light Scandinavian literature in the twentieth century: *herrgårdsromantik* (Danish, *herregårdsromantik*)–the 'romanticism of life on an estate.'[150] He also uses other compounds with *romantik*, notably *röfverromantik*[151] – doubtless a translation of German *Räuberromantik* – and *fängelseromantik* ('prison romanticism').[152] Although Levertin could use *romantik* in the sense of motion-picture advertisements in the later twentieth century ('the 54-year-old man took as his bride a 17-year-old girl, a proof of his unquenchable fire and that shimmer of romanticism age cast upon his figure'[153]) he also used it in a sense that has become popular in Scandinavia in recent decades: romanticism is the ingredient of happy experiences, which make life worth living. Thus, in 1898, he could write of 'the romanticism of all of existence with the intoxicating storms and the shining stars'/*'hela tillvarons romantik med de berusande stormar och de strålande stjärnor ...*'[154] and of an old maid, 'her romanticism which, achieved late, had quickly frozen'/*'hans gamla svenska fröken och hennes sent vunna, men hastigt förfrusna romantik ...*'[155] Levertin also associated *romantisk* with two concepts, the classical and the realistic, which the nineteenth century had used frequently as foils for the 'unromantic.' Thus, in 1904, he spoke of 'Runeberg's time and its romantically beautified antiquity ...'/*'Runebergs tid och dess romantiskt förskönade antik ...*'[156] and remarked of a play by Gunnar Heiberg that it was 'romantic and realistic, without time or space'/*'Det är romantiskt och realistiskt, utan tid och rum.*'[157]

Levertin applied the identification *romantisk* generously. Zola, Flaubert, and Jens Peter Jacobsen were romantic – but not the Swedish poet, Carl Snoilsky: 'He who calls him a romantic has in principle never understood the nature of romanticism'/*'Den har aldrig i hufvudsak förstått romantikens väsen, som kallar honom romantiker.*'[158] The peremptory quality of Levertin's conviction about

Snoilsky seems a bit odd in view of the fact that Snoilsky's primary orientation was toward Byron and Heine.

On the whole, the post-Brandesian (and post-Levertinian) critics in Scandinavia up to World War II tend to use the terms *romantisk* and *Romantik* loosely and uncritically, but clearly reflect the attitudes and biases visible in Brandes' *Œuvre*. Probably the two most prolific and widely read critics of the 1920s and '30s are the Swede, Frederik Böök, and his somewhat younger Danish contemporary, Paul V. Rubow; they may be taken to exemplify Scandinavian criticism between the two world wars. In 1918, Böök published a work on 'The Romantic Age' in which he enumerated the component parts of that age:

the great delight in poetry; the acceptance of the world of the poem as a higher reality, an eternal world of idea; the patriotic enthusiasm, love of myth, saga, and history; the romantic quietism in Atterbom's manner; the bold optimism, which contains an echo of Tegners' *Sången*; in short, all the traces which the great romantic creative spirits made upon Swedish culture.

... den starka hänförelsen för poesien; uppfattningen av diktens värld som en högre verklighet, en evig idévärld; den patriotiska högstämningen, kärleken till myt, saga och historia; den romantiska kvietismen i Atterboms stil; den frejdige optimismen, som rymmer ett eko av Tegnérs Sången; *kort sagt, alla de spår, som de stora romantiska nydanarna satt i svensk kultur.*[159]

Oddly enough, on the very same page Böök declares Runeberg to be the great realist who overcomes romanticism / '*Romantikens övervinnare är hos oss Runeberg, den store realisten ...*'[160] Romanticism for Böök had apparently to be associated with a reaction against rationalism. Tegnér's ideas were wholly romantic, according to Böök, for in them 'antirationalism finds clear expression.'[161] Yet, on page 4 of the same work, Böök had written that 'the romantic age is the age of renewed science, new humanism'/'*Den romantiska tidsåldern är de förnyade vetenskapernas, nyhumanismens.*'[162] Another example of contradiction within Böök is his assessment of the Swedish poet, Sven Lidman, in *Resa kring svenska Parnassen*. We read on page 122 that 'all his lyrics are the song of the blood, a wild romantic orgy,' and three pages later that he was a realist.

Paul V. Rubow wrote in *Georg Brandes' Briller* (1932) that Brandes 'had begun his grand crusade against the philosophy and art of romanticism'[163] in 1871, but identified Brandes himself as a romantic many times, even in the very same work, where he spoke of

Brandes' romantic prejudices (p. 21) or criticized Brandes' book on Shakespeare as 'an expression of his time's romantic view of the poetry of the past.'[164] In passing, Rubow, echoing Brandes' own opinion, called Kierkegaard's *Either-Or* a 'true product of the romantic school'/'... *dette ægte Produkt af den romantiske Skole ...*'[165] In this connection it is worth mentioning the stimulating article 'Krisen i nordisk romantikk' ('The Crisis in Scandinavian Romanticism') by the Norwegian cultural historian, Paulus Svendsen, from the year 1941. Svendsen denied the tenet that the romantics had no sense for the real problems of life/'*Et absolutt feilsyn er det når en tror at romantikerne ikke hadde* interesse for livets oppgaver.'[166] He called such an attitude—Brandes' attitude—absolutely mistaken. Svendsen nevertheless agreed that Kierkegaard was a 'true romantic.' He even felt that Kierkegaard saw 'with unique clarity what romanticism consisted of'/'*Han ser med enestående klarhet hvori romantikkens vesen består ... Om sitt forfatterskap taler han som en ekte romantiker ...*'[167]

In the face of the mass of contradictory opinion and utterances that have been cited in the present essay, Professor Svendsen seems to have been overly optimistic in his belief that the nature of romanticism could be defined.

If one would analyse the *being of romanticism* [he wrote] one must not stop at the longing for infinity or the view of art, of nature and history ... romanticism is ... *a uniform weltanschauung.*

Dersom en vil analysere romantikkens vesen ... *må en ikke stanse ved dens uendelighetslengsel eller ved dens syn på kunsten, på naturen og historien ... romantikken er ... en enhetlig verdensanskuelse.*[168]

In a circular argument, Professor Svendsen insisted that

one can speak of the romantic man ... Of course there have always been variants of this type in the development of our culture. But only once has this type had the chance to create a complete, admirable attitude toward life. This is the time we call 'romanticism.'

En kan tale om det romantiske menneske ... Selvsagt har det alltid vært varianter av denne type i vår kulturutvickling. Men bare én gang har denne type hatt sjansen til å skape en fullstendig fullverdig livsholdning. Det er den tiden vi kaller 'romantikken.'[169]

Despite occasional scepticism about the value of employing the term *romantisk*, it remained ubiquitous in Scandinavian criticism. Paul V. Rubow can be used again as a whipping-boy. In a collection of Rubow's essays published in 1958 (*Herman Bang og flere kritiske*

Studier), the reader comes upon many word combinations that include *romantisk* or *Romantik*, as, for example, 'the great name [Sibbern] in romantic philosophy,' 'the curse of the romantic generation,' 'the flaring up of romanticism in these years [i.e., about 1890],' "national romantic drama [in Norway],' 'the call, the *idée fixe* of romantic poetry,' 'medieval romanticism,' '[Sainte-Beuve] had acquired the romantic sickness,' and 'The romantic cloak was a splendid finery for Chateaubriand' / '*den romantiske Filosofis store Navn*' (p. 40), '*den romantiske Slægts-Forbandelse*' (p. 65)' '*den opblussende Romantik i disse Aar*' (p. 74), '*nationalt romantisk Drama*' (p. 91), '*Kaldet, den romantiske Poesis Kæphest*' (p. 92), '*den middelalderlige Romantik*' (p. 101), '*havde modtaget den romantiske Syge,*' '*Den romantiske Kaabe var en prægtig Pynt for Chateaubriand*' (p. 130). No demonstrable limited meaning evolves from Rubow's use of *romantisk*; nor is there a chronological limitation determinable for the word, which he seems to employ much in the same way that Brandes did during the last decades of the nineteenth century.

In an effort to achieve greater terminological precision and specifically to distinguish between phases of literary developments previously lumped together under the heading 'nineteenth-century romanticism,' recent Danish critics have used the French term *romanticisme* as the label for much of the literature between about 1830 and 1850. The word had been used earlier as a synonym for *Romantik*. Thus, in a letter to his mother of 20 June 1870, Brandes had called romanticism *Romantisme* and characterized it as

(a) *a breach with Latin and Greek antiquity* ... (b) *Sturm-und Drang* period. Its merging with the revolution of 1830 ... the god of romanticism is *passion*. (c) romanticism is a continuation of *Rousseau*.

(a) Brud med den latinske-græske Oldtid ... (b) Sturm-und Drang Periode. *Dens Sammenfald med Revolutionen 1830 ... Romantismens Gud er Lidenskaben.* (c) *Romantismen er* Rousseau's *Fortsættelse* ...[170]

In his history of Danish literature (1886), P. Hansen (who based his book on N. M. Petersen's earlier work) declared that Oehlenschläger's 'awakening *Anti-Romantisme*' '... *Digterens vaagnende Anti-Romantisme* ...'[171] was visible in *Palnatoke* – from the year 1809. He did not employ the adjective *romantisk* about Oehlenschläger after 1809. His successors in producing a standard history of Danish literature, Vilhelm Andersen and Carl S. Petersen (in *Illustreret dansk Litteraturhistorie* [1916] – 1934), however, used *romantisk* in treating the literature of the early nineteenth century and *Romantisme* about the writers of the 1830s. In discussing Oehlenschlager's *Sct. Hansaftenspil*, Vilhelm Andersen wrote that it contained 'all the elements of Danish romanticism: nature and love and youth, history and art.'/'... *alle den danske Romantiks Elementer: Natur og Kærlighed og Ungdom, Historie og Kunst ...*'[172]

Paul V. Rubow was probably responsible for the currency that *Romantisme* has enjoyed in Danish: In his dissertation on nineteenth-century Danish literary criticism (1921), he explained the French influence on Danish literature as the advent of *Romantisme*, which he set off from *Romantik*. 'In these authors,' Rubow wrote,

we have found agreement with the literary direction which started con-temporaneously with romanticism, but which merged only partly with it: *romantisme*. Romanticism is a Central European movement, whereas *romantisme* is at home among the western powers. Really doctrinaire *romantisme*, which is a French or Parisian product, never fully penetrates Danish criticism ... Truer *romantisme* is found in P. L. Møller's otherwise unclear *Œuvre*, which corresponds in *belles-lettres* to authors like Aarestrup, Carl Bagger and Christian Winther, and to a certain degree also to Hans Christian Andersen. *Romantisme* hovers over Goldschmidt's criticism, which, however, corresponds to no other imaginative writing than his own.

Vi har hos disse Forfattere fundet en Overensstemmelse med en poetisk Retning, der er opstaaet samtidig med Romantikken, men kun til Dels falder sammen med den: Romantismen. Romantikken er en centraleuropæisk Bevægelse, mens Romantismen hører hjemme blandt Vestmagterne. Den egentlig doktrinære Romantisme, som er et fransk eller parisisk Produkt, vinder dog aldrig rigtig Indpas i dansk Kritik ... Mere ægte Romantisme findes i P. L. Møllers ellers uklare Forfatterskab, der i Skøn-litteraturen nærmest svarer til Forfattere som Aarestrup, Carl Bagger og Chr. Winther, til en vis Grad ogsaa H. C. Andersen. Romantismen spøger ligeledes i Goldschmidts Kritikker, der dog ikke svarer til anden Poesi end hans egen.[173]

After reflecting on this statement, the reader is puzzled to find that Steen Steensen Blicher, the poet of the Jutland heath whose work was published between about 1814 and 1840, belongs, in Rubow's opinion, to Danish *romantisme* because of his prose: '*Denne Digter hører ved sin Prosa den danske Romantisme til ...*'[174]

F. J. Billeskov Jansen, following Arthur O. Lovejoy's example, speaks of many romanticisms; he differentiates between *Romantik* and *Romantisme* in *Danmarks Digtekunst* (III, 1958) and distinguishes between the two on the basis of chronology and foreign influences.

Romantik he identifies as German-orientated literature from about 1800 to 1825; *romantisme*, as French-orientated literature from about 1825 to 1850. In contrast, his colleague, Sven Møller Kristensen, writing in 1966, states that 'it was heretical *romantisme* which came again with Brandes' / '*Det var den forkætrede romantisme der kom igen med Brandes* ...'[175] In retrospect, then, *Romantisme* was no more definitive than *Romantik* up to the First World War, but has acquired a chronological delimitation since.

Since the Second World War, several books and monographs have appeared in Scandinavia which have *romantisk* or *Romantik* in their titles. A few examples indicate the continued breadth and vagueness of the terms:

C. I. Scharling, *Grundtvig og Romantikken* / 'Grundtvig and Romanticism' (Copenhagen., 1947).

Ole Koppang, *Romantikk og romantisme. Sammelikning mellem fransk og tysk romantikk* 'Romanticism and *romantisme*. Comparison of French and German romanticism' (Oslo, 1951).

Bror Eriksson, *En romantiker i en oromantisk tid. Ungdoms-och studieårs ... i Fredrik Vetterlunds diktning* 'A romantic in an unromantic time. Youth and student years in Fredrik Vetterlunds poetry' (Stockholm, 1952).

Ingvar Holm, *Ola Hansson. En studie i åttiotalromantik* 'Ola Hansson, a study in the romanticism of the 1880s' (Lund, 1957).

L. Longum, *To Kjærlighetsromantikere. En studie i G. Heibergs og H. Krogs erotiske dramatik* 'Two love romantics. A study in Gunnar Heiberg's and Helge Krog's erotic drama' (Oslo, 1960).

S. Reimann, *John Steinbeck. Realist og romantiker* (Copenhagen, 1962).

Sven Møller Kristensen, *Den dobbelte Eros. Studier i den danske Romantik* / 'Double Eros. Studies in Danish romanticism' (Copenhagen, 1966). Contains, among others, essays on Hans Christian Andersen, Frederik Paludan-Müller, Søren Kierkegaard, and Meir Goldschmidt.

Despite the forthrightness of these titles, the authors of the several studies have not always themselves been certain what they meant by *romantisk*. One example will suffice. At the beginning of his book, Bishop Scharling debates the question whether Grundtvig was a romantic, points out that scholars disagree on the matter, and explains the divergence of opinion as ascribable to the 'lack of clarity about the word *Romantik* itself.'[176] At the conclusion of his book, Bishop Scharling has decided that Grundtvig was not a romantic, because the 'strong characteristics of his spiritual heritage and of his own personality hindered this' / '*Og dog blev Grundtvig ikke Romantiker. Stærke Træk i hans aandelige Fædrenearv og i hans egen Personlighed hindrede dette.*'[177]

In order to seek evidence of the current use of *romantisk* and *Romantik* in Scandinavia, we shall glance at recent volumes of three representative and comparable critical periodicals: the Danish *Kritik* i (1967); the Norwegian *Edda* LXVI (1966); and the Swedish *Samlaren* LXXXVII/1966 (1967). We find that the occurrences of *romantisk/Romantik* can be put into three categories: (1) indiscriminate use of the terms either alone or in phrases or compounds; (2) circumscribed use of the terms in explanatory statements; and (3) critical discussion of the terms themselves.

In the first category one finds phrases which range from the trite and generally accepted to the original and poetic, as, for example, 'national romanticism,' 'romantic music';[178] 'romantic woods and ruins illuminated by the light of the moon,'[179] 'a romantic landscape painting,' 'romantic uncertainty,' and 'romantic decoration';[180] 'romantic nature mythology' and 'romantic attitude toward life';[181] 'the romantic's naïve warmth' and 'the taste of *romantisme*';[182] 'romantic pantheism,'[183] 'the Norwegian new romantics' (of the late nineteenth century),[184] 'a romantic dreamer,'[185] 'erotic romanticism,'[186] 'pre-romanticism,'[187] 'post-romanticism,' and the 'romanticism that is Italy.'[188]

In the second category are more explicit statements, such as 'certain types of romantic thought, which look upon the individual as but a practitioner of the creative power of collectivity (of the people, etc.),' or 'romanticism's pansympathetic feeling for life,' or 'There is romantic language, romantic philosophy, even phosphorism in Stagnelius' Narcissus,' or, '*The Little Mermaid* – Hans Christian Andersen's treatment of a typical romantic motif – is a rejection of the pantheistic monism of romanticism,' or, 'the destruction by the Enlightenment and Romanticism of the natural relationship to tradition, for example, to the Bible, classical literature, or Roman law,' or 'the archromantic conjunction of nature and man becomes in this poem a *Biedermeier* opposition of country and city, a Sunday realism,' or, 'In postwar [i.e., World War I] literature ... the view of love is the same: It is first romantic, then out of hand, and finally tragedy,' or, 'where romantic subjectivism has been melted down into classicistic formal language,' or, 'Rilke's romantic appearance, the burning, dark sorrowful eyes in the pale beard-framed face.'

visse typer romantisk tænkning, der ser individet som blot udøver af kollektivet
(*folkets, etc.*) *skaberkraft* ...[189]

romantikens pansympatiske livsfornemmelse.[190]

Det finns romantiskt språk, romantisk filosofi, t.o.m. fosforism i Stagnelius'
Narcissus ...[191]

Den lille Havfrue – *H. C. Andersens behandling af et typisk romantisk motiv – er*
en afvisning af romantikens panteistiske monisme.[192]

oplysningstidens og romantikkens ødelæggelse af det selvfølgelige forhold til
overleveringen, f. eks. til bibelen, den klassiske litteratur eller romerretten.[193]

højromantikkens sammenstilling af natur og menneske bliver i dette digt en Bieder-
meier-modstilling af land og by, en søndagsrealisme.[194]

I den etterkrigslitteraturen ... *er synet på kjærligheten det samme: Den blir først*
romantisk, så over evne og til slutt tragedie.[195]

hvor romantisk subjektivisme er smeltet ned i et klassisistisk formsprog.[196]

Rilkes romantiske utseende, de brinnande, mörka, sorgsna ögonen i det bleka,
skägginramade ansiktet ...[197]

The third category may be eloquently represented by two
quotations from *Samlaren* for 1966 (1967). In a review of Bengt
Lewan's *Drömmen om Italien* ('The dream of Italy,' Lund, 1966),
Ulla-Britta Lagerroth wrote,

Lewan not only fails to delineate the concept 'the romanticism that was
Italy,' but he also employs the term romanticism carelessly ... In a confusing manner, the adjective *romantic* is applied to descriptions now by the
actual romantics, now by all the travellers to Italy who are mentioned
(including the realists!); now and then the adjective is quite simply
synonymous with anything enthusiastic said about countries to the south.

Lewan inte bara försummar att utreda begreppet Italiaromantik, utan han handskas
också lättsinnigt med termen romantik ... *På ett något förvirrande sätt får*
adjektivet 'romantisk' hänföra sig till skildringar av de egentliga romantikerna, än
till samtliga de behandlade Italienresenärerna (också realisterna!) : då och då blir
adjektivet helt enkelt synonymt till det som innebär något entusiastiskt om landet i
söder.[198]

In an article critically sceptical of Wellek's defense of the term
romanticism, Lars Gustafsson states in words reminiscent of Atterbom
in 1808, of Tegnér in 1822, and of Heiberg in 1827 (see p. 376, 380*f.*),

The more concentrated the study of traditional, classicistic poetics has become, the more we have discovered how many ostensibly romantic ideas are contained in those poetics, and the greater has become the need for making sharper distinctions in the history of ideas and for a more differentiated terminology.

Ju mera studiet af den traditionella, klassicistiska poetiken har fördjupats, ju mera det har upptäckts hur mycket av föregivet romantiska idéer som ryms inom denne poetik, desto större har behovet blivit av skarpare idéhistoriska distinktioner och en mera differentierad terminologi.[199]

Icelandic usage is equally inconsistent. In his above-mentioned lecture on poetry from the year 1888, the Icelander, Benedict Gröndal, had complained that nobody really knew what romanticism was and that the word was as misused as the term *idealism*. He himself nevertheless characterized his fellow poet, Bjarni Thorarensen, as 'the greatest romantic and idealist whom we have' *('hann er sá mesti rómantíker og idealisti, sem vér eigum.*'* Their countryman, Professor Einar Ólafur Sveinsson, writing in 1956, contradicted the common assumption of a century – and Gröndal as well – when he declared that Old Icelandic literature had very little of the romantic.[200]

Thus, a hundred years after Meir Goldschmidt put the question, 'what do you understand by romanticism?' Scandinavian criticism still provides no satisfactory answer. Even the divisions into four or five principal meanings of *romantik* and *romantisk* in the major Scandinavian dictionaries fail to clarify the confused application of the words in the last hundred and fifty or more years. *Romantisk* still evokes many connotations both pleasant and unpleasant – as it did for Goldschmidt. Its denotations remain numerous and elusive. *Romantisk* may still mean the picturesque or the exciting, the medieval or the modern, the radical or the reactionary, the erotic, the exotic, and the fantastic, the non-classical or the nationalistic, the desirable or the impractical, the grand or the nonsensical. The term remains conveniently imprecise – if a bad penny, nevertheless a part of common speech as well as of the schooled language of the critic and literary historian.

Even apprised of these divergencies of meaning, today's reader

* Benedikt Gröndal, *Ritsafn* IV (Reykjavik, 1953): 228, 242. The noun *rómantíker* as applied to a person in written Icelandic is found only in Gröndal, according to the records of the Icelandic dictionary being edited by Dr. Jakob Benediktsson, although the noun *rómantík* and the adjective *rómantískur* are in use. Despite the strong tendency to purism in modern Icelandic, there has been no attempt to create Icelandic equivalents for the two words.

may feel disconcerted by a remark made by the Danish poetess, Cecil Bødker, in an interview in 1966:

Naturally I am a romantic ... And I am not absolutely certain that what I understand as romanticism will have any attraction whatsoever for normal romantics. My special type of romanticism finds expression in cleaning out the chicken coop and cultivating tomatoes in the manure – it has nothing to do with poetic enthusiasm.

Naturligvis er jeg romantiker ... Og jeg er aldeles ikke sikker på, at det jeg selv opfatter som romantisk vil have nogensomhelst tiltrækning på normale romantikere. Min særlige form for romantik giver sig udslag i at muge ud under hønsene og dyrke tomater i gødningen – det har intet med poetisk sværmeri at gøre ...[201]

NOTES

1 *Breve fra og til Meir Goldschmidt*, ed. Morten Borup, II (Copenhagen, 1963): 156.
2 Frederik Sneedorff, *Samlede Skrifter* I (Copenhagen, 1794): 196 *f.*
3 *Breve fra og til Meir Goldschmidt* I: 195.
4 *Thomas Thorilds Bref*, ed. Lauritz Weibull, III (1902): 174.
5 Gunnar Reinhard, ' "Romanesk," "romantisk," "romantik" i svensk literatur till omkring år 1810,' *Samlaren* N.S. XXV (1945): 86.
6 Cited by G. Reinhard, *Samlaren* N.S. XXV (1945): 87.
7 Henrik Steffens, *Indledning til philosophiske Forelæsninger i København*, 1803, ed. B. T. Dahl (Copenhagen, 1905), p. 108.
8 Esaias Tegnér, *Filosofiska och estetiske skrifter* (Stockholm, 1913), p. 329.
9 17 February 1811, in Esaias Tegnér, *Brev*, ed. N. Palmberg, I [Malmö, 1953]: 196.
10 *Polyfem*, supplement to number 21 (1810).
11 Christian Molbech, *Blandede Skrifter* II (Copenhagen, 1854): 234.
12 *Swensk Literatur-Tidning*, 1821, col. 117.
13 P. L. Møller, *Kritiske Skizzer* I (Copenhagen, 1847): 122.
14 *Polyfem* (1810), no. 23.
15 C. A. Ehrenswärd, *Swensk Literatur-Tidning*, 1814, col. 807.
16 Repr. in Daniel Andreæ (ed.), *Svensk Litteraturkritik* (Stockholm, 1964), p. 44.
17 Repr. in *Blandede Skrifter* III (1855): 161.
18 Esaias Tegnér, *Samlade Skrifter* IV (Stockholm, 1920): 162.
19 Ibid., p. 162 *f.*
20 Ibid., p. 163.
21 Ibid., p. 164.
22 Ibid.
23 Ibid., p. 165.
24 Ibid.
25 Johan Ludvig Heiberg, 'Tegnérs Frithiof,' repr. in *Prosaiske Skrifter* V (Copenhagen, 1861): 20.
26 Ibid., pp. 22 *f.*
27 Møller, *Kritiske Skizzer* I: 56.
28 Ibid., II: 159.
29 Ibid., II: 183.
30 Ibid., II: 184.

31 *Swensk Literatur-Tidning*, 1813, col. 352. Cf. F. Schlegel's definition, 'Ein Roman ist ein romantisches Buch' (*Kritische Ausgabe* II: 335).
32 *Swensk Literatur-Tidning*, 1813, col. 352.
33 Oehlenschläger, in *Athene* I (1813): 295.
34 Fredric Cederborgh, *Ottar Trallings Lefnads-Målning*, 1814, repr. Stockholm, [1951], pp. 130 f.
35 Tegnér, *Brev* I: 245.
36 Christian Molbech, in *Athene* VIII (1817): 85.
37 Ibid., IX (1817): 170.
38 Axel Garde, *Stille Øjeblikke* (Copenhagen, 1944), p. 64.
39 Christian Molbech, in *Athene* IX (1817): 172.
40 Ibid.
41 Oscar Levertin, repr. in *Nordisk litteratur* (Stockholm, 1909), p. 229.
42 Christian Molbech, in *Athene* VIII (1817): 84; review of J. L. Heiberg, *Dristig vovet*.
43 Ibid., IX (1817): 480; review of J. M. Thiele, *Prøver af danske Folkesagn.*
44 Ibid., p. 171.
45 Peder Hjort, in *Athene* V (1815): 405.
46 *Swensk Literatur-Tidning*, 1815, col. 832.
47 Ibid., 1816, col. 97, in a review of *Flykten till Spetsbergen* I–II (Stockholm, 1815).
48 *Swensk Literatur-Tidning*, 1813, col. 648.
49 Ibid., 1814, col. 188.
50 Ibid., 1816, col. 416.
51 Christian Molbech, in *Athene* VIII (1817): 80; review of J. L. Heiberg's *Dristig vovet*.
52 Carsten Hauch, in *Athene* VIII (1817): 438 f.
53 Ibid., p. 424.
54 *Swensk Literatur-Tidning*, 1818, col. 439.
55 Ibid., 1823, col. 162.
56 Ibid., 1825, col. 724.
57 Christian Molbech (1827), repr. in *Blandede Skrifter* II: 205.
58 Ibid., p. 192.
59 J. L. Heiberg, 'Cervantes' Don Quixote' (1830), repr. in *Prosaiske Skrifter* V (1861): 79.
60 P. L. Møller, review of J. L. Heiberg's *Syvsoverdag*, in *Kritiske Skizzer* I (1847): 110.
61 *Swensk Literatur-Tidning*, 1813, col. 387.
62 Ibid., 1814, col. 167.
63 Ibid., 1816, col. 354.
64 Ibid., 1820, col. 809 f.
65 Tegnér, *Samlade Skrifter* IV: 168.
66 *Swensk Literatur-Tidning*, 1821, col. 39.
67 Tegnér, repr. in *Samlade Skrifter* IV (1920): 165.
68 Peder Hjort, *Athene* V (1815): 89.
69 Ibid.
70 Ibid.
71 Ibid., p. 422.
72 Ibid.
73 Ibid., VI (1816): 158.
74 Ibid., p. 160.
75 Ibid., p. 165.
76 *Swensk Literatur-Tidning*, 1816, col. 703.
77 Ibid., col. 766.
78 Ibid.
79 *Athene* VII (1816): 100.
80 *Swensk Literatur-Tidning*, 1817, no. 46, col. 719.

81   Ibid., 1819, no. 21, col. 335.
82   Ibid., 1820, col. 816.
83   Ibid., col. 825.
84   Cf. above, pp. 147 f.
85   Molbech, *Blandede Skrifter* II: 191n.
86   Ibid.
87   Christian Molbech, *Nordisk Tidsskrift for Historie* II (1827): 187.
88   'Cervantes' Don Quixote,' repr. in J. L. Heiberg, *Prosaiske Skrifter* v (1861): 70.
89   Carsten Hauch, 'Bidrag til Belysningen af nogle æsthetiske Stridspuncter,'
     repr. in *Afhandlinger og æsthetiske Betragtninger* (Copenhagen, 1855), pp. 291, 274.
90   P. L. Møller, 'Lidt om Calderon,' in *Kritiske Skizzer* I: 194.
91   See. for example, *Kritiske Skizzer* II: 110.
92   E. Tegnér, *Samlade Skrifter* IX (Stockholm, 1925): 312.
93   B. Björnson, *Brevveksling med Danske* I (Copenhagen, 1953): 240.
94   Ibid., I: 242.
95   Ibid., II: 199.
96   *Swensk Literatur-Tidning*, 1819, col. 199.
97   Ibid., col. 596.
98   Repr. in Oscar Levertin, *Utländsk Litteratur* (Stockholm, 1909). p. 34.
99   Repr. in Oscar Levertin, *Essayer* II (Stockholm, 1907): 75.
100 'Öfwersigt af Sweriges nuwarande Dagblads-Literatur,' *Swensk Literatur-Tidning*,
     24 December 1821, col. 753 ff., esp. col. 764.
101 H. Wergeland, *Skrifter* II (Oslo, 1960): 31.
102 Repr. in Christian Molbech, *Blandede Skrifter* (1832), II: 348.
103 H. Wergeland, *Skrifter* (1837), III: 176.
104 Møller, *Kritiske Skizzer* I (1841): 45.
105 Ibid., p. 49.
106 E. G. Geijer, repr. in D. Andreæ, *Svensk Litteraturkritik* (Stockholm, 1964),
     pp. 57 f.
107 Fredrik Böök, *Resa kring svenska parnassen* (Stockholm, 1926), p. 144.
108 Paul V. Rubow, *Dansk Litterær Kritik* (Copenhagen, 1921), p. 59.
109 Møller, *Kritiske Skizzer* II: 231.
110 C. F. Blixen Finecke to Goldschmidt, *Breve fra og til Meir Goldschmidt* I: 278.
111 Ibid., II: 48.
112 *Samlede Verker* (Oslo, 1922 ff.), XV: 29.
113 Ibid., IV: 145.
114 Ibid., p. 153.
115 Ibid., VI: 478.
116 Ibid., III: 33.
117 *Folkekalender for Danmark* (1853), p. 110.
118 Ibid., 1859, p. 34.
119 Ibid., p. 55.
120 Georg Brandes, *Samlede Skrifter* IV (1900): 207.
121 Ibid., p. 206.
122 Ibid., p. 208.
123 See A. Ruge and Th. Echtermeyer, 'Der Protestantismus und die Romantik ...
     Ein Manifest,' *Hallische Jahrbücher für deutsche Wissenschaft und Kunst*, 1839, no.
     245 – 1840, no. 64.
124 Brandes, *Samlede Skrifter* IV: 450.
125 Ibid., p. 200.
126 Ibid., VI: 23.
127 George Brandes, 'Paul Heyse,' in *Det Nittende Aarhundrede* (1874/5), pp. 107 f.
128 Henrik Jæger, *Literaturhistoriske Pennetegninger* / (Christiania, 1878), pp. 157 f.
129 Ibid., p. 216.
130 Ibid., p. 203.
131 Herman Bang, *Realism og Realister*, 1879 (new ed., Copenhagen, 1966), p. 15.

132 Ibid., pp. 84, 50.
133 Ibid., p. 154.
134 Ibid., p. 164.
135 Valdemar Vedel, *Guldalderen* (2nd ed., Copenhagen, 1948), p. 133.
136 Ibid., p. 146.
137 Ibid., p. 127.
138 Ibid., p. 147.
139 Ibid., p. 150.
140 Valdemar Vedel, *Svensk Romantik* (Copenhagen, 1894), p. 149.
141 Ibid., p. 159.
142 Vedel, *Guldalderen*, p. 216.
143 Hans E. Kinck, 'Evnene til Længsel,' in *Rormanden overbord* (Kristiania, 1920), p. 247.
144 A. Strindberg, 'Konstakademiens utställning 1877,' repr. in *Samlade Skrifter* (Stockholm. 1912–19), IV: 161.
145 Ibid., XIV (1913): 24.
146 Ibid., p. 18.
147 Ibid., p. 35.
148 Cited by Daniel Andreæ (ed.), *Svensk litteraturkritik* (Stockholm, 1964), p. 97.
149 Oscar Levertin, in 'Bertel Gripenberg' (1904), repr. in *Nordisk Litteratur* (Stockholm, 1909), p. 34.
150 Oscar Levertin, in an essay written in 1904 and repr. in *Essayer* I (Stockholm, 1907): 147.
151 Oscar Levertin in a review of a book by Paul Bourget, 1900, repr. in *Utländsk Litteratur* (Stockholm, 1909), p. 37.
152 Oscar Levertin, in a review of Strindberg, *Nya svenska öden*, repr. in *Svensk Litteratur* I (Stockholm, 1908): 73.
153 Oscar Levertin, *Essayer*, I: 163.
154 Oscar Levertin, in *Utländsk Literatur*, p. 46.
155 Oscar Levertin, in *Svensk Litteratur* I: 249.
156 Oscar Levertin, in *Nordisk Litteratur*, p. 65.
157 Ibid., p. 100
158 Oscar Levertin, 'Snoilskys utveckling,' 1906, repr. in *Essayer* I: 237.
159 Frederik Böök, *Den romantiska tidsaldern* (Stockholm, 1918), p. 14.
160 Ibid.
161 Ibid., p. 32.
162 Ibid., p. 4.
163 Paul V. Rubow, *Georg Brandes' Briller* (Copenhagen, 1932), p. 189.
164 Ibid., p. 230.
165 Ibid., p. 133.
166 Paulus Svendsen, *Edda* XLI (1941): 409.
167 Ibid., p. 416.
168 Ibid., p. 410.
169 Ibid.
170 *Georg Brandes' Breve til Hjemmet 1870–1871* (Copenhagen, 1938), pp. 60 f.
171 P. Hansen, *Illustreret dansk Litteraturhistorie* II (Copenhagen, 1866): 312.
172 Vilhelm Andersen, in *Illustreret dansk Litteraturhistorie* III (Copenhagen, 1924): 35.
173 Paul V. Rubow, *Dansk litterær Kritik* (Copenhagen, 1921), p. 270 (hereafter cited as *Kritik*).
174 Ibid., p. 75.
175 S. M. Kristensen, *Den dobbelte Eros* (Copenhagen, 1966), p. 288.
176 C. I. Scharling, *Grundtvig og Romantiken* (Copenhagen, 1947), p. 7.
177 Ibid., p. 242.
178 E.g., *Edda* LXVI: 336, 344.
179 Ibid., p. 242.

180 *Kritik* I, 2: 91, 96, 99.
181 *Kritik* I, 1: 74.
182 *Kritik* I, 3: 89.
183 *Kritik* I, 1: 75.
184 *Edda* LXVI: 206.
185 Ibid., p. 291.
186 Ibid., p. 415.
187 Ibid., p. 381 *et passim.*
188 'Italiaromantiken,' *Samlaren* LXXXVII: 189.
189 *Kritik* I, 1: 36.
190 Ibid., p. 75.
191 *Samlaren* LXXXVII: 53 *f.*
192 *Kritik* I, 1: 74.
193 *Kritik* I, 4: 90.
194 *Kritik* I, 2: 100.
195 *Edda* LXVI: 84.
196 *Edda* LXVI: 289.
197 *Edda* LXVI: 305.
198 Ulla-Britta Lagerroth, *Samlaren* LXXXVII: 194.
199 Lars Gustafsson, *Samlaren* LXXXVII: 34.
200 Einar Ólafur Sveinsson, *Við uppspretturnar* (Reykjavik, 1956), p. 259.
201 *Digtere i forhør 1966*, ed. Claus Clausen (Copenhagen, 1967), p. 132.

SIGRID McLAUGHLIN

Russia /
Romaničeskij – Romantičeskij –
Romantizm

1791–1820

Romanticism is like a phantom. Many people believe in it; there is a conviction that it exists, but where are its distinctive features, how can it be defined, how can one put one's finger on it?

Romantizm kak domovoj. Mnogie verjat emu, ubeždenija est', čto on suščestvuet, no gde ego primety, kak oboznačit' ego? Kak natknut' na nego palec?[1]

These words were written in 1824 by P. A. Vyazemsky. Puskhin repeats this complaint when he says in a letter of 25 May 1825: 'I've noticed that everybody [in Russia], even you, has only the vaguest notion of romanticism'/*Ja zametil, čto vse, daže ty, imejut u nas samoe temnoe ponjatie o romantizme.*'[2] Belinsky, two decades later, echoes Pushkin: '... the problem has not become clarified [from all these disputes] and romanticism, as before, has remained a mysterious and enigmatic subject'/*... ot vsego ètogo [spory] vopros ne ujasnilsja i romantizm po-prežnemu ostalsja tainstvennym i zagadočnym predmetom.*'[3]

Eighty years later, A. I. Beletsky has not discovered any improvement. In 1927 he writes: 'Hundreds of pages of scholarly investigations ... have not dispersed the mist which this term brought into the history of literature, in particular, Russian literature'/ '*Sotni stranic v naučnyx issledovanijax ... ne razvejali tumana, vnesennogo ètim terminom v istoriju literatury, v častnosti russkoj.*'[4] In 1959, Meylakh repeats: '... it is common knowledge that in no other area of literary criticism do so many contradictions, such discordance exist as in that of the interpretation of romanticism'/*Izvestno, čto ni v odnoj oblasti literaturovedenija net stol'kix protivorečij, takoj rasnogolosicy, kak v oblasti ponimanija romantizma.*'[5] Finally, in 1967, Pospelov summarized the present situation: 'The word romanticism grew into a homonymic tree in a little over a hundred years' / '*V takoe omonimičeskoe drevo vyroslo za sto s lišnim let i slovo romantizm.*'[6]

Thus, for one and a half centuries the problem of a definition of romanticism has been posed by scholars of Russian literature. In the course of these years, the word 'romantic' not only has produced numerous cognates – the *Dictionary of the Contemporary Russian Literary Language* lists eighteen – but has come to mean so many, often contradictory, things that its meaning can be determined only from the context, if at all. An examination of when and in what semantic contexts the cognates were introduced should throw light on the logical relationships between them, on the complexity of the historical shift in consciousness, values, and aesthetic standards involved, and on the kinds of limitations 'romantic' has if used as a literary term.

In Russian, several words exist to render the English word 'romantic': *romaničeskij, romantičeskij, romaničnyj.* The word that was the first to come into usage was *romaničeskij,* which made its first appearance in Karamzin's *Letters of a Russian Traveller,* published in 1791–2 in the *Moscow Journal (Moskovskij Žurnal).** Karamzin finds in Rousseau's *New Heloise* '... much that is unnatural, exaggerated – in a word, romantic.' He speaks of his desire to visit the locations where Rousseau placed his 'romantic lovers' (*romaničeskix ljubovnikov*),[7] and writes that he

surely will walk up the terrace of the local church in order to sit for a while between the tomb stones, under the gloomy shade of one-hundred-year-old trees, in order to follow the setting sun with his eyes ... and to observe the falling of the dense nightly shadows upon the romantic picture of the surroundings of Vevey.

... Vzojdet, konečno, na terrasu zdešnej cerkvi, čtoby posidet' meždu grobami, pod mračnoj ten'ju stoletnix derev'ev, provodit' glazami zaxodjaščee solnce ... i videt' sguščenie nočnyx tenej na romaničeskoj kartine Vevejskix okrestnostej.[8]

---

*   See G. A. Višnevskaja, 'Iz istorii russkogo romantizma (Literaturno-teoreti-
     českie suždenija N. M. Karamzina 1787–92 gg.),' *Voprosy romantizma v russkoj
     literature, Sbornik* II (Kazan, 1964): 82. V. Zhirmunsky ('Romantizm,'
     Enciklopedičeskij slovar' XXXVI, ed. V. Y. Zhelezov, Moscow, 1909, p. 267) asserts
     that the word *romantičeskij* came into wide use at the beginning of the nineteenth
     century, but it is unclear whether he speaks of European literature including
     Russian or not. If he intended the former he should have referred to *romaničeskij*
     rather than *romantičeskij.*

When Karamzin describes the marriage of Haller's granddaughter, he mentions her unexpected meeting with her future husband in unusual circumstances and summarizes it by saying that everything took place 'in the most romantic manner'/'*samym romaničeskim obrazom*'.[9]

In 'My Confession' ('Moja ispoved'') of 1802, 'romantic' is associated with 'emotional' and becomes a quality of the heart. The heroine's name, Emilia, like the title of the story, points to the source of this usage, Rousseau. Generalizing about Emilia, the narrator says:

The most romantic woman can in certain circumstances become tempted by wealth, but wealth loses for her all its value with the first movement of the heart.

Ženščina samaja romaničeskaja v nekotoryx obstojatel'stvax možet prel'stit'sja bogatstvom, no bogatstvo terjaet dlja nee vsju cenu pri pervom dviženii serdca.[10]

In 'A Knight of Our Time' ('Rycar' našego vremeni,' 1802), Karamzin has his narrator say: 'I do not like my readers to yawn, and therefore I shall relate the romantic story [*romaničeskuju istoriju*] of one of my friends instead of an historical novel [*vmesto istoričeskogo romana*].'[11] Later the same narrator says: 'Leon was occupied more with events, the connections of things and events, than with the feelings of romantic love [*ljubvi romaničeskoj*].'[12]

Karamzin seems to have distinguished between two kinds of novels/'*romany*' – novels concerned with the moral nature of man, such as those of Richardson, Rousseau, and Fielding,[13] and novels of a less realistic type, which he characterized by calling them 'invented'/'*vymyšlennyj*'. Broadly speaking, this distinction corresponds to Clara Reeve's famous distinction between 'novels' and 'romances,' and Karamzin obviously primarily associated the romantic/'*romaničeskij*' with the latter type, using the adjective with respect to the state of mind produced by reading romances, with picturesque landscapes of the type described in romances, with the heart rather than reason, and quite generally with improbability, fantasy, or flights of the imagination.*

At that time, the *roman* was held in very low esteem by most literary theoreticians.[14] In the 1800s, Zhukovsky spoke with contempt of this genre, which implied for him 'nonsense, foolhardiness,

---

* Karamzin implies the distinction between *roman* and *istorija* or *byl'* when he asks in 'Poor Liza': 'Why do I write, not a novel, but a sad story of the past?' ('Dlja čego pišu ne roman a pečal'nuju byl'?'). N. M. Karamzin, *Sobranie sočinenij* I (Moscow-Leningrad, 1964): 619.

dream, and insignificance' / '*vzdor, bezrassudnost'*, *mečta, ničto žestvo*.'[15] The *New Explanatory Dictionary* (*Novyj slovotolkovatel'*) of 1803–6 also characterized the novel negatively:

Most of these works narrate amorous adventures ... Good and prudent parents and educators certainly will make every effort to keep this evil out of the hands of their children and students by making them understand the danger of novels. How many young people's heads did they not turn, and how many of the very best hearts corrupt? A writer ... must have nothing else in his mind than ... to improve people ... If his work does not achieve this goal, it is not worthy of being published and the writer deserves universal contempt.[16]

In line with this definition of *roman*, the *New Explanatory Dictionary* defined *romaničeskij* as 'fictitious, amorous, fabulous, fantastic, chimerical, like romantic imaginings' / '... *vymyšlennyj, ljubovnyj, basnotvornyj, skazočnyj, ximeričeskij, kak romaničeskie voobraženija*.'

This is also the meaning of *romaničeskij* in the ironic 'Conversation' in *Pleasant and Useful Spending of Time* (*Prijatnoe i poleznoe preprovoždenie vremeni*) of 1798:

Enough romanticizing, my dear friend! I notice that some novel attracted you with its truthfulness and inflamed the great desire in you to play the romantic role of a lover. Nowadays this love is already out of fashion, and is considered nothing but a satire on stupid, old-fashioned manners.

Polno, ljubeznyj drug moj, romaničestvovat'! Ja primečaju, čto kakoj-nibud' roman prel'stil tebja svoeju vernost'ju i velikoe želanie vospalil v tebe sygrat' romaničeskuju rol' ljubovnika? Nyne uže èta ljubov' ne v mode, i ona teper' priznaetsja ne za inoe čto, kak za satiru na glupye starinnye nravy.[17]

With the same connotations, *romaničeskij* is found again in the phrase 'romantic havens of bliss' / '*romaničeskie ubežišča blaženstva*' in Izmaylov's story of 1804, 'Lake Rostov.'[18]

In 1805 a rather inaccurate Russian translation of an anonymous German article, 'On Opera,' was published in *Severnyj Vestnik* (pt. IV, no. 4, pp. 16–27), which associates *romaničeskij* with music and otherworldliness:

The romantic [*romaničeskoe*] is *per se* the marvellous, and everything marvellous is *per se* the poetic ... The romantic must be expressed in a manner that is appropriate for it; the most fitting means for this is the union of music with poetry. Music is always an echo of another world, a world of magic which we can neither understand nor feel exactly. It [music] echoes loudly in us; but this response, it seems, comes from higher spheres. In exactly such a content [do you find] the romantic. It lies in ourselves, in the world of our feelings, in our beliefs, in our inner meditations; and it must be connected with emotional adventure ...

Romaničeskoe est' samo po sebe čudesnoe, a vse čudesnoe est' samo po sebe stixotvorčeskoe ... Romaničeskoe trebuet svojstvennogo emu vyraženija; udobnejšee že k tomu sredstvo est' soedinenie muzyki s stixotvorstvom. Muzyka vsegda est' otgolosok drugogo mira, mira volšebnogo, kotorogo my ni točno ponjat', ni čuvstvovat' ne možem. Gromko otzyvaetsja ona v nas; no otzyv ee, kažetsja, nisxodit ot vysšix stran. V takom že točno soderžanii i romaničeskoe. Ono naxoditsja v nas, v mire našix čuvstv, v našem verovanii, vo vnutrennem našem rassmatrivanii; a čtob emu živoe imet' nad nami dejstvie, – nadobno, čtob ono svjazano bylo s čuvstvennymi priključenijami, s čudesnymi javlenijami, s predmetami i razgovorami.[19]

This explanation is, however, criticized in a footnote by an unnamed editor, who offers a definition of his own:

If everything romantic [*romaničeskoe*] is marvellous, two thirds of the best Spanish novels contain nothing romantic. The romantic is possibility refined for poetic effect, and this refinement does not require an admixture of the marvellous. An object becomes romantic when it acquires the appearance of the marvellous without thereby losing its [inner] truth.

Esli vse romaničeskoe est' čudesnoe, to dve tretie doli lučšix gišpanskix romanov ne zaključajut v sebe ničego romaničeskogo. Romaničeskoe dlja stixotvorčeskogo dejstvija est' utončennaja vozmožnost', i utončenie sie ne trebuet smešenija s čudesnym. Romaničeskim delaetsja predmet, kogda priobretaet on vid čudesnogo, ne terjaja pritom svoej istiny.[20]

This problem of sustaining an illusion of reality in a fictional work that abounds in objects, situations, and characters described as *romaničeskij* also occupied P. Shalikov. The narrator of 'Adelanda and Ariston, or the Colonists' (1810) wonders whether his heroes become unrealistic when he gives them 'romantic names' / *romaničeskie imena*. At the same time he tries to clarify the connection between *romaničeskij*, *romanizm*, and *roman* when he asks whether his characters must be immoral and ridiculous when described as *romaničeskij*: '*Ja govoril: romaničeskoe namerenie, romaničeskie kolonisty, romaničeskij domik: i sprašivaju odnakož, est' li v istorii six ljudej takoj roman ili romanizm, kotoryj byl by dostoin nasmešlivoj ulybki, ili osnovatel'nogo poricanija?*'[21] The cognates still seem to form a conceptual unit for him: the romantic is the novel-like (*das Romanhafte*).

The meanings derivative from *roman* remained prevalent in the

1810s. Thus, the hero of Narezhny's *A Russian Gil Blas* (1814) is 'a person of the most romantic disposition' / *čelovek samogo romaničeskogo duxa*,[22] and Vyazemsky attributes the 'romantic color' / *cvet romantizma* of Ozerov's poetry to his reading of *romany*.[23]

In the second decade of the nineteenth century, the situation became more complicated with the introduction of the word *romantičeskij* as both a synonym for *romaničeskij* and as a term to refer to a new kind of poetry. Thus, in 1810, the narrator of V. M. Prevoshchikov's story, 'Modest and Sofya,' believes that experience has destroyed his 'romantic dreams' / *'romantičeskie sny.'* *Romantičeskij* here means the same as *romaničeskij*: unrealizable, beautifully fantastic, ideal.*

From 1813 on, 'obscure rumours about some romanticism' / *'o kakom to romantizme'* began to creep into the Russian journals.[24] Not much later, Mme de Staël's *De l'Allemagne* became known in Russia, and in 1815 a critical review of A. W. Schlegel's *Course of Dramatic Literature* was printed in *The Spirit of Journals* (*Dux Žurnalov*). In 1816 and 1817, articles against Mme de Staël and Schiller's *Maria Stuart* continued the critical discussion of what was labelled *romantičeskij*.[25] In 1817, followers of the romantic school / *'romantiki'* were called 'literary schismatics [*raskol'niki literatury*] [who] surrendered with body and soul to the depraved muses of the romantic Parnassus [*romantičeskogo Parnassa*].'[26]

In 1819, *The Messenger of Europe* (*Vestnik Evropy*) printed a translation of an article, 'About Classical and Romantic Works' ('O tvorenijax klassičeskix i romantičeskix'), by the Polish professor Sniadecki, who condemned the romantics' return to a poetic folklore of the past as a sign of ignorance and as a departure from classical rules. He called romanticism a 'school of treason and a plague,' 'a new ideology full of incomprehensible mysteries,' and a 'threat to science.'[27] *Romantičeskij* and *romantizm* thus entered the Russian language ambiguously as synonyms of the older *romaničeskij* and *romanizm*, and also as terms referring to post-classical and contemporary, i.e., modern as opposed to classical or ancient, literature.

By 1820, two literary forms, the ballad and the *poèma*, had become known as 'romantic genres' / *'romantičeskie rody.'* As early as

---

* V. M. Prevoščikov, 'Modest i Sofija,' *Cvetnik* (1810), p. 289, cited by *Brang*, pp. 27, 251. This seems to be the first time *romantičeskij* is used in Russian. R. A. Budagov ('Iz istorii slov: ROMANTIČESKIJ i ROMANTIZM,' *Izvestija Akademii Nauk SSSR-Serija literatury i jazyka*, 1968, XXVII, vyp. 3, p. 251) credits the *Messenger of Europe* of 1821 with the first occurrence of *romantičeskij*.

1810, for instance, in a letter to A. Turgenev, Zhukovsky identified features of his *poèma*, 'The Twelve Sleeping Maidens,' as romantic: 'It will be heroic,' he says, 'what the Germans call *romantisches Heldengedicht*; thus I allowed myself ... a mixture of all kinds of inventions'/'*Poèma že budet geroičeskaja, a to, čto nazyvajut nemcy romantisches Heldengedicht; sledovatel'no ja pozvolil sebe ... smes' vsjakogo roda vymyslov.*'[28] In 1817 Vyazemsky attempted to prove that Ozerov's tragedies must be regarded as belonging 'to the most recent dramatic genre, the so-called romantic style /'*tak nazyvaemomu romantičeskomu [rodu]*', which the Germans adopted from the Spaniards and the English.' He justified this conclusion on the grounds that 'in their very errors they [Ozerov's tragedies] constitute digressions from the rules – digressions filled with life and bearing a mark of their own':

... *k novejšemu dramatičeskomu rodu, tak nazyvaemomu romantičeskomu, kotoryj prinjat nemcami ot ispancev i angličan ... v samyx pogrešnostjax svoix [oni] predstavljajut nam otstuplenija ot pravil, ispolnennye žizni i nosjaščie svoj obraz.*[29]

1820 – 40

The appearance of Pushkin's 'Ruslan and Lyudmila' in 1820 called forth from various existing literary factions critical articles which tried to account for the novelty of this work and to relate it to the 'new (romantic) poetry.' Both 'liberal' groups were puzzled because it went far beyond what they considered to be romantic.* Voeykov's characterization (in 1820) of 'Ruslan and Lyudmila' as belonging to the 'romantic genre of poetry'/ '*romantičeskij rod poèzii*' because of its mixture of the heroic, the comic, and the marvellous well illustrates the existing confusion.[30] That the new ideas from the West were not yet clearly associated with the term *romantičeskij* and that this word was felt to be synonymous with *romaničeskij* is evident from N. F. Ostolopov's *Dictionary of Old and New Poetics* of 1821, where both cognates are listed, but only *romaničeskij* is defined:

*   In 1820 two groups of Russian *literati* existed that were favourably disposed to 'romanticism,' as they understood it. One group, the followers of Karamzin, considered the essence of romanticism to be the exploration of the individual and his rights. The other group, the followers of Shishkov and members of his *Assembly of Lovers of the Russian Word* (*Beseda ljubitelej russkogo slova*) – Katenin, Griboedov, Kyukhelbeker – focussed on ideas of folklore and national-mindedness as central ideas of romanticism. These groups fought over the concept of romanticism among themselves as well as with their classicist opponents. See *Mordovčenko*, pp. 146 f., 165.

A romantic verse tale is a narrative in verse about some knightly event, which consists of a mixture of love, courage, and piety, and which is based on miraculous acts.

Poèma Romaničeskaja est' stixotvorčeskoe povestvovanie o kakom-libo proisšestvii Rycarskom, sostavljajuščem smes' ljubvi, xrabrosti, blagočestija i osnovannom na dejstvijax čudesnyx.[31]

Pushkin's verse tale became the starting point of a debate concerning the meaning of 'romantic' as a literary term that was to last almost two decades.

Since the various *literati* who called themselves romanticists/ '*romantiki*' or romantic poets/ '*romantičeskie poèty*' had the most varied conceptions of what 'romantic' meant, it is best to let each of them have his say. Yet one conviction was common to all of these authors – the conviction that the romantic was the opposite of the classical. But what was meant by 'classical'? the ancient? French neo-classicism? the timeless qualities of a work of art? A definition of 'romantic' inevitably depended on how 'classical' was characterized.

P. A. Vyazemsky searched for a definition of the word *romantic* in two essays of 1822 and 1824, which were then considered programmatic for the new school. The first was about Pushkin's 'Prisoner of the Caucasus'; the second was occasioned by Pushkin's 'The Fountain of Bakhchisaray.' Vyazemsky admitted that for most Russians 'romantic' still was a 'strange name, considered predatory and lawless' / '... *nazvanie dikoe i počitaemoe za xiščničeskoe i bezzakonnoe*'[32] and that it implied for them 'capricious anarchy' and the destruction of 'rules sacred through age and veneration' / '*Na romantizm smotrjat kak na anarxiju svoevol'nuju, razrušitel'nicu postanovlenij, osvjaščennyx drevnostiju i sueveriem.*'[33] In contrast to these popular views, Vyazemsky, however, found two positive meanings in the term. 'Romantic' meant to him close to or derived from nature; also, it implied local colour, the mark of national history and national spirit, and, implicitly, the rejection of classical, eternal, and universal norms of art.

Although Vyazemsky held that the 'foundation' of romantic poetry 'lies in nature' / '*Načalo ee v prirode*,'[34] this did not mean for him absolute freedom and lawlessness. One of the most essential features of romanticism, he asserted, was that it 'accepts necessities while liberating itself from some relative rules. It must have uniformity, but this is the uniformity of nature which is always new and attractive':

Osvoboždajas' ot nekotoryx uslovnyx pravil, on [romantizm] pokorjaetsja potrebnostjam. V nem dolžno byt' odnoobrazie, no èto odnoobrazie prirody, kotoroe zavsegda novo i zamančivo.[35]

The poet is, however, subject only to the laws of nature and beauty.[36]

This closeness to nature has an effect on the language of poetry. Vyazemsky defends the use of new words that were banned from the *Dictionary of the Russian Academy* 'without due process and for no known crime':

Look at nature! Human faces, which are composed of the very same parts, are not all molded into one physiognomy; and expressiveness is the physiognomy of words.

Smotrite na prirodu! Lica čelovečeskija, sostavlennyja iz odnix i tex že častej, vylity ne vse v odnu fiziognomiju, a vyraženie est' fiziognomija slov.[37]

Variety in nature should be paralleled by variety in language. Just as nature is not all explicit and rounded off, the romantic mood is characterized by 'slight hints' and 'nebulous enigmas' / '... *legkie nameki, tumannyja zagadki – vot materialy izgotovlennye romantičeskim poètom...*'[38] This mood is heightened by fragmentariness: 'The action is only slightly indicated, the reader ... must ... fill in for the author' / '*Po obyknoveniju romantičeskomu, vse èto dejstvie tol'ko slegka oboznačeno ...*'[39]

The romantic is also synonymous with national-mindedness. It is the local colour of 'The Fountain of Bakhchisaray,' 'with all its freshness and brightness,' that makes it a romantic work. 'Homer, Horace, and Aeschylus have more affinity and connections with the main figures of the romantic school than do their cold slavish followers [the classicists]' / '*Gomer, Goracij, Èsxil imejut gorazdo bolee srodstva i sootnošenij s glavami romantičeskoj školy, čem s svoimi xolodnymi rabskimi posledovateljami.*'[40] Thus, romanticism may be an attribute of any national literature at any time. Its characteristic feature is 'folk-character' / '*narodnost'*.'[41] For Vyazemsky, indigenous national content and formal originality inspired by nature constituted the positive essence of romantic poetry. Romanticism in his view became inevitably linked with the search for a new national literature.

F. Bulgarin interpreted the term *romantic* along one of the lines indicated by Vyazemsky. He defended romantic poetry as 'natural poetry,' though 'nature' had different connotations for him:

In the wild and varied beauties of nature, amidst storms and blizzards, between mountains and cliffs, in impenetrable thickets, there is no related plan, but there is harmony, this mutual agreement and correspondence of heterogeneous things ... And similarly in poetry that nowadays is called romantic (and which I call natural) one must in my opinion not look for a plan, but for general harmony or agreement of the whole; not for a complete description of characters, but for spiritual impulses which originate in character. If in a work events are not connected with one another, it is a shortcoming in the activity of nature, and the poet covers up the intervals.

V dikix i raznoobraznyx krasotax prirody, sredi bur' i v'jugi, meždu gor i utesov, v neproxodimyx debrjax net svjaznogo plana, no est' garmonija, èto vzaimnoe soglasie i sootvetstvennost' raznorodnyx predmetov ... I tak v poèzii, nazyvaemoj nyne romantičeskoju (kotoruju ja nazovu prirodnoju), dolžno iskat', po moemu mneniju, ne plana, no obščej garmonii ili soglasija v celom; ne polnogo očertanija xarakterov, no duševnyx dviženij, zaimstvujuščix xarakter. Esli v sočinenii proisšestvija ne svjazany meždu soboju, èto nedostatok prirodnogo dejstvija, i poèt nakryvaet pokrov na promežutki.[42]

V. N. Olin criticized Bulgarin for calling romantic poetry 'natural' when he actually meant 'without plan'/'*besplannyj*'. Whereas Bulgarin considered the romantic to be synonymous with poetic nature, Olin wanted to include the *prosaic* aspects of reality as well:

As regards your opinion that the romantic poet does not draw prose into the nets of art [Olin writes to Bulgarin], I tell you that the laws of art derive directly from nature ... art is a copy of nature, or, in other words, art and nature are of synonymous meaning.

Čto že kasaetsja do mnenija Vašego, čto Romantičeskij Poèt NE VOVLEKAET PROZU V SETI ISKUSSTVA: *ja ... ; skažu Vam, čto pravila iskusstva ... izvlekajutsja neposredstvenno iz samoj Prirody;* ISKUSSTVO *est' kopija Prirody; ili govorja inače, iskusstvo i Priroda sut' značenija sinonimnyja ...**

Orest Somov in his article, 'About Romantic Poetry' (1823), suggested a definition still broader than those just discussed:

Some deduce this name, romantic poetry, from romances sung by ancient troubadours, or, like the romances themselves, from the

---

*   *Russkij Invalid*, 1825, no. 52, p. 209; quoted from *Russkaja kritičeskaja literatura o proizvedenijax A. S. Puškina* III. ed. V. Zelinskij (Moscow, 1901): 4. On the polysemy of 'nature' and its significance for romanticism, see A. O. Lovejoy, ' "Nature" as Aesthetic Norm,' *Essays in the History of Ideas* (New York, 1960), pp. 66–77.

Romance language (*langue romance*); others deduce it from the structure of novels, that is, narratives, invented by imagination, in which historica truth is mixed with invention. Incidentally, this name is perhaps entirely arbitrary; but in agreement with common usage, we will call romantic the most recent poetry which is not based on the mythology of the ancients and does not follow their rules.

Nazvanie sie, poèzija romantičeskaja, odni proizvodjat ot romansov, petyx drevnimi trubadurami, ili kak i samye romansy, ot jazyka romanskogo (langue romance); *drugie – ot vedénija romanov, to est' povestej, izobretennyx voobraženiem ili v koix istoričeskaja dostovernost' smešana s vymyslom. Vpročem, nazvanie sie možet byt' soveršenno proizvol'noe; no my, soglasujas' s obščim upotrebleniem, stanem nazyvat' novejšuju poèziju, ne osnovannuju na mifologii drevnix i ne sledujuščuju ix pravilam, poèziej romantičeskoj.*[43]

Somov disagreed with the definition of romanticism as Christian and medieval because not all European nations were familiar with knightly concepts. For the Slavic nations, for example, the 'main charm' of romantic poetry lay, according to him, in 'national and local colour' / '*v narodnosti i mestnosti*,'[44] It was not its Christian, spiritual content, but its originality and novelty, its imaginative and especially its national quality that made literature romantic. Thus, the 'first people who had romantic poetry were undoubtedly the Arabs or Moors ... Among the European nations, the Italians,' while 'the Spaniards were the founders of romantic taste in dramatic poetry':

Pervyj narod, imevšij poèziju romantičeskuju, byl neosporimo araby ili mavry ... Iz evropejskix narodov ital'jancy ... Ispancy, kažetsja, byli osnovateljami vkusa romantičeskogo v poèzii dramatičeskoj ...[45]

Somov considered Corneille's *Le Cid* to be the first French romantic drama. 'The first known period of English poetry, beginning with Shakespeare and Spenser, was marked by romantic taste.'[46] Milton, Pope, Byron, Moore, Southey, and Walter Scott were also regarded as English romantics. His account of German poetry paraphrases Mme de Staël; Schiller and Goethe are included among the romantics.

Concerning Russian romantic poetry, Somov named Derzhavin, Zhukovsky, and Pushkin's southern *poèmy* as representative, on the grounds that their works were national and had their roots in folk traditions. In addition to folk tradition, Somov seems, however, to have required a particular setting for romantic poetry, offering 'grandiose horrors' and 'brilliant charms' of nature; for it is these qualities that, according to Somov, inspire a poet to create works full of national and local colour. He pleads with the Russian poets not to ignore the qualities of Russian nature, which possesses such romantic areas as the Ukraine, the Caucasus, the Crimea, and Siberia. This emphasis on the national element is characteristic of Somov's notion of romantic poetry, which he calls 'a folk poetry that is neither imitative nor dependent on foreign traditions'/'... *narodnoj poèzii, nepodražatel'noj i nezavisimoj ot predanij čuždyx.*'*

V. K. Kyukhelbeker distinguished between a true and false romanticism. According to him, romanticism had become a fashionable literary trend that had been taken up by untalented poets who imitated foreigners:

[In Russia] people from high society even now cringe before these foreign rules in spite of the romantic babblings with which they have been bombarding everybody who came their way. For now, naturally, it is the duty of every gentleman to be, or at least to seem, a romantic.

U nas ljudi svetskie i ponyne rabolepstvujut pered simi čužezemnymi zakonami, vopreki romantičeskomu lepetaniju, koim s nekotorogo vremeni b'jut v uši vstrečnomu i poperečnomu, ibo teper', konečno, byt' ili, po krajnej mere, kazat'sja romantikom, objazannost' vsjakogo ljubeznika.[47]

For Kyukhelbeker, Zhukovsky and Batyushkov were the leading figures of a school which 'is represented as romantic' / '*vydajut nam za Romantičeskuju.*'[48] But whereas in the rest of Europe 'all poetry which is free and national is called romantic,' the elegics of Zhukovsky and Batyushkov are not romantic at all in this sense of the word, but imitations of German and French works. 'What is our romanticism?' Kyukhelbeker asks – using here *romantika* instead of *romantizm*. He answers as follows:

We have no strength, only murky, effeminate, colourless works that define nothing. Everything here is *dream* or *spectre*, everything is *imagined* and *seems*, and *appears*; everything is only *as if, might, something, somewhat* ... Feelings have not existed for a long time: the feeling of despondency has devoured all others. We all compete in grieving for our lost youth; we dwell endlessly on this grief and, for a break, we show off our faint-heartedness. If this sadness were not simply a rhetorical figure, somebody might think – judging from our Childe-Harolds who have barely

* Somov, p. 147. Somov seems to forget about his own definition when he discusses Schiller's *Wallenstein* and claims that this playwright was able to evoke romantic sympathy (*učastie romaničeskoe*) by creating the characters of Max Piccolomini and Thekla, who love each other in spite of their parents.

grown out of their diapers – that in Russia poets are born as old men. The pictures are everywhere the same: the *moon*, which is, of course, *melancholic* and *pale*; cliffs and oak forests where none ever existed; a forest behind which the sinking sun is pictured a hundred times; sunset; at times long shadows and ghosts; something invisible, something unknown; common-place allegories; pale, tasteless embodiments of *Work, Sweet Bliss, Peace, Grief, Laziness* of the writer and *Boredom* of the reader; and especially mist – mist above water, mist above a forest, mist over fields, mist in the head of the writer.

U nas net sily, tol'ko mutnye, ničego ne opredeljajuščie, iznežennye, bescvetnye proizvedenija. U nas vse mečta *i* prizrak, *vse* mnitsja *i* kažetsja *i* čuditsja, *vse tol'ko* budto by, kak by, nečto, čto-to ... *Cuvstv u nas uže davno net : čuvstvo unynija proglotilo vse pročie. Vse my v zapuski toskuem o svoej pogibšej molodosti; do beskonečnosti žuem i pereževyvaem ètu tosku i na pereryv ščegoljaem svoim malodušiem. Esli by sija grust', ne byla prosto retoričeskoj figuroj, inoj, sudja po našim Čajl'dam Garol'dam, edva vyšedšim iz pelen, mog by podumat', čto u nas na Rusi Poèty uže roždajutsja starikami. Kartiny vezde odni i te že:* luna, kotoraja – razumeetsja – unyla *i* bledna, skaly i dubravy, gde ix nikogda ne byvalo, les, za kotorym sto raz predstavljajut zaxodjaščee solnce, večernjaja zarja; izredka dlinnye teni i prividenija, čto-to nevidimoe, čto-to nevedomoe, pošlye inoskazanija, blednye bezvkusnye olicetvorenija* Truda, Negi, Pokoja, Pečali, Leni *pisatelja i* Skuki *čitatelja; v osobennosti že tuman: tumany nad vodami, tumany nad borom, tumany nad poljami, tumany v golove sočinitelja.*[49]

Romanticism, to Kyukhelbeker's thinking, had been compromised by the recent poets who were very 'cold-blooded, very unromantic romantics and imposters'/'... *ves'ma xladnokrovnye, ves'ma ostorožnye, ves'ma ne romantičeskie samozvancy-romantiki.*'[50] It must be liberated from the falseness and superficiality which it acquired when it became fashionable, and it must again become synonymous with high art, which transforms reality.

True romanticism, according to Kyukhelbeker, originated in Provence; under its influence Dante threw off the yoke of imitation.[51] It had nothing in common with Byron. In the introduction to his dramatic sketch, 'The Spirits of Shakespeare' (1825), he offered as examples of true romanticism Shakespeare's *Midsummer Night's Dream* and *The Tempest* with their 'romantic fabulousness'/'*s romantičeskim basnosloviem*'[52] and P. A. Katenin's ballads. Kyukhelbeker suggested that a new 'romantic mythology' should be invented; that romantic poetry should help the renaissance of mankind. Such 'true' romanticism would be identical with idealism.

His criteria for defining it were freedom of imagination and lofty, idealistic content.

K. F. Ryleev defined romanticism as

... original, independent poetry; and in this sense Homer, Aeschylus, Pindar – in a word all the best Greek romantic poets, as well as the most outstanding works of the most recent poets, written according to the rules of the ancients, but whose subjects were taken from ancient history, are romantic works.

... *poèziju original'nuju, samobytnuju, a v ètom smysle Gomer, Èsxil, Pindar – slovom, vse lučšie grečeskie poèty-romantiki, ravno kak i prevosxodnejšie proizvedenija novejšix poètov, napisannye po pravilam drevnix, no predmety koix ne vzjaty iz drevnej istorii, sut' proizvedenija romantičeskie.*[53]

For Ryleev 'neither romantic nor classical poetry exists';[54] instead, one should distinguish between ancient and modern poetry, for 'true poetry has always been the same ... It differs only in the essence and forms which are lent to it in different ages by the spirit of the time, the degree of enlightenment, and the location of the country where it appears.'

A. A. Bestuzhcv-Marlinsky was at first close to Vyazemsky's views on romanticism. He took exception to an article by Katenin, in which novelty of *form* was considered to be the essential feature of romanticism, and insisted on novelty of *content*. According to Bestuzhev, the romantic writer was concerned with national history. Thus, for example, he regarded Zhukovsky as a member of the romantic school, but as a translator rather than an author. Batyushkov he considered to have written only three pieces in the romantic style: 'The Crossing of the Rhine,' 'The Prisoner,' and 'The Castle in Sweden':

Žukovskij prinadležit k škole romantičeskoj, no bolee kak perevodčik, neželi kak avtor; čto že do Batjuškova, to v romantičeskom rode u nego napisany tol'ko tri p'esy: 'Perexod čerez Rejn,' 'Plennyj,' i 'Zamok v Švecii.'[55]

In the same article, Bestuzhev placed Ryleev's *dumy* 'in the category of purely romantic poetry'/'*v razrjad čisto romantičeskoj poèzii.*'[56] The feature that united these writers was their concern with national historical themes.

Bestuzhev's ideas concerning romanticism seem to have undergone a slight modification in his longest article devoted to the topic, 'About Romances and Romanticism' ('O romansax i romantizme') of 1833. This article, occasioned by N. Polevoy's novel, *The Oath at the Lord's Grave*, deals with the social and historical necessity of romanticism and its place in the history of culture and literature. The nature of romanticism is elucidated by an investigation of the history of the human spirit:

Here is the key to the dual – romantic-historical – direction of literature ... By romanticism, I understand the aspiration of the infinite human spirit to express itself in finite forms. Therefore I consider it of the same age as the human soul. And therefore I think that in spirit and essence there are only two literatures: the literature before and the literature since Christianity. I would call the first the literature of *fate*, the second the literature of *freedom*. In the first, emotions and material images prevail; in the second, the soul reigns, thoughts are victorious. The first is a place of execution where fate is the hangman, man the victim; the second is a battlefield where passions fight with free will, [a battlefield] over which at times the shadow of the hand of providence passes. Insignificant incidents gave the name classical to ancient literature and the name romantic to new literature ... What do we care that the romance troubadours took the fairy tales and refrains everywhere; what do we care whether classes [*klassy*] or Romance countries [*Romanija*] gave names to the two literatures.

Vot ključ dvojstvennogo napravlenija sovremennoj slovesnosti: romantičesko-istoričeskogo ... pod imenem romantizma razumeju ja stremlenie beskonečnogo duxa čelovečeskogo vyrazit'sja v konečnyx formax. A potomu ja sčitaju ego rovesnikom duše čelovečeskoj. A potomu ja dumaju, čto po duxu i suščnosti est' tol'ko dve literatury: èto literatura do xristianstva i literatura so vremen xristianstva. Ja nazval by pervuju literaturoj sud'by, vtoruju – literaturoj voli. V pervoj preobladajut čuvstva i veščestvennye obrazy; vo vtoroj carstvuet duša, pobeždajut mysli. Pervaja – lobnoe mesto, gde rok palač, čelovek – žertva; vtoraja – pole bitvy, na koem sražajutsja strasti s voleju, nad koim poroj mel'kaet ten' ruki providenija. Ničtožnye slučajnosti dali drevnej literature imja klassičeskoj, a novoj imja romantičeskoj ... kakoe nam delo, čto romanskie trubadury raznesli povsjudu svoi skazki i pripevy; kakoe nam delo: klassy li, Romanija li dali imja dvum slovesnostjam! ...[57]

The Christian spirit of the Middle Ages with its inward orientation, its preoccupation with the soul, its otherworldliness and its disregard of the external details of everyday life is thus identified with the essence of romanticism. When speaking of the spirit of the Christian knights of the Middle Ages, Bestuzhev asks rhetorically:

This union of souls, this immutable aspiration to the object of one's passion, this marvellous ability to feel, to see one thing in all nature – isn't this practical romanticism, romanticism in action?

Ètot duxovnyj sojuz duš, èto neizmennoe stremlenie k predmetu svoej strasti, èto čudnoe svojstvo vo vsej prirode čuvstvovat' odno, videt' odno – ne est' li praktičeskij Romantizm, Romantizm na dele?[58]

Implicit here is another feature of the meaning of romanticism: spiritual longing, insatiability, preoccupation with ideals, with absolutes and abstractions, with the dissolution of the present for the sake of infinite goals. This is the meaning given to *romantičeskij* when Bestuzhev exclaims (referring to the hero of Polevoy's novel):

What a lofty romantic idea [*romantičeskaja mysl'*] it was to portray a man who sacrificed to devotion all joys of life, all worldly ambition, even hope after the grave.

Kakaja vysokaja romantičeskaja mysl' byla izobrazit' čeloveka, otdavšego v žertvu vse radosti žizni, vse čestoljubie sveta, daže nadeždu za grobom, – predannosti![59]

This spirit had been revived, according to Bestuzhev, in the present.

We live in the age of romanticism. There are people ... who imagine that romanticism is a fashion for readers, a caprice for authors, and not at all the need of our age, the craving of the peoples' mind, the call of the human soul ...

My živem v veke romantizma ... Est' ljudi ... kotorye voobražajut, čto romantizm v otnošenii k čitateljam moda, v otnošenii k sočiniteljam pričuda, a vovse ne potrebnost' veka, ne žažda uma narodnogo, ne zov duši čelovečeskoj ...[60]

Romanticism and idealism are interchangeable: 'Romanticism was victorious! Idealism was victorious!'/'*Romantizm pobedil, idealizm pobedil.*'[61] For Bestuzhev, the Gospel was a 'type of romanticism,' a prototype of the new literature, and the 'first hotbed of idealism'/ '*Evangelie est' tip romantizma ... bylo pervoobrazom novoj slovesnosti, pervym rassadnikom idealizma.*'[62]

Bestuzhev's historical derivation of the meaning of romanticism gives the term ethical and spiritual rather than aesthetic and literary overtones. Yet he seems to have been aware of the artistic consequences of this new spiritual orientation: 'From that time [the Crusades] on, prophetic mysticism, Oriental ornateness of descriptions, allegories, and solemnity of language, took hold of all poetry'

/ '*S ètix por proročeskij misticizm, vostočnaja roskoš' opisanij, inoskazanija i toržestvennost' jazyka zavladeli vseju poèziej.*'[63] Bestuzhev even discovers formal romanticism in a work that is not romantic in content: he regarded Walter Scott as

... a romantic not as a result of his subject-matter, but ... because of his presentation, his forms, the Sterne-like spirit of analysis of all movements of the soul, of all acts of the will.

... *ne romantik po predmetu, no ... po izloženiju, po formam, Sternovskomu duxu analiza vsex dviženij duši, vsex postupkov voli.*[64]

All this leads Bestuzhev to a rather vague and excessively broad classification of various writers as romantic. His list includes Rabelais, Montaigne, Byron, Schiller, Shakespeare, and Scott. In Russia, according to Bestuzhev, it was Derzhavin who founded romanticism

... not only in spirit, but also in the daring of his images and the novelty of his forms. Read 'The Swallow,' 'God,' 'To Happiness,' 'Felicia,' 'The Magnate,' 'The Waterfall,' and you will call them romantic poems.

Deržavin pervyj položil kamen' russkogo romantizma, ne tol'ko po duxu, no i po derzosti obrazov, po novosti form. Pročtite 'Lastočku,' 'Bog,' 'Na sčastie,' 'Felicu,' 'Vel'možu,' 'Vodopad,' i vy nazovete ix Romantičeskimi poèmami.[65]

Karamzin 'instilled in the Russians romantic dreaminess' / '*Romantičeskuju mečtatel'nost'*.[66] Zhukovsky 'transplanted romanticism into the virgin soil of Russian literature;' but Pushkin, whom many consider the most important representative of romanticism in Russia, had for Bestuzhev 'very little idealism – that is, romanticism' / '... *ves'ma malo imeet v sebe ideal'nogo, to est', romantičeskogo.*'[67] Thus it seems that Bestuzhev classifies the works of various writers as romantic on the basis of their idealistic content and certain characteristics of their form; nevertheless, a precise account of the criteria that make a work romantic is wanting.*

*   The absence of a clear concept of the meaning of 'romantic' is evident also from Bestuzhev's inconsistent use of the words *romantizm* and *romanizm* . On the one hand, Bestuzhev is impatient with those who use the Russian cognates for 'romantic' and 'romanticism' indiscriminately. Thus, he indignantly addresses one of his opponents with the question: 'Does he perhaps assume that *romanizm* and *romantizm* are the same?' (*Syn Otečestva*, 1823, IV: 179.) On the other hand, he writes of Bulgarin's novel *Dmitry the Imposter*: 'Po dorožke protorennoj ego samozvancem, kinulis' djužiny pisatelej na peregonku, budto sorevnuja konskim ristanijam, pojavivšimsja na Rusi vo odno vremja s ROMANIZMOM' (*Moskovskij Telegraf*, 1833, XV: 339). And several paragraphs later, speaking of the general trend of thought in his day, he writes: 'We live in the century of romanticism

N. Polevoy, whom Belinsky called the leader of Russian romanticism, attempted to unite the two basic conceptions of 'romantic' then current in Russia: romantic as descriptive of the spirit and art of the Middle Ages, and romantic as anti-classical and true to nature. It is especially in the development of the second conception that Polevoy added to romantic aesthetics by shifting the emphasis from a mimetic to an expressive critical theory. Romantic poetry was 'natural' to Polevoy because 'the secret and cause of so-called romantic poetry was [to be found] in the indefinite, inexplicable state of the human heart' / '... *v neopredelennom, neiz" jasnimom sostojanii serdca čelovečeskogo zaključena i tajna i pričina tak nazyvaemoj romanticeskoj Poèzii*.'* A truly romantic work should aim only at revealing man's character; the plot should serve this sole purpose and be truthful in itself.

These views are applied and elaborated in Polevoy's long article on M. Pogodin's historical novel, *The Plague (Černaja nemoč')*. Comparing this novel with the historical novels of Walter Scott, Polevoy argued that there existed a certain 'incongruity'/*'nesoobraznost' '* in Pogodin's work because it lacked historical vision and insight. He reproached Pogodin for depicting unnatural (untruthful) events, caricaturing great men, and failing to present an historically accurate background for his characters. Polevoy pleaded for a truthful portrayal of important historical events and their presentation in a popular form.[68] 'What does it mean to base a romantic story [novelistic narrative?] on an historical event?' he asks. It means to have 'historical perspective,' to produce 'a unified creation,' 'a portrayal of the human spirit in general.'/*'Čto značit osnovat' na istoričeskom sobytii romaničeskij rasskaz? ... istoričeskij vzgljad, obščnost' sozdanija ... predstavlenie čelovečeskogo duxa voobšče.'*[69] These are the qualities that make a work of art worthy of being called romantic, and it is on the basis of these criteria that Polevoy determines which writers should be placed in this category:

With respect to truth, expressiveness, language befitting the characters, the truthful portrayal of the characters and of the spirit of the time ... the

(*romantizma*), and in an historic century.' Bestuzhev's own practice seems to have been to use *romanizm* when speaking of novels and *romantizm* when speaking of contemporary literature in general. Bestuzhev's all-inclusive definition of *roman* points to F. Schlegel's influence: 'Roman ... est' ne čto inoe, kak poèma i drama, lirizm i filosofija i vsja poèzija v tysjače granej svoix, ves' svoj vek na obe korki' (*Moskovskij Telegraf*, 1833, xvi: 540).

* *Russkaja kritičeskaja literatura o proizvedenijax A. S. Puškina* II, ed. V. Zelinskij (Moscow, 1899): 13. This typological conception of romanticism anticipates Belinsky's views.

classical Homer was as much a romantic as Schiller, Goethe, Walter Scott and others.

Votnošenii k istine, k vyrazitel'nosti, k jazyku, priličnomu dejstvujuščim licam, k vernomu izobraženiju xarakterov, duxa vremeni opisyvaemoj èpoxi, klassičeskij Omir byl takoj že romantik kak Šiller, Gete, Val'ter Skott i drugie.[70]

Mere disregard of the classical rules, Polevoy maintained elsewhere, did not entitle a writer to be called romantic:

Polagajut, čto ne-nabljudenie trex edinstv v tragedii, otčuždenie vozzvanija k Muzam v poèmax i upotreblenie pjatistopnogo jamba vmesto Aleksandrijskogo dajut polnoe pravo na nazvanie romantičeskogo pisatelja.[71]

Nor, in his conception, should the 'truth' of a romantic work be identified with the truthfulness of realism. Instead, Polevoy recommended that only poetical subjects be presented and that man's moral and spiritual make-up, rather than his physical characteristics, be discussed. Thus he rejected the 'furious [French] romantics'/'*neistovye romantiki*' and Pushkin's *Tales of Belkin*.[72] A new demand on the romantic poet made by Polevoy was that he should be an inspired individual interested exclusively in persuading his readers through his art to pursue high moral goals: '*Čto dolžen delat' zdes' poèt? ... ne rešat' ničego ot sebja i udalit' sja daže ot vsex sentencij. Polnotoju xaraktera ... i polnotoju dejstvija ukazyvaet on na nravstvennuju cel'.*'[73]

A. S. Pushkin is considered by many to have been the greatest Russian romantic writer. Indeed, while writing his Southern Poèmy, he did regard himself as a romantic and his works as 'a romantic enterprise' / '*romantičeskuju lavočku,*'* though he was not quite sure of what he understood by the word. He defined romanticism in 1824 as 'absence of all rules but not of all art,'[74] as 'Parnassian atheism,'[75] or as an approach that considered inspiration the only rule / '*... romantičeskij tragik prinimaet za pravilo odno vdoxnovenie.*'[76] Other qualities associated by Pushkin with the term *romantic* in 1825 were 'passion and tenderness in love, a leaning toward the marvellous and the rich eloquence of the Orient,' 'the piety and

---

* A. S. Pushkin, *Polnoe sobranie sočinenij* xii (Moscow, 1937–49): 28. Like his contemporaries, Pushkin did not distinguish between *romaničeskij* and *romantičeskij* as literary terms. Thus, he refers to the 'new romantic school' as *romaničeskaja škola* (xii: 71). The use of *romaničeskij* in combination with 'school' can be observed as late as 1856, when Nekrasov writes that 'The old romantic school [*romaničeskaja škola*] did much harm' (*Russkie pisateli o literature*, ed. B. Bursov a.o., Leningrad, 1955, ii: 173). On Pushkin's definition of *romantizm*, see John Mersereau, Jr., "Pushkin's Concept of Romanticism," *Studies in Romanticism* 2 (1963): 24–41.

simplicity' of the knights and their ideas of 'heroism and the loose-
ness of manners':

*Mavry vnušili ej [romantičeskoj poèzii] isstuplenie i nežnost' ljubvi,
priveržennost' k čudesnomu i roskošnoe krasnorečie vostoka; rycari soobščili svoju
nabožnost' i prostodušie, svoi ponjatija o gerojstve i vol'nosti nravov ... Takovo
bylo smirennoe načalo romantičeskoj poèzii.*[77]

In 1828, Pushkin's conception of romanticism began to take
more definite and rather different shape:

Examining the critical articles in our journals more attentively, I began
to suspect that I was cruelly deceived in thinking that an aspiration toward a romantic transformation was apparent in our literature ... Having
voluntarily refrained from the advantages offered to me by an aesthetic
system warranted by experience and affirmed by habit, I tried to replace
this perceptible shortcoming by a truthful portrayal of characters and of
the times, and by the development of historical characters and events –
in a word, I wrote a truly romantic tragedy [*Boris Godunov*].

*... vnimatel'nee rassmatrivaja kritičeskie stat'i, pomeščaemye v žurnalax, ja načal
podozrevat', čto ja žestoko obmanulsja, dumaja, čto v našej slovesnosti obnaružilos'
stremlenie k romantičeskomu preobrazovaniju ... Otkazavšis' dobrovol'no ot vygod,
mne predstavljaemyx sistemoju iskusstva, opravdannoj opytami, utverždennoj
privyčkoju, ja staralsja zamenit' sej čuvstvitel'nyj nedostatok vernym izobraženiem
lic, vremeni, razvitiem istoričeskix xarakterov i sobytij, – slovom, napisal tragediju
istinno romantičeskuju.*[78]

Since romanticism meant something different to his contemporaries,[79] Pushkin felt that his concept and his drama were anachron-
isms. To him romanticism included both a rejection of governance
by classical rules and a truthful description of reality or history.
'Our timid taste,' he wrote, 'cannot bear true romanticism'/'*Robkij
vkus naš ne sterpit istinnogo romantizma.*'* Such deliberations led
Pushkin to conclude that definitions of romanticism on the basis of

---

* Pushkin, *Polnoe sobranie sočinenij* III: 228. N. V. Gogol in a draft of 'Petersburg
Notes of 1836' (*Polnoe sobranie sočinenij*, Moscow, 1937–52, VIII: 553 f.) seems
to express an essentially similar view when he says that romanticism was
'nothing more than an attempt to move closer to our society' since 'we had
been totally estranged from it by the imitation of the society and people who
appeared in the creations of the writers of antiquity.' But to Gogol this
'romantic audacity' caused excesses and chaos, unless restrained by a great
talent who 'turned what was romantic into what is classic, or better into a
graphic, clear, majestic creation.' See Carl R. Proffer, "Gogol's Definition of
Romanticism," *Studies in Romanticism* 6 (1967): 120–7.

the content or spirit of a work would not work. Rather, form should be the sole criterion:

The French, who led Russian critics astray, usually considered everything romantic that seemed to them marked by dreaminess and German ideology or that was based on the prejudices and traditions of common people. This is a most inexact definition. A poem may have all of these characteristics, yet belong to classical literature. We should consider classical only those poems whose forms were known to the Greeks and Romans or whose images they left to us. If instead of the form we take only the spirit in which a poem is written as a basis [for calling it romantic] we will never disentangle the definitions ... Which kinds of poems should be considered romantic? Those which were not known to the ancients, and those in which the earlier forms have been changed or replaced by others.

Sbivšie s tolku russkuju kritiku francuzy obyknovenno otnosjat k romantizmu vse, čto im kažetsja oznamenovannym pečat'ju mečtatel'nosti i germanskogo ideologizma, ili osnovannym na predrassudkax i predanijax prostonarodnyx. Opredelenie samoe netočnoe. Stixotvorenie možet javljat' vse èti priznaki, a meždu tem prinadležat' k rodu klassičeskomu. K semu rody dolžny otnosit'sja te stixotvorenija, koix formy izvestny byli grekam i rimljanam, ili koix obrazy oni nam ostavili. Esli že vmesto formy stixotvorenija budem brat' za osnovanie tol'ko dux, v kotorom ono napisano, to nikogda ne vyputaemsja iz opredelenij ... Kakie že rody stixotvorenij dolžny otnest' k poèzii romantičeskoj? Te, kotorye ne izvestny drevnim, i te, v koix prežnie formy izmenilis' ili zameneny drugimi.[80]

Pushkin's growing scepticism as to the meaning of the term *romantic* is evident from the frequently ironic context in which *romantičeskij* and *romaničeskij* appear in his works. Pushkin sensed that romanticism was turning into those very things it had rebelled against: it was becoming standardized and normative like classicism, although in a different manner; it had developed a stereotyped language and stereotyped situations and characters. He could not but rebel against these new fetters placed on free imagination. In *Eugene Onegin* and especially in the *Tales of Belkin*, ironic, mocking uses of romantic clichés abound.

Pushkin's ridicule points to two rather different aberrations that had occurred within the romantic movement. One, embodied in Lensky (*Eugene Onegin*), is the idealism that inspired a naïve lifestyle that romanticized the world. It simplified reality, ignoring or overlooking its problems and contradictions. Under the influence of German idealist philosophy, Lensky had tried to realize his ideals (love, friendship) on earth, but had failed because he did not see the world as it was:

He sang of separation and sadness, and of something, and of the misty distance and of romantic roses.

> *On pel razluku i pečal'*
> *I nečto, i tumannu dal'*
> *I romantičeskie rozy.*[81]

He wrote thus (incomprehensibly and without spirit), what we call romanticism, although I do not see any here; but what does it matter?

> *Tak on pisal* (temno i vjalo),
> *Čto romantizmom my zovem,*
> *Xot' romantizma tut ni malo*
> *Ne vižu ja; da čto nam v tom?*[82]

The second aberration of romanticism is embodied in Pushkin's Onegin and ascribed to Byron, who 'with successful whim vested himself in doleful romanticism and hopeless egoism.'/'*Lord Bajron prixot'ju udačnoj*ı*Oblek v unylyj romantizm*ı*I beznadežnyj egoizm.*'[83] Here another romantic style of life is implied. While Lensky's manner of 'romantic living' was serious and genuinely felt, the Byronic romantic manner of life, according to Pushkin, was false, narcissistic, and a trivialization of the concerns of Lensky's romanticism. Lensky's feeling of isolation becomes in Onegin a cult of solitude; Lensky's faith in ideals is in Onegin nihilism and egoism. Lensky's world-weariness and longing is transformed into Onegin's ennui, his eternal homelessness, his immoral and cynical flirtation with life and death. It becomes a fashionable game. These Byronesque qualities are even more saliently parodied in Pushkin's 'Lady Turned Peasant' of 1830, where Aleksey, a simple, good-hearted youth, pretends to be a romantic hero and consequently acts as if he were gloomy and disappointed, speaks of lost joys and faded youth, and wears a black mysterious ring with a skull.*

* Lermontov's Grushnitsky (1841) is one of the last satiric portrayals of the tragic romantic attitudinizing: 'He is one of those people who, for every occasion in life, have ready-made pompous phrases, whom unadorned beauty does not move, and who solemnly drape themselves in extraordinary emotions, exalted passions, and exceptional sufferings. To produce an effect is rapture to them; romantic provincial ladies go crazy over them ... His coming to the Caucasus is likewise a consequence of his fanatic romanticism. I am sure that on the eve of his departure he told some pretty neighbour, with a gloomy air, that he was going ... not merely to serve there, but that he was seeking death because ...

Among the classicists of the period, there is also a great divergence of opinion, although they did agree in using 'romantic' as a term of literary, political, and moral criticism. It was synonymous for them with political, aesthetic, and ethical anarchy. It meant a vague, careless, obscure, disorganized, and disharmonious style in works of art; immorality in ethics; liberalism and rebellion in politics. Polevoy summarized the classicists' attitude when he said that they liked 'to wail over [the romantics'] depravity and the ruin of taste' and considered romanticism to be identical with 'Atheism, Schellingism, Liberalism, Terrorism, the offspring of unbelief and revolution'/'... *vopijat' o razvrate, o pogibeli vkusa ... iskussno soedinjat' s ètim mysl', čto romantizm est' to že, čto Ateizm, Šellingizm, Liberalizm, Terrorizm, čado bezverija i revoljucii.*'[84]

The conservative *literati* considered romantic art to be opposed to the formal perfection and sublime content of classical works. In 1820, Voeykov, in a discussion of recent ballads and of Pushkin's 'Ruslan and Lyudmila,' spoke of the 'deviation of many poets from the true path leading to perfection' and of the 'boundless imitation of the brilliant, often false charms of German – if I am not wrong – *romanticism*, rather than of the immortal beauty of the classics, which are totally forgotten in Russia'/'... *imel ja v vidu ... uklonenie mnogix poètov ot istinnogo puti, veduščego k soveršenstvu; bezmernoe podražanie blestjaščim, neredko ložnym prelestjam* ROMANTIZMA, *esli ne ošibajus'* GERMANIČESKOGO.'[85]

Prince N. Tsertelev, a leading exponent of classical ideals, claimed in 1823 that the romantic poet was characterized by the fact that he

... does not know limits, his ardent imagination embraces the whole universe, his genius is a despot which orders everything according to its whim; his taste differs from that of others; his manner of expressing himself is special, if you like, strange, and sometimes even not easily intelligible, because this very vagueness has its charms; in his creation one can notice the carelessness of genius, and therefore his work does not have a definite colour but gathers all colours, so to speak.

..*' ne znaet predelov, plamennoe voobraženie ego obemlet vsju vselennuju, ego genij – despot, raspolagajuščij vse po svoemu proizvoleniju; vkus ego otličen ot drugix; obraz vyraženija osobennyj, esli xotite strannyj i daže inogda neudobo-*

and here, probably he would cover his eyes with his hand and continue thus ...'
M. Lermontov, *A Hero of Our Time* (Doubleday Anchor Original, 1958), pp. 84 f. For the original Russian, see Lermontov, *Sobranie sočinenij* IV (Moscow 1958): 70 f.

ponjatnyj, ibo samaja temnota imeet svoju prelest'; v tvorenii ego vidna genial'naja nebrežnost', i ot sego-to ono ne imeet opredelennogo cveta, no slivaet v sebe, tak skazat', vse cvety.[86]

Tsertelev pointed to other formal shortcomings of romantic works when he wrote that 'slavicisms, gallicisms, mysticisms, romanticisms, deviltries alternately attacked her [Russian poetry], as the Tartar hordes attacked Russia'/'*Slavjanizmy, gallicizmy, misticizmy, romantizmy, d'javolizmy napali na nee [russkuju poèziju] ... poperemenno, kak ordy tatarskie na Rossiju.*'[87] Romanticism was equated by him with literary anarchy, with the rejection of the 'legislative power of good taste' and the 'advocacy of the absolute freedom of genius.'* It implied to its classical opponents not only a poor certificate as to literary loyalty, but to any other loyalty, especially political. 'Romantic' and 'Freemason' were often used synonymously, to indicate the 'presence of secret social endeavours of not conservative colouring in a person.'[88] In a statement on the literary policy of the journal *Blagonamerennyj* (*The Loyalist*), Tsertelev declared: 'The voluptuous Bacchanalian and even liberal poems of our young spoiled poets [the romantics] will not find a place in *The Loyalist*'/'*Ne budut imet' mesto v 'Blagonamerennom' ... sladostrastnye, vakxičeskie i daže* LIBERAL'NYE *stixotvorenija molodyx našix balovnej-poètov.*'[89]

N. E. Nadezhdin provided a most elaborate negative analysis of contemporary romanticism in 1830, in his dissertation, later published as an essay, *De Poësi Romantica*, which showed a good knowledge of the West European critical literature on the subject. (Both A. W. Schlegel and Mme de Staël are quoted and paraphrased.) His thesis was that current romantic literature resembled the true romanticism of the Middle Ages as little as eighteenth-century pseudo-classical literature resembled Greek literature, and that nothing but an aesthetically insignificant pseudo-romanticism was possible in our time. As he used the term, *romantičeskij* referred to the spirit of medieval Christian literature such as Dante's *Divine Comedy*. Like everything truly romantic, this work, in Nadezhdin's view, displayed 'an inner harmony of spiritual existence' that

---

*   *Vestnik Evropy* (1829), VIII: 287–90; X: 130. Such a critique of 'romantic' art by the classicists was not entirley unjustified. The ballad writer Katenin, whom Pushkin considered the most important among the founders of romanticism, wrote in 1823: 'It is too bad that people with true talent do not always have what is even more necessary, good judgment; it seems that it is the fault of one word: *romantique*. This magic word permits the writing of nonsense and the gain of praise ...' ('Vsemu vinovato odno slovo: *romantique*. S ètim volšebnym slovom daetsja volja pisat' bessmyslicu i priobretat' poxvalu.') Babkin and Shendecov, op. cit. (as in note 28 below), p. 1136.

affected both the 'inner structure of poetic forms and the external structure of mechanical versification.' A romantic poet derived his material from the 'inner world of concepts, sensations, and desires.' According to Nadezhdin,

romantic poetry is distinguished from classical poetry as far as poetic invention is concerned by the fact that the former is more human, whereas the latter is more natural. The world of classical poetry is a heroic world or ennobled nature; and the world of romantic poetry is a knightly world, or enlightened humanity.

Poèzija romantičeskaja otličaetsja ot klassičeskoj v otnošenii k poetičeskomu izobreteniju tem, čto ona bolee čelovečeskaja, togda kak poslednjaja bolee estestvenna. Mir poèzii klassičeskoj est' mir geroičeskij, ili oblagoražennaja priroda, a mir poèzii romantičeskoj est' mir rycarskij, ili čelovečestvo prosvetlennoe.[90]

From this it followed that

the means of expression of romantic poetry must naturally be more varied and more involved than those of classical poetry ... The romantics thus had a special passion for the ornamentation of speech. The whole range of tropes and figures was sounded out by them and its wealth was put into circulation.

Otsjuda vyraženie poèzii romantičeskoj estestvenno, dolženstvovalo byt' bolee raznoobrazno i zaputanno, neželi vyraženie poèzii klassičeskoj ... Romantiki imeli osoboe pristrastie k ubranstvu i ukrašeniju reči. Vsja oblast' tropov i figur byla imi izmerena, i vse bogatstvo eja puščeno v oborot.[91]

In the course of time, romantic poetry

... either dissolved in the soap bubbles of bombastic emotionalism or plunged into the dense darkness of impenetrable mysticism, or – disregarding the laws of visible nature – absolutely destroyed poetic truth itself in monstrous and ugly inventions, which were composed according to the capricious whim of a quaint fantasy.

... ona ili razrešalas' v myl'nye puzyri napuščennoj čuvstvitel'nosti, libo pogružalas' v gustoj mrak nepronicaemogo misticizma, ili ne obraščaja vnimanija na zakony vidimoj prirody, rešitel'no razrušala samuju poètičeskuju istinu v čudoviščnyx i urodlivyx vymyslax, sostavlennyx po kapriznoj prixoti pričudlivoj fantazii.[92]

Such is the case, Nadezhdin says, with the 'new or pseudo-romanticism'/ *'novyj romantizm, lže-romantičeskaja poèzija.'* Therefore it is

... not surprising that the name romantic [*imja romaničeskogo*], which is usually attached to its [romantic poetry's] spurious remains, has been and still is considered something ridiculous and abusive.

... *neudivitel'no, čto imja romaničeskogo* (romanesque), *pripisyvaemoe oby-knovenno poddel'nym ego ostatkam, do six por počitalos' i počitaetsja čem-to smešnym i ponosnym.*[92]

Nadezhdin protested against the view that all post-classical poetry was 'romantic' and distinguished between the two adjectives available to him. In the positive sense, in which it characterized the Christian content and the harmonious forms of medieval art, he used *romantičeskij*. In the negative sense, when writing of what seemed to him the exaggeration, artificiality, imitative nature, and formlessness of so much contemporary literature, he used *romaničeskij*.

By 1840, then, the cognates *romaničeskij, romantičeskij, romanizm, romantizm, romantika,* and *romantiki* had acquired non-technical denotations such as 'emotional,' 'unusual,' 'lofty,' 'fantastic,' 'idealistic,' which users did not necessarily and readily connect with the original root word *roman* and which they applied in vastly generalized contexts. These meanings speedily developed evaluative connotations (frequently negative) and submeanings: *politically*, 'romantic' implied liberal, independent, and even subversive; *philosophically*, it suggested the spirituality or sensibility created by Christianity and by German idealist philosophy; *characterologically*, it referred to melancholic, dreamy, idealistic individuals who sentimentally surrendered to visions, reveries, moonlight and tombstones, like Lensky, and thrived on lofty emotions of friendship, love, etc., but also to disillusioned, cynical, ironic, despondent egoists like Onegin who filled their lives with amorous adventures, often in contempt of established 'civilized' mores. The characterological and philosophical connotations anticipated the typological conception of romanticism as an ahistorical universal category of the mind developed later by Belinsky and spilled over into the literary-technical usage of the cognates.

As *literary* terms the cognates could refer to (a) post-classical, Christian, and medieval literature, (b) modern, contemporary West-European and Russian literature, (c) all original, indigenous poetry or prose imbued with love of the nation's past, regardless of when it was written, (d) all prose or poetry that abounded in the passionate and fantastic, that concentrated on lofty emotions and on the description of places that suggested divine grandeur and invited the soul's aspiration toward it, (e) poetry or prose that reflected human life, nature, history in their fullness, diversity, and richness of contrasts, i.e., more truthfully than classical norms had permitted, (f) all works in a form unknown to the ancients, (g) disregard of rules and precedents, naturalness, naiveté, and hence, universal aesthetic validity, (h) a new style which permitted, in poetry, enjambments, mobile caesuras, and other liberties; in epic works, a mixture of 'the tragic and the comic, the lofty and the lowly, the sacred and the profane, the metaphysical generalization and the physical detail,'* and which, in general, abounded in picturesque figures of speech and in colourful, exotic detail. These fumbling, motley definitions reflect a fundamental change in sensibility and, concomitantly, in literary conventions. No wonder that the meaning of 'romantic' and its cognates, forced to absorb the complexities of such a change, expanded enough to include a whole gamut of views on what constituted a work of art and on how it should relate to the universe, the artist, and the public.†

1840–80

By the time the dispute over the meaning of *klassičeskij* and *romantičeskij* ended, the two words were opposed to one another no longer primarily as words referring to contemporary literary works with certain qualities, but as words which designated general qualities of literature at all times. The groping towards a definition of contemporary works had led those concerned to look beyond the boundary of the specific historical phenomenon they started out with. The result was that the chances for a technical definition of literary works around 1820–40 became slimmer, and a vague typological, non-technical use of *romantičeskij* gained increasing prevalence. It was Belinsky in particular who completed this process and established this usage for subsequent writers.

Two ideas of *romantizm* are expressed in Belinsky's writings: He used the word to refer not only to a timeless state of mind, but also to literary movements – Greek, medieval, and modern. The relation of these two concepts in his writings can at times be confusing, and his

---

*   Vladimir Nabokov paraphrasing Pushkin in his edition of *Eugene Onegin in English with Commentary* ... (New York, 1964), III: 34. See also Nabokov's discussion of the eleven 'varieties and phases' of romanticism, ibid., pp. 32–7.
†   Some of the essays containing the critical views on romanticism discussed in this section have become available in English in Carl R. Proffer, *The Critical Prose of Alexander Pushkin with Critical Essays by Four Russian Romantic Poets* (Bloomington, 1969).

attitude to the phenomena described by the word underwent significant changes.*

In 'Russian Literature of 1841,' Belinsky wrote of a timeless *romantizm* immensely beneficial to humanity:

Romanticism is the inner world of man, the world of the soul and the heart, of feelings and beliefs, the world of impulses towards the infinite, the world of mysterious visions and contemplations, the world of heavenly ideals. The soil of romanticism is not history, not real life, not nature, and not the external world, but the mysterious laboratory of the human heart, where questions about the world and eternity, death and immortality, the fate of the individual, the mysteries of love, bliss, and suffering are born incessantly ... The development of romantic elements is the first condition of our humanity.

Romantizm èto mir vnutrennego čeloveka, mir duši i serdca, mir oščuščenij i verovanij, mir poryvanij k beskonečnomu, mir tainstvennyx videnij i sozercanij, mir nebesnyx idealov. Počva romantizma ne istorija, ne žizn' dejstvitel'naja, ne priroda i ne vnešnij mir, a tainstvennaja laboratorija grudi čelovečeskoj, gde neumolkaemo roždajutsja voprosy o mire i večnosti, o smerti i bessmertii, o sud'be ličnogo čeloveka, o tainstvax ljubvi, blaženstva i stradanija ... Razvitie romantičeskix elementov est' pervoe uslovie našej čelovečnosti.[94]

One year later, he used the word with a more narrowly contemporary reference, claiming that *romantizm*

... had cleansed the arena [of our literature] that was cluttered with the trash and dregs of pseudo-classical prejudices and ... thus prepared the possibility of an indigenous literature.

I naš romantizm ... rasčistil ee [našej literatury] arenu, zavalennuju sorom i drjazgom psevdoklassičeskix predrassudkov ... i tem predugotovil vozmožnost' samobytnoj literatury.[95]

---

* As Budagov suggests, these changes may be due partly to Hegel's lectures on aesthetics, which gradually penetrated to the Russian 'circles' in the late '30s and in the '40s. In these lectures Hegel provided both an historical and a typological characterization of romanticism. 'With Hegel,' Budagov writes, 'the typological definition of these word-concepts turned out to be much richer and more subtle than a purely historical definition. From an historical position, romanticism constituted for the German philosopher the literature and art of the new age; classicism was that of the ancient world ... Hegel attempted to deepen the typological definition of romanticism ... Hegel gave a broad analysis of the individual features of romanticism independently from the historical setting of the 1820s and '30s: loftiness, lyricism, musicality, penetration of the inner life of the individual, etc.' Budagov, op. cit. in note 31, p. 253; cf. also B. G. Reizov, *Meždu klassicizmom i romantizmom* (Leningrad, 1962), pp. 5–15.

In the same year, he seems to have come to regard romanticism as ethically harmful; in a letter of 7 November 1842, he wrote:

Some time ago a great change took place in me; for a long time now I have dismissed romanticism [*romantizma*], mysticism, and all 'isms' ... I understand that he [M. Bakunin] belongs to the left wing of Hegelianism ... and understands the pitiful romantic Schelling who died during his lifetime. The path upon which he set out now must bring him to rebirth, for only romanticism allows man to feel beautifully, think loftily, and act badly.

S nekotorogo vremeni vo mne proizošel sil'nyj perevorot; ja davno uže otrešilsja ot romantizma, misticizma i vsex 'izmov.' ... Ja znaju, čto on ['Mišel'' Bakunin] prinadležit k levoj storone gegelianizma ... i ponimaet žalkogo zaživo umeršego romantika Šellinga ... Pritom že doroga, na kotoruju on vyšel teper', dolžna privesti ego ko vsjačeskomu vozroždeniju, ibo tol'ko romantizm pozvoljaet čeloveku prekrasno čuvstvovat', vozvyšenno rassuždat' i durno postupat'.[96]

This negative evaluation of romanticism is, however, not reflected in Belinsky's second essay of 1843 on Pushkin. Here, his historical conception of romanticism is discussed at length:

The essence of romanticism is contained in its idea, not in the arbitrary fortuitousness of external form ... [for] the heart of man is the mysterious source of romanticism; feeling, love is the manifestation or the effect of romanticism; and therefore almost every man is a romantic.

Suščnost' romantizma zaključaetsja v ego idee, a ne v proizvol'nyx slučajnostjax vnešnej formy ... V serdce čeloveka zaključaetsja tainstvennyj istočnik romantizma; čuvstvo, ljubov' est' projavlenie ili dejstvie romantizma, i potomu počti vsjakij čelovek romantik.[97]

Since, however, the manner of feeling and thought changes with time, romanticism changes. Thus, there is a Greek romanticism, a medieval romanticism, and a modern romanticism. Belinsky discusses these romanticisms in terms of their treatment of love, 'which is primarily a romantic feeling'/*'romantičeskoe čuvstvo'*.[98] Greek romanticism is supposed to have been dominated by a notion of love 'as sensual aspiration which is enlightened and spiritualized by the idea of beauty'/*'Tam ona [ljubov'] – čuvstvennoe stremlenie, prosvetlennoe i oduxotvorennoe ideeju krasoty.'*[99] Euripides was Greece's most romantic poet and Plato her romantic philosopher.[100] The elegy is the 'ultra-romantic genre of poetry'/*'Romantičeskaja lira Ellady umela vospevat' ne odno tol'ko sčastie ljubvi, kak strastnoe i izjaščnoe naslaždenie, ona umela plakat' ešče i nad urnoju milogo praxa, i ELEGIJA – ètot ul'tra-romantičeskij rod poèzii-byla sozdana eju že* ...'[101] Nonetheless, in the same context, romanticism is called the 'exclusive property of the Middle Ages that even bears the name of the nations of Romance origin.' Whereas in Greece it was a 'dark force' always defeated by the Olympic gods, 'in the Middle Ages ... romanticism constituted an unparalleled, independent force which ... attained utmost extremes in contradictoriness and nonsense'/'*V srednie veka, naprotiv, romantizm sostavljal besprimernuju, samobytnuju silu, kotoraja ... došla do poslednix krajnostej protivorečija i bessmyslicy.*'[102] In this medieval romanticism,

... everything lived and breathed by a feeling without reality, by an impulse without attainment, by an aspiration without satisfaction, by hope without realization, by desire without fulfilment, by passionate, restless activity without goal and result.

Vse žilo i dyšalo čuvstvom bez dejstvitel'nosti, poryvaniem bez dostiženija, stremleniem bez udovletvorenija, nadeždoju bez soveršenija, želaniem bez vypolnenija, strastnoju, bespokojnoju dejatel'nostiju bez celi i rezul'tata.[103]

The romanticism of the present age is then characterized by Belinsky as follows:

The romanticism of our time is the descendent of the romanticism of the Middle Ages, but it is also very akin to Greek romanticism ... Our romanticism is the organic fullness and entirety of the romanticism of all centuries and of all phases of the development of mankind ... Society still adheres to the principles of the old, medieval romanticism which has already turned into empty forms since their content has been outlived; but the people ... already try to realize the ideal of the new romanticism. Our time is the epoch of a harmonious balancing of all aspects of the human spirit.

Romantizm našego vremeni est' syn romantizma srednix vekov, no on že očen' srodni i romantizmu grečeskomu ... Naš romantizm est' organičeskaja polnota i vsecelost' romantizma vsex vekov i vsex fazisov razvitija čelovečeskogo roda ... Obščestvo vse ešče deržitsja principami starogo, srednevekovskogo romantizma, obrativšegosja uže v pustye formy za otsutstviem umeršego soderžanija: no ljudi ... uže siljatsja osuščestvit' ideal novogo romantizma. Naše vremja est' èpoxa garmoničeskogo uravnovešenija vsex storon čelovečeskogo duxa.[104]

Although the 'exalted romanticism' of the Middle Ages must be superseded, this does not mean 'a negation of all idealism' and 'submersion in the prose and dirt of life.'[105]

Discussing contemporary European romanticism, Belinsky counts most German and some French romantics (Hugo, Lamartine)

among the medieval type, but refers to Byron as the 'champion of the new romanticism.'[106] Of the Russians, Derzhavin's anacreontic poems contain sparks of Greek romanticism. Zhukovsky spiritualized Russian literature by introducing it to the 'mysteries of the romanticism of the Middle Ages';[107] he possessed the art 'to paint landscapes and to invest them with romantic life' / '... *živopisat' kartiny prirody i vlagat' v nix romantičeskuju žizn'.*'[108] Thus the romanticism of the Middle Ages

... did not die, but only was transformed. Our most recent romanticism does not think of rejecting love as a natural aspiration of the heart, but only demands that this aspiration be not a subterranean, dark, hellish force ... Our romanticism, without depriving feeling of its freedom, demands that feeling, in its turn, should not take man's freedom away.

On [romantizm] ne umer posle srednix vekov, a tol'ko preobrazilsja. I tak, naš novejšij romantizm ne dumaet otricat' ljubvi, kak estestvennogo stremlenija serdca, no tol'ko trebuet, čtob èto stremlenie ne bylo podzemnoju, temnoju, adskoju siloju ... Ne otnimaja u čuvstva svobody, naš romantizm trebuet, čtob i čuvstvo ne otnimalo u čeloveka svobody ...[109]

By 1845 Belinsky's evaluation of romanticism had changed drastically, as had his political views. Now the 'true expression of the romantic movement' were the tales of Bestuzhev-Marlinsky and Polevoy's stories, 'The Painter,' 'The Bliss of Insanity,' and 'Emma.'

Romanticism contained the 'phraseology of German-bourgeois dreaminess, along with poorly understood German philosophical sophistry, and our supposedly national boldness in feelings and expressions.'

Istinnym vyraženiem romantičeskogo napravlenija byli povesti Marlinskogo, s dopolneniem k nim povestej, vrode 'Živopisca,' 'Blaženstva bezumija,' 'Emmy' ... V nem byla i otčajannaja frazeologija nemecko-bjurgerovskoj mečtatel'nosti, popolam s ploxo ponjatym nemecko-filosofskim mudrovaniem, i naša budto by narodnaja udal' čuvstv i vyraženij.[110]

Belinsky now spoke with contempt of 'romantics of life' / '*romantiki zizni*' who had been created by romantic literature, had no contact with reality, and lived in a dream world.[111] In 'A Survey of Russian Literature in 1847' Belinsky used the hero of Goncharov's *A Common Story*, Aduev, the 'romantic little animal' / '*romantičeskij zverek*,' as a point of departure for his attack on the 'romantic' phenomena of egoism, self-indulgence, isolation from reality, idealism, and self-importance. 'Romantic' now had acquired the connotation of aloofness from social problems and of conservatism – a use which has continued until today.*

In 'Romantic Dilettantes' of 1842, A. Herzen developed Belinsky's views. Romanticism and classicism are here discussed as general world views that constitute the basis of the corresponding literary trends. Classicism, which is associated with the ancient world, is characterized by admiration of nature, empiricism, and a practical utilitarian orientation, whereas romanticism, associated particularly with the Middle Ages, is distinguished by spiritualism, contempt for nature, and remoteness from the practical interests of life. The two world views are eternal possibilities of the human spirit, and yet belong, or ought to belong, to the past:

Romanticism and classicism had to find their grave in the new world ... and their immortality ... The eternal classical and romantic elements are alive. They belong to two genuine and necessary moments in the temporal development of the human spirit. They are two phases, two world views of different ages and relative truth. Youth, the time of first love, of ignorance of life, predisposes to romanticism, which is beneficial at that time: it purifies, ennobles the soul, burns out its animality and coarse desires. Those who are endowed with a bright intellect rather than a sensitive heart are classicists in their internal spiritual make-up; contemplative, tender, and languid rather than reflective people are ignorant romantics rather than classicists.

Romantizm i klassicizm dolžny byli najti svoj grob v novom mire, i ... svoe bessmertie ... Večnye elementy, klassičeskie i romantičeskie, živy. Oni prinadležat dvum istinnym i neobxodimym momentam razvitija duxa čelovečeskogo vo vremeni. Oni sostavljajut dve fazy, dva vozzrenija, raznoletnie i otnositel'no istinnye. Junošestvo, vremja pervoj ljubvi, nevedenija žizni, raspolagaet k romantizmu, romantizm blagotvoren v èto vremja: on očiščaet, oblagoraživaet dušu, vyžigaet iz nee životnost' i grubye želanija. Ljudi, odarennye svetlym umom bolee, neželi čuvstvitel'nym serdcem, – klassiki po vnutrennemu stroeniju duxa, tak, kak ljudi sozercatel'nye, nežnye, temnye bolee, neželi mysljaščie, – skoree romantiki, neželi klassiki.[112]

---

* As Belinsky devoted so much effort to an interpretation of *romantizm*, one would expect him to differentiate between *romantičeskij* and *romaničeskij*. Indeed, he seems to use *romaničeskij* only in the old meaning of 'amorous,' 'novel-like.' Compare, for example, the following passages from his discussion of Lazhechnikov's novel, *Ledjanoj dom*, of 1839: 'Po pročtenii romana dlja čitatelja ostaetsja zagadkoju i istoričeskij i romaničeskij Biron.' '... čisto romaničeskaja čast'' romana razvita i opravdana ...' (Ibid., III: 15, 18).

At present, 'mankind has entered such an epoch of maturity that the attempt to turn it back to classicism or romanticism has become simply ridiculous.' 'The vigorous school of neo-romanticism [which] appeared after Napoleon,' can, according to Herzen, only be shortlived 'because the feelings which called it forth were exclusively temporal':

Čelovečestvo vošlo v takuju èpoxu soveršennoletija, čto prosto smešno sdelalos' pritjazanie obratit' ego v klassicizm ili romantizm ... posle Napoleona javilas' sil'naja škola neoromantizma ... no tak kak čuvstva, vyzvavšie neoromantizm, byli čisto vremennye, to sud'bu ego možno bylo legko predvidet'.[113]

Neoromanticism is a stage inimical to the development of mankind; it is reactionary:

Dreamy romanticism began to hate the new movement [the natural school] because of its realism.

Mečtatel'nyj romantizm stal NENAVIDET' *novoe napravlenie za ego* REALIZM.[114]

The romantic view [*romantičeskoe vozzrenie*] is almost exclusively the property of catholicism ... A nebulous fantasy, inclined to contemplation and mysticism ... spiritualism and transcendentalism are the foundations of romanticism. For it [romanticism], spirit and matter are seen not in a harmonious development, but in a struggle ... Nature is a lie, not something truthful; everything natural is rejected.

Romantičeskoe vozzrenie ... počti isključitel'naja prinadležnost' katolicizma ... Tumannaja, naklonnaja k sozercaniju i misticizmu fantazija ... spiritualizm, transcendentnost' – osnova romantizma. Dux i materija dlja nego ne v garmoničeskom razvitii, a v bor'be ... Priroda – lož', ne istinnoe; vse estestvennoe otrinuto ...[115]

Romantičeskij and *romaničeskij* are used by Herzen as synonyms, as is shown, for example, by a comparison of the preceding quotation with the following passage from 1843:

The romantic view [*romaničeskoe vozzrenie*] presents, like a telescope, the whole world upside down; the internal is presented as distant, the spiritual full of sensuality; sensuality is spiritualized.

Romaničeskoe vozzrenie predstavljaet, kak teleskop, ves' mir vverx nogami; vnutrennee u nego postavleno vdali, duxovnoe ispolneno čuvstvennosti, čuvstvennost' oduxotvorena ...[116]

The negative connotation of 'romantic' as a political and anti-realistic view is maintained by the 'radical' literary critics of the

1860s, and by some writers throughout the second half of the nineteenth century.

N. G. Chernyshevsky distinguished between a specific 'romantic school' and an eternal romantic disposition. He also made a distinction between a German, idealistic, spiritualizing trend and a French, anti-classicist, liberalizing trend in Russian romanticism, regarding the latter as dominant. In his 'Outline of the Gogolian Period in Russian Literature' of 1855–6, Chernyshevsky wrote that 'the romantics became the enemies of common sense and artificially excited their imagination to the point of pathological stress'/ '*Romantiki sdelalis*' *vragami zdravogo smysla i iskusstvenno razdražali fantaziju do boleznennogo naprjaženija.*'[117] Thus

... the critical literature of the Gogolian period arose against romanticism as an expression of a strained, exalted, false understanding of life, as a perversion of the intellectual and moral forces of man, which leads to dreaminess, vulgar pettiness, self-delusion and conceit. The essence of pseudo-romanticism consists, not in the breaking of aesthetic rules, but in a distorted understanding of the conditions of human life.

Kritika gogolevskogo perioda ... vosstala na romantizm, kak na vyraženie natjanutyx, èkzaltirovannyx lživyx ponjatij o žizni, kak na izvraščenie umstvennyx i nravstvennyx sil čeloveka, veduščee k fantazerstvu i pošlosti, samoobol'ščeniju i kičlivosti ... Suščnost' pseudoromantizma zaključaetsja ne v narušenii èstetičeskix uslovij, a v iskažennom ponjatii ob uslovijax čelovečeskoj žizni.[118]

Similarly, D. I. Pisarev in 'A Promenade through the Gardens of Russian Literature' of 1864 used 'romanticism' with reference to a resigned disposition and a passive attitude to the world:

Decrepit romanticism is ridiculous and disgusting to our healthy youth, but nonetheless romanticism exists in belles-lettres as well as in the criticism of our routine journals.

*Drjaxlyj romantizm smešon i gadok dlja našej zdorovoj molodeži, no tem ne menee romantizm suščestvuet kak v belletristike, tak i v kritike našix rutinnyx žurnalov.**

The dictionaries published from about 1840 to 1880 do not reflect the multitude of connotations 'romantic' had developed since the turn of the century. In the conservative *Dictionary of the Old*

---

*   *Russkie pisateli*, p. 563. Pypin, elaborating the views of these 'radical critics,' considered the romantic school a reflection of a world view which arose after the French revolution (A. N. Pypin, *Xarakteristiki literaturnyx mnenij ot 20-x do 50-x godov*, St. Petersburg, 1890, p. 26).

Church Slavonic Language of 1847, for example, romanticism is defined as 'the particular quality of works in which nature – not always refined – is imitated and the examples of classical writers are discarded'/'*Romantizm: osobennoe svojstvo sočinenij, v kotoryx, ne sleduja primeram klassičeskix pisatelej, podražajut prirode, ne vsegda izjaščnoj.*'[119] The most thorough and detailed definition, covering two pages in Starchevsky's *Encyclopedic Reference Book* of 1854, refers exclusively to a literary school, derived from medieval spirituality. The word *romantic* is traced to 'everything that has to do with the literature written in the Romance languages'/'*Tak nazyvaetsja vse, čto kasaetsja do literatury romanskix jazykov.*'[120] Recent developments in Russian literature are interpreted as attempts to introduce this spirit into art. The 'romantic movement'/'*romantičeskoe napravlenie*' is said to comprise all the literature of medieval spirituality. The negative bias of the writer of this article is evident from the fact that he refers to the founders of romanticism as 'culprits.' Starchevsky's definition was summarized ten years later in *The Table Reference Book for All Branches of Knowledge*, where romanticism is identified with the spirit of 'fanaticism, mysticism, fatalism, [and] suppression of individualism.'[121]

The *Dictionary of the Old Church Slavonic and Russian Language*, in its second edition of 1867, offers a surprisingly scanty definition of romanticism. *Romantizm* is even misspelled: 'Romanticism/romantic [*romantism/romantičeskij*]: one says of belles lettres: unrestrained, free, uninhibited by conventional rules, imitative of daily life or nature; opposite of classicism'/'*Romantism* [sic]/*romantičeskij: govorjat ob izjaščnyx sočinenijax: vol'nyj, svobodnyj, ne stesnennyj uslovnymi pravilami, podražajuščij bytu, libo prirode, protivopoložnyj klassicizmu.*'[122]

The *Explanatory Dictionary* of 1871 offers an even more surprising explanation. *Romantizm* is derived, according to this source, from the Latin word *romanus*, and is defined as an 'aesthetic feeling or love for art and literature'/'*... èstetičeskoe čuvstvo ili ljubov' k iskusstvu i literature.*'[123] This definition is echoed ten years later in the *New Explanatory Dictionary* where romanticism is taken to mean 'love for poetry, music, art, and literature; that is, artistic taste, inclination to abstractness'/'*... ljubov' k poèzii, muzyke, iskusstvu i k literature, to est', xudožestvennyj vkus, sklonnost' k otvlečennosti.*'[124]

A socially and politically orientated definition is given in Berezin's *Russian Encyclopedic Dictionary* of 1877. Romanticism is said to have appeared 'when people began noticing shortcomings in the life of society, which limited personal freedom.'[125] According to this source, romanticism in Russia existed only for ten years and was successful in spite of the vagueness of its ideas, its shaky judgments and self-contradictions, and the scarcity of literary models.

Side by side with the vague and mutually contradictory technical meanings our cognates had acquired in the literary criticism of the period from 1840 to 1880, the full range of earlier meanings of course survived – a fact which can be illustrated conveniently by quoting from works of fiction. Very frequently the basic meaning of 'romantic' (and, *mutatis mutandis*, of 'romanticism') was 'idealistic,' either with the negative connotation of being incapable of seeing things as they really are or with the positive one of refusing to give in to reality, of clinging to one's ideals in spite of seemingly insuperable odds and the promptings of common sense. Thus, Nekrasov wrote in *The Life and Adventures of Tikhon Trostnikov* (1843): 'My heart experienced its epoch of romanticism ... I wanted a higher goal than those which usually absorbed my activity, but what kind of goal I did not know myself'/'*Serdce moe pereživalo svoju èpoxu romantizma ... Mne xotelos' kakoj-nibud' celi vyše tex, kotorye obyknovenno pogloščali moju dejatel'nost', no kakoj imenno – sam ja ne znal ...*'[126] Quite similarly, we read in Pisemsky's *A Thousand Souls* (1858): 'Not your commerce ... created and invented the railroad and the screw: romanticism in science created them'/'... *Ne kommercija vaša ... sozdala i izobrela železnuju dorogu i vint: ix sozdal romantizm v nauke.*'[127] A closely related, but less positive usage occurs in Dostoevsky's *The Insulted and Injured* (1860):

Nikolay Sergeevich was one of those very good-natured and naïvely romantic people who – if they come to like somebody – surrender their whole being, extending their attachment at times to the point of becoming comic.

Nikolaj Sergeevič byl odin iz tex dobrejšix i naivno-romantičeskix ljudej, kotorye, esli už poljubjat kogo, to otdajutsja emu vsej dušoj, prostiraja inogda svoju privjazannost' do komičeskogo.[128]

In the same novel, Dostoevsky also used a neologism, the verb *romantizirovat'*, meaning 'to have impracticable idealistic aspirations': 'I did this [built a hospital] when I romanticized ['*romantiziroval*'], when I wanted to be the benefactor of mankind and found a philanthropic society' / '*Èto ja sdelal, kogda romantiziroval, xotel byl' blagodetelem čelovečestva, filantropičeskoe obščestvo osnovat'.*[129]

Romaničeskij continued to be used with such meanings as amorous, fabulous, unusual, mysterious, exotic, unreal, but often it was semantically indistinguishable from *romantičeskij*. Thus

Tolstoy wrote in *War and Peace* (1867) : 'High society received him amicably, because he was a prospective bridegroom, rich and noble, and almost a new face with the aura of the romantic story of his supposed death and his wife's tragic end' / '... *s oreolom romaničeskoj istorii o mnimoj smerti i tragičeskoj končine ženy.*'[130] *Romaničeskij*, however, occurred less frequently than *rom antičeskij*.

1880 – 1920

By the end of the nineteenth century, literary historians made the first attempts at tidying up the prevailing confusion in the usage of the cognates by studying the history of the Russian novel and the literary and critical works of the 'romantic school.' V. V. Sipovsky, in his *Sketches of a History of the Russian Novel* (1890), seems to have been the first scholar to introduce a neutral, technical use of *romaničeskij*, in the sense of 'novelistic,' 'pertaining to the novel.' He called the heroes of the novels he discussed *romaničeskie geroi* and wrote of their 'novelistic names' / *romaničeskie imena.**

Most of the efforts to reduce the polysemy of the cognates achieved no more, however, than, at best, to call attention to the complexity of the issue; at worst, they further increased the muddle. I. Zamotin, by incorporating the existing typological and literary definitions of romanticism in his work – designating it as an idealist world view that consisted of romantic individualism, nationalism, and universalism – failed to elucidate the concept. He could, therefore, write indiscriminately of the romanticism of Euripides, Petrarch, Racine, Dickens, the brothers Schlegel, Novalis, and Schelling, as well as of a formidable array of Russian writers: Aleksey Tolstoy, Polonsky, Gogol, Lermontov, Bakunin, K. Leont'ev, Dostoevsky, Tolstoy, Ostrovsky, Gorky, L. Andreev, and the symbolists.[131]

Other critics approached the problem through studies of

---

* V. V. Sipovskij, 'Očerki po istorii russkogo romana,' *Zapiski istoriko-filologičeskogo fakul'teta imperatorskogo St. Peterburgskogo universiteta* xcvii (St. Petersburg, 1909). p. 16. In *Bajron i Puškin* (Leningrad, 1924), V. Zhirmunsky continues the use of this distinction between *romantičeskij* and *romaničeskij*. Thus, in describing eighteenth century novels, he talks of 'romaničeskaja fabula, neobyčajnye xaraktery, potrjasajuščie i neredko melodramatičeskie duševnye pereživanija, èffektnye žesty i rozy, èkzotičeskaja obstanovka dejstvija ... vse èti elementy suščestvovali do Bajrona' (p. 98). Or: 'Sravnenie sposobstvuet ritoričeskoj emfaze, usileniju, preuveličennoj èkspresivnosti; ono okružaet predmety ... atmosferoj emocional'no povyšennogo, neobyčajnogo romaničeskogo' (p. 163).

specific writers that had been termed 'romantic.' A. N. Pypin defined romanticism in his history of Russian literature by way of discussing Zhukovsky, in his view a romantic. A. N. Veselovsky made a similar attempt, but concluded that Zhukovsky was not clearly a romantic. At the turn of the century, greater attention to literary history and its periodization led to the investigation of 'secondary' writers of the 'romantic' period. Kozmin's studies of Polevoy (1903) and Nadezhdin (1912) brought to light the complexity of opinions on romanticism in the 1820s and '30s.[132]

When sensibilities and literary conventions changed again between 1890 and 1910, observers compared these changes to those of 1820–40, often calling the new literary trend 'neo-romanticism'. It was inevitable that, in this context, the problem of defining 'romantic' should arise with fresh urgency. The new definitions placed the emphasis on the typological, i.e., universal, ahistorical aspects of 'romantic,' but suffered from vagueness, tautology, and confusing circumscriptions. Thus, A. Blok, a major representative of the new literary school, wrote in his rather opaque essay, 'About Romanticism' (1919), that 'genuine romanticism' was not just a literary trend but

... attempted to be and became for a while a new form of sensibility, a new manner of experiencing life. [It was] no renunciation of life; on the contrary, genuine romanticism was filled with an avid thirst for life; [romanticism] seems now indeed nothing but a new way of living with ten-fold strength ... all other features of romanticism as a literary move ment are entirely arbitrary; that is, secondary ... Romanticism is the conventional designation of the sixth sense.

Romantizm stremilsja stat' i stal na mgnovenie novoj formoj čuvstvovanija, novym sposobom pereživanija žizni ... podlinnyj romantizm ne byl otrešeniem ot žizni; on byl naoborot, preispolnen žadnym stremleniem k žizni ... [on] okazyvaetsja teper' na samom dele ne čem inym kak novym sposobom žit' udesjaterennoj siloj, sleduet, čto vse ostal'nye priznaki romantizma kak literaturnogo tečenija vpolne proizvol'ny, to est', vtorostepenny ... Romantizm – uslovnoe oboznačenie šestogo čuvstva.[133]

Romanticism also meant closeness to nature for Blok. He called any human connection with the elements a 'romantic connection' (for instance, *Čelovek ot veka svjazan s prirodoj, so vsemi stixijami ... èta svjaz' so stixiej est' svjaz' romantičeskaja*).[134] He saw romanticism as the forerunner of realism/ '*Podlinnyj realizm zaključaetsja ... v preobraženii prirody, to est' podlinnyj realizm – naslednik romantizma.*'[135]

In his article, 'About Classical and Romantic Poetry' (1920), V. Zhirmunsky attempted to construct a new definition of romanticism that would include the literary school of the 1820s and '30s as well as the neoromantic symbolists of the 1890s and 1900s. He viewed romanticism as an 'eternal extra-temporal type of poetic creativity.' With obvious dependence on Friedrich Schlegel, he claimed that 'romantic art strives towards the interesting, the individual, the characteristic, seeks new and forceful impressions' and 'knows no general law of the beautiful.'[136] According to him, Bryusov, Blok, and Bely 'epitomize the tradition of romanticism.'

At the same time, a more social and political definition of romanticism was being constructed by Gorky and Lenin. In his *History of Russian Literature* of 1909, Gorky distinguished between a negative 'individualistic romanticism' and a positive 'social' or 'collective' romanticism. The former, according to Gorky, derives 'ideological material from the soul, from individual experience'; the latter 'originates as a result of man's awareness of his link with the world and the sensation of his creative force called forth by this awareness.' This second variety of romanticism, according to Gorky, is just forming; its receptacle is the proletariat. 'With this term ... I define only the heightened militant mood of a proletarian.'[137] Gorky evaluated the romantics of the beginning of the nineteenth century positively in so far as they protested against the 'forms of bourgeois morality.' 'Contemporary romanticism,' on the other hand, is 'a purely reactionary phenomenon, caused by the fear of the inevitable social crisis.'[138]

Gorky's distinction (which later took the form of 'active' or 'revolutionary' versus 'passive' romanticism)[139] was also made by Lenin in an article of 1910, 'Concerning the Characterization of Economic Romanticism,' about the reactionary romanticism of Sismondi and the populists. Lenin's theory of two cultures within one national culture became the foundation for his definition of two kinds of romanticism: progressive and conservative. Sismondi's economic system he considers conservatively romantic because Sismondi offers 'hopelessly antiquated social forms of the past as remedies for [contemporary] reality.' But if romanticism is the dream of a desirable future, it is progressive and synonymous with 'racing ahead and visualizing ... that creation as completed which just begins to grow under one's hands.'[140]

In general usage, meanwhile, a further broadening of the meanings of the cognates took place. If *romantizm* had come to be widely used with the connotations of idealism, visionariness, loftiness, or lyricism in general from the 1840s on, it could now also mean 'emotionality' or 'elatedness' in general (*'romantizm bor'by, romantičeskie mečty'*).[141] Korolenko, in 'On a Cloudy Day,' even used a new cognate to convey this meaning: 'Youth is romantic [*'romantična'*] ... And what can be more romantic [*'romantičnee'*] than the bygone old times that were present to our mothers and fathers?'/ *'Molodost' romantična ... A čto možet byt' romantičnee isčeznuvšej stariny, kotoraja byla nastojaščim dlja našix materej i otcov.'*[142] Yet at the same time one can find *romantičeskij* (like *romaničeskij* formerly with Karamzin) used in reference to landscape, with the meaning of 'picturesque,' 'attractive.' Skitalets (S. G. Petrov) wrote in *Stages* (1908): 'One could think well under the harmonious roar of the waterfall, contemplating this romantic little corner of nature ...'/ *'Xorošo dumalos' pod garmoničeskij šum vodopada, sozercaja romantičeskij ugolok prirody ...'*[143] In the same year, Gumilyov called a collection of his exotic poems of adventure *Romantic Flowers* (*Romantičeskie Cvety*). *Romaničeskij* was also used in the old sense of 'amorous,' for example, when Anton Chekhov complained in 'Verochka' (1887): 'I have been alive for 29 years, but I've never had one amorous adventure [*'roman'*]. In my whole life not a single romantic [*romaničeskoj*] liaison'/*'živu ja na svete 29 let, no u menja v žizni ni razu romana ne bylo. Vo vsju žizn' ni odnoj romaničeskoj istorii.'*[144]

Dictionaries and encyclopedias continued to combine technical and non-technical, historical and universal criteria of romanticism. Pavlenko's *Encyclopedic Dictionary* of 1913 defined romanticism as

... a movement in art in general, and poetry in particular, the distinctive feature [of which] is the element of the miraculous, unusual, infinite as opposed to the clarity, naïvety, and calm of ancient art.

Romantizm – napravlenie v iskusstve voobšče, i v častnosti v poèzii. Otličitel'naja čerta romantizma – èto element fantastičeskogo, neobyčnogo, beskonečnogo v protivopoložnost' jasnosti, naivnosti, spokojstvija v iskusstve antičnom ...[145]

1920 TO THE PRESENT: THE SOVIET PERIOD

A. Gurevich summarized the official attitude to romanticism in the Soviet Union when he said in 1964:

Romanticism still remains – as Pushkin jokingly defined it – Parnassian atheism ... [For] all those who write about romanticism unanimously point to its anti-educational character and consider it as identical with anti-social retreat into the self, into the emotional world of a self-contained individual.[146]

Gorky's and Lenin's sociologically grounded distinctions of the two kinds of romanticism became the basis of Soviet definitions. Whether used in reference to the historical 'romantic school' of 1820–40, to later historical, or to contemporary manifestations of romanticism, *romantičeskij*, *romantizm*, *romantik* now primarily connoted 'counter-revolutionary,' 'anti-progressive,' 'impractical,' 'subversive': romanticism was seen as an escape from the facts and needs of Soviet reality.*

When used in reference to a work of literature, 'romantic' frequently meant 'outdated,' 'reactionary.' Romanticism was considered pre-realism, an inferior stage of realism. Thus, A. Fadeev in 1929 wrote: 'The method of proletarian realism does not need any romantic admixture, on the contrary, is basically inimical to them' / '*Metod proletarskogo realizma ne nuždaetsja ni v kakix romantičeskix primesjax, naoborot, on v korne vraždeben im.*'[147] P. S. Kogan and V. M. Friche similarly define romanticism by contrasting it to realism. Kogan, for example, wrote:

If I see in this table an item which I perceive only with my sensory organs ... I am a realist. But if I declare that I sense something in this table about which neither my sight, hearing, nor touch gives information ... I am a mystic, a romantic.

Esli ja vižu v ètom stole predmet, kotoryj ja vosprinimaju tol'ko svoimi organami čuvstv ... – ja realist. No esli ja zajavljaju, čto v ètom stole ja oščuščaju nečto, o čem ne govorit mne ni moj glaz, ni slux, ne osjazatel'noe čuvstvo ... ja javljajus' mistikom, romantikom.[148]

Friche noted that 'romanticism considered the ideal world more real than the real world' / '*Romantizm sčital ideal'nyj mir bolee real'nym, čem real'nyj mir.*'[149] P. N. Sakulin asserted similarly that the essence

---

*   In his evaluation of B. Pilnyak, Leon Trotsky wrote in 1924: 'Pilnyak does not present a picture of the Revolution, but only its base and background ... The proletarian Revolution can be technically and culturally completed and justified only through electrification, not through a return to the candle, through the materialist philosophy of a working optimism, and not through woodland superstitions and stagnant fatalism ... This results in a deviation from the most important aspects of reality, and in a reduction of everything to the primitive, to the socially barbaric ... Further on, before you know it, it will lead to mysticism and to mystic hypocrisy (as per the passport of a romanticist), which is the complete and final death. Even now Pilnyak shows his romanticist passport every time he is in difficulty ...' Trotsky, *Literature and Revolution* (Ann Arbor Paperback, 1960), pp. 86 *f.* See also Olesha, *Envy* (Anchor Books, 1967), pp. 22, 32.

of romanticism is in 'irrealism'/'*Osnovnaja suščnost' romantizma zaključaetsja v irrealizme.*'[150] and V. F. Pereverzev wrote that 'Romanticism is the aspiration to what is impossible in reality'/ '*Romantizm – èto stremlenie k tomu, čto nevozmožno v dejstvitel'nosti.*'[151]

Even so, Gorky's and Lenin's positive meaning of romanticism as the dream of a realizable future remained current. The literature of the 1920s about the Revolution and the Civil War was described as full of 'revolutionary romanticism' / '*revolucionnaja romantika*', the belief in an attainable future ideal which was being fought for. When in the 1930s phrases such as 'we began to need heroic romanticism [*geroičeskoj romantike*] again'[152] were heard, the reference was clearly to the politically militant civil war spirit absent during the time of collectivization and the purges. But in the 1920s romanticism was also discussed by literary scholars, especially some formalists, outside the framework of Gorky's and Lenin's conception. A. I. Beletsky, for example, found that 'one should look for the essence of romanticism above all in a work's style,' the source of which he saw to be 'a world view the distinctive feature of which was dualism'/'*Suščnost' romantizma prežde vsego nužno bylo by iskat' v samom stile ... ego [stil'] istočnikom javljaetsja mirovozzrenie, otličitel'naja čerta kotorogo dualizm.*'[153] He singled out the prevalence of metaphor as the essential feature of romantic style, a criterion also suggested by D. Chizhevsky and Roman Jakobson.

With the introduction of socialist realism in 1932–4, 'revolutionary romanticism' became an ingredient or, at times, even a synonym for this new literary doctrine. Developing the ideas of Gorky and Lenin, literary theoreticians used both *romantika* and *romantizm* to denote the ability to see the ideal, not in the future, but already realized in the present. It represented an ability to 'romanticize reality, to support its leading positive tendencies'/'... *romantizirovat' dejstvitel'nost', to est', podderživat' ee veduščie položitel'nye tendencii, ee pafos.*'[154] It was only a short step, however, from this to a new negative meaning, 'the embellishment, the lacquering' of reality/'... *lakirovka ... priukrašenie ...*'[155] Gradually, *romantičeskij*, *romantizm*, and *romantika* became associated with falsity, unreality, cloying sweetness (curiously enough, obsolete connotations of *romaničeskij*). I. M. Dubrovina in 1967 characterized romanticism as

an entirely innocent concept [which] was in some measure compromised by the pseudo-romantic embellishment of life. It is not difficult to understand why some people began to have a guarded or even sceptical attitude toward romanticism.

Ni v čem ne povinnoe ponjatie bylo v kakoj-to mere skomprometirovano ložno-
romantičeskim podrumjanivaniem žizni. I netrudno ponjat', počemu koe-kto stal
otnosit'sja k romantike nastoroženno, a to i skeptičeski.[156]

Recent approaches to romanticism depended to a great extent
on the degree to which scholars followed the interpretation of
Gorky and Lenin. Following their line closely, V. B. Korzun distinguished in 1953 between 'a reactionary romantic method
essentially inimical to realism [and] a progressive, revolutionary
method [that is] an original form of the manifestation of realism.'[157]
E. Tsoy in 1964 almost deprived romanticism of its independent
existence when he wrote: 'Critical realism absorbed and developed the best achievements of romanticism ... In that sense
realism in general is "romantic".' [158] But hereby he also justified its
existence.

The less orthodox literary critics concentrated their efforts on
searching for a definition of the historical phenomenon of the
'romantic school.' Typological and literary-linguistic criteria
intermingle in these attempts. For G. A. Gukovsky romanticism
was equivalent to an individualism that 'manifests itself, in the
romantic method and style, as subjectivism.' L. I. Timofeev called
romanticism the 'transforming principle' as opposed to the
'mimetic principle' of realism, but hesitated to associate these
principles with any particular period. A. M. Gurevich pointed to
the 'absolute nature of ideals and the awareness that their realization in a given reality is impossible,' i.e., to the 'dual nature of
existence,' as the fundamental feature of romanticism and explained it as a 'reaction against eighteenth-century rationalism.'[159]
For V. I. Kuleshov, romanticism was one of the varieties of what
Belinsky called ideal poetry, i.e., a manner of expressing a conception of life with the help of fictive, imaginary subjects, so that
the real and the fantastic overlap; a manner that has its own logic,
truth, necessity, and probability, which the reader agrees to accept
when he begins reading.[160] G. N. Pospelov, in turn, called romanticism a type of creativity that represented life according to a
specific set of norms that dominated in the 1820s and '30s. This
conception led him to speak of 'normatively romantic creativity'
/ *normativno-romantičeskoe tvorčestvo*.[161] B. Reizov defined romanticism
as 'a system and process of interpretation that in each country leads
to different, nationally and historically qualified results'; and
consequently – like Lovejoy in the United States – spoke of 'romanticisms' / *'romantizmy'* in the plural.[162]

Attempts at clarification were reflected in such new usages as 'pre-romanticism' / '*predromantizm*' or 'romantic tendencies' / '*romantičeskie tendencii*' in reference to the works of Batyushkov and Karamzin, and 'romantic realism' / '*romantičeskij realizm*' used by G. Byaly with reference to writers of the 1880s. Yet the terminology remained vague enough for such Soviet writers as Bagritsky, Paustovsky, Prishvin, Gorbatov, Dovzhenko, and Kazakevich to be called romantic, and for L. P. Egorova to speak of 'the romantic school within socialist realism.'[163]

The problem of the word's multiple meanings in contemporary Soviet usage is humorously presented in I. M. Dubrovina's booklet, *Romanticism in Art* (*Romantika v iskusstve*), of 1967. She begins with the curious statement that 'the need for romanticism is a need of the present,'[164] and continues with some quotations from contemporary articles that reveal the prevailing confusion. One finds such combinations as 'on romantic sails' / '*na romantičeskix parusax*,' 'romanticism of humaneness' / '*romantika čelovečnosti*,' 'the iron romantics of the epoch' / '*železnye romantiki èpoxi*,' the 'gold of romanticism' / '*zoloto romantiki*,' 'romanticism of a detective' / '*romantika detektiva*,' 'plebeian democratic romanticism' / '*plebejskaja demokratičeskaja romantika*,' 'the romanticism of crimson epaulettes' / '*romantika alyx pogon*,' 'exotic-romantic camels' / '*èkzotičeski-romantičeskie verbljudy*,' 'super-romantic conventionality' / '*sverx-romantičeskaja uslovnost*',' 'romantic clichés' / '*romantičeskie štampy*,' 'revolutionary irrealistic romanticism' / '*revolujucionnaja, irrealističeskaja romantika*,' and 'pseudo-romantic falsity' / '*psevdo-romantičeskaja fal'š*'.'[165]

From the above quotations it becomes clear that *romantika*, *romantizm*, and *romantičnost*' are used interchangeably in reference to an historical period, a universal creative method, or a general feeling about life. Several scholars in recent years, however, attempted to differentiate between the meaning of these cognates. Dubrovina, for example, wishes to use *romantika* as meaning 'the ability to awaken a special relationship to the world which can manifest itself in the art of various epochs and in various schools' / '... *ta sposobnost' probuždat' osoboe otnošenie k miru, kotoroja možet projavljat'sja v iskusstve raznyx èpox i raznyx napravlenij*.'[166] Pospelov writes in a similar vein:

The romantic school [*romantizm*] is a phenomenon of the past, but the romantic spirit [*romantika*] was reborn again and again in various literary movements. It lives now, too, in the works of many Soviet writers.

Romantizm davno ušel v prošloe, a romantika vse snova i snova vozroždalas' i žila v raznyx literaturnyx tečenijax. Ona živet i v naše vremja v proizvedenijax mnogix sovetskix pisatelej. [167]

P. I. Grazhis, in a dissertation entitled 'Turgenev and Romanticism,' tries to 'explain the relationship between the romantic spirit [*romantika*] and the romantic principles of figurative representation' / '... *vyjasnit' sootnošenie romantiki i romantičeskix principov obraznogo otraženija.*'[168] Here, then, Belinsky's definition of romanticism as an eternal human trait reappears attached to the cognate *romantika*, rather than to *romantizm*, which has an historical meaning.

Similarly, attempts are being made to differentiate between the adjectives *romantičnyj* (associated with *romantika*) and *romantičeskij* (associated with *romantizm*). Dubrovina writes that 'in the romantic [*romantičnom*] image lyricism and the ideal are inseparable' ı'*V romantičnom obraze liričnost' i ideal nerazryvny.*'[169] Vanslov likewise seems to use *romantičnyj* with a meaning derived from *romantika* and different from that of *romantičeskij*, for example, in the following passage:

The above-named works of various writers and composers are romantic [*romantičeskimi*], not because they are linked with one another, but on the contrary because bonds of mutual influence arose among them, so that they are all essentially romantic [*romantičnyj*] (possess an [identical] ideological artistic conception).

Ne potomu vse nazvannye proizvedenija različnyx pisatelej i kompozitorov javljajutsja romantičeskimi, čto svjazany meždu soboj, a naoborot, potomu i voznikli meždu nimi niti vzaimovlijanij, čto vse oni po suščestvu romantičny (obladajut obščnost'ju idejno-xudožestvennoj koncepcii).[170]

But however helpful such distinctions might be, common usage does not adhere to them. *Romantizm*, as Vanslov points out, still has the same meaning as *romantika* for the general public. It is associated with 'rosy, impractical dreams,' 'spiritual nobility,' 'lofty dreaminess,' and 'poetic love.' With romanticism are linked such ideas as 'altruism,' 'dream of a better future,' 'intensive emotional life,' 'artistic giftedness.'[171]

The confusion that still prevails is reflected in the vague and undifferentiated definitions offered by the *Dictionary of the Contemporary Russian Literary Language* of 1961, which lists eighteen cognates: *romantika, romantičnyj, roman, romanizirovanie, romanizm, romanizovat', romanist, romaničeskij, romannyj, romanskij, romantizacija,*

romantizirovat',' romantizm, romantik, romantička, romantičeskij, ro-
maničeskij, romaničnost'.[172]

In this dictionary, *romaničeskij* is regarded as an adjective from *roman* (novel), meaning 'novelistic,' and *roman* (romance), meaning 'amorous'. The new adjective *romannyj* is listed with the exclusive meaning of 'novelistic.' The old meaning of *romaničeskij* (extra-ordinary, fabulous, causing an emotional and lofty attitude, inclined to dreaming and idealization of people and life) is noted as obsolete. *Romanizm* now can only mean a turn of speech borrowed from a Romance language.

Romantičeskij is presented as an adjective associated with (1) *romantizm* (romanticism), referring to (*a*) 'a cultural movement at the beginning of the nineteenth century that fought classicism, emphasized the individual and emotion, and used historical and national poetic themes' or (*b*) 'a movement in literature and art, permeated by optimism and the attempt to show the high purpose of man in bright images; (2) *romantik* (romanticist), referring to persons inclined to dreaminess and idealization of life; (3) *romantika* (romantic spirit), meaning 'emotionally elevated,' 'unusual,' 'fabulous'; and (4) *romantičnost'* (romantic spirit), with the same meaning as (3) and having its own adjective, *romantičnyj.*

Such a cataloguing, descriptive, chronological study of the semasiology of *romantičeskij* suggests a number of concluding comments.

The semantic development of the Russian cognates of 'romantic' was not organic, unless one argues only from a strictly linguistic point of view that all these cognates are related to the root word *roman.* The process by which the diverse meanings of the cognates developed was almost alogical, often associative. The meanings were often unrelated to each other; they depended on indigenous literary traditions, the literary and critical context, and the political and social situation of the time. In fact, one hesitates to speak of a semantic *development* between 1815 and 1840, since meanings also amorphously accumulated as a result of the increased influence of Western writings. Diverse literary and intellectual phenomena received, often coincidentally, the same designation. Thus, Pospelov's metaphor of a 'homonymic tree of romanticism' is somewhat misleading.

Though there seems to be no principle of order in the chaotic attempts at definitions in the first decades during which the cognates were used, there is some 'logic' that one can discover behind the ascription of meanings to them: a progression from definitions of *roman* and the adjective *romaničeskij* to definitions of 'modern' (i.e. contemporary) poetry and literature in terms of the *roman*, and from there to the new cognates *romantičeskij* and *romantizm*, which were used to designate that same recent literature.

The root word *roman*, which until the end of the eighteenth century retained the flavor of a foreign word in Russia, had the meaning of 'love-affair' as well as 'novel.' But *roman* as 'novel' tended to connote to a Russian something imagined and alien to the realities of life, while the more neutral Russian equivalent *povest'* suggested a didactic prose narrative based on true events. *Roman* was therefore not discussed by neoclassicist theoreticians, whereas the didactic *povest'* was at times mentioned under the heading 'oratory.' As late as 1822, N. I. Grech entered *roman* in his *Textbook of Russian Literature* (*Učebnaja kniga rossijskoj slovesnosti*) under 'oratory' or 'rhetoric' and discussed it in the section 'historical genres' as 'novelistic poetry' / *romaničeskaja poèzija*. Until far into the nineteenth century *roman* was associated with such unfavourable features as exaggerated feelings, exotic locations and names, bizarre events, complicated plots, and endless love adventures always crowned with good fortune.[173] It was inevitable that the adjective *romaničeskij*, when it appeared in 1791, much later than *roman*, carried these connotations along with imported meanings such as 'picturesque' and 'sentimental.' Soon both the meanings derived from the indigenous aesthetics of the novel and those derived from imported literary works were found to be applicable to a very large part of recent literature, which included drama and poetry and was before long designated by a new cognate, *romantičeskij*.

When *romantičeskij* appeared in 1810 in a literary context, it was simply a synonym of *romaničeskij*, an apparently thoughtless rendering of the German *romantisch* and the French *romantique*. From 1815 on, paralleling Russian acquaintance with West European theoretical writings on recent or 'romantic' literature, *romantičeskij* and the cognates *romantizm, romantika, romantik* absorbed historical, philosophical, and aesthetic connotations. The numerous definitions that Russian critics offered can be reduced to two approaches to the problem, which immediately became two further sources of ambiguity: the typological-philosophical, content-oriented and the aesthetic-technical, form- and rule-oriented search for criteria of *romantizm*.

Before taking up these two approaches to defining the cognates, it should be pointed out that the simplified interpretation of *romantičeskij* as an organic branch on the homonymic tree *roman* co-existed with the other definitional approaches. This simplification was related to the negative connotations of *roman* and at the same time to F. Schlegel's positive derivation of romantic poetry from the exemplary qualities of a large number of verse epics, romances, and novels all of which, as was explained in an earlier essay of this volume, were comprised in the broad category denoted in the usage of that time by the German word *Roman*.[174] Thus V. N. Olin, betraying a rather shallow knowledge of Schlegel's theories, wrote in 1825:

Romantic poetry can be also called poetry of the novel, because all circumstances, all situations that are proper for the novel are also proper for the romantic verse tale. Therefore, a romantic verse tale is a novel in verse, or in other words, a poetic novel.

Poèziju romantičeskuju možno inače nazvat' romaničeskoju, potomu čto vse obstojatel'stva, vse položenija priličestvujuščie romanu, priličny takže i poème romantičeskoj. Itak poèma romantičeskaja est' roman v stixax, ili govorja inače, roman poètičeskij.[175]

The philosophical-typological approach to defining *romantičeskij* reflects the critics' scarch for what constituted the spiritual content of contemporary literature. It was an attempt to verbalize the shift in values, consciousness, and the conception of the world and man, the cultural crisis that was in the air. In order to prove the positive value and desirability of a new, freshly coherent system of beliefs, the critics cited earlier writers who to them most fully anticipated what they felt to be the charactcristics of 'modern' literature. That is, the past was used to ennoble, justify, and define the present. This approach opened a Pandora's box of definitions. The critics overlooked, underemphasized, and obscured the historical particularities of the conceptual changes of their own time. Instead of elucidating the new concept by contrasting it with related past phenomena, the critics obfuscated it by finding superficial resemblances.

Other pitfalls lay in store for those critics who concentrated on what we would now call aesthetic theory to explain 'romanticism.' When 'romantic' became identified with 'natural' and contrasted with 'classical' or 'neoclassical,' it soon was evident that these words had as many meanings as users. To give some examples: for

Vyazemsky, whom some called the head of Russian romanticism, 'natural' meant, on the one hand, spontaneous, original, varied, diverse, daring, independent, and inspired (for nature and genius followed only inspiration in their creations); on the other hand, it also implied 'national' (*narodnyj*) since the 'national' is intimately and commonly familiar and inspiring. Furthermore, 'natural' was associated for Vyazemsky with the preponderance of simple feeling as the spontaneous, common, and therefore most natural element in human nature. 'Natural,' however, by no means signified imitation of nature, i.e., truthfulness to external material reality, for Vyazemsky. He was concerned with internal truthfulness and found, in fact, that the more imaginative a work was, the more truth it communicated: 'Here [in romanticism] we are not concerned with positive truth (*istina*), nor with reality (*suščestvennost'*), but with the truth of feelings. Here truth (*istina*)is a synonym for correctness (*vernost'*).[175] For Bulgarin 'natural' meant planless, heterogeneous, bizarre, but harmonious. Olin, in turn, considered it the artist's task to copy nature, and 'natural' therefore meant to him imitative of nature or of external reality. For Polevoy, being 'natural' connoted truthfulness to one's feeling, a subjective response to nature. Worst of all, the critics were quite unaware of the polysemy.

In the case of 'classical' the same multiplicity of meanings is apparent. To some, it meant almost exactly what 'romantic' meant to others – 'natural.' For Nadezhdin, for instance, 'classical' meant 'natural' in the sense of being oriented toward the external world, while 'romantic' connoted inner-orientedness. For Ryleev, 'classical' meant exemplary, but also blindly imitative of ancient masterpieces; for Gogol, graphic, clear, majestic; for Bestuzhev it indicated the reign of fate, the prevalence of emotions and material images. 'Classical' could also be used as a synonym of 'pseudo-classical' or 'neo-classicist,' which, in turn, meant anything from adherence to Boileau's *Art Poétique* to conformity with an average image of the world, objective beauty, symmetry, simplicity, lack of ornament, and the depiction of ideal or general types. Stylistic definitions of supposedly 'romantic' works suffered equally from vagueness. The identification of the 'romantic' with ornateness, fragmentariness, diversity, allusiveness, and wealth and bizarreness of images did not preclude the characterisation of literary works of earlier times in terms of these qualities. The naiveté with which many of these definitions were offered as definitive and lucid is striking.

The lack of sophistication that such largely uncritical repetitions of West European definitions reflects points to some of the factors that were responsible for the amorphousness and muddiness of Russian discussions of *romantičeskij* and its cognates between 1815 and 1840 – factors that ought to be studied carefully if one wants to grasp the 'romantic' phenomenon in Russia in connection with the semasiology of the term. Underlying the issues of romanticism/ classicism were such vital problems as that of the literary language, the state and function of Russian literature, national identity and *narodnost'*,* and the state of criticism.

During the first two decades, the controversy over the meaning and value of 'romanticism' (as opposed to 'classicism') overlapped with the (slightly earlier) controversy concerning the 'old style' and the 'new style.' The latter expression referred to the French-oriented linguistic innovations of the sentimentalist Karamzin (simplification of syntax, loan-translations from French, the use of a pleasant, but effeminate and bland, language in literary works that imitated the language of polite society); defending what he called the 'old style,' Shishkov insisted that neologisms should be derived from Slavic roots and archaisms should be used to enrich contemporary language.† Karamzin and his followers tended to be linked with romanticism, Shishkov and his followers with classicism. But issues became more confused when 'romantics' claimed *narodnost'* for their works, an orientation that the Shishkovites had been boasting of, and when morality – the goal of literature – became associated with the Shishkovites and with classicism. Associations of Karamzinists (followed by defenders of romanticism) with liberalism and of Shishkovites (identified with classicists) with conservatism were quick to form (often unjustly) and gave the controversies political overtones.

The semantic fate of 'romantic' was influenced, furthermore, by the state of literary criticism. The beginnings of criticism in Russia coincided with the controversy concerning *romantizm*. Literary criticism was not a profession, and the best critics were

*   *Narodnost'* is a difficult word to translate. *Narod* means people or nation, *narodnost'* something like the German *Volkstümlichkeit*, i.e., national essence or identity, national character, people-mindedness.

†   The controversy indicates the unsatisfactory state of the Russian literary language. As late as 1829 Vyazemsky could remark that it was interesting to translate the 'refined, metaphysical, and subtly sensitive *Adolphe* [Benjamin Constant's novel] into our uncouth language and to study it, feel it out and to make experiments, if not torments [untranslatable pun *popytki/pytki*] with it' (*Wytrzens*, p. 127).

themselves poets. Such criticism as there was consisted chiefly of subjective, impressionistic remarks about new literary works, of discussions of their patriotic qualities and their proper or improper subject matter, of biographical and bibliographical information, of listings of typographical errors and of statements about the quality of the paper on which the works were printed. Issues were frequently treated as political and personal matters and led to denunciations to the censor. Literary polemics often deteriorated into undignified, vicious personal attacks. Views were presented arrogantly and naïvely. A writer's social class could be cause enough to despise his views, to suspect him politically, and to question his motives. With the beginning of professional criticism in the late 1820s and '30s, that is, when educated men from classes other than the nobility began to edit journals, class animosity became even more pronounced in literary issues. In such a context *romantizm* acquired overtones peculiar to the state of cultural affairs in Russia.

The issues that occupied Russian educated minds were for the most part discussed in journals, but few of these existed long enough to provide any consistency in literary arguments and to make a lasting impact. Certain journals quickly came to represent specific attitudes to the new system of beliefs, paralleling their political outlook; one might even speak of polarization. *The Spirit of Journals (Dux žurnalov)*, the first periodical to speak of West European romanticism, did so, in 1815–17, in the form of attacks on (genuinely or supposedly) German romantic aesthetics and philosophy (A. W. Schlegel, Fichte, Kant, Schiller) and resorted to translations from *Journal des Débats*. *The Messenger of Europe (Vestnik Evropy*, 1802–30) and M. P. Pavlov's *Athenaeum (Atenej*, 1828–30) followed in line. Kyukhelbeker's and Odoevsky's *Mnemozina* (1824–5) became a spokesman for 'true' romanticism, relying on German romantic theory; M. P. Pogodin's *Moscow Messenger (Moskovskij Vestnik*, 1827–30) also favoured romanticism, following German models, while N. A. Polevoy's *Moscow Telegraph (Moskovskij Telegraf*, 1825–34) primarily represented French and English views of romanticism.

The ambiguities and confusions that pervade the discussions concerning romanticism in these journals have continued to exist until the present day, with the difference that more recent critics are aware of the complexities involved. In the remaining decades of the nineteenth century typological definitions dominated, but varied in accordance with the philosophical, political, and social circumstances of the time. The typological definitions of *romantičeskij* are also most widely implied in the current usage of the word. When M. Bulgakov in *The Master and Margarita* (completed in 1940) has his hero called 'thrice romantic' (*triždy romantičeskij*), this is not, as one might suspect in the light of all the ambiguities of the term, an entirely meaningless appelation. *Romantičeskij* in literary usage now generally refers to a universal philosophical attitude to man and the world. This attitude implies a superiority of vision and intuition, even madness, over rational analysis and factual, empirical data; a greater importance of the individual (the part, the subject) than the state (the whole, the object); and the appreciation of imagination at the expense of common sense, which is regarded as trivial and banal. It also implies that one should live by values and ideals that are intangible and cannot be proven by empirical evidence, such as love, the improvement of mankind, and moral freedom, that there is an elusive supernatural world, and that the world and the evil in it have a secret symbolic significance.

When used as technical term, however, *romantičeskij* has remained relative, comparative, devoid of the exactness that such a term should have. Unless one conceptualizes the diversity it hides, unless one explores the specific literary and aesthetic manifestations that it is intended to refer to in a given case, and unless one correlates a precisely defined, historically conditioned system of beliefs with the various artistic expressions it finds, *romantizm* and *romantičeskij* are empty labels.

NOTES

1 Cited by G. N. Pospelov, 'Čto že takoe romantizm?' *Problemy romantizma* (Moscow, 1967), p. 41 (hereafter cited as *Pospelov*).
2 A. S. Puškin, *Polnoe sobranie sočinenij* XIII (Moscow, 1937–49): 183.
3 V. Belinskij, *Polnoe sobranie sočinenij* VII (Moscow-Leningrad, 1952–9); 144.
4 A. I. Beleckij, 'Očerednye voprosy izučenija russkogo romantizma,' *Russkij romantizm – sbornik statej* (Leningrad, 1927), p. 5 (hereafter cited as *Russkij romantizm*).
5 A. N. Sokolov, 'K sporam o romantizme,' *Voprosy literatury* (1963), VII: 122.
6 *Pospelov*, p. 42.
7 G. A. Višnevskaja, 'Iz istorii russkogo romantizma,' *Voprosy romantizma v russkoj literature*, Sbornik II (Kazan, 1964): 82 (hereafter cited as *Višnevskaja*).
8 Ibid., pp. 82 f.
9 Ibid.
10 N. M. Karamzin, *Izbrannye sočinenija* I (Moscow-Lenningrad, 1964): 737 (hereafter cited as *Karamzin, Izbrannye*).

11 Ibid., p. 755.
12 Ibid., p. 764.
13 *Višnevskaja*, p. 93.
14 See P. Brang, *Studien zur Theorie und Praxis der russischen Erzählung 1770–1811* (Wiesbaden, 1960), pp. 37–44 (hereafter cited as *Brang*).
15 N. I. Mordovčenko, *Russkaja kritika pervoj četverti XIX veka* (Moscow-Leningrad, 1959), p. 122 (hereafter cited as *Mordovčenko*).
16 N. M. Janovskij (ed.), *Novyj slovotolkovatel'* (St. Petersburg, 1803–6).
17 V. V. Sipovskij, 'Očerki po istorii russkogo romana,' *Zapiski istoriko-filologičeskogo fakul'teta imperatorskogo Sanktpeterburgskogo universiteta* XCVII (St. Petersburg, 1909): 16.
18 *Brang*, p. 250.
19 Cited by *Mordovčenko*, pp. 113 *f*. The German source, stated neither in *Severnyj Vestnik* nor by Mordovčenko, is the article 'Über die Oper' in *Der Freimütige*, 28 January 1805), no. 20, pp. 77 *ff*. The anonymous author is Christian Schreiber.
20 *Mordovčenko* ascribes the footnote to the editor of *Severnyj Vestnik*, I. I. Martynov; it is, in fact, an inaccurate translation of an editorial note on the original article and must be ascribed to the editor of the *German* periodical, Garlieb Merkel. See Eichner, pp. 123 *f*. above.
21 See *Brang*, p. 254.
22 V. T. Narežnyj, *Rossijskij Žilblaz ili poxoždenija knjazja Čistjakova* II (Moscow, 1938): 234.
23 P. A. Vjazemskij, *Polnoe sobranie sočinenij* I (St. Petersburg, 1878): 28 *f*. (hereafter cited as *Vjazemskij*).
24 *Mordovčenko*, p. 143.
25 Ibid., pp. 144 *f*.
26 *Dux Žurnalov* (1817), XXVII: 111.
27 *Mordovčenko*, p. 145.
28 A. M. Babkin and V. V. Šendecov, *Slovar' inojazyčnyx slov, upotrebljajuščixsja v russkom jazyke bez perevoda* (Moscow-Leningrad, 1966), p. 1136.
29 *Vjazemskij*, p. 49.
30 A. F. Voejkov, 'Ruslan i Ljudmila,' *Syn Otečestva* (1820), XXXVI: 15.
31 N. Ostolopov, *Slovar' drevnej i novoj poèzii* (St. Petersburg, 1821) III: 28–30, cited by R. A. Budagov, 'Iz istorii slov: ROMANTIČESKIJ i ROMANTIZM,' *Izvestija Akademii Nauk SSSR-Serija literatury i jazyka* (1968), XXVII, vyp 3, p. 251.
32 *Vjazemskij*, pp. 73 *f*..
33 Ibid., p. 170.
34 Ibid.
35 Ibid., p. 331.
36 Ibid., p. 226.
37 Ibid., p. 168.
38 Ibid., p. 172.
39 Ibid.
40 Ibid., p. 169.
41 G. Wytrzens, *Pjotr Andreevič Vjazemskij. Studien zur russischen Literatur – und Kulturgeschichte des 19. Jahrhunderts* (Wien, 1961), p. 102.
42 *Literaturnye Listki* (1824), VII: 267 *f*.; cited by *Mordovčenko*, pp. 211 *f*.
43 O. Somov, 'O romantičeskoj poèzii,' *Sorevnovatel' prosveščenija i blagotvorenija* (St. Petersburg, 1823), pt. 23, I: 43–59; II: 151–69; III: 263–306; pt. 24, II: 125–47.
44 Ibid., pp. 156 *f*.
45 Ibid., pp. 157–9.
46 Ibid., p. 160.

47 *Syn Otečestva* (1825), XVII: 77 *f.*
48 *Mnemozina* (1824), II: 34.
49 Ibid., pp. 36 *f.*
50 *Syn Otečestva* (1825), XVII: 71.
51 *Mnemozina* (1824), II: 34.
52 Cited by *Mordovčenko*, p. 409.
53 Ibid., p. 229.
54 Ibid.
55 *Syn Otečestva* (1823), IV: 179.
56 Ibid., pp. 183 *f.*
57 A. A. Bestužev-Marlinskij, 'O romansax i romantizme,' *Moskovskij Telegraf* (1833), XV: 406.
58 Ibid., XVI: 546.
59 Ibid., XVIII: 106; also A. A. Bestužev-Marlinskij, *Sočinenija* II (Moscow, 1958): 607.
60 *Moskovskij Telegraf* (1833), XV: 401; XVII: 105. See also Bestužev-Marlinskij, *Sočinenija*, II: 562, 594.
61 *Moskovskij Telegraf* (1833), XVII: 104.
62 *Mordovčenko*, p. 370.
63 *Moskovskij Telegraf* (1833), XVI: 554.
64 Ibid., XV: 506.
65 Ibid., XVII: 96.
66 Ibid., p. 97.
67 Cited by *Mordovčenko*, p. 364.
68 *Moskovskij Telegraf* (1829), XV: 326.
69 Ibid., pp. 318 *f.*
70 Ibid. (1830), XXXII: 233.
71 Ibid., p. 229.
72 Ibid. (1826), VIII: 70 *f.*; (1832), XLVII: 568 *f.*
73 Ibid. (1826), IX: 141.
74 A. S. Puškin, *Polnoe sobranie sočinenij* XII (Moscow, 1937–49): 39.
75 Ibid., II: 267.
76 Ibid., XIII: 57.
77 Ibid., XI: 37.
78 Ibid., XI: 67 *f.*
79 Ibid.
80 Puškin, XI: 36.
81 Ibid., (*Eugene Onegin*), V, ch. 2, stanza 10.
82 Ibid., V, ch. 6, stanza 23.
83 Ibid., V, ch. 3, stanza 17.
84 *Moskovskij Telegraf* (1830), X: 227.
85 A. F. Voeykov, *Vestnik Evropy* (1820), XVI: 287.
86 *Mordovčenko*, p. 187.
87 Ibid., p. 188.
88 A. P. Pjatkovskij, *Knjaz' Vladimir F. Odoevskij* (St. Petersburg, 1880), pp. 5 *f.*
89 *Blagonamerennyj* (1823), XXI: 224.
90 Cited by N. K. Kozmin, *Nikolaj Ivanovič Nadeždin* (*Žizn' i naučno-literaturnaja dejatel'nost' 1804–1836*) (St. Petersburg, 1912), p. 203.
91 Ibid., pp. 205 *f.*
92 Ibid., p. 203.
93 Ibid., p. 221.
94 V. Belinskij, *Polnoe sobranie sočinenij* (Moscow-Leningrad, 1952–9), V: 548, 549.
95 Ibid., VI: 522.
96 Ibid., XII: 114.

97   Ibid., VII: 145.
98   Ibid., p. 146.
99   Ibid., p. 147.
100 Ibid., pp. 154, 158.
101 Ibid., p. 150.
102 Ibid., p. 154.
103 Ibid., p. 155.
104 Ibid., p. 158.
105 Ibid., p. 161.
106 Ibid., p. 165.
107 Ibid., p. 166.
108 Ibid., p. 215.
109 Ibid., pp. 173 f.
110 Ibid., IX: 384.
111 Ibid., p. 387.
112 A. I. Gercen, 'Dilettanty-romantiki,' *Sobranie sočinenij* III (Moscow, 1954): 37.
113 Ibid., pp. 28, 38.
114 Ibid., p. 28.
115 Ibid., p. 31.
116 *Russkie pisateli o literaturnom trude* II, ed. B. Bursov a.o. (Leningrad, 1955): 74 (hereafter cited as *Russkie pisateli*).
117 N. G. Černyševskij, *Polnoe sobranie sočinenij* III (Moscow, 1947): 26.
118 Ibid., p. 188.
119 *Slovar' cerkovno-slavjanskogo i russkogo jazyka* III (St. Petersburg, 1847).
120 *Spravočnyj ènciklopedičeskij slovar'* IX, ed. A. Starčevskij (St. Petersburg, 1854): 136 f.
121 F. Toll', *Nastol'nyj slovar' dlja spravok po vsem otrasljam znanija* III (St. Petersburg, 1864): 339.
122 *Slovar' cerkovno-slavjanskogo i russkogo jazyka* (2nd ed., St. Petersburg, 1867).
123 *Slovotolkovatel' 3000 inostrannyx slov, vošedšix v sostav velikorusskogo jazyka s označeniem ix kornej*, ed. I. F. Burdon and A. D. Mixel'son (3rd ed., Moscow, 1871).
124 *Novyj slovotolkovatel' 85 000 inostrannyx slov vošedšix v russkij jazyk* II (Moscow, 1881): 120.
125 *Russkij ènciklopedičeskij slovar'*, ed. I. N. Berezin (St. Petersburg, 1877), p. 288.
126 *Russkie pisateli*, p. 167.
127 Ibid., p. 1450.
128 *Slovar' sovremennogo russkogo literaturnogo jazyka* XII (Moscow-Leningrad, 1961): 1450.
129 Ibid., p. 1449. For further examples of the literary usage of the cognates from 1840–80, see pp. 1444–54.
130 Ibid., p. 1446.
131 I. Zamotin, *Rannie romantičeskie vejanija v russkoj literature* (Warsaw, 1900); discussed by A. I. Beleckij, *Russkij romantizm*, p. 6 (see note 4 above).
132 A. N. Pypin, *Xarakteristiki literaturnyx mnenij ot 20-x do 50-x godov* (St. Petersburg, 1890); A. N. Veselovskij, *V. A. Žukovskij. Poèzija čuvstva i serdečnogo voobraženija* (St. Petersburg, 1904); N. K. Kozmin, *Nikolaj Ivanovič Nadeždin* (*Žizn' i naučno-literaturnaja dejatel'nost'* (*1804–1836*) (St. Petersburg, 1912); N. K. Kozmin, 'Novoe opredelenie romantizma,' *Žurnal Ministerstva Narodnogo prosveščenija* (1908), V: 223–9; N. K. Kozmin, *Očerki iz istorii russkogo romantizma* (*N. S. Polevoj kak vyrazitel' literaturnyx napravlenij sovremennoj emu èpoxi*) (St. Petersburg, 1903). For references to literature on romanticism see K. D. Muratova (ed.), *Istorija russkoj literatury – Bibliografičeskij ukazatel'* (Moscow-Leningrad, 1962), pp. 58 ff.

133 A. Blok, *Sobranie sočinenij* VI (Moscow-Leningrad, 1962): 364 *ff.*
134 Ibid.
135 Ibid., p. 370.
136 V. Žirmunskij, 'O poèzii klassičeskoj i romantičeskoj,' *Voprosy teorii literatury* (The Hague, 1962), p. 180.
137 *Russkie pisateli* VI: 44.
138 Ibid.
139 Ibid., pp. 54, 56, 73, 85.
140 Cited by B. Reizov, 'O literaturnyx napravlenijax,' *Voprosy literatury* (1957), IV: 93 *f.* (herafter cited as *Reizov*).
141 Budagov, op. cit. in note 31, p. 254.
142 Ibid., p. 1453.
143 *Slovar' sovremennogo russkogo literaturnogo jasyka* XII: 1452.
144 Ibid., p. 1446.
145 F. Pavlenko, *Enciklopedičeskij slovar'* (St. Petersburg, 1913), p. 2164.
146 A. Gurevič, 'Žažda soveršenstva,' *Voprosy literatury* (1964), IX: 133.
147 *Problemy romantizma – Sbornik statej.* ed. U. R. Foxt (Moscow, 1967), p. 7 (hereafter cited as *Problemy romantizma*).
148 P. S. Kogan, *Glavnye napravlenija v Evropejskoj literature XIX veka* (Moscow, 1930), p. 6.
149 V. M. Friče, *Očerk zapadnyx literatur* (Moscow, 1930), p. 135.
150 P. N. Sakulin, *Russkaja literatura* (Moscow, 1929), p. 351.
151 V. F. Pereverzev, 'K voprosu o social'nom genezise tvorčestva Gončarova,' *Pečat' i Revoljucija* (1923), I: 42.
152 L. P. Egorova, *O romantičeskom tečenii v sovetskoj proze* (Stavropol', 1966), p. 14 (hereafter cited as *Egorova*).
153 A. I. Beleckij, op. cit. in note 7, pp. 11, 13, 15.
154 *Egorova*, pp. 14–16.
155 Ibid.
156 I. M. Dubrovina, *Romantika v iskusstve* (Moscow), 1967), p. 10 (hereafter cited as *Dubrovina*).
157 V. B. Korzun, 'K voprosu o romantizme kak xudožestvennom metode,' *Učenye Zapiski Groznenskogo Pedagogičeskogo Instituta* (1953), VIII: 6, 11. Cited from A. N. Sokolov, 'K sporam o romantizme,' *Voprosy literatury* (1963) VII: 134.
158 E. Coj, 'Opirajas' na živoj opyt literatury,' *Voprosy literatury* (1964), IX: 128.
159 *Problemy romantizma*, pp. 27 *f.*
160 V. I. Kulešov, 'Zum gegenwärtigen Meinungsstreit über den Begriff der Romantik in der sowjetischen Literaturwissenschaft,' *Wissenschaftliche Zeitschrift der Universität Rostock* XIV (1965), no. 3, p. 230.
161 G. N. Pospelov, 'Možet li byt' romantizm bez romantiki?' *Voprosy literatury* (1961), IX: 117.
162 *Reizov*, pp. 94, 98.
163 *Egorova*, p. 3.
164 *Dubrovina*, p. 5.
165 Ibid., pp. 3, 8, 9, 17, 23. See also F. Svetov, *Ušla li romantika* (Moscow, 1963).
166 *Dubrovina*, p. 10.
167 *Pospelov*, p. 117.
168 P. I. Gražis, *Turgenev i romantizm (o projavlenijax principov romantičeskogo iskusstva v tvorčestve I. S. Turgeneva zrelogo perioda)* (Moscow diss., 1956), p. 7.
169 *Dubrovina*, p. 22
170 V. V. Vanslov, *Èstetika romantizma* (Moscow, 1966), p. 19.
171 Ibid., pp. 44 *f.*
172 *Slovar' sovremennogo literaturnogo russkogo jazyka* XII: 1444–54.

173 *Brang*, pp. 28, 41.
174 See pp. 104–16 (esp. 109 f.) above.
175 V. N. Olin in *Russkij Invalid* (1825), no. 52, pp. 208 ff.; quoted from *Mordovčenko*, p. 213.
176 *Wytrzens*, pp. 101–8.

HENRY H. H. REMAK

Trends of Recent Research on West European Romanticism

The writer confesses that he is responsible for two previous essays on West European romanticism which he will try not to duplicate (Remak, 1961, 1968). His emphasis will therefore be on post-1960 scholarship but not to the exclusion of scholarship in the 1950s and even earlier which he either had not discovered before or which had to be alluded to again. Scholarship on romanticism harking back to the decades prior to the 1950s and 1960s but recently reprinted is also considered. Republication of scholarship many years after its first appearance is rare and a convincing sign of its continuing relevance. Such a repeat performance gains a new crop of readers and is, in this sense, a 'new' publication at a time often very different from the ambiance in which it first saw the light. The re-issuing in the last decade or two of a number of scholarly works on romanticism dating back as far as the 1920s is a sure sign of the timeliness of what romanticism stands for.

I have limited myself mainly to works dealing with a *West European* aspect of romanticism. Inclusion of works on a nationally circumscribed romanticism is exceptional and occurs only when the particular investigation, often quite unintentionally, seemed capable of extension to pan-European problems. It is only too probable that many other such studies exist. What I have been able to give are samples, no more.

Scholars trying to justify their claim to printed space on a subject are often tempted to announce that they have come to rescue 'their' subject from shameful neglect, but research on romanticism is, if anything, overdeveloped.* The general plethora of scholarship on romanticism does not prevail everywhere, however. Wellek (1963)† has noted the relative dearth of research on romanticism in Germany since 1945. This may be a reaction against the abundance of such scholarship and a certain idolizing of Romanticism in German *Literaturwissenschaft* characteristic even of the pre-Hitler era (Schanze, pp. 13–14). To some extent, Hitler's exploitation and prostitution of romantic, post-romantic, and pseudo-romantic thoughts, motifs, and symbols has probably injected political considerations which have led to this 'flight from romanticism,' and certainly to second thoughts on the subject. Fritz Strich is a telling illustration. In his influential *Deutsche Klassik und Romantik* (1922), he expounded seductive dialectic generalisations about romanticism, which, in his post-war (1948) foreword to the fourth edition, he repudiated, influenced, no doubt, by his tenure of a professorship in Switzerland during the Hitler era. The very title ('The Romantic *Relapse*') of Fambach's anthology is revealing.

But even for politically oriented studies of romanticism balanced models are now available. Lion's account of 'Romanticism as the German Destiny,' published immediately after the Second World War, proves that a realistic synthesis of romanticism as a later nineteenth-century phenomenon in German politics is possible, that the politico-cultural executorship of romanticism by Richard Wagner, Bismarck, and William II, and particularly the failure of the latter to fuse modern with historizing-mythologizing tendencies, *can* be elucidated with a modicum of righteous indignation.

The general dilemma of romanticism (rationality vs mysticism) has certainly been that of latter-day Germany, including modern German literary scholarship before 1945, but Thorlby is, I think,

---

*   In view of this fact my essay can hope, at best, to offer illustrations of significant trends, not a comprehensive coverage of relevant publications.

†   In order not to clutter up the essay with too much bibliographical information, I have relegated the full bibliography to the end, referring to it in the text by the last name of the writer and, if necessary, year only. When relevant, the page number of a particular reference is added. Authors whose studies are not listed in the bibliography may ordinarily be found in my 1961 bibliography. To the best of my knowledge and memory, all items listed have been examined unless otherwise indicated.

quite right when he follows Richard Benz (*Lebenswelt der Romantik*, 1948) in saying that 'any more detailed analysis of actual romantic authors shows them to have held views irreconcilable with Nazi aims or propaganda' (p. 65). Laini (p. 798) observes that, much irrationalism in the romantic baggage notwithstanding, one of the canons of romanticism, the emancipation of the individual, is diametrically opposed to Hitlerism. Bearing out Schenk, Fortier has shown in his article on Gobineau's connection with German racism that even from this ill-reputed romantic ancestor the Nazis could derive but little comfort. Reiss, who is not above apodictic statements on the reactionary impact of German Romantic thought, denies a necessary causal connection between German romanticism and Nazism (p. 82); so does Schenk (p. 223), a rather stern task-master of romanticism, who nevertheless cannot overlook 'the long and painful process of deterioration and perversion which Romantic ideals underwent between the middle of the nineteenth century and the aftermath of the First World War.'

If the temporary German alienation from romanticism can perhaps be best explained as a political reaction, France, partly for 'political' or 'anti-political' reasons also, reacted inversely. Throughout the nineteenth century and during the first decades of the twentieth century, romanticism suffered from double jeopardy in France: attacked from the left for its supposed anti-rationalistic, anti-enlightenment, anti-Cartesian complexion and from the right as a foreign, notably Anglo-German, 'Protestant' subversion of the monarchic-Catholic concepts of law and order (political, religious, literary) incarnated in the Golden Age of Louis xiv (Neubert), romanticism was bound to run afoul of the classicistic preferences of both wings. Legion are the names of the French poets, critics, philosophers, academics, and 'hommes de lettres' who have vented their *Haßliebe* on romanticism: Brunetière, Lemaître, Faguet, Bourget, Barrès, Maurras, Lasserre, Seillière, Léon Daudet, Louis Reynaud etc.

Literary history is in the fortunate, rare position of being able to pinpoint the very year when the peripeteia took place: 1937, a hundred years after German romanticism had reached its first peak of penetration in France. A special issue of the *Cahiers du Sud* devoted to German romanticism and Béguin's memorable and moving study on the impact of German romanticism on French poetry mark this turning point.

The resurrected 'blue flower' of German romanticism did not wilt in the years of German occupation of France. On the contrary, writers of the French resistance reacted to the Nazi twisting and besmirching of German literature by going back to the sources. They read, translated, and defended the cultural heritage of Germany, particularly writers who, without being 'straight' romantics themselves, represented or inherited the most substantial, humanistic features of romanticism: Goethe, Hölderlin, Nietzsche, Rilke, and Hofmannsthal.* After the war, interest sharpened in the German romantics *per se* (Kleist, Novalis, Jean Paul) as well as in French contemporaries vitally affected by German romanticism (Gérard de Nerval, Charles Nodier). Béguin's two-volume 'essay' on the profound changes worked by the dreams of German romanticism in French poetry (1937) has been extended geographically by Bousquet (1964) to a study of the dream in French, English, and German romanticism. In the preface to the second edition of his book (1939, p. vi; see also pp. 399 *f.*), Béguin had felt it necessary to offer assurances that he was not a lobbyist for dreams and the subconscious at the expense of consciousness. This would seem not only superfluous but absurd today. French poetry absorbed German romanticism long ago; now French criticism and scholarship have followed suit.

Reduced to primitive dimensions, the French acceptance of German romanticism may be viewed as a need of prevailing rationalism for poetic disorder and metaphysical speculation. A comparable factor with a somewhat different psychological twist may also account, in part, for the astoundingly plentiful and substantial American (including Canadian) scholarship on romanticism, particularly in the last twenty years.† There is in romanticism an anti-pragmatism, a neo-utopianism, an extolling of poetic substance in life that seems to correspond to the deep-seated feelings of academic humanists resentful of the business society which does not 'understand' and 'appreciate' them and which, in turn, our academic humanists (unless they happen to be in administrative positions) make little effort to appreciate and understand themselves. The basic sympathy for the student activists shown, for example, by many younger members of English Departments surely has its origin, to some extent, in this latent romanticism,

* See Konrad F. Bieber, *L'Allemagne vue par les écrivains de la Résistance française* (Geneva and Lille, 1954).
† Cf. the revealing analyses of comparative literature programmes and dissertations in *Yearbook of Comparative and General Literature*, xii (1963): 70–5; xiii (1964): 130–4; and xvi (1967): 60–78, which show that few are the graduate students writing dissertations on the practical Enlightenment in comparison to those earning their spurs with a thesis on Romanticism.

confirmed by the surprisingly clear lifelines between current youth movements (active and passive) on the one hand and romanticism on the other hand (see S. N. Eisenstadt, *Essays on Comparative Institutions*, New York, 1965, p. 157, and Peter F. Drucker, 'The Romantic Generation,' *Harper's*, May 1966, pp. 12–22). When Marion Gräfin Döhnhoff, in *Die Zeit* of 9 January 1968, entitles a perceptive article on German student unrest 'The Rebellion of the Romantics' (*'Die Rebellion der Romantiker'*), she is confirming just that, not only in the title but in the analysis itself, which works with precisely the same epithets traditionally applied to romanticism: vague, emotional, passionate, irrational, unrealistic, anti-technological, folkloristic.

Turning from activists to 'passivists,' never before has the neoromantic Hermann Hesse, with his uncompromising distaste for politics, materialism, and war, his Oriental sympathies for relaxed contemplation and utopianism (expressed, it must be emphasized, in a prose language of exemplary lucidity), fared so well with sensitive American high school and college youngsters. Hesse is the bible of numerous Hippies. Love and peace and the lotus flower, aversion to gainful employment, guruism, 'Taugenichtse' in the image of Eichendorff and Hesse's Knulp, Nirwana and LSD, 'Gammler' and pot, shades of Coleridge and DeQuincey have become a startling reality, an unexpected romantic plant in what seemed just a few years ago the most unlikely soil for it, the rational, pragmatic, sensible constitutionalism of the Republic founded by Benjamin Franklin and George Washington. (A little more than fifteen years ago, when Colin Wilson wrote *The Outsider*, devoting most of his chapter on 'The Romantic Outsider' to Hesse, 'four out of five of the major novels had been out of print in England for several years and none of the earlier novels had been translated into English.')

Never has a knowledge of romanticism been so imperative to understand the activities of the most interesting (certainly not the most sensible) of our youth, which we see reflected in newspaper headlines every other morning. It is perhaps not farfetched to say that only an empathy with romantic symbolism enables us to know what is happening on our campuses today.

It has been observed that our student activists are trying to implement, one hundred and fifty years late, the *leftist* political potential of romanticism which was frustrated (particularly in Germany) in the nineteenth century. There are, to be sure, all kinds of other elements mixed up in student militancy that may have little to do with romanticism (e.g. Jacobinism, Marxism, anarchism), there are also striking analogies with *Sturm und Drang* and Expressionism, and I want to say emphatically that anti-intellectualism and aversion to historical scholarship are by no means characteristic of romanticism.

II   SUBJECTIVITY IN ROMANTIC SCHOLARSHIP

Despite the cardinal tenet of scholarship, viz., utmost objectivity in assaying the evidence and letting the facts determine one's evaluation, human nature is not capable of totally excluding subjectivity. Furthermore, in literature the evidence often permits divergent interpretations – demands it, in fact. Personal involvement is especially strong in scholarship on romanticism. It is impossible to read Béguin's admirable study on *L'Ame Romantique et le Rêve* without sensing the total commitment of his personality to this attempted (and successful) breakthrough in France. Involvement is apparent not only in the vigour of the language of scholars committed to romanticism, like Peckham and Fogle, but it is noticeable even in the apologetic attitude displayed by some American scholars as they try to define romanticism. They, like Béguin (pp. 395 *f.*), seem to shudder a bit before making bold to define the 'undefinable,' as if they expected to be called to account for this unromantic endeavour by the departed souls of romantic writers. (The temptation, however, nearly always proves stronger than the bad conscience, and we are the richer for it.) Schueller notes that some scholars describe the phenomenon of romanticism but avoid the term. He displays a typical syndrome when he says that it is temerity to define romanticism, but then ventures a definit on anyway. However, perhaps to deflect the wrath of his departed heroes, he cushions the shock by making the definition very broad (he sees romanticism as opposed to confines, including human confines, as subjectivism). Gleckner, Newton, Prang, Shroder, and Whalley are among other scholars exhibiting hesitancy. For Shroder, romanticism is not a period but a set of ideas which is to be explored not by analysis and synthesis but by the jelling of a myth, like Icarus the artist.

Romanticism is, for many scholars, more than a case: it is a cause. And a faith – an intelligent, nuanced faith, but a faith nevertheless. The personal involvement shows up in the language and tone of relevant scholarship. It manifests itself in the defense of the revolutionary uniqueness of romanticism by Northrop Frye and in such affectionate nouns as 'rebellion' lavished on the movement by

Newton and Pesch. It is evident in the loaded terms Peckham inflicts on the Enlightenment (the Enlightenment is not just inadequate, it 'collapses'; it does not reassert itself during or after romanticism but there is a 'regression' to it) whereas he greets the chieftains of romanticism as a 'small embattled alienated group of cultural leaders throughout Europe' and their product as the 'profoundest cultural transformation in human history since the invention of the city,' while conceding that Communism and Fascism are the two great heirs of romantic transcendentalism (in *Romanticism. The Culture of the nineteenth century.* 1965; see also Peckham, 1967). Subjectivism appears in such extravagant epithets as the 'imperishable universe of art' (Gleckner and Enscoe), in Harold Bloom's *The Visionary Company*, and even in more restrained appraisals of romanticism such as Peters'.

Let it not be said, however, that the bias of scholarship is all on the side of romanticism. Although the opposition to romanticism may have diminished in France since the last war, it is far from silent in England and America. It is noteworthy that the traditional strictures on romanticism expressed in the 1920s and 30s by Abercrombie and Lucas have been reprinted in the 1960s. But these reservations are by no means limited to the pre-war period. We find guarded reservations in Bowra's 'The Romantic Achievement,' the last chapter in his *The Romantic Imagination* (1949, reissued in 1961), which has much to say about the dangers and limitations of romanticism. Romanticism is even taken to task by Bowra for being vague about the Beyond!

In the 1940s and 50s, Fairchild, Havens, and Ryals continue to worry about certain romantic traits. The common denominator of many of these criticisms by literary scholars seems to have bases other than literary: political (Lucas), religious (Fairchild, Schenk), ethical-humanistic (Babbitt, Lasserre).

The political heritage and risks of romanticism elicit concern in works published in the west (Friederich, Lion, Lucas) as well as in the east (Fambach, Jelistratowa). Romanticism in such criticism is associated with irrationalism* in politics, with political movements thriving on symbols and myths, with a self-sufficient aestheticism that is blind to social, political, and economic causes of human misery, and to ethics, Christian or otherwise. Although romanticism

* There is, one senses, something irrational, obsessed about anti-romanticism itself, although almost all scholars in this general category strain hard to give romanticism at least literary credit wherever possible (Lucas, Fairchild).

is, on these scores, a *prima facie* suspect to Marxist scholarship, Marxist scholars like, on the other hand, to claim from romanticism whatever may fit, or is made to fit, the Hegel-Marx line. Jelistratowa, for example, defends Byron and Shelley as 'progressive' thinkers against the criticisms of Eliot, Leavis, and Spender. Lukács credits Sir Walter Scott with historicist innovation in his view of the Middle Ages. The patent dogmatic bias of Marxist criticism should not prevent us from recognizing the real connections that undoubtedly exist, at least in method, between romantic historicism and Marx's interpretation of an organic 'grand design,' a necessary development of history.

Even those who approve of English romanticism (a pretty safe romanticism to approve of), like Thorpe, Baker, and Weaver (1957, 1964), imply that they would look askance at it if certain characteristics like sentimentalism and escapism 'that no one can approve or admire' were predominant (p. xv).

Perhaps nowhere today is there so much guardedness about romanticism, even by scholars who have made this period a main concern, as in England (see, for example, Thorlby, p. 65). An at times almost belligerent attitude towards romanticism is adopted particularly by Germanic scholars in Great Britain (E. M. Butler, Ronald Gray, Roy Pascal, Tymms, Van Abbé). It is difficult not to connect this marked phenomenon with the long memory the British have kept of the Third *Reich*.

III RANGE OF ROMANTIC SCHOLARSHIP

Turning from attitude to range, one notes with some regret that departmental traditions continue strong in research on romanticism (and presumably in teaching practices also). Despite the 'European' approach to romanticism of De Man, Laini, Oppel, Peckham, Poulet, Thorlby, Thorslev, Van Tieghem, Weintraub, Wellek, etc., for most scholars romanticism seems to be limited to one department. To have, e.g., an encyclopedic scholar like Bowra take so off hand a view of romanticism outside England is disappointing.

It is encouraging, however, that bilateral studies in romanticism have increased, particularly on Anglo-German relations during the romantic period – an area of prime interest because of the importance of both literatures as romantic seeders. There are, in addition to the Beyer, Thorslev and Wimsatt studies, Bowra, Mason, Oppel, and Wellek (1964), who stress the difference between English and German romanticism without ignoring basic affinities, and

Hartman and Hirsch, who stress basic affinities without ignoring differences.

The interrelations between Germanic and Romance literatures in the romantic period seem to have benefitted relatively little from clarification in the last decade. So solid, clear, cautious, and directive a synthesis as Ole Koppang's comparison between the German and French romantic movements (1951) has found few followers. Similarly neglected remain the 'little' countries, despite the prominent place their connections occupied at the Utrecht Congress of Comparative Literature in 1961 (see *Proceedings*, Mouton, The Hague, 1962). All too rare are such studies as de Deugd's which acquaint the reader with so significant a thinker as Bilderdijk, practically unknown in the western scholarly world outside the Netherlands. Investigations involving such 'little' or neglected countries as Belgium, Holland, Denmark, Norway, Sweden, Finland, the Baltic countries, Portugal, Hungary and Czechoslovakia should be deliberately fostered. With less nationalistic resistance both in literature and in literary scholarship, they are open to influences from all sides and constitute a testing ground for inter-European confrontations *par excellence*. Yet, when a rare article with the promising title of 'Nordic Past and European Currents in Scandinavian Romanticism' (by Billeskov-Jansen) comes along, it gives only elementary information on some Scandinavian writers and no European picture at all. Wellek (1949) has rightly called attention to the predictability of romantic trends in these smaller literatures as an essential corroboration of any pan-European theory of romanticism. Even when they are derivative and artistically inferior, they are most important as historical evidence, particularly for political and folkloristic implications of romantic literature.

But even such more 'common' foreign literatures as those of Italy and Spain do not figure much either in non-departmental courses on romanticism or in scholarship. Little relevant research seems to have come out of Spain since Pujals (1951), and, although Italy is more productive, the items noted have been disappointing (e.g., Petronio). We cannot hope to have an approximately comprehensive view of European romanticism until the necessary linguistic and literary spade work is done on the undergraduate or early graduate levels on this continent which would open up the neglected European languages and cultures to future scholars. My incompetence in a Slavic language has limited my access to studies on Slavic romanticism to such books as the elementary introduction to Czech romanticism by Souckova.

Unless we are to give up any ambition to arrive at a synthesis, we must venture into co-operative research. The most substantial new results in research on romanticism in the next decade are likely to come from a meticulous combing of its linguistic patterns: phonetics, syntax, vocabulary (see, for example, Thalmann, 1967). The linguistic structure of West European romanticism can, I venture to say, never be explored without collective action by institutions (universities, academies, foundations) comprising *all* scholars (in the old sense: students and teachers) as well as statistical equipment (let the horrible word *computer* finally be articulated). The romantics themselves seem to have exhibited less prejudice towards the sciences (Coleridge, de Quincey, Evariste Galois, Goethe, Schelling, Novalis, Baader, Carus, Johann Wilhelm Ritter, Stendhal, etc.) and towards team-work (Goethe and Schiller, Wackenroder and Tieck, Wordsworth and Coleridge, Arnim and Brentano, etc.) than their professorial progeny. The several volumes on English romanticism sponsored by the Modern Language Association of America (edited by Bernbaum; Raysor, Thorpe; Baker and Weaver; C. W. and L. H. Houtchens) are proof that collective labours are needed and workable. Jones, in his unorthodox study, which Wellek (1963) dismisses too lightly, supports the 'team-work' idea. The 'History of European Literature' projected by the International Comparative Literature Association might well be the proper medium in which such an experiment could be launched.

IV   HOW ROMANTIC IS ROMANTICISM?

Is romanticism *sui generis* or not? Newton (1962) answers in the affirmative, distinguishing clearly between romanticism, its predecessor (classicism) and successor (realism). Although Wellek (1963) and Peckham (*PCTE*, 1965, p. 47–50) find that Earl Wasserman's own language is turgid rather than subtle, they accept his conclusion that romanticism itself is subtler. And yet, the more romantic works one reads, the less one-sided he finds them, and the best seem, as Croce said long ago, also to be the best balanced (see also Eichner, p. 214; Whalley, p. 239).

In much scholarship, the classicism-romanticism antithesis is still being stressed (Read, 1926, 1963; Nicolson; Brion; Gleckner; Behler; Newton, p. 205–6; George [in music]; etc.), at times for pedagogical, 'presentational' reasons, and occasionally from very new angles (Antal). The contradistinction has actually been fortified through such pinpointing confrontations of movements, authors, and genres as Brown's (Pope and satire vs Shelley and the lyric) or such extensions as Salop's finding that romanticism creates a major musical change towards greater intensity in the early decades of the nineteenth century, and George's conclusion that classical music is more structural, inclined towards generalized emotion, whereas romantic music is more expressive, tending towards personal emotion.

Schenk still sees romanticism as a revolt against the eighteenth century. The enlightenment-romanticism antithesis, sharply formulated by Peckham in 1951 (see also Frodsham, pp. 17–18) has been somewhat qualified by him (1961), but without detracting from his view of romanticism as an epochal, almost millennial event.

In the last section of this essay I shall assert that we have made very substantial progress towards the definition of the essential features of West European romanticism. Scholars not quite so optimistic (Peckham, *PCTE*, 1965) will agree that we have made considerable advances in at least reducing the alternatives. This progress will permit research to turn increasingly towards the gradual evolution of romanticism, in its initial and ultimate phases, from Enlightenment and Classicism to Realism and Symbolism.

Thorlby (p. 165) stresses what the romanticism of Wordsworth, Goethe, Novalis, and Kleist has carried over from the Enlightenment. For Schueller, romanticism embraces both classical and romantic elements, 'health' and 'sickness.' Ottino della Chiesa sees in the neoclassical and in the romantic two faces of the same coin. Sengle tends to see (German) Enlightenment, *Sturm und Drang*, classicism and romanticism as *one*, complementary, 'Deutsche Bewegung,' an unfortunate and not very meaningful term. Eichner downgrades 'classical' and 'romantic' as antonyms (p. 214), preferring an historical approach tracing the use of the terms 'classical' and 'romantic' in literary criticism. Whalley is sceptical about the romantic-classical antithesis. Forty years ago, J. G. Robertson pitted German classicism *and* late romanticism against realism. Abercrombie sets off romanticism against realism rather than classicism.

At the other end (romanticism evolving into realism), it is to be hoped that differentiated transition analyses like Fanger's of *Dostoevsky and Romantic Realism* (1965) will be followed by an increasing and, more importantly, equally good number of analogous studies. Erich Auerbach, in his *Mimesis*, had already established an affinity between 'atmospheric historicism and atmospheric realism'

(Chapter XVIII, on Stendhal, Balzac, and Flaubert; see Thorlby, pp. 95–6). That real progress is being made may be gathered from the charming lamentation of Fairchild (in Thorpe et al., 1957, 1964, p. 27) that 'nowadays, however, it is dubious strategy to glorify the romantic poets solely as seers and mystics; they must also be honored at our MLA conventions for their "realism".' Scholars still working – and effectively so – with such tripartite divisions as classical-romantic-realistic, such as Newton (1962), are careful to give them not timeless but only historic value: Newton states that this tripartite division breaks down with the abstract, nonphenomenal art of the twentieth century.

This *rapprochement* must not, however, mean the effacement of romanticism, or the minimizing of preceding or following movements or currents to the disproportionate advantage of romanticism. Kahn is quite justified in protesting against Wellek's reduction of the impact and continuity of German classicism, and few scholars will follow Barzun (1961) in swallowing up realism, symbolism, and naturalism as the last three of the 'four phases of romanticism.'

V   CURRENT ROMANTIC SCHOLARSHIP

Recent scholarship on West European romanticism has been strong on the investigation of specific romantic elements, particularly images and metaphors, in one or more writers, but usually, alas, of the same nationality: wheel and sea (Auden), water and shipwreck (Blume), waterfall (Cizevskij), boat (Frye), wind (Abrams), as well as the conventional ones: sun, moon, stars, flowers. It has been strong in studies on the distribution, use, and variety of the shadings of certain phenomena and themes: dreams (Béguin, Bousquet), time (Poulet), improvisation (Weintraub), the artist (Shroder), the French Revolution (Abrams, Schenk, and, more indirectly, Trilling). The image of the city in romanticism is a particularly timely and still unresolved topic (Fanger; Peckham; Thalmann, 1965, 1967; Reiss; Kohlschmidt, pp. 226–31). One could easily think of others: mines or mining, jewels, winter, silence, etc. These are excellent subjects, affording crystallization as well as breadth, contributing simultaneously to literary criticism and literary history.

We have also been very enterprising on the other end of the scale, the open-ended one: the relevance of romanticism to the later nineteenth and twentieth centuries (Peckham, *passim*; Peyre, 1954, 1969). Even so mundane a medium as the contemporary detective novel has been charged to romanticism (Laini, p. 770). Speaking of the impact on 'serious' literature only, Béguin has analyzed the links between Brentano and Baudelaire; Weinberg, the affinities between Heine, Baudelaire, and Mallarmé; Vordtriede (Novalis), Kermode, and Thalmann (1967), those between romanticism and French Symbolism; and Thorpe, the romantic heritage of symbolism, contrasts, irony, and paradox in subsequent literature, and its executor, Yeats.

A particularly complex problem is the relationship of the New Criticism to romanticism. Several scholars, including Wellek (*A History of Modern Criticism* I, 1955, pp. 1–5), have had a field day tracing the romantic virus in New Critics who claim to be immune to it (Hardy names Eliot, Richards, Blackmur, Brooks, Ransom, Vivas, Wimsatt, Tate, Warren, Heilman). Fogle, Foster, and Foakes, with some assistance from Thorpe, Baker, and Weaver (in their introduction) and Miss Nitchie, have been particularly successful in unfrocking the New Critics as romantics in their own right, at least in part, in suggesting that *Haßliebe* may play a role in the feelings entertained by the new Critics toward their romantic ancestors, a phenomenon undoubtedly true of the French anti-romantics discussed earlier. When New Critics oppose romanticism, it is often difficult to tell whether they do so for reasons primarily political (that is, conservative: Eliot, Tate, Ransom), intellectual (romanticism is depicted as fuzzy, soft, and moist as against the dry, ironic, urbane literary ideal of the New Criticism), or literary (romanticism is equated with formlessness).

It is gratifying to note that much attention has been given to synaesthetic and interdisciplinary implications of romanticism (Peckham, *passim*; Trilling), a topic which, while difficult, is highly welcome in view of the danger of departmentalizing subjects. Brion, Newton, Canaday (see Schueller), Lucas, Béguin, Réau, Peckham, de Keyser (wild!), Heller, Thalmann (1967), Weisstein, and Pesch have all linked romantic literature with painting. Skira and Courthion and Schlenoff have provided effective teaching materials for the comparison of romantic literature with romantic painting. Such lifelines have been particularly noted in German romanticism (Eichner, Pesch, Peckham, and Heller, the last two particularly interested in Caspar David Friedrich), but they must certainly be applicable also in other romantic movements, particularly the French one (Delacroix, Géricault – see Antal). Lucas and Béguin call attention to the romantic features of surrealism. Larrabee's 'classic' study of English (especially romantic) poets and their relatedness to Greek sculpture (1943) was re-issued in 1964. Réau gives some attention to sculpture.

The affinity between romantic literature and music has attracted the attention of Chantavoine and Gaudefroy-Demombyne, Peckham, Newton, Weisstein, Schenk, Thalmann (1967), Steiner (p. 43), and Salop. For Wellek (1964), the amusicality of English romanticism is one of the qualities that most strikingly distinguish it from German romanticism. Music need not be looked at exclusively as an extension of or analogy to literary romanticism; it can also be seen in opposition to it. Schenk calls dissonance a 'characteristic of the Romantic movement as a whole' (p. 233) whereas Harold Schönberg (see Schueller) views twentieth-century music as a reaction against romanticism.

Peckham (especially 1966) has extended his interest from romantic literature to architecture (see also Newton, Réau, Ottino della Chiesa, de Keyser), and, along with Béguin (p. 395 f. – Novalis!), Jones and Fairchild, to science (see also Eichner, pp. 226–8), particularly biology, physiology, and psychology.

Romanticism's role in the history of ideas and of criticism forms the nucleus of Wellek's various contributions to the subject. De Deugd has given us a very substantial if rather inconclusive volume on romanticism in philosophy and the history of ideas; Schenk, a rather condescending chapter on Schelling; Hirsch, an exemplary application of an analogy (not influence) approach to 'romantische Weltanschauung' in his analysis of the astonishing spiritual closeness of Wordsworth and Schelling; Benoit, an attempted synthesis of Poulet's and Gérard's ideas, e.g., a synthesis of time with matter, eternity with spirit; Jones, a methodological alternative in grasping the ideological structure of romanticism; Peckham, many somewhat bewildering leads in cultural ideology; Weber, a good textbook on European thought from romanticism to existentialism.

The religious and political colouring of recent scholarship on romanticism has been alluded to before. Schenk has written a very readable, conservative, and, particularly in the second part, rather episodic and biographical sampling of European romanticism's struggle with Christianity. The sum total conservative political stance of German romanticism has been established by Reiss (texts, 1955; interpretation, 1966) and Droz (texts, 1963; interpretation, 1966), but the 'Other Romanticism' edited by Schanze opens up a more liberal side, which, although secondary, must not be ignored as it usually is (e.g., by Steiner, p. 351). An extension of these surveys to the political thought of other European countries during the romantic period, followed by a co-ordinated synthesis, is needed not only to clarify one of the least resolved questions of European romanticism but to shed light on our political quandaries of today.

Scholarship has thus run strong laterally, at both ends of the scale: in the analysis of very specific elements (but usually only in one literature), and in the relevance of romanticism to related disciplines and future epochs. Little headway has, however, been made in the centre: in systematically following up a particular literary phenomenon (image, metaphor, theme) throughout Europe within the romantic period. When we consider that Van Tieghem gave us the basic approach and the raw materials for such investigations over twenty years ago (*Le Romantisme dans la littérature européenne*, 1948), this lack of initiative is disappointing. References to *European* romanticism are frequent but fitful in Abercrombie, cursory and sweeping in Bowra.

Almost all the motifs covered within a literature I have mentioned in this section lend themselves to analysis and synthesis in European romanticism as a whole (wheel, water, boat, wind, etc.). Following the sensible guidelines set down by Trousson (1965) and exemplified in his own study of the European history of the Prometheus myth (1964), other myths should be followed up to permit wider conclusions on romanticism as well as on the evolution of the myths themselves. Hartman suggests that certain myths and motifs converge in what we might want to call a super-myth. Thus Cain, Ahasuerus, the Ancient Mariner, and Faust move within the scope of the Solitary, or Wandering Jew theme, highly developed by and since the romantic period. An excellent beginning for the European exploration of romantic Satanism has been made by Thorslev and by Guthke; of the romantic hero, by Garber (see also Howard Hugo, pp. 147 *f.*, and Peckham, 1967). Less specific themes should follow: inner vs outer direction, the insider-outsider tension, intensity in general, incest, and particularly irony (Behler, pp. 124–6; the excellent Strohschneider-Kohrs study is entirely limited to German thought). We particularly commend comparative genre studies in European romanticism which provide a 'safe' structural, literary basis; the ballad, the historical novel, the novella, the lyric (see, e.g., Brown). The temper of our time suggests that sociologically oriented studies of literary movements, still in their infancy, will appeal especially to younger scholars. *Wirkungs-geschichte* need not be limited to an array of facts and statistics. It should incorporate some of the sociological and politicological models recently developed by experts in these fields insofar as they lend themselves to this kind of 'mixed' study. It seems absurd that comparative literature scholars should not take advantage of or at least be cognizant of the significant surge of comparative studies in the social sciences. We cannot very well inveigh against provincialism within literary scholarship and refuse to examine related (of course, not identical) developments in other cognitive fields. The recent founding of West European Studies programmes in a number of European and American universities will perhaps contribute to this interaction. A study of the romantic clientele (reading, seeing, hearing) is not only vital to the historical impact of romanticism but of relevance to the critique of the work *per se*, for literature is written to be read, seen, or heard, or else it would not have been written.

VI THE DEFINITION

The final question is, have we achieved any kind of consensus on what we mean by (European) romanticism? Miraculously enough, we have. Wellek (1963, p. 131) states:

in all of these studies [of the last fourteen years] ... convincing agreement has been reached: they all see the implication of the imagination, symbol, myth, and organic nature, and see it as a part of the great endeavor to overcome the split between subject and object, the self and the world, the conscious and the unconscious. This is the central creed of the great romantic poets in England, Germany, and France.

There is, of course, no unanimity on the subject. Some learned writers insist on fighting simplistic bugaboos such as 'a unified school of European Romanticism' (Furst). Germanic scholars seem particularly reluctant to agree to the European integration of 'their' romanticism. Some of this is scepticism in principle about highly inclusive *post factum* definitions (Eichner, Kahn; see also Whalley); some of it seems to be a misunderstanding of what Wellek means by 'norms' (Kahn), some of it is the refusal even to try *some* integration, which may lead to a different, more accurate definition (Reiss). But for each of Wellek's elements we could cite chapter and verse in support. To name just a few: for the imagination, Bowra and Hugo; for the symbol, Newton, Foakes, Kermode, Auden, Bateson, Sørensen, and David Perkins; for myth, Hartman and Shroder; for organic nature, Lovejoy, Fogle, and Fairchild. And for all of these, there is strong evidence in de Deugd, although he is very hesitant in drawing conclusions himself. Further support of efforts at synthesis are found in Behler, Eichner (pp. 230–1), Foakes, Fogle, Remak (1968), Thorlby (p. 55), and, with qualifications, in Peckham's 'positive romanticism' (1951), as well as in Schueller.

It is especially encouraging that Wellek's validated criteria stay remarkably close to those basic ingredients of romanticism propounded by Béguin in his 'breakthrough' of 1937: Dream (night), the subconscious (including the collective subconscious), symbol, and myth as a way of communication with the absolute; poetry as absolute truth representing a series of magic gestures (poetry = magic language). It is likewise encouraging when scholars like Eichner and Whalley, very reluctant to categorize, nevertheless come through with 'features' or 'considerations' analogous to Béguin's and Wellek's (Eichner, p. 230; Whalley, pp. 240–2).

Of course, we can nibble at and quibble with the verdict. We can say that the question of the metaphysical or anti-metaphysical coherence and consistency of romanticism has not been solved, despite the impressive testimony for a West European romantic metaphysics marshalled by de Deugd in his monumental study, which deals, however, with romantic ideas, philosophy, and criticism rather than with romantic literature. Or we could add, as not yet conclusively substantiated, the shift from outer-directedness to inner-directedness as a cardinal tenet of romanticism.

Literary scholarship must be based on a painstaking reading of texts and a knowledge of 'external' but relevant facts. Yet, its interpretive, subjective, speculative top will always remain the best part of it, provided it is firmly rooted in knowledge. Complete agreement is impossible; a certain consensus is desirable. We have reached this consensus on romanticism. Whether we will have it five or ten years from now is another matter.*

*   I wish to thank the John Simon Guggenheim Foundation for its generous support during the period when this essay was cast into formal shape. While the fellowship was mainly awarded for another project, it liberated the time used for this secondary undertaking. I also want to thank my research assistant, Frederick Betz, iii, for the capable help he has given me in this effort.

BIBLIOGRAPHY

Abercrombie, Leslie. *Romanticism.* New York: Barnes & Noble, 1963 (first published by Secker: London, 1926). 142 pp.

Abrams, M. H. 'English Romanticism: The Spirit of the Age,' in *Romanticism Reconsidered.* New York: Columbia University Press, 1963. Pp. 26–72

Antal, Frederick. 'Classicism and Romanticism,' in *Classicism and Romanticism With Other Studies in Art History*. New York: Basic Books. 1966. Pp. 1–45

Banaševič, Nikola. 'La Note serbo-croate dans le romantisme européen' (summary of a paper) in *Proceedings of the IIId International Comparative Literature Association Congress*. The Hague: Mouton, 1962. P. 334

Béguin, Albert. *L'Ame romantique et le rêve. Essai sur le romantisme allemand et la poésie française*. Nouvelle édition, Paris: Corti, 1939 (first edition, 1937)

Behler, Ernst. 'The Origins of the Romantic Literary Theory.' *Colloquia Germanica* (1968): nos. 1/2, pp. 109–26

Benoit, Raymond Paul. 'Romanticism: A Reinterpretation.' Diss., University of Oregon, 1965. In *Dissertation Abstracts* XXVI: 6018

Beyer, Werner W. *The Enchanted Forest*. Oxford: Blackwell, 1963. 273 pp.

Billeskov-Jansen, F. J. 'Nordische Vergangenheit und europäische Strömungen in der skandinavischen Hochromantik,' in *Tradition und Ursprünglichkeit*. Berne: Francke, 1966. Pp. 39–52

Bloom, Harold. *The Visionary Company. A Reading of English Romantic Poetry*. Garden City, New York: Doubleday, 1961

Bousquet, Jacques. *Les Thèmes du rêve dans la littérature romantique (France, Angleterre, Allemagne)*. Paris: Didier, 1964. 656 pp.

Bowra, C. M. *The Romantic Imagination*. New York: Oxford University Press, 1961 (first published by Harvard University Press: Cambridge, Mass., 1949). 306 pp.

Brion, Marcel. *L'Allemagne Romantique*. Two volumes. Paris: Michel, 1963
— 'Le Romantisme et la recherche de l'infini.' *Revue de Paris* LXVI (September 1959): 62–76

Brown, Calvin. 'Toward a Definition of Romanticism,' in *Varieties of Literary Experience. Eighteen Essays in World Literature*, ed. Stanley Burnshaw. New York: New York University Press, 1962. Pp. 115–35

Chantavoine, Jean, and Jean Gaudefroy-Demombynes. *Le Romantisme dans la musique européenne*. Paris: Michel, 1955

Cizevskij, Dmitrij. *On Romanticism in Slavic Literatures*. The Hague: Mouton, 1957. 63 pp.

Courthion, see Skira

de Deugd, Cornelis. *Het Meta-fysisch Grondpatroon van het Romantische Literaire Denken. De Fenomenologie van en Geestesgesteldheid* (with a summary in English). Groningen: Wolters, 1966. 516 pp. (no. 10 in *Studia Litteraria Rheno-Traiectina*). See also his 'The Unity of Romanticism as an International Movement. A Phenomenological Approach,' in *Proceedings of the Fifth Congress of the International Comparative Literature Association*. Belgrade and Amsterdam: Swets & Zeittinger, 1969. Pp. 173–89

Droz, Jacques. *Le Romantisme allemand et l'Etat. Résistance et collaboration dans l'Allemagne napoléonienne*. Paris: Payot, 1966. 310 pp.

— (ed.) *Le Romantisme politique en Allemagne. Textes choisis et présentés*. Paris: Colin, 1963. 210 pp.

Eichner, Hans. 'The Genesis of German Romanticism.' *Queen's Quarterly* LXXII (Summer 1965): no. 2, pp. 213–31

Fairchild, Hoxie N. 'Romanticism: Devil's Advocate,' in *Major English Romantic Poets*, ed. Thorpe, Baker, and Weaver (see under Thorpe), pp. 24–31

Fambach, Oscar. *Der romantische Rückfall in der Kritik der Zeit. Die wesentlichen und die umstrittenen Rezensionen aus der periodischen Literatur von 1806 bis 1815, begleitet von den Stimmen der Umwelt*. Berlin: Akademie-Verlag, 1963. 797 pp.

Fanger, Donald L. 'Romanticism and Comparative Literature.' *Comparative Literature* XIV (1962): 153–66.

— *Dostoevsky and Romantic Realism. A Study of Dostoevsky in Relation to Balzac, Dickens, and Gogol*. Cambridge, Mass.: Harvard University Press, 1965. 307 pp.

Foakes, R. A. 'The Commitment to Metaphor: Modern Criticism and Romantic Poetry,' in *British Romantic Poets. Recent Revaluations*. New York: New York University Press, 1966. Pp. 22–32 (first published in R. A. Foakes, *The Romantic Assertion*. New Haven: Yale University Press, 1958)

— 'Order out of Chaos: The Task of the Romantic Poet,' in *Romanticism. Points of View*, ed. Robert F. Gleckner (see there), pp. 238–46 (first published in R. A. Foakes, *The Romantic Assertion*, see above)

Fogle, Richard H. 'Romantic Bards and Metaphysical Reviewers,' in *Romanticism Points of View*, ed. Robert F.

Gleckner (see there), pp. 151–67, first published in *Journal of English Literary History* XII (1945): 221–50

— 'A Note on Romantic Oppositions and Reconciliations,' in *Major English Romantic Poets*, ed. Clarence D. Thorpe (see there), pp. 17–23

Fortier, Paul, 'Gobineau and German Racism.' *Comparative Literature* XIX (Fall 1967): no. 4, pp. 341–50

Foster, Richard. *The New Romantics. Reappraisal of the New Criticism*. Bloomington: Indiana University Press, 1962. 238 pp.

Friederich, Werner P. 'The Political Failure of German Late Romanticism.' *Jadavpur Journal of Comparative Literature* I (March 1961): 1–9

Frodsham, J. D. *Nature Poetry: Chinese and English*. Petaling Jaya: Sharikat Malayan Printers, 1965

Frye, Northrop. 'Foreword' and 'The Drunken Boat: The Revolutionary Element in Romanticism,' in *Romanticism Reconsidered*. New York: Columbia University Press, 1963. Pp. v–ix, 1–25

— 'The Romantic Myth,' in *A Study of English Romanticism*. New York: Random House, 1968. Pp. 3–49

Furst, Lilian R. 'Romanticism in Historical Perspective.' *Comparative Literature Studies* V (June 1968): no. 2, pp. 115–43

Garber, Frederick. 'Self, Society, Value, and the Romantic Hero.' *Comparative Literature* XIX (Fall 1967): no. 4, pp. 321–33

Gaudon, Jean. 'Réflexions sur le romantisme.' *Le Français dans le monde* (April–May 1964): no. 24, pp. 16–19

George, Graham. 'Towards a Definition of Romanticism.' *Queen's Quarterly* LXXII (Summer 1965): no. 2, pp. 253–69

Gleckner, Robert F., and Gerald E. Enscoe (eds.). *Romanticism. Points of View*. Englewood Cliffs, New Jersey: Prentice-Hall, 1962. 259 pp.

Guthke, Karl S. 'Der Mythos des Bösen in der Westeuropäischen Romantik.' *Colloquia Germanica* (1968): nos. 1/2, pp. 1–36

Hardy, John Edward. *The Curious Frame. Seven Poems in Text and Context*. Notre Dame, Indiana: The University of Notre Dame Press, 1962. 196 pp.

Hartman, Geoffrey H. 'Romanticism and "Anti-Self Consciousness." ' *The Centennial Review* VI (1962): 553–65

Havens, George R. 'Pre-Romanticism in France.' *L'Esprit Créateur* VI (1966): 63–76

Heller, Erich. 'The Romantic Expectation,' in *The Artist's Journey into the Interior*. New York: Random House, 1965. Pp. 73–86

Hirsch, E. D., Jr. *Wordsworth and Schelling. A Typological Study of Romanticism*. New Haven: Yale University Press, 1960. 217 pp.

Houtchens, Carolyn W. and Lawrence H. (eds.). *The English Romantic Poets and Essayists. A Review of Research and Criticism*. New York: The Modern Language Association of America, 1957. 363 pp. (companion volume to Raysor)

Hugo, Howard E. (ed.). *The Portable Romantic Reader. The Age of Romanticism (1756–1848) Mirrored in Poetry and Prose from England, France, Germany, and America*. New York: The Viking Press, 1957. 621 pp.

Jelistratowa, A. A. 'Probleme der englischen Romantik in der reaktionären Literaturwissenschaft,' in *Falschmünzer der Literatur*. Berlin: Dietz, 1962, pp. 78–125

Jones, W. T. *The Romantic Syndrome. Toward a New Method in Cultural Anthropology and History of Ideas*. The Hague: Nijhoff, 1961. 255 pp. (also in paperback)

Kahn, Robert L. 'Some Recent Definitions of German Romanticism, or the Case against Dialectics.' *Rice University Studies* L (1964): 3–26

de Keyser, Eugénie. *The Romantic West, 1789–1850*. Geneva: Skira, and Cleveland: The World Publishing Company, 1965. 210 pp.

King, Edmund L. 'What is Spanish Romanticism?' *Studies in Romanticism* II (1962): 1–11

Kohlschmidt, Werner. 'Aspekte des Stadtmotivs in der deutschen Dichtung,' in *Un dialogue des nations*. Albert Fuchs zum 70. Geburtstag. Munich: Hueber, and Paris: Klinksieck, 1967. Pp. 219–37 (on romanticism: pp. 226–31)

Koppang, Ole. *Romantikk og Romantisme*. Oslo: Akademisk Forlag, 1951

Kumar, Shiv K. (ed.). *British Romantic Poets: Recent Revaluations*. New York: New York University Press, 1966

Laini, Giovanni. *Il Romanticismo Europeo*. Two volumes. Florence: Vallecchi, 1959. 806 pp.

Larrabee, Stephen A. *English Bards and Grecian Marbles*. Port Washington, New York. Kennikat Press, 1964 (first published by Columbia University Press: New York, 1943). 312 pp.

Lion, Ferdinand. *Romantik als deutsches Schicksal*. Stuttgart: Kohlhammer, 1963 (first published by Rowohlt: Hamburg, 1947)

Lucas, F. L. *The Decline and Fall of the Romantic Ideal*. Cambridge, England: Cambridge University Press, 1963 (first edition, 1936, second edition, 1948). 236 pp.

Matlaw, Ralph D. (ed.). 'Romantic Fiction.' Proceedings of the Conference on Slavistics and Comparative Literature at the MLA Meeting in Philadelphia, 1960, in *Yearbook of Comparative and General Literature* x (1961): 70–3

Neubert, Fritz. 'Der Kampf um die Romantik in Frankreich' and 'Der französische Kreuzzug gegen die Romantik im 20. Jahrhundert,' in his *Studien zur vergleichenden Literaturgeschichte*. Berlin: Duncker & Humblot, 1952. Pp. 11–53

Newton, Eric. *The Romantic Rebellion*. London: Longmans, 1962. 224 pp.

Nicolson, Harold. 'The Romantic Revolt.' *Horizon* III (1961): 58–88

Nitchie, Elizabeth. 'Form in Romantic Poetry,' in *Major English Romantic Poets*, ed. Thorpe (see there), pp. 3–16 (first published in 1957)

Ottino della Chiesa, Angela. 'Neoclassico e Romantico in Europa.' *Veltro* IX (1965): 23–32

Peckham, Morse. 'Aestheticism to Modernism: Fulfilment or Revolution?' *Mundus Artium* I (Winter 1967): no. 1, pp. 36–55

— *Beyond the Tragic Vision. The Quest for Identity in the Nineteenth Century*. New York: Braziller, 1962. 380 pp.

— *Man's Rage for Chaos*. Philadelphia: Chilton, 1965. 339 pp.

— 'The Place of Architecture in Nineteenth-Century Romantic Culture.' *Yearbook of Comparative and General Literature* xv (1966): 36–49

— (ed.) *Romanticism. The Culture of the Nineteenth Century*. New York: Braziller, 1965. 351 pp.

— 'Romanticism: The Present State of Theory.' *Bulletin of the Pennsylvania Council of Teachers of English (PCTE Bulletin)* (December 1965): no. 12, pp. 31–53

Peer, Larry. 'New Perspective on the Theory of the Novel in European Romanticism.' Ph.D. dissertation, University of Maryland, 1969

Perkins, David. *The Quest for Permanence: The Symbol of Wordsworth, Shelley, and Keats*. Cambridge: Harvard University Press, 1959

Pesch, Ludwig. *Die romantische Rebellion in der modernen Literatur und Kunst.* Munich: Beck, 1962. 227 pp.

Peters, Robert L. 'Toward an "Un-definition" of Decadent as Applied to British Literature of the 19th Century.' *Journal of Aesthetics and Art Criticism* XVIII (1959): 258–64

Petronio, Giuseppe. 'Proposte e ipotesi di lavoro per uno studio sul Romanticismo.' *Beiträge zur romanischen Philologie* II (1963): 116–26

Peyre, Henri. 'The Originality of French Romanticism.' *Symposium* (Fall–Winter 1969): 333–45

— 'Romanticism and French Literature Today. Le Mort Vivant.' *Modern Language Quarterly* XV (1954): 3–17

Poulet, Georges. 'Timelessness and Romanticism.' *Journal of the History of Ideas* XV (1954): 3–22. Also in *Ideas in Cultural Perspective*, ed. Philip P. Wiener and Aaron Noland. New Brunswick: Rutgers University Press, 1962. Pp. 658–77

— *Les Métamorphoses du cercle.* Paris: Plon, 1961. 523 pp.

Prang, Helmut. 'Einleitung,' in *Begriffsbestimmung der Romantik*, vol. CL in *Wege der Forschung*, ed. Prang. Darmstadt: Wissenschaftliche Buchgesellschaft, 1968. Pp. 1–6

Pujals, Esteban. *Espronceda y Lord Byron*, Madrid: Consejo Superior de Investigaciones, 1951. 510 pp.

Raysor, Thomas M. (ed.). *The English Romantic Poets: A Review of Research.* Revised ed., New York: Modern Language Association of America, 1956 (first edition, ed. Ernest Bernbaum, 1950). 307 pp.

Read, Herbert. *Reason and Romanticism. Essays in Literary Criticism.* New York: Russell and Russell, 1963 (first published in 1926). 229 pp.

Réau, Louis. 'L'Ere Romantique,' *Les Arts Plastiques.* Paris: Michel, 1949. 301 pp.

Reiss, Hans. *Politisches Denken in der deutschen Romantik.* Berne: Francke, 1956 (Dalp-Taschenbücher 386). 96 pp. (Revised and enlarged version of Introduction to *The Political Thought of the German Romantics (1793–1815).* Oxford: Blackwell, 1955)

Remak, Henry H. H. 'West European Romanticism: Definition and Scope,' in *Comparative Literature: Method and Perspective*, ed. Newton P. Stallknecht and Horst Frenz. Carbondale: Southern Illinois University Press, 1961. Pp. 223–59

— A Key to West European Romanticism?' *Colloquia Germanica* (1968): nos. 1–2, pp. 37–46. Slightly modified

German version of this essay, 'Ein Schlüssel zur Westeuropäischen Romantik?' in vol. CL of 'Wege der Forschung,' *Begriffsbestimmung der Romantik*. Darmstadt: Wissenschaftliche Buchgesellschaft, 1968. Pp. 427–41

Reynaud, Louis. *La Crise de notre littérature. Des Romantiques à Proust, Gide et Valéry*. Paris: Hachette, 1929

de Ryals, Clyde. 'Toward a Definition of Decadent as Applied to British Literature of the 19th Century.' *Journal of Aesthetics and Art Criticism* XVII (1958): 85–92

— 'The 19th Century Cult of Inaction.' *Tennessee Studies in Literature* IV (1959): 51–60

Salop, Arnold. 'Intensity as a Distinction Between Classical and Romantic Music.' *Journal of Aesthetics and Art Criticism* XXIII (1964–5): 358–71

Schanze, Helmut (ed.). *Die andere Romantik. Eine Dokumentation.* Sammlung Insel 29. Frankfurt am Main: Insel, 1967. 216 pp.

Schenk, Hans G. *The Mind of the European Romantics. An Essay in Cultural History*. London: Constable, 1966. 303 pp.

Schlenoff, Norman. *Romanticism and Realism*. New York: McGraw-Hill, 1965. 47 pp. and 24 slides

Schueller, Herbert M. 'Romanticism Reconsidered.' *Journal of Aesthetics and Art Criticism* XX (1962): 359–68

Sengle, Friedrich. 'Zur Einheit von Literaturgeschichte und Literaturkritik. Ein Vortrag.' *Deutsche Vierteljahrsschrift für Literaturwissenschaft und Geistesgeschichte* XXXIV (1960): 327–37

Shroder, Maurice Z. *Icarus: The Image of the Artist in French Romanticism*. Cambridge, Mass.: Harvard University Press, 1961. 287 pp.

Skira, Albert (ed.). *Le Romantisme.* Text by Pierre Courthion. Milan: Skira, 1961. 139 pp.

Sørensen, Bengt A. *Symbol und Symbolismus in den ästhetischen Theorien des 18. Jahrhunderts und der deutschen Romantik.* Copenhagen: Munksgaard, 1963. 332 pp.

Souckova, Milada. *The Czech Romantics.* The Hague: Mouton, 1958. 168 pp.

Steiner, George. *Language and Silence. Essays on Language, Literature, and the Inhuman.* New York: Atheneum, 1967. 426 pp.

Strohschneider-Kohrs, Ingrid. *Die romantische Ironie in Theorie und Gestaltung.* Tübingen: Niemeyer, 1960. 446 pp.

Thalmann, Marianne. *Romantiker entdecken die Stadt.* Munich:

Nymphenburger Verlags-
buchhandlung, 1965. 146 pp.
— *Zeichensprache der Romantik.*
Heidelberg: Lothar Stiehm,
1967. 115 pp.
Thorlby, Anthony K. *The Roman-
tic Movement.* London: Long-
mans Green, 1966. 176 pp.
Thorpe, Clarence D., Carlos
Baker, and Bennett Weaver
(eds.). *The Major English
Romantic Poets. A Symposium in
Reappraisal.* Carbondale:
Southern Illinois University
Press, 1957 (Arcturus paper-
back, 1964). 269 pp.
Thorslev, Peter L., Jr. 'The
Romantic Mind Is Its Own
Place.' *Comparative Literature*
xv (1963): 250–68
Trilling, Lionel. 'The Fate of
Pleasure: Wordsworth to
Dostoevsky,' in *Romanticism
Reconsidered* (see Northrop
Frye, ed.), pp. 73–106
Trousson, Raymond. *Le Thème
de Prométhée dans la littérature
européenne.* Two volumes.
Geneva: Droz, 1964
— *Un Problème de littérature
comparée: les études de thème.
Essai de méthodologie.* Paris:
Minard – Lettres Modernes,
1965

Vordtriede, Werner. *Novalis und
die französischen Symbolisten.*
Stuttgart: Kohlhammer,
1963. 196 pp.

Weber, Eugen (ed.). *Paths to the
Present. Aspects of European
Thought from Romanticism to
Existentialism.* New York and
Toronto: Dodd, Mead, 1960.
453 pp.
Weinberg, Kurt. *Henri Heine,
'Romantique défroqué,' héraut du
symbolisme français.* New
Haven: Yale University
Press, and Paris: Presses
Universitaires de France,
1954. 303 pp.
Weintraub, Wiktor. 'The Prob-
lem of Improvisation in
Romantic Literature.' *Com-
parative Literature* xvi (1964):
119–37
Weisstein, Ulrich. 'Romanticism.
Transcendentalist Games or
"Wechselseitige Erhellung
der Künste"?' *Colloquia
Germanica* (1968): nos. 1/2,
pp. 47–69
Wellek, René. 'Romanticism Re-
Examined,' in *Romanticism
Reconsidered,* ed. Northrop
Frye. New York: Columbia
University Press, 1963. Pp.
107–33
— 'German and English Ro-
manticism: A Confrontation.'
Studies in Romanticism iv
(1964): 35–56. (Reprinted in
Wellek, *Confrontations.* Prince-
ton: Princeton University
Press, 1965)
Whalley, George. 'Literary Ro-
manticism.' *Queen's Quarterly*
LXXII (1965): 232–52
Wimsatt, William K. *Hateful
Contraries. Studies in Literature*

and Criticism. Lexington:
University of Kentucky Press
1965. 260 pp. (Particularly
ch. 1, 'Horses of Wrath:
Recent Critical Lessons')
Winner, Thomas G. (ed.).
    'Dostoevsky and Romantic
Aesthetics.' Proceedings of
the Conference on Slavistics
and Comparative Literature
at the MLA Meeting in
Chicago, 1961, in *Yearbook of
Comparative and General Literature* XI (1962): 36–9

Chronology

The left column lists works and events of importance in the history of the word *romantic* and its cognates. The right column records works and events of importance in the history of the romantic movement in the countries discussed in the text of this book. Many of the titles listed could have been placed with equal justice in either column, but the editor feels nonetheless that the arrangement in two columns will be a help to quick orientation. The few titles listed in parenthesis in the right-hand column were included as being of particular importance to the history of pre-romanticism. D = Denmark; E = England; F = France; G = Germany; I = Italy; N = Norway; R = Russia; SP = Spain; SW = Sweden.

1650

E: First recorded occurrence of 'romantic': *Herba Parietis or the Wall Flower*. As it grew out of the Stone Chamber belonging to the Metropolitan prison of London, called Newgate. Being a history which is partly true, partly romantick, morally divine. Whereby a marriage between reality and fancy is solemnized by divinity. Written by T.[homas] B.[aily], D.D., whilst he was a prisoner there.[1]

1661
F: First recorded occurrence of
'romanesque.'[2]
1663
E: 'Romantic' applied to landscapes.
G: First recorded occurrence of
'romansch,' 'romanisch.'[3]
F: Molière (*L'Étourdi*, line 31):
'Vous êtes romanesque avecque
vos chimères.'[4]
1669
F: Jean Chapelain contrasts
'poésie romanesque' and 'poésie
héroïque.'[5]
1673
F: René Rapin writes of the
'poésie romanesque' of Pulci,
Boiardo, and Ariosto.[6]
1674
E: Thomas Rymer, translating
Rapin, uses the phrase 'Romantick Poetry.'[7]
1685
I: First occurrence of 'romanesco.'[8]
1694
F: Isolated occurrence of 'romantique,' but 'romantic' continues
to be translated by 'romanesque' or 'pittoresque' in all
contexts.[9]
1698
G: First occurrence of 'romantisch.'[10]
1722 *ff.*
F: 'Romanesque' used of romance-
like landscapes.[11]
1730
E: Increasing popularity of the
English garden.

1731
I: First occurrence of 'romanzesco.'[12]

1740
E: (Joseph Warton, *The Enthusiast*.)

1742–5
E: (Edward Young, *Night
Thoughts*.)

1754
E: Thomas Warton, *Observations
on the Faerie Queen*.

1760 ff.
E: The English garden becomes
increasingly popular on the continent.
G: 'Romantisch' used frequently
by Wieland, Gerstenberg, and
Herder.

1760
E: (James Macpherson, *Fragments of Ancient English Poetry*.)

1761
F: (Rousseau, *La Nouvelle
Héloïse*.)

1762
E: Richard Hurd, *Letters on
Chivalry and Romance*.

1764
SP: First use of 'romanesco.'[13]

1765
E: (Thomas Percy, *Reliques of
Ancient English Poetry*.)

1766–7
G: Gerstenberg, *Briefe über die
Merkwürdigkeiten der Literatur*.

1772
F: A. L. Thomas: 'Jamais le mot
romanesque ne dut être si à la
mode.'[14]

1772
I: (M. Cesarotti, *Le poesie di
Ossian*.)

1773
G: (J. G. Herder, *Von deutscher Art
und Kunst*. J. W. Goethe, *Götz von
Berlichingen*. G. A. Bürger,
'Lenore.')

1774
E: Thomas Warton, *The Origin of Romantic Fiction in Europe.*

1774
G: (Goethe, *Werthers Leiden.*)

1776
F: Letourneur and Girardin use 'romantique.'[15]
SP: First occurrence of 'romancesco.'[16]

1778
D: O. E. Müller uses 'romantisk.'[17]

1778–9
G: (Herder, *Volkslieder.*)

1781
E: Thomas Warton calls Dante's *Divina Commedia* a 'wonderful compound of classical and romantic fancy.'[18]

1781
G: (Friedrich Schiller, *Die Räuber.*)

1782
F: Posthumous publication of Rousseau's *Rêveries du promeneur solitaire.*

1790
G: First recorded occurrence of 'Romantik.'[19]

1791
F: Panckoucke's *Encyclopédie méthodique* distinguishes between *Le romanesque* ('ce qui appartient au roman') and *Le romantique* ('ce qui lui convient ou qui a l'air de lui appartenir.')[20]
R: First recorded occurrence of 'romaničeskij.'[21]

1791–2
R: (Nikolai Karamzin, *Pis'ma russkogo puteshestvennika.*)

1794
G: (J. G. Fichte, *Wissenschaftslehre.*)

1795–6
G: Schiller, 'Über naive und sentimentalische Dichtung.'

1795–6
G: Ludwig Tieck, *William Lovell.*

1796
E: (William Taylor's translation of Bürger's 'Lenore' published.)

1797
E: Coleridge begins 'Ancient Mariner' and writes first part of 'Christabel' and (?) 'Kubla Khan.' M. G. Lewis, *The Monk*.
G: Wackenroder and Tieck, *Herzensergießungen eines kunstliebenden Klosterbruders*.

1798
G: Friedrich Schlegel's first definition of 'romantische Poesie.'
F: 'Romantique' admitted to the Dictionary of the *Académie Française*.

1798
E: [Wordsworth and Coleridge,] *Lyrical Ballads*.[22]
G: Tieck, *Franz Sternbalds Wanderungen*. A. W. and F. Schlegel, *Athenäum* (1798–1800).

1799–1800
G: Tieck, *Romantische Dichtungen*.

1800
G: Friedrich Schlegel's definition of 'romantische Poesie' in his 'Gespräch über die Poesie.' Explicit statement of the 'classic/romantic' dichotomy.

1801
G: Schiller, *Die Jungfrau von Orleans. Eine romantische Tragödie*. The phrase 'New School' used by Henry Crabb Robinson, evidently as a translation of 'neue Schule.' A. W. Schlegel's Berlin lectures (1801–4; published in 1884).

1801
R: (V. Zhukovsky, translation of Gray's 'Elegy in a Country Churchyard.')

1802
E: The 'new school of poetry' (i.e., the Lake School) identified by F. Jeffrey in a review of Southey's *Thalaba*.
G: First occurrence of 'Romantik' in the typological sense.
D: Henrik Steffens returns from Germany to Copenhagen and there introduces the German technical meaning of 'romantisk.'

1802
E: *Lyrical Ballads* published with revised preface and appendix on poetic diction.
G: Novalis, *Heinrich von Ofterdingen* published posthumously.
F: Chateaubriand, *Génie du christianisme*.
I: Ugo Foscolo, *Le ultime lettere di Jacopo Ortis*.[23]
D: Adam Oehlenschläger, *Digte*.[24]

1803

G: Novalis called a 'romantischer Dichter' in a review in the *Allgemeine Literatur-Zeitung* (12 September).

1804

G: 'Romantik' used extensively by Jean Paul, with reference both to old masters and to contemporaries.

1805

E: John Foster, 'On the Application of the Epithet Romantic.'

1807

F: A. W. Schlegel presents the antithesis 'classical/romantic' to French readers.

1807–8

G: 'Romantik,' 'Romantiker' used extensively with specific reference to contemporary authors.

1808

E: Coleridge's first course of lectures on literature.[25]

G: A. W. Schlegel lectures in Vienna on Dramatic Art and Literature (published in 3 vols., 1809–11).

sw: First occurrence of the noun *romantik*.

1810

F: Mme de Staël, *De l'Allemagne* (suppressed).

R: First recorded use of 'romantičeskij.'[26]

1803

G: Zacharias Werner, *Die Söhne des Tals* (2 pt., 1803–4).

1804

G: Tieck, *Kaiser Oktavianus*.

F: Senancour, *Obermann*.

1805

E: Walter Scott, *The Lay of the Last Minstrel*.

G: Arnim and Brentano, *Des Knaben Wunderhorn* (3 vols., 1805–8).

1807

E: Wordsworth, *Poems in Two Volumes*.

1808

R: V. Zhukovsky's translation of Bürger's 'Lenore.' V. Zhukovsky, 'Svetlana.'

D: N. F. S. Grundtvig, *Nordens Mytologi* (revised ed., 1832).

1809

E: Byron, *English Bards and Scotch Reviewers*.

I: Ugo Foscolo, *Dell'origine e dell' ufficio della letteratura*.

1810

G: H. v. Kleist, *Erzählungen*; *Das Käthchen von Heilbronn*; *Der Prinz von Homburg*.

1810 (*cont.*)
sw: The journal *Phosphorus*
(1810–13).
1811
sw: E. G. Geijer publishes the
first of his 'Gothic' poems in
Iduna.

1812
E: First occurrence of the phrase
'Lake Poets.'

1812
E: Byron, *Childe Harold's Pilgrimage: a romaunt*, I, II. (III, 1816; IV,
1818).
sw: P. D. A. Atterbom,
Blommorna.[27]

1813
E, F: Mme de Staël, *De l'Allemagne* published in London, both
in the original and in English
translation. Sismonde de Sismondi, *De la littérature du midi
de l'Europe*. Mme Necker de
Saussure's translation of
A. W. Schlegel's Vienna
lectures.

1813
E: Shelley, *Queen Mab*.
G: E. T. A. Hoffmann, *Phanta-
siestücke in Callots Manier* (4 vols.,
1813–15).

1814
E: Hazlitt's review of A. W.
Schlegel's Vienna lectures.
F: Paris edition of *De l'Allemagne*.
I: Bertolotti's translation of *De
l'Allemagne*, rendering 'romanti-
que' by 'romanzesco.' First
occurrence of 'romantico.'
SP: Böhl von Faber introduces
A. W. Schlegel's theories, using
'romancesco' in Schlegel's sense of
'romantic.'

1814
E: Wordsworth, *The Excursion*.
Scott, *Waverley*.
G: Chamisso, *Peter Schlemihl*.
sw: A. A. Afzelius, *Svenska
folkvisor* (1814–16).

1815
E: A. W. Schlegel's Vienna lectures translated.

1815
E: Wordsworth, *Poems, including
Lyrical Ballads*.
G: J. v. Eichendorff, *Ahnung und
Gegenwart*. E. T. A. Hoffmann,
Die Elixiere des Teufels (2 vols.,
1815–16.)

1816

F: 'Romantisme' first used in its present ('contemporary') sense.[29]

1817

I: Gherardini's translation of A. W. Schlegel's Vienna lectures, based on the French edition, rendering 'romantique' by 'romantico.'

1818

F: Stendhal refers to himself as a 'romantic' – apparently the first Frenchman to do so.[31]
I: Earliest occurrence of 'romanticismo.'[32]
SP: Earliest occurrence of 'romántico.'[33]

1819

G: The phrase 'romantische Schule' used frequently in vol. XI of Bouterwek's *Geschichte der Poesie und Beredsamkeit*.
I: 'Romantico' first used of a contemporary school of writing.

1820

E: Byron writes to Goethe on the classic-romantic distinction.
G: Heine, 'Die Romantik.'
I: Manzoni, *Lettre à M.C*** sur l'unité de temps et de lieu dans la tragédie* (published 1823).

1815 *(cont.)*

I: Silvio Pellico, *Francesca da Rimini*. Alessandro Manzoni, *Inni sacri*.[28]

1816

E: Coleridge's *Christabel* volume.[30] Shelley's *Alastor*.
F: Benjamin Constant, *Adolphe*.
I: Translation of Mme de Staël's 'De l'esprit des traductions,' published in the *Biblioteca italiana*. Berchet's pamphlet on Bürger's ballads.

1817

E: Coleridge, *Sibylline Leaves*, *Biographia Literaria*. Keats, *Poems*. Byron, *Manfred*.
I: Leopardi, *Zibaldone di pensieri* (written 1817–32, published 1898–1900).

1818

E: Keats, *Endymion*.
I: Leopardi, *Discorso di un italiano intorno alla poesia romantica* (first published in 1906).

1819

E: Byron, *Don Juan* (Cantos 1–2)
F: Chénier, *Œuvres posthumes*.
I: Manzoni, *Il Conte di Carmagnola*. Leopardi, *L'infinito*.

1820

E: Keats, *Lamia* volume, including 'The Eve of St. Agnes.'
G: E. T. A. Hoffmann, *Lebensansichten des Katers Murr* (2 vols., 1820–2; written in 1818 and 1821).

1820 (*cont.*)

F: Lamartine, *Méditations poétiques.*

1821

R: Yevgeny Baratynsky, Elegies and Verse Tales. Nikolai Yazykov, Ballads.

1822-7

R: Pushkin, *Yuzhnye poemy* (written 1820-4).

1823

F: Stendhal, *Racine et Shakespeare* (I). 'Romantique' used widely by the opponents of the movement.
I: Manzoni, *Sul Romanticismo. Lettera al marchese Cesare d'Azeglio* (published in 1846).

1823

F: Victor Hugo, *Han d'Islande.*

1824

sw: E. J. Stagnelius, *Samlade skrifter* (1824-6).

1825

F: Stendhal, *Racine et Shakespeare* (II).

1825

sw: Esaias Tegnér, *Frithiofs Saga.*[34]
R: Pushkin, *Boris Godunov* (published 1831); *Evgeny Onegin* (published in instalments 1825-32, in book form 1833). Kondraty Ryleev, *Voynarovsky.*

1826

G: Eichendorff, *Aus dem Leben eines Taugenichts.*
F: Vigny, *Poèmes antiques et modernes; Cinq-Mars.*
I: Tommaso Grossi, *I Lombardi alla prima Crociata.* Leopardi, *Operette morali.*[35]

1827

F: Hugo, Preface to *Cromwell*; the term 'romantisme' adopted by the French romantics.

1827

F: Hugo, *Cromwell.*
I: Manzoni, *I promessi sposi.*[36]

1829

F: Hugo, *Les Orientales.*
R: Zagoskin, *Yuri Miloslavsky.*

1830
July Revolution in Paris.[37]
E: Tennyson, *Poems Chiefly Lyrical.*
F: Hugo, *Hernani.* Lamartine,
Harmonies poétiques et religieuses.
Musset, *Contes d'Espagne et d'Italie.*

1831
E: Carlyle laments the English
failure to take up German romanticism.[38]
I: Manzoni, *Del Romanzo storico e,
in genere, de'componimenti misti di
storia e d'invenzione.*[40]

1831
F: Hugo, *Les Feuilles d'automne.*
I: Leopardi, *Canti.*[39]
R: Vladimir Odoevsky, *Povesti*
(1831–7).

1832
I: Silvio Pellico, *Le mie prigioni.*

1833
E: W. Maginn refers to Coleridge
as the 'founder of the romantic
school of poetry,' but the term
does not catch on.[41]

1833
N: Andreas Faye publishes the
first collection of Norwegian
folklore.
R: Nesto Kukol'nik, *Torkvato
Tasso.*

1834
SP: Return of the exiled writers.
Alcalá Galiano distinguishes between historical romanticism and
the 'romanticismo actual' of his
contemporaries.

1834
G: Eichendorff, *Dichter und ihre
Gesellen.*
I: *Tommaso Grossi, Marco Vis-
conti.*
SP: Rivas, *El moro expósito.* First
performances of Martínez de la
Rosa's *La conjuración de Venecia* and
of Larra's *Macías.*

1835
F: Vigny, *Chatterton.* Hugo, *Les
Chants du crépuscule.*
SP: First performance of Rivas'
Don Álvaro.
D: Hans Christian Andersen,
Eventyr, fortalte for Børn (1835–72).
R: Lermontov, *Maskarad.* Gogol,
Mirgorod. Aleksandr Bestuzhev-
Marlinsky, *Russkie povesti i
rasskazy* (1836–7).

1836
G: Heine, *Die romantische Schule*.[42]

1836
SP: First performance of Gutiérrez' *El Trovador*.

1837
G: Eichendorff, *Gedichte*.
F: Hugo, *Les Voix intérieures*.
SP: First performance of Hartzen-busch's *Los amantes de Teruel*.

1838
F: Lamartine, *La Chute d'un Ange*.

1840
F: Hugo, *Les Rayons et les ombres*.
R: First small collection of Ler-montov's poems.

1841
SP: Espronceda, *El diablo mundo*. Zorrilla, *Cantos del trovador*. Rivas, *Romances históricos*.

1842–4
N: Asbjörnsen and Moe, *Norske Folkeeventyr*.

1843
F: Hugo, *Les Burgraves*.

1844
SP: Zorrilla, *Don Juan Tenorio*.

1846
G: Eichendorff, *Zur Geschichte der neueren romantischen Poesie in Deutschland*.[43]

1846
G: Brentano, *Märchen* (posthu-mous)[44]

1849
E: Thomas Shaw, *Outlines of English Literature*, speaking of 'romanticism' and 'romanticists' in connection with Scott, Byron, etc.[45]

1852
E: D. M. Moir's *Sketches of the Poetical Literature of the Past Half Century* declares M. G. Lewis leader of the 'purely romantic school.'

1853 ff.
D: *Danmarks gamle Folkeviser*, ed.
S. Grundtvig et al.

1855
D: Christian Winther, *Hjortens Flugt.*

1863
E: W. Rushton, *Afternoon Lectures on English Literature* places Scott and Wordsworth in the 'Romantic School of English Literature'.

1871
E: English translation (2 vols., 1871–2), of Taine's *Histoire de la littérature anglaise* (5 vols., 1864–9) uses the phrase 'English Romantic School.'

1887
E: Lady Eastlake's translation of Alois Brandl, *Coleridge und die romantische Schule in England.*

1889
E: Walter Pater's 'Postscript' to *Appreciations.*

NOTES

1 *British Museum General Catalogue of Printed Books* XIII (London, 1965), col. 213. Cited by F. Baldensperger, ' "Romantique," ses analogues et ses équivalents,' *Harvard Studies and Notes in Philology and Literature* XIX (1937): 16 (hereafter cited as *Baldensperger*).
2 *Baldensperger*, p. 20.
3 Grimms *Deutsches Wörterbuch* VIII (Leipzig, 1893): 1155. Cf. p. 55 above.
4 See Alexis François, 'Où en est "Romantique," ' *Mélanges d'histoire littéraire générale et comparée offerts à Fernand Baldensperger* (Paris, 1930), 1: 323.
5 *Baldensperger*, p. 22.
6 Ibid., p. 24.
7 Ibid., p. 26
8 Ibid., p. 31.
9 Ibid., p. 34; cf. Alexis François, 'Romantique,' *Annales de la Sociéte Jean-Jaques Rousseau* V (1909): 204 ff.
10 Richard Ullmann and Helene Gotthard, *Geschichte des Begriffes 'romantisch' in Deutschland* (Berlin, 1927), p. 16.
11 Cf. François Jost, 'Romantique: la leçon d'un mot,' *Essais de littérature comparée* II (Urbana, 1968): 212 (hereafter cited as *Jost*).
12 Ibid., p. 226.
13 Shaw, p. 342 *f.* above.

14 *Jost,* p. 213, n. 3.
15 Immerwahr, p. 386 above.
16 Shaw, pp. 342 *f.* above.
17 Mitchell, p. 373 above.
18 *History of English Poetry* III (London, 1781): 241; cited by René Wellek, *Concepts of Criticism* (New Haven and London, [1963]), p. 132.
19 Eichner, p. 142 above.
20 Shroder, p. 268 above.
21 McLaughlin, p. 419 above.
22 Published anonymously; 2nd ed. 'by William Wordsworth,' 1800, with Preface. (Preface revised in edition of 1802 and appendix on poetic diction added; essay supplementary added in 1815.)
23 Revised editions, 1816 and 1817; an earlier incomplete version had begun to appear in 1799.
24 Published in December 1802 with imprint 1803.
25 Followed by others in 1811–12, 1812, 1812–13, 1813, 1818, 1818–19.
26 McLaughlin, pp. 419 n. and 423 above.
27 The complete sequence of these poems was first published in Atterbom's *Samlade dikter,* 1837–8.
28 Only the first four of the *Inni sacri* appeared at this time. The first of them, 'La Risurrezione,' had been written in 1812; the complete sequence was published in 1822.
29 See Shroder, p. 276 above.
30 The poem was completed in 1800 except for the 'Conclusion to Part II,' added in 1801.
31 Letter to Baron de Mareste, 14 April 1818. Cf. Wellek (as in n. 18), p. 141.
32 Ragusa, pp. 314 *f.* above.
33 See Shaw, p. 346 above.
34 Definitive edition; four of the romances of the cycle had appeared in 1820.
35 Only the first three of the *operette* were published at this time; others appeared between 1827 and 1845.
36 3 vols. with imprint 1825–6; revised edition, 1842 with imprint 1840. An early version, 'Fermo e Lucia,' was written 1821–3.
37 German historians of literature tend to date the end of the romantic movement in Germany from the July Revolution and its repercussions in Germany. It is well to keep in mind, however, that the 'Young Germans,' who dominated the literary scene in the 1830's, had much in common with the 'liberal' and 'realistic' wing of French romanticism. Contemporary critics saw this quite clearly. A. Ruge and T. Echtermayer, at the end of their manifesto 'Der Protestantismus und die Romantik' (1839–40), provide a survey of German romanticism in which they distinguish four stages: (1) 'Die *Progonen* der Romantik' (the authors of the *Storm and Stress,* etc.) (2) '*Die eigentlichen Romantiker*' (F. and A. W. Schlegel, Tieck, Wackenroder, Werner, Arnim, Brentano, etc.) (3) '*Die zahlreiche Epigonenschaft*' (Uhland, Kleist, Eichendorff, Hoffmann, etc.) (4) '*Die französierenden Romantiker, das junge Deutschland.*' (*Hallische Jahrbücher für deutsche Wissenschaft und Kunst,* 1840, no. 64, col. 511 f.)
38 Whalley, pp. 238 *f.* above.
39 Some of these poems had appeared earlier; the first were composed in 1816.
40 Begun 1828, published 1851.
41 Whalley, pp. 220, 234 *f.* above.
42 Based on a series of essays published in *L'Europe littéraire* in 1833; expanded German version completed in 1835.
43 Serial in *Historisch-politische Blätter*; republished as a book in 1847.
44 Written for the most part before 1818.
45 For this and the following entries, see Wellek (as in n. 18), p. 150, and Whalley, pp. 246–9 above.

Index

In its general arrangement the Index follows the Catalogue of the British Museum, except that ä and ü are alphabetized throughout as ae and ue, and ö and ø are alphabetized throughout as oe.

The Chronology (pp. 501–513) is not included in the Index.

André, John 272&n
Andreev, Leonid Nikolaevich 454
Anne (of England) 9n
Anson, Admiral George 25f, 55n
Antal, Frederick 484, 487, 492
Anti-Jacobin, The 217, 221&n
Antogina, A. 325
Apel, Johann August 117, 132, 140n
Apollon 146n, 153n48
Apollonio, Carla 295n, 306n, 308n, 336f
Arabian Nights Entertainments 207
Arese, Antonietta Fagnani 309n
Ariosto, Ludovico 6, 43, 49, 50, 57n, 71, 109, 110n, 111, 114, 120, 122, 296, 307, 308n, 310&n, 321n, 351, 377
Aristophanes 158n, 206
Aristotle 110
Arnim, Achim von 9n, 13, 141n, 143n, 144–8, 484
Arnold, Benedict 272
Arnold, Matthew 236, 237, 239n, 240–2&n, 244, 245, 247, 250, 253, 262n135
Arrieta, García de 343
Arthur, King 319
Artista, El 350
Assézat, Jules 285
Ast, Friedrich 116, 118, 120, 126, 128, 131, 144, 148, 154n78
Atenej 468
Athenaeum 98, 112, 114, 116, 136, 144, 203
Athene 377, 383, 387
Atterbom, Per Daniel Amadeus 376f, 387, 396, 402, 405, 411
Attiret, (Frère) Jean-Denis 41
Aubrey, John 20
Auden, Wystan Hugh 486, 490
Auerbach, Erich 485
Auger, Louis-Simon 276, 281
Aurora, eller den Norrska Flickan 386
Aynard, Joseph 355, 370n30

Baader, Franz Xaver von 484

Babbitt, Irving 481
Bach, Johann Sebastian 22n
Bäumer, Max L. 96n225
Bagehot, Walter 249–51, 252, 254, 255
Bagger, Carl 408
Baggesen, Jens 89, 146n, 147f, 392f, 397
Bagritsky, Eduard Georgievich 461
Baillie, Joanna 248n
Baker, Carlos 482, 484, 487
Bakunin, Mikhail Aleksandrovich 446, 454
Balaun (Balazun, troubador) 84
Baldensperger, Fernand 17, 18, 87n, 90n5
Balderston, Katharine Canby 222n
Balmes, Jaime 365f, 371nn39&40
Balzac, Honoré de 266, 274, 322n, 486
Banashevich, Nikola 492
Bang, Herman 401f
Banville, Théodore de 286
Baour-Lormian, Marie-François 281&n
Baretti, Giuseppe 295f, 305n
Barrès, Maurice 477
Barzun, Jacques 486
Bateson, Frederick W. 490
Battaglia, Salvatore 334n
Battisti, Carlo 307, 319n, 334n
Batyushkov, Konstantin Nikolaevich 429, 431, 461
Baudelaire, Charles 274, 283f, 287, 335, 487
Bayly, Thomas Haynes 19, 245 (misspelled Bailey)
Beattie, James 248n
Beaumont, Francis 46, 168n
Beaumont, Sir George 179n, 198n, 221n, 260n75
Becher, Herbert 343n, 369n5, 370nn9&10
Beckford, William 46–8, 52, 75, 94n119
Beers, Henry A. 253

Brandes, Georg 398, 399–401, 403, 405f, 407, 409
Brandl, Alois 246
Brang, Peter 470n14
Brauser, E. R. 148
Breitinger, Johann Jacob 55, 124f
Breme, Ludovico Di 306, 308–11, 313, 317, 325n
Brentano, Clemens 9n, 12, 13, 116, 125, 141&n, 143n, 144–8, 150n, 155n120, 484, 487
Breughel, Pieter 33
Bridges, Robert 244f&n
Brifaut, Charles 276
Bril, Paul 33
Brillat-Savarin, Anthelme 272n
Brion, Marcel 484, 487, 492
Bronson, Bertrand Harris 125n
Brooks, Cleanth 487
Brown, Calvin 485, 489, 492
Brown, Dr. John 33f, 35, 42
Brown, Launcelot ('Capability' Brown) 37, 38, 43
Browning, Elizabeth Barrett 246
Browning, Robert 237&n, 246, 250, 254
Bruce, James 26, 27
Brüggemann, Werner 369n2
Bruneau, Charles 263
Brunetière, Ferdinand 253n, 281, 477
Brydone, Patrick 41, 55n
Bryusov, Valery Yakovlevich 456
Buchholtz, Carl August 387
Budagov, Ruben Aleksandrovich 423n, 444–5n
Budde, Wilhelm 117n
Büchner, Georg 151
Bückeburg, Count von, see Schaumburg-Lippe
Bürger, Gottfried August 11, 128, 158, 257n1, 306, 311
Bulgakov, Mikhail Athanas'evich 469
Bulgarin, Thaddey Venediktovich 426f, 434–5n, 466
Bulle, Oscar 306n, 311n, 322

Burgos, Carmen de 360n
Burke, Edmund 36, 37, 38, 270
Burlington, Richard Boyle, Third Earl of 41
Burne-Jones, Sir Edward 245
Burney, Fanny (Madame D'Arblay) 54&n
Burns, Robert 224, 237n, 247, 248n, 251, 262n146
Bursov, Boris Ivanovich 436n
Burton, Robert 203n
Butcher, Samuel Henry 242f
Butler, Eliza Marian 482
Butler, Samuel 247n
Byaly, Grigory Abramovich 461
Byron, George Gordon Noel, Lord 4, 10, 48, 76, 102, 104, 161, 162f, 163f, 166, 195f, 202&n, 209, 214, 216, 219, 224, 225&n, 226, 228&n, 232f&n, 245, 246, 247&n, 248&n, 251, 254, 258n11, 261nn102&104, 262n146, 314, 325, 330, 346, 347, 349, 352, 364, 368, 405, 428, 429f, 430, 434, 439, 448, 449n, 454n, 482

Cain 489
Calcaterra, Carlo 309n, 311n, 313n, 316n, 320n, 321n, 332n
Caldera, E. 370n14
Calderón de la Barca, Pedro 8, 16n7, 114, 137, 344, 346, 349, 352, 364, 385, 394, 400
Caleppio, Trussardo 308, 314
Camoens, Luis 346
Campbell, Thomas 209&n, 214n, 216, 225&n, 245f, 248
Camus, Albert 288
Canaday, Nicholas 487
Canova, Antonio 334n
Canzoniere, see Petrarca
Caravaca, Ferdinand 370n18
Carducci, Giosuè 302n, 329
Carli, Plinio 309n
Carlyle, Thomas 202n, 214, 237–40, 242, 253, 254, 257n1

Carrilla, Emilio 356
Cartas a un escéptico 365, 366
Cartas Españolas 350
Carter, Elizabeth 29
Carus, Carl Gustav 484
Casalduero, Joaquín 342, 354, 359, 369, 370n24
Casarotti, Ilario 325, 326
Castelnau, Julien 279
Cattaneo, M. J. 370n14
Cederborgh, Fredrik 383
Cervantes Saavedra, Miguel de 12, 22, 43, 56f, 57n, 107, 109, 114, 115, 119, 166, 173, 321n, 343, 388, 394
Chalmers, Alexander 236
Chambers, William 43f, 44n, 45, 52, 55n, 85
Chamisso, Adelbert von 148
Chantavoine, Jean 488, 492
Charlemagne 52, 320
Charles XII (of Sweden) 402f
Charrel, H. 314n
Chase, Isabel W. U. 92n64
Chateaubriand, François-René de 8, 266f, 271, 272, 328, 346, 407
Chatterton, Thomas 166n, 248n
Chaucer, Geoffrey 51, 52, 174
Chekhov, Anton Pavlovich 457
Chénier, André 279
Chernyshevsky, Nicolay Gavrilovich 451
Chiari, Alberto 323n
Chizhevsky, Dmitry 459, 486, 492
Choderlos de Laclos, Pierre 266, 320
Cicero 294, 334
Cieco d'Adria, *see* Groto, Luigi
Clarkson, Thomas 177
Claude Lorraine (Claude Gelée) 5, 31, 32, 34, 35, 37, 128, 195, 197, 198, 219, 260nn75&76
Claudian 225&n
Cleopatra 141
Coburn, Kathleen 158n, 208n, 257n1

Coleridge, Ernest Hartley 257n2, 259n69
Coleridge, Henry Nelson 204n, 217, 220, 223n, 230n, 231–3, 234f, 249, 260nn82&83
Coleridge, John 162
Coleridge, John Taylor 223
Coleridge, Mrs S. T., née Fricker 182, 221n
Coleridge, Samuel Taylor: *use of romantic* 177–83, 183–94, 209; cf. 173f, 213f; *and A. W. Schlegel* 199–216, 260nn82&96; *as 'Romantic'* 220, 234f, 246, 247, 248&n, 251&n, 254, 258n25, 261n104; *on Gothic romance etc.* 158&n, 160n, 189, 207; *Ancient Mariner* 159, 190, 215, 222n, 226, 227, 232&n, 249, 259n54, 262n130; *Christabel* 159&n, 161, 175, 220, 224, 226f, 232&n, 233, 249, 262n130; *Kubla Khan* 161, 167, 177, 180, 181f, 184&n, 185, 227, 232n, 249; *other* 4, 8, 25n, 26, 44, 49, 125n, 157, 159, 161f, 164n, 166, 168n, 175, 176, 191–3, 197f, 203n, 216f, 218n, 219, 221n, 222, 225&n, 226, 227, 228n, 231, 233, 236n, 243&n, 250, 256, 258n3, 260nn76&94, 261n104, 479, 484; *see also Lyrical Ballads*
Coleridge, Sara 168n, 200
Collins, William 248n
Colomb, Romain 281
Colón, Germán 4n
Comelati, Guglielmo 305–6n
Conciliatore, Il 276, 313, 314, 338n21
Condé, Louis Joseph de Bourbon, prince de 273
Consoli, Domenico 338n10
Constant, Benjamin 467n
Cook, James 26
Corneille, Pierre 115, 428
Corregio, Antonio (Allegri) 378
Corriere delle dame 308

Goethe (*cont.*)
293, 296, 297n, 298, 306n, 311,
316, 320, 322n, 330, 331n, 335,
377, 428, 436, 478, 484, 485
Gogol, Nikolay Vasil'evich 451,
454, 466
Goldschmidt, Meir 372f, 397, 408f,
412
Goldsmith, Oliver 219
Goncharov, Ivan Aleksandrovich
448
Goncourt, Edmond *and* Jules de 286
Gonzáles Ruiz, Nicolás 357, 370n32
Gorbatov, Boris Leont'evich 461
Gordon, George 254n
Gorky, Maxim 454, 456, 458, 459,
460
Gothein, Marie Luise 93n104
Gottfried von Strassburg 119
Gotthard, Helene 17, 53–5, 57n,
62n, 90n1, 98n, 102, 152n5
Grand Larousse encyclopédique 284,
288n
Grande Almanacco romantico, Il 314
Grassi, Giuseppe 306n
Grattan, Colley 210
Gravina, Gian Vincenzo 309
Gray, Ronald 482
Gray, Thomas 34, 35, 42, 46, 157,
235, 248n, 298
Grazhis, P. I. 462
Grech, Nikolay Ivanovich 464
Greever, Garland 158n
Griboedov, Aleksandr Sergeevich
424n
Griggs, Earl Leslie 201n, 257n1
Grigson, Geoffrey 182, 258n39
Grillparzer, Franz 130
Grimm, Hermann 149n
Grimm, Jacob *and* Wilhelm
(*Wörterbuch*) 4n, 102n, 144
Grimm, Reinhold 149n
Grimm, Wilhelm 149n
Gröndal, Benedikt 397, 412
Grossi, Tommaso 237, 324f, 328
Groto, Luigi ('Cieco d'Adria') 377

Grundtvig, Nicolai Frederik Severin
409
Guarini, Giovanni Battista 114
Guérin, Maurice de 240&n, 244,
247
Gukovsky, Grigory Aleksandrovich
460
Gumilev, Nikolay Stepanovich 457
Gurevich, A. M. 457, 460
Gustafson, Lars 411f
Guthke, Karl S. 489, 494

Hackert, Philipp 40
Hadley, Michael 142n
Händel, Georg Friedrich 222n
Hagen, Friedrich Heinrich von der
148
Haller, Albrecht von 374
Hallische Jahrbücher 143n, 151n
Hammersköld, Lorenzo 384
Hansen, Peter 407
Hansson, Ola 409
Hardenberg, Friedrich von, *see*
Novalis
Hardenberg, Georg Anton von
148
Hardenberg, Karl von 147f
Hardy, John Edward 487, 494
Hartman, Geoffrey H. 483, 489,
490, 494
Hartzenbusch, Juan Eugenio 356,
358, 361, 363
Hauch, Carsten 387, 394, 402
Haug, Johann Christoph Friedrich
146f, 156n136
Havens, George R. 481, 494
Hawtrey, Edward Craven 243
Haydn, Joseph 133
Haydon, Benjamin Robert 161,
163, 195&n, 258n5
Hazlitt, William 163, 196–9&n,
203n, 210–13, 217n, 222, 223n,
228&n, 232n, 236, 249, 255n,
261n124
Hebbel, Friedrich 143n
Heely, Joseph 42f, 53, 55n

Loew (=Loeben?) 148, 156n140
Lollis, Cesare de 335
London Magazine 228n, 259n68, 261n124
Londonio, C. G. 308n
Longinus 36
Longman's Magazine 162n
Longum, Leif 409
López Soler, Ramón 347f, 370n14
Lorraine, *see* Claude Lorraine
Louis xiv 477
Lovejoy, Arthur O. 11, 93n104, 354, 370n25, 408, 427n, 460, 490
Lovell, Robert 221&n
Lower, William 19
Lowes, John Livingston 26, 44n, 91n42, 258n37
Lucács, Georg 482
Lucas, Edward V. 257n1
Lucas, Frank Lawrence 481, 487, 496
Lucian 58
Luther, Martin 221, 239n
Lyceum der schönen Künste 107
Lyrical Ballads 125n, 161, 175, 188, 192, 216, 217–19, 220, 223n, 226, 227, 228&n, 233, 236, 252, 257, 259n54, 261n106

Macaulay, Thomas Babington 9n, 233f, 236&n, 249, 253
McFarland, Thomas 200n, 201n
Mackintosh, Sir James 202, 260n83
Macpherson, James 6, 37, 45, 50f, 52, 75, 80, 82, 243, 248n, 271, 272, 298
Maggi, Gian Antonio 314
Maginn, William 220, 234f
Maier, Enrico 296f, 297n, 303n, 307n
Majer, Friedrich 101, 104n
Mallarmé, Stéphane 487
Malte-Brun, Conrad 279, 303f
Man, Paul de 482
Mann, Thomas 99, 102n, 143n
Manning, Thomas 176, 177

Manso, Johann Caspar Friedrich 100, 110n, 154n67
Manwaring, Elizabeth 31, 92n61
Manzoni, Alessandro 8&n, 10, 11, 12, 237, 297, 299, 306, 307, 313, 316, 317, 319&n, 322&nn, 323, 324, 325, 327, 329, 330, 331, 335, 346
Marcazzan, Mario 294n, 306, 308n, 324f, 337n8, 339n64
Mareste, Adolphe, Baron de 13, 276, 279
Marivaux, Pierre Carlet de Chamblain de 266
Marlowe, Christopher 214n
Marmontel, Jean-François 273, 274, 275, 314, 339n38
Marsia (by Pagani?) 314, 339n38
Martegiani, Gina 332, 340n79
Martens, Otto 145, 147
Martínez de la Rosa, Francisco 8, 356–8, 359
Martynov, Ivan Ivanovich 470n20
Marx, Karl 479, 482
Mary Magdalene 22
Mason, Eudo C. 482
Mason, William 42
Masson, Charles-François-Philibert 267
Mathew, George Felton 194, 196
Matlaw, Ralph D. 496
Maturin, Charles Robert 158n
Maupassant, Guy de 335
Maurice, Thomas 26f, 53
Maurras, Charles 477
Mazzini, Giuseppe 329f
Mazzoni, Guido 322n
Meiners, Christian 81, 82
Meini, Giuseppe 299n
Meisling, Simon 377
Mendelssohn, Moses 69n
Mendès, Catulle 286
Menzel, Wolfgang 151n
Mercier, Louis-Sébastien 268, 275
Mercurio Gaditano, El 369n6
Meredith, George 254

Merkel, Garlieb 101, 123, 124&n, 470n20
Mersereau, John, Jr. 436n
Mesonero Romanos, Ramón de 365n
Metford, John C. J. 370n22
Meylakh, B. S. 418
Michaelis, Salomon Heinrich Karl 117, 134, 145
Michelangelo Buonarotti 310
Michiels, Alfred 278
Millin, Aubin-Louis 265n
Milton, John 22, 41, 49, 50, 130, 222n, 224, 229, 235f, 236n, 245, 428
Mnemozina 468
Mnioch, Johann Jacob 116, 143, 144n, 153n42
Moe, Jørgen 401
Møller, Peder Ludvig 378, 382, 394, 396f, 408
Mörike, Eduard 25n
Moir, David Macbeth 246
Molbech, Christian 378f, 384f, 387, 393, 396
Molière (Jean-Baptiste Poquelin) 276, 292n77
Molitor, Joseph Franz 119, 149n
Momigliano, Attilio 325n
Monglond, André 263
Monk, Samuel H. 36n, 91n22
Montaigne, Michel Eyquem 434
Montalvo, Garci-Rodríguez de 320
Monteggia, Luigi 10, 346f, 348, 351, 364
Montesinos, José F. 344, 353f
Montgomery, Gerard, *see* Coleridge, Henry Nelson
Montgomery, James 261n104
Monthly Review 202, 223, 261n126
Monti, Vincenzo 300f, 316n, 321n, 324
Moore, Thomas 216, 224, 225&n, 227, 232, 245, 247, 248, 428
Mora, José Joaquín de 343f, 351, 369n6

Mordovchenko, Nikolay Ivanovich 470n15
More, Hannah 45f
More, Henry 20
Morgan, Lady Sydney, née Owenson 198f
Morgenblatt für gebildete Stände 117, 141, 143n, 144–7, 149n, 155n118
Moritz, Karl Philipp 73f, 80
Morley, Edith J. 260nn80&84
Morning Post 168n
Morris, William 245, 254
Mosconi, Clarina 316n
Moskovskij Telegraf 434–5n, 468
Moskovskij Vestnik 468
Mozart, Wolfgang Amadeus 133
Mudford, William 208
Müller, Adam 141n, 148
Müller, Otto Frederik 373
Müller von Itzehoe, Johann Gottwerth 142
Munárriz, José Luis 343
Munch, Charlotte 374
Muoni, Guido 329, 333, 339n67
Murray, John 203n, 209n, 225, 247
Musaeus, Johann Karl August 214n
Musset, Louis Charles Alfred de 247n, 263, 268, 282, 284

Nabokov, Vladimir 444n
Nachtwachen ('von Bonaventura') 125n, 144, 152n117
Nadezhdin, Nikolay Ivanovich 441–3, 455, 466
Nagarajara, Chetana 155n108
Napoleon Bonaparte 202, 450
Narezhny, Vasily Trofimovich 423
Necker de Saussure, *see* Saussure
Negri, Renzo 305n
Neiman, Fraser 242n
Nekrasov, Nikolay Alekseevich 436n, 453
Nerval, Gérard de 478
Neubert, Fritz 477, 496
Neue Teutsche Merkur, Der 55n, 56n

Shakespeare, William 8, 9, 12, 28, 43, 63, 64, 66, 73, 86, 87, 103, 106, 107, 109, 110n, 111, 114, 119, 130, 137, 144n, 151, 152n, 155n123, 158n, 169, 199–208, 215, 229, 238, 241, 242n, 243, 245, 252, 253n, 265, 276, 283, 295, 303&n, 310, 335, 346, 349, 352, 364, 373, 406, 428, 430, 434
Shalikov, Petr Ivanovich, Prince 422
Shaw, Thomas Budd 247–9
Shawcross, John 158, 200
Shedd, William G. T. 125n
Shelley, Percy Bysshe 4, 125n, 161, 163, 216, 233&n, 240, 242n, 243n, 245, 246, 247n, 248&n, 249, 250n, 254, 261n104, 482, 485
Shelvocke, George 25
Shishkov, Aleksandr Semenovich 424n, 467
Shroder, Maurice Z. 480, 486, 490, 498
Sibbern, Frederik Christian 397, 407
Sidney, Philip 20, 21, 50
Silva, Raúl 365n
Silverstolpe, Gustaf Abraham 374
Simpliciad, The 192
Singer, Samuel 214n
Sipovsky, Vasily Vasil'evich 454
Sismondi, Jean-Charles-Léonard Simonde de 263, 277, 279, 302n, 304, 309n, 456
Skira, Albert 487, 498
Skitalets (S. G. Petrov) 457
Smith, Elsie 217n
Smith, Horace and James 261n106
Smith, Logan Pearsall 17, 57n, 90n3, 256, 289n5
Smith, Sir William 247–9
Sneedorf, Friedrich 373f
Sniadecki, Jan 423
Snoilsky, Carl 404f
Søetoft, Niels Bierfreund 384f, 391

Sørensen, Bengt A. 490, 498
Soldin, Salomon 377
Somov, Orest 427–9
Sophocles 107, 112, 114, 158n, 162n, 252, 312, 335
Souckova, Milada 483, 498
Southey, Robert 9n, 158, 161, 164n, 167n, 183f, 189, 202, 209, 216, 217, 218n, 220, 221, 222n, 223n, 224n, 225&n, 231, 232, 235, 236, 243n, 246, 247, 248 &n, 253f, 254, 258n3, 261n104, 428
Spectateur, Le 303
Spectator 22
Spender, Stephen 482
Spenser, Edmund 49, 50, 52n, 64, 103, 110n, 157, 159, 174, 182, 194, 246, 248n, 428
Spettatore, Lo 303, 304f&n
Spingarn, Joel Elias 255n
Staël-Holstein, Anne-Louise-Germaine de 7, 8, 12, 117, 137, 160, 202f&n, 208, 209n, 214, 228, 239, 260n84, 263, 276, 278, 279, 280n, 288, 294, 296, 302–4, 306, 307n, 308, 310, 313, 320, 323, 379, 423, 428, 441
Staffeldt, Adam Wilhelm Schack von 385
Stagnelius, Erik Johan 379, 410
Stapfer, Philippe-Albert 275f
Starchevsky, Adalbert Vikentievich 452
Steele, Richard 21
Steffens, Henrik 376, 399, 401
Steig, Reinhold 143n, 149n
Steinbeck, John 409
Steiner, George 488, 498
Stella, Antonio 303n
Stendhal (Henry Beyle) 8, 10, 11, 13, 273, 276, 279, 281, 282f, 285, 316, 323n, 395, 484, 486
Sterne, Laurence 58, 157, 159, 197, 434
Stevenson, Robert Louis 162n

Storm, Edvard 373
Strich, Fritz 132n, 476
Strindberg, August 403f
Strohschneider-Kohrs, Ingrid 489, 498
Sulzer, Johann Georg 110n
Suphan, Bernhard 69, 95n175
Sveinsson, Einar Ólafur 412
Svendsen, Paulus 406
Swensk Literatur Tidning 374, 377–395 *passim*
Swenska Mercurius 375
Swift, Jonathan 321n
Swinburne, Algernon Charles 246, 251n, 254
Swinburne, Henry 35f, 40
Sydow, Anne von 80n

Taine, Hippolite 240n, 246&n, 252
Tait's Edinburgh Magazine 213, 259n70
Talfourd, Sir Thomas Noon 248n, 261n128
Talmud 312
Tarr, Frederick Courtney 349, 353, 355, 362, 369
Tassie, James 195
Tasso, Torquato 6, 43, 49, 50, 85, 107, 110, 111, 296, 307, 320, 377
Tate, Allen John 487
Taylor, Henry 248n
Taylor, William, of Norwich 158, 202, 257n1
Tegnér, Esaias 377, 380f, 384f, 389f, 394f, 396f&n, 402, 405, 412
Telemaco (Les Aventures de Télémaque), *see* Fénelon
Temple, William 22, 41f
Templeman, William Darley 38n
Tennyson, Alfred, Lord 195, 236, 237&n, 246, 250, 254, 261n104, 262n146
Tennyson, Hallam 237n
Teutsche Merkur, Der 55n, 56n, 58, 60, 111n

Thalmann, Marianne 125n, 484, 487, 488, 498
Thicknesse, Philip 40, 55n
Thomas de Celano 146
Thomson, James 32f, 198n, 218, 248n, 298, 306n
Thorarensen, Bjarni 412
Thordarson, Sturla 100
Thorild, Thomas 374f
Thorlby, Anthony K. 476, 482, 485, 486, 491, 499
Thorpe, Clarence D. 482, 484, 486, 487, 499
Thorslev, Peter L., Jr. 482, 489, 499
Tieck, Ludwig 8, 9n, 10, 39, 56, 103, 119, 125n, 128, 141&n, 148, 151n, 203n, 209, 238, 239&n, 262n140, 376, 396, 484
Times, The 159n
Timofeev, Leonid Ivanovich 460
Titian (Tiziano Vecelli) 58, 195, 198, 199
Tolstoy, Aleksey Konstantinovich 454
Tolstoy, Leo Nikolaevich 194, 454
Tommaseo, Niccolò 11, 299–302, 319n, 321–2n, 329
Tooke, Andrew 195
Trahard, Pierre 287
Transactions of the Royal Society of Literature 210
Trilling, Lionel 486, 487, 499
Trissino, Giangiorgio 351
Trotsky, Leon 458n
Trousson, Raymond 489, 499
Tsertelev, N. A. 440f
Tsoy, E. 460
Tubino, Francisco M. 368, 369
Tuckermann, Henry Theodore 247n
Turgenev, Aleksandr Ivanovich 424
Turgenev, Ivan Sergeyevich 462
Tymms, Ralph 482
Tytler, James 158

Uhland, Ludwig 131f, 144
Ullmann, Richard 17, 53–55, 57n, 62n, 90n1, 98n, 101n, 102, 152n5
Urfé, Honoré d' 21

Valentini, Francesco 305n, 306n
Valera, Juan 368
Valéry, Paul 281, 287, 288
Van Abbé, Derek 482
Vandervelde, Willem 260n75
Van Dyck, Sir Anthony 198
Van Laun, H. 240n, 247n
Vanslov, Viktor Vladimirovich 462
Van Tieghem, Paul 482, 489
Vapor, El 365
Variedades de Ciencia, Literatura y Artes 343
Varus 65
Vaughan, Charles Edwyn 253
Vedel, Anders Sørensen 378
Vedel, Valdemar 402
Vega, Ventura de la 366, 367
Verlaine, Paul 284
Veselovsky, Aleksandr Nikolaevich 455
Vestnik Evropy 423&n, 441n, 468
Vetterlund, Fredrik 409
Viaje de España 343
Vigny, Alfred de 8, 286
Villers, Charles de 275, 277, 278
Villon, François 335
Virgil 24, 25, 228, 253n, 294, 334, 346
Visconti, Ermès 276, 316–21, 322
Vishnevskaya, G. A. 419n, 469n7
Vitet, Ludovic 11, 282, 285
Vivas, Eliseo 487
Voeykov, Aleksandr Fedorovich 424, 440
Vogtberg, G. de 305n
Voltaire, François-Marie Arouet de 87, 277n, 324
Vordtriede, Werner 487, 499
Voss, Heinrich 147
Voss, Johann Heinrich 100, 145–9

Vyazemsky, Petr Andreevich, Prince 11, 418, 423, 424, 425f, 431, 466, 467n, 470n23

Wackenroder, Wilhelm Heinrich 9n, 25n, 484
Wagner, Richard 476
Wain, John 261n104
Walpole, Horace 10n, 19, 29, 31f, 42, 43&n, 53, 157, 254n
Walter, Richard 25, 26
Walzel, Oskar 153n
Warren, Robert Penn 487
Wartburg, Walther von 18n
Warton, Joseph 19, 33, 198n
Warton, Thomas 6, 12, 19, 51–3, 60, 62n, 63, 84, 104, 157, 235, 248n
Washington, George 272&n, 320, 479
Wassermann, Earl 484
Watelet, Claude Henri 84f
Watteau, Jean Antoine 268
Weaver, Bennet 482, 484, 487
Weber, Eugen 488, 499
Weber, Ferdinand Adolf 306n
Weinberg, Kurt 487, 499
Weintraub, Wiktor 482, 486, 499
Weisinger, Herbert 199n, 203n, 261nn98, 100, 101
Weisser, Friedrich 146, 150n, 155n118
Weisstein, Ulrich 487, 488, 499
Wellek, René 9n, 11n, 15&n1, 49n, 52, 200&n, 201&n, 202n, 203, 214, 240&n, 246, 260n81, 261nn102&104, 262nn136&150, 294, 304n, 370n26, 411, 467, 482, 483, 484, 486, 487, 488, 490, 491, 499
Werden, A. *and* J. 153n48
Wergeland, Henrik 396, 401
Werner, Zacharias 120, 144
West, Richard 32
Whalley, George 4, 480, 484, 485, 490, 491, 499

This book
was designed by
ANTJE LINGNER
under the direction of
ALLAN FLEMING
and was printed by
R & R CLARK, LTD
EDINBURGH
for
University of
Toronto
Press